THE MAKING AND RE-MAKING OF PUBLIC LAW

This volume originates from the fourth Public Law Conference, held in Dublin in 2022. Leading scholars and judges from across the common law world presented papers on the making (and re-making) of public law across country studies, historical studies and studies of contemporary and future issues.

The book has three broad categories of contribution: country studies which consider the evolution of public law within a particular jurisdictional context; historical studies, which shed light on the foundations of public law; and studies of contemporary and future issues, namely populism, COVID-19, protection of Indigenous peoples, and the public–private divide.

The Making and Re-Making of Public Law

Edited by
Eoin Carolan
Jason NE Varuhas
and
Sarah Fulham-McQuillan

• HART •
OXFORD • LONDON • NEW YORK • NEW DELHI • SYDNEY

HART PUBLISHING

Bloomsbury Publishing Plc

Kemp House, Chawley Park, Cumnor Hill, Oxford, OX2 9PH, UK

1385 Broadway, New York, NY 10018, USA

Bloomsbury Publishing Ireland Limited, 29 Earlsfort Terrace, Dublin 2, D02 AY28, Ireland

HART PUBLISHING, the Hart/Stag logo, BLOOMSBURY and the Diana logo are trademarks of Bloomsbury Publishing Plc

First published in Great Britain 2025

A catalogue record for this book is available from the British Library.

Library of Congress Cataloging-in-Publication data

Names: Public Law Conference (4th : 2022 : Dublin, Ireland), author. | Carolan, Eoin, editor. | Varuhas, Jason NE., editor. | Fulham-McQuillan, Sarah, editor.

Title: The making and re-making of public law / edited by Eoin Carolan, Jason NE Varuhas, and Sarah Fulham-McQuillan.

Description: Oxford ; New York : Hart Publishing, 2025. | Includes bibliographical references and index. | Summary: "This volume originates from the fourth Public Law Conference, held in Dublin in 2022. The volume has three broad categories of paper: country studies which consider the evolution of public law within a particular jurisdictional context; historical studies, which shed light on the foundations of public law; and studies of contemporary and future issues, namely populism, Covid-19, protection of Indigenous peoples, and the public-private divide"—Provided by publisher.

Identifiers: LCCN 2024043001 (print) | LCCN 2024043002 (ebook) | ISBN 9781509970056 (hardback) | ISBN 9781509970094 (paperback) | ISBN 9781509970063 (Epub) | ISBN 9781509970070 (ebook)

Subjects: LCSH: Public law—Congresses.

Classification: LCC K3150.A6 P83 2022 (print) | LCC K3150.A6 (ebook) | DDC 342—dc23/eng/20240913

LC record available at https://lccn.loc.gov/2024043001

LC ebook record available at https://lccn.loc.gov/2024043002

ISBN: HB: 978-1-50997-005-6
ePDF: 978-1-50997-007-0
ePub: 978-1-50997-006-3

Typeset by Compuscript Ltd, Shannon

For product safety related questions contact productsafety@bloomsbury.com

To find out more about our authors and books visit www.hartpublishing.co.uk. Here you will find extracts, author information, details of forthcoming events and the option to sign up for our newsletters.

Contents

List of Contributors .... *vii*

Introduction *1*
Eoin Carolan, Jason NE Varuhas and Sarah Fulham-McQuillan

PART I
THE MAKING OF PUBLIC LAW IN THE COMMON LAW WORLD

1. *A Court and the World* *9*
Donal O'Donnell

2. *The Power of Narrative – Shaping Aotearoa New Zealand's Public Law* *29*
Helen Winkelmann

3. *Justice Devolved – Milestones in Northern Ireland Constitutional Law Since 2010* *51*
Siobhan Keegan

4. *Making and Re-Making of Public Law: The Canadian Way* *69*
Sheilah L Martin

5. *The Building of South Africa's Constitution on the Ruins of its Past: The Remodelling of Public Law in Post-Apartheid South Africa* *85*
Steven Majiedt

6. *Double Act: Assessing Constitutional Entrenchment and Codification in the Re-Making of Administrative Law in Democratic South Africa* *109*
Catherine O'Regan

7. *South Africa's Transformative Constitution as 'Non-Reformist Reform'?* *121*
Nomfundo Ramalekana

PART II
MAKING PUBLIC LAW IN THE COMMON LAW TRADITION

8. *The Beginnings of Judicial Review* *147*
John Baker

9. *Good Counsel as a Constitutional Imperative* *165*
Janet McLean

10. *Private Rights and Public Wrongs* *185*
Brian Murray

11. *Long Waves of Constitutional Principle in the Common Law* 203
Philip Sales

12. *Why Does Ireland Have a System of Judicial Review of Legislation? The Legacy of the Irish Free State Constitution of 1922* 221
Gerard Hogan

PART III
RE-MAKING PUBLIC LAW: CONTEMPORARY CHALLENGES AND THE FUTURE

13. *Legislating for Emergencies: Insights from the Pandemic* 233
Cheryl Saunders

14. *Administrative Law and the Pandemic* 247
Gillian E Metzger

15. *Populism and Administrative Law* 271
Carol Harlow and Richard Rawlings

16. *Populism and Constitutional Democracy: Feature or Bug?* 297
Neil Walker

17. *'You Can't Go Home Again': Constitutional Fidelity and Change in Post-Brexit Britain* 315
Colm Ó Cinnéide

18. *Public Faces: Indigenous Law Today and Through the Futuristic Looking Glass* 335
Val Napoleon

19. *Public Law and the Future: A Sustainable Jurisprudence?* 353
Peter C Oliver

Index 381

List of Contributors

Sir John Baker is Downing Professor Emeritus of the Laws of England at the University of Cambridge, UK.

Eoin Carolan is Professor at University College Dublin, Ireland.

Sarah Fulham-McQuillan is Assistant Professor at University College Dublin, Ireland.

Carol Harlow is Emeritus Professor at London School of Economics, UK.

Gerard Hogan is a Justice of the Supreme Court of Ireland.

Dame Siobhan Keegan is the Lady Chief Justice of Northern Ireland.

Janet McLean is Professor at the University of Auckland, New Zealand.

Steven Majiedt is a Justice of the Constitutional Court of South Africa.

Sheilah L Martin is a Justice of the Supreme Court of Canada.

Gillian E Metzger is Harlan Fiske Stone Professor of Constitutional Law at Columbia University, USA.

Brian Murray is a Justice of the Supreme Court of Ireland.

Val Napoleon is Professor and Law Foundation Chair of Indigenous Justice and Governance at the University of Victoria, Canada.

Colm Ó Cinnéide is Professor at University College London, UK.

Donal O'Donnell is the Chief Justice of Ireland.

Catherine O'Regan is Director of the Bonavero Institute of Human Rights at the University of Oxford, UK.

Peter C Oliver is Professor at the University of Ottawa, Canada.

Nomfundo Ramalekana is a Senior Lecturer at the University of Cape Town, South Africa.

Richard Rawlings is Professor of Public Law at University College London, UK.

Philip Sales (Lord Sales) is a Justice of the UK Supreme Court.

Cheryl Saunders is Laureate Professor Emeritus at the University of Melbourne, Australia.

Jason NE Varuhas is Professor at the University of Melbourne, Australia.

Neil Walker is Regius Professor of Public Law and the Law of Nature and Nations at the University of Edinburgh, UK.

Dame Helen Winkelmann is the Chief Justice of New Zealand.

Introduction

EOIN CAROLAN, JASON NE VARUHAS AND
SARAH FULHAM-McQUILLAN

THIS COLLECTION ORIGINATES from the 2022 Public Law Conference, a major international conference hosted by the Centre for Constitutional Studies at University College Dublin, and co-organised by University College Dublin and the University of Melbourne. The title of this collection, *The Making and Re-Making of Public Law*, mirrors the conference theme, and invites engagement with a range of issues concerning how public law in common law systems develops and changes over time.

The 2022 Public Law Conference was the fourth in an ongoing biennial series of major international conferences. Previous conferences have been held in Cambridge, in 2014 and 2016, and Melbourne in 2018. The 2020 conference was to be held in Ottawa, but was cancelled due to the global pandemic. We are therefore delighted that Ottawa is the host of the 2024 conference.

This collection is the fourth book in an ongoing series, following on from those collections from the previous conferences: *Public Law Adjudication in Common Law Systems: Process and Substance*,[1] *The Unity of Public Law? Doctrinal, Theoretical and Comparative Perspectives*,[2] and *The Frontiers of Public Law*.[3]

The motivation for the Public Law Conference series is to provide a leading international forum for public lawyers from a broad range of jurisdictions to discuss and debate the most important public law issues facing common law jurisdictions, and through this enterprise to foster a community of public lawyers drawn from multiple jurisdictions and from the academy, judiciary, practice and government. The sense of community, collegiality and intellectual fellowship that has grown up around the conference series has become one of its defining features.

The conference series moves around the common law world, being held in a different place each time. Moving the conference carries forward the goals of the series, bringing in a wider range of perspectives and participants from different jurisdictions and focusing attention on public law issues pertinent to different countries and regions.

* * *

With the 2022 conference being the first time the Public Law Conference had been held in Ireland, the conference's focus on the making and re-making of public law was apt.

[1] J Bell, M Elliott, JNE Varuhas and P Murray (eds), *Public Law Adjudication in Common Law Systems: Process and Substance* (Hart Publishing, 2016).

[2] M Elliott, JNE Varuhas and S Wilson Stark (eds), *The Unity of Public Law? Doctrinal, Theoretical and Comparative Perspectives* (Hart Publishing, 2018).

[3] JNE Varuhas and S Wilson Stark (eds), *The Frontiers of Public Law* (Hart Publishing, 2020).

2022 was the centenary of both Ireland's independence and its first Constitution.[4] The conference formed one of a series of events through 2022 which marked this important anniversary, with the significance of the conference acknowledged by its inclusion in the official national programme of centenary events.

For an event rooted in the common law tradition, this was a centenary of particular interest. Events in Ireland up to and including 1922 had implications for public law in many of the other common law jurisdictions represented at the conference and in this collection. It was, for example, in the context of the Treaty between the United Kingdom (UK) and Ireland, and debates on that agreement in the UK House of Commons, that the concept and precise scope of 'Dominion status' came to be first discussed (and contested) in constitutional terms.[5] That Ireland's relationship with Britain descended into conflict, military action and ultimately independence was a striking development for Westminster, the empire and their respective authority.[6] Yet, equally, the fact the Treaty compelled Ireland's efforts to move from Free State to full independence by a gradual and incrementalist expansion in what it meant to be a self-governing Dominion meant that Ireland's efforts had not just symbolic but also practical legal consequences for other common law jurisdictions.[7] McDonagh, for example, has argued that 'Ireland became an influential legal and political reference point for later British/Dominion constitutional arrangements over a wide range of issues'.[8]

Moreover, the efforts by Ireland in and after 1922 to develop, apply and adapt a model of written constitutionalism to a common law culture was also influential in several states that were later confronted with the same challenge, some of whom engaged in a degree of constitutional borrowing from elements of the Irish experience. In fact, a volume on *Select Constitutions of the World* which was prepared for the Irish Constituent Assembly in 1922 was widely circulated amongst countries which were instituting a written constitution in the post-1922 and (in particular) post-1945 periods. The volume was specifically relied on in a number of jurisdictions such as India and Burma when they came to draft their own first constitutions.[9]

There were also several aspects of how Ireland came to diverge from the common law tradition that, in some respects, anticipated the questions and challenges which would arise for public lawyers in the century to follow. While the 1922 Constitution retained Westminster's effectively fused model of executive-legislative relations, it also marked a significant break with the Diceyan model of parliamentary supremacy. It not only included a guarantee of fundamental rights but also made provision for referendums

[4] On which, see L Cahillane and DK Coffey (eds), *The Centenary of the Irish Free State Constitution* (Palgrave MacMillan, 2024).

[5] P Oliver, '"Dominion Status": History, Framework and Context' (2019) 17 (4) *International Journal of Constitutional Law* 1173–91.

[6] DK Coffey, '1916, 1921 and the "Destruction of the Legal Unity of the British Empire"' (2016) *Dublin University Law Journal*.

[7] T Mohr, 'George Gavan Duffy and the Irish Free State on the International Stage, 1921–1923' (2021) 32 *Irish Studies in International Affairs* 261–78.

[8] L McDonagh, 'Losing Ireland, Losing the Empire: Dominion Status and the Irish Constitutions of 1922 and 1937' (2019) 17 (4) *International Journal of Constitutional Law* 1192–1212.

[9] DK Coffey, 'The Drafting of the Constitution of the Union of Burma in 1947: Dominion Status, Indo–Burmese Relations, and the Irish Example' (2023) 41 *Law and History Review* 253–72.

to be held, thereby acknowledging an ongoing role for the People as the sovereign and constituent power. These conceptual and practical tensions between parliamentary and popular sovereignty, legal and political constitutionalism, plebiscitary will and political representation, and constituent and constituted power continue, of course, to be prominent in our public law debates.

The conference theme had additional and specific resonance, however, given the political, legal and social circumstances in which independence and the 1922 Constitution came to be. Ireland, at the time, was emerging from a military conflict with a colonial power while still experiencing the ongoing effects of a divisive civil war over the future of the state and its relationship with that power. The leaders of the fledgling state were faced with the significant challenge of, in effect, creating the structures for a new nation. In the first months and years of independence, the Provisional Government would have to draft a new Constitution,[10] pass legislation to establish an entirely new court structure,[11] devise new systems of electing and organising local and central government,[12] construct and regulate a variety of new public agencies,[13] establish new defence and police forces,[14] create and regulate a new civil service[15] – and, in at least some of these matters, secure the agreement of a Westminster Government which was anxious about the implications of Irish actions for the empire.

Moreover, they had to do so in a context where there were deep divisions over questions of national, religious and constitutional identity; and residual uncertainty over the precise legal relationship between an independent Ireland (or Free State as it was formally known), the new Northern Ireland, Britain and the empire. Amongst the myriad tasks confronting them were formal ones like the drafting of a new constitution, the creation and design of novel governing structures and the establishment of a new judiciary and court system; as well as more political but equally pressing concerns such as how – especially in the face of identitarian divisions and recent social conflict – to secure and maintain the authority and legitimacy of the new state and these structures.

These are questions that recur and resonate across time and jurisdictions as public law is forced to adapt to changes in the social, political and constitutional context of the structures and territories to which it applies. How is a system of public law established? How does public law generally, or the common law tradition in particular, adapt to local context, indigenous culture or historical traditions? By what methods, or through which actors, should it be developed? How is it legitimised? How is that legitimacy maintained? How does it deal with constitutional transitions or transformations? Can it, or should it, adapt to social and political changes? How does public law deal with radical challenges to its sovereignty or authority? What role do theories or claims to sovereign and constituent authority play? How are the People represented within the system? What are the methods

[10] Constitution of the Irish Free State (Saorstát Éireann) Act 1922.
[11] Courts of Justice Act 1924.
[12] Local Government Electors Registration Act 1924.
[13] Fisheries Act 1924.
[14] Garda Siochana (Temporary Provisions) Act 1923; Defence Forces (Temporary Provisions) Act 1923; Garda Siochana Act 1924.
[15] Civil Service Regulation Act 1923; Ministers and Secretaries Act 1924.

and processes by which popular engagement can be encouraged or controlled? How does, or should, a public law system treat minority or other under-represented views? How can common law systems adapt to a post-colonial or post-imperial political settlement? These are all issues that confronted Ireland in 1922; and that continue to challenge public law and its practitioners a century on.

These persistent questions underpinned many of the papers presented at the conference, and are engaged with in this collection. The chapters that follow present varied perspectives on these same challenges, including finding common ground and building consensus in the face of social change, fragmentation of values, and political division and conflict. The chapters consider how public law and public lawyers can, across different times and contexts, respond to such challenges with appeals to narrative, identity or notions of sovereignty, democracy or constitutional fidelity, as well as more formal techniques of legal structure, process or adjudication.

* * *

Turning to the collection itself, the chapters are organised into three Parts, which broadly reflect three key themes relating to how public law develops and changes in common law systems, that is, how it is made and re-made, though all three themes find reflection throughout the collection. The three themes are: (i) *plurality*: the plural nature of public law across the common law world, including variety in the different contextual forces that have shaped legal development in different jurisdictions; (ii) *the common law tradition*: while there is significant variety across the common law world, there are also commonalities associated with a shared common law tradition, which includes historical, substantive and methodological dimensions; and (iii) *contemporary challenges and the future*: examining challenges of context and conflict faced across common law jurisdictions, how public law has responded, and how public law might best be adapted or re-imagined.

The chapters in Part I address the making of public law in the common law world. They chart trajectories of legal development in different parts of the common law world, and the ways in which contextual features of each jurisdiction have shaped that legal development so as to produce distinct variants of common law public law. The narratives that emerge reinforce the importance of contextual features in shaping and also understanding the law of particular jurisdictions, but there are also, at a higher level of abstraction, common themes that emerge about the nature of legal change within common law systems.

Part II addresses the making of public law in the common law tradition. The chapters interrogate core aspects of public law in the common law tradition, including formative stages in the early history of common law public law (as much to understand core aspects of the tradition as to inform the future), the historical absence of a public-private division in the common law tradition, and how constitutional change occurs according to common law method.

Part III addresses the re-making of public law, interrogating how public law in common law systems has responded to and can be adapted to meet contemporary and future challenges of context and conflict, from calls to better integrate Indigenous traditions and minority identity; to efforts to preserve legal and democratic unity in the face of division and discord over issues such as COVID-19, climate change, or populism.

* * *

The significance of the Irish centenary, and of having the conference at University College Dublin during the centenary year, was reflected in the generous support given by a number of parties to the event. The conference was supported by the Government of Ireland under the Decade of Centenaries Programme 2012–2023; by University College Dublin under its own Decade of Centenaries Programme; and by the University College Dublin Centre for Constitutional Studies funding scheme.

We are also extremely grateful to the Department of An Taoiseach and the Department of Tourism, Culture, Arts, Gaeltacht, Sport and Media for their assistance in securing St Partrick's Hall in Dublin Castle as a venue for part of the conference programme. Given this was the seat of British imperial power in Ireland, and the site of the formal handover of power to the new Provisional Government in 1922, this was an especially meaningful venue for the conference programme.

The conference also benefitted from the generous support of Mason Hayes and Curran LLP, a major law firm with offices in Dublin, San Francisco, New York and London and which has a leading presence in public law and litigation in Ireland and elsewhere. Mason Hayes and Curran were the sponsors of the conference welcome reception, and we very much appreciate their support.

We are grateful to Hart Publishing, the principal sponsor of the 2022 Public Law Conference, for its ongoing commitment to, and support of the conference series. Hart played a critical role in the establishment of the conference series, has been the principal sponsor of each conference in the series, and has published an edited collection from each conference. In particular we have greatly appreciated the support of Sinead Moloney, Hart's Director and General Manager, Kate Whetter, Senior Commissioning Editor, and Verity Stuart, Assistant Editor. We are delighted that Hart were present at and exhibited at the conference, and that Kate addressed the conference delegates at the opening plenary session.

In terms of the organisation of the event, we would like to thank a number of people whose support and efforts were critical to its success. In University College Dublin, the events team from the Sutherland School of Law, especially Una Kelly and Laura McLoughlin, were enormously supportive over the many months of preparation. The Dean of the School of Law, Niamh Howlin, and the University's then Vice-President of Research (and now President), Professor Orla Feely, were also very supportive throughout, for which we are immensely grateful. Felicitas Odemer and Ronan Flood from Advantage Group handled the logistics and administrative organisation of the event, and did so with dedication, professionalism and good humour.

The Public Law Conference continues its strong commitment to supporting and promoting the work of early career scholars. In common with previous conferences the 2022 conference included dedicated doctoral panels, and a fee-waiver programme for doctoral speakers. The Richard Hart Prize for the best paper by an early career scholar, first established at the 2016 conference, was again offered at the 2022 conference. We are grateful to Mr Richard Hart, the founder of Hart Publishing, for his continued support of the prize. The 2022 winner was Sam Bookman, a SJD candidate at Harvard Law School, for his paper entitled 'Creativity and Climate Rights in Common Law Jurisdictions: A Comparative Analysis'. The runner-up was Meghan Finn, a doctoral candidate at the University of Witwatersrand, for her paper entitled 'Reconstituting the Public/Private Divide in South African Anti-Discrimination Law'. We are grateful to the members of the judging panel: Professor Cora Hoexter (University of Witwatersrand), Lord Sales (UK Supreme Court) and Mr Justice Brian Murray (Irish Supreme Court).

Finally, we would also like to express our sincere appreciation to the Chief Justice of Ireland, Mr Justice Donal O'Donnell, and his colleague on the Supreme Court, Mr Justice Brian Murray, for their generosity and hospitality in hosting a welcome lunch for participants in the conference at the Honourable Society of King's Inns.

Part I

The Making of Public Law in the Common Law World

1

A Court and the World

DONAL O'DONNELL

I. COURTS IN AN INTERCONNECTED WORLD

IN OTHER CIRCUMSTANCES, the title of this chapter might risk an action for passing-off as, given the substitution of the indefinite for the definite article, it copies the title of a relatively recent book published by then Justice Stephen Breyer, then a justice of the United States (US) Supreme Court.[1] The book, which was published in 2015 to respectful reviews, was written against a backdrop of a debate that had arisen in the US Supreme Court at that time. It had been contended by a number of Justice Breyer's colleagues that the US Supreme Court should not entertain the citation of authorities from other jurisdictions. *The Court and the World* is a book-length scholarly response, which commences by detailing those areas of law where the US Supreme Court necessarily deals with matters either beyond the territorial limits of the US or within those limits, but which are nevertheless affected by events, and consequently law, outside its boundaries. Examples include the exercise of the Executive Power in respect of foreign relations, the treaty power and its impact upon law within the federal and state system, international commercial transactions, the alien tort statute and the capacity to sue in the US for breaches occurring outside the States, child custody and family law matters which necessarily cross borders and may require interaction and cooperation with foreign jurisdictions, investment treaties protecting investments by US companies outside the US, and offering corresponding protection to foreign companies investing in that jurisdiction. The theme of the book is that, in an ever-increasingly interconnected world, where issues of commerce, protection of the environment and security give rise to problems which can only be dealt with on an international and supranational scale, it is not feasible or, if feasible, not sensible, to attempt to deal with such matters in a form of splendid isolation from other legal systems. Justice Breyer also discusses the benefits he has found in his annual engagement with judges and academic lawyers from other jurisdictions and explains why he disagrees with the argument that the US courts should not have regard to decisions from other constitutional courts.[2]

[1] S Breyer, *The Court and the World: American Law and the New Global Realities* (Knopf, 2015).
[2] ibid 254–62.

II. IRELAND'S LEGAL ECONOMY

Ireland, we are often told, is a small open economy which has benefited from world trade and is both particularly open to influence and susceptible to change from developments in other economies. To a large extent this is true also of the legal economy. Ireland was the 'first adventure of the common law',[3] which arrived in Ireland with the Normans after 1169. Article 8 of the Act of Union (Ireland) 1800 provided that appeals from the Irish courts lay to the House of Lords.[4] The decisions of that body were thereafter formally binding on the Irish courts, but the decisions of other courts in the rest of the United Kingdom (UK) were also treated as having a high degree of persuasive authority in the Irish courts. Even after independence in 1922, the continued application of the common law in the Free State and, perhaps, the prevalence of textbooks published in the UK, meant that authority, which was now technically foreign and persuasive only, was nevertheless regularly cited, analysed and often applied in the Irish courts. Even when there was, from the 1960s onwards, a very conscious attempt to assert a form of national independence in legal matters, that only resulted in the citation of additional authority from more jurisdictions rather than a retreat towards isolation. Accession to the European Union (EU) and the increase in importance of the European Convention on Human Rights (ECHR) have both been credited with encouraging changes in Ireland in areas such as social matters, gender equality, and the protection of the environment, but have also provided opportunities for lawyers so that there is a relatively high degree of communication with, and interaction between, the Irish courts, the Court of Justice of the European Union (CJEU) and the European Court of Human Rights (ECtHR).[5] In addition, graduates of Irish universities have increasingly studied abroad and sometimes pursued careers as practising lawyers or academics in other legal systems.

III. PROPORTIONALITY: A CASE STUDY OF INTERNATIONAL JURISPRUDENTIAL INFLUENCE

Returning to *The Court and the World* then, after demonstrating the degree to which international matters are unavoidably part of the everyday function of the Court, Justice Breyer offers a particular example (which, to me at least, seems slightly underwhelming) of a positive benefit that might accrue to the US system if it were more open to developments in other jurisdictions.[6] He suggests that the concept of proportionality as applied in the law of the EU might usefully be employed in the analysis of cases under the First Amendment.[7] While acknowledging that the application of proportionality analysis 'may seem in part subjective', he argues that the balancing exercise, whereby the judge 'inevitably considers countervailing effects, degrees of harm and of importance', is made more explicit and transparent so that it can be seen and criticised.[8] I lack the

[3] WJ Johnson, 'The First Adventure of the Common Law' (1920) 36 *LQR* 9.
[4] S Henchy, 'Precedent in the Irish Supreme Court' (1962) 25 *MLR* 544.
[5] Breyer (n 1) 254.
[6] ibid 254–62.
[7] ibid 254.
[8] ibid 257.

expertise to analyse whether the proportionality analysis would provide better results, either in substance, or in the process by which they are arrived at, than those made under the approach which has grown up incrementally in the US, but I think anyone familiar with the operation of proportionality in those jurisdictions where it is regularly adopted might think that there is an element of 'far-off fields' about the argument. However, since proportionality analysis is employed in Irish courts, in large part due to the influence of developments in other jurisdictions, it provides a useful departure point for my consideration of some broader issues.

As it happens, the concept of proportionality as assisting the analysis of the consistency of any challenged legislation with the requirements of the Constitution can be found at a relatively early stage in Irish law, and in one of the landmark cases on the development of our constitutional jurisprudence: *Ryan v Attorney General* (*Ryan*),[9] where Kenny J said that a court could interfere with and set aside legislation where '[t]here is no reasonable proportion between the benefit which the legislation will confer on the citizens or a substantial body of them and the interference with the personal rights of the citizen'.[10] But the suggestion, if that is what it was, was not taken up in the immediate aftermath of *Ryan* and the widespread use of proportionality as a tool of analysis can generally be traced to the judgment of Costello J (as he then was) in the High Court in *Heaney v Ireland* (*Heaney*),[11] and an extra-judicial article by the same judge entitled 'Limiting Rights Constitutionally'.[12]

In *Heaney*, Costello J adopted a proportionality test, observing that

> … the courts in this country and elsewhere have found it helpful to apply the test of proportionality, a test which contains the notions of minimal restraint on the exercise of protected rights, and of the exigencies of the common good in a democratic society.[13]

He noted that it had been adopted by the ECtHR, citing *The Sunday Times v United Kingdom*,[14] and that the test had recently been formulated by the Supreme Court of Canada in *R v Chaulk* (*Chaulk*),[15] in terms which he adopted:

> The objective of the impugned provision must be of sufficient importance to warrant overriding a constitutionally protected right. It must relate to concerns pressing and substantial in a free and democratic society. The means chosen must pass the proportionality test. They must: (a) be rationally connected to the objective and not be arbitrary, unfair or based on irrational considerations; (b) impair the right as little as possible, and (c) be such that their effects on rights are proportional to the objective.[16]

Here we have, therefore, a very clear example of what Justice Breyer hoped for in the US: the adoption of the test of proportionality, by an explicit reference to international authority, in this case looking to the east in the shape of the ECtHR and to the north in

[9] *Ryan v Attorney General* [1965] IR 294.

[10] ibid 313.

[11] *Heaney v Ireland* [1994] 3 IR 593.

[12] D Costello, 'Limiting Rights Constitutionally' in J O' Reilly (ed), *Human Rights and Constitutional Law: Essays in Honour of Brian Walsh* (Round Hall Press, 1992).

[13] Heaney (n 11) 607.

[14] *The Sunday Times v United Kingdom* [1979] 58 ILR 490.

[15] *R v Chaulk* [1990] 3 SCR 1303, 1335–36.

[16] *Heaney* (n 11) 607.

the shape of the Canadian Supreme Court, but, as is evident from Justice Breyer's discussion, the Court might as easily have looked to the CJEU, and, if his suggestion had been adopted and acted upon, the decisions of the US Supreme Court.[17]

At this point, it is worth noting a curious feature of the *Heaney* decision. Anyone familiar with the jurisprudence of the Supreme Court of Canada will be aware that the proportionality test in that jurisdiction can be traced to the major early Canadian Charter of Rights and Freedoms case, *R v Oakes* (*Oakes*).[18] *Chaulk* is a relatively minor case which merely adopts and applies the *Oakes* test in the context of criminal law, which was of course the context in which *Heaney* was decided.

Heaney was approved on appeal by the Irish Supreme Court.[19] This marked the introduction of proportionality into the mainstream of constitutional analysis in this jurisdiction, and it was adopted and applied enthusiastically, and almost routinely, thereafter. It was observed from time to time that the test was applied with varying degrees of rigour, sometimes relatively loosely, when it seemed almost a synonym for reasonableness, and sometimes very strictly. One observer noted that in Canadian jurisprudence the proportionality test is a form of strict scrutiny which involves quite a structured analysis, whereas in Ireland the overall application of the test was more fluid and not as demanding.[20]

Almost inevitably this percolated into the jurisprudence of the Irish courts. Perhaps the most obvious point of difference between the Canadian jurisprudence on proportionality and the application of the test in Ireland was the fact that, in Canada, the onus of proof is reversed. In essence, once it was established that the Canadian Charter-protected right was affected by a provision, the onus shifted to the State party, whether federal or provincial, to prove that the interference was proportionate, that it was justified by concerns pressing and substantial on a free society, that it was rationally connected to the objective, not arbitrary, impaired the right as little as possible, and was proportionate to the objective.[21]

The possible distinction between the Canadian approach and that which was adopted in Ireland, was touched on in two Supreme Court cases, *PJ Carroll & Co v Minister for Health and Children*[22] and *Fleming v Ireland* (*Fleming*)[23] without being resolved. It might be noted that both of these cases are examples of what might be described as horizontal subject matter comparison: in each case, the subject matter of the proceedings (prohibition on tobacco advertising, on the one hand, and a right to die, on the other) was an area in which there was existing Canadian authority dealing with the same issue by reference to the Canadian Charter.[24] The subject matter appears to have brought the doctrinal approach to the attention of the Irish courts, rather than the other way around.

[17] Breyer (n 1) 257.
[18] *R v Oakes* [1986] 1 SCR 103.
[19] *Heaney v Ireland* [1996] 1 IR 580, [1997] 1 ILRM 117.
[20] D Kenny, 'Proportionality and the Inevitability of the Local: A Comparative Localist Analysis of Canada and Ireland' (2018) 66 *American Journal of Comparative Law* 537; D Kenny, 'Proportionality, the Burden of Proof, Some Signs of Reconsideration (2014) 52 *The Irish Jurist* 141.
[21] Kenny, 'Proportionality and the Inevitability of the Local' (n 20) 557–58.
[22] *PJ Carroll & Co v Minister for Health and Children* [2006] IESC 36, [2006] 3 IR 431.
[23] *Fleming v Ireland* [2013] IESC 19, [2013] 2 IR 417.
[24] See *RJR-MacDonald Inc v Canada (Attorney General)* [1995] 3 SCR 199 (Tobacco Advertising); *Carter v Canada (Attorney General)* [2015] 1 SCR 331 (Right to Die).

In the event, the Irish courts were cautious about adopting the Canadian approach. In *Fleming*, a Divisional Court of the High Court had appeared to accept that an onus shifted to the State to justify any limitation, but this was disapproved of by the Supreme Court, which said:

> … an argument was advanced, derived it appears from Canadian jurisprudence, suggesting that the court should approach the question by first determining in general whether a right existed, whereupon the onus shifted to the State to justify by evidence any limitation whatsoever on the general right asserted, by reference to the principle of proportionality … It should be observed that there is no support in the jurisprudence of this Court for such an approach. Accordingly, this court expressly reserves for a case in which the issue properly and necessarily arises, and is the subject of focussed argument and express decision in the High Court, whether the approach to proportionality urged by the appellant … is required by, or compatible with, the Constitution.[25]

The issue has arisen and been considered in two Supreme Court appeals, in which decisions have been delivered recently: *Donnelly & ors v The Minister for Social Protection & Ors* (*Donnelly*)[26] and *O'Doherty & Waters v The Minister for Health & ors* (*O'Doherty*).[27] In both cases, the Supreme Court decisively refused to follow the Canadian approach. The Court set out a number of reasons for coming to its conclusion:

- In the first place, the point was not as clear cut in Canadian Charter jurisprudence as might be thought.
- Onus-shifting in Canada was derived from a textual analysis of the Canadian Charter provisions which were structured as a guarantee of certain fundamental rights subject to a limitation contained in section 1 of the Canadian Charter which guaranteed such rights 'subject only to such reasonable limits prescribed by law as can be demonstrably justified in a free and democratic society'. This naturally suggested that limitations had to be demonstrably justified and that the burden of so demonstrating lay on the State. There was, however, no basis for importing such an approach into the different text and structure of the Irish Constitution, and to do so could strain credibility and undermine legitimacy.
- As Professor Peter Hogg, in his book *Constitutional Law of Canada* pointed out, there is a connection between the scope of the right protected and the extent of a limitation on that right.[28] Rights may be broadly expressed but subject to broad limitation, or narrowly expressed and subject to very limited qualification. The end point in terms of the extent of the right protected may be exactly the same, whichever approach is taken, but it is dangerous to mix the approaches.
- The onus-shifting approach is, and was recognised by Canadian authority, as incompatible with any presumption of constitutionality. However, the presumption of constitutionality had been established in Irish jurisprudence almost since the enactment of the Constitution; it can be traced to *Pigs Marketing Board v Donnelly*,[29] which was the first case in which a statute was challenged under the new Constitution.

[25] *Fleming* (n 23) [140].
[26] *Donnelly & ors v The Minister for Social Protection & Ors* [2022] IESC 31.
[27] *O'Doherty & Waters v The Minister for Health & ors* [2022] IESC 32.
[28] P Hogg, *Constitutional Law of Canada*, 5th edn (Thomson Carswell, 2007) 38.4–38.5.
[29] *Pigs Marketing Board v Donnelly* [1939] IR 413.

- The presumption of constitutionality in Irish law has been deduced from the separation of powers identified in the Constitution. It would, therefore, be a significant alteration of the perceived balance of the separation of powers established by the Constitution to alter that.
- The Canadian approach had further consequences for the traditional model of adversarial adjudication which applied in Ireland and was arguably contemplated by Article 34 of the Constitution. Thus, it was accepted in Canadian jurisprudence that courts should distinguish between primary facts, and what were described as social facts or legislative facts which did not require proof in the same way. Furthermore, findings of fact by a trial court were not subject to the same deference in Canadian Charter litigation, and appellate courts had greater liberty to substitute their own conclusions for those of the trial courts.[30] These are substantial differences from the established practice of the Irish courts.

These were all powerful considerations against the simple adoption of the Canadian approach. However, advocates of that approach suggested that it avoided the possibility of injustice. The judgments of the Supreme Court doubted, however, that a shifting of the onus of proof would be of significant practical benefit in resolving cases in fact, and that plaintiff challenges would not be significantly disadvantaged by requiring them to discharge the onus of proof. All of this casts the omission in *Heaney* of any reference to *Oakes* in a different light. It may be that Costello J was cautious about fully embracing the *Oakes* test.

The outcome of both *Donnelly* and *O'Doherty* might, at a superficial level, look like the approach advocated recently in the US Supreme Court (and which Justice Breyer criticised), of a reluctance to consider or follow foreign precedent. However, on closer analysis, this reading does not hold up. The reasoning of the Supreme Court in *O'Doherty* was heavily reliant on a detailed consideration of the Canadian jurisprudence and influenced, in particular, by academic commentary such as that contained in the magisterial work of the late Professor Peter Hogg.[31] While the particular argument failed, the conclusion of the Supreme Court is not consistent with a position of 'less foreign law'; if anything, its lesson is that such arguments require *more* analysis of foreign jurisprudence. The cases show a move from a basic comparative analysis looking only at decisions on similar subject matter, towards more detailed consideration of the jurisprudence cited so as to understand those cases against the background of the foreign legal system.

IV. IRELAND'S OUTWARD-LOOKING COURTS OF THE 1960s AND 1970s

Mention of the US Supreme Court brings me to another aspect of this topic. While, at one level, it could be said that Irish courts have always been open to influence by foreign jurisprudence in the sense that Irish courts generally received and applied the common law decisions of UK courts, that was a largely passive exercise which became increasingly recognised as such, and as undesirable, in the period which followed independence.

[30] Hogg (n 28) 60.2.
[31] ibid.

The 1960s saw an upsurge in activity in the Irish Supreme Court during the period it was presided over by Chief Justice Cearbhall Ó Dálaigh. This period was characterised by increasing scepticism of authority from the UK, a strong insistence on the independence and integrity of national jurisprudence, and a very deliberate invocation of the decisions of courts of other jurisdictions, the US Supreme Court in particular.

These pressures were building up in the early 1960s and the dam burst in a memorable case in 1964. The received wisdom among lawyers was that Chief Justice Ó Dálaigh was a quiet, cultured, and polite man, but it is said that he was red in the face with anger when reading the judgment in *State (Quinn) v Ryan*.[32] The case involved a man arrested on foot of a British warrant but who had succeeded in securing his release. He was then removed from the jurisdiction of the Irish courts by arrangement between An Garda Síochána and members of the British Police Force to permit his prosecution in Great Britain. He had been taken by car to Northern Ireland and handed over there to members of the Royal Ulster Constabulary and transferred to England for prosecution. There was no doubt that this course had been taken to avoid a further application for *habeas corpus*. However, the arrangements which then operated for the surrender of suspects to the UK were contained in a pre-independence statute, ie, section 29 of the Petty Sessions (Ireland) Act 1851 (the 1851 Act), and which permitted what was described as the 'backing of British warrants' in Ireland and the immediate removal of the person sought to the jurisdiction of the courts in Great Britain and vice versa and so this course was, on the face of it, lawful. As Ó Dálaigh CJ said, the speedy removal of the individual was the purpose of the Act when it was enacted:

> Ireland was then part of the entity known as the United Kingdom of Great Britain and Ireland and was in enjoyment of the benefits of the Act of Union. One of these benefits was the free interchange of alleged offenders subject to the formality of local backing of warrants.[33]

As he said:

> the whole pattern (understandably in what was a homogenous political system) is a pattern of domestic dealing; and no question could arise of an arrested person not being in a position to have access to the courts; the Queen's courts were as much, if not more so, in Britain as in Ireland.[34]

Furthermore, the validity of this provision of the 1851 Act had been upheld in two decisions of the Supreme Court: *State (Dowling) v Kingston (No 2)*,[35] and *State (Duggan) v Tapley*.[36] This all appeared to add up to a formidable hurdle to any challenge, but the Supreme Court unanimously held that the provisions of section 29 of the 1851 Act were invalid having regard to the Constitution and that the Gardaí respondents were guilty of contempt of court. In what was, and is, a powerful statement of the impact of the Irish Constitution, Chief Justice Ó Dálaigh said:

> It was not the intention of the Constitution in guaranteeing the fundamental rights of the citizen that these rights should be set at nought or circumvented. The intention was that rights

[32] *State (Quinn) v Ryan* [1965] IR 70.
[33] ibid 119.
[34] ibid.
[35] *State (Dowling) v Kingston (No 2)* [1937] IR 699.
[36] *State (Duggan) v Tapley* [1952] IR 62.

> of substance were being assured to the individual and that the Courts were the custodians of these rights. As a necessary corollary it follows that no one can with impunity set these rights at nought or circumvent them, and that the Court's powers in this regard are as ample as the defence of the Constitution requires. Anyone who sets himself such a course is guilty of contempt of the Courts and is punishable accordingly.[37]

These comments sent seismic tremors through the Irish legal system. It is significant therefore that it was in this case that Walsh J also said:

> I reject the submission that because upon the foundation of the State our Courts took over an English legal system and the common law that the Courts must be deemed to have adopted and should now adopt an approach to Constitutional questions conditioned by English judicial methods and English legal training which despite their undoubted excellence were not fashioned for interpreting written constitutions or reviewing the constitutionality of legislation. In this State one would have expected that if the approach of any Court of final appeal of another State was to have been held up as an example for this Court to follow it would more appropriately have been the Supreme Court of the United States rather than the House of Lords.[38]

These sentiments illustrate much of the energy of the Supreme Court in that era and led both to the regular citation of US authority in Irish courts and a steady trickle of Irish lawyers choosing to pursue post-graduate studies in the US. The closeness of the connection, and the impact upon Irish law, can be illustrated by reference to perhaps two cases.

In *People v O'Brien*,[39] the Supreme Court had to consider the question of the exclusion of both illegally obtained evidence, and evidence which, it was contended, had been obtained in breach of a constitutional right. This involved a wide-ranging consideration of authority. The judgment of Walsh J made reference to several US authorities, including *Mapp v Ohio*,[40] and two later cases, *Silverman v US*[41] and *Fahy v Connecticut*[42] and a decision of the Supreme Court in *Stoner v State of California*,[43] which at that time was unreported and had been delivered on 23 March 1964. What is noteworthy about this, is that none of these cases were cited in argument, nor could they have been. They were all decided, and judgments delivered, in the period between the arguments in the Supreme Court and the eventual delivery of judgment.[44] This was in an era before the sort of instantaneous communication we now take for granted and, indeed, the extensive coverage of affairs in other countries (particularly the US) which is part of our daily lives.

This brings us to *McGee v Attorney General* (*McGee*),[45] decided almost a decade later and described recently, as a rose among many thorns in the constitutional jurisprudence of Ireland.[46] In December 1973, by a majority of four to one, the Supreme

[37] *State (Quinn) v Ryan* (n 32) 122.
[38] ibid 100 ILTR 105.
[39] *People v O'Brien* [1965] IR 142.
[40] *Mapp v Ohio* (1961) 367 US 643.
[41] *Silverman v US* (1961) 365 US 505.
[42] *Fahy v Connecticut* (1963) 375 US 85.
[43] *Stoner v State of California* (1964) 376 US 483.
[44] R Mac Cormaic, *The Supreme Court* (Penguin, 2016) 83 details the close relationship between Walsh J and Justice William Brennan and that Brennan sent Walsh three judgments on the exclusionary rule shortly after they met in 1963.
[45] *McGee v Attorney General* [1974] IR 283.
[46] B Dickson, *The Irish Supreme Court: Historical and Comparative Perspectives* (Oxford University Press, 2019).

Court held that the provisions of section 17 of the Criminal Law (Amendment) Act 1935, which prohibited the importation or sale of contraceptives, was unconstitutional. This case has particularly contemporary resonance because the US authority which was to the very forefront of the case was the decision of the US Supreme Court in *Griswold v Connecticut* (*Griswold*),[47] which has been much discussed recently. Counsel for the appellant, Mrs McGee, took what was then the unusual step of submitting a written summary of their submissions which was reproduced in the report of the case, and which made it clear that *Griswold* and *Eisenstadt v Baird* (*Eisenstadt*)[48] were central to their case:

> 11. The American Federal Supreme Court has ruled certain State laws against contraception to be unconstitutional as an invasion of the right of privacy of marriage people: *Poe v Ullman*; *Griswold v Connecticut: Eisenstadt v Baird.*
> 12. The same line of reasoning supports the authority claimed for parents at paragraph 5 and the rights claimed at paragraph 9.
> 13. The American cases also decided that laws which interfere with the family and with the private laws of married people require special justification. No such justification has been offered in the present case.[49]

However, the case is perhaps more significant for what authority was not cited. As we all know, *Roe v Wade* (*Roe*),[50] which relied on the precedents of *Griswold*[51] and *Eisenstadt* which had been decided earlier in that same year on 22 January 1973 and had made international headlines provoking immediate criticism from the US Catholic bishops and even the Vatican, all of which had been reported in Ireland.[52] *Griswold* was relied on by Henchy J in the majority judgment, but was even more obvious by its absence from the judgment of Walsh J who, while referring to *Poe v Ullman*,[53] *Griswold* and *Eisenstadt*, said

> my reason for not referring to them is not because I did not find them helpful or relevant, which indeed they were, but because I found it unnecessary to rely upon any of the dicta in those cases to support the views which I have expressed in this judgment.[54]

It seems plausible that this was an attempt both to protect the decision in *McGee* from the accusation that it was reliant on a line of jurisprudence which had led to *Roe*, and at the same time to seek to prevent the reasoning in *McGee* from being adapted and used to promote an argument in favour of a right to abortion.

While *McGee* is, therefore, an extremely important case in Irish constitutional law in its own right, it is also like a snapshot which gains significance because of the figures captured in the background; in this instance developments in US constitutional law at what has transpired to be a critical juncture in the development of the jurisprudence of the US Supreme Court, and its position in the culture and politics of the US.

[47] *Griswold v Connecticut* (1965) 381 US 479.
[48] *Griswold* and *Eisenstadt v Baird* (1972) 405 US 438.
[49] *McGee* (n 45) 295 (citations omitted).
[50] *Roe v Wade* (1973) 410 US 113.
[51] *Griswold* (n 47).
[52] Mac Cormaic (n 44) records that Brennan had arranged for Walsh to be sent a copy of all decisions of the US Supreme Court, so it is probable he had a copy of *Roe*.
[53] *Poe v Ullman* (1961) 367 US 497.
[54] *McGee* (n 45) 319.

V. LAW AND POLITICS

This brings us to the most recent book written by Justice Stephen Breyer: *The Authority of the Court and the Peril of Politics*.[55] In this book, Justice Breyer argues that, notwithstanding the sharp divisions in the Supreme Court, it is jurisprudential rather than political differences that divide the current members of the Supreme Court and that this is critical because the belief that law is just, even when it does not deliver the results for which you hope, is essential in creating legal obedience which every state requires. This was not as well received as *The Court and the World*. I was particularly struck by one criticism contained in an article, 'Politicians in Robes' in *The New York Review of Books* of 10 March 2022.[56] Commentary on legal matters, even in sophisticated reviews, tends to be at too high a level of generality to be of interest to a specialist public law audience, but this article was authored by Laurence Tribe, the 81-year-old constitutional scholar and author of *American Constitutional Law*,[57] and who has appeared on more than 30 occasions before the Supreme Court. The article is a stinging attack on Breyer and his book, describing it as containing 'a self-serving series of what can only be called platitudes' and showing 'apparent contempt for his readers' and most of all for not acknowledging that the decisions of the Supreme Court, including *Brown v Board of Education*[58] and other controversial cases, are 'basically expressions of political and moral views filtered through legal categories and conveyed in a legal voice'.[59]

Tribe also discusses the Presidential Commission on the Supreme Court of the US, on which he served. This was a body of constitutional scholars and lawyers which were requested by President Biden to consider various proposals to address concerns about the US Supreme Court, including enlarging the Court by adding new members;[60] imposing term limits on judges; requiring rotation between the Supreme Court and the lower Federal Courts; and creating separate chambers of the Supreme Court, requiring a super majority for invalidation of congressional acts, or indeed, removing that jurisdiction from the Supreme Court altogether. These and other proposals were described by the Commission as measures designed to 'reduce the power of the Supreme Court or of the judicial branch as a whole'[61] and 'designed to shift power to resolve major social political and cultural issues from the Court to the political branches'.[62] It is not, of course, unprecedented for such discussions to take place in the US, but it is still noteworthy that these matters have reached the level of a formal Presidential Commission asked to analyse and report upon the possible options.

[55] S Breyer, *The Authority of the Court and the Peril of Politics* (Harvard University Press, 2021).

[56] LH Tribe, 'Politicians in Robes' (*The New York Review of Books*, 10 March 2022), available at www.nybooks.com/articles/2022/03/10/politicians-in-robes-justice-breyer-tribe/?lp_txn_id=1391227. Tribe subsequently struck a more moderate tone in the same pages: LH Tribe, 'Constrain the Court – Without Crippling It' (*The New York Review of Books*, 17 August 2023), available at www.nybooks.com/articles/2023/08/17/constrain-the-court-without-crippling-it-laurence-h-tribe/.

[57] LH Tribe, *American Constitutional Law*, 3rd edn (The Foundation Press, 2000).

[58] *Brown v Board of Education* (1954) 347 US 483.

[59] Tribe, 'Politicians in Robes' (n 56).

[60] In this regard, the Commission included Ireland among one of its comparators.

[61] *Presidential Commission on the Supreme Court of the United States* (Final Report, December 2021) 8, available at www.whitehouse.gov/wp-content/uploads/2021/12/SCOTUS-Report-Final-12.8.21-1.pdf.

[62] ibid 9.

Tribe appears to consider that none of these proposals, however radical, are a sufficient remedy for the problem he sees in the current jurisprudential cast of the Supreme Court. Instead, he advances an almost apocalyptic view. Citing a number of scholars who gave evidence to the Commission,[63] he states:

> These scholars made a persuasive case that throughout our history, and especially in its current configuration, the Supreme Court has by no means been a friend to politically underrepresented minorities, an ally to the rights of the least powerful among us, or a defender of the rights of all to full and equal participation in the project of self-government – the only reasons sufficient, in the minds of many, to warrant entrusting a power so vast to so politically unaccountable an institution. They have argued that giving the nation's highest court not just the power of judicial review but of judicial supremacy – the final word on the meaning and application of a flawed by aspirational Constitution – has repeatedly been harmful to the cause of freedom and equality, with infamous decisions being the rule rather than the exception.[64]

This is a conclusion not merely that the Supreme Court in its current configuration is arriving at decisions of which these scholars profoundly disapprove, but a rereading of almost the entire history of the Supreme Court to conclude that the exercise of judicial review since *Marbury v Madison*[65] has been fundamentally harmful and damaging. *Brown v Board of Education* and the decisions of Chief Justice Earl Warren's court are, on this view, a lonely aberration, which cannot justify the power which the Court has exercised for more than 200 years.

Tribe must still address the fact that some recent decisions cannot fit neatly into an ideological box, perhaps most notably, the decision on same sex marriage, *Obergefell v Hodges*[66] or *Bostock v Clayton County*,[67] which has, Tribe observes, surprised most court observers when a statutory ban on discriminating on the basis of sex was held to cover anti-transgender discrimination. Tribe considers, however, that

> such decisions reveal only that the justices are, in the end, masters of their craft and know that their power requires them to act as lawyers. But the sad truth remains that 'law's constraints are no match for power's voracious appetite.[68]

These developments go some way to explain why decisions of the US Supreme Court are no longer cited in Irish courts as routinely as they were in the 60s and 70s: the paths have diverged in ways that might not have been foreseen then.

If so, this is important in its own way and raises a further question of the value of reference to jurisprudence from other jurisdictions. It might indeed be said to provide some support for those in the US Supreme Court, who took the view that the US courts should not consider the jurisprudence of other courts dealing with constitutional or human rights issues. To adapt an image employed by Justice Scalia in the context of statutory interpretation, the process of looking to foreign authority can be reduced all

[63] Nikolas Bowie, Michael Klarman and Samuel Moyn among others.

[64] On this reading, a series of much criticised cases, *Dred Scott v Sandford* (1856) 60 US 393; *Plessy v Ferguson* (1893) 163 US 537; *Lochner v New York* (1905) 198 US 45; *Korematsu v US* (1944) 323 US 214 become the rule rather than the exception.

[65] *Marbury v Madison* (1803) 5 US (1 Cranch) 137.

[66] *Obergefell v Hodges* (2015) 576 US 644.

[67] *Bostock v Clayton County* 590 US _, 140 S Ct 1731 (2020).

[68] Tribe, 'Politicians in Robes' (n 56).

too easily to a process of looking over a crowded room to find a few friends. Tribe's remark that 'the law's constraints are no match for power's voracious appetite' suggests that, while all lawyers share common values and in turn value certain skills, and that these values and skills might be thought to constrain judges' power to merely do what they want to do, those constraints are in the end no match for the irresistible gravitational pull of the prospect of the exercise of naked power. Moreover, Tribe appears to suggest that this is, in truth, what animated, and even more strikingly has always animated, the US Supreme Court.[69]

VI. THE UK EXPERIENCE

Coming closer to home, recently however, the position of the UK courts and, indeed, the ECtHR, have become an issue in political debate. In the UK, the Conservative Party manifesto before the last election promised to look at '... the broader aspects of our constitution: the relationship between the Government Parliament and the Courts ...'[70] and to '... update the Human Rights Act ... to ensure that there is a proper balance between the rights of individuals, our vital national security and effective government'.[71] In late November 2020, it was suggested that there were plans to reform the Supreme Court by measures such as replacing the current Supreme Court bench with a large pool of appeal judges, renaming the highest court as the upper Court of Appeal, or reverting to the appellate committee of the House of Lords.[72]

A Panel was established under the chairmanship of Sir Peter Gross, a retired judge of the Court of Appeal to review the operation of the Human Rights Act 1998 ('the 1998 Act'). The Panel included a distinguished Irish academic lawyer and held meetings with other courts including members of the Irish Supreme Court.[73] The report[74] made a number of interesting proposals which were reasonably uncontroversial and well received. It proposed an educational campaign to explain the function of the 1998 Act. More specifically it proposed a provision requiring domestic law remedies to be considered before considering remedies under the 1998 Act and, furthermore, that the UK should enter dialogue with other Convention states on the question of the extraterritorial application of the Convention, which it considered was a matter of concern. The majority of the members of the Panel stopped short, however, of recommending any change to the interpretative obligation under section 3 of the Act.[75] Nor did the majority of the Panel suggest any change to the approach to the margin of appreciation.

[69] ibid.

[70] Conservative and Unionist Party, *Manifesto 2019* (2019), available at www.conservatives.com/our-plan/conservative-party-manifesto-2019> accessed 07 November 2022.

[71] ibid.

[72] J Murphy, 'UK Supreme Court Reform: Combating Smoke with Fire' (*The Oxford University Undergraduate Law Journal Blog*, 5 July 2021), available at https://blogs.law.ox.ac.uk/ouulj/blog/2021/07/uk-supreme-court-reform-combating-smoke-fire.

[73] I was one of the members of the Court who met the Commission.

[74] The Panel of the Independent Human Rights Act Review, *The Independent Human Rights Act Review 2021* (December 2021).

[75] As interpreted and applied in *Ghaidan v Godin-Mendoza* [2004] UKHL 30.

Recently, however, the UK Supreme Court delivered an important judgment, *R (on the application of Elan – Cane) v Secretary of State for the Home Department*,[76] in which, in a judgment of Lord Reed, the Court disapproved of *dicta* in *Re G Adoption (unmarried couple)*[77] and concluded that the obligation was to treat the Act as a domestic or remedial regime in respect of the rights to which the UK was subject in international law under the ECHR. Interestingly, the judgment made reference to the Irish European Convention on Human Rights Act 2003 which explicitly defines domestic obligations imposed by reference to compatibility with the State's obligations under the Convention.[78]

More recently, the UK Government has introduced a Bill which would amend the 1998 Act.[79] It may be deduced from the terms of the Bill that the Government wishes to go further than the recommendations of the Independent Human Rights Act Review. The Bill would take some steps by further enhancing the obligation of the courts to give particular effect to freedom of speech, and also by providing further protection for journalistic sources. However, the thrust of the Bill is directed towards reversing the trend of interpretation and application of the 1998 Act. Perhaps most notably, the UK courts were to be precluded from going beyond Strasbourg case law in their interpretation of the Convention but would be permitted to depart from it. The Bill would also reverse the decision of the UK Supreme Court in *Ghaidan v Godin-Mendoza*[80] and limit the interpretive obligation under the Act to an interpretation where the words were, as a matter of law, capable of bearing the Convention compliant interpretation. If this was not possible, the Court could not go further, but would be limited to making a declaration of incompatibility.

These changes are not, perhaps, dramatic in themselves and it is not my function to discuss these proposals on their merits and it is not at all clear that they will proceed.[81] However, the detail of the change is perhaps less important than the direction of travel. It seems that the objective of the Bill, while framed in terms of supporting and reinforcing the role of the UK Supreme Court and directed more obviously towards limiting the direct impact of decisions of the Strasbourg Court, is nevertheless aimed at reducing the extent to which decisions of the Courts, both in the UK and abroad may have an impact on governmental or parliamentary decisions.

These developments, while significant, are not limited to the political arena. Concerns have been expressed in legal circles. Shortly after his retirement from the UK Supreme Court, Lord Sumption delivered the Reith Lectures on BBC, entitled 'Law's Expanding Empire', arguing that the law was taking over the space once occupied by politics.[82] Significantly, in particular, he argued that judges, especially those of the ECtHR, had usurped power by expanding the interpretation of human rights law. Notably, one of the lectures was recorded in Washington and compared the US and UK's constitutional

[76] *R (on the application of Elan – Cane) v Secretary of State for the Home Department* [2022] 2 All ER 1 (SC).

[77] *Re G Adoption (unmarried couple)* [2009] 1 AC 173 (HL).

[78] These matters are discussed by me in D O'Donnell, 'The ECHR Act 2003: Ireland and the Post War Human Rights Project' (2022) 6(2) *Irish Judicial Studies Journal* 1.

[79] Bill of Rights HC Bill (2022–23) [117].

[80] *Ghaidan v Godin-Mendoza* [2004] 2 AC 557 (HL).

[81] Indeed, the Bill was withdrawn on 27 June 2023.

[82] J Sumption, 'Law's Expanding Empire' (2019) Reith Lectures, BBC Radio 4, delivered 21 May 2019, available at www.bbc.co.uk/programmes/m00057m8.

model. He argued that the UK should learn from the US and be careful about rights which were put beyond democratic choice. He referred to *Griswold* and *Roe*.[83] While the lectures are both thoughtful and stimulating, the discussion was perhaps a little less sure-footed when discussing the US position. Perhaps an unnoticed and beneficial side effect of the encouragement in Ireland of reference to US authority in the 1960s is a greater opportunity for engagement by academic and practising lawyers with the extraordinarily rich literature in the US and study built up over more than two centuries. Nevertheless, the drawing of a connection to developments in the US was interesting. The developments in the UK are of a different order to what is occurring in the US, but they are interesting straws in the wind and, taken together with developments in some EU Member States, amount to something of which we should take note. More recently again, Martin Loughlin, professor of Public Law at London School of Economics has published an important book placing scepticism of the approach to the Human Rights Act in a broad historical and international context.[84]

VII. INTERNATIONAL STORM CLOUDS

It is rarely helpful however and, in any event would be inconsistent with the theme of this chapter, to seek to make some high-level generalisation about these developments. It would certainly be wrong to draw the complacent conclusion that, since the concept of judicial enforcement of rights is being assailed from all sides, it must be in a reasonably stable position. But it is, however, surely noteworthy, particularly so far as Ireland is concerned, that two major common law jurisdictions, both in different ways long-standing standard bearers in the field of human rights and the application of the rule of law, are jurisdictions in which official government reports have been directed towards the question of restriction of the role of courts, with voices calling for more serious change up to and including completely removing the power of courts to review the compatibility of legislation with the Constitution or Convention and/or to withdraw from conventions providing international protection for rights within national territories. Even more tellingly, this wave of scepticism about the exercise of judicial review comes from opposite ends of the political spectrum. When we put that together with the difficulties the EU is experiencing in upholding the guarantee of the protection of the rule of law, and the stresses facing the ECtHR and Council of Europe, and developments in Israel in relation to proposed changes to the judiciary's power to review acts of the legislature, and elsewhere more generally it is, I think, possible, and not alarmist to see that the post-war model of judicial protection of human rights is under more challenge today in more significant ways and in more locations than at any time since 1945.

In these turbulent international waters, it may appear sensible to withdraw to our national harbours and concentrate on the domestic in the hope that the international storm clouds will dissipate and not make landfall here. That would, however, be a

[83] J Sumption, 'Rights and the Ideal Constitution' (2019) Reith Lectures, BBC Radio 4, delivered 11 June 2019, available at www.bbc.co.uk/programmes/m0005t85.

[84] M Loughlin, *Against Constitutionalism* (Harvard University Press, 2022). Disappointingly, however, the book does not address the position in Ireland.

mistake – at least in my view. We have important lessons to learn and perhaps some things to teach. I do not accept that it is somehow inevitable that decisions on constitutional matters should be seen as merely the expression of moral or political views in a legal voice. Nor do I accept that law imposes no real or effective constraints on the exercise of judicial power. But if the protection of rights by judicial review is to be sustained, it must be placed on a firmer footing than a particular decision that is temporarily popular with the general population, or indeed that smaller section that constitutes the legal academic community or opinion formers more generally. A fundamental function of the Court under the Irish Constitution, and indeed any court with a duty to protect rights, is, if required to do so, to make decisions which may be unpopular since, by definition, they are capable of reversing the will of a popularly elected parliament. In Alexander Bickel's famous phrase, the power is, in essence, counter-majoritarian.[85]

In Ireland, we have been fortunate that, with some exceptions, a debate about the role of courts has not yet gained real traction, and certainly not to the point of questioning the exercise of the power of judicial review contained in the Irish Constitution. This may be partly because much of the legislation which has been challenged and struck down in the exercise of the power was in fact not the product of a contemporary political majority, but rather old legislation out of step with contemporary views. Other decisions, while temporarily controversial, have not provoked a reaction resulting in scrutiny of the process. There has been an important history of the exercise of the power over nearly a century and an equally important and underrated tradition of general acceptance of the decisions of the Supreme Court by the other branches of government, even when those decisions were more than inconvenient. The fact that the Constitution can be amended and has been amended to remove or reverse the effect of some decisions, also has an important consequence in promoting acceptance of decisions and, more broadly, the power to make them. However, we cannot assume that the stars will always be aligned in this way, and, in any event, it is important that we discuss and debate the nature and power of judicial review and, where appropriate, its boundaries, in a context which is insulated from the pressures which can arise in a political crisis.

In that regard, I think that what is indicated is greater study of other jurisdictions, and more in-depth analysis of the case law and jurisprudence. In particular, I think it is unfortunate that more attention has not been paid here, or indeed in the broader context of the ECHR, to the vast theoretical literature that has grown up in the US particularly in the latter half of the twentieth century and a study of which could only, I think, deepen discussion on this side of the Atlantic. Let me take our one example, which is illuminating, I think, because the charge of exceeding the constraints of the law came from a different quarter and involved those cases and developments which Tribe exempts from his criticism.

Much of the debate, in so much as it is discussed in popular discourse, particularly on this side of the Atlantic, is characterised as a choice between judicial activism and judicial restraint. The idea of judicial restraint is associated with the great US Judge Learned Hand and his 1958 Oliver Wendell Holmes lectures at Harvard now published in book

[85] See, eg, RL Brown, 'Accountability, Liberty, and the Constitution' (1998) 98(3) *Columbia Law Review* 531 for a contrarian account.

form as *The Bill of Rights*.[86] It was important that concerns were expressed with the direction of travel of the Warren court by such a significant figure and the vivid and forceful expressions contained in the lecture have made it easily quotable. The lecture crystallised a growing concern about the extent of the exercise of the power of constitutional interpretation by the Supreme Court. However, for me it is something of a frustration that any note of caution about what might be described as ambitious interpretation of a constitution or convention is characterised as judicial restraint, sometimes with references to Hand. His approach, whatever its merits, is not easily translated to other jurisdictions. A central theme in his argument was that since judicial review was not explicit in the Federal Constitution but can only be deduced from it by a process of necessary implication as had occurred in *Marbury v Madison*,[87] it was a legitimate threshold question for the Court whether, in any given case, it should exercise the power.

It must be apparent that this is not a form of reasoning easily applicable to any other jurisdiction, still less one like Ireland which since 1922 has had a judicial review expressed in the Constitution.[88] Indeed, if the underlying analysis is accepted, it might tend in an entirely opposite direction here. Hand's argument is that there are no inbuilt limits on what the Court can do and, therefore, judges should exercise restraint. The courts *can do* what they like in the interpretation of the Constitution but *should not*. Anyone who accepts the first step in this analysis and who disagrees with the second, or indeed its application in a particular case, would have a charter for the very type of interpretation which concerned Hand.

The grouping of all concerns with expansive interpretation of the Constitution or Convention under the heading of judicial restraint does not do justice to the many different approaches which expressed anxiety about the direction of jurisprudence in the Warren court, even while often sympathising with the outcomes of the cases. One influential voice, for example, was Alexander Bickel. Two major books, *The Least Dangerous Branch*,[89] and *The Supreme Court and the Idea of Progress*,[90] traced the arc of his growing disenchantment with the approach of the Court, and in particular the manner in which it purported to reach its conclusions.

Judge Hand's lecture also provoked a response from another quarter, again, sympathetic to the causes espoused by the Warren court, but troubled both by the method the Court adopted, and by the criticism Judge Hand had advanced. In 1959, the Holmes lecture was delivered by Professor Herbert Wechsler. That lecture, 'Towards Neutral Principles of Constitutional Law',[91] came to mind when considering Justice Breyer's book, and Professor Tribe's contention that law and the legal method was not a constraint, or a sufficient constraint, on the exercise of raw power. Wechsler disagreed that judicial review was a mere interpolation and not grounded in the language of the Constitution. It was instead a duty grounded in the Constitution.

[86] Learned Hand, *The Bill of Rights* (Harvard University Press, 1958).

[87] *Marbury v Madison* (1803) 5 US (1 Cranch) 137.

[88] Article 65 of the Irish Free State Constitution: 'The judicial power of the *Irish Free State* shall extend to the validity of any law having regard to the Constitution'; see also, Article 34.3.2° Bunreacht na hÉireann.

[89] A Bickel, *The Least Dangerous Branch: The Supreme Court at the Bar of Politics* (Yale University Press, 1978).

[90] A Bickel, *The Supreme Court and the Idea of Progress* (Yale University Press, 1978).

[91] H Wechsler, 'Towards Neutral Principles of Constitutional Law' (1959) 73(1) *Harvard Law Review* 1.

The duty to interpret and enforce the Constitution is 'to decide the litigated case and to decide it in accordance with the law, with all that that implies as to a rigorous insistence on the satisfaction of procedural and jurisdictional requirements …'.[92] The 'political question' doctrine[93] for example was not, in Wechsler's analysis, a prudential decision to refrain from interfering in a politically complex area, but rather a more limited conception so that 'all the doctrine can defensibly imply is that the courts are called upon to judge whether the Constitution has committed to another agency of government the autonomous determination of the issue raised, a finding that itself requires interpretation'.[94] Difficult as the process of interpretation was, it was something courts were obliged to undertake and by the standards that govern the interpretive process generally. That was something entirely different from a broad discretion to abstain or intervene. Later, Wechsler made an observation that should still resonate with those who are inclined to criticise or defend judgments by reference to their outcome:

> The man who simply lets his judgment turn on the immediate result may not, however, realize that his position implies that courts are free to function as a naked power organ that, that it is an empty affirmation to regard them, as ambivalently he so often does, as courts of law.[95]

These observations have many modern resonances and cast an interesting light on Tribe's criticism of Breyer. The heart of the lecture was that something more was required from the courts:

> I put it to you that the main constituent of the judicial process is precisely that it must be genuinely principled, resting with respect to every step that is involved in reaching judgment on analysis and reasons quite transcending the immediate result that is achieved. To be sure, the courts decide, or should decide only the case they have before them. But must they not decide on grounds of adequate neutrality and generality, tested not only by the instant application but by others that the principles imply? Is it not the very essence of judicial method to insist upon attending to such other cases, preferably those involving an opposing interest, in evaluating any principle avowed?[96]

The lecture had an immediate and deserved impact.[97] Perhaps like other impressive departures it received more acclaim, and had more claimed for it, than it could reasonably sustain. Some sought to draw a connection between Hand and Bickel and Justices Stewart and Harlan, and suggested that there was an emerging school of thought, which shared a commitment to what was described as reasoned elaboration.[98]

There was, of course, an inevitable reaction. The standing army[99] of constitutional scholars in the US were quick to point out, with some merit, that what Wechsler

[92] ibid 6.

[93] See, in an Irish context, PA McDermott, 'The Separation of Powers and the Doctrine of Non-Justiciability' (2000) 35 *The Irish Jurist* 280.

[94] H Wechsler, *Principles, Politics and Fundamental Law Selected Essays* (Harvard University Press, 1961).

[95] Wechsler (n 91) 12.

[96] ibid 15.

[97] Surveyed in K Greenawalt, 'The Enduring Significance of Neutral Principles' (1978) 78 *Columbia Law Review* 982.

[98] GE White, 'The Evolution of Reasoned Elaboration: Jurisprudential Criticism and Social Change' (1972) 59 *Virginia Law Review* 279. White, a noted legal historian, withdrew the suggestion of a school of jurisprudence some years later in his magisterial book, *The American Judicial Tradition* (Oxford University Press, 1976).

[99] Patrick Kavanagh was reputed to have said, rather scornfully, that the standing army of Irish poets (that is, those who liked to think of themselves as poets) never numbered less than 10,000.

was insisting on was essentially a process of reasoned analysis and that the search for neutral principles in the sense of judgments that could command absolute agreement was illusory.[100] It was entirely possible to construct two judgments, coming to opposite conclusions, which nevertheless complied with Wechsler's prescription. If there was a school of thought committed to reasoned elaboration, it fell far short of a comprehensive theory of law.

The argument also suffered from unfortunate timing in two respects. Wechsler worried publicly about the analysis of the Supreme Court in the desegregation cases, the so-called restrictive covenant case in *Shelley v Kramer*[101] and *Brown v Board of Education*[102] itself.[103] But anything that seemed to question what most of us saw, and still see, as one of the great achievements of the US Supreme Court, was likely to face resistance. Perhaps as importantly, when he spoke, the Warren court's revolution was getting into gear, and there were few, particularly in universities, who did not feel the thrill of the period and revel in the idea that constitutional law could be a powerful agent of change. As Judge J Skelly Wright, a supporter of the Warren court, put it rather bluntly, young lawyers 'see no point in querulous admonitions that the Court should restrain itself from combatting injustice now, in order to preserve itself to combat a coup later on'.[104] So the Warren court and its supporters pressed on and commentators as sober as Bickel were led to conclude that the Warren court 'relied on events for vindication more than on the method of reason for contemporary validation',[105] and Philip Kurland could conclude that the opinions of the Court 'have tended towards fiat rather than reason' and that the Court had 'failed abysmally to persuade the people that its judgments have been made for sound reasons'.[106]

These observations were made in 1970, and before *Roe*. It is certainly possible to argue that Wechsler's complaint was that the courts had failed to create law in the image of a thoughtful law professor so that a good judgment had the characteristics of a good law review article and that as such it may not even be a comprehensive account of the ideal judicial craft. But it is also possible to regret, I think, that these concerns were swept away so comprehensively, particularly in the universities, and to wonder how matters would have developed, if more value had been laid upon those lawyerly virtues of careful reasoning and rigorous analysis which most common law jurisdictions share. In one sense, this is, I think, what Breyer was referring to when he argued that decisions like *Brown* won acceptance and ultimately obedience because the legal rather than political character of the decision was recognised, which promoted respect for the Court and its authority. Laurence Tribe implicitly acknowledges that the lawyer's craft is capable of operating as a constraint on the attractions of the exercise of power.[107] If so, then we should attempt at every point to reinforce rather than undermine those constraints.

[100] *Shelley v Kramer* 334 US 1, 68 S Ct 836 (1948).
[101] *Shelley v Kramer* 349 US 294, 75 S Ct 753 (1955).
[102] *Brown v Board of Education of Topeka* 349 US 294, 75 S Ct 753 (1955).
[103] Wechsler (n 91) 29–30.
[104] J Skelly Wright, 'Professor Bickel, The Scholarly Tradition, and the Supreme Court' (1971) 84(4) *Harvard Law Review* 769.
[105] Bickel (n 90) 12.
[106] PB Kurland, *Politics the Constitution and the Warren Court* (University of Chicago Press, 1970).
[107] Tribe, 'Politicians in Robes' (n 56).

In this regard, the judgments in *Griswold* and the majority judgment in *McGee* deserve some consideration. Justice Douglas' opinion in *Griswold* is at one and the same time frustrating and tantalising. It shows an enviable confidence about what the Constitution should be understood as protecting, is almost impatient to reach its conclusions, and makes little, if any, reference to precedent. It is tantalising precisely because many of the things it says so brusquely and dismissively may be correct, and valuable. But it gives no hint that it recognises that a significant conceptual step is being taken, nor does it evince much sense of being obliged to explain or justify it.

In many ways, the decision in *McGee* involved a potentially greater leap, since, as was observed, it appeared to be wrung from a constitution which was perceived as having a strong Catholic flavour.[108] To my knowledge, however, the majority decision of Henchy J has not been subject to much, if any, criticism in the succeeding half century.[109] The acceptance of the outcome in *McGee* has of course many sources, not least that the development of public opinion was moving in favour of the availability of contraceptives. The acceptance of the decision, even by those who were opposed to the result, may also owe something to inertia perhaps, but also to the fact that the decision stood upon a relatively long history of acceptance of the decisions of the Supreme Court in the interpretation and application of the Constitution. However, some part of the response to the judgment over the last 50 years is, I think, that the judgment so clearly attempts to explain how its conclusion that the Constitution protected a right to privacy was to be deduced from the Constitution, and largely succeeded in doing so, in a passage which has been repeated and expanded on in subsequent decisions.

VIII. CONCLUSION

These thoughts lead me to some tentative if not, perhaps, remarkable conclusions. First, consideration of authority from other common law jurisdictions should not be limited to the search for the chimera of a precisely similar decision addressing the same subject matter. The value of international authority is enhanced if it comes with an awareness of the theoretical background to the decisions. When it does, then even when courts decide that foreign authority is not an appropriate guide to a particular decision, the exercise of assessing and analysing that authority can add an important degree of rigour and depth to the judgment, and locate it more soundly, on firmer foundations.

Second, the post-war enterprise of judicial protection of human rights through constitutions and international conventions,[110] is now being challenged perhaps more fundamentally than at any time since the Second World War, and from more surprising quarters than could have been anticipated even a decade or two ago. The vulnerability of that system is now more apparent than any other period. It is important not to simply

[108] JH Whyte, *Church and State in Modern Ireland 1923–79* (Gill & Macmillan, 1979).

[109] The judgment of Walsh J, although sometimes treated (wrongly) as the majority judgment, has perhaps been less successful. See generally, D O'Donnell, 'The Sleep of Reason' (2017) 40 *Dublin University Law Journal* 191.

[110] P Sales, 'Strasbourg Jurisprudence and the Human Rights Act: a Response to Lord Irvine' (2015) *Public Law* 253.

bemoan those developments. We should address ourselves to what lawyers can do. One thing is to recognise that the perception that courts' decisions are driven by ideology is easily propagated and difficult to shake off once it gains traction. If that system of protection of human rights, both domestic and international, is to be able to weather the challenges, it is important that it finds a firm footing and we develop a shared understanding of the place of judicial decision-making and communicate it more generally. In that regard, international examples, even unhappy, and the rich theoretical literature that is built up, particularly in the US, is particularly valuable, both in the domestic setting and in relation to the ECHR and the EU Charter of Fundamental Rights. Engagement with that thought can lead to a more sophisticated analysis, without having to experience the sometimes-bruising real world developments that have given rise to the commentary. In this regard, the borderline between provocative academic debate and corrosive public commentary is often very fine. In my view, however, admittedly from a jurisdiction with a Constitution which is capable of amendment, and a strong common law tradition, commentary tends to exaggerate the scope of judicial decision-making and underestimates the significant constraints upon it. I do not accept that judicial decisions can be reduced to an expression of moral or political views in a legal voice. Nor do I accept that law and the legal method do not constrain the ability of courts to act as an unelected and uncontrolled engine of political power. The scholarly and lawyerly qualities of attention to detail, rigorous analysis, cautious and incremental development, tolerance of opposing views, and a willingness to entertain the possibility that you are wrong, and a commitment to the law are not merely admirable but old-fashioned virtues: they are important and real constraints upon the possibility of the type of decision-making that can give rise to challenges to the entire process. This suggests more, rather than less, depth of analysis, more, rather than less, thought, discussion and respectful exchange of views, and more, rather than less, recourse to international comparisons.

2

The Power of Narrative – Shaping Aotearoa New Zealand's Public Law

HELEN WINKELMANN*

WHEN WE LOOK for the forces at work in the making of Aotearoa New Zealand's public law, it is right, as some commentators have done, to acknowledge the importance of a national psyche and culture which favours pragmatism and simplicity over complex theoretical frameworks.[1] This is a culture that values compliance with the law and representative government but is not necessarily all that interested in what it is that secures the rule of law.[2]

It is important also to describe New Zealand's constitutional history. Its initial reluctance to accept full nationhood and its search for a place in the international order. The relative informality of much of its constitutional structure and in particular the absence of a formal constitutional charter. This leaves a constitutional landscape that is constantly being reshaped – by legislation, by court decisions, and by significant events. The lack of a constitutional charter means that, as Professor Geiringer puts it, 'we are constantly reconstituting ourselves. There is no constitutive moment: just a series of constitutive iterations'.[3]

It is relevant to understand that there are few formal barriers to accessing the courts in the realm of public law (I say nothing of obstacles created by expense and complexity of law). Statutory bars or barriers to seeking judicial review are few, the principles applied as to standing are fairly described as permissive, and the courts have taken a broad view as to what is amenable to judicial review.[4] Some scholars have remarked also upon what they see as a feature of our public law – a tendency (regrettable on their account) of New

* I am also deeply indebted to the work of my clerk, Josie Butcher, for her assistance in the preparation of this chapter.

[1] M Taggart, 'The New Zealandness of New Zealand Public Law' (2004) 15 *Public Law Review* 81.

[2] See, eg, S Elias, 'Transition, Stability and the New Zealand Legal System' (2004) 10 *Otago Law Review* 475, 475; G Palmer, 'The Bill of Rights Fifteen Years On' (Ministry of Justice Symposium, Wellington, 10 February 2006) para 39; J Priestley, 'Chipping Away the Judicial Arm?' (2009) 17 *Waikato Law Review* 1, 23.

[3] C Geiringer, 'What's the Story? The Instablility of the Australasian Bills of Rights' (2016) 14(1) *International Journal of Constitutional Law* 156, 171. See also J Mclean, 'The Unwritten Political Constitution and its Enemies' (2016) 14(1) *International Journal of Constitutional Law* 119.

[4] S Elias, 'Judicial Review and Constitutional Balance' (2019) 17 *New Zealand Journal of Public and International Law* 1, 9. See also MSR Palmer and DR Knight, *The Constitution of New Zealand* (Hart Publishing, 2022) 168.

Zealand judges to under-theorise issues such as grounds of review or intensity of review[5] – a legacy, perhaps, of a search for simplicity and accessibility in the law.[6]

As a working judge my interest is inevitably captured by the issues the courts are being called upon to decide and by the arguments we hear. This has led me to the reflection that it is historical and social forces, operating as they do within a system without a constitutional charter, that are today the major forces shaping New Zealand's public law. These forces operate more directly than they might if mediated through the language and structure of a written constitution. In this chapter I consider how Te Tiriti o Waitangi (the Treaty which lies at the beginning of the story of New Zealand as a nation), tikanga (New Zealand's first law), our statutory bill of rights and New Zealand's commitment to the international order have all shaped and continue to shape our public law. I describe how it is that these forces have shaped and reshaped dynamics between Parliament, the Executive and the courts. Their impact can be seen in the development of common law presumptions guiding statutory interpretation, in the reassessment of the requirements of comity between the branches of government and in the development of remedial responses to breaches of our statutory bill of rights.

I. A LITTLE HISTORICAL AND CONSTITUTIONAL CONTEXT

A. The Creation of a New Nation

English settlers began to arrive in New Zealand in numbers in the early part of the nineteenth century. They found that the land was already occupied by Māori, who had sophisticated social structures, strong tribal affiliations, and complex rules regarding social relations, their relationship with the land, and the achieving of balance following any wrong. These customs, rules, and values are collectively referred to as tikanga. They had (and continue to have) such status in Māori society that tikanga is now recognised as New Zealand's first law.[7]

In 1840 the British Crown entered into a treaty with Māori Rangatira (chiefs), representing various hapū (subtribes). Drafted by Crown officials with the assistance of Anglican missionaries, it was prepared in both the English (this version is commonly referred to as the Treaty) and Māori language (referred to as Te Tiriti). Te Tiriti was signed by 540 rangatira, but only 39 of those signed the English version.

In the English text of the Treaty Māori ceded to the Queen all rights of sovereignty which they possessed and granted to the Crown rights of pre-emption in relation to their lands. Māori were guaranteed in return 'the full exclusive and undisturbed possession of

[5] DR Knight, *Vigilance and Restraint in the Common Law of Judicial Review* (Cambridge University Press, 2018) 255–56. See also Elias (n 4) 4.

[6] Referring to Lord Cooke's quest for a fairness and simplicity in Aotearoa New Zealand's public law: R Cooke 'The Struggle for Simplicity in Administrative Law' in M Taggart (ed), *Judicial Review of Administrative Action in the 1980s* (Oxford University Press, 1986). For further explanation of Lord Cooke's influence in New Zealand's public law, see DR Knight, 'Simple, Fair and Discretionary Administrative Law' (2008) 39 *Victoria University of Wellington Law Review* 99, 102.

[7] J Williams, 'Lex Aotearoa: An Heroic Attempt to Map the Māori Dimension in Modern New Zealand Law' (2013) 21 *Waikato Law Review* 1, 2–5. See also *Re Edwards (Te Whakatōhea No 2)* [2021] NZHC 1025 [69]; *Ngawaka v Ngāti Rehua-Ngātiwai ki Aotea Trust Board (No 2)* [2021] NZHC 291, [2021] 2 NZLR 1 [2], [43]; *Ellis v R* [2022] NZSC 114, [2022] 1 NZLR 239 [22], [107], [172].

their Lands and Estates, Forests, Fisheries and other properties which they may collectively or individually possess' and the rights and privileges of British subjects.[8]

However, the document written in te reo Māori (Te Tiriti), conveyed different concepts. It guaranteed Māori tino rangatiratanga (unqualified chieftainship) over their lands, villages and all their treasures (taonga). It ceded to the British, only kāwanatanga, which could be construed as governorship. The exact terms of what was agreed has been the subject of debate since that time.

The history that ensued did see the Crown establish sovereignty over the country, with New Zealand becoming a colony within the British Empire.[9] Within this new colony land became a flash point in relations between Māori and settlers.[10] Settlers wished to acquire land from Māori, but in accordance with tikanga, land was not a commodity to be bought or sold. The loss of land by Māori lies near the beginning of a long and complex history of dispossession, leading to the economic and social marginalisation of the Māori people. Their social structures were damaged or destroyed, particularly through the loss of chiefly authority (tino rangatiratanga) and damaging of iwi (tribes) and hapū (subtribes) communities. The cumulative effect of this history is now seen today in the inequitable outcomes for Māori across almost every aspect of social and political life, with Māori becoming the most imprisoned people in New Zealand.[11]

B. A Calling to Account for Past and Present Wrongs

Although Māori have maintained calls for justice for breaches of the promises made to them in 1840, for a long time there was little political interest in admitting these wrongs, confronting these consequences, and attempting to address them. This began to change with the creation of the Waitangi Tribunal, established in 1975 under the Treaty of Waitangi Act 1975, to enquire into breaches of the Treaty. The Tribunal's jurisdiction was expanded in the 1980s to enquire into historical wrongs. The work of the Waitangi Tribunal undoubtedly contributed to the role Te Tiriti/the Treaty has played as a major engine driving the development of public law in New Zealand. Along with this has been the question, asked more insistently in the last decade, as to the place of the first law of New Zealand, tikanga, in our legal order.

C. Constitutional Settlement

Representative government was established in New Zealand in 1853. Although full self-government was offered by the Statute of Westminster in 1931, New Zealand can be said

[8] Treaty of Waitangi 1840, art 2 (English text).

[9] The Waitangi Tribunal has concluded that the Crown did not acquire sovereignty through the signing of Te Tiriti – whilst also acknowledging that sovereignty had been acquired at some point: Waitangi Tribunal, *He Whakaputanga me te Tiriti: The Report on Stage 1 of the Te Paparahi o Te Raki Inquiry* (Wai 1040, 2014) 526–27.

[10] With the British forces ultimately bringing arms against iwi in order to pursue the colonial project leading to significant loss of life and land for Māori.

[11] Te Uepū Hāpai i te Ora | Safe and Effective Justice Advisory Group, *He Waka Roimata – Transforming our Criminal Justice System* (Ministry of Justice, 2019) 6.

to have moved reluctantly to independence from England, waiting 16 years to take up that opportunity. Even then, the New Zealand Parliament was not fully independent from the United Kingdom (UK) until the Constitution Act was passed in 1986.

The New Zealand court system waited longer for full independence. It was not until 1 January 2004 that the right to appeal to the Privy Council was removed and a final court of appeal established within New Zealand – the Supreme Court.[12] The establishment of the court was recognition, in the words of the relevant legislation, that New Zealand is an independent nation. The court was established with the intention that it 'would enable important legal matters, including legal matters relating to the Treaty of Waitangi, to be resolved with an understanding of New Zealand conditions, history, and traditions'.[13]

D. A Late Addition to Our Constitutional Settlement – A Statutory Bill of Rights

The enactment of the New Zealand Bill of Rights Act in 1990 certainly created the potential for a judicial voice to be heard more loudly in relation to New Zealand's constitutional settlement. The purpose of the Act was to affirm, protect and promote the rights and freedoms recorded there and to give effect to New Zealand's commitments under the International Covenant on Civil and Political Rights (ICCPR).[14] It was conceived as a supreme law, but not enacted in that form. As enacted, the Bill of Rights excludes the possibility of legislation being repealed, amended or disapplied by reason only of inconsistency with the Act's provisions.[15] New Zealand is one of six commonwealth jurisdictions to have adopted a statutory bill of rights – along with Canada (its statutory Bill of Rights was superseded by the Canadian Charter of Rights and Freedoms), the UK, the Australian Capital Territory, and the Australian states of Victoria and Queensland.

E. Constitutional Culture

Aotearoa's unicameral Parliament and its lack of any federal constitution means that its constitutional arrangements are different to those of the UK, Australia and Canada, contributing to a powerful Executive branch. Academics such as David Williams and Mark Hickford argue that as a result of Aotearoa's unwritten constitution, constitutional matters are largely governed by what they refer to as 'political constitutionalism'.[16] Political constitutionalism refers to the effect of the constitution in terms of its political operability in practice rather than its legal description in positive law terms.[17]

[12] Supreme Court Act 2003, s 42. There were transitional provisions, see ss 50–51. This Act has since been repealed, however, these provisions have been retained in the Senior Courts Act 2016, sch 5, pt 1.

[13] Supreme Court Act 2003, s 3(1).

[14] New Zealand Bill of Rights Act 1990, long title.

[15] ibid s 4.

[16] DV Williams, 'Justiciability and Tikanga: Towards "Soft" Legal Constitutionalism' (2021) 29 *New Zealand Universities Law Review* 649, 650 referring to the use of the term in M Hickford, 'The Historical, Political Constitution – Some Reflections on Political Constitutionalism in New Zealand's History and its Possible Normative Value' [2013] *New Zealand Law Review* 585, 586. See also E Willis, 'Political Constitutionalism: The "Critical Morality" of Constitutional Politics' (2018) 28 *New Zealand University Law Review* 237, 238.

[17] Hickford (n 16).

Academics suggest that as a result of the enhanced role of politics in our constitutional settlement, judges in Aotearoa tend to show considerable 'judicial restraint' and deference.[18] Sir Geoffrey Palmer characterises the judiciary as 'cautious' and 'leery of' constitutional issues.[19]

Whilst history may record few constitutional showdowns between Parliament, the Judiciary and the Executive,[20] there have been points of tension. An examination of recent history shows occasions in which court decisions have led to a swift legislative response to undo or limit their effect.[21] However, there are also instances, some discussed in this chapter, where other branches of government have responded constructively to court decisions bearing upon the functions and responsibilities of those branches.

Some have perceived a change in recent times – a movement away from judicial restraint or at least toward a 'soft version of legal constitutionalism'.[22] Any judge would be 'leery of' (to steal Sir Geoffrey's expression) making such generalisations. But in the cases I touch upon below, there is also an undeniable articulation of common law principle by the courts with structural implications for how statute law will be applied by the courts, and a determined assertion of their constitutional role to interpret and apply the law.

II. THE STORY OF THE TREATY/TE TIRITI IN NEW ZEALAND'S PUBLIC LAW

In his article 'What a Difference a Treaty Makes', Paul McHugh comments:[23]

> In the common law jurisdictions of North America and Australasia at the close of the 20th century, no area of public law matched the growth of activity in the aboriginal sphere. Aboriginal law grew like the proverbial beanstalk; its pitch sometimes frenzied, its direction and purpose often difficult to gauge.

McHugh describes how the different legal pathways followed in each jurisdiction can be traced to the existence or non-existence of treaties, and their status in domestic law. The first nations of Australia lack the protection of treaty rights. Canada's Constitution Act 1982 provides for express reference to 'existing aboriginal and treaty rights'.[24] Ultimately,

[18] See, eg, Williams (n 16) 659; C Geiringer and A Geddis, 'Judicial Deference and Emergency Power: A Perspective on *Borrowdale v Director-General*' (2020) 31 *Public Law Review* 376, 382–83.

[19] G Palmer, 'What the New Zealand Bill of Rights Act Aimed to Do, Why It Did Not Succeed and How It Can Be Repaired' (2016) 14 *New Zealand Journal of Public and International Law* 169, 175.

[20] In the most famous case in which the courts articulated the limits of Executive power, the judge declined to make any remedial orders, allowing rather for a political solution: *Fitzgerald v Muldoon* [1976] 2 NZLR 615 (SC). See Justice S Kós, 'The Judiciary and the Executive: Robert Muldoon and the Judges' in J Burrows and J Finn (eds), *Challenge and Change: Judging in Aotearoa New Zealand* (LexisNexis, 2022).

[21] See, eg, *Attorney-General v Ngāti Apa* [2003] 3 NZLR 643 (CA) and the Foreshore and Seabed Act 2004; *Attorney-General v Leigh* [2011] NZSC 106, [2012] 2 NZLR 713 and the Parliamentary Privilege Act 2014; *Ministry of Health v Atkinson* [2012] NZCA 184, [2012] 3 NZLR 456 and the New Zealand Health and Disability Amendment Act 2013; *D (SC 31/2019) v New Zealand Police* [2021] NZSC 2, [2021] 1 NZLR 213 and the Child Protection (Child Sex Offender Government Agency Registration) Amendment Act 2021.

[22] Williams (n 16) 652. See also C Geiringer, 'The Constitutional Role of the Courts under the NZ Bill of Rights: Three Narratives from *Attorney-General v Taylor*' (2017) 48 *Victoria University of Wellington Law Review* 547.

[23] PG McHugh, 'What a Difference a Treaty Makes – The Pathway of Aboriginal Rights Jurisprudence in New Zealand Public Law' (2004) 15 *Public Law Review* 87, 88 (fnn omitted).

[24] In the United States there has also, to some extent, been statutory protection of existing treaty rights: ibid 98–99.

McHugh suggests, although there are distinctive 'national hues' there are also strong parallels between the different jurisdictions.[25]

As to the position in New Zealand, the case of *Te Heuheu Tūkino v Aotea District Māori Land Board* stands as authority for the proposition that Te Tiriti is not directly enforceable in New Zealand courts except in so far as it is made so by legislative authority.[26]

It was social and political pressure which ultimately led to a political response to the issues of historical and racial justice in New Zealand. The creation of the Waitangi Tribunal in 1975 by the Waitangi Tribunal Act was part of that response. That legislation used for the first time, at least in statutory form, the expression the 'principles of the Treaty' – principles which it did not define. Jurisdiction was conferred on the Tribunal to inquire into whether 'certain matters' were inconsistent with those undefined principles. The Act was statutory recognition that the Crown had obligations to Māori under the Treaty (an idea on which there was no public consensus at that time) and that breaches of those obligations should at least be avoided, even if the legislation stopped short of conferring remedial powers on the Tribunal.[27]

It is hard to overstate the significance of this Act. It ensured that public resource would be devoted to investigating breaches, including, when its jurisdiction was extended in 1986, historical breaches. The historical accounts that were and continue to be recovered and documented by the Tribunal have contributed to our national understanding of these issues and have altered the political landscape.

The concept of 'free floating' Treaty principles, not pinned to any expression in the text, broke a log jam created by the conflict between the language of the Treaty and Te Tiriti, and created a path forward through a contested space. As I come to, while the historical and legal legitimacy of these principles is now the subject of debate,[28] the use of the phrase 'the principles of the Treaty' has led to a body of jurisprudence which has reinforced Te Tiriti as a document of constitutional status.

The courts' engagement with the Treaty began in earnest in 1987, sparked by a reference to the principles of the Treaty in the State-Owned Enterprises Act 1986, an Act to enable government activities and assets to be owned and dealt with through companies. The Act raised the possibility that assets subject to Treaty claims could be transferred out of Crown ownership and so beyond the reach of Treaty claimants. Section 9 of the Act included, on the recommendation of the Waitangi Tribunal, that 'nothing in this Act shall permit the Crown to act in a manner that is inconsistent with the principles of the Treaty'. In a case – commonly referred to as the *Lands* case – the Court of Appeal found that this provision did indeed require the Crown to act consistently with Treaty principles when transferring state assets which could be subject to a Treaty-based claim to state-owned enterprises.[29] The Court found that the Treaty created an enduring relationship of

[25] ibid 89–92.

[26] *Te Heuheu Tūkino v Aotea District Māori Land Board* [1941] NZLR 590 (PC).

[27] Although limited remedial powers were conferred by amendments to the Act in 1989. For an explanation of the legislative history see *Haronga v Waitangi Tribunal* [2011] NZSC 53, [2011] 2 NZLR 53 [56]–[77].

[28] See, eg, the view expressed in A Mikaere, 'The Treaty of Waitangi and Recognition of Tikanga Māori' in M Belgrave, M Kawharu and D Williams (eds), *Waitangi Revisited: Perspectives on the Treaty of Waitangi* (Oxford University Press, 2005) 330, 341–42.

[29] *New Zealand Maori Council v Attorney General* [1987] 1 NZLR 641 (HC and CA) (*Lands* case).

a partnership with responsibilities akin to fiduciary duties, with each party accepting a positive duty to act in good faith, fairly, reasonably and honourably toward one another.[30]

The *Lands* case could have been a point of constitutional conflict. The decision is one of the most consequential in New Zealand's history. The relief granted included a requirement that the Crown formulate a scheme of safeguards to ensure that lands or waters were not transferred to state-owned enterprises in such a way as to prejudice Māori claims under the Treaty and that this scheme then be submitted to the court for approval.[31]

Still more significant was how the President of the Court of Appeal, Justice Cooke, framed the decision:

> … The prosaic language of the Court's formal orders should not be allowed to obscure the fact that the Maori people have succeeded in this case. Some might speak of a victory, but Courts do not usually use that kind of language. At the outset I mentioned that each member of the Court was writing a separate judgment. It will be seen that approaching the case independently we have all reached two major conclusions. First that the principles of the Treaty of Waitangi override everything else in the State-Owned Enterprises Act. Second that those principles require the Pakeha and Maori Treaty partners to act towards each other reasonably and with the utmost good faith. That duty is no light one. It is infinitely more than a formality. If a breach of the duty is demonstrated at any time, the duty of the Court will be to insist that it be honoured.[32]

But Cooke P also described the Court's actions as the orthodox application of statutory provisions – it was the legislature after all which had bound the Crown to the principles.[33] No constitutional showdown ensued – the Executive complied with the process set out in the decision. Parliament did not repeal section 9. Far from it – Parliament has continued to refer to 'Treaty principles' in legislation. These provisions are now referred to as a category as 'Treaty clauses'.

Following the *Lands* decision, the Executive and then Parliament began in earnest the work of understanding and acknowledging breaches of the principles of Te Tiriti and then, through the Treaty settlement process, providing some form of recompense for those breaches (whether or not adequate). This process has extended far beyond the scope of the initial focus of the *Lands* case – a process usually, although not always, initiated by the Waitangi Tribunal historic claims process.[34]

Over the 35 years since the *Lands* case the courts have also continued to play a role in adjudicating between the Crown and Māori in relation to the rights and obligations arising from Te Tiriti. The impact of the Treaty principles in the area of public law, and in society has been profound.

I highlight two aspects of the engagement by the courts in this area. First, in statutory interpretation. Second, in adjudicating between the Crown and iwi in relation to negotiated Treaty settlements. Each has implications for our constitutional landscape and our public law.

[30] ibid 664.
[31] ibid 667–68.
[32] ibid 667.
[33] ibid 659.
[34] MSR Palmer and DR Knight, *The Constitution of New Zealand: A Contextual Analysis* (Hart Publishing, 2023) 218–19.

A. Te Tiriti and Statutory Interpretation

Today at least 35 statutes[35] contain explicit references to the Treaty. Under those statutes, public officials are required to act consistently with its principles – a requirement which has given rise to a steady diet of judicial review proceedings in which the Treaty is invoked directly to challenge Executive decision-making.[36] An example of a treaty clause is section 4 of the Conservation Act 1987 which provides: 'This Act shall so be interpreted and administered as to give effect to the principles of the Treaty of Waitangi.'

The inclusion of clauses such as this affect the interpretation of the Act itself, and of course, the obligations of decision-makers under it, including the matters that they are obliged to consider, and the processes to be followed.

In recent years there has been a drafting trend towards including in statute how it is that the statutory scheme fulfils the Crown's responsibility under the Treaty.[37] But this trend toward more specificity in statutory expression has not diminished the extent of the obligations that have been found to arise under the Treaty – the courts developing a principle of statutory interpretation that legislation is to be interpreted with reference to the principles of Te Tiriti unless a contrary intention is made clear.[38]

This development began not long after the creation of the Waitangi Tribunal. It was accepted, at least at first instance level, that the Treaty and its principles were relevant to the interpretation of statutes, and that the principles of the Treaty were implicit relevant considerations in the exercise of statutory powers affecting Māori interests.[39] In the case of *Huakina Development Trust v Waikato Valley Authority*[40] Chilwell J said of the Treaty that it was part of the fabric of New Zealand society and 'therefore part of the context' in which the court is to interpret and apply legislation.[41] This was an approach which did not turn on the existence of Treaty clauses.

In the recent Supreme Court decision of *Trans-Tasman Resources Ltd v Taranaki Whanganui Conservation Board (Trans-Tasman)*, the impact of this development was made still more explicit.[42] That case concerned an application by Trans-Tasman Resources for consent to undertake seabed mining off New Zealand's west coast. This would involve extracting seabed material from the region's iconic black sands.

[35] See PA Joseph, *Joseph on Constitutional and Administrative Law*, 5th edn (Thomson Reuters, 2021) 89.

[36] The Treaty has featured extensively in the law of judicial review in New Zealand. I will not attempt to add to the scholarship of Matthew Palmer in which he provides an analysis of 53 cases in which the Treaty was directly invoked in judicial review proceedings: MSR Palmer, 'Indigenous Rights, Judges and Judicial Review in New Zealand' in JNE Varuhas and SW Stark (eds), *The Frontiers of Public Law* (Hart Publishing, 2020) 135.

[37] RI Carter, *Burrows and Carter Statute Law in New Zealand*, 6th edn (LexisNexis, 2021) 697. See also MSR Palmer, *The Treaty of Waitangi in New Zealand's Law and Constitution* (Victoria University Press, 2008) 96–101, 183–84; Legislation Design and Advisory Committee, *Legislation Guidelines* (September 2021) ch 5.

[38] See N Coates, 'The Rise of Tikanga Māori and Te Tiriti o Waitangi Jurisprudence' in J Burrows and J Finn (eds), *Challenge and Change: Judging in Aotearoa New Zealand* (LexisNexis, 2022) 81 referring to the comments of the Supreme Court in *Trans-Tasman Resources Ltd v Taranaki-Whanganui Conservation Board* [2021] NZSC 127, [2021] 1 NZLR 801 [151] (*Trans-Tasman*).

[39] P Rishworth, 'Writing Things Unwritten: Common Law in New Zealand's Constitution' (2016) 14 *International Journal of Constitutional Law* 137, 151.

[40] *Huakina Development Trust v Waikato Valley Authority* [1987] 2 NZLR 188 (HC). See also *Barton-Prescott v Director General of Social Welfare* [1997] 3 NZLR 179 (HC).

[41] *Huakina Development Trust* (n 40) 210.

[42] *Trans-Tasman* (n 38).

Up to 50 million tonnes of seabed material would be permitted to be extracted annually under that licence.

Local iwi and conservation groups objected to the proposal. One of the principal issues for the Court was the relevance of tikanga values and Te Tiriti-based customary rights and interests – how were those interests to be weighed in the consenting process, indeed were they to be weighed at all?

The relevant statute, the Exclusive Economic Zone and Continental Shelf (Environmental Effects) Act 2012 (EEZ Act) contained a bespoke treaty clause, which particularised the sections that had been included in the Act '[i]n order to recognise and respect the Crown's responsibility to give effect to the principles of the Treaty of Waitangi for the purposes of [the] Act'.[43]

The appellant argued it was significant to the interpretation of the EEZ Act that there was no general direction requiring the decision-maker to give effect to the principles of the Treaty of Waitangi, like that contained in the Conservation Act. And that this different articulation reflected a deliberate choice on the part of Parliament. In rejecting that argument, the Court said:

> … the move to finely tuned subtle wording does not axiomatically give support to a narrow approach to the meaning of such clauses. Indeed, the contrary must be true given the constitutional significance of the Treaty to the modern New Zealand state. The courts will not easily read statutory language as excluding consideration of Treaty principles if a statute is silent on the question … An intention to constrain the ability of statutory decision-makers to respect Treaty principles should not be ascribed to Parliament unless that intention is made quite clear.[44]

It has been suggested that this analysis brings the principles of the Treaty into the group of values and rights protected by the principle of legality in New Zealand.[45] I reserve my views on that issue for when it arises for decision.

B. Te Tiriti and Constitutional Comity

Although this was not the case in the early days of the process, Treaty settlements in New Zealand now take place in accordance with carefully worked out and published treaty settlement policies, complete with complex fiscal considerations.[46] Settlements that are concluded are then given effect by legislation.

Not infrequently, Treaty settlements give rise to disputes – including in relation to the mandate of those who purport to reach agreement on behalf of potential claimants, and in relation to overlapping claims. The courts have on occasion taken the view that issues are non-justiciable where implementation of the settlement includes legislation (which it usually will), invoking the principle of non-interference in parliamentary proceedings.

[43] ibid [140] referring to s 12 of the EEZ Act.

[44] ibid [151] (footnotes omitted).

[45] Coates (n 38) 81.

[46] For a fuller account of these policies see Williams (n 16) fn 23 referring to Office of Treaty Settlements, *Healing the Past, Building a Future: A Guide to Treaty of Waitangi Claims and Negotiations with the Crown/Ka tika ā muri, ka tika ā mua: He Tohutohu Whakamārama i ngā Whakataunga Kerēme e pā ana ki te Tiriti o Waitangi me ngā Whakaritenga ke te Karauna* (Office of Treaty Settlements, March 2015).

In his article 'Justiciability and Tikanga', David Williams describes a narrowing of the areas of recognised non-justiciability in recent cases before the courts.[47]

While there are a number of cases that could be discussed in this area,[48] I focus on two: one at the beginning of the story – *Te Runanga o Wharekauri Rekohu Inc v Attorney General* (also referred to as the *Sealords* case)[49] – and one, at the end point (end point only in the sense that it is the most recent in time) – *Ngāti Whātua Ōrākei Trust v Attorney-General*.[50]

The first, the *Sealords* case, was one of several critical decisions which have, at least until recent times, shaped the relationship between Te Tiriti, Parliament, the Executive and the courts. In *Sealords*, a challenge was brought by iwi representatives who opposed a settlement deed between the Crown and other Māori representatives. The deed was expressed to be between the Crown and all Māori and to settle fisheries claims. The settlement was of historic dimensions – it would settle Te Tiriti-based claims by Māori to commercial fishing rights.

The deed contemplated the introduction to Parliament of legislation which would carry many of the terms of settlement into effect and, when enacted, would bind all Māori. In an affidavit filed in the proceedings, the responsible Minister said the Government intended to proceed, as it was contractually obliged to, by introducing legislation to Parliament.

The deed did not define who Māori were, and those who negotiated the deed did not claim to have a mandate on behalf of all Māori, and certainly not on behalf of the claimants in the proceedings. The claimants argued that they were not bound, and that proper process had not been followed to secure their agreement to the settlement.

The relief sought in the High Court and Court of Appeal included declaratory orders that the settlement was not binding or enforceable against Māori, was a breach of the Treaty of Waitangi and/or a breach of the Crown's fiduciary duties. They also sought prohibition orders restraining the Crown and Ministers from introducing legislation to implement the settlement.

Writing for the Court, Cooke P accepted that the deed was 'a most unusual document and, perhaps even designedly, obscure in some major respects', observing that the signatories for Māori did not claim to have authority for or intention to bind all Māori.[51] But he reasoned, the deed was plainly not intended to bind the Crown to introduce legislation. Once that was understood, it was clear the proceedings were misconceived, because the deed was non-binding on all signatories. As to the relief sought, he continued that it would be 'wrong and almost inconceivable for the Courts to attempt to dictate, by

[47] Williams (n 16) 659–60.

[48] See, eg, *Te Runanga o Wharekauri Rekohu Inc v Attorney-General* [1993] 2 NZLR 301 (CA) (*Sealords*); *Ngati Apa Ki Te Waipounamu Trust v Attorney-General* [2004] 1 NZLR 462 (CA); *Milroy v Attorney-General* [2005] NZAR 562 (CA); *Ngāti Te Ata v Minister for Treaty of Waitangi Negotiations* [2017] NZHC 2058.

[49] *Sealords* (n 48).

[50] *Ngāti Whātua Ōrākei Trust v Attorney-General* [2018] NZSC 84, [2019] 1 NZLR 116 (*Ngāti Whātua*). Since this paper was delivered the Supreme Court also discussed this issue, albeit only briefly, in *Wairarapa Moana ki Pouākani Inc v Mercury NZ Ltd* [2022] NZSC 142 [46]–[47] (Winkelmann CJ, Glazebrook and Williams JJ).

[51] *Sealords* (n 48) 307.

declaration or a willingness to award damages or any other form of relief, what should be placed before Parliament'.[52]

There are other cases that touched upon where the boundary of this principle of non-interference in parliamentary proceedings lay. But for the purposes of this chapter, I fast forward to *Ngāti Whātua*, a case which again arose in the context of a treaty settlement. The iwi Ngāti Whātua had settled its claims in respect of Tāmaki Makaurau Auckland. It sought to challenge ministerial decisions to transfer land in that region (in which it claimed mana whenua[53]) in order to settle other iwi claims – settlements which would be carried into effect by legislation. Ngāti Whātua challenged both the ministerial decisions involved and the Crown's settlement policy as to how settlements were to be undertaken in areas where there were overlapping interests. It argued that the settlements were inconsistent with its rights arising in accordance with tikanga and under the Treaty. It challenged the application of the Crown's overlapping claims policy in relation to land that was the subject of the settlements, arguing that Treaty and tikanga rights must be determined prior to the making of a settlement offer. The Crown sought to strike-out the claim on the basis of non-justiciability – the relief sought would interfere with parliamentary proceedings.

The Court took a fine-grained approach to assessing whether the claim as formulated, or as it could be reformulated, engaged the principle of non-interference with parliamentary proceedings. Ellen France J, writing for the majority, endorsed the view that it 'is a matter of assessing on which side of the line a particular proceeding falls'.[54] Analysing the nature of the claims and the remedies sought, she identified those in respect of which the Court would be called upon to do no more than fulfil its usual function of declaring rights. And, in so doing, she signalled a re-setting of that line from where earlier decisions had placed it:

> It is, nonetheless, appropriate to sound a note of caution at the extent to which the principle of non-interference in parliamentary proceedings has been held to apply to decisions somewhat distant from, for example, the decision of a minister to introduce a Bill to the House or from debate in the House. It would be overbroad to suggest that the fact a decision may, potentially, be the subject of legislation would always suffice to take the advice leading up to that decision out of the reach of supervision by the courts. That would be to ignore the function of the courts to make declarations as to rights.[55]

What emerges clearly from *Ngāti Whātua* is how important the formulation of the claim is. Seeking declarative relief as to rights or interests, or even as to the lawfulness of the application of the very policy engaged in a settlement, may not fall on the wrong side of the line if the relief is not directed to parliamentary proceedings, nor to the very decisions

[52] ibid 308.

[53] Mana whenua can be broadly described as authority over a particular territory associated with possession and occupation of tribal land: JC Moorfield, *Te Aka Māori Dictionary* (online edn), available at https://maoridictionary.co.nz. Note, however, there is significant debate as to how mana whenua is defined and applied. See, eg, HM Mead, *Tikanga Māori: Living by Māori Values* (Huia Publishers, 2019) ch 17; R Benton, A Frame and P Meredith, *Te Mātāpunenga: A Compendium of References to the Concepts and Institutions of Māori Customary Law* (Victoria University Press, 2013) 178.

[54] *Ngāti Whātua* (n 50) [44] citing *Te Ohu Kai Moana Trustee Ltd v Attorney General* [2016] NZHC 1798, [2016] NZAR 1169 [24] (Simon France J).

[55] *Ngāti Whātua* (n 50) [46].

(the ministerial decisions to settle) which led to the initiation of those proceedings.[56] The courts will not be precluded by the principle of non-interference with parliamentary proceedings from declaring the law merely because contemplated legislation lies somewhere in the factual matrix of the dispute between the parties.

C. Te Tiriti and the Future

This narrative makes clear that while the principle in *Te Heuheu* (that the Treaty is not directly enforceable before the courts unless incorporated by statute) remains part of our law, the tide of public law has flowed around it. One commentator has described the principle in *Te Heuheu* as 'a crumbling façade'.[57] Today, few would challenge Te Tiriti as one of the engines driving developments in our public law.

Perhaps the next chapter has already been written with the creation of the 2019 Cabinet Circular, 'Te Tiriti o Waitangi Guidance'.[58] The circular sets out guidelines agreed by Cabinet for policy-makers to consider the Treaty in their work.

In New Zealand, the Cabinet Manual is perhaps the most authoritative statement in a single document of how our constitution works in practice. It guides and shapes the actions of Ministers and public servants.[59] Although it does not create justiciable rights,[60] the Cabinet Manual has been treated as relevant to assessing the lawfulness of ministerial actions.[61]

The Manual lists the Treaty as one of the 'major sources of the constitution' and describes the ways in which the Executive must take the Treaty into account in formulating policy and when submitting bills. The 2019 Cabinet Circular signals a deliberate move away from the concept of the free-floating Treaty principles guiding executive action, and toward a focus upon the text: 'whilst the courts and previous guidance have developed and focussed on the principles of the Treaty, this guidance takes the text of the Treaty as its focus'.[62]

III. TIKANGA

Any discussion of the development of the law in New Zealand to meet the needs of this nation must address the status of tikanga as a source of law. The story is one of delayed

[56] And on the other side of the coin, in the determination of the remitted proceeding *Ngāti Whātua Ōrākei Trust v Attorney-General (No 4)* [2022] NZHC 843 Palmer J at [609] cautioned that it would be inconsistent with the honour of the Crown were the Crown to attempt to cloak its actions in Parliamentary proceedings for the deliberate purpose of avoiding judicial review of actions it knew were inconsistent with the Treaty of Waitangi.

[57] Coates (n 38) 81.

[58] Cabinet Office, *Te Tiriti o Waitangi/Treaty of Waitangi Guidance* (Cabinet Office Circular, CO19/5, 22 October 2019).

[59] Cabinet Office, *Cabinet Manual 2017* (Department of Prime Minister and Cabinet 2017).

[60] *Rabson v Attorney-General* [2016] NZHC 2876.

[61] See, eg, *Peters v Attorney General* [2021] NZCA 355, [2021] 3 NZLR 191.

[62] Cabinet Office, *Treaty of Waitangi Guidance* (n 58) para 17.

development. In the century and a half after the signing of Te Tiriti, tikanga's status as law, and even its existence was seldom acknowledged by the courts.

There is now a reckoning with this history. In case after case, tikanga's status as a source of values, and even of law, is acknowledged.[63] It is acknowledged that tikanga was the first law of New Zealand and was not displaced or extinguished by the arrival of the English common law, the latter applying 'only insofar as it is applicable to the circumstances of New Zealand'.[64] Tikanga is acknowledged as relevant to the development of the common law because tikanga has continued to shape and regulate the lives of iwi, hapū and whānau up until the present day.[65] Increasingly, it has also shaped the values of the broader New Zealand society particularly in relation to attitudes to the environment and to family.[66] In the public law realm it is especially relevant because of the extent to which statutes require decision-makers to take into account tikanga, or particular aspects of tikanga.[67] For example, in the Education and Training Act 2020, school boards are required under sections 9 and 27 to ensure their schools' curriculum and policies reflect tikanga Māori, mātauranga Māori (Māori knowledge) and te ao Māori (the Māori world).

The place and force of tikanga in Aotearoa's common law is now evolving quickly. The cases in which tikanga values are mandatory or discretionary considerations are fertile grounds for judicial review, requiring judges to engage in this area. But even where it is not a stipulated consideration, it has been argued and accepted that aspects of tikanga can be relevant to statutory decision-makers. In *Tukaki v Commonwealth of Australia*, for example, the Court of Appeal accepted that tikanga precepts that guided and shaped the applicant's life were relevant to the Court's assessment of whether he was ineligible for surrender on the grounds that to order it would be oppressive.[68] Another recent example is the decision of Palmer J in *Sweeney v Prison Manager, Spring Hill Corrections Facility*, in which, following a successful judicial review of a prison manager's decision to revoke a prison permit, the judge explicitly granted relief on the basis that the decision affected the mana of the plaintiff.[69]

Significant milestones in the development of jurisprudence relating to tikanga in the common law also include two recent Supreme Court decisions – *Trans-Tasman* (again) and *Ellis v R*.[70] In *Trans-Tasman*, a case that involved a question of statutory interpretation, all five judges agreed that tikanga formed part of the statutory words 'any other

[63] See, eg, *Takamore v Clarke* [2012] NZSC 116, [2013] 2 NZLR 733 [94]; *Ngāti Whātua* (n 50) [77]; *Mercury NZ Ltd v Waitangi Tribunal* [2021] NZHC 654, [2021] 2 NZLR 142 [103]; *Sweeney v Prison Manager, Spring Hill Corrections Facility* [2021] NZHC 181, [2021] 2 NZLR 127; *Trans-Tasman* (n 38) [167]; *Ellis v R* (n 7) [108] (Glazebrook J), [171] (Winkelmann CJ), [257] (Williams J), [279] (O'Regan and Arnold JJ).

[64] *Takamore v Clarke* (n 63) [150] (Tipping, McGrath and Blanchard JJ) citing *Paki v Attorney-General* [2012] NZSC 50, [2012] 3 NZLR 277 [18] (Elias CJ, Blanchard and Tipping JJ), [105] (McGrath J). See English Laws Act 1858, s 1; English Laws Act 1908, s 2, the effect of which is preserved by the Imperial Laws Application Act 1988, s 5.

[65] *Tukaki v Commonwealth of Australia* [2018] NZCA 32454, [2018] NZAR 1597.

[66] Williams (n 7) 17–26.

[67] See, eg, Oranga Tamariki Act 1989; Resource Management Act 1991; Marine and Coastal Area (Takutai Moana) Act 2011.

[68] *Tukaki* (n 65) [38].

[69] *Sweeney v Prison Manager, Spring Hill Corrections Facility* (n 63).

[70] *Trans-Tasman* (n 38); *Ellis v R* (n 7).

applicable law'.[71] The later case of *Ellis* concerned how a common law test to determine whether an appeal should continue after the appellant's death should be formulated. Of note, the appeal did not involve Māori parties or interests. Nevertheless, all judges considered tikanga in the course of addressing the particular application,[72] with two judges utilising tikanga in formulating the test and deciding the application.[73] Further, by a majority, the Court rejected the application of the colonial tests for incorporation of custom into the law as applicable to tikanga,[74] concluding simply that the relationship between tikanga and the common law should develop on a case-by-case basis.[75]

A. Tikanga and the Future

There is debate about the place of tikanga within New Zealand's common law and the methodology the courts should use in applying tikanga to the facts of any case and in the development of principle. Much of that debate is about the risk of eroding the integrity and content of tikanga.[76] I make no comment about how these issues will be resolved – that is a task for the common law method. In *Ellis* the Court warned that judges should be alive to the reality that tikanga exists as a system in its own right and therefore must ensure that when engaging with tikanga they employ processes and practices which help preserve the integrity of tikanga as a cohesive system.[77] The process adopted by counsel in *Ellis*, where a wānanga[78] of tikanga experts was convened and a joint statement of tikanga determined, is an example of that care.

David Williams argues that the recent appellate decisions in *Ngāti Whātua* and *Trans-Tasman*, along with other recent decisions, set the stage for further evolution in Aotearoa's treatment of the Treaty and tikanga Māori, particularly in the public law sphere. As Williams argues:

> … there are now two threads of authority that suggest a definite sea change in constitutional jurisprudence and somewhat less concern for constructive abeyance. First, there are cases where the courts have been less deferential to the executive and to the Waitangi Tribunal than heretofore in litigation involving Treaty of Waitangi settlement disputes. Secondly, there is a steady flow of decisions that indicate tikanga Māori is a source of the common law in this realm, and one or two decisions where application of tikanga has been determinative of the

[71] *Trans-Tasman* (n 38) [169] (William Young and Ellen France JJ), [237] (Glazebrook J), [296]–[297] (Williams J), [332] (Winkelmann CJ).

[72] *Ellis v R* (n 7) [142]–[145] (Glazebrook J), [315] (O'Regan and Arnold JJ).

[73] Winkelmann CJ and Williams J preferred a different test for continuation from the majority, explicitly shaping their test by reference to tikanga concepts: ibid [210]–[211]. Glazebrook J made clear that tikanga could be relevant at each point of her test, and that her consideration of tikanga reinforced her view as to the application of that test: ibid [144]–[146].

[74] *Ellis v R* (n 7) [113]–[116] (Glazebrook J), [177] (Winkelmann CJ), [260] (Williams J), rejecting the test set out in *The Public Trustee v Loasby* (1908) 27 NZLR 801 (SC).

[75] *Ellis v R* (n 7) [116], [119], [127] (Glazebrook J), [183] (Winkelmann CJ), [261] (Williams J).

[76] N Coates, 'The Recognition of Tikanga in the Common Law of New Zealand' [2015] *New Zealand Law Review* 1.

[77] *Ellis v R* (n 7) [120], [122] (Glazebrook J), [181] (Winkelmann CJ), [270]–[272] (Williams J).

[78] A forum to meet and discuss issues, traditionally in relation to important cultural matters: Moorfield, *Te Aka Māori Dictionary* (n 53).

outcome in the case. It is suggested that the new developments in these two lines of authority are interconnected.[79]

I have no doubt that the place of tikanga in the development of public law will continue to evolve. We have yet to see much in the way of public law challenge to decision-making by the various types of incorporated bodies which administer and hold iwi assets, and settlements.[80] Or to see explored the impact of tikanga on notions of procedural fairness – a critical aspect of tikanga is the tika (right) way to go about binding hapū and iwi members to decisions, reaching agreement, and resolving disputes.

One aspect that has undoubtedly slowed the development of the law has been a lack of knowledge on the part of judges and lawyers of tikanga concepts and values, or knowledge of the processes by which tikanga is applied to assist decision-making and resolve disputes. It is only in recent years that Māori have been joining the profession in numbers – still more recent has been the appointment of Māori in numbers to District and Senior Courts.[81] It is only in the last seven years that judges have been receiving education in relation to tikanga. I believe that the profession has lagged further behind in this regard, but this is about to change. The seventh of May 2021 was a historic day – the day on which the New Zealand Council of Legal Education resolved that te ao Māori (Māori worldview) concepts, particularly tikanga Māori, would be taught in each of the core law subjects in New Zealand universities.[82]

IV. THE NEW ZEALAND BILL OF RIGHTS ACT

The long title to the New Zealand Bill of Rights Act 1990 states that it is an Act to affirm, protect and promote human rights and fundamental freedoms in New Zealand and to affirm New Zealand's commitment to the ICCPR. As mentioned earlier, its original conception as supreme law was not carried into effect. And unlike other statutory bills of rights, the Act did not provide expressly for declarations of inconsistency.

The story of the Bill of Rights Act is a complex one in New Zealand's public law. Sir Geoffrey Palmer, the architect of the original Bill, has expressed disappointment that, after what seemed a promising start, the courts have failed to realise the potential, as he saw it, of the Act.[83] There are certainly many narratives to be explored in relation to it. There is the impact on the development of the law of the decision *R v Hansen*, in which the New Zealand Supreme Court eschewed the robust approach of the House of Lords to a statutory presumption of rights-consistency even though section 3 of the UK Human Rights Act 1998 was modelled on our own section 6 (which directs the courts to

[79] Williams, 'Justiciability and Tikanga' (n 16) 662.

[80] Williams, 'Lex Aotearoa' (n 7) 31–32.

[81] For a breakdown of the current diversity within the judiciary, see Chief Justice of New Zealand | Te Tumu Whakawa o Aotearoa, *Annual Report: 1 January 2020–31 December 2021* (Te Tari Toko i te Tumu Whakawa | The Office of the Chief Justice, March 2022) 11–16.

[82] The Council is an independent statutory body with responsibility for, amongst other things, setting the educational requirements for admission as a barrister and solicitor in New Zealand, and the quality and provision of legal education: Lawyers and Conveyancers Act 2006, pt 8.

[83] Palmer (n 19).

give an enactment a meaning that is consistent with the rights and freedoms contained in the Bill whenever that can be done).[84] There is the, perhaps related, on-going exploration of the relationship between the principle of legality and the section 6 direction.[85] And there is the impact the Act has had on administrative decision-making, which has yet to be fully settled.[86]

An important narrative is the courts' development of remedies for breaches of the Bill of Rights Act. The courts quite quickly moved to develop the remedy of damages for breaches by the Crown of protected rights.[87] However, the courts took a far more cautious approach to asserting the right to make formal declarations of inconsistency in the absence of a statutory provision conferring that power. The possibility of that step was first discussed by Cooke P in 1992, shortly after the enactment of the Bill of Rights Act, in the decision of *Temese v New Zealand Police*.[88] In *Moonen v Film and Literature Board of Review*, the Court of Appeal came close to deciding that it had the power to make such a declaration but declined to finally determine the issue.[89] Sir Geoffrey has summarised the case law after *Moonen* as exhibiting a 'pronounced judicial reluctance' to make any such declaration.[90] In the *Saxmere* case, Hammond J even pondered that it was 'curious' no courts in Aotearoa had issued a declaration of inconsistency.[91]

The issue finally came to a head in *Attorney-General v Taylor*.[92] In that case, several prisoners challenged the Bill of Rights consistency of a statutory blanket ban on voting. The Attorney-General's report to Parliament, required under section 7 of the Bill of Rights Act, reported that the ban was an unjustified limit on the right to vote under section 25 of the Act.[93] The prisoners sought a declaration of inconsistency. Each of the

[84] *R v Hansen* [2007] NZSC 7, [2007] 3 NZLR 1 in which the Court unanimously departed from the approach in *R v Lambert* [2001] UKHL 37, [2002] 1 AC 545. However, the approach in *Hansen* has been the subject of some academic critique. See, eg, A Butler, 'Interface between the Human Rights Act 1998 and Other Enactments: Pointers from New Zealand' (2000) 3 *European Human Rights Law Review* 249, 251; C Geiringer, 'The Principle of Legality and the Bill of Rights Act: A Critical Examination of *R v Hansen*' (2008) 6 *New Zealand Journal of Public and International Law* 59, 73.

[85] See, eg, *D v New Zealand Police* [2021] NZSC 2, [2021] 1 NZLR 213 [75]–[82] (Winkelmann CJ and O'Regan J), [165]–[167] (Glazebrook J); *Fitzgerald v R* [2021] NZSC 131, [2021] 1 NZLR 551 [51]–[57] (Winkelmann CJ), [207]–[217] (Arnold and O'Regan JJ), [251] (Glazebrook J), [327] (William Young J).

[86] For initial predictions as to the impact, see J McLean, P Rishworth and M Taggart, 'The Impact of the New Zealand Bill of Rights on Administrative Law' in Legal Research Foundation, *The New Zealand Bill of Rights Act 1990* (Legal Research Foundation seminars, Auckland, 24 August 1992, Wellington, 25 August 1992). For discussion of the application to administrative decision-making, see J McLean, 'The Impact of the Bill of Rights on Administrative Law Revisited: Rights, Utility, and Administration' [2008] *New Zealand Law Review* 377; C Geiringer, 'Sources of Resistance to Proportionality Review of Administrative Power under the New Zealand Bill of Rights Act' (2013) 11 *New Zealand Journal of Public and International Law* 123; H Wilberg 'The Bill of Rights in Administrative Law Cases: Taking Stock and Suggesting Some Reassessment' (2013) 25 *New Zealand Universities Law Review* 866.

[87] *Simpson v Attorney-General* [1994] 3 NZLR 667 (CA) (*Baigent's Case*). See also *Taunoa v Attorney-General* [2007] NZSC 70, [2008] 1 NZLR 429.

[88] *Temese v Police* (1992) 9 CRNZ 425 (CA) 427.

[89] *Moonen v Film and Literature Board of Review* [2000] 2 NZLR 9 (CA).

[90] G Palmer, 'The Bill of Rights after Twenty-One Years: The New Zealand Constitutional Caravan Moves On?' (2013) 11 *New Zealand Journal of Public and International Law* 257, 287.

[91] *Wool Board Disestablishment Co Ltd v Saxmere Co Ltd* [2010] NZCA 513, [2011] 2 NZLR 442 [140].

[92] *Taylor v Attorney-General* [2014] NZHC 1706, [2015] 3 NZLR 791; *Attorney-General v Taylor* [2017] NZCA 215, [2017] 3 NZLR 24; *Attorney-General v Taylor* [2018] NZSC 104, [2019] 1 NZLR 213.

[93] C Finlayson, 'Report of the Attorney-General under the New Zealand Bill of Rights Act 1990 on the Electoral (Disqualification of Convicted Prisoners) Amendment Bill' (House of Representatives, 2010).

High Court, Court of Appeal and Supreme Court accepted arguments that there was jurisdiction for such declaration to be made, and that this was a correct case in which to exercise that power.

The majority in the Supreme Court emphasised the importance of having a judicial response to a breach of rights, adopting what has been called the 'no right without a remedy' approach.[94] Glazebrook and Ellen France JJ characterised the exercise of declaratory powers as nothing more than a natural extension of the existing law.[95] Chief Justice Elias said that the need to declare inconsistencies was a matter of 'constitutional obligation'.[96] She said that the availability of declaratory relief followed from the scheme of the Bill of Rights Act and its requirement that the rights recognised apply to the acts of the legislature. While issuing a declaration of inconsistency is 'constitutional innovation', it was a consequence of the enactment of section 3 of the Act which made clear that the Act applied to the legislative branch.[97]

The majority distinguished the approach taken by the High Court of Australia in *Momcilovic v R* in which the Court held that granting a declaration of inconsistency under the Victorian Charter of Human Rights and Responsibilities Act 2006 was not a judicial function.[98] Both majority judgments held that *Momcilovic* had limited relevance given Australia's 'very different constitutional and legislative circumstances'.[99] As noted by Philip Joseph, 'the constitutional separation of powers in Australia lacks any comparison under New Zealand's flexible constitutional arrangements'.[100]

The decision is also notable for the argument advanced for the Attorney-General in the hearing that there was no breach of rights in the enactment of inconsistent legislation since the legislation itself in abridging the right had changed the scope of the right preserved in the New Zealand Bill of Rights Act. In rejecting the argument, the Chief Justice said it denied the fundamental nature of the enacted rights and said it was:

> ... inconsistent with indications, contained for example in the Cabinet Manual, that legislation such as the New Zealand Bill of Rights Act, occupies a position properly described as 'constitutional'. Nor is the argument easy to reconcile with the principle of legality, which requires Parliament to speak unmistakably when limiting fundamental rights recognised by the common law.[101]

This echoes the remarks of Laws LJ in *Thoburn v Sunderland City Council* that while ordinary statutes may be impliedly repealed, constitutional statutes may not.[102]

In response to the Supreme Court's decision, Parliament has enacted the New Zealand Bill of Rights (Declarations of Inconsistency) Amendment Act 2022. The purpose of the Act is to provide a mechanism by which Parliament can consider, and if it wishes to, respond to a declaration of inconsistency made by the courts under either the Bill of

[94] A Geddis, 'Prisoner Voting in New Zealand's Supreme Court' (2019) 30 *Public Law Review* 3, 3.
[95] *Attorney-General v Taylor* (NZSC) (n 92) [53].
[96] ibid [117].
[97] ibid.
[98] *Momcilovic v The Queen* [2011] HCA 34, (2011) 245 CLR 1.
[99] *Attorney-General v Taylor* (NZSC) (n 92) [111] (Elias CJ), [60]–[63] (Glazebrook and Ellen France JJ).
[100] PA Joseph, 'Declarations of Inconsistency under the New Zealand Bill of Rights Act 1990' (2019) 30 *Public Law Review* 7, 9.
[101] *Attorney-General v Taylor* (SC) (n 92) [103] (Elias CJ).
[102] *Thoburn v Sunderland City Council* [2003] QB 151, [2002] EWHC 195. See also Joseph (n 100) 10.

Rights Act or the Human Rights Act (the latter Act having provision for the making of such declarations in limited circumstances).[103] The explanatory note of the Bill of Rights (Declarations of Inconsistency) Amendment Bill as introduced to Parliament states that one of its purposes is to 'further the constitutional relationship of mutual respect between Parliament and the Judiciary'. The explanatory note acknowledges that declarations of inconsistency are of high public and constitutional significance, and that it is vital that in creating laws and administering them the legislative and executive branches, respectively, are both seen by the public to (and do in fact) consider such declarations properly. It is significant that the Act had broad cross-party support.

The enactment of this Act illustrates the gradual and collaborative elaboration between Parliament and the courts of New Zealand's constitutional arrangements – an elaboration born in part of the courts' assertion of their constitutional role (obligation) to determine and apply the law, even to the extent of declaring an Act of Parliament inconsistent with statutorily-affirmed rights.

V. THE ROLE OF INTERNATIONAL LAW IN AOTEAROA'S PUBLIC LAW

New Zealand exists in a far-flung part of the globe. As noted by Sir Geoffrey Palmer, it 'is a country impelled by its circumstances to be internationalist in outlook'.[104] It eventually accepted the offer of independence contained in the Statute of Westminster, although, as mentioned earlier, it did so reluctantly. Today it is international law and not colonial law that dominates as a source of extra territorial inspiration.[105] In the area of public law, the influence of international law is seen most clearly in statutory interpretation and in the area of administrative law. New Zealand courts apply a principle of statutory interpretation that domestic statutes ought to be interpreted, so far as possible, consistently with New Zealand's international obligations.[106] This presumption applies whether the source of the international obligation is a treaty or lies within customary international law.[107] In contrast to some jurisdictions, there is no requirement that there be any ambiguity in the statute for the presumption to be enlivened.[108]

[103] The Human Rights Review Tribunal was given the power to make declarations, but only in relation to unjustified breaches of the right in s 19 of the New Zealand Bill of Rights Act to freedom from discrimination: See Human Rights Act 1993, s 92J, introduced by the Human Rights Amendment Act 2001.

[104] G Palmer, 'Rethinking Public Law in a Time of Democratic Decline' (2021) 52 *Victoria University of Wellington Law Review* 414, 428.

[105] J McLean, 'From Empire to Globalization: The New Zealand Experience' (2004) 11 *Indiana Journal of Global Legal Studies* 161, 167.

[106] *Ye v Minister of Immigration* [2009] NZSC 76, [2010] 1 NZLR 104; *Helu v Immigration and Protection Tribunal* [2015] NZSC 28, [2016] 1 NZLR 298; *Ortmann v United States of America* [2020] NZSC 120, [2020] 1 NZLR 475 [96], citing *New Zealand Air Line Pilots' Assoc Inc v Attorney-General* [1997] 3 NZLR 269 (CA).

[107] T Dunworth, 'Sources of International Law in Aotearoa New Zealand' in A Hertogen and A Hood (eds), *International Law in Aotearoa New Zealand* (Thomson Reuters, 2021) 22–23, referring to numerous cases affirming this approach.

[108] *New Zealand Air Line Pilots' Assoc Inc v Attorney General* (n 106); *Wellington District Legal Services Committee v Tangiora* [1998] 1 NZLR 129 (CA); *Sellers v Maritime Safety Inspector* [1999] 2 NZLR 44 (CA). Contrast with the approach in Australia: *Minister for Immigration and Ethnic Affairs v Teoh* (1995) 183 CLR 273 (HC) 287 (Mason CJ and Deane J); *Plaintiff (S157/2002) v Commonwealth* (2003) 211 CLR 476 (HC) [29] (Gleeson CJ) and the approach in the UK: *Assange v Swedish Prosecution Authority* [2012] UKSC 22, [2012] 2 AC 471; *R (Yam) v Central Criminal Court* [2015] UKSC 76, [2016] AC 771.

The presumption of consistency with unincorporated international instruments has been applied to restrict or expand the meaning of general words or provisions conferring discretionary powers. In *Sellers v Maritime Safety Inspector*, the Court of Appeal found that general words conferring a discretion on the Director of Maritime Safety under the Maritime Transport Act 1994 should be read down to comply with international law as to freedom of the high seas.[109] And, it commented, that reading could only be widened to the extent that international law allowed. Keith J, writing for the Court, made clear just how significant a principle this was:

> To repeat, for centuries national law in this area has been essentially governed by and derived from international law with the consequence that national law is to be read, if at all possible, consistently with the related international law. That will sometimes mean that the day-to-day (or at least year-to-year) meaning of national law may vary without formal change.[110]

In *Zaoui v Attorney-General (No 2)*, the Court addressed the relationship between New Zealand's obligations under international law and the requirements of domestic statutes. Mr Zaoui was a refugee, but the Minister wished to deport him on the grounds he was a threat to national security. Mr Zaoui feared that on return to his home country he would be subject to the threat of torture or the arbitrary deprivation of his life. An issue for the Court was the relationship between New Zealand's non-refoulement obligations under Article 33 of the United Nations Convention Relating to the Status of Refugees 1951 and section 72 of the Immigration Act 1987, which allowed the relevant Minister to order deportation where they considered the refugee's continued presence constituted a threat to national security. The Supreme Court noted the interplay between the interpretive presumption in section 6 of the Bill of Rights and international law:

> As directed by s 6 of the Bill of Rights, s 72 is to be given a meaning if it can be, consistent with the rights and freedoms contained in it .... Those rights in turn are to be interpreted and the powers conferred by s 72 are to be exercised, if the wording will permit, so as to be in accordance with international law, both customary and treaty-based.[111]

The Court found nothing in the words of section 72 or the scheme of the Immigration Act preventing section 72 being read consistently with New Zealand's obligations under the ICCPR, the Convention Against Torture and the Bill of Rights Act.

Again, the question arises, does this statutory presumption provide yet another national hue to the principle of legality? Claudia Geiringer suggests that the Supreme Court in *Zaoui* treated the presumptions in section 6 of the Bill of Rights Act and the presumption of consistency with New Zealand's international obligations as of essentially the same character.[112] But against that we have to weigh the careful contextual analysis that Keith J outlined in *New Zealand Air Line Pilots' Association Inc v Attorney-General* as relevant to the operation of the presumption.[113]

[109] *Sellers v Maritime Safety Inspector* (n 108) 62.

[110] ibid 62. For example, in *TUV v Chief of New Zealand Defence Force* [2022] NZSC 69 [94] Winkelmann CJ and O'Regan J found that the presumption of consistency with New Zealand's obligations applies retrospectively to legislation enacted before the ratification of the relevant treaty.

[111] *Zaoui v Attorney-General (No 2)* [2005] NZSC 38, [2006] 1 NZLR 289 [90] (fn omitted).

[112] C Geiringer, 'International law through the lens of Zaoui: Where is New Zealand at?' (2006) 17 *Public Law Review* 300, 317.

[113] *New Zealand Air Line Pilots' Assoc Inc v Attorney-General* (n 106).

Concluding on this point, as Andrew Geddis points out, the push and pull effect of these various presumptions on the relationship between the different branches of government can be seen in the Government's own *Legislation Guidelines*, which are intended to provide best practice advice for those involved in the creation of proposed legislation. The relevant part of the guidelines state that:

> Fundamental constitutional principles and values in New Zealand law and practice run so deep that the courts will often draw on them when interpreting legislation or otherwise deciding cases. If new legislation is inconsistent with or challenges one of these fundamental principles, it will become the subject of concern and increased scrutiny of Parliament, the public, and often the courts.[114]

The courts have also been prepared to apply international law as a constraint on the exercise of administrative power. The role of international law in judicial review has been described by Treasa Dunworth as 'the central aspect of the relationship between international law and New Zealand domestic law'.[115]

Just how important international law would be in this context was established in *Tavita v Minister of Immigration*.[116] In that case, Mr Tavita sought judicial review of the Minister's decision to issue a removal warrant. The Crown argued the Minister was entitled to ignore Aotearoa's international treaty obligations relating to the rights of the child and rights to a family.[117] In rejecting this argument, the Court of Appeal affirmed that 'some international obligations are so manifestly important that no reasonable Minister could fail to take them into account'.[118]

The Court was not required to finally decide the matter in *Tavita* as it was adjourned so the Minister could consider the interests of the child. However, the comments made by the Court about the relevance of international instruments have been seminal in the development of judicial review jurisprudence. In many cases after *Tavita*, international human rights norms and international instruments have been held to be mandatory considerations for ministers and officials in the exercise of discretion.[119]

VI. CONCLUSION

As I stated at the outset of this chapter, my understanding of and perspective on Aotearoa's public law is necessarily conditioned by my position as a working judge. Judges address the issues that arise in the cases that come before them and strive to find, in accordance with the law, a resolution that serves today's society.

[114] A Geddis, 'Parliament and the Courts: Lessons from Recent Experiences' in J Burrows and J Finn (eds), *Challenge and Change: Judging in Aotearoa New Zealand* (LexisNexis, 2022) 139.

[115] Dunworth (n 107) 24.

[116] *Tavita v Minister of Immigration* [1994] 2 NZLR 257 (CA).

[117] ibid 261 referring to Arts 23(1) and 24(1) of the ICCPR (adopted 16 December 1966, entered into force 23 March 1976) 999 UNTS 171.

[118] ibid 266.

[119] See, eg, *Elika v Minister of Immigration* [1996] 1 NZLR 741 (HC); *Mil Mohamud v Minister of Immigration* [1997] NZAR 223 (HC); *Patel v Minister of Immigration* [1997] 1 NZLR 252 (HC); *Ye v Minister of Immigration* (n 106).

But my reflections today have all returned to the same point: Aotearoa's history. The history of our nation – as home to Māori, as a settler colony, as an independent nation finding its place in an international order, and in the South Pacific – continues to be played out in our society. As such, it has had, and will continue to have, a profound effect on the shaping of our public law. The topics I have touched upon, of common law presumptions in statutory interpretation, judicial review, the application of statutory bills of rights, and of international law, are all recognisable to any common law audience. But as the cases I have discussed show, these areas of law are now acquiring a distinctive Aotearoa New Zealand hue.

My final reflection is that the task of ensuring that our public law continues to be fit to regulate our institutions and to serve the people of Aotearoa New Zealand requires lawyers and judges to be grounded in the present but with a deep understanding of what has come before.

3

Justice Devolved – Milestones in Northern Ireland Constitutional Law Since 2010

SIOBHAN KEEGAN

In law, 'context is everything'. For this discussion, context is an important framing feature. However, the Northern Ireland context is also nuanced, complex, delicate and shifting. In one of the earliest constitutional cases, *Robinson v Secretary of State for Northern Ireland and Others (Northern Ireland)*,[1] Lord Bingham described the 'staccato nature' of devolution arrangements in Northern Ireland whilst also striving to find solutions to preserve it.

It is clear that Northern Ireland has an exceptional constitutional arrangement. This chapter looks at developments in the constitutional framework of Northern Ireland in recent times and considers the role the courts have played in the unique landscape of Northern Ireland constitutional law.

I. THE CONSTITUTIONAL STRUCTURE OF NORTHERN IRELAND

First to some history. The constitutional history of Northern Ireland begins over a century ago in May 1921 with the implementation of the Government of Ireland Act 1920. This created the jurisdiction of Northern Ireland as part of the then United Kingdom of Great Britain and Ireland. The Parliament of Northern Ireland was established in June 1921 and exercised its functions until 1972 when, in the early years of the period of our history known as 'the Troubles', it was suspended and 'direct rule' from Westminster imposed.

Direct rule remained in place until, in 1998, the Good Friday, or Belfast, Agreement was reached, laying the foundations for devolution of powers once again to a locally elected Northern Ireland Assembly. Related to this domestic political agreement was the international British-Irish Agreement between the governments of the United Kingdom (UK) and the Republic of Ireland. These agreements, which comprise commitments, have consistently been used to interpret our constitutional arrangements. Imprimatur is found in *Robinson* insofar as it recognises the Good Friday Agreement 1998, a political agreement which does not itself have the force of law, as an interpretative aid to the Northern Ireland Act 1998 (NIA 1998). This approach was also confirmed in *Re McCord*.[2]

[1] *Robinson v Secretary of State for Northern Ireland and Others (Northern Ireland)* [2002] UKHL 32, [2002] NI 390.

[2] *Re McCord* [2020] NICA 23.

The NIA 1998 gave effect to the Good Friday Agreement 1998 by providing the framework for the Northern Ireland devolution settlement. The NIA 1998 provides for the devolution of powers to a power-sharing Northern Ireland legislative assembly, with Northern Ireland departments being led by Northern Ireland Ministers and a system of Assembly Committees, including an Executive Committee comprising all the Northern Ireland Ministers.

The Northern Ireland Assembly has legislative and executive competence for all matters that are transferred to it under powers in the NIA 1998. These are known as 'transferred matters' and effectively comprise all matters with which central government is concerned, save those 'reserved' or 'excepted'[3] by the respective iterations of Schedules 2 and 3 to the NIA 1998 at any given time. Excepted matters include international relations and defence and foreign policy. Reserved matters include domicile and civil aviation.

Uniquely among the legislatures of the UK, Ireland and beyond, the NIA 1998 contains safeguards for minority rights, through the requirement for Assembly members, known as 'members of the legislative assembly' (MLAs), to designate as 'unionist', 'nationalist' or 'other'[4] and the 'Petition of Concern' procedure[5] which, in broad terms, allows for cross-community voting on any issue if at least 30 members so petition. While the first Northern Ireland Assembly sittings took place in 1998, it was not until 2010 that responsibility for justice and policing was transferred to the Assembly.

Northern Ireland Ministers have competence for transferred matters. The prerogative powers of His Majesty The King and executive authority in Northern Ireland in relation to transferred matters is exercisable by Ministers or departments.[6] Additionally, Ministers may have individual statutory powers.[7] By virtue of Article 4(3) of the Departments (Northern Ireland) Order 1999, Ministers may exercise the powers of their Department.

The NIA 1998 links the functions of Ministers to the functions of the Northern Ireland departments which were already in existence.[8] Accordingly, Northern Ireland Ministers act individually, not collectively.

This constitutional structure of individual ministerial responsibility is a key distinguishing feature of the Northern Ireland arrangements, differing from the structures pertaining within the UK Government and within the devolved administrations in Scotland and Wales, where Ministers act collectively and powers may be exercised by any Minister, irrespective of their portfolio. Individual ministerial responsibility is an important facet of the devolution settlement, creating what have been termed ministerial 'silos' and acting as the foundation for the exercise of executive authority on a cross-community basis.

This new structure was complemented by continuance of the historical practice under the Government of Ireland Act 1920 of conferring statutory powers upon specific Ministers or specific departments, rather than upon Ministers collectively. The structure was maintained during the period of direct rule (1972–1999) when the Northern

[3] Northern Ireland Act 1998, ss 4, 5 and 6.
[4] ibid ss 4(5), and Standing Orders.
[5] ibid s 42.
[6] ibid s 23.
[7] ibid s 22.
[8] ibid s 17(1) and (3).

Ireland Parliament was prorogued and the executive powers of Ministers transferred to the Secretary of State.[9] This foundation enabled the new power-sharing institutions to be grafted onto the existing structure of government in Northern Ireland. It also avoided a complete re-write of the Northern Ireland statute book which must have caused a hearty sign of relief.

The number of departments and ministerial portfolios was increased in 1999, essentially to create sufficient 'seats at the table' for executive powers to be spread across the political spectrum. There were originally 10 departments and two junior ministers.[10] This was reduced in 2015 to seven departments. That in itself has attracted comment as it might be argued that Northern Ireland could function with fewer departments but sufficient 'seats at the table' are still required to ensure cross-community representation in the Executive Committee of the Assembly.

The First Minister (FM) and deputy First Minister (dFM) were originally appointed jointly, by a single vote of the Assembly on a cross-community basis.[11] These are separate offices, however, uniquely, their powers are exercised jointly with one another. There are very few express statutory recognitions of the joint nature of the office. It is not expressly recognised in the NIA 1998. Article 2 of the Departments (Northern Ireland) Order 1999 provides for the Executive Office to be under the direction and control of the FM and dFM acting jointly. Many other specific statutory functions are conferred upon the FM and dFM acting jointly, such as appointing the Attorney-General for Northern Ireland.

Ministerial appointments made by the nominating officer of a political party represented in the Assembly are made in accordance with the mathematics of the 'D'Hont Formula'.[12]

The Executive Committee, commonly referred to as 'the Executive', is a committee of the Assembly. It comprises all Northern Ireland Ministers.[13] Originally, the functions of the Executive were limited to those set out in paragraphs 19 and 20 of Strand 1 of the Good Friday Agreement, ie agreeing a common position on matters 'cutting across responsibility of two or more ministers', prioritising legislative proposals, external relations and agreeing a Programme for Government linked to a budget. Importantly, it is a 'forum for discussion of and agreement upon' matters by Ministers. The Executive does not have executive powers with executive authority being conferred on Ministers and departments.[14]

As mentioned, policing and justice functions were not initially devolved, that was as a result of ongoing disputes about decommissioning of paramilitary weapons. In the early years, the Democratic Unionist Party (DUP) took up ministerial posts but would not sit in the Executive with Sinn Féin Ministers. This led to some early Minister versus Minister litigation when Ministers Morrow and Campbell of the DUP sought a judicial review of a decision by the FM and dFM to refuse to circulate copies of an Executive paper to them.[15]

[9] Northern Ireland (Temporary Provisions) Act 1972, s 1.

[10] See Article 3 of the Departments (Northern Ireland) Order 1999 (as originally enacted) and the Departments (Transfer and Assignment of Functions) Order 1999.

[11] Northern Ireland Act 1998, s 16.

[12] ibid s 18(3).

[13] ibid s 20(1).

[14] See *Re Solinas* [2009] NIQB 43 [30].

[15] *Re Campbell and Morrow* [2001] NIQB 13.

This brings me to the authority vested in the Executive and the parameters of power. First, it is of note that the Northern Ireland Executive does not itself have executive authority. Authority is vested solely in individual ministers who have responsibility for individual departments. The role of the Executive is therefore limited to approving (or not) the exercise of ministerial power by the relevant Minister. The point is explained in the case of *Re Solinas*:

> It is, however, important to recognise that the Executive Committee has not and never has had executive power or the entitlement to exercise executive power. By virtue of s 23(2) of the 1998 Act it is Ministers or Northern Ireland departments who have the right to exercise executive power although there were certain savings in respect of the Northern Ireland Civil Service and the Commissioner for Public Appointments for Northern Ireland. That position has not been altered by the 2006 Act.[16]

The devolved institutions collapsed in 2002 as a result of allegations that a 'spy ring' was operating in Northern Ireland governmental structures. The UK Government responded by re-introducing direct rule, as provided for in the Northern Ireland Act 2000 (NIA 2000). Using the power in section 1 of that Act, the Assembly was suspended. Northern Ireland legislation was to be made using the Order in Council procedure[17] and the powers of Northern Ireland Ministers were exercisable by the Secretary of State.[18] Direct rule remained in place until 2007 when the institutions were reinstated as a result of the St Andrews Agreement 2006 in which Sinn Féin and the DUP agreed to share power.

The St Andrews Agreement included a number of important structural and procedural changes to the devolved institutions,[19] implemented by amendments to the NIA 1998 brought in by the Northern Ireland (St Andrews Agreement) Act 2006 (SAA 2006). The changes included the inclusion of deadlines for the formation of an Executive, later extended by the Northern Ireland (St Andrews Agreement) Act 2007 (SAA 2007). The NIA 2000 was repealed by the SAA 2006, thereby removing the default safety net of direct rule from the statute book.

Under the St Andrews Agreement, the FM and dFM are now appointed separately by the nominating officers of the largest two parties in the Assembly. Both offices were to be filled within seven days following the election of an Assembly, extended to 14 days in 2016.[20] Other Ministers continue to be appointed by the nominating officers of parties.[21]

This brings me to what I will describe as an unusual arrangement for Ministers ceasing to hold office. The FM or dFM could resign at any time, resulting in the other ceasing to hold office. This happened in February 2022 when then First Minister Paul Givan resigned as part of the DUP's protests against the Ireland/Northern Ireland Protocol. Otherwise, the FM and dFM held office until immediately before the offices were next filled.[22] However, the remaining Northern Ireland Ministers ceased to hold office upon the election of the next Assembly.[23]

[16] *Re Solinas* (n 14) [30].
[17] Northern Ireland Act 2000, Sch 1, para 1.
[18] ibid para 4.
[19] Agreement at St Andrews, Annex A.
[20] Northern Ireland Act 1998, s 16A.
[21] ibid s 18.
[22] ibid ss 16A(10) and 16B.
[23] ibid s 16A(1)–(3).

The provisions relating to ministerial resignations and appointment have two interesting consequences. Firstly, the combination of the provisions enabled a 'gap' in ministerial control in the event of a failure to appoint the FM and dFM following an election. It led directly to the prolonged stalemate following the March 2017 election, called by the Secretary of State, following the resignation of the dFM in January 2017. The provisions have since been amended so that there is now a period of up to 24 weeks after an election for an Executive to be formed. Ministers remain in office until new Ministers are appointed.[24] Secondly, the power of Ministers to resign and for appointments to be made by the nominating officer of the party enabled a so-called 'ministerial merry-go-round' as a form of protest, without bringing down the Executive whereby Ministers resigned in a co-ordinated sequence and were then individually re-appointed just before expiry of the statutory period.

The SAA 2006 also contained amendments to the ministerial Pledge of Office to include a pledge to uphold the rule of law and to participate fully in the Executive Committee, the North/South Ministerial Council and the British/Irish Council,[25] along with new provisions for the nomination of Ministers to attend the North South Ministerial Council and duty to attend.[26] There was also a requirement for a new Ministerial Code[27] reinforced by a statutory obligation for ministers to comply with the Code.[28] Ministers have 'no ministerial authority' to act in a manner contrary to the Ministerial Code.[29] The functions of the Executive Committee were amended to include discussion of, and agreement on, 'significant or controversial matters' which were either 'clearly outside' the Programme for Government or determined by the FM and dFM as matters to be decided by the Executive.[30] There was also a new procedure for 30 MLAs to require a decision of a Minister to be referred to the Executive.[31]

The SAA 2006 inserted a new section 21A into the NIA 1998 which conferred upon the Assembly power to establish a new department for the purpose of exercising policing and justice functions. This was done by way of the Department of Justice Act (Northern Ireland) 2010 which came into operation in April 2010. A suite of secondary legislation transferred a range of existing statutory powers and functions to the new Department of Justice.[32]

The Minister of Justice is appointed by a different procedure to other Ministers. On the proposal of a MLA, the Minister of Justice is approved by a resolution of the Assembly, with cross-community support.[33] To date, no member of the main nationalist or unionist parties has held the post, the three post-holders being: David Ford (2010–2016; Alliance Party, designated as Other); Clare Sugden (2016–2017; Independent, designated as Unionist); Naomi Long (2020 – present, designated as Other).

[24] Northern Ireland (Elections, Ministers and Petitions of Concern) Act 2022, s 2.
[25] St Andrews Agreement Act 2006, Sch 4.
[26] ibid s 52A – 52C.
[27] Northern Ireland Executive Ministerial Code.
[28] St Andrews Agreement Act 2006, s 28A(5).
[29] ibid s 28A(10).
[30] ibid s 20(4).
[31] ibid s 28B.
[32] See, eg, The Northern Ireland Act 1998 (Devolution of Policing and Justice Functions) Order 2010.
[33] Department of Justice Act (Northern Ireland) 2010, s 2.

II. LEGAL OBLIGATIONS ARISING UNDER THE MINISTERIAL CODE

From this background, I move to the growing body of Northern Ireland jurisprudence relating to the legal obligations arising under the Ministerial Code. While there has always been a Ministerial Code, the combined effect of the ministerial obligation to comply with the Code[34] and the lack of ministerial authority to act in a manner contrary to it[35] have given its content significant legal effect. These are very important obligations, with potent legal effects. Expansion of the circumstances in which Executive approval is required can also have significant political consequences. It can slow the pace of political decisions. It can also trigger political 'trading' in which Executive parties either seek compromise on the proposal or on other proposals.

The Ministerial Code confers responsibility for setting the Executive agenda upon the FM and dFM acting jointly.[36] Even where an obligation to refer a decision arises, there may be a lack of agreement between the FM and dFM and the matter may not make it onto the agenda – at least for some time.

The FM and dFM have a duty under the Code to seek consensus on decisions. Discharge of this duty can delay matters getting onto the agenda. They also have a duty to put matters to a vote in the Executive. If three Ministers require, a proposal must achieve cross-community consensus to pass.[37]

Paragraph 2.4 of the Ministerial Code places an obligation upon Ministers to refer to the Executive those matters which fall within its functions. These provisions are intended to prevent ministerial 'solo runs'. To date, the courts have interpreted the obligation widely. In every case in which the issue has been raised, the court has found that the Minister was subject to an obligation to refer.

Re Buick is an important constitutional case in Northern Ireland where these issues came into sharp focus during a time of governmental stasis.[38] In the absence of a Minister in charge due to ongoing political difficulties, a senior civil servant took a decision on behalf of the Department of Infrastructure to grant planning permission for a major waste treatment centre and incinerator. This led to a challenge by a member of the community who, assisted by lawyers, raised issues of competence in decision-making within our constitutional structures.

At first instance, the High Court held that, in the absence of a Minister in charge, the Department did not have power to grant the permission. At appeal, the Court of Appeal focused on whether planning permission for a regional waste incineration plant was cross-cutting, a point which had not occupied much space at first instance. It held that the matter was cross-cutting, based on the fact that the decision engaged the 'interests' of the Minister with responsibility for the Department of Agriculture, Environment and Rural Affairs. This is different from the statutory language of 'responsibilities of two or more ministers'. Previously, planning decisions had not been considered to engage the responsibilities of other ministers.

[34] ibid s 28A(5).
[35] ibid s 28A(1).
[36] Ministerial Code, para 2.11.
[37] ibid para 2.12 and s 28A(8).
[38] *Re Buick* [2018] NIQB 43, [2018] NICA 26.

This decision led swiftly to legislation in the form of the Executive Committee (Functions) Act (Northern Ireland) 2020, which amended section 20 of the NIA 1998 to make provision concerning the decisions which may be made by Ministers without recourse to the Executive Committee.

Also in receipt of court attention is paragraph 2.3(vi) of the Ministerial Code which provides that the Executive Committee shall provide a forum for discussion of and agreement upon significant or controversial matters that are clearly outside the scope of the agreed programme for government. This has been interpreted broadly and thus given rise to an increase in the number of decisions which must go to the Executive.

An illustration of this is the case of *Re Minister of Finance & Personnel*,[39] it was found that a decision to allow a proportion of EU Common Agricultural Policy funding for direct payments to farmers to be transferred to fund rural development projects was both 'significant' and 'controversial'. The Minister for Agriculture and Rural Development should have brought the matter to the attention of the Executive Committee and therefore had made the decision in breach of the Ministerial Code. There was no authority to make the decision and therefore it was quashed.

In both *Re Central Craigavon*,[40] and *Re SAFE Electricity*,[41] the Court considered that the issue of whether a matter was 'controversial' should be considered by reference to the views of other Ministers. However, in *Re Buick*, it may be argued that the Northern Ireland Court of Appeal took a broader approach and considered the question by reference to the level of public interest in (and opposition to) the proposed incinerator. This is an issue which the courts may be asked to consider more closely in forthcoming litigation: 'public controversy' may not be the same as 'politically controversial'.

There have also been occasions where the Executive has failed to agree a Programme for Government. In *Re Central Craigavon*, it was held that, in the absence of a Programme for Government, not all significant or controversial decisions might need to be referred. In *Re Buick*, the Court of Appeal reached the opposite conclusion. It concluded that the correct interpretation was for all significant or controversial decisions to be referred unless within the Programme for Government. Section 20 of the NIA 1998 has now been amended to reflect the *Buick* interpretation.[42]

Paragraph 2.3(vii) of the Ministerial Code provides that the Executive Committee shall provide a forum for discussion of and agreement upon significant or controversial matters which the FM and dFM acting jointly have determined should be considered by the Executive. Under paragraph 2.4(vi) of the Ministerial Code, where the FM and dFM have so determined, a Minister is under a duty to bring the matter to the attention of the Executive to be considered by it.

Elucidation of this is readily found in *Re Minister for Enterprise, Trade and Investment*,[43] the Minister for Environment adopted the Belfast Metropolitan Area Plan, a statutory area development plan which took approximately seven years to prepare, without Executive approval. The FM and dFM had jointly determined that the matter

[39] *Re Minister of Finance & Personnel* [2013] NIQB 137.
[40] *Re Central Craigavon* [2012] NI 60.
[41] *Re SAFE Electricity* [2021] NIQB 93, [2022] NICA 61.
[42] Executive Committee (Functions) (NI) Act 2020, s 1(2).
[43] *Re Minister for Enterprise, Trade and Investment* [2016] NIQB 26, [2017] NICA 28.

should be considered by the Executive on the basis that it was both significant and controversial. The Minister did so refer but the Executive did not agree and there were ongoing objections from other Ministers. The Minister eventually proceeded unilaterally to direct his department to adopt the Plan and this was challenged by the Minister for Enterprise, Trade and Investment in judicial review proceedings. The decision was found to have been unlawful on the basis that the Environment Minister had no power to make a decision in violation of the Ministerial Code.

The case of *Re Solinas* provides an interesting contrast. This case related to departmental funding for certain post-conflict community organisations. The FM and dFM decided that the matter should come before the Executive. It was considered and the Executive decided how the decision-making process should then conclude. The Minister proceeded in a manner that was not in accordance with how the Executive had determined the matter should proceed. The Court found no breach of the Ministerial Code, however, it quashed the Minister's decision on the basis of the procedural error.

I now move to consider North–South relations within our constitutional structure. The North South Ministerial Council (NSMC) was established under the Good Friday Agreement to develop consultation, co-operation and action within the island of Ireland in relation to six 'Areas of Co-operation', namely agriculture, education, environment, health, tourism and transport.

Paragraph 3.11 of the Ministerial Code requires appropriate Ministers, or nominees, to participate in NSMC meetings. There are two interesting legal cases in which this has arisen, reflecting both sides of the obligation. They straddle the St Andrews Agreement reforms and each is an example of a case where the court has intervened to enforce ministerial obligations.

In *Re De Brun*,[44] the FM refused to nominate Sinn Féin Ministers to attend NSMC meetings (for which they were the responsible Ministers), with a view to encouraging them to exercise influence to achieve decommissioning. A Sinn Féin Minister successfully sought a judicial review of the decision, which was quashed on the ground that the power to nominate Ministers to attend had been exercised for an improper purpose – it was a straightforward application of the principle in *Padfield v Minister of Agriculture, Fisheries and Food*.[45]

More recently, in *Re Napier*,[46] DUP Ministers followed a party policy of refusing to participate in NSMC meetings in protest at the Ireland/Northern Ireland Protocol. The Court found that this was a breach of ministerial obligations and of the Pledge of Office. The Court expressed itself in strong terms as to the propriety of this however, ultimately it did not order mandatory relief. The Court however found that the refusal to nominate Ministers to enable participation was an exercise of power for an improper purpose.

Pursuant to paragraph 2.14 of the Code, the Executive can give retrospective approval for decisions. This does not feature heavily in the case law as the decisions tend to be of a contentious nature and frequently Executive approval might not be forthcoming. In *Re Minister for Enterprise, Trade and Development*, the Executive had given retrospective

[44] *Re De Brun* [2001] NI 442.
[45] *Padfield v Minister of Agriculture, Fisheries and Food* [1968] AC 77 (HL).
[46] *Re Napier* [2021] NIQB 86 and [2021] NIQB 120.

approval for the entirety of the Belfast Metropolitan Area Plan (BMAP), save for a contentious proposed planning policy which related to retail development at the Sprucefield site outside Lisburn. In the High Court, this was sufficient to prevent an order for *certiorari*. However, the remedies decision was overturned in the Court of Appeal and the adoption decision was quashed.

Where the courts have found a breach of the obligation to refer a decision to the Executive Committee, they have invariably quashed the decision. The BMAP case is a good example which illustrates the potency of the provision.

That said there are some examples of decisions which were not quashed which I will also reference. In *Re Central Craigavon*, the Minister had written in advance to colleagues and received supportive comments from most Ministers. The Court concluded that the contravention of the Code was technical in nature and inadvertent. This was sufficient not to quash the planning policy on this ground. On appeal, the issue had fallen away as the policy was withdrawn.

In *Re SAFE Electricity*, the Court considered that the Minister had kept the Executive apprised of her proposed conduct, even if she did not seek express approval. It also concluded that the disempowering effect of section 28A(10) of the NIA 1998 only applied to a contravention of the Code prepared under section 28A(5), which in turn required referral to the Executive of matters which, by reason of its functions under section 20(3) or (4) of the NIA 1998, fell within its responsibilities. By the time of the decision, the Assembly had amended section 20 to exempt planning decisions from its responsibilities. Accordingly, the Court held that section 28A(5) did not apply. The Minister had therefore acted in breach of the Code, but had not been deprived of authority. The decision was therefore not quashed.

The decision in *Re SAFE Electricity* was overturned by the Northern Ireland Court of Appeal in October 2022.[47] Prior to that, it was applied with most significance in a decision relating to the development of a football stadium at Casement Park in Belfast. In *Mooreland and Owenvarragh Residents Association Application*,[48] the first instance Court, despite what was described as a 'full frontal attack' on the decision in *SAFE Electricity*, applied it. The Court took this course on the basis of judicial comity and the precedent of the earlier decision but also because it felt that the argument that the Assembly could itself amend the Ministerial Code was an attractive one. The Court thought that if section 20(7) was not effective, this could 'potentially subvert the constitutional arrangements since it would be in the hands of the Executive to decide when and to what extent primary legislation would be in force'.[49]

A further interesting question relates to standing. To date, the courts have not considered the question of whether individuals (as opposed to members of the Executive) have standing to bring challenges based upon a lack of Executive approval. So far, third party challenges such as in *Re Solinas* and *Re Central Craigavon* have been accepted and determined without dispute on standing.

This body of case law illustrates the perhaps unique consequence of Northern Ireland Ministers having individual rather than collective responsibility. In the absence

[47] *Minister for Infrastructure v Safe Electricity Ltd and the Executive Office* [2022] NICA 61.
[48] *Mooreland and Owenvarragh Residents Association Application* [2022] NIQB 40.
[49] ibid [48].

of agreement within the Executive, the concept of collective ministerial responsibility is heavily modified in Northern Ireland. There is now a long tradition of Ministers suing one another, something which is unheard of in other jurisdictions.

III. PROCEDURAL DEADLOCKS

The above discussion also highlights a phenomenon I will term 'procedural deadlocks', which has exercised the courts in dealing with constitutional issues.

On this, I can do no better than the analysis of the Good Friday Agreement and the NIA 1998 by Lord Bingham in *Robinson*.[50] He summarises the minority safeguards within the constitutional arrangements in Northern Ireland. These have changed slightly over the years, but arrangements and institutions are still founded upon the need for consent and agreement across the political spectrum. They can be broadly categorised as follows:

- Assembly: Assembly is elected by proportional representation, ensuring cross-community representation. The requirement for a cross-community vote, where required by 30 MLAs.[51]
- Executive: Ministerial offices are filled using the D'Hont system, thus ensuring mandatory coalition. Cross-community voting within the Executive can be required by three Ministers.[52]
- FM and dFM: This office lies at the heart of the devolved arrangements. They are separate offices, but the functions are exercised jointly.

Inevitably, all of these protections for minority interests give rise to multiple opportunities for procedural deadlock. The general principle is that unless there is agreement on a position, there is no agreement and hence no position. This can manifest itself in multiple ways: a backlog of proposals within the Executive, papers not making it onto the Agenda, failure to provide instructions to courts and legal advisors, sometimes even failure to agree on correspondence.

There are relatively few cases in which these issues have been raised or analysed. In *Re Hughes*,[53] the Minister for Justice brought forward a proposal for funding the Lord Chief Justice's legacy inquest plan. The then FM refused to put it on the agenda as she considered that the proposal should be more 'balanced' and that legacy proposals should embrace a range of other measures. This debate took place in the context of an existing Article 2 duty to hold inquests in cases where they had been ordered (or opened). In that case Lord Justice Girvan ultimately found that the action was unlawful. There are important aspects of the decision as follows. It was found that it was impermissible for the FM to take account of other factors and proposals, rather than the proposal made by the Minister.

This case arose on the borders of law and politics. The Court analysed the actions of the FM on an individual basis, rather than the joint position. The Court recognised the

[50] *Robinson* (n 1).
[51] Northern Ireland Act 1998, s 42.
[52] ibid s 28A(8).
[53] *Re Hughes* [2020] NI 257.

entitlement of the FM and dFM to disagree, but found that they must first engage in bona fide discussion on a proposal, rather than blocking it. This raises the difficult question about how hard the FM and dFM must try before failing to reach agreement and also the extent to which the courts are prepared to exercise supervisory jurisdiction over both the process and the reasons for disagreement and when the boundary is crossed.

One possible boundary is a refusal by a FM or dFM to consider an issue and hence to perform a function of the office. This issue was explored in some detail in the second judgment in *Re Napier*, where there was an effective refusal by the FM to discharge the function of nominating Ministers to attend the NSMC or agree the agenda. However, the case did proceed on the assumption that the Court could exercise supervisory jurisdiction over the actions of the FM alone and also that there was a legal duty to discuss and consider proposals on the merits. The facts of *Re Napier* and the reasons for refusal were therefore different to those in *Re Hughes*.

IV. GOVERNING IN THE ABSENCE OF AGREEMENT

Impasses in government in Northern Ireland have also resulted in the Westminster Parliament stepping in to make legislation. Abortion is an example of an area where Parliament acted not to fill a gap in the devolution settlement but where deadlock among the devolved authorities resulted in a failure to vindicate recognised rights.

Section 9 of the Northern Ireland (Executive Formation etc) Act 2019 imposed a statutory power and obligation upon the Secretary of State to make provision for abortion in Northern Ireland. The Secretary of State did so by way of regulations. This solution was less than perfect, however, as the Secretary of State did not have executive authority to direct and control the devolved health authorities. Giving effect to the regulations therefore required action by the devolved authorities and Executive agreement. Further deadlocks were inevitably experienced and further regulations passed conferring additional powers to direct Northern Ireland authorities.

There are two important features of the events. Firstly, primary legislation was required to empower the Secretary of State to exercise legislative and executive authority in Northern Ireland in relation to a transferred matter. Secondly, this is the first example of Parliament empowering the Secretary of State to act, at a time when an Executive was in place. Parallel executive authority is a constitutional novelty. The issues are still the subject of ongoing litigation (*Re SPUC*).[54]

In addition, I mention that section 8 of the 2019 Act required the Secretary of State to make regulations providing for same sex marriage. However, section 8 has not given rise to litigation.

Another area where a bespoke solution was required as a result of a failure to reach agreement is social welfare. Welfare is a transferred matter and in 2015, the Northern Ireland parties reached a deadlock over welfare reform. A new legislative structure was enacted which enables the Secretary of State to legislate for welfare, while leaving open the

[54] *Re SPUC* [2022] NIQB 9. Since the time of writing this chapter, the Northern Ireland Court of Appeal dismissed an application for judicial review; *In the Matter of an Application by SPUC Pro-Life Limited for Judicial Review v The Secretary of State for Northern Ireland and Others* [2023] NICA 35.

option of the devolved authorities doing so if future agreement is reached. The chain of legislative provisions is explained in the reference by the Attorney General for Northern Ireland of devolution issues to the Supreme Court pursuant to paragraph 34 of Schedule 10 to the Northern Ireland Act 1998, relating to Universal Credit.[55]

Section 1 of the Welfare Reform (Northern Ireland) Act 2015 (UK legislation) provides that Her Majesty may legislate by Order in Council for social security and child support in Northern Ireland. An Order in Council was made providing that either the Secretary of State or a Northern Ireland department may make regulations dealing with welfare provisions. However, until such time as the Secretary of State appoints, the power can only be exercised by the Secretary of State. This enables contentious welfare reforms to be made by the Secretary of State, without deadlock occurring, but keeps open the option of future departmental action, either in specific cases or generally. The role of the Secretary of State is also important to ensure parity in welfare provision across the UK and thus prevent 'welfare tourism'.

V. GOVERNING IN THE ABSENCE OF POWER-SHARING

A further watershed in our constitutional functioning was in early 2017 when the dFM resigned. Under the legislative framework pertaining at the time, this meant that the FM and Northern Ireland Ministers were no longer in post. That remained the case until 2020. During this period, there were two challenges which concerned the powers of departments to act in the absence of Ministers.

In *Re Hughes*, the Court made the *obiter* comments that the requirement in Article 4 of the Departments (Northern Ireland) Order 1999 for departments to be under the control of a minister 'at all times' must be read subject to the qualification 'provided there is a Minister in place'.[56] The Court also accepted that during the statutory period for formation of an Executive, authority for devolved matters did not revert to the Secretary of State.

The Court of Appeal and the High Court took a different approach on this issue in *Re Buick*. The Court of Appeal held that the NIA 1998 must be interpreted in accordance with constitutional principle. Civil servants could not act without Ministers and the NIA 1998 should not be interpreted in a manner which permitted departments to function without Ministers. The potential result was a significant gap in governance for Northern Ireland departments during periods when Ministers were not in place. The contrary argument was that section 23(2) of the NIA 1998 expressly referred to devolved executive authority being exercisable by 'any Minister or Northern Ireland Department'.

Article 4 of the Departments (Northern Ireland) Order 1999 also permitted the statutory powers of a department to be exercised by a Minister or senior civil servant. It was argued that Parliament could not have intended that departments would be unable to exercise any functions during a period when Ministers were not in place. The NIA 1998 also expressly anticipated gaps in Ministers in the period following elections.

[55] *Attorney General of Northern Ireland's Reference* [2020] UKSC 2.
[56] Departments (Northern Ireland) Order 1999, Art 4, para 63.

There were two significant practical problems associated with the contrary argument, the first being that it was unclear how long Parliament intended this stalemate could continue, when the House of Lords in *Robinson* had recognised that the Secretary of State's duty to call an election contained flexibility and did not necessarily crystallise immediately after the statutory period for an election lapsed. The second was that there was no clear principled basis on which the Court could decide which statutory powers could be exercised by departments and in which circumstances, for example, were there decisions which would otherwise go to the Executive?

Buick is a clear example of a situation in which the court considered that the 'gap' in the Northern Ireland constitutional arrangements was too significant and that it required a legislative solution. Parliament responded swiftly to the problem in two separate statutes. The Northern Ireland (Executive Formation and Exercise of Functions) Act 2018 addressed the immediate problem by both (a) setting fixed (but extendable) periods for formation of an Executive[57] and (b) expressly permitting departments to exercise all statutory functions in the absence of Ministers, including decisions which would otherwise go to the Executive. Statutory guidance by the Secretary of State required departments to carry out a public interest assessment prior to exercising functions. In practice, some departments with a Permanent Secretary who had a greater appetite for risk and was willing to take significant decisions, did so, while others were less willing. This was a 'short term solution' insofar as the arrangements came to an end once an Executive was formed.

The Northern Ireland (Ministers, Elections and Petitions of Concern) Act 2022 contained a longer-term solution. The rules are complex, but in summary, existing Ministers now remain in place until new Ministers are appointed, even if the FM and dFM are not in place. Accordingly, even if the Executive cannot meet, departments have Ministers and can function.[58] The Assembly (on a cross-community vote) can resolve for Ministers to cease to hold office. Additionally, the period for formation of an Executive following an election is six weeks, extendable up to 24 weeks (subject to a period of 48 weeks since a gap in the offices of the FM and dFM). There is no permanent 'fall back' solution within the 2022 Act for departments to exercise functions in the absence of Ministers. From a constitutional perspective, the 'gap' in the constitutional arrangements for governance in Northern Ireland was addressed by Parliament and not the courts.

In other circumstances, solutions have been found by an interpretative route. The example I give is that the courts in Northern Ireland have twice considered the duty upon the Secretary of State to call an election. In *Robinson*, there was a fixed period within which the Assembly was required to elect a FM and dFM. If there was no appointment, the Secretary of State had a duty to call an election. In this case, the resolution was passed two days late.

The House of Lords held that the appointment was valid. The NIA 1998 was, in substance, a constitution for Northern Ireland and should be interpreted 'generously and purposively' in light of the objectives of restoring peace and devolved government in Northern Ireland. It found that the duty to call an election was triggered as soon as the

[57] The period for formation of an Executive was extended by the Northern Ireland (Executive Formation etc) Act 2019.

[58] Northern Ireland (Ministers, Elections and Petitions of Concern) Act 2022, s 2.

statutory time period elapsed, but that the Secretary of State had some flexibility and was entitled to exercise his political judgment about the timing of a new election, subject to there being 'no prolonged vacuum'.

Another recent case of import which led to a legislative solution is *In Re JR 80*.[59] In that case the applicant wished to see the establishment of the Historical Institutional Abuse Redress Board. It was not possible in the absence of Ministers and the Assembly. The conduct of the case coincided with the enactment of the Northern Ireland (Executive Formation and Exercise of Functions) Act 2018. This aspect of the case therefore fell away. However, the case is important insofar as the applicant contended that the Secretary of State for Northern Ireland was under a duty to act.

The Court found that the Secretary of State had no executive authority in Northern Ireland in relation to 'transferred' matters. He had no power to direct and control Northern Ireland departments and had no prerogative functions. The 'safety net' provisions which were contained in the Northern Ireland Act 2000 had been repealed. The result was a gap in executive authority in Northern Ireland. This followed on from the decision in *Re Hughes*. The case ultimately came to an end when the Secretary of State secured enactment by Parliament of the Historical Institutional Abuse (Northern Ireland) Act 2019.

VI. SOVEREIGNTY ISSUES IN NORTHERN IRELAND

To complete this discussion, I must also mention the consent principle which is tied to issues of sovereignty. The constitutional status of Northern Ireland within the UK is recognised expressly in section 1 of the NIA 1998. It may only change following a border poll conducted in accordance with Schedule 1 to that Act. A border poll may take place in two circumstances, both of which involve the exercise of political judgment by the Secretary of State:

i. The Secretary of State has a discretion to call a border poll at any time (ie an assessment of public interest).[60]
ii. The Secretary of State has a duty to call a border poll if he considers that a majority are likely to vote in favour (ie an assessment of public opinion).[61]

The Secretary of State may not order a poll until seven years have lapsed since a previous poll.[62]

There are two cases in which the issue of a border poll has arisen in Northern Ireland. *Re Agnew*[63] and *Re McCord* involved cases which arose from disputes as to the 'constitutional requirements' which govern a decision by the UK to withdraw from the European Union under Article 50 of the Treaty of the European Union. The Supreme Court rejected the submission that a change in the constitutional status of Northern Ireland would

[59] *In Re JR 80* [2019] NIQB 43.
[60] Northern Ireland Act 1998, Sch 1, para 1.
[61] ibid Sch 1, para 2.
[62] ibid Sch 1, para 3.
[63] *Re Agnew* [2017] UKSC 5.

require the consent of the people of Northern Ireland. It was confirmed that the Good Friday Agreement and the NIA 1998 relate only to the question of whether Northern Ireland remains in the UK or forms part of a united Ireland.

In *Re McCord*, the applicant contended that the Secretary of State was under an obligation to promulgate a policy governing the circumstances in which he might call a border poll, the factors which he would take into account and the sources of evidence he would rely upon. The High Court and Court of Appeal rejected the submission. The Court of Appeal held that this was an intensely politically sensitive power and that the judgments which the Secretary of State must form were broad. It was stated that he should be allowed flexibility, rather than be constrained by a policy formulated at one point in time or by reference to fixed sources of evidence. A policy which contained 'built-in' flexibility would be of little value. Permission to appeal to the Supreme Court was refused.

Critically the Court was influenced in its interpretation of the NIA 1998 by the content of the British-Irish Agreement (an international treaty) which was entered into at the same time as the Good Friday Agreement. A draft of the British-Irish Agreement is annexed to the Good Friday Agreement. It contains guarantees such as the principle of consent and dual citizenship rights. It also contains a commitment by the Secretary of State to discharge his political functions in Northern Ireland with 'rigorous impartiality'.

VII. DEVOLUTION ISSUES AND THE ATTORNEY GENERAL'S REFERENCE

I have been referencing cases which come to the courts by way of judicial review applications. Another mechanism exists for the resolution of constitutional issues which I will briefly mention. Under section 22 of the Justice (Northern Ireland) Act 2002, since justice and policing was devolved in 2010, it has been the duty of the FM and dFM to appoint the Attorney General for Northern Ireland. There have been two Attorney Generals in Northern Ireland in that time – John Larkin QC (May 2010 – June 2020) and Dame Brenda King (June 2020 – present).

The Attorney General has a mix of common law powers and specific statutory powers in relation to transferred matters which form part of the devolution settlement. She must exercise her functions independently of any other person.[64] The Advocate-General for Northern Ireland retains functions in respect of excepted and reserved matters. The common law powers of the Attorney General are those traditionally associated with the public interest functions of a law officer. These include acting as the chief legal advisor to the Executive; providing advice to Ministers/departments; acting for departments in litigation, where instructed; and relator actions.

By virtue of Schedule 10, paragraph 5 to the NIA 1998, the Attorney General is put on notice of any court case in which a devolution issue under the NIA 1998 arises and they may participate in the litigation. She may also institute proceedings for the determination of a devolution issue and may defend any such proceedings.[65] The Attorney may 'require' any court or tribunal to refer a devolution issue which it is considering to the

[64] Justice (Northern Ireland) Act 2002, s 22(5).
[65] Northern Ireland Act 1998, Sch 10, para 4.

Supreme Court[66] and she has power to refer any devolution issue which is not the subject of proceedings to the Supreme Court for determination.[67]

The powers of the Attorney General in respect of devolution issues have given rise to a small body of jurisprudence. The Supreme Court has twice rejected a freestanding reference where there were not proceedings. In the first, *Attorney General of Northern Ireland's Reference*,[68] the Attorney referred questions about the power of Northern Ireland departments to exercise functions in the absence of ministers. The Supreme Court refused to accept the reference on the ground that there were a number of cases then pending before the courts in Northern Ireland in which those issues had been raised. The Court declined to answer the questions, preferring to do so 'against the background of a clear factual matrix, rather than as theoretical or academic issues of law'.[69] The role of the Court on a reference under paragraphs 33 or 34 was to 'provide authoritative legal guidance on the questions of law which arise on the reference. It is central to the exercise of this function that the reference be made on a devolution issue'.[70]

Secondly, in *Attorney General of Northern Ireland's Reference*,[71] the Attorney General made a paragraph 34 reference in relation to questions about the compatibility of universal credit legislation in Northern Ireland with the European Convention on Human Rights. The Supreme Court again rejected the reference on the ground that there was no 'act' by a Northern Ireland department. The legislation had been made by the Secretary of State. While the Department for Communities had facilitated the legislation by publishing lists of districts and a geographical sequence for phasing in the benefits, this was not sufficiently connected to its substance which was the true target.

The Attorney General has a statutory duty to scrutinise every Bill passed by the Assembly (both Executive Bills and Bills initiated by individual MLAs) to determine whether the provisions of those Bills are within the legislative competence of the Assembly. Under section 11 of the NIA 1998, the Attorney General may refer an Assembly Bill to the Supreme Court to determine if it would be within legislative competence. This power has been exercised on one occasion by the Attorney, in relation to the Damages Asbestos Related Conditions Bill, but the reference was ultimately withdrawn.

A recent Attorney General's reference will be heard this month by the Supreme Court in relation to clause 5(2)(a) of the Abortion Services (Safe Access Zone) (Northern Ireland) Bill. The question is whether the Bill is outside the legislative competence of the Northern Ireland Assembly as it disproportionately interferes with the rights of persons who wish to express their opposition to the provision of abortion treatment in Northern Ireland.[72]

[66] ibid Sch 10, para 33.
[67] In accordance with ibid Sch 10, para 34.
[68] *Attorney General of Northern Ireland's Reference* [2019] UKSC 1.
[69] ibid [28].
[70] ibid [2].
[71] *Attorney General of Northern Ireland's Reference* (n 55).
[72] Since the time of writing, the Supreme Court unanimously held that clause 5(2)(a) of the Bill was compatible with the European Convention on Human Rights and that, accordingly, the impugned clause was within the legislative competence of The Assembly: [2022] UKSC 32; [2023] AC 505. The Bill was subsequently passed and received Royal Assent on 6 February 2023 (Abortion Services (Safe Access Zones) Act (Northern Ireland) 2023 c. 1.

VIII. CONCLUSION

I have reached the end of this discussion, acknowledging that much more could be said on this engaging topic. Of course I have not even touched on Brexit and the implications for Northern Ireland which have come before our courts in cases which question the Northern Ireland Protocol within the constitutional structure.[73] These cases highlight the fear and uncertainty which pervades this issue, and highlight the changing landscape since our devolved arrangements were made nearly 25 years ago. Debate on those issues, however, is for another day.

With that I return to my opening gambit concerning context. The current landscape of Northern Ireland constitutional law is informed by the unique history of the jurisdiction since its formation in 1921 and especially so since the devolved institutions were established under the Good Friday/Belfast Agreement, which cemented the peace settlement. Within this constitutional framework, the role of the courts is as it always has been, to determine whether powers have been exercised and duties fulfilled in accordance with the law. In undertaking this task the courts are also aware of the often delicate equilibrium of our constitutional arrangements, the potential effects of decision-making, and the context in which the administration of justice prevails in Northern Ireland.

[73] *Allister and Others v The Prime Minister, Secretary of State for Northern Ireland and Chancellor of The Duchy of Lancaster* [2022] NICA 15. Since the time of writing this chapter, the Supreme Court unanimously dismissed the subsequent appeal: [2023] UKSC 5; [2023] 2 WLR 457.

4

Making and Re-Making of Public Law: The Canadian Way

SHEILAH L MARTIN

I. INTRODUCTION

A CONSTITUTION IS an expression of a nation's fundamental values. It reflects what a nation is, and what it aspires to become.[1] It carries with it the stories of a country's people.[2] When the conference organisers speak of 'indigenising' public law they are directing attention to how constitutions around the world adapt to and reflect historical relationships and local influences including cultural, social, linguistic and political conditions.[3] In Canada, this process continues to this day, as our public law is constantly challenged to respond to society's evolving needs. Of fundamental value to Canadians is our understanding of the Constitution as 'a living tree which, by way of progressive interpretation, accommodates and addresses the realities of modern life'.[4]

In this chapter I explore three stages of Canada's legal development that illustrate our constitution's constant ability to redefine its identity. The first concerns Canada's adaptation of traditions and laws from venerable constitutional regimes to fit the Canadian experience. The longstanding institutions of constitutional monarchy and parliamentary democracy are foundations of the constitutional democracy that Canada is today. The second occurred in 1982 when Canada once again transformed its constitutional landscape

[1] AW MacKay, 'Merging Public Law Silos and Canada's Evolving Constitutional Landscape' in E Mendes (ed), *Canada's Constitutional Democracy: The 150th Anniversary Celebration* (LexisNexis, 2017) 207.

[2] E Adams, 'Canadian Constitutional Identities' (2015) 38(2) *Dalhousie Law Journal* 311, 311.

[3] In Canada, the term 'indigenisation' is used to recognise the validity of Indigenous worldviews, knowledge and perspectives. In order to respect the Canadian discourse, I only use the term 'indigenisation' when referring to the incorporation of Indigenous ways of knowing and doing into Canadian public law; see AS Chan, 'Decolonizing and Indigenizing Discourses in a Canadian Context' in H Wright and M Høyen (eds), *Discourses We Live By: Narratives of Educational and Social Endeavour* (Open Book Publishers, 2020); Many academic institutions seeking to reconceptualise their pedagogy make note of their efforts to both indigenise and decolonise; see A Gaudry and D Lorenz, 'Indigenization as Inclusion, Reconciliation, and Decolonization: Navigating the Different Visions for Indigenizing the Canadian Academy' (2018) 14(3) *AlterNative* 218; see, eg, 'Decolonizing and Indigenizing' (*Queen's University Office of Indigenous Initiatives*), available at www.queensu.ca/indigenous/decolonizing-and-indigenizing/defintions; 'Indigenizing and Decolonizing Teaching and Learning' (*University of Alberta Centre for Teaching and Learning*), available at www.ualberta.ca/centre-for-teaching-and-learning/teaching-support/indigenization/index.html; 'Indigenization' (*University of Saskatchewan Teaching and Learning*), available at https://teaching.usask.ca/curriculum/indigenization.php.

[4] *Reference re Same-Sex Marriage* 2004 SCC 79 [22]. See also *R v Blais* 2003 SCC 44 [40].

by introducing the Canadian Charter of Rights and Freedoms,[5] which entrenched rights and remedies that went to the core of its values and also enabled the State to justify breaches of certain rights. That courts were now defining rights, crafting remedies and balancing rights and state interests brought about new dimensions to judicial review and to the separation of powers between legislatures and courts.

The term 'indigenising' has a distinct meaning in the Canadian experience. As I discuss at the third stage, indigenisation refers to the re-conceptualisation of the Constitution to account for the prior occupation of Canada by Indigenous nations and their continued place, influence and role.[6] As Canada's constitutional landscape continues to develop, the country is confronted with sources and voices historically absent from the recorded narrative of our Constitution's history. Now, Canada is called upon to acknowledge the nation-to-nation relationships between Indigenous peoples and the Crown and to address the limits of the British and French contributions that represent the two-nation theory of Canada's history. In the final portion of this chapter, I explore how Canada's indigenisation of constitutional law must take into account that Indigenous peoples were this country's first occupants, and how it is called upon to incorporate Indigenous knowledge systems into legal regimes built on traditionally western systems.[7]

II. CANADA'S CONSTITUTION: INSPIRED BY A TAPESTRY OF NATIONS

The very inception of Canada's Constitution reflects how historical relationships shaped our understanding and interpretation of constitutional principles. The amalgamation of British, American, and French sources and influences led to an original constitutional document that is distinctly Canadian and which responded to the needs of this newly founded nation.

Until the arrival of French and British expeditions in the late fifteenth, and sixteenth centuries, the land that is present-day Canada was occupied by numerous Indigenous nations since time immemorial. Great Britain and France quickly began to build colonies in Canada and the early European settlers relied upon the traditional knowledge and skills of the Indigenous population to survive in a cold and harsh land. As both Great Britain and France vied for global gain, their colonial presence in North America ultimately ended in war. The British-French conflict culminated in 1763, at which time France ceded its territory to Great Britain through the Treaty of Paris, leaving Great Britain as the dominant power and commencing the age of British rule over Canadian colonies.[8]

[5] Canadian Charter of Rights and Freedoms, Part I of the Constitution Act, 1982, being Schedule B to the Canada Act *1982* (UK), 1982, c 11.

[6] *Delgamuukw v British Columbia* [1997] 3 SCR 1010 [114].

[7] See, eg, Gaudry and Lorenz (n 3). See also, DM Conway, 'Indigenizing Intellectual Property Law: Customary Law, Legal Pluralism, and the Protection of Indigenous Peoples' Rights, Identity and Resources' (2009) 15 *Texas Wesleyan Law Review* 207.

[8] The legal effect of the Treaty of Paris of 1763 was described by the Judicial Committee of the Privy Council in *Attorney General for Canada v Cain* [1906] AC 542, 545–46:

> In 1763 Canada and all its dependencies, with the sovereignty, property, and possession, and all other rights which had at any time been held or acquired by the Crown of France, were ceded to Great Britain. Upon that event the Crown of England became possessed of all legislative and executive powers within the

More than a century later in 1867, through what has come to be known as Confederation, the Dominion of Canada was born from the union of three colonies (the Provinces of Canada, Nova Scotia and New Brunswick).[9] At this time, Canada's foundational constitutional document, the Constitution Act, 1867, was drafted.[10] Drafters looked to the unwritten constitution of the United Kingdom for inspiration, and as a consequence, the legal and institutional structure of the new nation was remarkably similar to that of the British legal regime.[11] In fact, the preamble to the Constitution Act, 1867 declares that the founding provinces were to be joined together under one Dominion, 'with a Constitution similar in principle to that of the United Kingdom'.[12] The 'Britishness' of Canada's Constitution is found in both the written text and unwritten conventions, through such features as the preservation of the Monarch, the bicameral composition of the legislature, the formal workings of the Westminster tradition of parliamentary government, and the dominance of parliamentary supremacy.[13]

Critical to Canada's constitutional design was also the experiences of its neighbour to the south. Canada departed from British law when it incorporated the American principle of federalism.[14] Because of this, Canada's Constitution included balancing two heads of power through the division of competencies among federal and provincial governments, with courts acting as arbiters in the case of disputed jurisdiction.

But Canada's version of federalism did not mirror its neighbour's. Unlike the United States' Constitution, Canada chose to 'vest the national government with extensive powers over matters affecting the nation as a whole' in order to safeguard against 'America's experience with "states' rights" that ultimately led to the Civil War'.[15] In so doing, Canada 'drew upon what [it] considered the best features of the United States Constitution, while avoiding those aspects which conflicted with traditional notions of English parliamentary government'.[16] This new federal structure preserved a degree of localised provincial autonomy, while also responding to the prevalence of regionalism that de-stabilised pre-Confederation politics.

> country so ceded to it, and, save so far as it has since parted with these powers by legislation, royal proclamation, or voluntary grant, it is still possessed of them.
>
> (citations omitted).

[9] *R v Comeau* 2018 SCC 15 [1].

[10] Constitution Act, 1867 (UK), 30 & 31 Vict, c 3. At the time of its enactment, the Constitution Act, 1867 was originally titled the British North America Act 1867 (UK), 30 & 31 Vict, c 3, but was renamed at patriation in 1982.

[11] WJ Newman, 'The Rule of Law, the Separation of Powers and Judicial Independence in Canada' in P Oliver, P Macklem and N Des Rosiers (eds), *The Oxford Handbook of the Canadian Constitution* (Oxford University Press, 2017) 1032.

[12] Constitution Act, 1867 (n 10) preamble. See *Reference re Remuneration of Judges of the Provincial Court of Prince Edward Island; Reference re Independence and Impartiality of Judges of the Provincial Court of Prince Edward Island* [1997] 3 SCR 3 [94].

[13] MP Harrington, 'The Post-Confederation Era' in E Mendes (ed), *Canada's Constitutional Democracy: The 150th Anniversary Celebration* (LexisNexis, 2017) 29; *Remuneration of Judges* (n 12) [92]–[106].

[14] As P Daly describes, 'at the time of Confederation, no major change was effected to the traditional English approach: parliamentary sovereignty was simply divided between the federal and provincial levels of power with each level supreme on those "matters that fall within their respective spheres of jurisdiction"': see P Daly, 'Divergence And Convergence in English And Canadian Administrative Law' in M Ramsden and S Jhaveri (eds), *Indigenizing Administrative Law* (Cambridge University Press, 2020) 2.

[15] Harrington (n 13) 29.

[16] ibid.

Finally, a historical overview of Canada would not be complete without discussion of Quebec's uniquely French identity. The Constitution Act, 1867 marked the beginnings of legal bilingualism and bijuralism in the nation. Section 133 required that federal and Quebec legislation be printed in both languages, and made it possible to use English and French in federal Parliament, the Legislature of Quebec, as well as in federal courts and those in the province of Quebec.[17] Similarly, section 92(13) of the Constitution Act, 1867 granted provincial legislatures the authority to legislate regarding 'property and civil rights'. This enabled the province of Quebec to maintain the pre-eminence of the French civil law tradition in matters relating to property and civil rights, which was first established by the Quebec Act in 1774, in an otherwise common law country.[18]

Over time, more provinces joined the Dominion. Still, Canada lacked full legal autonomy, remaining under British rule. Even after the Statute of Westminster gave Canada and other Commonwealth nations legislative equality with the United Kingdom in 1931, the country was unable to amend the Constitution Act, 1867 independent of legislative action by the British Parliament.[19] Following the Second World War, the quest for true legal independence began. This resulted in the enactment of the Constitution Act, 1982, which 'retrieved' Canada's Constitution from the British Parliament and 'patriated' it as our own.[20] In so doing, the Constitution Act, 1982 transferred full and exclusive constitutional competency to Canada, marking our nation's final step in its peaceful transition from a British colony to an independent country.[21]

With the Constitution Act, 1982 came two important reforms to Canada's Constitution which exemplify its willingness to redefine its story. The first was the entrenchment of the Canadian Charter of Rights and Freedoms. The second was the recognition and affirmation of Aboriginal and treaty rights through section 35 of the Constitution Act, 1982.[22] Each of these proved to be pivotal chapters in the Canadian constitutional story that continue to contribute to Canada's unique constitutional identity.

III. THE EMERGENCE OF A CONSTITUTIONAL DEMOCRACY THROUGH THE CHARTER

The story of Canada's patriation is often told with a strong focus on the role played by then-Prime Minister Pierre Elliott Trudeau. However, while the Prime Minister, provincial premiers, and their advisers spearheaded the project, ordinary Canadian citizens and

[17] Constitution Act, 1867 (n 10) s 133. See *Re Manitoba Language Rights* [1985] 1 SCR 721.

[18] *Laurentide Motels Ltd v Beauport (City)* [1989] 1 SCR 705. The Quebec Act, 1774 (UK) was the first of many enactments seeking to protect the language and culture of a particular group. The Constitutional Act, 1791 (UK) (also called the Quebec Act, 1791) is often seen as a further watershed in the development of French Canadian nationalism as it provided for a province (Lower Canada) which French speakers considered to be their own, separate from the predominantly English-speaking province of Upper Canada.

[19] Statute of Westminster 1931 (UK).

[20] Constitution Act, 1982, being Schedule B to the Canada Act, 1982 (UK), 1982, c 11; BL Strayer, 'The Constitution Act, 1982: the Foreseen and Unforeseen' (2007) 16(2) *Constitutional Forum* 51, 51.

[21] M St-Hilaire, PF Baud and ES Drouin, 'The Constitution of Canada as Supreme Law: A New Definition' (2019) 28(1) *Constitutional Forum* 7, 7.

[22] See generally Strayer (n 20).

interest groups greatly influenced the final product.[23] The vital involvement of individuals, minority interest organisations, and Indigenous groups moved the Charter's objective of protecting purely individual rights to one that also guarantees collective rights like freedom of association, language rights, gender equality, and cultural protections.[24] It was the people who understood that an essential part of an individual's identity are the groups they belong to and who brought this unique dimension to Canada's Charter.

The resulting Charter is a uniquely Canadian product that reflects the nation's deep devotion to plurality. It continued the Canadian tradition of protecting minority rights, which began with the Quebec Act, 1774,[25] was carried forward in the Constitution Act, 1867,[26] and has persisted through Canada's political reality as a multicultural nation. Canada's identity is built on, and strengthened by, immigration. As a democratic nation with Indigenous, cultural and linguistic minorities, Canada has had to develop pluralistic approaches to ethnicity, race, language, culture and rights, which include group rights that serve to safeguard our diverse cultural mosaic from discrimination and allow our differences to survive and thrive.[27] Hence, the final versions of the Constitution Act, 1982 and the Charter, born from political negotiations and engaged everyday citizens, flowed directly from Canada's history and commitment to pluralism as the country's *modus vivendi*.

The enshrinement of individual and collective rights under the Charter, and the jurisprudence that followed, helped shape Canadian society. It was through the application of the Charter that the Supreme Court of Canada found, for example, that: a criminal prohibition against abortion was unconstitutional as it posed increased health risks to women and deprived women of the right to security of the person under section 7 of the Charter;[28] that the failure to include sexual orientation as a prohibited ground of discrimination in provincial human rights legislation was a violation of the equality guarantee under section 15;[29] that Criminal Code provisions prohibiting assistance in dying unjustifiably infringed the section 7 rights to life, liberty and security of the person;[30] and that freedom of association protects activities such as trade unions which are inherently collective and inconceivable at the individual level.[31]

[23] L Harder and S Patten, 'Looking Back on Patriation and Its Consequences' in L Harder and S Patten (eds), *Patriation and its Consequences: Constitution Making in Canada* (University of British Columbia Press, 2015) 11–12.

[24] Group rights include, for example, those under s 15 (equality rights), s 23 (minority language education rights), s 27 (preservation and enhancement of the multicultural heritage of Canadians) and s 28 (rights guaranteed equally to both sexes).

[25] The Constitutional Act, 1791 (also called the Quebec Act, 1791) is often seen as a watershed in the development of French Canadian nationalism as it provided for a province (Lower Canada) which the French considered to be their own, separate from English-speaking Upper Canada. The Quebec Act 1791 was the first of many enactments seeking to protect the language and culture of a particular group.

[26] Similarly, the Constitution Act, 1867 sought to protect the French minority outside of the Quebec and the English minority within Quebec. See the discussion in B McLachlin, 'Remarks of the Right Honourable Beverley McLachlin, PC, Chief Justice of Canada: Canadian Rights and Freedoms: 20 Years Under the *Charter*' (17 April 2002), available at www.scc-csc.ca/judges-juges/spe-dis/bm-2002-04-17-eng.aspx.

[27] As the European Court of Human Rights has observed, '[p]luralism, tolerance and broadmindedness are hallmarks of a "democratic society"': *Sahin v Turkey* App no 44774/98 (ECtHR, 10 November 2005) 25.

[28] *R v Morgentaler* [1988] 1 SCR 30.

[29] *Vriend v Alberta* [1998] 1 SCR 493.

[30] *Carter v Canada (Attorney General)* 2015 SCC 5.

[31] *Dunmore v Ontario* [2001] 3 SCR 1016; *Health Services and Support-Facilities Subsector Bargaining Assn v British Columbia* [2007] 2 SCR 391.

The reach of Charter rights, however, is not unbounded. The Charter acknowledges the limit of rights, and that tensions exist between specific individual and group interests versus those of the collective.[32] The Charter thus recognises – in its very structure – Canada's historical commitment to a positive relationship between the exercise of individual and group rights and the state. As noted by former Chief Justice of the Supreme Court of Canada Beverley McLachlin, unlike its neighbour to the south, 'Canada was born not of revolution but evolution'. The consequence is that while '[t]he United States constitution casts rights in absolute terms, making no mention of the need to balance them against the collective interest', the Canadian Charter 'acknowledges the need to balance individual and collective interests'.[33]

Generally, the Charter demands that such tension be resolved not by *suppressing* one interest at the expense of the other through denial, but primarily by *balancing* competing interests through a process of justification.[34] It does so in its very first provision which states that Charter rights can be limited by law so long as those limits can be shown to be reasonable in a free and democratic society. The Government has the onus of demonstrating that a limitation on a right is reasonable by establishing that it fulfills a pressing and substantial objective and is proportionate. The proportionality analysis involves three questions:

1. Is there a rational connection between the infringement and the objective?
2. Do the means chosen to further the objective interfere as little as reasonably possible with the right that has been infringed?
3. Do the benefits of the infringing measure outweigh its negative effects?[35]

This justification provision is the reason why, for example, a provincial requirement that all licensed drivers be photographed was found to be a justifiable limit on Hutterites' right to freedom of religion, a group who sincerely believes that the Second Commandment prohibits them from having their photograph willingly taken.[36] It is also why the criminal prosecution of a teacher for making antisemitic- and hateful statements to his students was deemed to be a reasonable and justifiable limitation on his freedom of expression.[37] In both cases, society's objectives outweighed the harm to individual rights.

As these examples illustrate, the arrival of the Charter in 1982 tasked Canadian judges with a novel role of boiling down broad and universal values into precise, clear, and functional doctrine while also finding the appropriate balance between conflicting individual rights and collective interests, all in the absence of precedent.[38] The importance of context, policy and philosophy in judgments heightened.[39] While judges have always taken these matters into consideration, the demands of Charter adjudication brought this

[32] McLachlin (n 26).
[33] ibid.
[34] Section 33 permits Parliament or the Legislature of a Province to expressly declare, for a five-year period, that its laws shall operate notwithstanding sections 2 and 7–15 of the Charter.
[35] *R v Oakes* [1986] 1 SCR 103, 138–40.
[36] *Alberta v Hutterian Brethren of Wilson Colony* 2009 SCC 37.
[37] *R v Keegstra* [1990] 3 SCR 697.
[38] B McLachlin, 'The *Charter*: A New Role for the Judiciary' (1991) 29(3) *Alberta Law Review* 540, 542–45.
[39] See R Sharpe, 'Role of Judging in a Constitutional Democracy' in R Sharpe (ed), *Good Judgment: Making Judicial Decisions* (University of Toronto Press, 2018).

type of judicial thinking to the forefront. It led judges to openly acknowledge that before making a decision that affects people's lives or government policy, they must understand the circumstances and context of the problem as well as the implications their decision will have. They equally appreciate that judicial decisions can have important policy ramifications, and that some understanding of philosophy may be of assistance when faced with difficult issues.[40]

In addition to altering judicial thinking, the provisions of the Charter and the Constitution Act, 1982 expanded the scope of judicial review.[41] Until 1982, the role of the court in constitutional adjudication was largely that of an umpire in federal-provincial jurisdictional disputes that arose under the division of powers doctrine of the Constitution Act, 1867.[42] The judicial oversight role grounded in federalism broadened, however, when the Charter added a new set of constitutional provisions that could invalidate inconsistent laws and called on Canadian courts to review legislation and government action for compliance with the Charter's various rights and guarantees.[43] By doing so, the Charter transformed Canada from a parliamentary democracy (predicated on the British notion of parliamentary supremacy) to a constitutional democracy, 'in which Government [is] constrained not only by institutional structures, but also by the human and civil rights belonging to the people' – many of which were previously protected primarily under the common law.[44] The metamorphosis brought on by the protections under the Charter was crystallised in section 52 of the Constitution Act, 1982, which expressly codified constitutional supremacy, noting 'any law that is inconsistent with the provisions of the Constitution is of no force or effect'.[45]

The expansion of judicial review that accompanied post-Charter judging caused some to raise questions about the proper scope of the judicial role. Of course, the debate about the role of the judiciary in a constitutional democracy is neither novel nor unique to Canada. However, with the ambit of the rights and remedies in the Charter, what would have been widely regarded as falling within the preserve of politics prior to 1982, was now endowed with a legal/constitutional dimension. Charter litigation called upon courts to assess the merit of politically-charged questions in a manner not contemplated previously, thereby 'mak[ing] the Court's role as lawmaker more explicit, more pronounced, and more controversial'.[46]

The traditional criticism levied against judicial review is that judicial institutions run counter to our conceptions of democracy.[47] Proponents of this view maintain that

[40] See McLachlin (n 38) 542–45. See also R Dworkin, 'Must Our Judges Be Philosophers? *Can* They Be Philosophers?' (New York Council for the Humanities Scholar of the Year Lecture, 11 October 2000) 15.

[41] Some viewed this expansion as predictable, and indeed inevitable: see McLachlin (n 38) 541–42. Others commented that the scope of the extent of the expansion was unexpected: see, eg, Strayer (n 20) 51–56.

[42] P Hogg, *Constitutional Law of Canada* (Thomson Reuters, 2020) 864.

[43] ibid.

[44] N Hassan, 'Three Theories of "Principles of Fundamental Justice"' (2013) 63 *Supreme Court Law Review* 339, 343. See also C Milne, J Greiss and D Boswell, 'Symposium Summary: The State of Canada's Constitutional Democracy' (2016) 25(3) *Constitutional Forum* 1, 6–7.

[45] *Reference re Secession of Quebec* [1998] 2 SCR 217 [72].

[46] See CA Fraser, 'Constitutional Dialogues between Courts and Legislatures: Can We Talk?' (2005) 14(3) *Constitutional Forum* 7, 8–9. See also McLachlin (n 38) 542.

[47] See, eg, J Waldron, 'The Core of the Case against Judicial Review' (2006) 115(6) *Yale Law Journal* 1346.

legislatures 'are more legitimate, egalitarian, and participatory than courts ... and so embody crucial democratic rights and values to an extent that is impossible for the [courts] to imitate'.[48] Critics argue that the Charter's emphasis on group rights and remedial provisions that demand the balancing of rights against societal interests are policy-laden inquiries that courts are ill-placed to embark upon. They accuse courts of having stepped outside their proper judicial role and into the role of law-maker.[49] Put in another way, critics claim that judges are engaging in judicial activism, in what is an impermissible intrusion on the supremacy of an elected legislature.[50]

Critics also question the legitimacy of courts to the extent their decisions constrain the course of state conduct and/or direct government spending – a complaint which is often loudest and harshest when made against equality-related decisions that affirm the rights of minorities or other disadvantaged groups. This is so even though other types of court decisions may impose great restrictions or costs on the state. Take, for example, the finding in *Stinchcombe* that the Crown had a duty to disclose all relevant information in its possession to the accused by virtue of an accused's right of full answer and defence.[51] The compliance cost across the country was enormous and yet this change to the criminal process, based as it was in individual rights, did not engender the same type of debate or derision as the declaration that sexual orientation was a protected ground of discrimination or that same-sex marriage was constitutional.[52]

Such criticisms and challenges tend to rest on an overly restrictive definition of both democracy and the role currently assigned to courts. Democracy is not merely premised on majoritarianism, but a set of aspirational ideals.[53] At its core, democracy is about equality and equal participation.[54] As Justice Rosalie Abella has noted,

> [t]he most basic of the central concepts we need back in the conversation is that democracy is not – and never was – just about the wishes of the majority. What pumps oxygen no less forcefully through vibrant democratic veins is the protection of rights through courts, *notwithstanding* the wishes of the majority.[55]

[48] A Lever, 'Democracy and Judicial Review: Are They Really Incompatible?' (2009) 7(4) *Perspectives on Politics* 805, 805. See also A Bickel, *The Least Dangerous Branch: The Supreme Court at the Bar of Politics*, 2nd edn (Yale University Press, 1986).

[49] See B McLachlin, 'Respecting Democratic Roles' (2005) 14(3) *Constitutional Forum* 15, 17–20.

[50] Others call this '*Charter* Revolution', referring to what they describe as an active law-making role taken by the Supreme Court of Canada since the adoption of the Charter: see FL Morton and R Knopff, *The Charter Revolution and the Court Party* (Broadview Press, 2000). Those who take a different view to the propriety of judicial review use the term 'dialogue theory': see PW Hogg and AA Bushell, 'The *Charter* Dialogue Between Courts and Legislatures (or Perhaps the Charter of Rights Isn't Such a Bad Thing After All)' (1997) 35(1) *Osgoode Hall Law Journal* 75.

[51] *R v Stinchcombe* [1991] 3 SCR 326. See similarly *R v Stillman* [1997] 1 SCR 607, which significantly curtailed the scope of police search powers upon arrest.

[52] *Vriend* (n 29); *Reference Re Same-Sex Marriage* 2004 SCC 79.

[53] As noted in *Reference re Secession of Quebec* (n 45) [76]–[77], 'Canadians have never accepted that ours is a system of simple majority rule. Our principle of democracy, taken in conjunction with the other constitutional principles discussed here, is richer ... our belief in democracy may be harmonized with our belief in constitutionalism.'

[54] Indeed, equality for all has been described as an 'associated tenet' of Canadian democracy: *Harper v Canada (Attorney General)* 2004 SCC 33 [12].

[55] R Silberman Abella, 'The Judicial Role in a Democratic State' (2000) (8)(1)–(3) *Canada Watch* 8, 10, cited in Fraser (n 46) 9.

Viewed in this light, judicial institutions are an *essential* part of the overall democratic makeup of the Canadian system, and the theme of plurality that underpins our society.[56] Whereas ballot boxes give the citizenry the right to vote, legal contestation before the courts confers a broader right of participation to all individuals – citizens or not – whose rights have been violated or who otherwise wish to hold their democratically-elected representatives to account through judicial scrutiny.[57]

While the legislatures are dominant players in shaping society, judicial institutions have an important role to play in maintaining Canadian democracy.[58] Despite assertions to the contrary, the judiciary has not inappropriately encroached upon legislative policy-based law-making because 'the political character of *Charter* adjudication is implicit in the very structure of the analysis contemplated'.[59] Both the substantive sections of the Charter, as well as the remedial provisions envisage an independent arbiter.[60] Further, the substantive rights, remedial provisions and justification clause under section 1, were all purposeful choices of an elected Parliament. As the Supreme Court of Canada noted in *Vriend*,

> our Charter's introduction and the consequential remedial role of the courts were choices of the Canadian people through their elected representatives as part of a redefinition of our democracy .... So courts in their trustee or arbiter role must perforce scrutinize the work of the legislature and executive not in the name of the courts, but in the interests of the new social contract that was democratically chosen.[61]

[56] Courts are an additional mode of access for citizen input into the political system, and in this sense, are extensions of more traditional democratic institutions. See, eg, Lever (n 48) 813.

[57] Academics like Monahan envisage a potential role for judicial review in promoting democratic participation. His theory of judicial review views judges as responsible for the implementation of democratic values and the promotion of political participation. He asserts that two principles of judicial review should be adopted: (1) the judiciary ought to be guided by the 'right of equal access to and participation in the political process', acknowledging that 'formal access does not guarantee equal access', and (2) judges should 'ensure that all social arrangements are subject to meaningful debate and transformation through the political process': see PJ Monahan, *Politics and the Constitution: The Charter, Federalism and the Supreme Court of Canada* (Carswell, 1987) 124–25. While some may view this theory as antithetical to democracy as providing some groups with an inequitable advantage through the adversarial system of the courts, the focus on substantive merits prevents litigants from gaining extra or unfair political influence that they would not otherwise have had: see C Lafont, *Democracy without Shortcuts: A Participatory Conception of Deliberative Democracy* (Oxford University Press, 2020) 230.

[58] Others justify the scope of judicial review on the basis that '[i]n selecting some rights and freedoms for inclusion in the *Charter* there was no intention to create a hierarchy of rights in the sense that the rights included in that document were more important than others. Rather, the rights and freedoms chosen for inclusion in the *Charter* were selected because it was reasonable to give the courts a role in their enforcement': see A Blakeney, 'The Notwithstanding Clause, the *Charter*, and Canada's Patriated Constitution: What I Thought We Were Doing' (2010) 19(1) *Constitutional Forum* 1, 4.

[59] P Monahan, 'Judicial Review and Democracy: A Theory of Judicial Review' (1987) 21(1) *University of British Columbia Law Review* 87, 89.

[60] For example, 's. 7 of the *Charter* speaks of no denial of the rights therein except in accordance with the principles of fundamental justice, which include the process of law and legislative action': *Vriend* (n 29) [137]. Similarly, the justification clause under section 1 provides that rights can be limited only where those limits can be shown to be reasonable in a free and democratic society, reflecting an overarching interest 'to ensure respect for legislative action and the collective or societal interests represented by legislation': *Vriend* (n 29) [137]. Section 24 of the Charter, and section 52 of the Constitution Act, 1928, create remedial mechanisms that must be given effect by courts. Subsection 24(1), for example, specifies that '[a]nyone whose rights or freedoms, as guaranteed by this Charter, have been infringed or denied *may apply to a court of competent jurisdiction to obtain such remedy as the court considers appropriate and just in the circumstances*' (emphasis added).

[61] *Vriend* (n 29) [134]–[135]. See also Fraser (n 46) 8.

Since the 1929 Judicial Committee of the Privy Council decision that established that women are eligible to be appointed to the Senate,[62] the constitutional doctrine of the 'living tree' has been carried through Canadian constitutional jurisprudence and has enabled the Constitution to change and evolve over time while still staying true to its original intentions. Hence, what may be considered as forward thinking decisions are necessary products of the established constitutional regime in Canada, which permits evolution of the written text. Indeed at the time of designing the Charter, drafters rooted substantive rights and remedial provisions in widely worded and expansive language, with a firm understanding of the living tree doctrine.[63] Accordingly, in Canada, even a purportedly originalist view of the Constitution means that the Charter was devised to be remedial and to be read purposively, with the flexibility necessary to respond to changing times.

IV. RECONNECTING CANADA TO ITS THREE-NATION PAST[64]

In addition to the entrenchment of the Charter, patriation marked the constitutional recognition of Indigenous rights under section 35 of the Constitution Act, 1982.[65] Section 35 did not create rights. Rather, its effect was to give constitutional status to the existing rights of the Indigenous peoples of Canada, which, prior to 1982, had no constitutional protection but were recognised in the common law.[66]

Section 35 was not the first constitutional provision relating to Indigenous peoples. Canada's constitutional framework has, since Confederation, acknowledged the Indigenous presence. Before section 35, section 91(24) of the Constitution Act, 1867 granted the federal Government exclusive legislative authority over 'Indians, and lands reserved for the Indians' in the division of powers between the federal and provincial governments. But many have argued that at its heart, section 91(24) embodied assimilationist and colonial policies aimed at the 'Indian problem'.[67] It was criticised for morphing 'Indigenous judicial independence', or the creation of resolution processes independent of Canadian Government, into 'legal subjecthood'.[68] The constitutional status of

[62] *Edwards v Attorney-General for Canada* [1930] AC 124.

[63] See *Reference Re Provincial Electoral Boundaries (Sask)* [1991] 2 SCR 158, 180, *citing Edwards* (n 62) 136 (PC). It must be noted that, as the Supreme Court of Canada wrote in *Parry Sound (District) Social Services Administration Board v Ontario Public Services Employees Union* [2003] 2 SCR 157 [39], there is a 'presumption that the legislature does not intend to change existing law or to depart from established principles, policies or practices'.

[64] I use the term 'three-nation' as a foil to Canada's two founding nations of Britain and France, discussed above. The third nation represents Canada's Indigenous population which in fact includes hundreds of distinct nations with their own language, culture and worldview. See, eg, J Borrows, 'Indigenous Legal Traditions in Canada' (2005) 19 *Washington University Journal of Law and Policy* 167.

[65] Though they are described as 'Aboriginal and treaty rights' in the text of the provision.

[66] *Calder v Attorney-General of British Columbia* [1973] SCR 313; *R v Sparrow* [1990] 1 SCR 1075; *Delgamuukw* (n 6).

[67] H LaForme, '150 Years of Canadian Confederation: Is There Reason for Indigenous People to Celebrate?' in E Mendes (ed), *Canada's Constitutional Democracy: The 150th Anniversary Celebration* (LexisNexis, 2017) 5; G Starblanket, 'Constitutionalizing (In)justice: Treaty Interpretation and the Containment of Indigenous Governance' (2019) 28(2) *Constitutional Forum* 13, 14.

[68] LaForme (n 67).

section 35 rights thus renewed hopes for a new chapter in the relationship between Canada and its first occupants where they would be more than subjects of the Crown.

The Supreme Court of Canada understood section 35 to be 'a solemn commitment [which] must be given meaningful content', noting that the provision warrants a 'generous, large, and liberal interpretation' to give full effect to its purpose.[69] The Court found section 35 to engage the honour of the Crown, and to ground a fiduciary relationship between the Crown and Indigenous peoples. It described the objective of section 35 in a purposive manner, characterising it as 'the reconciliation of aboriginal people and non-aboriginal peoples and their respective claims, interests and ambitions'[70] and '[t]he reconciliation of Aboriginal and non-Aboriginal Canadians in a mutually respectful long-term relationship'.[71]

As the body of section 35 case law has developed, the Supreme Court has interpreted the section 35 language of 'existing aboriginal and treaty rights' flexibly, affirming those rights 'in a contemporary form rather than in their primeval simplicity and vigour' to permit their evolution over time.[72] This includes the recognition of Canada's prior occupation by organised, autonomous societies and the need to reconcile their modern-day existence within the Crown's assertion of sovereignty. It is because the Indigenous presence predated the imposition of provincial and territorial boundaries that the Supreme Court has recognised that Aboriginal rights claimants under section 35 do not need to be citizens or residents of Canada.[73] And similarly, that the province of Quebec must have jurisdiction in the part of an Innu group's traditional territory situated in the separate province of Newfoundland and Labrador to prevent an awkward patchwork of constitutional protection for Indigenous rights across the country.[74]

Section 35 has enabled communities to continue practices, customs and traditions based on prior use and occupation of the land because when Europeans arrived in North America, Indigenous peoples were already here, living in communities on the land, and participating in distinctive cultures, as they had done for centuries.[75] Under this rubric, the Supreme Court recognised a wide range of Indigenous practice-related rights including: the right to hunt/fish for particular species,[76] the right to fish for food, social and ceremonial purposes,[77] the right to fish and to sell fish for moderate community livelihood,[78] and the right to harvest wood for domestic use.[79] The Supreme Court has also held that the section 35 right includes a right to Aboriginal land title, which is *sui generis*, or of its own kind.[80] This produced a duty on the Crown to consult with the rights-holding

[69] *Sparrow* (n 66) 1108. See also *R v Van der Peet* [1996] 2 SCR 507 [142].

[70] *Mikisew Cree First Nation v Canada (Minister of Canadian Heritage)* 2005 SCC 69.

[71] *Beckman v Little Salmon/Carmacks First Nation* 2010 SCC 53.

[72] *Sparrow* (n 66).

[73] *R v Desautel* 2021 SCC 17; the case concerned an American citizen living in Washington State who claimed that he had an Aboriginal right to hunt in his ancestors' traditional territories near Castelgar, British Columbia.

[74] *Newfoundland and Labrador (Attorney General) v Uashaunnuat (Innu of Uashat and of Mani-Utenam)* 2020 SCC 4.

[75] See *Van der Peet* (n 69).

[76] *R v Gladstone* [1996] 2 SCR 723.

[77] *R v Nikal* [1996] 1 SCR 1013.

[78] *R v Marshall*; *R v Bernard* 2005 SCC 43.

[79] *R v Sappier* 2006 SCC 54.

[80] See *Calder* (n 66); *Delgamuukw* (n 6).

group – and, where appropriate, accommodate the rights in question – when it is contemplating conduct that could have an adverse impact on section 35 and treaty rights.[81]

The elevation of Indigenous rights to a constitutional status was 'a real achievement'[82] as it afforded some protections and recognition to section 35 rights.[83] However, section 35 was an opportunity to pave the path forward for a post-colonial Canada, and many academics contend that it failed to pass muster.[84] Scholars have observed that while courts and politicians alike have made advances in their understanding of Indigenous rights and traditions – for example, by appreciating the need to adjust evidentiary rules to respond to oral history evidence[85] – the deep attachment to western-Eurocentrism acts as an impediment to truly understanding Indigenous people, their histories, and their political and legal institutions.[86] As Dr Kiera Ladner has put it: 'Indigenous constitutional orders are currently incomprehensible to and incompatible with the Canadian constitutional order, with its roots in common law, civil law, and the "legal magic" of colonialism'.[87]

The Supreme Court decision of *Ktunaxa*[88] showcases some of the complexities in interpreting Indigenous rights in a federal, Charter-bound state. The Court was asked to address an assertion of Indigenous spirituality and the guarantee of freedom of religion under the Charter. The majority found that the Minister of Forests, Lands and Natural Resource Operations' decision to approve the building of a ski resort in a body of sacred land that the Ktunaxa people sincerely believed to be inhabited by the Grizzly Bear Spirit did not violate their Charter right to freedom of religion because the Charter protects the freedom to worship and not 'the spiritual focal point of worship'.[89] Legal counsel for the Ktunaxa people described the outcome as a failure of the legal system at the highest level, as it did not recognise the spiritual relationship Indigenous peoples have with their territories.

For many Indigenous leaders and scholars, decisions like this *Ktunaxa* illustrate why Canada must make room for Indigenous law in its existing constitutional framework. They urge Canada to acknowledge Indigenous legal orders and laws as necessary parts of this country's governance.[90] As Indigenous scholar John Borrows explains, all people benefit from understanding and applying Indigenous norms and all three of Canada's legal traditions may be improved and strengthened as a result of increased knowledge, comparison and cross-pollination.[91]

The concept of a three-nation Canada is not new. The Supreme Court recognised that the early periods of Indigenous/non-Indigenous diplomacy in what is now Canada

[81] See *Haida Nation v British Columbia (Minister of Forests)* 2004 SCC 73; *Mikisew Cree* (n 70).

[82] K Ladner, 'An Indigenous Constitutional Paradox: Both Monumental Achievement and Monumental Defeat' in Harder and Patten (eds) (n 23) 271.

[83] ibid 270.

[84] See, eg, Ladner (n 82); L Mandell and L Hall Pinder, 'Tracking Justice: The Constitution Express to Section 35 and Beyond' in Harder and Patten (eds) (n 23) 197.

[85] See *Delgamuukw* (n 6) [87]. See similarly *Mitchell v MNR* 2001 SCC 33 [3], [30], [37], [39].

[86] Ladner (n 82) 285.

[87] ibid, citing P Russell, *Constitutional Odyssey*, 3rd edn (University of Toronto Press, 2004).

[88] *Ktunaxa Nation v British Columbia (Forests, Lands and Natural Resource Operations)* 2017 SCC 54.

[89] ibid [71].

[90] V Napoleon, 'Thinking About Indigenous Legal Orders' (2007) *Research Paper for the National Centre for First Nations Governance*, 19.

[91] J Borrows, *Canada's Indigenous Constitution* (University of Toronto Press, 2010) 10.

were forged through treaty-making and built upon recognition of the Indigenous people's autonomy and their independence.[92] As Lamer J (as he then was), writing for the unanimous Court, observed over three decades ago:

> … the Indian nations were regarded in their relations with the European nations which occupied North America as independent nations. The papers of Sir William Johnson (The Papers of Sir William Johnson, 14 vol.), who was in charge of Indian affairs in British North America, demonstrate the recognition by Great Britain that nation-to-nation relations had to be conducted with the North American Indians.[93]

During this time period, the Royal Proclamation, 1763 – which was issued by George III to establish the form of civil government applicable to British colonies – recognised the intention of early treaties to declare peaceful co-existence.[94] As many scholars have noted, these early relations were 'characterized by a deeper and more mutual respect for legal pluralism'.[95]

However, these original partnerships failed to endure. Instead, expanding economic objectives and the desire for settler sovereignty led to shifts in policies that divided Indigenous people and their former settler partners. As many have observed, the 'colonial government determined that [Indigenous] self-government had to end', and the pre-existing respect and recognition of Indigenous legal and social systems 'was gradually replaced by a vision of Canada in which "a minority of 'civilized' farming Indians would survive in the midst of a 'nourishing settler colonial economy'"'.[96] Cooperative relations were superseded by what former Chief Justice Beverley McLachlin described as an attempt at 'cultural genocide' and the worst stain on the nation's history.[97] From this shift also emerged a version of history that downplayed the autonomous partnership between Indigenous peoples and European settlers. Instead, a two-nation theory of Canada's history was advanced and while the union of the French and English into a bilingual and bijural country is an important aspect of Canada's development, it tells only part of our national story.

As the under-inclusive two-nation theory took hold of historical accounts and collective amnesia minimised the presence of Indigenous nations in Canada since time immemorial, the Indigenous assertion of self-governance and a demand for change did not waver. Indigenous organisations and communities consistently championed the issue. Further, two federal commissions, the Royal Commission on Aboriginal Peoples and the Truth and Reconciliation Commission of Canada (TRC), recommended governmental policies aimed at reconciliation with Indigenous peoples and substantial modification

[92] See also Royal Commission on Aboriginal Peoples, *Report of the Royal Commission on Aboriginal Peoples*, vol 1: 'Looking Forward, Looking Back' (Canada Communication Group, 1996) 42, 114–20.
[93] *R v Sioui* [1990] 1 SCR 1025, 1052–53.
[94] PJ Monahan, B Shaw and P Ryan, *Constitutional Law*, 5th edn (Irwin Law, 2017) 474.
[95] Starblanket (n 67) 14.
[96] LaForme (n 67) 10 citing J Milloy, 'Indian Act Colonialism: A Century of Dishonor, 1869–1969' (2008) *Research Paper for the National Center for First Nations Governance* 6–7. Starblanket (n 67) 14, citing P McHugh and L Ford, 'Settler Sovereignty and the Shapeshifting Crown' in L Ford and T Rowse (eds), *Between Indigenous and Settler Governance* (Routledge, 2014) 25.
[97] S Fine, 'Chief Justice says Canada Attempted "Cultural Genocide" on Aboriginals' (*The Globe and Mail*, 28 May 2015), available at www.theglobeandmail.com/news/national/chief-justice-says-canada-attempted-cultural-genocide-on-aboriginals/article24688854/.

to the *status quo*. The need to give effect to Indigenous self-government underlies both Commission reports.

In its five-volume report issued in 1996, the Royal Commission acknowledged that mutually beneficial relations between Canada and Indigenous peoples had been replaced with policies intended to remove Indigenous peoples from their lands, suppress nations and their government, undermine culture and stifle Indigenous identity. The report called for a complete restructuring of the Crown-Indigenous relationship in order to acknowledge and respect Indigenous peoples as *nations* with distinct cultures and values, and with the inherent right to self-determination.[98]

Nearly 20 years later, the TRC, established as part of the Indian Residential Schools Settlement Agreement, issued a final report. It detailed the grave and assimilationist consequences of the church and state-run residential schools, which separated Indigenous children from their families, minimised and weakened family ties and cultural linkages, and indoctrinated children into a new culture.[99] With its report, the TRC also issued 94 calls to action ranging from child welfare and health to language and culture in order to further reconciliation between Canadians and Indigenous peoples. Much like the Royal Commission, the TRC's proposed framework is built upon awareness of the past, acknowledgement of the inflicted harm, atonement for the causes, and action to change behaviour. The report also forcefully demands that Canada's legal system be transformed and that Indigenous laws be recovered, restored and reinvigorated in recognition of the fact that Indigenous peoples have always had their own laws and legal traditions.

Today, a three-nation theory of Canada is resurfacing and the restoration and recognition of Indigenous law as a legitimate system of law is well underway. Canada endorsed the United Nations Declaration on the Rights of Indigenous Peoples in 2016,[100] and subsequently enacted the United Nations Declaration on the Rights of Indigenous Peoples Act that seeks to 'affirm the Declaration as a universal international human rights instrument with application in Canadian law'.[101] It has also encouraged grassroots initiatives such as the Idle No More movement.[102] All of this demonstrates Canada's will to re-conceptualise its legal system in a way that incorporates Indigenous self-government and legal orders.[103]

[98] Crown-Indigenous Relations and Northern Affairs Canada, 'Highlights from the Report of the Royal Commission on Aboriginal Peoples', available at www.rcaanc-cirnac.gc.ca/eng/1100100014597/1572547985018.

[99] Crown-Indigenous Relations and Northern Affairs Canada, 'Truth and Reconciliation Commission of Canada', available at www.rcaanc-cirnac.gc.ca/eng/1450124405592/1529106060525. Truth and Reconciliation Commission of Canada, 'Honouring the Truth, Reconciling for the Future: Summary of the Final Report of the Truth and Reconciliation Commission of Canada' (2015) v, 23.

[100] *United Nations Declaration on the Rights of Indigenous Peoples*, GA Res 61/295, UN GAOR, 61st Sess, Supp No 49, UN Doc A/RES/61/295 (13 September 2007). See *R v Sayers* 2017 ONCJ 77 [49]; *Sheck v Canada (Minister of Justice)* 2019 BCCA 364 [85].

[101] *United Nations Declaration on the Rights of Indigenous Peoples Act*, SC 2021, c 14. Bill C-15, *An Act respecting the United Nations Declaration on the Rights of Indigenous Peoples*, 2nd Sess, 43rd Parl, 2020, cl 4(a) (first reading 3 December 2020).

[102] The 'Idle No More' movement began in November 2012 in protest of the Canadian Government's dismantling of environmental protection laws, which it was claimed endanger First Nations who live on the land. The movement calls for the rebuilding of nation-to-nation relationships. Idle No More quickly 'grew into an inclusive, continent-wide network of urban and rural Indigenous working hand in hand with non-Indigenous allies to build a movement for Indigenous rights and the protection of land, water, and sky'. See 'About the Movement' (*Idle No More*), available at https://idlenomore.ca/about-the-movement/.

[103] As Indigenous legal scholar Val Napoleon explains, Indigenous laws are a crucial resource for Indigenous peoples to both imagine and manage themselves as self-determining peoples.

Further, legislative preambles that recognise Indigenous self-determination are emerging.[104] Policies such as the 'Principles respecting the Government of Canada's relationship with Indigenous peoples', and directives like 'The Attorney General of Canada's Directive on Civil Litigation Involving Indigenous Peoples',[105] are recognising Canada's commitment 'to achieving reconciliation with Indigenous peoples through a renewed, nation-to-nation, government-to-government, and Inuit-Crown relationship based on recognition of rights, respect, co-operation, and partnership as the foundation for transformative change'.[106]

As of 2021, Canada had 1.67 million Indigenous inhabitants, including over 630 communities of First Nations representing more than 50 Nations and 50 Indigenous languages, 53 communities of Inuit residing across the northern regions of Canada in Inuit Nunangat, and various Métis settlements.[107] Approximately 70 historic treaties signed between 1701 and 1923, as well as nearly 100 modern treaties (otherwise known as comprehensive land claim agreements) entered into after 1973 form the basis of the Crown-Indigenous relationships, though parts of Canada remain untreatied and numerous modern treaty negotiations have yet to be concluded.[108] The path forged moving forward should be responsive to the unique needs of each of the differing nations and communities. To this end, advocates urge for the mutually respectful and beneficial relations of pre-Confederation times to be reinstated, which 'will require transformative constitutional change rooted in new understandings of constitutional histories, sovereignties, Indigenous nationalisms, and Indigenous constitutional orders'.[109] This is a crucial task because, in the words of the Supreme Court in *Delgamuukw*: 'Let us face it, we are all here to stay'.[110]

V. CONCLUSION

Canada covers a vast and diverse mass of land. It is home to a pluralistic and dynamic population. Canadians are constantly negotiating how to live together and our constitution is thus constantly challenged to redefine itself.

In the very beginning, Canada took inspiration from other countries to create its own unique version of a constitution. Then in 1982, it took the conscious and progressive step

[104] See, eg, *United Nations Declaration on the Rights of Indigenous Peoples Act* (n 101). See similarly, *An Act respecting First Nations, Inuit and Métis Children, Youth and Families*, SC 2019, c 24.

[105] Department of Justice (Canada), *Principles Respecting the Government of Canada's Relationship with Indigenous Peoples* (Department of Justice, 2021), available at www.justice.gc.ca/eng/csj-sjc/principles-principes.html; Department of Justice (Canada), *Attorney General of Canada's Directive on Civil Litigation Involving Indigenous Peoples* (Department of Justice, 2019), available at www.justice.gc.ca/eng/csj-sjc/ijr-dja/dclip-dlcpa/litigation-litiges.html.

[106] *Principles Respecting the Government of Canada's Relationship with Indigenous Peoples* ibid 3.

[107] 'Indigenous Peoples and Communities' (*Crown-Indigenous Relations and Northern Affairs Canada*), available at www.rcaanc-cirnac.gc.ca/eng/1100100013785/1529102490303; 'First Nations' (*Crown-Indigenous Relations and Northern Affairs Canada*), available at www.rcaanc-cirnac.gc.ca/eng/1100100013791/1535470872302; 'Inuit' (*Crown-Indigenous Relations and Northern Affairs Canada*) (2021).

[108] 'Treaties and Agreements' (*Crown-Indigenous Relations and Northern Affairs Canada*), available at www.rcaanc-cirnac.gc.ca/eng/1100100028574/1529354437231.

[109] Ladner (n 82) 287.

[110] *Delgamuukw* (n 6) 186.

of instituting the Charter. The unique opportunity to constitutionalise such a document as a fully developed nation is very distinctive to Canadian culture and attests to Canada's will to constantly redefine its story.

Canada's constitutional history has thus far proven our nation's ability to respond to changing needs and emerging challenges. Perhaps the biggest challenge Canada will face as a nation in the next chapter of making its public and constitutional law its own will be to recognise Indigenous peoples not only as rights-holders, but as *law-makers*. History has proven that Canada is capable and ready to redefine its story in a way that includes Indigenous legal traditions among its own. Indeed, these traditions have never left. As indicated by scholars, 'Canada is a young country with ancient roots. Indigenous laws and legal systems are the deepest roots of our living tree of Confederation'.[111]

[111] Mandell and Pinder (n 84) 199.

5

The Building of South Africa's Constitution on the Ruins of its Past: The Remodelling of Public Law in Post-Apartheid South Africa

STEVEN MAJIEDT

I. INTRODUCTION

A CONSTITUTION REFLECTS a country's soul and is a mirror in which it views itself.[1] This is because constitutions, by their nature, capture and record the collective memory and past fears of a country, while simultaneously espousing the hopes, vision and ambitions of the future. South Africa's Constitution is no different.[2] It is a constitution that is acutely mindful of the racist, sexist and oppressive ruins of the apartheid regime and which sets the foundation for a country that is based on equality, dignity and freedom. The interim Constitution of South Africa characterised itself as a

> historical bridge between the past of a deeply divided society, characterised by strife, conflict, untold suffering and injustice, and a future founded on the recognition of human rights, democracy and peaceful co-existence and development opportunities for all South Africans.[3]

This powerful imagery persists and carries through to the current Constitution. Recognising the reflective nature of a constitution, the former Chief Justice of South Africa, Justice Ismail Mohamed, remarked:

The constitution of a nation is not simply a statute which mechanically defines the structures of government and the relations between the government and the people, it is a 'mirror of the national soul', the identification of the ideals and aspirations of the nation, the articulation of the values binding its people and disciplining its government.[4]

[1] J Hatchard, 'Some Lessons on Constitution-Making from Zimbabwe' (2001) 45 *Journal of African Law* 210; H Ebrahim, *The Soul of a Nation* (Oxford University Press, 1998).

[2] The Constitution of the Republic of South Africa, 1996 (the Constitution).

[3] The Constitution of the Republic of South Africa Act 200 of 1993 (the interim Constitution). See also E Mureinik, 'A Bridge to Where? Introducing the Interim Bill of Rights' (1994) 10 *South African Journal on Human Rights* 31.

[4] Hatchard (n 1) 210.

Our Constitution is not bereft of feeling, value and purpose. It calculatedly implores those applying and interpreting it, to ensure transformation in the social and economic spheres of life. Judges are thus duty-bound to remould our society from one ravaged by the ruinous effects of the brutal repressive apartheid regime to that visualised by the Constitution with its founding values of dignity, equality, human rights and freedom and the supremacy of the Constitution and the rule of law.

The notion that a constitution reflects the soul of a nation is a simple but powerful proposition. It implicitly illustrates the importance of domesticating or indigenising public law generally and constitutions specifically. Van der Vyver cautioned that the mere imposition of constitutional principles, without domestication, may cause a legitimacy crisis as those principles may not address the real needs and conditions of the particular jurisdiction it purports to govern.[5] The notions of justice, freedom, dignity and equality as enshrined in any constitution must resonate and be in harmony with the overriding indigenous juridical principles of that jurisdiction.

This chapter attempts to explore this idea – the domestication of constitutions and the value that this adds to their legitimacy. Allied to this idea is how the past of a country shapes its understanding and interpretation of a constitution and the general public law. By domestication or indigenisation of a constitution and public law, I am referring to the act of altering the 'DNA' or composition of those laws in order for them to reflect the prevailing social, political and economic conditions of a particular jurisdiction. Wholly transplanting legal systems without more will most likely not be seen as legitimate and may be rejected. For the transposition to be successful, the recipient society must view the laws as legitimate, practicable and relevant and the law must be consistent with the prevailing socio-cultural norms of that society and not misunderstand the systems of that society. To advance this central argument, I focus specifically on South Africa. The chapter will be divided into three parts.

Section II examines South Africa's oppressive apartheid past, which was predicated on parliamentary sovereignty. After detailing the past, it then provides, in section III, an exposition of the current Constitution, which has been lauded as one of the most progressive constitutions in the world. Here, there will be a discussion of some of the salient features of the Constitution, which illustrate the importance of indigenising public law, through the notion of transformative constitutionalism, constitutional supremacy and the South African legal principle of *ubuntu*. Section IV is a discussion of selected cases which demonstrate some of the points raised in section III, while section V concludes. These cases concern socio-economic rights such as housing and the election regime in South Africa. What will be illustrated in this chapter is that in South Africa, indigenisation takes place through laws passed by the legislature or through the interpretation of laws by the judiciary.

[5] J van der Vyver, 'Constitutional Options for Post-Apartheid South Africa' (1991) 40 *Emory Law Journal* 745, 822.

II. THE LONG ROAD[6] TO CONSTITUTIONAL SUPREMACY

To properly understand South Africa's Constitution, it is necessary to consider the oppressive legal order that operated in South Africa prior to its adoption. This is particularly unavoidable, because the Constitution was intended to be a decisive break[7] from the past and usher in a future based on human rights.[8] In this sense, it is a backward- and forward-looking Constitution. This is evident in numerous provisions that are historically self-conscious.[9] For instance, the Preamble of the Constitution recognises the need to redress the injustices of the past and honour those who struggled for freedom for South Africa.[10] The Constitution is backward looking because the contours of justice (today and in the future) is informed, in part, by the peculiar injustices of the past.[11] Perforce, I take a moment to reflect on South Africa's history.

A. The Legal Nature of Apartheid: Parliamentary Sovereignty

Prior to the advent of the Constitution, South Africa adhered to the doctrine of parliamentary sovereignty and the principle of executive prerogative. These were inherited from the British monarchical system under colonialism. Parliamentary sovereignty empowered the legislature to make any statute or measure it deemed necessary, without regard to their arbitrariness or unreasonableness. Thus, the legislature was the supreme law-making body and there was no law or measure beyond its purview. The import of this doctrine was captured by AV Dicey in the following terms:

> Parliament has under the English constitution the right to make or unmake any law whatever, further that no person or body is recognised by the law of England as has a right to override or set aside the legislation of Parliament.[12]

[6] For a personal, enthralling account of the prolonged struggle against apartheid, which resulted in the end of apartheid in 1994 and the beginning of a democratic South Africa, see N Mandela, *Long Walk to Freedom: The Autobiography of Nelson Mandela* (Little Brown & Co, 1995).

[7] In *S v Makwanyane and Another* 1995 (3) SA 391 (CC) [220], Justice Langa held that:

> When the Constitution was enacted, it signalled a dramatic change in the system of governance from one based on rule by parliament to a constitutional state in which the rights of individuals are guaranteed by the Constitution. It also signalled a new dispensation, as it were, where rule by force would be replaced by democratic principles and a governmental system based on the precepts of equality and freedom.

[8] Justice Mahomed, at [262], in *Makwanyane* ibid, remarked:

> The South African Constitution is different: it retains from the past only what is defensible and represents a decisive break from, and a ringing rejection of, that part of the past which is disgracefully racist, authoritarian, insular, and repressive and a vigorous identification of and commitment to a democratic, universalistic, caring and aspirationally egalitarian ethos, expressly articulated in the Constitution. The contrast between the past which it repudiates and the future to which it seeks to commit the nation is stark and dramatic.

[9] The notion of 'historical self-consciousness' is taken from K Klare, 'Legal Culture and Transformative Constitutionalism' (1998) 14 *South African Journal on Human Rights* 146, 155.

[10] P de Vos 'Looking Backward, Looking Forward: Race, Corrective Measures and the South African Constitutional Court' (2012) 79 *Transformation: Critical Perspectives on Southern Africa* 144.

[11] K Asmal, 'Peace, Multiculturalism and Development' in J Hume, TG Fraser and L Murray (eds), *Peacemaking in the Twenty-First Century* (Manchester Scholarship Online, 2013) 190.

[12] AV Dicey, *Introduction to the Study of the Law of the Constitution*, 10th edn (St Martin's Press, 1959) 70.

Apartheid[13] was a complex arrangement of legal, social, political and economic practices of subjugation, oppression and domination. Its aim was to segregate people on the basis of race and gender and it discriminated on those grounds.[14] It denied people who were classified as 'non-Europeans' basic rights and stripped them of their humanity.[15] As noted by the Constitutional Court in *Brink v Kitshoff NO*,[16] apartheid systemically, through law and policies, discriminated against Black people in every facet of life, literally from the cradle to the grave. Black people were prohibited from attending well-resourced schools and were denied the opportunity of attending university. Their access to public transport, libraries and civic amenities were severely restricted and, in some instances, entirely denied.[17] A simple pleasure of walking on a public beach was something 'non-Europeans' were not permitted.[18] Black people were also legally prohibited from owning land, and in certain instances, were proscribed from residing on land that was reserved for white people. The enforcement of discriminatory land and spatial legislation caused mass dispossession and forced removals of Black people, resulting in white people owning nearly 90 per cent of land in South Africa.[19] In many respects, dispossession, for Black people, was nine-tenths of the law[20] and many of them were rendered strangers in their own country.[21]

There was no facet of social life that was left untouched by apartheid. The Prohibition of Mixed Marriages Act 55 of 1949 prohibited marriages between 'whites' and 'non-whites'. Accordingly, the law dictated who individuals could permissibly marry. Similarly, the Immorality Act 23 of 1957 proscribed sexual intercourse or 'immoral or indecent acts' between white people and people who were not white. All these statutes were based on and made possible by the Population Registration Act 30 of 1950, which imposed a

[13] Apartheid means 'apartness' in Afrikaans.

[14] MS McDougal, HD Lasswell and L Chen, *Human Rights and World Public Order* (Oxford University Press, 1980) 523.

[15] J Dugard, *Human Rights and the South African Legal Order* (Princeton Legacy Library, 1978) 93–94; M Higginbotham, L Higginbotham and S Ngcobo, 'De Jure Segregation in the United States and South Africa: The Difficult Pursuit for Racial Justice' (1990) 4 *University of Illinois Law Review* 763.

[16] *Brink v Kitshoff NO* 1996 (4) SA 197 [40].

[17] ibid. See also *Minister of Finance v Van Heerden* 2004 (6) SA 121 (CC) [74].

[18] See JM Rogerson, 'Kicking Sand in the Face of Apartheid" Segregated Beaches in South Africa' (2017) 35 *Bulletin of Geography: Socio-economic Series* 93.

[19] Land dispossession in South Africa first occurred through the barrel of the gun and trickery and then subsequently through an array of oppressive legislation such as the Native Land Act 27 of 1913; Native Trust and Land Act 18 of 1936; Group Areas Act 41 of 1950; Prevention of Illegal Squatting Act 52 of 1951; Group Areas Act 36 of 1966. See also *Western Cape Provincial Government In Re: DVB Behuising (Pty) Ltd v North West Provincial Government* 2001 (1) SA 500 (CC) [41]; *Daniels v Scribante* 2017 (4) SA 341 (CC); *District Six Committee v Minister of Rural Development & Land Reform* [2019] 4 All SA 89 (LCC); R Davenport, 'Some Reflections on the History of Land Tenure in South Africa, Seen in the Light of Attempts by the State to Impose Political and Economic Control' (1985) *Acta Juridica* 53; R Hamilton, 'Role of Apartheid Legislation in the Property Law of South Africa' (1987) 10 *National Black Law Journal* 152; B Atuahene, 'Paying for the Past: Redressing the Legacy of Land Dispossession in South Africa' (2011) 45 *Law & Society Review* 955; SB Nxumalo, 'Revisiting the Relationship Between Property Rights and Land Reform Legislation in South Africa: Grobler v Phillips and Others' (*Oxford Property Law Blog*, 22 December 2021), available at www.law.ox.ac.uk/research-and-subject-groups/property-law/blog/2021/12/revisiting-relationship-between-property; B Bhandar, *Colonial Lives of Property* (Duke University Press, 2018); T Ngcukaitobi, *Land Matters* (Penguin Random House, 2021).

[20] *Port Elizabeth Municipality v Various Occupiers* 2005 (1) SA 217 (CC) [9].

[21] S Plaatje, *Native Life in South Africa* (Picador Africa, 2007) 21.

duty on people to identify and register as one of the four distinct racial groups created by the apartheid state: white, Coloured, Black and other.[22] There was a plethora of statutes passed by the apartheid state to further its racist and gendered ideology, including segregating even graveyards based on race.[23]

B. The Common Law under Apartheid

Outside of legislation, another important source of law was the common law, which still operates today.[24] South Africa's common law is a mix of Roman-Dutch law and English law, which has been applied and developed through the courts.[25] This amalgamation of the common law is a result of two conquests – the arrival of the Dutch East India Company at the Cape in 1652, which led to imposition of the Dutch-inspired legal system, underpinned by Roman law;[26] and the British conquest of the Cape in 1795, which interrupted Dutch rule.[27] The Court of Kings Bench in *Campbell v Hall* held that the Dutch legal system should remain in place, subject to incremental alterations made by the British colonial authorities.[28] Thus, Roman-Dutch law persisted and English common law was introduced incrementally, particularly in the areas of court procedure, the structures of government as well as criminal and mercantile law.[29] While English law had little to no impact on the law of persons, the English administrators introduced changes to various definitions of crimes and delicts and imposed the notion of a 'reasonable man' and 'the duty of care'.[30]

[22] The Population Registration Act was not a model of clarity and was poorly drafted. In s 1, it defined the four distinct races in the following terms:

> 'Black' means a person who is, or is generally accepted as, a member of any aboriginal race or tribe of Africa;
>
> 'coloured person' means a person who is not a white person or a Black;
>
> 'ethnic or other group' means a group prescribed and defined by the Governor-General in terms of sub-section (2) of section five;
>
> 'white person' means a person who-
>
> (a) in appearance obviously is a white person and who is not generally accepted as a coloured person; or
> (b) is generally accepted as a white person and is not in appearance obviously not a white person,
>
> but does not include any person who for the purposes of his classification under this Act, freely and voluntarily admits that he is by descent a Black or a coloured person unless it is proved that the admission is not based on fact.

[23] Reservation of Separate Amenities Act 49 of 1953; the provincial Reservation of Separations of Amenities by Local Authorities Ordinance of 1955.

[24] R Zimmermann and D Visser, 'Introduction: South African Law as a Mixed Legal System' in R Zimmermann and D Visser (eds), *Southern Cross: Civil Law and Common Law in South Africa* (Clarendon, 1996).

[25] H Corder, *Judges at Work: The Role and Attitudes of the South African Appellate Judiciary 1910-1950* (Juta & Co Ltd, 1984); J Sarkin, 'The Common Law in South Africa: Pro Apartheid or Pro Democracy' (1999) 23 *Hastings International and Comparative Law Review* 1.

[26] See J Wessels, 'The Future of Roman-Dutch Law in South Africa' (1920) 37 *South African Law Journal* 265; PJ Thomas, BC Stoop and GC van der Merwe, *The Historical Foundations of South African Private Law* (LexisNexis, 2000) 96–97; PT Mellet, *The Lie of 1652* (NB Publishers, 2020).

[27] E Zitzke, 'The History and Politics of Contemporary Common Law Purism' (2017) 23 *Fundamina* 185, 191.

[28] *Campbell v Hall* (1774) 1 Cowp 204, 98 ER 1045.

[29] HR Hahlo and E Kahn, *The South African Legal System and its Background* (Juta, 1968) 576–77.

[30] Sarkin (n 25) 2–3.

Some jurists are of the opinion that the common law, even under apartheid, was grounded in principles of justice, equality and fairness.[31] It was contended that absent the legislation promulgated by the apartheid state, the principles of justice, equality and fairness as espoused by the common law would have provided the guiding spirit of the law. Equality before the law and the protection and promotion of personal freedom by advancing certain rights and freedoms (such as the freedom of contract) were recognised. On this construction, the apartheid state did not rewrite the common law, but rather overrode the common law.[32] Recently, Nxumalo and Mafora remarked:

> [I]t is important to point out that the common law under apartheid was a social tool employed in the service of abhorrent and racist objectives but that that does not mean that the common law is itself essentially racist. It operated alongside legislation which was repressive and racist.
>
> Most of that legislation derogated from the common law and its application. However, everything is in flux and the law is no exception. It adapts itself to new environments, reflects the ideas and feelings of the society, contracts and expands, grows and declines.[33]

The common law was restricted by the repressive legislation in place at the time.[34] Notwithstanding this, the common law has a strong sense of justice. English law further entrenched principles of impartiality and natural justice.[35] In 1946, in *Mpanza v Minister of Native Affairs*, for instance, the Witwatersrand Local Division held that the right of personal liberty was a highly prized right, and our courts will always strive to uphold it.[36] However, this right could only operate and have force to the extent that it is permitted by an Act of Parliament. In other words, despite the importance of the right to personal liberty, the legislature could enact a statute that would have the effect of denying this right.[37]

C. The Role of the Courts During Apartheid

Both Roman-Dutch law and English law provided judicial recourse for any infringements on civil liberties. For instance, Roman-Dutch law provides an *interdictum de homine libero exhibendo*, a remedy to individuals who have been arbitrarily deprived of their liberty. Similarly, under English law, a person deprived of their liberty can approach a court and invoke a writ of *habeas corpus*. At the core of these remedies is the desire to protect personal freedom from undue, irrational and arbitrary government invasion. In 1916, the Transvaal Provincial Division unequivocally stated in *Principal Immigration Officer v Narayansamy* that everyone was entitled to invoke a writ of *habeas corpus*

[31] J Trengrove, 'Perspectives on the Role of Judges in a Deeply Divided Society' in H Corder (ed), *Democracy and the Judiciary* (IDASA, 1989) 125–26.

[32] Dugard (n 15) 382–83; J Dugard, 'Using the Law to Pervert Justice' (1983) 11 *Human Rights* 22.

[33] S Nxumalo and D Mafora, 'Mpofu-Walsh's Book "The New Apartheid" Misses the Point on Common and Contract Law' (*Mail & Guardian*, 22 August 2021), available at https://mg.co.za/opinion/2021-08-22-mpofu-walshs-book-the-new-apartheid-misses-the-point-on-common-and-contract-law/?utm_medium=Social&utm_source=Twitter#Echobox=1629659419-1.

[34] ibid.

[35] Sarkin (n 25) 3.

[36] *Mpanza v Minister of Native Affairs* 1946 WLD 225, 229.

[37] See Dugard (n 15) 108; Dugard (n 32) 38.

pursuant to Roman-Dutch and English law.[38] This was buttressed in *Wood v Ondangwa Tribal Authority*, where the Court held that an action of *habeas corpus* could be brought by any person on behalf of someone who has been imprisoned and that the laws pertaining to *habeas corpus* ought to be construed in favour of the liberty of an individual.[39] Regardless of these common law protections, the apartheid state enacted an assemblage of legislation that frustrated these protections.

This begs the question regarding the role of courts. During the apartheid era, the power of courts to review legislation and government action was significantly constrained. Courts were denuded of the power to review the substance of statutes. They could mostly adjudicate whether Parliament adhered to the prescribed procedure in the legislative process.[40] In *Johannesburg Consolidated Investment Co v Johannesburg Town Council*,[41] the Court held that the overarching justification for judicial intervention is the doctrine of ultra vires. Courts, according to this rationale, could only interfere on the basis that the state exercised power that went beyond its purview, as prescribed by Parliament. Courts were not allowed to second-guess the purported wisdom of the legislature. So, if the law was clear and certain, a court plainly did not have power to interfere with the propriety of the legislation.[42] Courts could not strike down or set aside laws that were morally unconscionable and unjust. As Centlivers CJ asseverated in *Ndlwana v Hofmeyr*, the 'court has no power to pronounce upon the validity of an Act of Parliament duly promulgated and printed and published by proper authority'.[43] In this regard, courts were inferior to the legislature and executive and were subordinate to them. Moreover, added to the rigid adherence to parliamentary sovereignty, was a strict fidelity to a literalist interpretive approach. Courts therefore had no latitude to strike down repugnant legislation, nor could they read down statutes to ameliorate their pernicious effect. Parliament ruled supreme and courts had to apply the law as they found it.

Unfortunately, the apartheid state was able to perpetrate many substantive injustices by merely following the correct procedure[44] and its successes were also exacerbated by a supine judiciary, which was not necessarily keen on upholding civil liberties, failed to guard its independence and permitted the legislature to step into its terrain.[45] Baxter described the South African judiciary under apartheid as an enigma, which was emasculated by a host of hostile legislation. He also stated that the judiciary had 'degenerated into a compliant auxiliary' of the other branches.[46] This criticism of courts can be seen in the so-called emergency cases, discussed next.

[38] *Principal Immigration Officer v Narayansamy* 1916 TPD 274.

[39] *Wood v Ondangwa Tribal Authority* 1975 (2) SA 294 (A).

[40] There are instances where courts attempted to invalidate laws on substantive grounds. See the landmark cases that formed part of the constitutional crisis of the 1950s: *Harris v Minister of the Interior* 1952 (2) SA 428 (A), *Minister of the Interior v Harris* 1952 (4) SA 769 (A); *Collins v Minister of the Interior* 1957 (1) SA 552 (A).

[41] *Johannesburg Consolidated Investment Company v Johannesburg Town Council* 1903 TS 111.

[42] M Du Plessis, 'The Legitimacy of Judicial Review in South Africa's New Constitutional Dispensation: Insights from the Canadian Experience' (2000) 33 *Comparative and International Law Journal of Southern Africa* 227, 228.

[43] *Ndlwana v Hofmeyr* 1937 AD 229, 231. See also E Griswold, 'The "Coloured Vote Case" in South Africa' (1952) 65 *Harvard Law Review* 1361.

[44] L Boulle, B Harris and C Hoexter, *Constitutional and Administrative Law: Basic Principles* (Juta, 1989) 131–43.

[45] Du Plessis (n 42) 228.

[46] L Baxter, 'A Judicial Declaration of Martial Law' (1987) 3 *South African Journal on Human Rights* 317, 317.

The Public Safety Act 3 of 1953 empowered the President to declare, by proclamation in the government gazette, that a state of emergency existed within the Republic or South West Africa (today Namibia) or any of their areas.[47] This broad power included the prohibition of gatherings and processions, the forced dispersal of illegal gatherings, the creation of broadly defined crimes and the suppression of publications and organisations.[48] Dugard argues that the Public Safety Act provided the apartheid state an unencumbered 'free hand' that permitted it to arrest anyone without warrant and detain without trial.[49] The apartheid state enthusiastically invoked this broad 'emergency' power and the case law reflects that the courts not only failed to recognise the injustice perpetuated by this Act, but actively aided the apartheid state. I briefly focus on three 'emergency' cases.

First, in *Minister of Law & Order v Dempsey*, a nun had been physically restrained by a policeman, who had assaulted a mourner at a funeral.[50] The nun was detained under emergency regulations. A *habeas corpus* application was sought to obtain the release of the nun. Under South African law, it was well-established that every invasion of personal liberty was *prima facie* unlawful and thus should be justified by the detainer. In other words, the burden of proof was on the detainer to prove that the detention was lawful and justified. However, in *Dempsey*, the Court held that the burden of proof rests with the applicant in *habeas corpus* proceedings. In other words, the nun had to prove that the state had abused its powers by detaining her.

Second, in *Omar v Minister of Law and Order*, a case involving our first Minister of Justice in the new democracy in President Mandela's Cabinet, Dullah Omar, the Court upheld certain regulations, which were promulgated under the emergency powers referenced above.[51] These regulations deprived emergency detainees of their right of access to counsel and their right to be heard before a decision was made to further their detention. Lamentably, the Court upheld these draconian regulations. Axiomatically, the rights of access to counsel and to be heard before a decision regarding continued detention is taken, are fundamental rights in many jurisdictions. Prior to this decision, the law was clear that any exercise of delegated legislation that infringed a fundamental right was impermissible. But, the Court overlooked this and held that Parliament could exclude the rights to *audi alteram partem* and legal counsel.

Finally, in *Staatspresident v United Democratic Front*, numerous emergency regulations were challenged on the basis that the term 'unrest', which had been used in the regulations, was so vague as to render the regulations null and void.[52] In terms of section

[47] Namibia was under South Africa's administration from 1915–1990 and was called 'South West Africa'. See J Dugard, *The South West Africa/Namibia Dispute: Documents and Scholarly Writings on the Controversy Between South Africa and the United Nations* (University of California Press, 1973); AM Fokkens, 'The Suppression of Internal Unrest in South West Africa (Namibia) 1921–1933' (2012) 40(3) *Scientia Militaria* 109.

[48] S Morton, 'States of Emergency and the Apartheid Legal Order in South African Fiction' (2010) 46 *Journal of Postcolonial Writing* 491, 492.

[49] Dugard (n 15) 110–11.

[50] *Minister of Law and Order v Dempsey* 1988 (3) SA 19 (A).

[51] *Omar v Minister of Law and Order; Fani and Others v Minister of Law and Order and Others; State President and Others v Bill* [1987] 4 All SA 556 (AD).

[52] *Staatspresident v United Democratic Front* 1988 (4) SA 830 (A). Another case that rejected the doctrine of ultra vires is: *Lipschitz v Wattrus* NO 1980 (1) SA 662 (T). See also C Forsyth, 'Of Fig Leaves and Fairy Tales: The Ultra Vires Doctrine, the Sovereignty of Parliament and Judicial Review' (1996) 55 *Cambridge Law Journal* 112.

5B of the Public Safety Act, courts were not competent to enquire into or to give judgment on the validity of these regulations. In other words, these regulations were subject to an ouster clause. The Court dismissed the challenge to these regulations and held that to be protected from being declared invalid by section 5B, a regulation does not have to comply with all the requirements for validity. Ergo, the doctrine of ultra vires was rejected in this case.

In summary, under apartheid, Parliament was sovereign and could make any law it deemed fit. These laws were oppressive and deeply unjust. Courts had no power to declare, let alone strike down, legislation invalid. It merely applied the law as it was, regardless of how unjust the law may be. Courts therefore merely served as a rubber stamp for the legislature. It is against the backdrop of these ruins that the Constitution must be understood.

III. A COUNTRY REIMAGINED: A CONSTITUTIONAL DEMOCRACY

The Constitution came about through a complex and protracted negotiation process including the Convention for a Democratic South Africa (CODESA), the adoption of the initial 34 Constitutional Principles, the interim Constitution and then the final Constitution which included two judgments of the Constitutional Court, certifying its provisions.[53] As alluded to in the Introduction, the South African Constitution carries a promise of a new society. The Preamble affirms the supremacy of the Constitution and declares that South Africa belongs to all those who live in it.[54] Importantly, it displaces parliamentary sovereignty. To this end, the Constitution signifies a break from a past characterised by inequality, oppression and exclusion to a future founded on justice, equality, dignity and equality.[55] Such a break must be understood in the context of 'transformative constitutionalism'. While there is no universally accepted definition of transformative constitutionalism,[56] Klare described it as:

> [A] long-term project of constitutional enactment, interpretation and enforcement committed (not in isolation, of course, but in a historical context of conducive political developments) to transforming a country's political and social institutions and power relationships in a democratic, participatory, and egalitarian direction.[57]

[53] *In re: Certification of the Constitution of the Republic of South Africa* 1996 (4) SA 744 (CC); *Certification of the Amended Text of the Constitution of the Republic of South Africa* 1997 (2) SA 97 (CC).

[54] Justice Mhantla in *Speaker of the National Assembly v Land Access Movement of South Africa* 2019 (6) SA 568 at [1] stated:

It aims to right historical wrongs, resolve unjust dispossession and heal the 'trauma of deep, dislocating loss of land' that has taken root in our country. It entails the practical disruption of racialised privilege in respect of land ownership. But it also incorporates a symbolic function of recognising histories and legacies of injustice that influence the lives of individuals, families and communities.

[55] AJ van der Walt, *Constitutional Property Clause* (Juta & Co, 1997) 79; AJ van der Walt, 'Transformative Constitutionalism and the Development of South African Property Law I' (2005) *Journal of South African Law* 655, 658.

[56] P Langa, 'Transformative Constitutionalism' (2006) 17 *Stellenbosch Law Review* 351, 351.

[57] K Klare, 'Legal Culture and Transformative Constitutionalism' (1998) 14 *South African Journal on Human Rights* 150. See also S Sibanda, 'Not Purpose-Made! Transformative Constitutionalism, Post-Independence Constitutionalism and the Struggle to Eradicate Poverty' (2011) 22 *Stellenbosch Law Review* 482, 486; J Brickhill and Y van Leeve, 'Transformative Constitutionalism – Guiding light or Empty Slogan?' (2015) *Acta Juridica* 141, 146.

The transformative nature of the Constitution means that there must be political, social and legal reform, with an awareness of the historical injustices which ought to be redressed. It is an enterprise of inducing large-scale social change through non-violent processes, grounded in law.[58] Transformative constitutionalism has two potential conceptions. First, transformation could refer to achievements of specific outcomes such as poverty reduction and eradicating inequality through adjudication. Second, it could refer to a fundamental change in institutions and systems, producing results.[59] At the heart of transformative constitutionalism is the demand for a change in legal culture and socio-economic conditions. Former Chief Justice Pius Langa plainly stated that our Constitution espouses the idea that 'we must change'.[60] In this sense, the Constitution is both backward-looking in that it is a break away from 'our socially degrading and economically exploitative apartheid past',[61] and forward-looking in that it facilitates the construction of a new political, social and economic order 'based on democratic values, social justice and fundamental human rights', which is concerned with bettering and improving the quality of life and freeing the potential of everyone.[62]

A. The Status of the Common Law in South Africa's Constitutional Supremacy

In light of the new constitutional order, what is the status of the common law? Did the common law collapse with apartheid? The short answer is no. The common law continues to occupy a central place in our country's legal landscape. That is because we apply the principle of subsidiarity, meaning that

> it does not follow that [resorting] to constitutional rights and values may be freewheeling or haphazard … The Constitution is primary but its influence is mostly indirect. It is perceived through its effects on legislation and the common law – to which one must look first.[63]

As it was articulated in *Du Plessis v De Klerk*, 'The common law is not to be trapped within the limitations of its past. It needs not to be interpreted in conditions of social and constitutional ossification'.[64] This is particularly so because there is a constitutional injunction that requires courts, when interpreting legislation and developing the common law, to promote the spirit, object and purport of the Bill of Rights.[65] Thus, the common law, once used to achieve racist and repressive ends, has now been re-invigorated and revitalised by the Constitution.[66] The interaction between the Constitution and the common law has been described by the Constitutional Court as a supplementation of the Constitution's written provisions by the common law. The latter derives its force from

[58] ibid.
[59] D Brand, 'Courts, Socio-Economic Rights and Transformative Politics', LLD thesis (University of Stellenbosch, 2009).
[60] ibid 352.
[61] D Moseneke, 'The Fourth Bram Fischer Memorial Lecture: Transformative Adjudication' (2002) 18 *South African Journal on Human Rights* 309, 315.
[62] S Liebenberg, *Socio-Economic Rights Adjudication Under a Transformative Constitution* (Juta, 2010) 27.
[63] *My Vote Counts NPC v Speaker of the National Assembly* 2016 (1) SA 132 (CC).
[64] *Du Plessis v De Klerk* 1996 (3) SA 850 (CC) [86].
[65] The Constitution s 39(2).
[66] *Barkhuizen v Napier* 2007 (5) SA 323 (CC).

the Constitution and must be developed to fulfil the Constitution's objectives. There is nonetheless only one system of law, with the Constitution as the supreme law and other laws must comply with it.[67]

In respect of the development of the common law, more particularly in remodelling public law,[68] it bears consideration that:

> There are notionally different ways to develop the common-law under section 39(2) of the Constitution, all of which might be consistent with its provisions. Not all would necessarily be equally beneficial for the common law. Before the advent of the [Interim Constitution], the refashioning of the common law in this area entailed 'policy decisions and value judgments' which had to 'reflect the wishes, often unspoken, and the perceptions, often but dimly discerned, of the people'. A balance had to be struck between the interests of the parties and the conflicting interests of the community according to what 'the [c]ourt conceives to be society's notions of what justice demands.' Under section 39(2) of the Constitution concepts such as 'policy decisions and value judgments' reflecting 'the wishes … and the perceptions … of the people' and 'society's notions of what justice demands' might well have to be replaced, or supplemented and enriched by the appropriate norms of the objective value system embodied in the Constitution.[69]

The need to develop the common law under section 39(2) could arise in at least two instances. The first would be when a rule of the common law is inconsistent with a constitutional provision. Repugnancy of this kind would compel an adaptation of the common law to resolve the inconsistency. The second instance would occur even when a rule of the common law is not inconsistent with a specific constitutional provision, but may fall short of its spirit, purport and objects. Then, the common law must be adapted so that it grows in harmony with the objective normative value system found in the Constitution.[70]

But there is a caveat to the development of the common law. It was expressed thus by the Constitutional Court in *Mighty Solutions CC t/a Orlando Service Station v Engen Petroleum Ltd and Another*:

> Our common law evolved from an ancient society in which slavery was lawful, through centuries of feudalism, colonialism, discrimination, sexism and exploitation. Furthermore, apartheid laws and practices permeated and to some extent delegitimised much of the pre-1994 South African legal system. Courts have a duty to develop the common law – like customary law – to accord with the Bill of Rights. … *Caution is called for though. It is tempting to regard precedents from the pre democratic era with suspicion. This may be more so when language is used, which some may regard as archaic and reminiscent of a patriarchal feudal era, as when the Court in* Kala Singh *said that 'it does not lie in the mouth of a lessee to question the title of his landlord'. However, the mere fact that common law principles are sourced from pre-constitutional case law is not always relevant. Age is not necessarily a reason to change. Some of the lessons gained from human experience over the ages are timeless and have passed the logical and moral tests of time. The Constitution indeed recognises the existing common law and customary law.* In *Zuma*, Kentridge AJ said that it is not the case that under our constitutional dispensation

[67] *Pharmaceutical Manufacturers Association of SA; In Re Ex Parte Application of the President of RSA* 2000 (2) SA 674 (CC) [49].

[68] One could also call it 'decolonising our common law'.

[69] *Carmichele v Minister of Safety and Security* 2001 (4) SA 938 (CC) [56].

[70] *Thebus and Another v S* 2003 (6) SA 505 (CC) [28].

> 'all the principles of law which have hitherto governed our courts are to be ignored. Those principles obviously contain much of lasting value'. Furthermore, legal certainty is essential for the rule of law – a constitutional value. It is also understandable that litigants who find themselves on the wrong side of the common law or customary law will – often at a late stage in proceedings – seek what they would call its 'development' (emphasis added).[71]

Thus, the common law is not inherently unconstitutional. Our courts are still required to robustly engage with the Constitution and its values. The Constitution must reinvigorate the common law to ensure that it is not at odds with constitutional promises. Excising the common law from our system of law would cause great uncertainty and disrupt our legal system. Developing the common law must take place when necessary and incrementally.

B. The Powers of the Judiciary under the Constitution

The Constitution entrenches a generous, and justiciable Bill of Rights, which includes the right to access to adequate housing,[72] the right to basic education[73] and the rights to healthcare, food, water and social security.[74] Further to this, it has clothed the judiciary with expansive powers to review legislation and governmental actions and strike them down where it is of the opinion that such action is constitutionally wanting. Van Schyff argues that judicial review is an integral part of a constitutional democracy. The constitutional text is open-ended and generously worded, giving courts the broad jurisdiction to interpret and give content to the constitutional text. While South Africa adheres to the separation of powers doctrine, the doctrine is not rigidly defined and is generally unfixed. In many instances, the courts themselves determine the content and meaning of the doctrine of separation of powers.[75] Recently, in *Mwelase*,[76] Justice Cameron cautioned that 'the bogeyman of separation of powers concerns should not cause courts to shirk from [their] constitutional responsibility'.[77]

The importance of the adoption of the Constitution was aptly summarised by Mureinik, who described it as a shift from a culture of authority to a culture of justification.[78] Under apartheid, the state acted through authority and punishment. It could enact repressive and unjust statutes without fear of being held accountable and needing to justify their exercise of public power.[79] Today, a culture of justification prevails, which requires courts to ensure that every Act or exercise of public power by the Government is

[71] *Mighty Solutions CC t/a Orlando Service Station v Engen Petroleum Ltd and Another* 2016 (1) SA 621 (CC) [36]–[37]. See *Kala Singh v Germiston Municipality* 1912 TPD 155, 160; *S v Zuma* 1995 (2) SA 642 [17].

[72] The Constitution s 26.

[73] ibid s 29.

[74] ibid s 27.

[75] See *Certification of the Amended Text of the Constitution of The Republic Of South Africa* 1997 (2) SA 97 (CC), 1997 (1) BCLR 1 (CC) [113]–[127]; *Justice Alliance of South Africa v President of Republic of South Africa* 2011 (5) SA 388 (CC); F Dube, 'Separation of Powers and the Institutional Supremacy of the Constitutional Court over Parliament and the Executive' (2020) 36 *South African Journal on Human Rights* 293.

[76] *Mwelase v Director-General for the Department of Rural Development and Land Reform* 2019 (6) SA 597 (CC).

[77] ibid [51].

[78] Mureinik (n 3) 33.

[79] ibid.

not only procedurally compliant, but substantively justifiable.[80] Thus, there is a constitutional demand on courts to ensure that the Bill of Rights is upheld and that the state does not act in any way that denigrates or makes inroads into these rights without providing substantive justification. Of considerable import, is that courts cannot be value-neutral or defer questions of social justice to other arms of government, because the Constitution is a repository of values that bind people.[81] These values are explicitly reflected in section 1 of the Constitution, and in particular include human dignity, the advancement of human rights and freedoms and the achievement of equality. As Justice Kriegler in *President of the Republic of South Africa v Hugo* put it, our Constitution is emphatically egalitarian,[82] and courts must be alive to this. Therefore, the arms of the state, including the courts, have the task of achieving social redistributive justice.[83] Courts, without more, are at the centre of the constitutional project. As Langa notes:

> Under a transformative Constitution, judges bear the ultimate responsibility to justify their decisions not only by reference to authority, but by reference to ideas and values. This approach to adjudication requires an acceptance of the politics of law. There is no longer place for assertions that the law can be kept isolated from politics. While they are not the same, they are inherently and necessarily linked.[84]

The Constitution therefore promotes a deliberative democracy through a constitutional dialogue between the three arms of government. All three arms of government are continuously engaged in a dialogue pertaining to the roles of each arm and their interaction with each other. Each arm is tasked with upholding the Constitution. The dialogue is continuous, because that permits for the role of each arm to be defined and redefined in light of the prevailing circumstances of the time. Thus, the South African Constitution is not a mere document that contains hallow shibboleths.[85]

C. The Indigenisation of the Constitution

South Africa's constitutional framework is deeply rooted in the recollection of its collective historical injustice. It is only logical that our public law is indigenised, through the Constitution, to take into account the memory of denial of certain people's humanness, which resulted in the undignified, unequal treatment of people considered to be not white. For example, the right to housing is specifically entrenched as a justiciable socio-economic right because of our long history of forced removals and dispossession. The Constitution's promise that everyone is entitled to basic education is based on the fact that education was reserved for a particular elite few. The demand for a progressively realisable right to healthcare is a response to centuries' systemic inequality that existed

[80] ibid. See also R Forst, 'The Justification of Human Rights and the Basic Right to Justification: A Reflexive Approach' (2010) 120 *Ethics* 711, 734; K Möller, 'Justifying the Culture of Justification' (2020) 17 *International Journal of Constitutional Law* 1078.

[81] Moseneke (n 61) 315; *Makwanyane* (n 7) 262.

[82] *President of the Republic of South Africa v Hugo* 1997 (4) SA 1 (CC) [74].

[83] Moseneke (n 61) 318.

[84] Langa (n 56) 352.

[85] The idea of 'hallow shibboleths' emerges from *Trop v Dulles* 356 US 86, 103 (1958).

under apartheid. If the Constitution did not directly confront these issues, it would have faced a legitimacy crisis. It would have led many to question who the 'people' referred to in the Constitution are, if it ignored the painful past of South Africa.[86]

A failure to indigenise public law generally, and the Constitution specifically, to reflect the domestic social, political and economic conditions may result in the vehement rejection of public law and the Constitution. Or at best, they may yield poor results. Thus, infusing the public law with local realities may enhance its normative force and legitimacy. Writing in the context of human rights, Mahao argues that:

> [T]he values underpinning the dominant rights paradigm are, by and large, removed from notions of justice as understood and lived by the vast majority of people previously colonised in places such as Africa. Thus, mainstreaming indigenous juridical principles in the legal system holds the promise of going some distance towards legitimising the system. Inherently, however, this entails an epistemological shift in world outlook.[87]

This proposition must be true even for constitutions and public law. It provides a complementary response to Lord Denning's observation that '[j]ust as with an English oak, so with the English common law. You cannot transplant it to the African continent and expect it to retain the tough character which it has in England'.[88] Legal systems of one jurisdiction cannot simply be transplanted in another jurisdiction without some form of domestication and infusing that legal system with some indigenous legal principles and doctrines.

One such indigenous principle, which has been interpreted into our constitutional framework, is the doctrine of *ubuntu*. It is a value of humaneness that undergirds the Constitution. The simplest formulation of *ubuntu* is the isiZulu expression, *umuntu ngumuntu ngabantu*, which literally means 'a human being is a human being through (the otherness of) other human beings'.[89] *Ubuntu* is a powerful concept, which emphasises the communal nature of society and espouses in it the ideas and notions of humaneness, social justice and fairness and envelopes the core values of group solidarity, compassion, respect, human dignity, conformity to basic norms and collective unity.[90] This principle has been accepted as a crucial value that underpins our Constitution. In *S v Makwanyane*, a landmark case that declared the death penalty unconstitutional, the Court held that the death penalty offended the principle of *ubuntu*, because of the value a community puts on life and human dignity. The death penalty is bereft of

[86] The Preamble of the Constitution refers to 'We the people of South Africa' acknowledge the injustices of the past.

[87] NL Mahao, 'Can African Juridical Principles Redeem and Legitimise Contemporary Human Rights Jurisprudence?' (2016) 49 *Comparative and International Law Journal of Southern Africa* 455, 456.

[88] *Nyali Ltd v Attorney-General* (1955) 1 All ER 646, 653.

[89] NM Kamwangamalu, 'Ubuntu: A Sociolinguistic Perspective to a Pan-African Concept' (1990) 12 *Critical Arts* 24; CBN Gade, 'What is Ubuntu? Different Interpretations Among South Africans of African Descent' (2012) 31 *South African Journal of Philosophy* 486.

[90] *Azanian Peoples Organisation v President of the Republic of South Africa* 1996 (4) SA 671 (CC) [3], [19], [48]; *Van Vuuren v Minister for Correctional Services* 2010 (12) BCLR 1233 (CC) [51]; *The Citizen 1978 (Pty) Ltd v McBride* 2011 (4) SA 191 (CC) [164]–[165], [168], [210], [216]–[218]; *Le Roux v Dey* 2011 (3) SA 274 (CC) [200]; Y Mokgoro, 'Ubuntu and the Law in South Africa' (1998) 4 *Buffalo Human Rights Law Review* 15; Y Mokgoro and S Woolman, 'Where Dignity Ends and Ubuntu Begins: An Amplification of, as well as an Identification of a Tension in Drucilla Cornell's Thoughts' (2010) 25 *Southern African Public Law* 400, 406.

ubuntu.[91] The principle of *ubuntu* has also been held to be a valid principle to govern contract law and possibly vitiate a contract found to be wanting on the grounds of *ubuntu*.[92] In *City of Johannesburg Metropolitan Municipality v Blue Moonlight Properties 39 (Pty) Ltd*,[93] the Constitutional Court recognised the concept of *ubuntu* as underlying the Constitution and the Prevention of Illegal Eviction from and Unlawful Occupation of Land Act 19 of 1998 (PIE Act), and that it is relevant to their interpretation. The Court referred to the following passage from *PE Municipality*[94] with approval:

> Thus, PIE expressly requires the court to infuse elements of grace and compassion into the formal structures of the law. It is called upon to balance competing interests in a principled way and to promote the constitutional vision of a caring society based on good neighbourliness and shared concern. The Constitution and PIE confirm that we are not islands unto ourselves. The spirit of ubuntu, part of the deep cultural heritage of the majority of the population, suffuses the whole constitutional order. It combines individual rights with a communitarian philosophy. It is a unifying motif of the Bill of Rights, which is nothing if not a structured, institutionalised and operational declaration in our evolving new society of the need for human interdependence, respect and concern.[95]

IV. CASES EVIDENCING THE INDIGENISATION OF PUBLIC LAW IN SOUTH AFRICA

The Constitutional Court has affirmed the relevance of our history in the process of interpreting the rights in the Bill of Rights.[96] In addition to the principle of *ubuntu* and development of the common law, the South African Constitution and its interpretation by the Constitutional Court has domesticated public law to reflect the material conditions of South Africa as well as the social, political and cultural realities through, amongst others, the right to access to adequate housing as well as the electoral regime in South Africa. I now turn to those two examples.

A. The Sisyphean Struggle for Housing

There is a housing crisis in South Africa.[97] As highlighted above, the right to exclude (given effect through the *rei vindicatio*), was used by the apartheid state to evict people,

[91] *Makwanyane* (n 7) [223]–[225]. A powerful passage by Mohamed DP at [263] is worth quoting:

> [Ubuntu] expresses the ethos of an instinctive capacity for and enjoyment of love towards our fellow men and women; the joy and the fulfilment involved in recognizing their innate humanity; the reciprocity this generates in interaction within the collective community; the richness of the creative emotions which it engenders and the moral energies which it releases both in the givers and the society which they serve and are served by.

[92] *Everfresh Market Virginia (Pty) Ltd v Shoprite Checkers (Pty) Ltd* 2012 (1) SA 256 (CC) [71]. See also the judgment of Victor AJ in *Beadica 231 CC v Trustees for the time being of the Oregon Trust* 2020 (5) SA 247 (CC).

[93] *City of Johannesburg Metropolitan Municipality v Blue Moonlight Properties 39 (Pty) Ltd* 2012 (2) SA 104 (CC).

[94] *Port Elizabeth Municipality v Various Occupiers* 2005 (1) SA 217 (CC) (*PE Municipality*).

[95] *Blue Moonlight* (n 93) [38].

[96] *Brink v Kitshoff* (n 16); *Prinsloo v Van der Linde* 1997 (3) SA 1012 (CC); *Department of Land Affairs v Goedgelegen Tropical Fruits* 2007 (6) SA 199 (CC).

[97] *President of the Republic of South Africa v Modderklip Boerdery (Pty) Ltd* 2005 (5) SA 3 (CC); NK Marutlulle, 'A Critical Analysis of Housing Inadequacy in South Africa and its Ramifications' (2021) 9 *Africa's Public*

and to establish and sustain unjust racial territorial segregation to advance its political objectives.[98] Thus, the right to exclude, bolstered by the oppressive legislative framework, operated not just to uphold ownership and the rights to own, use or exploit the land, but also to achieve particular ideological and political objectives on racial segregation.[99] In short, the right to exclude was politicised and was essential to the apartheid property regime.[100] This led to the dispossession of millions of indigenous people. It was a continuation of the dispossession that commenced at the beginning of colonialisation.[101] Justice Froneman eloquently explained this in *Shoprite Checkers (Pty) Ltd v Member of the Executive Council for Economic Development, Environmental Affairs and Tourism, Eastern Cape*:

> [T]he pre-constitutional conception of property entailed exclusive individual entitlement. Put simply, that is largely a history of dispossession of what indigenous people held, and its transfer to the colonisers in the form of land and other property, protected by an economic system that ensured the continued deprivation of those benefits on racial and class lines. That history of division probably explains the concerns both the previously advantaged and disadvantaged still have. The former fears that they will lose what they have; the latter that they will not receive what is justly theirs.[102]

Under apartheid, property law was characterised by abstract, syllogistic reasoning predicated on an immutable, hierarchal rights arrangement. Ownership reigned supreme at the top of the hierarchy. This meant that a property owner had the right to exclude and evict any person who had no right on the land from their property. The right to exclude was used in accordance with racial and class lines, which led to the mass and brutal dispossession of Black people.

The Constitution squarely confronts this issue through section 26.[103] Section 26(1) provides a right to access to adequate housing. Implicit in this statement is that there is a duty on the state and people not to interfere with this right. However, section 26(2) goes further and places a positive duty on the state to take reasonable legislative and other steps, within its available resources, to progressively realise this right. While this places a duty on the state, it also limits the right by the caveat of available resources. Recognising

Service Delivery and Performance Review 372; A Kumar and K Shika, 'South Africa's Housing Crisis: A New Breed of Honest Politicians is Needed to Unlock the Land' (*Daily Maverick*, 21 June 2021), available at www.dailymaverick.co.za/opinionista/2021-06-21-south-africas-housing-crisis-a-new-breed-of-honest-politicians-is-needed-to-unlock-the-land/.

[98] AJ van der Walt, 'Towards the Development of Post-Apartheid Land Law: An Exploratory Survey' (1990) 23 *De Jure* 1; Z Boggenpoel, '(Re)defining the Contours of Ownership: Moving beyond White Picket Fences" (2019) *Stellenbosch Law Review* 234.

[99] AJ van der Walt, 'Exclusivity of Ownership, Security of Tenure, and Eviction Orders: A Model to Evaluate South African Land-Reform Legislation' (2002) 2 *Journal of South African Law* 254, 261.

[100] ibid.

[101] Ngcukaitobi (n 19).

[102] *Shoprite Checkers (Pty) Ltd v Member of the Executive Council for Economic Development, Environmental Affairs and Tourism, Eastern Cape* 2015 (6) SA 125 (CC) [34].

[103] The Constitution, s 26 provides:

> (1) Everyone has the right to access to adequate housing.
> (2) The State must take reasonable legislative and other measures, within its available resources, to achieve the progressive realisation of this right.
> (3) No one may be evicted from their home, or have their home demolished, without an order of court made after considering all the relevant circumstances. No legislation may permit arbitrary evictions.

the constitutional importance of a person's place of abode, section 26(3) provides that no person will be evicted from their home without a court order and that no legislation may permit arbitrary evictions. To give effect to these constitutional promises, four interlocking statutes were enacted, two of which are the Extension of Security of Tenure Act 62 of 1997 and the PIE Act. As Justice Cameron recognises in *Mwelase*, these statutes were devised to 'fulfil the overall constitutional promise of restitution to those deprived of rights in land by racial subordination'.[104]

In the landmark decision of *President of the Republic v Grootboom*,[105] the Constitutional Court had to confront the harsh reality that the Constitution's promise of dignity and equality for all remains for many a distant dream. In this case, the applicants were living on a sports field, in deplorable conditions. The community was comprised of 390 adults and 510 children and the whole community lived in shacks.[106] There was no water, no refuse and sewage removal services and only five per cent had electricity. The land on which they lived was close to a main thoroughfare and was partly waterlogged.[107] The applicants approached the courts on the basis that these conditions limited their rights to access to housing, as well as the right of children to shelter as set out in section 28 of the Constitution. The High Court found in favour of the applicants and held that the state had failed in fulfilling its obligation to provide shelter to children and that the state had failed to take all reasonable legislative and other measures to achieve the right to adequate housing. However, the High Court only ordered that the state provide housing to children and their accompanying parents, but did not make an order relating to childless adults.[108]

On appeal, the Constitutional Court, in a unanimous decision, emphasised that the foundational values of human dignity, freedom, and equality are denied to those with no food, clothing or housing.[109] It held that the nationwide housing programme fell short of the obligations on the state under section 26 of the Constitution.[110] The state had dismally failed to take into account and make provisions for the immediate temporary amelioration of the circumstances of those in desperate need.[111] The Court, in its order, declared that section 26 of the Constitution imposes on the national government obligations to devise, fund, implement, and supervise measures to provide relief to those in desperate need. Of note, the Court expansively interpreted 'access to adequate housing' in these terms:

> Housing entails more than bricks and mortar. It requires available land, appropriate services such as the provision of water and the removal of sewage and the financing of all these, including the building of the house itself. For a person to have access to adequate housing all of these conditions need to be met: there must be land, there must be services, and there must be a dwelling. The right of access to adequate housing also suggests that it is not only the State

[104] *Mwelase* (n 76) [6].
[105] *Government of the Republic of South Africa v Grootboom* 2001 (1) SA 46 (CC).
[106] ibid [4], with reference to fn 2.
[107] ibid [7].
[108] *Grootboom v Oostenberg Municipality* 2000 (3) BCLR 277 (C).
[109] *South Africa v Grootboom* (n 105) [23].
[110] ibid [66].
[111] ibid [66]–[69].

> that is responsible for the provision of houses, but that other agents within society, including individuals themselves, must be enabled by legislative and other measures to provide housing.[112]

In *Grootboom*, the applicants argued that the right to access to housing comprised a minimum core.[113] In essence, a minimum core means that each right has a quintessential base, which requires the state to fulfil certain minimum essentials contained in the 'core' of the right, failing which the state is *prima facie* in violation of its obligations.[114] A minimum core obligation to rights necessitates recognising basic subsistence levels in respect of each socio-economic right and insisting that the provision of core goods and services enjoys immediate priority.[115] Therefore, this approach consists of finding the 'floor' of immediately enforceable entitlements, which are justiciable. Importantly, the minimum core ought to apply regardless of the availability of resources of the particular country or other factors and difficulties.[116]

The Court in *Grootboom*, and in subsequent cases,[117] decidedly rejected this approach and preferred the reasonableness approach. The Court has proffered at least four principal reasons for rejecting the minimum core standard:

a) the difficulty of defining the content of minimum core standard;
b) the needs and opportunities for the enjoyment of the minimum core vary and are diverse, depending on the economic and social history and circumstances of a particular country;
c) it is impossible to give everyone access to a 'core' service immediately; and
d) courts are not institutionally equipped to make the wide-ranging factual and political inquiries necessary for determining what the minimum core standards should be.

Furthermore, the Court held that a minimum core standard would be incongruent with the text of the Constitution, which provides that the positive obligation on the state is to take reasonable legislative and other measures to *progressively* realise the right of access to housing within available resources, and that in that section, there is no right to water or housing immediately.[118] Thus, the addition of the 'progressive realisation' caveat within the available resources makes it plain that rights cannot be achieved or enforced immediately.[119]

The Court further held that it would be institutionally inappropriate for a court to determine precisely what the achievement of any particular social and economic right entails and what steps government should take to ensure the progressive realisation of the

[112] ibid [35].
[113] ibid [18].
[114] D Bilchitz, 'Judicial Review in Practice: The Reasonableness Approach and its Shortcomings' in D Bilchitz, *Poverty and Fundamental Rights: The Justification and Enforcement of Socio-Economic Rights* (Oxford University Press, 2007) 140.
[115] M Pieterse, 'Resuscitating Socio-Economic Rights: Constitutional Entitlements to Health Care Services' (2006) *South African Journal on Human Rights* 473, 481.
[116] 'Masstricht Guidelines on Violations of Economic, Social and Cultural Rights' (Maastricht, 22–26 January 1997) para 9.
[117] *Minister of Health v Treatment Action Campaign* 2002 (5) SA 721 (CC) [26]–[39]; *Khosa v Minister of Social Development, Mahlaule v Minister of Social Development* 2004 (6) SA 5050 (CC); *Mazibuko v City of Johannesburg* 2010 (4) SA 1 (CC) [48]–[56].
[118] *Mazibuko* (n 117) [56].
[119] ibid.

right. Courts can enforce socio-economic rights in two ways. First, if government takes no steps to realise the rights, the courts will require government to take steps. Second, if the measures adopted by government are unreasonable, the courts will similarly require that they be reviewed so as to meet the constitutional standard of reasonableness.

The reasonableness approach is grounded in the explicit wording of the Constitution.[120] As the Court held in *Grootboom*, all that could be expected from the state was that it acts reasonably in progressively realising socio-economic rights.[121] The criteria for determining whether the state is acting reasonably were set out by the Court.[122] These include:

a) the allocation of responsibilities and tasks to the different spheres of government and ensuring that the appropriate financial and human resources are available;
b) policies and programmes that are reasonable both in their conception and their implementation;
c) a consideration of the challenges in their social, economic and historical context and the capacity of institutions responsible for implementation; and
d) understanding reasonableness in the context of the Bill of Rights as a whole.

Notably, the Court also emphasised that the reasonableness of the measures will be determined in light of the availability of resources.[123]

This is a domestication of public law in the sense that it differs substantially from international law instruments that embrace the minimum core standard. This standard was introduced by the United Nations Committee on Economic, Social and Cultural Rights (UNCESCR), to assess the compliance of states with the International Covenant on Economic, Social and Cultural Rights (ICESCR), when it issued its General Comment. To this end, the UNCESCR recognises that states have a minimum obligation to ensure the satisfaction of, at the very least, minimum essential levels of socio-economic rights (for instance rights to food, healthcare, housing and education and until recently the right to water).[124] It ought to be noted that the UNCESCR has started fleshing out the minimum content of rights in its General Recommendations. It has been argued that the specification of a minimum core is one of the key elements in finding an effective and feasible means of determining whether a state has violated its obligations under the ICESCR.[125]

Recently, the Constitutional Court dealt with a severe failure by the state in providing housing. In the matter of *Thubakgale v Ekurhuleni Metropolitan Municipality*, the

[120] Not all socio-economic rights in the South African Constitution are subject to the progressive realisation. For instance, the right to basic education is immediately realisable. See the Constitution, s 29.

[121] *South Africa v Grootboom* (n 105) [39]–[44].

[122] ibid.

[123] ibid [46].

[124] UNCESCR, 'General Comment No 3: The Nature of State Parties' Obligations' (14 December 1990) UN Doc E/1991/23.

[125] A Chapman, '"A Violations Approach" for Monitoring the International Covenant on Social, Economic and Cultural Rights' (1996) 18 *Human Rights Quarterly* 23, 43–55. Furthermore, following from the UNCESCR, the African Commission has also acknowledged the minimum core standard. See African Commission on Human and Peoples' Rights, 'Principles and Guidelines on the Implementation of Economic, Social and Cultural Rights in the African Charter on Human and Peoples' Rights' (African Commission on Human and Peoples' Rights, 2011) para 17; *Social and Economic Rights Action Centre and the Centre for Economic and Social Rights v Nigeria* (Communication 155/96) (2001) AHRLR 60, 65–66.

applicants were living in dire conditions, which in certain circumstances, consisted of houses of up to 10 people with little to no water, sanitation or electricity.[126] The applicants were terribly poor and did not have the financial means to sustain themselves. Without delving into the facts, which are a morass, the state had failed to provide the applicants with access to adequate housing for a period of 20 years. To make matters worse, the local authority had unlawfully given possession of the subsidised houses intended for the applicants, and to which they were still matched on the national housing database, to other residents, through either fraud or sheer incompetence.

The High Court made an order requiring the local authority to provide the applicants with housing. Ultimately, the state failed to comply with this court order and the applicants were in no better position. After various court proceedings in the lower courts, the applicants applied to the Constitutional Court for an order compelling the local authority to provide them with housing and then also for constitutional damages. I wrote the first judgment, which held that the local authority had failed to discharge its duties under section 26 of the Constitution. Thus, I found that the municipality had failed under the legislative framework to provide housing to the applicants. In my view, the matter was not the same as the case in *Grootboom*, where the question pertained to whether the content of the nationwide housing policy was reasonable. In this matter, the Court was concerned with the implementation of the legislative framework. In other words, the question to be determined was whether the state acted in accordance with its own legislative requirements. Thus, the Court was required to travel beyond the terrain covered in *Grootboom*.[127] Furthermore, I reasoned that the state had failed to comply with a court order which required it to provide housing. In light of the magnitude of the state's failures, I ordered the local authority to pay constitutional damages as an effective and appropriate remedy.[128] Unfortunately, mine was the minority decision.

My colleague, Justice Jafta, who penned the majority judgment, found that, despite the unlawfulness of the municipality's conduct, this was not a case that called for constitutional damages. In his view, constitutional damages are not appropriate in cases that concern breaches of socio-economic rights.[129] No proper case was pleaded for constitutional damages and there was no proof of any damages, let alone constitutional damages.[130] That second judgment has elicited fierce criticism from legal commentators, with some viewing it as a regressive step in the evolving of our socio-economic rights jurisprudence.[131]

The matter is currently before the High Court to allow the local authority to produce further evidence, and I cannot say more on it at this stage. However, it must be noted that this case illustrates that the substantive content of the right to housing has not been fully

[126] *Thubakgale v Ekurhuleni Metropolitan Municipality* [2021] ZACC 45.
[127] ibid [7].
[128] ibid [72]–[83].
[129] ibid [122].
[130] ibid.
[131] Professor Balthazar, 'The Jury is Still Out on Whether South Africa's Constitutional Democracy Will Survive Another 25 years' (*Daily Maverick*, 10 December 2021), available at www.dailymaverick.co.za/opinionista/2021-12-10-the-jury-is-still-out-on-whether-south-africas-constitutional-democracy-will-survive-another-25-years/; SB Nxumalo and T Jeewa, 'Thubakgale: Obscuring the Right to Access to Adequate Housing' (*Oxford Human Rights Hub*, 22 December 2022), available at https://ohrh.law.ox.ac.uk/thubakgale-obscuring-the-right-to-access-to-adequate-housing/.

delineated and is consistently being revisited in order to ensure that it is robust enough to address the changing circumstances facing South Africa. It illustrates that the flexible reasonableness standard encourages courts to recognise that there are various policy dimensions to the issues that South Africa faces and there must be a deliberate process between the state, the judiciary and the broader public. The struggle for a better society cannot solely be on the shoulders of courts. A democratic process requires an accountable state in all three of its different arms to act proactively, collaboratively and in line with the dictates of the Constitution.

B. The Electoral Regime in South Africa

Much like the right to housing explored above, the Constitutional Court's jurisprudence on political rights is similarly a site where South Africa's past informs the nature and scope of rights contained in the Bill of Rights. Political rights are enshrined in section 19 of the Constitution.[132]

Regarding the importance of the right to vote in our constitutional democracy, memorably, in *August v Electoral Commission*,[133] Justice Sachs declared that the vote of each and every citizen is a 'badge of dignity and personhood. Quite literally, it says that everybody counts'.[134] The precious value of the vote in South Africa arises in no small measure from a history in which the right to vote was denied to the majority of our citizens. Sachs J went on to note that in a country of great inequality such as South Africa, the right to vote declares that we all belong to the same nation and that 'our destinies are intertwined in a single interactive polity'.[135] This was later confirmed in *Richter*[136] where Justice O'Regan held:

> [T]he right to vote, and its exercise, has a constitutional importance in addition to this symbolic value. The right to vote, and the exercise of it, is a crucial working part of our democracy. Without voters who want to vote, who will take the trouble to register, and to stand in queues, as millions patiently and unforgettably did in April 1994, democracy itself will be imperilled. Each vote strengthens and invigorates our democracy. In marking their ballots, citizens remind

[132] The Constitution, s 19 provides:

> (1) Every citizen is free to make political choices, which includes the right—
>
> (a) to form a political party;
> (b) to participate in the activities of, or recruit members for, a political party; and
> (c) to campaign for a political party or cause.
>
> (2) Every citizen has the right to free, fair and regular elections for any legislative body established in terms of the Constitution.
>
> (3) Every adult citizen has the right—
>
> (a) to vote in elections for any legislative body established in terms of the Constitution, and to do so in secret; and
> (b) to stand for public office and, if elected, to hold office.

[133] *August v Electoral Commission* 1999 (3) SA 1 (CC).

[134] ibid [17].

[135] ibid.

[136] *Richter v The Minister for Home Affairs and Others (with the Democratic Alliance and Others Intervening, and with Afriforum and Another as Amici Curiae)* 2009 (3) SA 615 (CC).

> those elected that their position is based on the will of the people and will remain subject to that will. The moment of voting reminds us that both electors and the elected bear civic responsibilities arising out of our democratic Constitution and its values. We should accordingly approach any case concerning the right to vote mindful of the bright, symbolic value of the right to vote as well as the deep, democratic value that lies in a citizenry conscious of its civic responsibilities and willing to take the trouble that exercising the right to vote entails.[137]

With this historical context in mind, I will consider two further judgments regarding the importance of political rights in South Africa.

The first case is *My Vote Counts NPC v Speaker of the National Assembly*.[138] It was a matter concerning whether Parliament had failed to fulfil its constitutional obligation to enact national legislation which gives effect to the right of access to information by requiring political parties to disclose, proactively and regularly, the sources of their private funding. The Court considered the earlier judgment of *Ramakatsa v Magashule*[139] which highlighted the centrality of political parties in South Africa's constitutional democracy, stating that they are 'the veritable vehicles the Constitution has chosen for facilitating and entrenching democracy',[140] and that they are the 'indispensable conduits for the enjoyment of the right given by section 19(3)(a) to vote in elections'.[141]

The majority in *My Vote Counts* held that the Promotion of Access to Information Act[142] (PAIA) is the legislation – envisaged in the Constitution – meant to give effect to the right of access to information. As a result, the majority concluded that, in accordance with the principle of subsidiarity, the applicant should have attacked the constitutional validity of PAIA. This principle enjoins a litigant who is complaining about shortcomings in legislation enacted to give effect to a constitutional right to challenge the constitutional validity of that legislation instead of relying directly on the constitutional right. The majority judgment held that, since the essence of the complaint by the applicant was that PAIA has certain shortcomings, it ought to have attacked its constitutional validity in the High Court. Its failure to do so was dispositive of the case. The majority judgment accordingly dismissed the application.

The last case I consider here is *New Nation Movement NPC and Others v President of the Republic of South Africa and Others*.[143] It is a seminal judgment, giving scope to the nature of political rights enshrined in section 19 of the Constitution and further emphasises the break that these rights envisage from South Africa's apartheid history. The application concerned whether the Electoral Act was unconstitutional to the extent that it did not provide for adult citizens to be elected to the National Assembly and Provincial Legislatures as independent candidates. The argument advanced by the applicants was that the Electoral Act is unconstitutional for unjustifiably limiting the right to stand for public office and, if elected, to hold office, as conferred by section 19(3)(b) of

[137] ibid [53].
[138] *My Vote Counts NPC v Speaker of the National Assembly* 2016 (1) SA 132 (CC).
[139] *Ramakatsa v Magashule* 2013 (2) BCLR 202 (CC).
[140] ibid [67].
[141] ibid [68].
[142] Promotion of Access to Information Act 2 of 2000.
[143] *New Nation Movement NPC and Others v President of the Republic of South Africa and Others* 2020 (6) SA 257 (CC).

the Constitution. In addition, some applicants submitted that the Electoral Act infringes their right to freedom of association protected by section 18 of the Constitution.

Again, confirming *Ramakatsa*, Justice Madlanga emphasised:

> The scope and content of the rights entrenched by [section 19] may be ascertained by means of an interpretation process which must be informed by context that is both historical and constitutional. During the apartheid order, the majority of people in our country were denied political rights which were enjoyed by a minority. The majority of black people could not form or join political parties of their choice. Nor could they vote for those who were eligible to be members of Parliament. Differently put, they were not only disenfranchised but were also excluded from all decision-making processes undertaken by the government of the day, including those affecting them.[144]

Given the importance of political rights within the South African context and the far-reaching implications that such rights have on the right to human dignity, the first judgment held that the rights in sections 18 and 19(3)(b) of the Constitution must be interpreted generously, rather than restrictively. The Court held that the Electoral Act is unconstitutional to the extent that it requires that adult citizens be elected to the National Assembly and Provincial Legislatures only through their membership of political parties.

Political rights are therefore a clear example of how public law has been indigenised in South Africa, particularly in light of how political rights were used as a tool of exclusion under apartheid.

V. CONCLUSION: NEVER AGAIN

My aim in this chapter has been to explore the domestication of constitutions and the value this adds to their legitimacy. I have endeavoured to consider this, specifically in the case of South Africa, to show how the domestication of its public law has been shaped by its past. South Africa's Constitution signifies a decisive break from the past and has ushered in a future based on human rights. This is clear, not only from the wording of the constitutional text itself, but also through the jurisprudence of the Constitutional Court. South Africa is forever mindful of its past, having adopted a 'never again' paradigm. Justice Sachs eloquently puts it as follows: 'the "never again" principle, which I feel should be one of our guides to interpretation, applies not only to bitter experiences of former state enforced segregation, but also to those of past compulsory assimilation'.[145] Thereafter, in *Garvas*, the Constitutional Court confirmed that 'ours is a "never again" Constitution: never again will we allow the right of ordinary people to freedom in all its forms to be taken away'.[146] It is therefore South Africa's past that has provided the foundation for the domestication of its public law.

Having regard to events beyond our own shores, it bears emphasis that the rule of law and democratic gains must never simply be taken for granted. The calamitous reversal of

[144] *Ramakatsa* (n 139) [64].

[145] *Ex parte Gauteng Provincial Legislature: In re Dispute Concerning the Constitutionality of Certain Provisions of the Gauteng School Education Bill of 1995* 1996 (3) SA 165 (CC) [46].

[146] *South African Transport and Allied Workers Union and Another v Garvas* 2013 (1) SA 83 (CC) [63].

Roe v Wade by the US Supreme Court must be a clarion call to all of us to remain vigilant and steadfast in our endeavours to uphold democracy and the rule of law.[147] That is particularly true of my beautiful but troubled[148] beloved homeland. The gains made in 28 years of democratic rule and 27 years of widely admired constitutional jurisprudence must be zealously protected. Because today it may be the right to early termination of pregnancy and then tomorrow? Our revered global icon, Nelson Rolihlahla Mandela said at his inauguration, a glorious moment for South Africans:

> Never, never and never again shall it be that this beautiful land will again experience the oppression of one by another and suffer the indignity of being the skunk of the world.[149]

[147] *Roe v Wade*, 410 US 113 (1973); *Dobbs v Jackson Women's Health Organization*, 597 US ___ (2022).

[148] I say 'troubled' because not only are we the most unequal country in the world (see The World Bank *New World Bank Report Assesses Sources of Inequality in Five Countries in Southern Africa* (Press Release No 2002/055/AFE, March 2022), but a recent survey also suggests that only 32% of South Africans are satisfied with how democracy is working (J Steyn Kotze 'Democracy Loses its Glow for South Africans amid Persistent Inequality' (*The Conversation*, 25 April 2022), available at https://theconversation.com/democracy-loses-its-glow-for-south-africans-amid-persistent-inequality-181489).

[149] N Mandela, 'Inauguration Speech as President of the Republic of South Africa' (Pretoria, 10 May 1994), available at www.sanews.gov.za.

6

Double Act: Assessing Constitutional Entrenchment and Codification in the Re-Making of Administrative Law in Democratic South Africa

CATHERINE O'REGAN

FOLLOWING SOUTH AFRICA'S transition to democratic rule in the mid-1990s, two important steps were taken that resulted in the fundamental re-making of administrative law. First, both South Africa's transitional Constitution of 1993,[1] which paved the way for a constitution drafted and adopted by a democratically-elected Constitutional Assembly, and the 1996 Constitution that was the product of the work of the Constitutional Assembly, entrenched the right to administrative justice in the Bill of Rights.

The 1996 Constitution provides that, 'Everyone has the right to administrative action that is lawful, reasonable and procedurally fair' and that, 'Everyone whose rights have been adversely affected by administrative action has the right to be given written reasons'.[2]

The constitutional entrenchment of a right to administrative justice in a Bill of Rights is noteworthy in that the right to administrative justice is – unlike most rights entrenched in domestic constitutions – not drawn from international human rights treaties. In including administrative justice in its Bill of Rights, South Africa followed the lead of Namibia which entrenched administrative justice in its Constitution in 1990.[3]

[1] See section 24 of the Constitution of the Republic of South Africa, 200 of 1993 (the interim Constitution), which provided that:

> Every person shall have the right to -
>
> (a) lawful administrative action where any of his or her rights or interests is affected or threatened;
> (b) procedurally fair administrative action where any of his or her rights or legitimate expectations is affected or threatened;
> (c) be furnished with reasons in writing for administrative action which affects any of his or her rights or interests unless the reasons for such action have been made public; and
> (d) administrative action which is justifiable in relation to the reasons given for it where any of his or her rights is affected or threatened.

[2] The Constitution of the Republic of South Africa, 1996 (the Constitution), s 33.

[3] The text of Article 18 of the Namibian Constitution 1990 reads:

> Administrative bodies and administrative officials shall act fairly and reasonably and comply with the requirements imposed upon such bodies and officials by common law and any relevant legislation, and persons aggrieved by the exercise of such acts and decisions shall have the right to seek redress before a competent Court or Tribunal.

In the decades since, a period of intense constitution-making in southern and eastern Africa,[4] more constitutions in sub-Saharan Africa, have entrenched a right to administrative justice including those in Kenya,[5] Malawi[6] and Zimbabwe.[7]

The second step taken by South Africa was the enactment of the Promotion of Administrative Justice Act, 3 of 2000 (which South Africans call PAJA, but which for ease of reference I shall refer to as the 'administrative code') in early 2000, which was required by section 33 of the Constitution, and which codified administrative law, including the grounds of judicial review and administrative procedures.

Constitutional entrenchment and codification have been powerful drivers of the re-making of administrative law in South Africa over the last three decades. Given the growing practice of constitutional entrenchment across jurisdictions, as well as the ongoing debate about both the promise and pitfalls of codification, an assessment of South Africa's experience in the making of administrative law following constitutional entrenchment and codification may be of interest not only to South African administrative lawyers but to administrative lawyers elsewhere. This chapter assesses some of the successes and challenges of this fundamental re-making of administrative law in South Africa.

This chapter starts by providing a brief overview of administrative law as it had developed before the new Constitution came into force, to explain why South Africans opted both for the constitutional entrenchment of administrative justice and the codification of administrative law. Then the chapter turns to provide an overview of both the constitutional right to administrative justice and the administrative code, before offering an account of their successes and challenges.

I. ADMINISTRATIVE LAW IN SOUTH AFRICA BEFORE 1994

The development of administrative law in South Africa was heavily influenced by the common law,[8] a consequence of more than a century of British colonialism from the first decade of the 1800s to the twentieth century. In this regard, administrative law is unusual, for South Africa's common law system is Roman Dutch, inherited from 150 years of governance by the Dutch East India Company from the mid-seventeenth century to the early nineteenth century. Yet South Africa's administrative law is not a complete replica of the common law – particularly in the field of remedies.

[4] Of the 25 countries in southern and eastern Africa, 23 have adopted new constitutions since 1990: Angola (2010), Burundi (2005), Comoros (2001), Democratic Republic of Congo (2005), Djibouti (1992), Eswatini (2005), Ethiopia (1995), Eritrea (1997), Kenya (2010), Lesotho (1993), Madagascar (1998), Malawi (1994), Mozambique (1990), Namibia (1990), Rwanda (2003), Seychelles (1993), Somalia (2012), Somaliland (2000), South Africa (1996), South Sudan (2011), Uganda (1995), Zambia (1991) and Zimbabwe (2013). Only Botswana and Mauritius have not adopted new constitutions.

[5] The Kenyan Constitution 2010, Art 47. See C Hoexter, 'Administrative Justice in Kenya: Learning from South Africa's Mistakes?' (2018) 62 *Journal of African Law* 105; J Jowell, 'All Roads Lead to Rome: The International Convergence of Principles of Administrative Justice' (2015) 1 *Italian Journal of Public Law* 94.

[6] The Malawi Constitution 1994, s 43.

[7] The Zimbabwe Constitution 2013, s 68.

[8] See C Hoexter and G Penfold, *Administrative Law in South Africa*, 3rd edn (Juta, 2021) 17.

Before the transition to democracy in 1990, judicial review was one of the few tools available to those resisting the Government and its apartheid policies and it was frequently used. However, the courts' response was mixed.

In the last decade before the transition to democratic rule, both internal resistance by a range of civil society actors, including trade unions, religious organisations and civic organisations, and external resistance, were at their height. The Government responded with the declaration of successive states of emergency which gave sweeping powers to the State President 'to make such regulations as appear to him to be necessary or expedient for providing for the safety of the public, or the maintenance of public order'.[9] The State President enacted regulations containing a wide range of authoritarian powers including detention without trial.

Although initially there were some successful challenges to the emergency regulations particularly in Natal, a series of cases in the Appellate Division, then the highest court of appeal, mostly upheld the validity of the emergency regulations. Finding that detainees could be denied access to their legal representatives, Chief Justice Rabie reasoned that this was lawful because

> Parliament contemplated that the need to ensure the safety of the public or to maintain public order might necessitate the taking of extraordinary measures which might make drastic inroads into the rights and privileges normally enjoyed by individuals.[10]

If the courts' record in preventing abuse of power during the states of emergency in the 1980s was woeful, there were other moments when the courts did rely on the principles of administrative law to protect people against the misuse of power by government. For example, in the 1980s, the Appellate Division upheld two important challenges to the system of influx control, a cornerstone of the Government's apartheid policy, which denied African people the right of freedom of movement.[11] There were other victories too in other areas of governance. But on balance it is fair to say that judicial review did not provide a reliable bulwark against 'a legislature and executive bent on the abuse of powers for racial ends'.[12]

This history was undoubtedly important in the period of transition to democracy. Three lessons were drawn from the recent history of judicial review. First, that government power could be abused. Second, that the courts had not provided adequate protection against government abuses during the periods of apartheid or colonialism. Third, that courts could at times play an important role in protecting people from government abuse. It was these three lessons that led to the constitutional entrenchment of a right to administrative justice, and to the administrative code.

[9] The Public Safety Act, 3 of 1953, s 3(1)(a).

[10] *Omar and Others v Minister of Law and Order and Others*; *Fani and Others v Minister of Law and Order and Others*; *State President and Others v Bill* 1987 (3) SA 859 (A) 892. For a fuller discussion, see E Mureinik, 'Pursuing Principle: The Appellate Division and Review under the State of Emergency' (1989) 5 *South African Journal on Human Rights* 60.

[11] See *Komani NO v Bantu Affairs Administration Board, Peninsula Area* 1980 (4) SA 448 (A); *Oos-Randse Administrasieraad v Rikhoto* 1983 (3) SA 595 (A).

[12] See K O'Regan, 'Breaking Ground: Some Thoughts on the Seismic Shift in our Administrative Law' (2004) 121 *South African Law Journal* 424, 424.

II. KEY ELEMENTS OF CONSTITUTIONAL ENTRENCHMENT AND CODIFICATION

There are five key things to note about the constitutional provision (section 33) that entrenches the right to administrative justice. First, it hinges on the concept of 'administrative action', which triggers the entitlement to the right (discussed further below). Second, it entrenches a version of what might be described as Lord Diplock's *GCHQ* triptych in requiring administrative action to be lawful, reasonable and procedurally fair.[13] Third, it affords a right to written reasons to those whose rights have been adversely affected by administrative action. Fourth, it mandates Parliament to enact legislation to give effect to the right to administrative justice and to promote an efficient administration, within three years of the Constitution coming into force, which led (in the nick of time[14]) to the adoption of the administrative code. Fifth, like all rights in the Bill of Rights, the right to administrative justice is not absolute. It may be limited by law of general application as long as the limitation is reasonable and justifiable.[15]

There are six things to note about the administrative code. First, it seeks rather unsuccessfully to provide a definition of 'administrative action' – the core concept in the constitutional entrenchment.[16] Second, it seeks to codify the grounds of judicial review,[17] providing, in particular, a detailed provision regulating procedural fairness.[18] Third, it regulates the procedure of judicial review, perhaps most notably setting a time limit of 180 days within which proceedings must be launched.[19] Fourth, it provides in a non-exhaustive manner for the remedies which may be made in judicial review proceedings.[20] Fifth, it regulates the provision of written reasons to those whose rights have been materially and adversely affected by administrative action, on the basis that they must be requested within 90 days of the person becoming aware of the action and the administrator then has 90 days to respond.[21] Sixth, it provides that when administrative action will materially and adversely affect the rights of the public, a decision-maker must decide whether to institute a notice-and-comment procedure or a public hearing or some other form of appropriate procedure.[22]

III. SUCCESSES OF CONSTITUTIONAL ENTRENCHMENT

The constitutional entrenchment of administrative justice has been valuable in three key respects. First, it has provided a coherent constitutional basis for judicial review.[23]

[13] See *Council of Civil Service Unions v Minister for the Civil Service* [1985] AC 374.

[14] The Act was published on 3 February 2000, having been enacted by Parliament and signed by the President, just making the three-year deadline which would have expired at midnight on 4 February. It came into force on 30 November 2000.

[15] See the Constitution, s 36.

[16] See the Promotion of Administrative Justice Act, 3 of 2000 (PAJA), s 1.

[17] ibid s 6.

[18] ibid s 3.

[19] ibid s 7(1).

[20] ibid s 8.

[21] ibid s 5.

[22] ibid s 4.

[23] See C Hoexter, 'The Constitutionalization and Codification of Judicial Review in South Africa' in C Forsyth and others (eds), *Effective Judicial Review: A Cornerstone of Good Governance* (Oxford University Press, 2010) 46.

Second, it has made clear that limitations on judicial review, such as ouster clauses, will be constitutionally impermissible unless they are shown to be reasonable and justifiable under the general limitations clause in the Bill of Rights.[24] Thirdly, it has made clear that administrative action must be lawful, reasonable and procedurally fair and that there is an entitlement to written reasons when one's rights have been adversely affected by administrative action.

To start with the first, before 1994, there was a bitter debate in South Africa (and elsewhere in the Commonwealth) about the legal and constitutional basis of judicial review. The orthodox view was that judicial review was based on a broad principle of *ultra vires*, that Parliament in conferring powers upon administrators intends the administrators to act within the scope of their powers and to observe the principles of natural justice. The orthodox view was not unanimously held in South Africa. At least one leading administrative law scholar proposed an alternative account[25] and in the late 1980s the Appellate Division delivered a judgment which suggested that not all judicial review would be founded on the broad principle of *ultra vires*.[26]

There are undoubtedly difficulties with the orthodox view. As Christopher Forsyth has acknowledged, it is improbable that Parliament does indeed form the intention that administrators should comply with the evolving principles of administrative law as they have been developed by the courts over the last half century when it enacts legislation.[27] In South Africa, where Parliament often enacted repressive legislation, that implication seemed even more far-fetched.

Another difficulty with the orthodox view is that judicial review is available even when the powers being exercised do not flow from legislation.[28] In the United Kingdom (UK), difficulties with the orthodox view have led scholars to propose that judicial review arises from the common law,[29] or from several founding principles, including the rule of law, the separation of powers and the sovereignty of Parliament,[30] and not from the implied intentions of Parliament. This approach of course is based on an acknowledgement that administrative law is judge-made law, which has its own challenges.

A great benefit of the constitutional entrenchment of administrative justice has been to end, for the most part, this debate, at least in South Africa. The constitutional roots of judicial review now lie in section 33 of the Constitution and the right to administrative action. Section 33 provides a constitutional remedy not only against all organs of state whether in the national, provincial or local sphere of government, but also against any other institution exercising a power or performing a function in terms of the Constitution or legislation.[31]

[24] The Constitution, s 36.

[25] See M Wiechers, *Administratiefreg*, 2nd edn (Butterworths, 1984). See also the discussion in South African Law Commission, 'Report on the Investigation into the Courts' Powers of Review of Administrative Acts Project 24' (Project 24, November 1992) paras 4.1.2ff.

[26] See *Staatspresident v United Democratic Front* 1988 (4) SA 830 (A). See also Mureinik (n 10).

[27] See C Forsyth, 'Of Fig Leaves and Fairy Tales: The Ultra Vires Doctrine, the Sovereignty of Parliament and Judicial Review' in C Forsyth (ed), *Judicial Review and the Constitution* (Hart Publishing, 2000).

[28] See D Oliver, 'Is the Ultra Vires Rule the Basis of Judicial Review?' in C Forsyth (ed), ibid.

[29] See P Craig, *Administrative Law*, 8th edn (Sweet and Maxwell, 2016) 13.

[30] See M Elliott, *The Constitutional Foundations of Judicial Review* (Hart Publishing, 2001).

[31] See definition of 'organ of state' in s 239 of the Constitution.

There may be a narrow exception to the clarity provided by constitutional entrenchment: that is where judicial review is available against the actions of a private actor, such as a club or a religious organisation, that cannot be said to have any public character.[32] Hoexter and Penfold consider that this form of judicial review is probably based on the principles of the common law,[33] which they acknowledge may be informed by the 'spirit, purport and values' of the Bill of Rights as contemplated by section 39(2) of the Constitution, an interpretive provision which requires courts, when developing the common law to promote the spirit, purport and objects of the Bill of Rights. For the moment, the foundations of judicial review against private actors remains unclear. No doubt further light will be shed on this question in the years ahead. For the rest, however, it is clear that constitutional entrenchment has largely clarified the constitutional basis of judicial review, which is without doubt a benefit not only to judges, but also to scholars, who have spent considerable ink on the question.

The second great benefit of the constitutional entrenchment of administrative justice is to make plain that if Parliament wishes to limit access to judicial review it must do so in a manner that is reasonable and justifiable under the general limitations clause in the Bill of Rights. In the apartheid period, the South African Government repeatedly sought to enact ouster clauses to restrict access to judicial review, although at times these were unsuccessful. Government will have to provide reasonable justification for any ouster clause enacted under the current constitutional framework. No such challenge has yet been brought.

The significance of this development can perhaps be illuminated by the debates in the UK that have followed in the wake of the Supreme Court decision in *R (Privacy International) v Investigatory Powers Tribunal*.[34] Privacy International challenged a decision of the Investigatory Powers Tribunal that had held that the Secretary of State could authorise computer hacking in respect of groups or categories of users. A provision in the empowering legislation appeared to block any such challenge as it provided that decisions of the Tribunal 'shall not be subject to appeal or be liable to be questioned in any court'.[35] In the Supreme Court, the majority took the view that the provision would only protect decisions of the Tribunal that were legally valid, giving rise to a lively debate about whether the UK's sovereign Parliament can ever enact an ouster clause.

The third benefit of constitutional entrenchment has been to provide greater clarity as to what administrative justice requires in several respects. First, before the advent of constitutional democracy, South African courts had not recognised reasonableness as a separate ground of review, save in the case of delegated legislation.[36] Section 33 made clear that reasonableness is a ground for review of administrative action. Second, section 33

[32] See, eg, *Theron v Ring van Wellington van die NG Sendingkerk in SA* 1976 (2) SA 1 (A).

[33] See Hoexter and Penfold (n 8) 165.

[34] *R (Privacy International) v Investigatory Powers Tribunal* [2019] UKSC 22.

[35] The Regulation of Investigatory Powers Act, 2000, s 67(8).

[36] The leading case was *Union Government v Union Steel Corporation* 1928 AD 220, 237 in which Stratford JA had held that unreasonableness is not a ground for review, unless the unreasonableness is 'so gross that something else can be inferred from it, either that it is "inexplicable except on the assumption of mala fides or ulterior motive" ... or that it amounts to proof that the person on whom the discretion is conferred has not applied his mind to the matter'. This ground of review came to be known as symptomatic unreasonableness, unreasonableness that is symptomatic of some other ground of review.

also makes clear that those whose rights are adversely affected by administrative action are entitled to written reasons. The right to written reasons had not been recognised in the years before constitutional democracy, so once again constitutional entrenchment has provided welcome clarity.

IV. THE ACHILLES HEEL OF CONSTITUTIONAL ENTRENCHMENT: THE CONCEPT OF ADMINISTRATIVE ACTION

Perhaps the greatest difficulty with the constitutional entrenchment of administrative justice has been in defining the scope of administrative action, which as mentioned above is the trigger for the right: a person is entitled to *administrative action* that is lawful, reasonable and procedurally fair. The administrative code provides a definition of administrative action, but long before it was enacted the courts had to grapple with what constituted administrative action because of the entrenchment of administrative justice in the interim Constitution.[37]

One of the first cases in which the question of what constitutes administrative action arose concerned the lawfulness of a municipal budget, in which municipal rates had been set, and adopted by the municipal council in Johannesburg.[38] Although the challenge was primarily based on the right to administrative justice in the interim Constitution, the Constitutional Court accepted an argument made by the Municipality that the resolutions were legislative rather than administrative action.

In reaching this conclusion, the Court noted that local government was recognised as a sphere of government by the Constitution, along with the national and provincial spheres of government and that like legislative bodies in other spheres of government, municipal councils are elected deliberative bodies. The question then arose whether there was any basis upon which the lawfulness of the municipal budget could be challenged if it were not administrative action. The Court held the rule of law was a founding constitutional principle that required any exercise of power by an organ of state to be lawful. The Court described this rule as the constitutional principle of legality.[39] It is important to distinguish this principle from the principle of legality in the UK, which is a principle of statutory interpretation that requires Parliament to use clear language if it intends to restrict or oust fundamental common law norms.[40] The South African constitutional principle of legality has been a source of significant development, which I shall return to below.

A second early case concerning the bounds of administrative action related to a challenge to the appointment of a Commission of Inquiry into the administration of rugby by President Mandela.[41] It was argued that the appointment of a Commission of Inquiry by

[37] The interim Constitution, s 24 is set out at n 1 above.

[38] *Fedsure Life Assurance Ltd and Others v Greater Johannesburg Transitional Metropolitan Council* [1998] ZACC 17.

[39] See ibid [57]–[58].

[40] For a discussion see J Varuhas, 'The Principle of Legality' 79 (2020) *Cambridge Law Journal* 578.

[41] *President of the Republic of South Africa and Others v South African Rugby Football Union and Others* [1999] ZACC 11.

the President under his constitutional powers as Head of State constituted administrative action, but the Constitutional Court disagreed. It held that in deciding whether action was administrative, the focus of the inquiry should be the function being performed rather than the functionary. The Court held that actions taken to implement legislation are clearly administrative action but determining whether other actions of government officials are administrative will need to be decided on a consideration of the relevant facts. It concluded that the power to appoint a Commission of Inquiry was a constitutional power conferred upon the President as Head of State, unrelated to the implementation of legislation, but instead 'an adjunct' to policy-making, providing a mechanism for the President to obtain information and advice. It concluded that appointing a Commission of Inquiry therefore did not constitute administrative action, although it would be bound by the constitutional principle of legality, and the President would be obliged to act in good faith and not misconstrue his powers.

The definition of administrative action in the administrative code draws on the principles set out in these judgments, and excludes from the ambit of administrative action many of the executive powers and functions of members of the executive in all three spheres of government (national, provincial and local), the legislative functions of government in all three spheres, and judicial functions. It also excludes decisions to institute or continue prosecutions, and decisions relating to the nomination, selection or appointment of judges by the Judicial Service Commission.[42]

But there are aspects of the definition in the code that are unhelpful and abstruse, notably its rather eclectic importation of unfamiliar principles of administrative law from disparate foreign jurisdictions. So, the code defines 'administrative action' as requiring a 'decision', apparently borrowing the definition at least in part from Australia,[43] and then requires the decision to have a 'direct, external legal effect', borrowing from German law.[44] The resulting definition has been described as 'cumbersome', which serves 'not so much to attribute meaning to the term as to limit its meaning by surrounding it within a palisade of qualifications'.[45] To my knowledge, there has never been a constitutional challenge to the definition in the code, but of course, like all legislation it must conform to the Constitution.

Answering the question what constitutes 'administrative action' thus continues to be challenging. One of the unanswered questions is whether enacting delegated legislation constitutes administrative action. In an important case four judges of the Constitutional Court held that delegated legislation would fall within the ambit of the definition of administrative action, but four of the five remaining judges in the matter held it was not necessary to decide the question in the case.[46] The question has arisen in several cases before the Supreme Court of Appeal but so far it remains an open question.[47]

[42] See PAJA, ss 1(b)(aa)–(hh).

[43] Australian Administrative Decisions (Judicial Review) Act 1977 (Cth), s 3(2).

[44] German Federal Law of Administrative Procedure 1976, s 35.

[45] *Greys Marine Hout Bay (Pty) Ltd and Others v Minister of Public Works and Others* [2005] ZASCA 43 [21].

[46] See *Minister of Health and Another v New Clicks South Africa (Pty) Ltd and Others* [2005] ZACC 14.

[47] For the most recent decision, see *Esau and Others v Minister of Co-operative Governance and Traditional Affairs* [2021] ZASCA 9.

Despite these continuing uncertainties, I would suggest that a core of clarity has emerged, perhaps best captured by the Supreme Court of Appeal when it held that administrative action

> is, in general terms, the conduct of the bureaucracy in carrying out the daily functions of the state which necessarily involves the application of policy, usually after its translation into law, with direct and immediate consequences for individuals or groups of individuals.[48]

But difficult questions of line-drawing remain. As a leading administrative scholar has noted, the definition of 'administrative action' has in some senses become the 'centre of gravity' of administrative law in South Africa.[49]

V. A WORRYING TREND: AVOIDANCE OF THE ADMINISTRATIVE CODE AND RELIANCE ON THE BURGEONING PRINCIPLE OF LEGALITY

The Constitutional Court has held that the principle of legality, which requires all exercises of public power to be lawful, applies to the exercise of public power that falls outside the ambit of administrative action. The Constitutional Court has developed a second principle that applies to all exercises of public power, and that is that they be performed in a rational manner. This requirement of rationality was established by the Constitutional Court, in a case brought by the President to set aside a decision he had made to bring legislation regulating medicines for human and animal use into force.[50] After the new legislation had been brought into force, it was realised that the decision had been premature because the necessary regulatory framework was not in place. The consequence of bringing the legislation into force was to leave a major legislative lacuna, because the earlier legislation was repealed but the new legislation, without its regulatory infrastructure was unworkable.

The Court held that the decision to bring the legislation into force was arbitrary and irrational, given that there was no reason to bring the legislation into force and it had been done mistakenly. The Court continued to say that rationality was 'a minimum threshold requirement'[51] applicable to the exercise of all public power, but that a finding of irrationality was only likely to be reached on rare occasions.

In fact, however, the principle of rationality, together with the principle of legality, have become mainstays of South African administrative law, and they often result in courts avoiding the application of the administrative code. A notable case in this regard concerned a challenge to a decision of the President to establish a special dispensation process to permit people who had committed politically motivated crimes during the apartheid period, but who had not sought amnesty from the Truth and Reconciliation Commission, to apply to the President for a pardon.[52] The Constitutional Court held, without considering whether the adoption of the special dispensation process constituted

[48] *Greys Marine Hout Bay* (n 45) [24].
[49] See Hoexter (n 5) 115.
[50] *Pharmaceutical Manufacturers' Association of South Africa and Another: In re Ex Parte President of the RSA and Others* [2000] ZACC 1.
[51] ibid [90].
[52] See *Albutt v The Centre for the Study of Vand Reconciliation and Others* [2010] ZACC 4.

administrative action, that the process established would be irrational on the basis of the principle of irrationality developed in the *Pharmaceuticals* case, if it did not permit victims of the relevant crime to be heard by the President before he decides whether to issue a pardon.

This case is illustrative of a worrying trend: the Court declined to decide whether the grant of a pardon by the President would constitute administrative action, and simply decided the case on the basis of the principles of legality and rationality. Cora Hoexter has described this case as dealing the administrative code 'a near fatal blow'.[53] This trend is increasingly common. Courts are often all too ready to avoid deciding cases under the administrative code preferring instead to decide them upon the basis of the principles of legality and rationality, which has led some commentators to refer to the principle of legality as 'the judges' darling'.[54]

Of course, avoidance of the administrative code is not only the fault of judges, it is also the fault of litigants who plead their cases on the basis of the principle of legality. Perhaps one of the reasons for litigants' choice of pleading is their desire to avoid the 180-day time limit for judicial review which has been enforced by the Constitutional Court, although it may be extended where the interests of justice so require.[55] Another may be that litigants wish to avoid the statutory requirement that they exhaust internal remedies before turning to judicial review.[56]

Why should we be worried about this trend? There are two reasons: the first is a separation of powers reason. The Constitution explicitly requires legislation to give effect to the right to administrative justice and thus preserves for Parliament a key role in developing the right to administrative justice, and by implication requires courts to respect Parliament's framework for the right, unless it can be shown that that framework constitutes an unreasonable or unjustifiable limitation on the right to administrative justice. Parliament has performed its constitutional task and enacted an administrative code to give effect to the constitutional right. And it now falls to courts to respect the legislation enacted by Parliament and apply it.

The second reason is that, although it is not perfect, the administrative code could assist in providing clarity on difficult questions of administrative law, including the grounds of review, procedural fairness, the right to written reasons and on processes to be followed.[57] It is true that its definition of administrative action is unhelpful, but slowly the courts have been bringing clarity to it, a process that will continue as long as courts, and litigants, grapple with the terms of the code.

VI. CONCLUSION

Constitutional entrenchment has largely been a success. It has ensured that administrative law will provide a bulwark against administrative abuse in the years ahead. The most

[53] See Hoexter (n 5) 126.
[54] See Hoexter and Penfold (n 8) 483.
[55] See PAJA, s 7(1). See also *Brummer v Minister for Social Development* 2009 (6) SA 323 (CC) [76]. With regard to an extension of the period, see PAJA, ss 9(1), (2).
[56] PAJA, s 7(2).
[57] See Hoexter (n 5) 116.

challenging aspect of the entrenchment has been defining the concept of 'administrative action' upon which the entrenched right hinges. That task has been made more difficult by a bewildering legislative definition in the administrative code, which of course could be amended by Parliament if it thought it appropriate.

Codification on the other hand has been more of a mixed blessing. Codification is often attempted to underpin the rule-of-law values of legal certainty, public accessibility and clarity, but so far that goal cannot be said to have been achieved. Of course, any codification is going to initially result in some uncertainty as cases concerning the new provisions explore and clarify the code. More than two decades in, however, that process is not yet complete in South Africa and if the trend to avoid application of the administrative code becomes more pronounced it may be imperilled.

One of the reasons for the avoidance of the administrative code may arise from the challenge of codifying any law in a common-law environment. In a recent assessment of the experience of Australia and South Africa with codification, Cheryl Saunders and I noted that:

> both in Australia and South Africa, lawyers and judges trained in the common law rules and practices of judicial review do not adopt reforms introduced by codification easily. In both systems, existing principles and practices of administrative law have continued to be drawn on and applied in the post-codification period.[58]

It is noteworthy that in both Australia and South Africa, constitutional avenues for judicial review, outside the respective administrative codes, have become increasingly important, if not dominant. Given the scant legislative framework for these avenues of judicial review, the possibility is that it will largely become judge-made law once again. In a newly established constitutional democracy, where Parliament's role in regulating the right to administrative justice was mandated in the constitutional text, this consequence must raise concerns. The solution, however, lies in the hands of judges who can insist that the administrative code be observed and respected, and not bypassed.

[58] See C Saunders and K O'Regan, 'Codification of Administrative Law in Common-Law Systems: Insights from Australia and South Africa: A Submission to the UK Independent Review of Administrative Law' (Bonavero Institute of Human Rights, Bonavero Report 6/2020, 28 October 2020) 31, available at <www.law.ox.ac.uk/sites/files/oxlaw/bonavero_report_6_2020_1.pdf.

7

South Africa's Transformative Constitution as 'Non-Reformist Reform'?

NOMFUNDO RAMALEKANA

> The non-reformist reform then provides a framework for demands that will undermine the prevailing political, economic, social system from reproducing itself, and to make more possible a radically different political, economic, social system.[1]

I. INTRODUCTION

At the centre of the call to decolonise the law in South Africa is an indictment of the 1996 Constitution as both an instrument of maintaining the hegemony of the white minority class and a tool for supporting the interests of the emerging Black elite.[2] This is the same Constitution that has been and, in some circles, continues to be lauded as the bulwark towards eradicating inequality and transforming society – the archetype of a 'transformative constitution'.[3] Within the context of the call to decolonise the law (especially constitutional law) and the commitment to a 'transformative constitution' in South Africa, two critical schools of thought are emerging.

The first school of thought is 'constitutional abolitionism'. A central tenet of constitutional abolitionism rejects the idea that the 1996 Constitution is 'transformative'. Instead, it argues that the Constitution is a negotiated settlement embedded in liberal legalism and

[1] A Akbar, 'Demands for a Democratic Political Economy' (2020) 134 *Harvard Law Review Forum* 90, 104.

[2] JM Modiri, 'Conquest and Constitutionalism: First Thoughts on an Alternative Jurisprudence' (2018) 34 *South African Journal on Human Rights* 300; N Dladla, 'The Liberation of History and the End of South Africa: Some Notes towards an Azanian Historiography in Africa, South' (2018) 34 *South African Journal on Human Rights* 415; S Sibanda, 'Not Yet Uhuru' – The Usurpation of the Liberation Aspirations of South Africa's Masses by a Commitment to Liberal Constitutional Democracy, PhD thesis (University of Witwatersrand, 2018); S Sibanda, 'Not Purpose-Made! Transformative Constitutionalism, Post-Independence Constitutionalism and the Struggle to Eradicate Poverty' (2011) 22(3) *Stellenbosch Law Review* 482; MB Ramose, 'Towards a Post-Conquest South Africa: Beyond the Constitution of 1996' (2018) 34 *South African Journal on Human Rights* 326; T Madlingozi, 'Social Justice in a Time of Neo-Apartheid Constitutionalism: Critiquing the Anti-Black Economy of Recognition, Incorporation and Distribution' (2017) 1 *Stellenbosch Law Review* 123.

[3] For comparative literature on transformative constitutionalism see, M Hailbronner, 'Transformative Constitutionalism: Not Only in the Global South' (2017) 65(3) *The American Journal of Comparative Law* 527; O Vihena Viera, U Baxi and F Vijoen (eds), *Transformative Constitutionalism: Comparing the Apex Courts of Brazil, India and South Africa* (Pretoria University Law Press, 2013); G Bhatia, *The Transformative Constitution: A Radical Biography in Nine Acts* (Harper Collins, 2019).

is thus incapable of repairing the harms of colonial and apartheid injustice or redressing present inequality. According to Modiri, for example, the Constitution

> embeds particular cultural and ideological values into its fold and as such works to consolidate and preserve particular arrangements and relations of power and knowledge. Understood in this way, the constitution must be implicated in the continuation of colonial-apartheid power relations, value systems and subjectivities.[4]

Constitutional abolitionists call for a new, 'post-conquest' constitution, a post-conquest South Africa.[5] The second school of thought, the 'institutional' critique, similarly questions the promise of transformative constitutionalism. However, proponents of this approach root the problem not in the text of the Constitution or whether it embodies liberal or other ideology, but in the failure of courts, the legislature, and the executive as the bodies tasked to give meaning and content to the Constitution (the enabling institutions).[6]

These two schools of thought frame the current discourse in South African public law, and they also map onto the debate about whether transformation should occur *via* revolutionary action or incremental reform.[7] Constitutional abolitionist argue for larger revolutionary change – a change that, according to constitutional abolitionists, cannot occur within the current constitutional paradigm. The institutionalist critique is more aligned with 'reformism' in the sense that it does not question existing constitutional arrangements, it merely critiques the failure to implement such arrangements. In this chapter, I suggest a shift away from the revolutionary versus reformist dichotomy – imagining a third way to understand the role that the Constitution *should* play in South Africa. In this way, we can begin to see the Constitution as an instrument that is neither revolutionary nor purely reformist; but as an enabler of non-reformist reform.[8]

Rooted in the work of the socialist philosopher Andre Gorz, non-reformist reforms are defined as strategies which work together to undermine or shrink a harmful system –

[4] Modiri (n 2) 305.

[5] A core tenet of constitutional abolitionism is the idea that colonialism never ended. Thus, justice demands a 'post-conquest' South Africa (and Constitution) – one that has 'responded concretely and effectively to the exigencies of justice with particular reference to disseizin or forcible expropriation of territory without compensation and, as a necessary consequence, the loss of sovereignty over it by its original indigenous owners from time immemorial.' See Ramose (n 2) 328.

[6] A sample of literature which tracks this approach includes: D Davis, 'Is the South African Constitution an Obstacle to a Democratic Post-Colonial State?' (2018) 34 *South African Journal on Human Rights* 359; D Davis, 'Transformation: The Constitutional Promise and Reality' (2010) 26 *South African Journal on Human Rights* 85; D Davis and K Klare, 'Transformative Constitutionalism and the Common and Customary Law' (2010) 26(3) *South African Journal on Human Rights* 403; to an extent S Hassim, 'Decolonising Equality: The Radical Roots of the Gender Equality Clause in the South African Constitution' (2018) 34 *South African Journal on Human Rights* 342; T Roux, 'Transformative Constitutionalism and the Best Interpretation of the South African Constitution: Distinction without a Difference' (2009) 20 *Stellenbosch Law Review* 258.

[7] I am particularly evoking the debates in the socialists tradition, see JD Stephens, 'Revolution and Reform' in JD Stephens, *The Transition from Capitalism to Socialism* (Palgrave, 1979).

[8] The possibility of this third path is not entirely inimical to the arguments made by constitutional abolitionist or the institutional critics. For example, a leading scholar in constitutional abolitionism in South Africa, Joel Modri, acknowledges the possibility of 'constitutionalisms from below' which are enacted by social movements and marginalised communities who engage in legal mobilisation strategies and court litigation to contest state power, issue change-oriented political demands and address immediate legal and socio-economic needs. Modiri (n 2) 323.

they work to reduce the power of an oppressive system.[9] As a socialist writing in the 1960s, Gorz was concerned that the kind of crisis capable of uniting the working class against capitalism was not imminent.[10] He observed that, 'In the foreseeable future there will be no crisis of European capitalism so dramatic as to drive the mass of workers to revolutionary general strikes or armed insurrection in defence of their vital interests.'[11] At the same time, it was clear that 'the bourgeoisie will never surrender its power without struggle, without being forced to do so by the revolutionary action of the masses'.[12] In those circumstances, Gorz argued that steps short of revolutionary change, but more than mere reform, should be taken to leave the path open for revolutionary change – non-reformist reforms. According to Gorz, 'The principal problem of a socialist strategy is to *create* the objective and subjective conditions which will make mass revolutionary action and engagement in a successful trial of strength with the bourgeoisie possible.'[13]

An attractive feature of non-reformist reforms is that they are not ends in and of themselves but a part of a larger vision for transformation.[14] They work towards shifting unequal power relations and clearing a path for more radical transformations.[15] While reformist reforms 'aim to improve, ameliorate, legitimate, and even advance the underlying system non-reformist reforms aim for political, economic, social transformation'.[16] Non-reformist reforms question, critique and undermine the status quo. Their core task is to reduce the scope, power, size and impact of structures; they should be capable of changing the balance of power and leave those mobilising in a better bargaining position than they would have been in but for these steps – they lay the path for the adjacent possible.

Relying on the concept of non-reformist reform, the chapter will argue that the Constitution has features that, if radically and persistently pursued, could pave the path towards the constitutional abolitionist's desired rupture from the prevailing social, economic and political arrangements on which deeply entrenched inequality in South Africa is rooted. I see this possibility in the small, though significant, departures that the Constitution makes from liberal constitutional design – departures that inspired the idea that the South African Constitution was transformative.

To chart this third path, I have divided the chapter into four sections. In the second section (II), I define transformative constitutionalism by exploring two important features from the early life (in the courts and academic commentary) of transformative constitutionalism. First, I explore the idea that the Constitution has features that depart from classical liberal constitutions. Second, I explore the idea that the Constitution invites the courts to interpret the provisions in the Constitution and exercise their judicial review

[9] See A Gorz, *Strategy for Labour: A Radical Proposal* (translated by MA Nicolaus and V Ortiz) (Beacon Press, 1967) 8; Akbar (n 1) 101; N Stump, '"Non-Reformist Reforms" in Radical Social Change: A Critical Legal Research Exploration' (2021) 101 *Boston University Law Review Online* 6, 12–13.

[10] A Gorz, 'Reform and Revolution' (1968) *The Socialist Register* 111 (translated by B Brewster), available at https://socialistregister.com/index.php/srv/article/view/5272/2173.

[11] ibid.

[12] ibid.

[13] ibid.

[14] According to Gorz, non-reformist reforms are a part of 'the preparatory phase which sets in motion a process leading to the edge of the crisis and the final trial of strength', ibid 112. See also, Akbar (n 1) 103.

[15] Akbar (n 1) 104.

[16] ibid.

powers in a manner that furthers the political goals of transformation – transformative adjudication. Having defined transformative constitutionalism, in the third section (III), I explore the abolitionist and institutional critiques of transformative constitutionalism. In the fourth section (IV), I explore the meaning of non-reformist reform and map a path for thinking about the Constitution as an enabler of non-reformist reform.

Before we begin, it is important that I note that this work is inspired by the work of the socialist who, facing the reality that a social revolution was not imminent, did not give up on the cause, instead, they diverted their attention to what could be done to create the conditions for the revolution to occur.[17] It is also inspired by the work of the prison abolitionists, who use non-reformist reform strategies to pave the path towards an abolitionist future.[18] I stand in this tradition with humility and hope for an alternative future.

II. DEFINING TRANSFORMATIVE CONSTITUTIONALISM

The demand for a new 'post-conquest' constitution and the institutional critique emerge in opposition to and as critiques of the leitmotif of South African constitutionalism, transformative constitutionalism. It is thus important to start with a broad analysis of what this concept, at least in the South African context, means.[19] South Africa comes from a history of colonial and apartheid domination and oppression – these institutions are the root of the prevailing, deeply entrenched structural inequality.[20] According to the South African Constitutional Court (Constitutional Court), transformation is aimed at redressing the historical imbalance caused by this past.[21] The constitutional commitment to transforming society through law, is evident in the Preamble of the Constitution which states that the Constitution was adopted in recognition of past injustice and to 'heal divisions of the past and establish a society based on the democratic values, social justice and

[17] Gorz (n 10); Gorz (n 9); N Fraser and A Honneth, *Redistribution or Recognition: A Political-Philosophical Exchange* (Verso, 2003).

[18] See, eg, M Stahly-Butts and A Akbar, 'Reforms for Radicals? An Abolitionist Framework' (2022) 68 *UCLA Law Review* 1544; R Reyes, 'Abolition Constitutionalism and Non-Reformist Reform: The Case for Ending Pretrial Detention' (2021) 53 *Connecticut Law Review* 667; Akbar (n 1) (and the work of social movements and community-led organisations discussed in these articles).

[19] As it is the preeminent approach to South African constitutionalism, there is a lot of literature on this concept, all defining different features of this idea and expressing diverging opinions on its value. A small sample includes K Klare, 'Legal Culture and Transformative Constitutionalism' (1998) 14 *South African Journal on Human Rights* 146; E Van Huyssteen, 'The Constitutional Court and the Redistribution of Power in South Africa: Towards Transformative Constitutionalism' (2000) 59 *African Studies* 245; A Van der Walt, 'Legal History, Legal Culture and Transformation in a Constitutional Democracy' (2006) 12 *Fundamina* 1; D Moseneke, 'Transformative Adjudication' (2002) 18 *South African Journal on Human Rights* 309; Justice Pius Langa, 'Transformative Constitutionalism' (2006) 3 *Stellenbosch Law Review* 351; Roux (n 6); J Brickhill and Y Van Leeve, 'Transformative Constitutionaslism – Guiding Light or Empty Slogan?' [2015] *Acta Juridica* 141.

[20] For an analysis of inequality in South Africa, see, 'Poverty Trends in South Africa: An Examination of Absolute Poverty between 2006 and 2015' (Statistics South Africa, 2017), available at www.statssa.gov.za/publications/Report-03-10-06/Report-03-10-062015.pdf; J Seekings and N Nattrass, *Policy, Politics and Poverty in South Africa* (Palgrave Macmillan, 2015); J Seekings and N Nattrass, *Class, Race, and Inequality in South Africa* (Yale University Press, 2005); S Terreblanche, *A History of Inequality in South Africa:1652–2002* (University of KwaZulu-Natal Press, 2003).

[21] *Bato Star Fishing (Pty) Ltd v Minister of Environmental Affairs and Tourism and Others* 2004 4 SA 490 CC [71], fn 43.

fundamental human rights' and to 'Improve the quality of life and free the potential of each person'.[22]

The idea that the new constitutional dispensation would bring or require transformation precedes the 1996 Constitution.[23] However, the American scholar, Karl Klare, popularised the term 'transformative constitutionalism' in relation to the Constitution in his 1998 article, 'Legal Culture and Transformative Constitutionalism'.[24] Rooting his analysis in the critical legal studies movement in the United States, Klare defined transformative constitutionalism as a 'long-term project of constitutional enactment, interpretation, and enforcement committed … to transforming a country's political and social institutions and power relationships in a democratic, participatory, and egalitarian direction'.[25]

There are many other definitions of transformation and transformative constitutionalism.[26] For Albertyn and Goldblatt, for example, transformation requires 'a complete reconstruction of the state and society, including a redistribution of power and resources along egalitarian lines'.[27] According to Liebenberg, the Constitution 'aims at facilitating the construction of a new political, social and economic order … this new order expressly envisages improving the quality of life and freeing the potential of each person'. This, she argues, will require redressing past injustice and 'a deep restructuring of the underlying institutional arrangements which generate various forms of political, economic and cultural injustice'.[28] Similarly, Van Huyssteen argues that the Constitution is transformative in the sense that:

> It expands the basis of popular participation in political decision making, entrenches government accountability, facilitates the redistribution of resources, and creates spaces for the legitimate expression of differences in the face of the nation-building imperative, it can provide the basis for the shifts in social, political and economic power relations.[29]

The definitions above have several important features to note. First, apparent in the breadth of the goals of transformative constitutionalism is the idea that transformation would not happen immediately – it is a long-term process. Second, transformation requires the engagement of all the branches of government – those who pass, implement, and interpret the law as well as society more broadly. No complete 'restructuring' as Albertyn and Goldblatt envisage,[30] could be possible without the commitment of all political and other social institutions. Third, while the term 'transformation' is value-neutral and says nothing about the *from* and *to* what of 'transform', transformative constitutionalism is tied to redressing the injustice rooted in South Africa's colonial and apartheid past (the from)

[22] Preamble, Constitution of the Republic of South Africa, 1996.

[23] Sibanda, 'Not yet Uhuru' (n 2) 194–200, for an analysis of references to transformation and constitutionalism prior to 1996 in South Africa.

[24] Klare (n 19).

[25] ibid 150.

[26] For an analysis of comparative approaches to transformative constitutionalism, see Hailbronner (n 3); Vihena Viera, Baxi and Vijoen (n 3).

[27] C Albertyn and B Goldblatt, 'Facing the Challenge of Transformation: Difficulties in the Development of an Indigenous Jurisprudence of Equality' (1998) 14 *South African Journal on Human Rights* 248, 249.

[28] S Liebenberg, *Socio-Economic Rights: Adjudication Under a Transformative Constitution* (Juta Ltd, 2010) 27.

[29] Van Huyssteen (n 19) 247–48.

[30] Albertyn and Goldblatt (n 27) 249.

and towards the goal of creating a democratic, participatory, and egalitarian society (to what). Fourth, it is concerned with altering unequal power relations in society and a fair distribution of resources.

The aims of transformative constitutionalism are clearly laudable. However, 29 years into our constitutional democracy, South Africa remains one of the most unequal societies in the world – an inequality that continues to map the fault lines of race, gender, and class.[31] The disconnect between the promise of transformative constitutionalism and prevailing inequality is the foundation that underlies the institutional, and the abolitionist critique of transformative constitutionalism. Before engaging with these critiques, I want us to explore why Klare and others consider the South African Constitution to be 'transformative'. This exploration will help set the scene for my analysis of the debate relating to transformative constitutionalism and serve as a foundation for the argument that ultimately, the Constitution has features which enable non-reformist reform.

A. A Departure from Classic Liberal Constitutions

The core of the argument that the Constitution is transformative is its 'post-liberal' features, which, according to Klare, invite 'a new imagination and self-reflection about legal method, analysis and reasoning consistent with its transformative goals'.[32] To understand the significance of this classification, I briefly discuss some features of what Klare considered to be aspects of a 'classic liberal constitution' and explore how the Constitution departs from these to constitute a *text* that is transformative.

At the core of classic liberal ideology is a commitment to individual freedom, autonomy, equality before the law and an abstentionist, neutral state.[33] As argued by Epstein, 'The classic liberal tradition … prized the protection of liberty and property under a system of limited government.'[34] For the purpose and function of constitutions, liberalism has three important ramifications which, reading Klare, characterise the classic liberal constitution: the neutrality of the state and the law, the public/private divide, and that rights give rise to negative as opposed to positive obligations. According to Klare, in contrast with 'classic liberal documents',[35] the Constitution was '*social, redistributive, caring, positive*, at least partly *horizontal, participatory, multicultural*, and *self-conscious* about its historical setting and transformative role and mission [emphasis added]'.[36]

Classic liberalism defines individual liberty in the negative sense – liberty is the absence of interference and coercion. Thus, liberal constitutions are 'most commonly'

[31] See the literature at n 20 above.

[32] Klare (n 19) 156.

[33] S Fredman, *Women and the Law* (Clarendon, 1997) for a detailed history of liberal ideology and its relationship with the right to equality, in particular, women's right to equality.

[34] R Epstein, *The Classic Liberal Constitution:The Uncertain Quest for Limited Government* (Harvard University Press, 2014) 17.

[35] Klare does not define what he means by classic liberal documents, but from the body of his argument, he identifies features including – the separation of law and politics, focus on individual rights and the focus on objectivity and neutrality in the interpretation and adjudication. 'The goal is to maintain the law/politics boundary by describing rational decision-procedures (deduction, balancing, purposive reasoning, etc) with which to arrive at determinate legal outcomes from neutral, consensus-based general principles expressed or immanent within a legal order', Klare (n 19) 158.

[36] ibid 153–55.

thought of as defining and limiting the reach of the state from interfering with individual liberty.[37] Under a classic liberal constitution, the respect for individual liberty, requires the state and the law to be neutral between persons and not intrude in the exercise of individual choices.[38] This understanding of the role of law and of the state means that the state cannot pursue any distributive or social justice aims – they must remain neutral and objective.[39] Rather than remain neutral, Klare argued that the Constitution recognised that the law could not be 'neutral with respect to the distribution of social and economic power and of opportunities for people to experience self-realization'.[40] For this, he primarily relied on section 9(2) of the Constitution, noting an express commitment to substantive equality which he defined as 'equality in lived, social and economic circumstances and opportunities needed to experience human self-realization'.[41] In addition to the commitment to substantive equality, the presence of a justiciable Bill of Rights, according to Klare, was emblematic of a commitment to ensure that persons have access to resources they need to exercise their political freedoms.[42]

Second, under classic liberalism, there is a divide between the public and the private. On this view, the state can only interfere with what is public, and not the private, largely defined as including the family and the marketplace. In relation to constitutions, this is 'the idea that the Constitution is especially concerned with the limitation of "public" power and, by the same token, that it is not ordinarily concerned with the regulation of other, "private," sources of power'.[43] This divide is often argued to be 'constitutive for constitutionalism'.[44] In his paper, Klare noted the express provision for both the horizontal and vertical application of rights in the Bill of Rights. Section 8(2) of the Constitution provides that the rights in the Bill of Rights bind 'natural or a juristic person if, and to the extent that, it is applicable, taking into account the nature of the right and the nature of any duty imposed by the right'.[45] Further, the prohibition of unfair discrimination in section 9 of the Constitution applies horizontally.[46]

[37] R Kay, 'The State Action Doctrine, the Public/Private Distinction, and the Independence of Constitutional Law' (1993) *University of Minnesota Law School: Constitutional Commentary* 329, 338, available at https://scholarship.law.umn.edu/cgi/viewcontent.cgi?article=1898&context=concomm.

[38] Fredman (n 33) 6.

[39] S Fredman, *Human Rights Transformed* (Oxford University Press, 2008) 11; Fredman (n 33) 7.

[40] Klare (n 19) 194.

[41] ibid 154, fn 15. For an analysis of the meaning of substantive equality and its relationship to transformation in South Africa, see C Albertyn, 'Contested Substantive Equality in the South African Constitution: Beyond Social Inclusion towards Systemic Justice' (2018) 34 *South African Journal on Human Rights* 441; C Albertyn, 'Substantive Equality and Transformation in South Africa' (2007) 23 *South African Journal on Human Rights* 253.

[42] For an analysis of the relationship between the ideal of transformative constitutionalism and socio-economic rights, see: Klare (n 19) 153; Liebenberg (n 28).

[43] Kay (n 37) 330.

[44] D Grimm, *Constitutionalism: Past, Present and Future* (Oxford University Press, 2016) 2.

[45] See *Khumalo and Others v Holomisa* 2002 8 BCLR 771. The Court confirmed that there is room for the direct, horizontal application of at least certain rights in the Bill of Rights, [33]. See also *Governing Body of the Juma Musjid Primary School & Others v Essay NO and Others* 2011 8 BCLR 761 CC. The Court held the purpose of section 8(2) of the Constitution was 'not to obstruct private autonomy or to impose on a private party the duties of the state in protecting the Bill of Rights' but to 'require private parties not to interfere with or diminish the enjoyment of a right', [58]. More recently, in *Daniels v Scribante and Another* 2017 8 BCLR 949 CC, Madlanga J extended this and opened the door for the horizontal application of rights even in relation to imposing positive obligations on private persons, [39].

[46] Section 9(4) of the Constitution of the Republic of South Africa, 1996 provides that, 'No person may unfairly discriminate directly or indirectly against anyone'. This provision has been used to pierce relationships

Third, and closely related to the public/private divide is the idea that under classic liberalism, rights can only give rise to negative obligations on the state. The state does not have a duty to act or ensure the realisation of rights. This is because such obligations would be seen as violating individual freedom and the exercise of choice. Instead, the state's obligations are negative. In order to protect individual liberty, it must refrain from violating or interfering with the enjoyment of rights. Thus, classic liberal constitutions tend to serve to protect persons from state intervention by placing duties of restraint rather than positive obligations on the state.[47] By contrast, Klare noted that the provisions in the Bill of Rights imposed positive obligations on the state 'to combat poverty and promote social welfare, to assist people in authentically exercising and enjoying their constitutional rights, and to facilitate and support individual self-realization'.[48]

Fourth, he argued that the Constitution was historically self-conscious in the sense that it was 'an instrument committed to social transformation and reconstruction'.[49] This contradicts the idea of law as static, neutral and objective. 'It rejects the fiction that the political community is founded at a single magic moment of 'social contract', thereby ratifying the pre-existing hierarchy and distribution of social and economic power'.[50]

For Klare, these departures from classic liberalism were an indication of the possibility of transforming South African society by working with the text of the Constitution. This brings us to the second aspect of Klare's argument. To be able to achieve the goals of transformation, he argued, there needed to be a change in the approach to working with the text and values which underlie the Constitution.[51] He thus advocated for *transformative adjudication* by judges as well as a change in the legal culture to make achieving the Constitution's transformative goals possible. In the section that follows, I discuss the meaning of transformative adjudication. I focus on the obligations that, according to Klare, transformative constitutionalism placed on the courts.

B. Transformative Adjudication

According to Klare, transformative adjudication is a method of adjudication that is politically engaged without amounting to 'illicit "judicial legislation"'.[52] The courts are required to interpret and apply the provisions in the Constitution in a manner that seeks to achieve the political goals embodied in the provisions.[53] This approach to adjudication is in contrast with the strict separation between law and politics and the idea that judges

historically considered to fall into the private realm – for example, finding a will unconstitutional because it unfairly discriminated against women, see *King NO and Others v De Jager and Others* [2021] ZACC 4; 2021 (5) BCLR 449 (CC).

[47] Fredman (n 39) 9.

[48] Klare (n 19) 154.

[49] ibid 155.

[50] ibid.

[51] ibid 156.

[52] ibid 150.

[53] M Pieterse, 'What Do We Mean When We Talk about Transformative Constitutionalism?' (2005) 20 *Southern African Public Law* 155, 164; Langa (n 19) 353. Former CJ Langa argues that 'Under a transformative Constitution, judges bear the ultimate responsibility to justify their decisions not only by reference to authority, but by reference to ideas and values.'

should 'check their politics at the courthouse door' and act as neutral and objective arbiters of legal disputes – what Klare called 'liberal legalism'.[54] Under this approach, it is understood that judges cannot keep their personal and political values from the interpretative and adjudicative process. These 'play a routine, normal, and ineradicable role in adjudication'.[55] Transformative adjudication contemplates 'new conceptions of judicial role and responsibility' and examines the prevailing judicial mindset and methodology to promote equality, a culture of democracy, and transparent governance.[56]

The Constitutional Court has sanctioned the commitment to transformative adjudication in its judgments,[57] as well as in extra-curial commentary by its judges.[58] According to Moseneke J, transformative constitutionalism demands that in fulfilling its mandate, the 'courts should search for substantive justice, which is to be inferred from the foundational values of the Constitution'.[59] These values include equality, human dignity and freedom.[60] However, the Constitutional Court has not been clear on its role in the process, with some judgments suggesting a deferent approach to other decision-makers on how to go about achieving the goals of transformation. For example, in *Bato Star*, O'Regan J held that because the 'goals of transformation can be achieved in a myriad of ways …. The manner in which transformation is to be achieved is, to a significant extent, left to the discretion of the decision-maker'.[61] She thus seems to envision a limited role for the courts in achieving the goals of transformation. However, some judgments see a more active, purpose-oriented role for the courts, exercising more or less deference in relation to the specific context of the case and what is at stake.[62]

In his article, Klare argued that one of the barriers to transformation in South Africa was its conservative legal culture. He defined legal culture as 'professional sensibilities, habits of mind, and intellectual reflexes' which determined the 'rhetorical strategies' used; the kinds of and range of possible arguments that are considered to be valid; the political and ethical commitments which influence professional discourse; the assumptions about politics, social life and justice.[63] The legal culture defines 'what qualifies as a proper legal problem, an authoritative legal rule or principle concerning that problem and a valid argument or methodology in applying the rule or principle to the problem'.[64] According to Klare, the South African legal culture was conservative in its 'strong faith in the precision, determinacy and self-revealingness of words and texts'.[65]

[54] Klare (n 19) 157.
[55] ibid 163.
[56] ibid 156.
[57] See, eg, *City Council of Pretoria v Walker* 1998 2 SA 363 [101] (Sachs J notes the need and the difficulty of creating a 'jurisprudence of transition').
[58] See Moseneke (n 19) 316; Langa (n 19) 354.
[59] Moseneke (n 19) 316.
[60] See South African Constitution, s 1 (Founding Provisions).
[61] *Bato Star* (n 21) [35].
[62] See Cameron J's majority in *Mwelase and Others v Director-General for the Department of Rural Development and Land Reform and Another* 2019 6 SA 597 CC. In the case, Cameron J took a very active role in crafting a remedy that would ensure a full vindication of the rights violations against harsh critique, including from the minority judgment by Jafta J that the remedy was violative of the separation of powers.
[63] Klare (n 19) 166–67.
[64] Van der Walt (n 19) 17; Klare (n 19) 166–67.
[65] Klare (n 19) 168.

This conservatism, Klare argued, led to a process of legal interpretation that was 'highly structured, technicist, literal and rule-bound'.[66] Further, he argued that these 'expressions of faith in the constraining power of legal texts and ritual invocation of the law/politics boundary' could induce 'intellectual caution that discourages appropriate constitutional innovation and leads to less generous or innovative interpretations and applications of the Constitution than are permitted by the text and drafting history'.[67] Classic liberal devices such as 'formalism, deference to legislative choices, and dichotomous conceptions of negative and positive rights, public and private law and politics',[68] hinder the possibility of transformation.[69] For Klare, the commitment to transformative constitutionalism, in particular, the shift from constraining liberal legalism, ways of seeing and lawyering would have to change to ensure that they did not limit the possibility of transformation.

Changing a legal culture is difficult – lawyers are trained to see the characteristics of the culture as normal.[70] The ignorance of the embeddedness in a legal culture prohibits critical reflection on how the prevailing legal culture can limit transformation.[71] As Van der Walt notes, under 'the hegemonic force' of legal tradition, 'new perspectives, alternative views and different arguments or ways of thinking are routinely or at least easily excluded or rejected and creative, alternative and unconventional solutions become difficult if not impossible to conceive, promote or defend'.[72] If an argument does not fit the legal culture, it is dismissed and considered as not possible. Thus, a conservative legal culture has a restraining effect on transformation.[73] The lack of self-consciousness, reflection, and reliance on culturally available tools and instincts from the past, according to Klare, 'exercise a drag on constitutional interpretation, weighing it down and limiting its ambition and achievements in democratic transformation'.[74] Klare's remedy for this limitation was that a 'searching and critical examination of the legal culture and its multifaceted and diffuse influences on interpretive practices' must be conducted to ensure that our legal culture does not have a restraining effect on transformation.[75]

Overall, transformative constitutionalism, as defined in this section, is rooted in the idea that there have been some departures from classic liberal constitutionalism, departures which empower the courts, more importantly, the broader community of enabling institutions – to pursue an approach to the Constitution that seeks to eliminate inequality and disrupt unequal power relations. However, as I noted earlier, it has been over

[66] ibid. See also Van der Walt (n 19) 18 who, drawing on Klare, defines legal culture/tradition as referring to a 'set of intellectual habits that are embedded in more or less uncritical acceptance of doing things the way they are usually done; the way they have been done for a long time'.

[67] Klare (n 19) 171.

[68] Liebenberg (n 28) 43.

[69] For an analysis of the tensions between the Constitution and the South African legal culture, see T Roux, *The Politics of Principle: The First South African Constitutional Court, 1995–2005* (Cambridge University Press, 2013) ch 5; Van der Walt (n 19); M Pieterse, 'Coming to Terms with Judicial Enforcement of Socio-Economic Rights' (2004) 20(3) *South African Journal on Human Rights* 383.

[70] Klare (n 19) 167.

[71] Van der Walt (n 19) 18.

[72] ibid.

[73] Van der Walt (n 19) 17, 30.

[74] Klare (n 19) 168.

[75] ibid.

two decades of the Constitution and the judicial and academic 'life' of transformative constitutionalism. During this time, levels of inequality, high unemployment amongst historically disadvantaged groups, and the abject poverty in which many South Africans find themselves have rightly placed the Constitution, more specifically, transformative constitutionalism, under intense scrutiny. In the section that follows, I explore strands of the abolitionist and 'institutional' critiques of transformative constitutionalism. Thereafter, I suggest that we draw on the departures of classic liberalism as tools that enable non-reformist reform.

III. A DEPARTURE WITHOUT RUPTURE?

As noted earlier in the chapter, the abolitionist critique culminates in the call for a new, post-conquest Constitution, a post-conquest South Africa.[76] Within this approach, there are three strands of argument. The first argument relies on the inclusion of classically liberal ideals (the separation of powers principle and the protection of private property, for example), as a basis on which to reject the characterisation of the Constitution as post-liberal.[77] The second argues that transformation is too reliant on interpretation and convergence in the ideological commitments of the community of legal interpreters – a commitment that, in the context of our conservative legal culture, does not exist.[78] The third rejects the idea that transformative constitutionalism heralds more than a limited, liberal constitutionalism.[79] Within this argument lies a specific critique of transformative constitutionalism as an ideal,[80] as well as a deeper critique of the Constitution as a negotiated settlement that, by design, entrenched the status quo of inequality, thus making transformation impossible.[81]

In the first strand, Sibanda's work challenges the idea that the Constitution marked a departure from the liberal tradition.[82] He distinguishes between an 'orthodox or liberal democratic approach to constitutionalism' and the 'transformative approach to constitutionalism'.[83] According to Sibanda, the latter is concerned with both political and

[76] According to Dladla, for example, a post-conquest South Africa 'will require nothing else than the restoration of title to territory to the indigenous people conquered in the unjust wars of colonisation, of the restoration of their encumbered sovereignty over it, as well as reparations for their unnecessary multi-century deprivation, suffering and preventable death. Dladla (n 2) 421.

[77] Sibanda, 'Purpose Made' (n 2).

[78] Sibanda, 'Not yet Uhuru' (n 2) ch 5.

[79] Madlingozi (n 2); Modiri (n 2); Ramose (n 2); Dladla (n 2); T Delport, 'An Ethical (Anti-)Constitutionalism? Transformation for a Transfigured Public' (2014) 46(3) *Acta Academica* 104.

[80] Sibanda, 'Not yet Uhuru' (n 2) ch 5.

[81] According to Modiri for eg, 'Each major concession the ANC made in the constitutional negotiations with regard to land, property, the power of the judiciary and the structure of the state ensured the survival of the old order in the new dispensation and legitimised the historical results of colonial-apartheid.' Modiri (n 2) 318–19. See also, Ramose (n 2); Dladla (n 2); Madlingozi (n 2).

[82] Roux (n 69) 203–208 makes the similar argument that, pointing at the inclusion of the separation of powers principle, core to liberal constitutionalism, the Constitution is not post-liberal. Instead, he argues that it is a species of liberalism aligned with uniquely South African values, including Ubuntu. In contrast with Sibanda though, Roux questions the post-liberal status to make the point that the goals of transformation can be achieved without the commitment to Klare's idea of transformative adjudication; see more of this discussion in Brickhill and Van Leeve (n 19) 255–56.

[83] Sibanda, 'Purpose Made' (n 2) 484–85.

socio-economic transformation, while the former is an ideal of having constitutional institutions and processes – an independent judiciary, the respect for the rule of law, free press, free and fair elections.[84] He then argues that while transformative constitutionalism may be a departure from 'liberal constitutionalism', it is still deeply embedded in liberal ideology.[85] For him, this embeddedness in liberalism means that despite the best intentions of those who interpret the Constitution, it 'has had the effect of defining the goods of constitutionalism in narrower terms than is in fact necessary or desirable for purposes of pursuing a truly transformative project of poverty eradication'.[86] Thus, he argues, the Constitution is 'ill-suited for achieving the social, economic and political vision it proclaims'.[87] At the core of Sibanda's argument is the fear that liberal constitutionalism's narrow focus on limiting state power will curtail the state from making radical interventions in favour of the poor.[88]

It would be disingenuous to disagree with the argument that the Constitution is embedded in liberal ideology and is a negotiated settlement. However, that the Constitution has liberal foundations should not be sufficient to conclude that it offers nothing to the project of transforming society. First, the text of the Constitution is not absolute and has not closed off the possibility of interpreting and applying it in ways that can, at the very least, disrupt systems of domination and oppression. Constitution-making is an ongoing process of construction and reconstruction, one in which different interpretive communities contribute.[89] As Van Huyssteen has argued, 'The Constitution provides the foundation for transformative constitutionalism, but the extent to which this potential is realised will depend on the nature and outcomes of social and political struggles and contestation, as well as of clashes before the Court'.[90] As I will illustrate in the next section, these struggles are not yet complete; they work through and with and against the law to transform society – this is constitution-making.

The second strand turns the focus to the relationship between the prevailing legal culture and the goals of transformative constitutionalism. As discussed in the previous section, one of Klare's arguments was that transformation could only occur with a real commitment to transformative adjudication and a sufficient change in the legal culture.[91] Drawing on this, Sibanda argues that the reliance on interpretation for transformation is a substantial barrier to achieving the purpose of transformation. In this regard, he notes that if the goals of transformative constitutionalism are primarily driven through the process of interpretation by lawyers and judges 'of different political persuasions and inclinations', these goals will be at risk of being undermined or becoming mere rhetoric.[92]

[84] ibid.
[85] ibid 486.
[86] ibid.
[87] ibid.
[88] ibid 498. S Sibanda, 'Not Quite a Rejoinder: Some Thoughts and Reflections on Michelman's "Liberal Constitutionalism, Property Rights and the Assault on Poverty"' [2013] *Stellenbosch Law Review* 329, 332. J Dugard, 'Courts and the Poor in South Africa: A Critique of Systemic Judicial Failures to Advance Transformative Justice' (2008) 24 *South African Journal on Human Rights* 214 (argument that the Constitutional Court's jurisprudence has not been pro-poor).
[89] Van Huyssteen (n 19) 247.
[90] ibid 247–48.
[91] Klare (n 19) 167–71.
[92] Sibanda, 'Purpose Made' (n 2) 493.

Essentially, Sibanda is concerned that transformative constitutionalism is too reliant on interpretation by a conservative legal community. This, together with its liberal 'roots', leaves the whole project susceptible to the limitations of liberal constitutionalism.[93] He thus argues that without 'a shared transformative consciousness deriving from the Constitution, its underlying values, rights framework and democratic institutions'[94] all that we have left 'is a prevailing system of liberal democratic constitutionalism with its emphasis on procedural democracy in the form of free and fair elections and the balancing of institutional power dynamics between the branches of government'.[95] More deeply, he argues that transformative constitutionalism's focus on the courts, lawyers, and legal academics enables 'elite capture by empowering courts and lawyers more broadly (especially academics) without expanding the possibilities of greater democratic participation in the project of constitutional meaning making'.[96] For Sibanda, transformative constitutionalism promises more than it can deliver. This is because its goals could only be realised 'in a political and legal community where there is a shared sense of a particular ideologically laden transformative consciousness, alongside value-laden, forward-looking and purposive interpretive approach by a transformed legal community'.[97] Absent this, the project's dependence on a particular mode of interpretation is for him its 'fatal weakness'.[98]

While it is true that the legal culture in South Africa remains largely conservative, this should not be the end of the story. The legal culture is capable of changing to better align with the commitment to transformative constitutionalism 'through critical awareness of and resistance against the hegemonic effect of legal culture and tradition'.[99] As Van der Walt argues, judges, lawyers and the community of constitutional interpreters 'should actively seek for and discover the dynamic potential for transformation inherent in the other, often marginal, experiences and interpretations of the law that are traditionally and routinely excluded or side-lined by mainstream legal consciousness and practice'.[100] As will be seen in the next section, this is already happening. Moreover, non-reformist reform requires actions, organising and movements beyond the work of lawyers and judges – even as they use law and legal instruments. I remain hopeful that the community of interpreters can work with the 'postliberal' features identified by Klare and, in the act of subverting the dominant legal culture and tradition, fashion new and novel arguments that push towards the goal of transformation.

It is important to note that transforming a legal culture is about more than changing the ways of thinking about law. It also requires a change in the composition of the legal community. As Sibanda illustrates, if a legal culture comprises of persons whose interests are threatened by transformation, they may not work towards it.[101] Thus, the inclusion of Black people, women, disabled people, people who come from other historically

[93] ibid 493–94. See also Pieterse (n 69) 398.
[94] Sibanda (n 88) 331.
[95] Sibanda, 'Purpose Made' (n 2) 494.
[96] Sibanda, 'Not yet Uhuru' (n 2) 194.
[97] ibid 220–21; For a similar argument, see Madlingozi (n 2) 144.
[98] Sibanda, 'Not yet Uhuru' (n 2) 221.
[99] Van der Walt (n 19) 31.
[100] ibid.
[101] Sibanda, 'Not yet Uhuru' (n 2) 220–22.

disadvantaged backgrounds can be instrumental in transforming the legal culture. In order to have a meaningful impact on legal culture, the inclusion of historically disadvantaged groups will have to occur alongside a change in legal education as well.[102] As Modiri has argued, despite the commitment to transformation, substantive equality, horizontality and social reconciliation, the approach to legal education in South Africa remains 'overwhelmingly dominated by formalism, legalism and liberalism'.[103] This kind of legal education prevents the possibility of 'questioning, resistance and transgression'.[104] It is a barrier to the commitment to transformation. Transformative constitutionalism requires a shift in our legal education to centre an approach that inspires students to think that the law can be used to transform society.[105] This work can and has been done in many law schools throughout the country.

In contrast with the critique discussed above, the third strand rejects not only transformative constitutionalism, or the possibility of achieving its aims within the current legal culture, but the Constitution itself.[106] Proponents of this strand of critique, what Cachalia calls 'postcolonial criticism',[107] argue that the Constitution entrenches colonial and apartheid privileges and power relations, necessarily making transformation impossible. According to Modiri, there exists a '(dis)continuity' between colonial conquest and settler colonialism and the current Constitution, a Constitution made in the image of 'western liberal democracy'.[108] This '(dis)continuity' explains the persisting injustices and the lack of transformation. Modiri's argument is not that nothing has changed, but rather that 'forms and visions of change being employed are not able to successfully dismantle the reigning order at the level of its constitutive or foundational structural elements'.[109] Thus, he notes that while the street names and government have changed, and apartheid laws are repealed, the 'arrangements of economic power, land and property ownership, spatial segregation, epistemic violence, Western imperialism, psychic trauma and labour exploitation' have not.[110] He thus argues that the 'failure to redress the structural continuity of colonial-apartheid renders the constitution's extension of universal suffrage, citizenship and human rights to Black people hollow and abstract'.[111]

Similarly, Madlingozi argues that the 'post-1994 constitutional re-arrangements are transforming society in ways that do not instantiate a fundamental rupture with the inherited, sedimented and bifurcated social configuration' – what he calls 'neo-apartheid constitutionalism'.[112] Drawing from African nationalist and black consciousness thought,

[102] JM Modiri, 'Transformation, Tension and Transgression: Reflections on the Culture and Ideology of South African Legal Education' (2013) 3 *Stellenbosch Law Review* 455, 457.

[103] ibid 456.

[104] ibid.

[105] Langa (n 19) 356.

[106] Madlingozi (n 2); Modiri (n 2); Ramose (n 2); Dladla (n 2).

[107] F Cachalia, 'Democratic Constitutionalism in the Time of the Postcolony: Beyond Triumph and Betrayal' (2018) 34(3) *South African Journal on Human Rights* 375, 378.

[108] Modiri (n 2) 6.

[109] ibid 16.

[110] ibid.

[111] Modiri (n 2)17.

[112] Madlingozi (n 2) 125. The opposite view has been put forward by many commentators, perhaps the most opposing language is that used by Ackerman, who argues that the new Constitution embodies a 'constitutional revolution' even while he acknowledges the embeddedness of the new Constitution in the past, noting that 'There was no discontinuous legal fracture with the old legal order. The revolution was commenced by a

he argues that within the current Constitutional order, 'an anti-black bifurcated societal structure' has emerged. On the one side of this structure are the privileged classes, white people and the Black middle class. This group is governed through a system of liberal democracy. On the other side, a system of 'patronage, appropriation, and repression remain politics *du jour*',[113] both of which keep the majority Black population impoverished and oppressed while legitimating the state in creating the mirage of transformation. Madlingozi powerfully notes:

> The discourse of post-apartheid constitutionalism enables beneficiaries of this elite transition to manufacture the consent that the year 1994 presaged both emancipation from racial domination and colonisation, and liberation to be post-racial and Afropolitan while in reality the majority of black people still suffer from systemic exclusion and institutionalised racism.[114]

In contrast to the democratisation framework within which the ideology of transformation and social justice is embedded, he argues for a decolonisation of the Constitution. For Madlingozi, democratisation serves the interests of the privileged classes – decolonisation would lead to the emancipation of the Black majority. At the core of Madlingozi's critique is that transformative constitutionalism will only benefit the historically privileged classes as well as the new black elite that is incorporated into the world of the other.[115]

I am partially persuaded by this strand of critique. However, the characterisation of the Constitution as a negotiated compromise is incomplete. Most constitutions are negotiated. Moreover, constitutions in democratic societies are provisional in the sense that their meaning is subject to contestation. Accordingly, 'Their legitimacy and efficacy have to be established in each generation through democratic politics'.[116] The Constitution is also a negotiating text. As Du Plessis has noted, the Constitution:

> [W]as not formulated to suggest that once its wording had been agreed upon, ideological tensions among the constitutional negotiators were settled, and that the negotiators were desirous for the written constitutional text to reflect such a settlement. Agreement on a written text was possible only on the condition that the ideological tensions would remain – and visibly so – to be negotiated and renegotiated every time the text is reread with an interpretive eye.[117]

The quote above makes it clear that the Constitution did not and was perhaps not meant to close off the ideological tensions that underlined the negotiating process. For example, the fact that the Constitution includes a property clause need not be the end of the question whether it can be interpreted in a manner that allows for large-scale land redistribution and compensation for the injustice of land dispossession under colonial and apartheid domination.[118] I will return to the 'land question' in the next section. For now,

parliamentary statute of that old order (namely, the IC) and controlled by it, and the Constitutional Court was created by it': see, L Ackermann, 'The Legal Nature of the South African Constitutional Revolution' (2004) *New Zealand Law Review* 633, 642–43.

[113] Madlingozi (n 2) 124–25.

[114] ibid 129.

[115] Madlingozi (n 2) 135.

[116] Cachalia (n 107) 381.

[117] Du Plessis Lourens, 'Interpretation' in S Woolman and M Bishop (eds), *Constitutional Law of South Africa*, 2nd edn (Juta Ltd, 2012) ch 32.3.

[118] See J Dugard and N Seme, 'Property Rights in Court: An Examination of Judicial Attempts to Settle Section 25's Balancing Act Re Restitution and Expropriation' (2018) 34(1) *South African Journal on Human*

I want to stress the point that, even as a negotiated settlement, the Constitution also embodies a culmination of multiple struggles for liberation in South Africa and other African countries, as well as larger global struggles against domination and oppression. For example, Hassim and Albertyn have shown how the right to equality is a product of women's fights against racial and gendered domination and oppression in South Africa. As Albertyn notes:

> Ideas of equality in South Africa emerged from the crucible of struggles against the deep political, social and economic inequalities that were inscribed and normalised in colonialism, segregation, apartheid, patriarchy and South Africa's particular brand of racialised accumulation and capitalism.[119]

Hassim points to the history of women's fight for liberation and illustrates how the right to equality was an important claim made by women, including Black women in articulating their demands.[120] Similarly, Cachalia has argued that though incomplete, the Constitution is a product of radical anti-colonial resistance.[121] While this history is partial and sits alongside other radical traditions in the struggle against colonialism and apartheid, we should not negate its value and importance.

From a pragmatic perspective, it's important to note that the Constitution is not the sole cause, nor the only remedy for prevailing inequality. As Cachalia argues,

> Questions of fundamental structural change present additional questions of political choice as well as of constraint on policy-making under conditions of global capitalism and democratic politics. Such questions cannot be treated simply as ones about the constitutional text and its interpretation.[122]

Further, as I discussed earlier in the chapter, transformation is a process,

> a way of looking at the world that creates a space in which dialogue and contestation are truly possible, in which new ways of being are constantly explored and created, accepted and rejected and in which change is unpredictable but the idea of change is constant.[123]

The text and the contested normative foundations of the Constitution did not lock us in time. The Constitution worked to get us through the negotiation of the democratic transition. The contents of the Constitution should not be seen as having closed the door for normative disagreement.[124] Rather, the Constitution has given us a 'framework for dealing with these unresolved questions through democratic practices of dialogue and contestation'.[125] The outcomes will depend on the work of grassroots social movements,

Rights 33: The authors review the Constitutional Court's s 25 judgments and argue that while there has been some progressive legal interpretation, the courts have yet to develop a comprehensive and coherent approach to realising the transformative potential in s 25, the property clause. See also N Sibanda, 'Amending Section 25 of the South African Constitution to Allow for Expropriation of Land without Compensation: Some Theoretical Considerations of the Social-Obligation Norm of Ownership' (2019) 35(2) *South African Journal on Human Rights* 129.

[119] Albertyn, 'Contested Equality' (n 41) 443.

[120] Hassim (n 6) 348.

[121] Cachalia (n 107) 389.

[122] ibid 388.

[123] Langa (n 19) 354.

[124] Cachalia (n 107) 383.

[125] ibid 385.

civil society, lawyers and judges, in the legislative choices made in Parliament, and decisions by the executive – all this against the background of larger global forces.

Finally, the institutional critique accepts Klare's vision of transformative constitutionalism. However, in examining the courts' jurisprudence, proponents of this approach argue that the courts have failed to realise the Constitution's transformative mission. According to Davis, the South African courts have not been faithful to the transformative mission of the Constitution.[126] In particular, he argues that 'the community of constitutional interpreters' has been subversive to the Constitution's transformative ambition.[127] This is because not much has been done 'to deconstruct the core of the South African legal system' and disrupt 'laws that have sustained dispossession and patterns of economic inequality that continue to run so markedly along race lines'.[128]

Overall, the ideal of transformative constitutionalism and its promises are rightly subject to a lot of contestations. As described above, the abolitionist critiques gesture towards a decolonised, post-conquest constitution that would eschew what proponents of this approach consider to be a Western, liberal, and Eurocentric ideology. Constitutional abolitionists are sceptical of the constitutional drafting process, the text of the Constitution, the Constitution's underlying ideology, and the community of interpreters tasked with giving effect to the Constitution. On the other hand, the institutional critiques accept the logic of the 1996 constitutional arrangements and limit their critique to the failure to implement and give effect to this vision. My argument is that we should move outside of this debate – and think of the South African Constitution and the project of transformative constitutionalism as enablers of non-reformist reform.

IV. NON-REFORMIST REFORM

> To believe that we can both work toward fundamental change while simultaneously engaging in incremental reform efforts requires that we identify what reforms move us toward transformational change, or at least those that do not move us away from it.[129]

As I have stated above, there is merit to the constitutional abolitionist and institutional critiques of transformative constitutionalism. That said, it is important for us to imagine a third path to thinking about and working with the Constitution. As public lawyers in South Africa, we should be stirred by the urgency of the need for the millions who live under the boot of exploitative and dehumanising systems of domination and oppression – racial capitalism, white supremacy, and patriarchy being salient. The abolitionist perspective renders all attempts at working with the Constitution futile. The institutional perspective overly centres on the failure to implement and give effect to the Constitution; it does not question or imagine the different ways in which the Constitution may itself be insufficient for transformative change. The proposal that follows seeks to shift us from the inertia that arises from the abolitionist and institutional critique of the Constitution. It bears emphasis that, as will be clear below, I do not believe that this third

[126] Davis (n 6).
[127] ibid 100.
[128] ibid 372.
[129] Stahly-Butts and Akbar (n 18) 1547.

path will deliver transformation, only that the Constitution has features that can pave the path for a transformed future – the use of these features in the design of non-reformist reforms is a worthwhile emancipatory project.

So, what is non-reformist reform? The best way to understand non-reformist reforms is to distinguish them from reformist reforms. First, according to Gorz, '[a] reformist reform is one which subordinates its objectives to the criteria of rationality and practicability of a given system and policy'.[130] What this means is that reformist reforms do not question the existing arrangements in society – they work within the system. They also 'reflect a liberal rather than fundamental critique' and thus conceive of problems 'as discrete rather than structural'.[131] By contrast, non-reformist reforms are 'conceived not in terms of what is possible within the framework of a given system and administration, but in view of what should be made possible in terms of human needs and demands'.[132] As explained by Evans, 'non-reformist reforms are those that push the boundaries of the possible, contributing towards changing the systems and structures within which they take place rather than shoring up the established order of things'.[133]

Second, while reformist reforms reify the status quo, non-reformist reforms seek to undermine existing power arrangements; they work to widen the cracks in the edifice of these arrangements.[134] According to Fraser, non-reformist reforms have a double face:

> [O]n the one hand, they engage people's identities and satisfy some of their needs as interpreted within existing frameworks of recognition and distribution; on the other hand, they set in motion a trajectory of change in which more radical reforms become practicable over time. When successful, nonreformist reforms change more than the institutional features they explicitly target. In addition, they alter the terrain upon which later struggles will be waged.[135]

Third, the goal of non-reformist reform is not the outcome of individual reforms – the 'reform is not the end goal; transformation is'.[136] By contrast, reformist reforms are less ambitious, the reforms are the goal. Non-reformist reforms are not concerned with what is possible within the given framework but with what *should* be made possible. Non-reformist reforms, 'seek to delegitimate the underlying system in service of building new forms of social organization'.[137] Further, 'they seek to create or sustain ideological crisis – as a way to provoke political action and develop consciousness among the public about the possibility of an alternative and our collective capacity to build it together'.[138]

While they are a step ahead of reformist reforms, non-reformist reforms are not in and of themselves going to lead to the kind of fundamental change and vision of transformation advocated in the abolitionist critique. However, they 'aid in the ongoing collective project of transformation'.[139] Fraser's typology provides a good illustration of how

[130] Gorz (n 9) 7–8.
[131] Stahly-Butts and Akbar (n 18) 1551.
[132] Gorz (n 9) 7–8.
[133] M Evans, 'Land and the Limits of Liberal Legalism: Property, Transitional Justice and Non-Reformist Reforms in Post-Apartheid South Africa' (2021) 48 *Review of African Political Economy* 646, 649.
[134] See the discussions in Stump (n 9); Akbar (n 1).
[135] Fraser and Honneth (n 17) 79–80.
[136] Akbar (n 1) 103.
[137] ibid 104.
[138] ibid.
[139] Stahly-Butts and Akbar (n 18) 1458.

non-reformist reforms differ from those interventions that are revolutionary or merely reformist. Seeking to answer the question, 'what remedies can help eradicate injustices related to the maldistribution of resources and recognition harms?', Fraser distinguished between affirmative and transformative strategies for achieving justice. According to Fraser, affirmative strategies 'aim to correct inequitable outcomes of social arrangements without disturbing the underlying social structures that generate them'.[140] In contrast, transformative strategies 'aim to correct unjust outcomes precisely by restructuring the underlying generative framework'.[141] The key difference is that 'whereas affirmation targets end state outcomes, transformation addresses root causes'.[142] While Fraser was clear that 'transformative strategies' were preferable, she noted that they were difficult to affect and rarely feasible.[143] Thus, she saw the value of some affirmative strategies – affirmative strategies that can have *transformative effects* if they are radically and consistently pursued – non-reformist reforms.[144]

According to Akbar and Stahly-Butts, 'The transformation sought through radical reforms will depend both on the critique of the underlying conditions and the horizon that motivates the organizing efforts.'[145] In our case, the latter is an upending of exploitative and dehumanising systems of domination and oppression, including racial capitalism, white supremacy, and patriarchy in the 'afterlife of colonial-apartheid' in South Africa.[146]

Now that we have clarity on the meaning of non-reformist reform and its purpose, it's important to note that the language and practice of non-reformist reforms can be co-opted into mainstream reformism. The question, then, is how can we tell whether reform is merely reformist or non-reformist? In their work on non-reformist reform and prison abolition, Akbar and Stahly-Butts have mapped a helpful list of features of non-reformist or what they call 'radical reform'. According to the authors:

> A radical reform: (1) shrinks the system doing harm … (2) relies on modes of political, economic, and social organization that contradict prevailing arrangements and gesture at new possibilities; (3) builds and shifts power into the hands of those directly impacted, who are often Black, brown, working class, and poor; (4) acknowledges and repairs past harm; and (5) improves, or at least does not harm, the material conditions of directly impacted people.[147]

Not every non-reformist reform will or needs to meet all five features described in the quote above.[148] At a minimum, a non-reformist reform should not worsen the material conditions of those affected. A non-reformist reform cannot pave the path towards future

[140] Fraser and Honneth (n 17) 74.

[141] ibid.

[142] ibid.

[143] According to Fraser, 'transformative strategies are highly vulnerable to collective action problems. In their pure form, at least, they become feasible only under unusual circumstances, when events conspire to wean many people simultaneously from current constructions of their interests and identities': Fraser and Honneth (n 17) 78.

[144] ibid.

[145] Stahly-Butts and Akbar (n 18) 1551.

[146] The term 'afterlife of colonial-apartheid' is borrowed from JM Modiri, *The Jurisprudence of Steve Biko : A Study in Race Law and Power in the 'Afterlife' of Colonial-Apartheid*, PhD Thesis (University of Pretoria, 2018), available at https://repository.up.ac.za/handle/2263/65693. I use it here to describe the continued impact of colonialism and apartheid in South African society.

[147] Stahly-Butts and Akbar (n 18) 1552.

[148] ibid.

transformation if, in the present, it worsens the material conditions of the oppressed. It bears repeating that the end goal of these individual reforms is not the reform itself; they serve to map the path for transformation. Further, 'No single reform can fundamentally change political, social, and economic conditions. The rubric is meant to contribute to analysis of whether, and how, a specific reform will assist in social transformation.'[149]

Looking back at the departures from 'classic liberal constitutions' identified by Klare, the Constitution offers opportunities for the design of non-reformist reforms. As an example, section 9(2) of the Constitution, which provides for the taking of positive and redistributive measures, is relied on to design and implement affirmative action measures which are remedial and restitutionary in nature.[150] These measures target and benefit Black people, women, and persons with disabilities. These measures have been most effective in the workplace, especially in the public sector.[151] Recently, this provision was relied on to justify COVID-19 relief policies, which gave preferential treatment to groups disproportionately affected by the COVID-19 pandemic – Black people and women.[152] This provision can also be used in the struggle for material reparations for the injustices of colonial and apartheid domination and oppression – this possibility is not foreclosed.[153] Section 9(2) of the Constitution has the potential to enable non-reformist reforms that meet at least three of Akbar and Stahly-Butts' criterion. First, it allows for reforms that shrink the system doing harm – mandating the redistribution of resources to the dispossessed, dominated and oppressed, and to those disproportionately affected by disaster and disease. Second, the provision is rooted in the acknowledgement of past harm and the need to repair it. It takes seriously historical colonial and apartheid domination and

[149] ibid 1564.

[150] In the landmark case, *Minister of Finance and Other v Van Heerden* 2004 6 SA 121 CC, the Constitutional Court held that measures taken under section 9(2) were not a breach of the right to equality, instead, 'such measures are not in themselves a deviation from, or invasive of, the right to equality guaranteed by the Constitution. They are not "reverse discrimination" or "positive discrimination"... They are integral to the reach of our equality protection'. See also *National Coalition for Gay and Lesbian Equality and Another v Minister of Justice and Others* 1999 1 SA 6 [61]; N Ramalekana, 'What's So Wrong with Quotas? An Argument for the Permissibility of Quotas under s 9(2) of the South African Constitution' (2020) 10 *Constitutional Court Review* 252; C Albertyn, 'Adjudicating Affirmative Action within a Normative Framework of Substantive Equality and the Employment Equity Act – An Opportunity Missed – South African Police Service v. Solidarity OBO Barnard' [2015] *South African Law Journal* 711; P De Vos, 'The Past Is Unpredictable: Race, Redress and Remembrance in the South African Constitution' (2012) 129(1) *South African Law Journal* 73.

[151] See the report from the 20th Commission for Employment Equity, 'Annual Report 2019–2020', available at www.labour.gov.za/DocumentCenter/Reports/Annual%20Reports/Employment%20Equity/2019%20-2020/20thCEE_Report_.pdf.

[152] For an analysis of the case law wherein the courts affirmed the constitutionality of the use of these criteria to distribute COVID-19 relief, see, C Albertyn, 'Section 9 in a Time of COVID: Substantive Equality, Economic Inclusion and Positive Duties' (2021) 37(2) *South African Journal on Human Rights* 205; V Myandazi, N Ramalekana and L Somolekae, 'An Equality-Sensitive Approach to Redressing the Disproportionate Socio-Economic Impact of Covid-19 on Vulnerable Groups in Botswana, Kenya, and South Africa' in J Mavedzenge (ed), *COVID-19 Pandemic and Socio-Economic Rights in Selected East and Southern African Countries* (Juta Ltd, 2020). For a sample of the case law see: *Solidarity Obo Members v Minister of Small Business Development and Others, Afriforum v Minister of Tourism and Others* (21314/20) (21399/2020) [2020] ZAGPPHC 133 (30 April 2020); *Democratic Alliance v President of the Republic of South Africa and Others* (21424/2020) [2020] ZAGPPHC 326 (29 July 2020).

[153] An example of emerging research on the use of the equality right for reparations is an argument for the introduction of a wealth tax. J Winchester, 'Too Taxing, Too Much Taxing, or Not Progressive Enough? The Introduction of a Wealth Tax as an Equality Imperative in South Africa' (2022) 37(4) *South African Journal on Human Rights* 512.

oppression and seeks to repair this.[154] Third, it improves the social and economic standing of its beneficiary classes.

A second example is the horizontal application of rights. As discussed earlier in this chapter, section 8(2) of the Constitution expressly provides for the horizontal application of rights.[155] This is an acknowledgement that apart from the state, private individuals and especially corporations, can exercise power over other individuals.[156] Without this acknowledgement, this power would remain unseen and unchallenged, but it would continue to be felt. This provision has been used to stop a private trust from evicting a school on privately owned property,[157] another private trust from preventing a tenant from improving the conditions of her home,[158] and it has also been used to strike down a will whose impact would perpetuate patriarchal notions of women's capacity and worth.[159] In this way, this provision can serve as reform that would meet at least four of the criterion suggested by Akbar and Stahly-Butts. First, the horizontal application of rights can shrink the system of private power and the harm it poses to individuals and communities. In the *Juma Musjid* case, for example, the recognition that private trusts have a negative obligation not to interfere with the exercise of the right to education is a bulwark against using private property rights against vulnerable communities.[160] Second, it shifts power into the hands of disadvantaged groups by creating obligations, both negative and positive, on the part of those who exercise private power.[161] This creates room for positive action and the basis for holding private actors accountable for their actions. Third, in acknowledging the institution of private power, the horizontal application of rights contradicts prevailing arrangements, creating possibilities where private power is not only felt but is seen, challenged and subject to control. Fourth, in the imposition of positive obligations and the remedies made possible by the horizontal application of rights, it can change the material conditions of people for the better.

Third, while the protection of private property in our Constitution is undeniably an instrument that has entrenched the spoils of colonial conquest and apartheid domination and oppression – this is not the end of the story. The Constitution mandates land

[154] In *Van Heerden* (n 150) [25] the Constitutional Court noted that 'our Constitution heralds not only equal protection of the law and non-discrimination but also the start of a credible and abiding process of reparation for past exclusion, dispossession, and indignity within the discipline of our constitutional framework'.

[155] According to s 8(2) of the Constitution, 'A provision of the Bill of Rights binds a natural or a juristic person if, and to the extent that, it is applicable, taking into account the nature of the right and the nature of any duty imposed by the right.'

[156] This understanding of the horizontal application of rights – that they apply in cases where the economic, social and/or cultural institution creates a power difference between parties draws on the work of G Bhatia, *Horizontal Rights: An Institutional Approach* (Hart Publishing, 2023) (pre-published manuscript viewed with permission from author).

[157] *Juma Musjid* (n 45).

[158] *Scribante* (n 45).

[159] *King NO and Others v De Jager and Others* (n 46).

[160] *Juma Musjid* (n 45) [60].

[161] That the horizontal application of rights applies in relation to positive and negative obligations was confirmed by the Constitutional Court in a judgment where Justice Madlanga held that 'Whether private persons will be bound depends on a number of factors. What is paramount includes: what is the nature of the right; what is the history behind the right; what does the right seek to achieve; how best can that be achieved; what is the "potential of invasion of that right by persons other than the State or organs of state"; and, would letting private persons off the net not negate the essential content of the right?' (and not whether the obligation at hand was positive or negative): *Scribante* (n 45) [39]–[41].

redistribution and reform. Section 26(5) of the Constitution requires the state to 'take reasonable legislative and other measures, within its available resources, to foster conditions which enable citizens to gain access to land on an equitable basis'. In the landmark *Adonisi* decision, grassroots social movements, including *Reclaim the City* and the non-governmental organisation *Ndifuna Ukwazi*, relied on section 26(5) to stop the City of Cape Town from selling publicly owned property to a private developer.[162] The core of this victory is the recognition, for the first time, that the state has an obligation to redress the legacy of 'spatial apartheid'.[163] According to the court,

> given the Constitution's broader goals of redress in relation to land in particular, and the advancement of substantive equality, the phrase 'on an equitable basis' must imply a pattern of access, holding, and the use of land that is designed to alleviate inequality in terms of race, gender and other relevant criteria.[164]

Further, section 26(7) of the Constitution provides that '[A] person or community dispossessed of property after 19 June 1913 as a result of past racially discriminatory laws or practices is entitled … either to restitution of that property or to equitable redress.' That these provisions have yet to completely alter the patterns of land ownership in South Africa sits alongside the victories of movements of landless and homeless people, who use and subvert these provisions to occupy land and fight for redressing spatial inequality rooted in apartheid segregationist policy.[165] Moreover, the conversation about land redistribution is not foreclosed. Recently, a bill was tabled before Parliament urging the expropriation of land without compensation.[166] While the bill did not pass into law, it is an example of the opportunities that remain open in the struggle to pave a path to transformation. These struggles occur alongside and against the protection of private property in the Constitution. They have the potential to pave the path for larger transformations by shrinking the meaning of 'ownership' and by creating space for new uses of land and new ways to re-acquire and repurpose land for the benefit of the dispossessed.

My core argument is that the promises in the Constitution cannot in and of themselves herald transformation. However, non-reformist reforms have the potential to undermine the subordination, domination and oppression inherent in exploitative and dehumanising systems of racial capitalism, white supremacy, and patriarchy. There is still room to work in the folds of the 'departures' from classic liberal constitutionalism outlined earlier in the chapter to recommit the community of constitutional interpreters to what I believe is still possible – eradicating inequality and redressing the injustice of past domination

[162] *Adonisi and Others v Minister for Transport and Public Works Western Cape and Others; Minister of Human Settlements and Others v Premier of the Western Cape Province and Others* (7908/2017) (12327/2017) [2020] ZAWCHC 87; (2021) 4 All SA 69 (WCC) (31 August 2020).

[163] For an analysis of the history of spatial apartheid in Cape Town, see ibid 95–103.

[164] ibid 71; For a critical discussion of this case and the latent possibilities in the Constitution's property clause, see M Shandu and M Clark, 'Rethinking Property: Towards a Values-Based Approach to Property Relations in South Africa' (2021) 11 *Constitutional Court Review* 39.

[165] I have in mind movements like Reclaim the City in Cape Town, who, alongside organisations like *Ndifuna Ukwazi*, have used protest action and the law in the struggle for affordable housing and dismantling spatial apartheid. To learn more about these movements see, 'Lessons for Change', available at www.lessonsforchange.org/reclaim-the-city/.

[166] The Expropriation Bill 2020 [Government Gazette No 43798]; For an analysis of the possibilities that expropriation without compensation would open, see Sibanda (n 118).

and oppression. A part of this is accepting the limitations of law, legal interpretation and process in effecting change while also constructively working to contribute to the legal culture necessary to allow for transformation. This is, to me, the promise of non-reformist reform. It is using the tools available to us to erode the structures and institutions on which prevailing inequality is based.

V. CONCLUSION

In this chapter, I have explored the meaning of transformative constitutionalism in South Africa. I illustrated that at the core of this approach to constitutionalism is a departure from some features of classic liberal constitutionalism. I explored the critique levelled against transformative constitutionalism and discussed the abolitionist and internal critiques of transformative constitutionalism. If we accept that 'every mode of reasoning used by lawyers, every application of legal principles to a specific scenario and every method of argumentation based on legal materials involves a normative and contestable vision of law and social and political life',[167] and if we agree that at the heart of the new Constitution is a commitment to transformation, to redress the past and ongoing racial, gender and forms of injustice, to *recover* what is lost and *recover* as a people, our ideas about what is possible through the Constitution can and should be guided by holding the tension between the promise of transformation and the known limitations of non-reformist reform. More importantly, I have argued that non-reformist reform requires a deep commitment from all enabling institutions and the people. We cannot give up now that we are faced with trouble bringing forth a new society. The struggles are a part of the work.

[167] Modiri (n 102) 471.

Part II

Making Public Law in the Common Law Tradition

8

The Beginnings of Judicial Review

JOHN BAKER

IT IS USUAL to trace the foundation of English liberties to Magna Carta, and the claims of the great charter to its place in history cannot justly be denied. Yet the resounding words of clause 39 (chapter 29 in the statutory version[1]) said nothing of remedies. It was not until the development of *habeas corpus* in the Elizabethan period that an adequate remedy was devised to protect the liberties of the subject, and that is the true beginning of judicial review in its modern form, followed soon after by the development of *mandamus* and *certiorari*. This important aspect of England's history has been largely ignored, since it has been hidden in manuscripts which few have cared to read.

The classical works on English constitutional history, including Maitland's lectures as printed posthumously,[2] tellingly used the language of 'constitutional history' rather than the history of constitutional *law*,[3] and they focused on the growth of Parliament and governmental institutions rather than on judicial decisions. There was little mention of cases before the seventeenth century, and nothing much on the prerogative writs before 1679, when the first Habeas Corpus Act seemed to be the main landmark. The few cases that did intrude were those generated by the events that led to the Civil War and then to the Glorious Revolution. Over the last 50 years we have become attuned to broader ideas of public law following the explosion of judicial review proceedings and the burgeoning scholarship of human rights. These innovations were still far off in Maitland's day; and throughout the twentieth century legal historians passed over public law to concentrate on land law, contract and tort. Yet judicial review has a longer history than is usually supposed. What has kept the story in the shadows is the dearth of relevant law reports.[4]

According to Sir John Dodderidge, king's serjeant, speaking in the House of Commons in 1610, the year books and law reports contained little public law, which had instead to be sought in the formal records of Parliament, Chancery and Exchequer. The year books,

[1] Lawyers in the early-modern period took no notice of the 1215 charter, which had no legal effect, whereas the revised charter of 1225 was received as a statute. See below, n 13.

[2] FW Maitland, *Lectures on Constitutional History: A Course of Lectures* (edited by HAL Fisher) (Cambridge University Press, 1908).

[3] There is, however, a discussion in Maitland's final lecture of the nature of constitutional law and whether it differed from administrative law (as Austin had supposed). Maitland's autograph lecture-notes in Cambridge University Library [CUL] (MSS Add 6996-6997) do not have a title; but the first lecture is headed 'Sketch of English *public law* at the end of Edward I's reign' (emphasis added).

[4] As far as the printed materials went, a thorough and valuable pioneering account was given by SA de Smith, 'The Judicial Writs' (1951) 11 *Cambridge Law Journal* 40–56.

he said, were 'nothing else for the most part but the reports of private suits'.[5] Reported cases on matters of public law were indeed rare before the time of Elizabeth I. Even the Elizabethan cases were not generally transmitted to posterity. Most reporters were students or barristers educated in a tradition which omitted public law from the curriculum – perhaps because it was politically risky, but also because it was remote from most barristers' professional concerns – and they put away their pens when such cases did occasionally come before the courts. There was therefore a self-perpetuating convention of exclusion, not unlike the myopia which affected English legal historians subsequent to Maitland. Nevertheless, the subject was of practical interest to judges and law officers, and it is chiefly from their long-unpublished notebooks that we are able to trace the beginnings of the story. There were some significant public-law cases in Dyer's reports, though they were cut out by the editors in 1585 and not printed until 1993.[6] Coke's notebooks, likewise, contained a good deal of public law which he did not feel able to publish. Some found its way into print in the 1650s,[7] while the rest has only just gone to press this year.[8] The shortage of information about public law in the courts, at any rate before the seventeenth century, helps to explain why most student books of constitutional sources – beginning with Bishop Stubbs's *Select Charters*[9] – were filled with bare documents, principally statutes and administrative records, rather than legal arguments and judgments. Even the voluminous case law of the seventeenth century, to the extent that it was noticed in the old books at all, came from the State Trials rather than the ordinary law reports; and the State Trials were compiled from pamphlets produced primarily for public consumption rather than professional use. It was understandable to suppose that constitutional law was not a subject for lawyers and courts.

The focus of early public law was the royal prerogative and the powers, whether executive or judicial, derived from it. The extent of those powers was a matter of law and not merely of usage. As *Bracton* observed, the king must be under the law, because it is the law which makes him king.[10] But the common law allowed the king certain prerogative powers, and it was the role of the king's courts to ensure that prerogative actions and functions did not stray over the boundaries. In that connection, the topics of concern in

[5] ER Foster (ed), *Proceedings in the Parliament of 1610* vol II (Yale University Press, 1966) 205. It is notable that Sir Matthew Hale's *The Prerogatives of the King* (edited by DEC Yale) (92 SS 1976), which was the first major treatise on English constitutional law (c 1660), made extensive use of records but none at all of unpublished case law.

[6] JH Baker (ed), *Reports from the lost Notebooks of Sir James Dyer* (110–111 SS 1994–95) ('*Dyer's Notebooks*'). Dyer was king's serjeant under Mary I and chief justice of the Common Pleas 1559–82.

[7] *The Twelfth Part of the Reports of Sir Edward Coke* (H Twyford and T Dring, 1658), containing cases from Coke's fourth and sixth notebooks; *Certain Select Cases in Law, reported by Sir Edward Coke* (J Sherly, H Twyford and T Dring, 1659), with cases from the fifth notebook. These were translations from the original Law French and contain errors. An extended new edition will appear in 2025.

[8] J Baker (ed), *Reports from the Notebooks of Edward Coke* (136–40 SS 2022–23) ('*Coke's Notebooks*'). These five volumes cover the period 1572–1600. The autograph notebooks continue to 1606 (when Coke was appointed to the bench) and two further volumes will complete the edition. Coke was solicitor-general 1592–94, attorney-general 1594–1606, knighted 1603.

[9] W Stubbs (ed), *Select Charters and Other Illustrations of English Constitutional History from the Earliest Times to the Reign of Edward the First* (Clarendon Press, 1870).

[10] Henry de Bracton, *On the Laws and Customs of England*, vol II (SE Thorne (trs)) (Harvard University Press, 1968) 33. It is no longer thought that Bracton was the author.

the medieval and early-modern periods presented themselves in different contexts from those of today. For instance, given the many different kinds of court – Coke listed over 70 species, most of them not statutory in origin[11] – a great part of public law was about jurisdictional boundaries and the general superintendency exercised by the King's Bench over other judicial institutions. However, it should be remembered that some important courts and tribunals – for instance the Exchequer, the Court of Wards, the Quarter Sessions, and the Commissions of Sewers – combined significant administrative responsibilities with judicial roles.[12] In controlling such authorities, the underlying issues were not fundamentally different from those which are now approached through the language of administrative law, judicial review and human rights. The problem is to uncover how they were dealt with, and when the basic principles emerged, given that none of this terminology existed until modern times.

I. THE RELATIVE INEFFECTIVENESS OF MAGNA CARTA

The principal starting point is chapter 29 of the charter of 1225. Although its wording was hardly changed from that of clauses 39–40 in the charter of 1215, King John's charter had never taken effect. It was the version of 1225 which was regarded by lawyers as the first English parliamentary statute. (Few modern historians acknowledge that; but it all depends on the definition of Parliament.[13]) Chapter 29, still in force today, contained the stirring if imprecise guarantee that no free person would be imprisoned, dispossessed or otherwise ruined except by judgment of his peers or by the law of the land, and that the king would not sell, deny or delay right and justice. In 2015 the world celebrated the eighth centenary of the great charter, and the Selden Society made its contribution by publishing an edition of some late-medieval lectures on Magna Carta in the inns of court. These long-forgotten commentaries turned out to reveal something more interesting than the specific contents.[14] By the fifteenth century, it seems, Magna Carta was not seen by lawyers as a constitutionally significant document. It was just a collection of technical legal principles, many of them obsolete, and most of them too vaguely worded to mean very much without a substantial gloss. In practical forensic terms, the commentators were right. Yet they had missed the potentiality of chapter 29, which they were content to explain with breath-taking literalism, and unthinking word-association, as being mainly about trial by peers in Parliament and not charging fees for writs of right or *justicies*. Selling justice, on this interpretation, was forbidden only in the case of manorial and county courts.

[11] They are discussed, one by one, in 4 Co Inst.

[12] It was not until 1888 that county government was removed from the justices of the peace in their Quarter Sessions.

[13] See J Baker, *The Reinvention of Magna Carta 1216–1616* (Cambridge University Press, 2017) 6–11. The previous versions might be seen as unilateral concessions, and the original version of 1215 had been unilaterally repudiated almost as soon as it was sealed. But the words towards the end of the 1225 charter state that it was granted in return for a fifteenth given to the king by the bishops, abbots, priors, barons, knights, freeholders and 'everyone of our realm', which can only have been the outcome of a major assembly in which everyone of the realm was deemed to be represented.

[14] J Baker (ed), *Selected Readings and Commentaries on Magna Carta 1400–1604* (132 SS 2015).

During the centuries when the great charter enjoyed its long slumber, the year books have little to tell us about public law in the courts. A notable exception was *Sir John Lee's Case* in 1368, when the chief justices sitting at Chelmsford expressed their indignation at a commission from the Chancery to arrest a named person and seize his chattels without due process.[15] Such a commission was simply void. The law report omitted to mention the current political background. Lee was already in the Tower of London, accused of extortion, and Parliament had only just reconfirmed Magna Carta and its requirement of 'due process and original writ, according to the old law of the land'.[16] The judicial indignation is more easily explained by that context than by any previous current of unwritten doctrine. But the brief report was embedded in the *Liber Assisarum*, first printed in 1514, and for legal purposes that was enough. It was almost the only medieval case on personal liberty which could be cited in succeeding centuries, and it was indeed cited over and over again as proving that the king could not authorise imprisonment or the confiscation of property outside the law of the land.

There were not enough reported cases of the like kind to create a medieval jurisprudence around chapter 29 of Magna Carta. The 1368 case was just an application of the principle – seldom spelt out explicitly – that the king could do no wrong. The idea has often caused mystification in recent times. I remember an external examination candidate in the 1960s writing: 'The queen can do no wrong. That is why she has ministers, to do the wrong for her.' There may have been a hint of truth underlying the howler. In fact, kings were better placed to do wrong *de facto* than anyone else, and were not above actually doing it; but the principle meant that kings could not *de jure* authorise wrongs, and therefore a commission, patent or administrative decision which threatened to harm a subject contrary to law could be treated as void for legal purposes. This principle prevented the king from granting authority to dispense with serious criminal offences or to pardon private wrongs for which subjects were entitled to a remedy. It prevented the use of a commission, as in the Chelmsford case, to seize a man's person or property without due process. It was deployed in 1406 to strike down a charter authorising the chancellor's court of Oxford University to proceed according to the Civil Law of Rome, since that would infringe the right of every subject to be governed by the common law of England.[17] And it was used in 1461 to strike down a writ of protection whereby a party on royal service at the Roman Curia was placed outside the reach of the law for three years, the legal limit for a protection being one year. As Moyle J observed, the king was bound by law to do right to all his subjects, and he was unable to do that if someone was granted exemption from legal proceedings for a lengthy period.[18] That was another way of saying that the king could do no wrong. If something wrong was done in his name, it could be quashed.[19]

[15] *Sir John atte Lee's Case* (1368) Lib Ass 42 Edw 3, pl 5; Baker (n 13) 58–60.

[16] 42 Edw 3, c 3.

[17] *Peddington v Otteworth* (1406) 88 SS 166. This was known to Coke: Yale Law School MS G R24.1, fo 190 (autograph note); Baker (n 13) 385 (citation in 1612). The same principle later denied Oxford University a jurisdiction in equity: *Perrot v Mathew* (1588) *Coke's Notebooks*, 137 SS 372.

[18] *Abbot of Glastonbury v Lax* (1461) YB Hil 39 Hen 6, fo 38, pl 3.

[19] This was clearly explained around 1660 by Hale (n 5) 14–15.

An ancillary principle of some importance was that the king could not acquire or part with real property except by matter of record. It required parchment, court-hand and Latin. Courts were thereby enabled, by reviewing the records in question, to strike down grants of things to which the crown was not entitled and to moderate the interpretations of royal grants. The courts could even grant relief where the relevant property was in the king's own hands: the remedy there was a petition of right,[20] which was a suit *to* the king rather than against him. No doubt property claims should generally be considered outside the scope of public law, even when the king was a party. But when real property included 'franchises' granted by the crown, and when these could include jurisdictional and administrative powers, the boundary seems less distinct, especially since such franchises could be taken away for misuse, disuse or abuse.[21]

II. ABSOLUTE AND ORDINARY ROYAL PREROGATIVES

Those, in outline, were the roots from which English public law grew; but they were a far cry from judicial review as we know it today. The administrative functions of both central and local government were largely beyond legal control, save in the daily work of the Court of Exchequer – a court rarely visited by law reporters (or by historians) and certainly not a tribunal minded to develop robust principles of judicial review. In the last resort, the coercive power of government was enforced by imprisonment. But imprisonment by the king or his ministers was hardly ever questioned before the sixteenth century, and we do not even know how common it was. The theoretical explanation, in the case of central government, is that decisions by the king and his council were *arcana imperii*, mysteries of state, akin to the exercise of powers under the absolute prerogative. The more practical explanation is that 'the crown' was not an entity separate from the king, and the king could not be sued in his own courts. Any remedy had to be indirect, as in the Chelmsford case,[22] and it was to little avail if authorities followed standard written procedures. It was said in the year books that the king could not personally arrest anyone, because there would be no way of challenging it.[23] But the reason given amounted to an admission that such an arrest was not justiciable.[24]

Nevertheless, we should not be tempted to suppose – as some modern commentators have done – that the starting point in the history of public law was a wide-ranging absolute royal prerogative, gradually chipped away at over the centuries. The very distinction between absolute and ordinary prerogatives, first encountered in English legal vocabulary in the Tudor period, proves that the absolute prerogative was circumscribed by law and had to be defined. Coke was fond of the expression, found in Plowden's *Commentaries*,

[20] Associated remedies to the same end were the *monstrans de droit* and the traverse to an inquisition. See further WS Holdsworth, 'Remedies against the Crown' in *History of English Law*, vol 9, 1st edn (Methuen & Co, 1926) 7–32.

[21] Here the public remedy against the franchise-holder was *quo warranto*, brought by the crown: see below.

[22] A noteworthy example not in the reports was *Bildeston's Case* (1344) KB 27/336, Rex, m 33 (82 SS 31), where a writ from the king himself to receive and detain a prisoner 'until we send you further order' was held invalid. This was cited by Selden in the debate on the liberty of the subject, 3 St Tr 109.

[23] *Anon* (1485) YB Mich 1 Hen 7, fo 4, pl 5.

[24] See *Serjeant Browne's Case* (1532) *Spelman's Reports*, 93 SS 183 (misdated 1540); below (n 35).

that the common law 'admeasured' the king's prerogative:[25] in other words, it set and controlled the boundaries. As he famously wrote in 1610, the king has no prerogative but that which the law of the land allows him.[26] By 'the law of the land', he meant the judges of the King's Bench and Common Pleas.

Coke identified only nine absolute prerogatives around 1600,[27] and the catalogue had not been significantly whittled down since the thirteenth century. They were: (1) a negative voice to any statute to be made; (2) dispensation with penal laws; (3) appointing judges and justices; (4) pardoning offences; (5) issuing coinage; (6) setting a value on the coin; (7) making treaties and declaring war; (8) summoning and dissolving Parliament; (9) making denizens. Of those nine, only the dispensing power has been completely abolished (in 1689), though the first is never exercised and some of the others have been modified or overtaken by Acts of Parliament. Coke's list was no doubt incomplete, perhaps deliberately selective. For instance, imprisoning people without showing the reason, declaring martial law, and even using torture, were still asserted (albeit controversially) as prerogatives until 1628;[28] the right to intercept communications was claimed as late as 1984; the prorogation of Parliament was regarded as an absolute prerogative until 2019; and the power to create peers remains unchecked to this day. It is nevertheless apparent that, although there have been some important reforms, the broad outlines of the absolute prerogative have not changed. As for the ordinary prerogatives of the crown, and the routine business which was managed through commissions, patents and writs under the king's seals, those were the subject of frequent litigation and reported cases throughout the medieval and early-modern periods.

The reason why medieval public law in the courts was limited to the scrutiny of letters patent, commissions and inquisitions is that judicial review (in so far as it existed[29]) was chiefly limited to matters of record. There was no effective remedy against the crown in respect of governmental functions which were exercised off the record, whether orally or on paper.[30] In any case, effective 'admeasurement' of the prerogative was dependent on the availability of remedies, and there were not many relevant remedies to be found in the old register of writs. It had been enacted in 1267 that actions for damages could be founded on Magna Carta, but for some reason this was not pursued.[31] The earliest known example of an action on Magna Carta was in 1501, when there began a number of challenges to the coercive jurisdiction of the new Court of Requests.[32] These were not exactly

[25] Plowd 236; 3 Co Inst 84. It was quoted four times in Coke's commonplace books: *Coke's Notebooks*, 136 SS cxli n 9.

[26] *Case of Proclamations* (1610) 12 Co Rep 74, 2 St Tr 723. This was not a decision in court, but the opinion of Coke CJ and three other judges on a reference from the Privy Council.

[27] *Coke's Notebooks*,138 SS 589.

[28] Coke was prominent in securing the Petition of Right 1628 (3 Car 1), which extinguished the first two unequivocally. Torture was judicially outlawed by *R v Felton* (1628) 3 St Tr 371 (with Coke's contemporary approval: 3 Co Inst 48).

[29] The term itself was originally used for the review of judgments by inferior courts, eg by writ of error or bill of review in Chancery. In its modern sense it may be no older than the twentieth century. Some earlier authors preferred to call it 'judicial control'.

[30] The petition of right and the closely similar *monstrans de droit* were limited to property and money claims and were predicated on previous records.

[31] Statute of Marlborough 1267 (52 Hen 3), c 5. Although actions could not be brought against the king, they could in theory have been brought against officials acting in the king's name.

[32] Baker (n 13) 97–99, 456–62.

actions against the central government, but they were challenges to the prerogative power with respect to the erection of new kinds of jurisdiction without parliamentary authority. Few of the actions resulted in judgment, and the formula devised in 1501 was not to be a vehicle for later development.[33] As with the action of trespass for false imprisonment, the main shortcoming of such actions was that they lay only for damages after the event; and it was not always obvious who to name as defendants. It was hardly politic in Tudor times to sue officers of state and ministers of the government, and it did not happen.

The difficulties were brought home in 1532 after a serjeant at law had been committed to prison on the orders of King Henry VIII for advising suspects in the Tower of London to sell their goods to avoid the possibility of forfeiture by attainder. The serjeant was soon released, but he complained to the Privy Council, and all the judges were summoned to give their advice whether the king could commit people to prison at his discretion. The judges were evidently embarrassed by the question, even though no remedy was being sought. They pointed out that it was against Magna Carta for the king to treat his subjects contrary to the law of the land, but they also pointed to an enactment of 1275 that a person committed by the king's command was not bailable:[34] so that *was* the law of land. They concluded that the king could send someone to prison, and that his discretion was not to be disputed, although in principle he ought not to do it without giving reasons.[35] A few years later the king sent the same serjeant and two other lawyers to the Tower for giving advice on tax avoidance, and kept them there until a legislative solution could be devised. Both cases were reported by Sir John Spelman, a King's Bench judge, but they were not printed until 1976.[36]

III. EXTENDING THE PREROGATIVE WRITS

A new chapter in public law began in the sixteenth century with the development of the three prerogative writs of *habeas corpus*, *mandamus* and *certiorari*. Unlike ordinary original writs emanating from the Chancery, these were issued by and returnable immediately in the common-law court which issued them. They had the further unusual feature that they were not brought against defendants but were orders to explain something in a 'return', so that the court could review the explanation. In the case of *habeas corpus* – the first of the three, historically – the order was to produce the body of a prisoner and certify the cause of his detention. In place of a judgment there was just another administrative order for discharge, bail or remand, given without recorded reasons. The absence of pleadings, jury trial, damages, or a judgment susceptible to a writ of error, might be seen as shortcomings of the procedure. But they were its strength. Since there was no defendant, the new procedure could be used to challenge coercive measures taken in

[33] An attempted revival in 1595, also aimed against the Requests, was stamped on by the Privy Council: *Parsons v Locke* (1595) CP 40/1540, m 401; British Library [BL] MS. Hargrave 7A, fo. 148v; other manuscript reports cited in Baker (n 13) 277–28, 484–87; 26 *Acts of the Privy Council* 92–93.

[34] Statute of Westminster I 1275 (3 Edw 1), c 15.

[35] *Serjeant Browne's Case* (n 24); Baker (n 13) 100–01.

[36] 94 SS 351. The lawyers all held office under the crown and were treated as having broken their oaths to serve the king; they were released the following month on paying fines and finding sureties. Spelman J noted this as a news story; there were no judicial proceedings.

the king's name, whether by central government or by the new prerogative jurisdictions, tacitly applying the old idea that the king could do no wrong. Such writs earned the name 'prerogative writs' in the early seventeenth century. It was a cleverly chosen name, devised to reinforce an ingenious if fragile underlying principle. In practice, they were often used to challenge exercises of prerogative authority, and that might seem a radical and daring innovation fraught with danger for the judges. But their use was made palatable to the sovereign by representing them as a way of exercising a higher prerogative, that of keeping all ministers, institutions and jurisdictions within the law. It was the practical mechanism whereby the king, through his own court,[37] discharged the duty of his coronation oath to uphold the law.[38] The proceedings were brought on behalf of the king, not against him. They were brought to fulfil the prerogative, not to destroy it. Even Stuart kings could accept that as an underlying principle.[39]

The main prototype was the medieval writ of prohibition, which was designed to keep ecclesiastical courts within their bounds. In the context of jurisdictional disputes with the Church, seen as a competing authority, it made sense for that writ to recite that encroachments on royal jurisdiction were 'against the king's crown and dignity'. Prohibition was also used against admiralty courts, which were likewise seen as competitors. Another prototype was *quo warranto*, initiated by the attorney-general to challenge encroachments on royal authority by those claiming franchises.[40] But these older writs were brought against defendants and were therefore not available to 'admeasure' the prerogative or to review the administrative actions of the crown.[41] The vehicle for most of the new development in the second half of the sixteenth century was, instead, the writ of *habeas corpus*.[42]

IV. *HABEAS CORPUS* IN THE TIME OF ELIZABETH I

It is difficult to attribute the new development to a single cause. Many of the cases reflect unease about the growing jurisdiction of new tribunals created under the prerogative, while others resulted from the actions of royal favourites who treated the law with contempt. No doubt Elizabeth I's personality was a factor in creating the right atmosphere, as was the sympathetic legal mindset of her enlightened chief minister William Cecil, Lord Burghley (ancient of Gray's Inn, secretary of

[37] The King's Bench was notionally held *coram rege seipso*, before the king himself. Coke made much of that, to emphasise its authority, though he took pains to ensure that James I did not take it literally and attend in person: *Prohibitions del Roy* (1608) 12 Co Rep 63. (The strange title 'Prohibitions del Roy' was a misreading by the editors of 1658; the case concerned writs of prohibition, and Coke's heading was 'Prohibitions. Roy'.)

[38] Hale (n 5) 14–15.

[39] Baker (n 13) 310–11, 485, 512–13.

[40] Since the obsolescence of the eyre, such proceedings were no longer commenced by writ but by an information in the nature of *quo warranto*. For Elizabethan examples see *Coke's Notebooks*, 136 SS introduction, cxxxvi.

[41] Coke, as attorney-general, opened up the possibility of a wider use for the procedure by using it to challenge exorbitant patents of monopoly: *Coke's Notebooks*, 136 SS introduction, cxxxix.

[42] The important study by PD Halliday, *Habeas Corpus from England to Empire* (Harvard University Press, 2010) makes full use of the records but begins the story later, with an important case of 1605 (see n 69, below).

state 1558–72, lord treasurer 1572–98).[43] We know from Coke's private notes, corroborated by a recollection of Thomas Egerton's, that the queen explicitly instructed her law officers on appointment not to stretch her prerogative beyond its legal bounds.[44] It is difficult to imagine her father doing the like. But the story of *habeas corpus* unfolded in Westminster Hall, not in the corridors of power. The start of the new era is revealed in the long-unpublished notes of the three chiefs at the beginning of the reign: Sir James Dyer (chief justice of the Common Pleas 1559–82), Sir Robert Catlin (chief justice of the King's Bench 1559–74) and Sir Edward Saunders (chief baron of the Exchequer 1559–76). It may not be a coincidence that they were all alumni of the Middle Temple, where William Fleetwood played a role in reawakening Magna Carta from its deep sleep, where Edmund Plowden wrote (in his *Commentaries*) of admeasuring the prerogative, and where (a few years later) Robert Snagge and James Morice would give lectures reintroducing Magna Carta and constitutional monarchy into everyday legal discourse.[45]

By the 1580s the whole profession was imbued with the new learning. Coke, as a junior barrister of the Inner Temple, reported a decision in 1587 that the King's Bench could never in justice deny a writ of *habeas corpus*, that the return had to be certain because it deprived a man of his liberty, that the return had to be sufficiently specific for its legal validity to be assessed, and that the court should adjudge solely upon the return without regard to extraneous circumstances. The authorities cited in the margin, perhaps added later, included chapter 29 of Magna Carta.[46] The connection between Magna Carta and *habeas corpus* – a legal connection, of course, rather than a historical mistake – had been made by Edmund Anderson of the Inner Temple in 1572.[47] But the beginning of the story may be traced beyond that.

Both Dyer and Saunders made detailed notes of a case in 1560 which set the judges thinking seriously about the potentiality of *habeas corpus*.[48] Mary I had unlawfully granted an office in the Common Pleas, while the chief justiceship was vacant, to a young courtier without the requisite technical knowledge.[49] Dyer CJ had rejected the grantee as an untrained layman and nominated an attorney called Scrogges. The earl of Bedford and Lord Dudley then used improper influence to procure a special commission to determine

[43] Burghley praised Magna Carta: *Att-Gen* v *Sheriffs of London* (1588) BL MS Harley 358, fo 201v, quoted in Baker (n 13) 268. He opposed self-incrimination through the oath *ex officio*, which he said was 'too much savouring of the Roman inquisition': J Strype (ed), *The Life and Acts of John Whitgift* (1718) app, 64, quoted in Baker (n 13) 260, fn 57.

[44] *Coke's Notebooks*, 138 SS 474, 573; 3 Co Inst 79; 2 Bulst 44. See also Baker (n 13) 149.

[45] For Fleetwood, see Baker (n 13) ch 6. Robert Snagge gave the first known reading devoted entirely to Magna Carta, c 29, in 1581: ibid 251–55. James Morice had prepared the way with an important reading on the prerogative in 1578. For Morice and the 'Puritan' lawyers serving in Parliament, see ibid 255–61. For Plowden see n 25, above.

[46] *Arundell's Case* (1587) *Coke's Notebooks*, 137 SS 324.

[47] *Marshall's Case* (1572) BL MS Hargrave 8, fo 163; CUL MS Hh.2.9, fo 61; Harvard Law School [HLS] MS 1192, fo 25. For the use made of Magna Carta, c 29, in legal arguments in the 1580s see Baker (n 13) 249–75.

[48] The parent King's Bench writ was of greater antiquity but it had chiefly been used to move prisoners, in order to alter their place of trial. The *corpus cum causa* form had long been used to remove private suits from London and other local courts into the Chancery.

[49] The office belonged to the chief justice to grant. It was a perquisite for which some consideration might be received, but it was always granted to a qualified person.

the title, with power to commit Scrogges if he refused to co-operate.[50] Since Scrogges did decline to co-operate, he was committed to the Fleet Prison for contempt and then applied to the Common Pleas for his release. The commissioners were exercising a newly invented, ad hoc power of imprisonment. But what could be done? Dyer CJ considered using a general *habeas corpus cum causa detentionis*, which he thought could be issued under the inherent jurisdiction of the court ('*ex officio curiae*'), though there was no reported precedent of it being used in the Common Pleas.[51] Such a writ was prepared but not sealed. On reflection it was thought better to rely on Scrogges's status as an attorney and release him on a writ of privilege, which was a well-established special form of *habeas corpus*. Scrogges was promptly rearrested by the commissioners, 'to be kept in close prison', and he remained in the Fleet for over five weeks until Sir Nicholas Bacon LK intervened with the commissioners to secure his release. The judges were deeply affronted by the high-handedness of the commissioners, and retrospectively declared the commission void. It was calculated, in Dyer's words, as 'a check to the law'. Saunders CB wrote with feeling about the case, adding in his report that 'all such of the judges of the Common Pleas as did learnedly and willingly agree to the awarding and executing of the same writ of privilege deserved the immortal fame of honourable and good judges'.[52] In the end, Scrogges was obliged to accept a compromise. But the current had been turned on.

Dyer and Catlin CJJ immediately began collecting and sharing precedents of general writs of *habeas corpus* whereby the King's Bench had in the past discharged or bailed prisoners committed by statesmen. The first example they found was in 1518 when Robert Sheffield, a bencher of the Inner Temple, was incarcerated by Cardinal Wolsey LC. What they did not know was that Sheffield had been rearrested and died in the Tower. Nor did they know that the true reason for the arrest seems to have been Sheffield's attempt to defend the rule of law against Wolsey's arbitrariness. It was enough that the return, showing a committal to prison by the lord chancellor without cause shown, had not precluded bail. Dyer CJ also found a case where the King's Bench judges had overturned a committal by Thomas Cromwell, though it seems they only performed this audacious feat shortly after Cromwell's fall and execution.[53] Dyer's collection was used by Coke after he came into possession of Dyer's notebook, and Coke went on to find many more precedents in the rolls of the Crown Office, some of them going back to the time of Henry VII. There were no reports of these cases, just records, and so the background to them was obscure; but the bare record was enough to show what the court could do when confronted with an inadequate return.

The newfound potential of *habeas corpus* was put to use in 1562, when the King's Bench granted an immediate discharge to a gentleman who had been committed to custody

[50] *Scrogges' Case* (1559–60) Dyer 175; 109 SS 34, 54–57; Baker (n 13) 156–57. In his answer, Scrogges relied on Magna Carta, c 29: BL MS Lansdowne 1057, fo 3.

[51] He found a formula in a 15th-century Common Pleas precedent book: 109 SS 54. It differed in some respects from the later formula, but it had the essential 'cum causa' clause, requiring the recipients to return the cause of detention to the court.

[52] *Saunders' Reports*, BL MS Hargrave 9, fo 22v. Saunders had been chief justice of the King's Bench from 1557 until January 1559, when he was demoted to chief baron.

[53] Baker (n 13) 161, tentatively identified as *Foster's Case* (1541) KB 29/174, m 38, which was known to Coke (Baker (n 13) 505).

by Sir Ambrose Cave, chancellor of the duchy of Lancaster, 'for various contempts within the duchy'.[54] As with the other cases, there must be more to the story than is revealed by the short entry on the roll. The main problem with all *habeas corpus* cases from the precedential point of view, as became notorious in the debates on the liberty of the subject in 1627–28, was the want of pleadings or any indication in the record why bail was given or withheld. But the 1562 case provided a clear precedent on the face of the record for discharge without bail where a return was inadequate.

Two important cases followed in 1565, both in connection with jurisdictional disputes. The first was that of John Lamburne, imprisoned by the Council of the North at York. The sheriff returned to Lamburne's *habeas corpus* that the archbishop had commanded his gaoler to disobey the writ and so the body could not be produced in the King's Bench. The court was dismayed by what appeared to be a direct snub, and Catlin CJ declared:[55]

> In this court we hold pleas before the queen herself, because this is the queen's highest court – whatever those of the Chancery might say – and it is of such dignity that, in whatever prison a man may be, we may command the officer to bring him here. Even if he is a prisoner in the Tower by command of the Council, we may send for him here by writ of *corpus cum causa* directed to the constable of the Tower … And we do not use to set out in the writ why we send for anyone, but reserve that in our breast, since it may be for treason or great conspiracy.[56]

The court not only ordered a further *habeas corpus*, but also a writ of attachment against both the archbishop and the gaoler.[57] The reports do not disclose that Lamburne was in fact a criminal who had turned queen's evidence against some robbers.[58] That, however, was not the point. The court had no judicial notice of the surrounding circumstances. It was for the King's Bench to decide on the lawfulness of an imprisonment, and without a proper return they could not do so.

The other case in 1565 provides the first instance of *habeas corpus* for a prisoner of the ecclesiastical High Commission, which was established in 1559. Edward Mytton, a Shropshire gentleman, was imprisoned for hearing mass (an indictable misdemeanour) and was released by the King's Bench on the grounds that the commissioners could not imprison. He was promptly rearrested; and this further example of high-handedness was 'much debated' by the judges, apparently without a satisfactory resolution,[59] though in the course of proceedings a valuable precedent of 1465 was discovered in the plea rolls showing that *habeas corpus* could be used in an ecclesiastical case.[60] Three years later, in

[54] *Robert Cooke's Case* (1562) KB 29/196, m 19 (translated). Cooke was nevertheless ordered to appear in the King's Bench from day to day.

[55] R Crompton, *L'authoritie et Jurisdiction des Courts* (1594), ff 78v–79 (tr). He cited the case of the imprisonment by Cardinal Wolsey, and Whiddon J referred to the story of Prince Henry (later Henry V) being committed to prison by Gascoigne, chief justice of the King's Bench.

[56] The point of this last remark was that the King's Bench was not restricted to using writs of privilege, which were only for its officers and litigants. The same point was made in *Arundell's Case* (1587) *Coke's Notebooks*, 137 SS 324. *cf* n 62, below.

[57] *John Lamburne's Case (*alias *Lambert)* (1565) KB 29/199, m 31. The case was noted as a precedent by Christopher Yelverton (BL MS Hargrave 430, fo 181) and by Coke (Baker (n 13) 506).

[58] See the archbishop's letter in MAE Green (ed), *Calendar of State Papers Domestic (Elizabeth): Addenda*, vol 12 (Her Majesty's Stationery Office, 1870) 554.

[59] *Mytton's Case* (1565) KB 29/199, m 31 (the same role as Lamburne); *Dyer's Notebook* 109 SS lxxix, 107. Mytton was subsequently indicted at common law, but died in 1568 before trial.

[60] *Kayser's Case* (1465) KB 27/818, m 143d; *Dyer's Notebook* 109 SS 108; Baker (n 13) 120. The *habeas corpus* here was a writ of privilege for a litigant. Coke knew of the case from Dyer's notebooks.

1568, the Common Pleas released a prisoner of the High Commission who had refused to incriminate himself upon the oath *ex officio*. Here, as in Scrogges's case, the prisoner was an attorney entitled to privilege, and this provided the formal justification for the involvement of the Common Pleas.[61] Though not reported in print, it stood as the first clear decision affirming the privilege against self-incrimination.[62] Thereafter the common-law courts were consistently opposed to the use of the oath in the case of laymen.[63]

During the same period, the King's Bench granted bail on *habeas corpus* to a person imprisoned by the Chancery for contempt,[64] and to a prisoner of the Court of Requests.[65] Dissatisfaction with the Requests, a newish jurisdiction with no statutory foundation, would lead the Common Pleas in 1598 to declare (without any real effect) that it had no coercive powers at all.[66] The Requests was not overcome at that time, because it was given protection by the Privy Council; but continued challenges from the common-law courts paved the way for its demise in the 1640s. The High Commission and the provincial councils were likewise subjected to numerous assaults by writs of *habeas corpus* over a period of some 80 years before their abolition in 1640.[67] These were prerogative courts – tribunals created under the royal prerogative rather than by statute[68] – but the remedies were given in the name of a superior prerogative and with the support of the law officers. In a *habeas corpus* case of 1605, Coke, attorney-general at that time, explained:

> Even if the king gives authority by his commission to some person to execute justice, or the law does so by Act of Parliament, nevertheless the examination thereof – as to what may be done by such authority – must remain in the absolute and supreme power of the king, that is, in his Bench, which is the proper seat of justice. And although there are no law reports to be found to prove this, yet he said that he had by search found infinite precedents to prove the continual use of it.[69]

He was referring to the precedents of *habeas corpus* found in the rolls of the clerk of the crown. But the great question was how far *habeas corpus* could reach towards the seat of government, the Privy Council, which was deemed to speak with the queen's own voice.

Dyer CJ expressed the view in 1577 that a general or unspecific return could not be reviewed in the case of a committal by the whole Privy Council, because there might

[61] In the 16th century only the King's Bench could use *habeas corpus* without reference to privilege. The assertion in Baker (n 13) 354 that the Common Pleas under Coke CJ began to award *habeas corpus* without a suggestion of privilege is probably mistaken. In the principal case of *Bulbrook* v *Roper* (1607) BL MS Lansdowne 1061, fo 47v, Roper was a Common Pleas litigant (in prohibition); moreover, although the Common Pleas approved a *habeas corpus*, he obtained a writ in the King's Bench (KB 21/3, fo 34v).

[62] *Thomas Lee's Case* (1568) *Dyer's Notebook* 109 SS 143; copy of the *habeas corpus*, tested by Dyer CJ, in BL MS Harley 7648, fo 267v; Coke's memorandum (1604) on Magna Carta, c 29, 132 SS 399; Baker (n 13) 506. It was frequently cited by Coke CJ in the following century.

[63] The clergy were not so fortunate: *Maunsell's Case* (1607): as to which see Baker (n 13) app 9.

[64] *John Astwyke's Case* (1566) KB 29/201, m 35d; cited in Moo 839.

[65] *Humfrey's Case* (1572) BL MS Add 35941 fo 30; 109 SS lxxxi n 67: as to which see Baker (n 13) 162 n 108.

[66] *Stepneth v Lloyd* (1598) *Coke's Notebooks*, 140 SS 950; 4 Co Inst 97.

[67] 16 Car 1, c 10. Sometimes called the Star Chamber Abolition Act, this also abolished the two provincial councils, the Duchy Court of Lancaster and the Exchequer of Chester. The High Commission was abolished by 16 Car 1, c 11.

[68] The High Commission was founded on the Act of Supremacy 1559, 1 Eliz 1, c 1, but it was contended that it had a wider jurisdiction derived from the inherent royal supremacy.

[69] *Whetherley v Whetherley* (1605) BL MS Lansdowne 1075, fos 101v–103v, translated in Baker (n 13) 512. This remark was in response to Francis Bacon's assertion that interference in this way with the Council in the Marches would damage the royal prerogative.

be secret reasons which it would not be appropriate to make public.[70] Nevertheless, the King's Bench in 1567 and again in 1578 granted bail to a prisoner sent to the Tower by the Privy Council without cause shown,[71] and in 1587 it held that anyone imprisoned by the whole Council was entitled to be brought before the court so that the lawfulness of the imprisonment could be examined.[72] Thus, as Catlin CJ had asserted in 1565, even the Privy Council could not place someone completely beyond the eyes of the law. But it was an empty remedy, since the judges formally conceded in 1592 that they could not review a general return in the case of an imprisonment by the queen or the full Council.[73] The prisoner had his day in court, but then had to be sent back to prison. Despite a lone protest from Walmsley J in 1601, this remained the position until the Petition of Right 1628.[74] The initial victory – and it was an important one – lay in outlawing arbitrary imprisonment by individual ministers, courtiers and officials, and ultra vires orders of committal by non-statutory tribunals. Most privy councillors probably accepted the justice of this, and when sitting in the Star Chamber they themselves kept a watchful eye on local magistrates and sheriffs to ensure that they did not exceed their duties.[75]

V. *MANDAMUS* AND *CERTIORARI*

Habeas corpus was, obviously, limited to restraints on bodily liberty. It was supplemented in the seventeenth century by the revival of *de homine replegiando* – originally devised to examine questions of villein status – since it lay in some cases where *habeas corpus* did not, and in appropriate cases offered the additional advantages of jury trial and compensation in damages. But there were other kinds of liberty which were not adequately protected (if at all) by *habeas corpus* or actions for damages.[76] The two further media of judicial review, *mandamus* and *certiorari*, were developed in the seventeenth century to fill some of the gaps.[77] They were originally aimed at local government: *mandamus* against municipal authorities, *certiorari* against the county administration. The first of them, chronologically, was *mandamus*. Fractious behaviour in urban government was commonplace by 1600 and sometimes resulted in arbitrary abuses of position by those in authority. A freeman might be disenfranchised, which would deprive him of a vote;

[70] *Hynde's Case* (1576–77) HLS MS 2071, fo 88; quoted in 109 SS lxxx n 61. *cf* 4 Leo 21 ('because it may concern the state of the realm, which ought not to be published').

[71] *Robert Constable's Case* (1567) KB 29/201, m 68; *John Brownyng's Case* (1578) KB 29/213, m 73d (Brownyng was perhaps the Cambridge Puritan).

[72] *John Howell's Case* (1587) 1 Leon 70; Baker (n 13) 166.

[73] *Memorial from the Judges* (1592) 1 And 297; Baker (n 13) 166–69, 496–98. An earlier version, signed in autograph by all the judges on 9 June 1591, is in the Burghley Papers, BL MS Lansdowne 67(87).

[74] *John Bate's Case* (1601) noted in J Baker, *English Law Under Two Elizabeths: The Late Tudor Legal World and the Present* (Cambridge University Press, 2021) 49–50.

[75] Baker, ibid 52–53, 75–76.

[76] Eg it was not decided until *Ashby* v *White* (1702) 2 Ld Raym 938, after much debate and dissension, that an action on the case lay against a returning officer for rejecting a valid vote in a parliamentary election.

[77] The story below is told mainly from the reported cases. The full story lies in the records. The original returns are in the King's Bench *recorda* files (KB 145 to 1689, then KB 16) and the proceedings in court may be followed in the controlment rolls (KB 29) and the rule books (KB 21). The pioneering study by EG Henderson, *Foundations of English Administrative Law* (Harvard University Press, 1963), made good use of the controlment rolls but did not use the files, which were not then available, or the manuscript reports.

an alderman, town-clerk or recorder might be removed on trumped-up or exaggerated charges of misconduct; an elected mayor might be kept out of office. *Mandamus* was nurtured as a 'writ of restitution' (its original name) in the time of Popham CJ (d. 1607) and his successor Fleming CJ (d. 1613).[78] It worked by ordering the municipal corporation to restore the applicant, whereupon the corporation could make a return justifying its conduct for the court to review. The command in the writ was not peremptory, but was a way of initiating a judicial review.[79]

The earliest reported example in the King's Bench, in 1606,[80] involved an element of *habeas corpus* as well as restitution, since the complainant had been imprisoned;[81] but *mandamus* rapidly became an independent procedure in regular use, and there were several reported cases in the next few years testing its limits.[82] It was a judicial invention; but in 1615 Coke CJ attributed it (like *habeas corpus*) to chapter 29 of Magna Carta – not as a matter of history, of course, but of legal doctrine – and went so far as to announce:

> To this court of King's Bench belongs authority not only to correct errors in judicial proceedings, but other errors and misdemeanours extrajudicial tending to the breach of peace or oppression of the subjects, or to the raising of faction, controversy, debate or any manner of misgovernment; so that no wrong or injury, either public or private, can be done but that it shall be reformed or punished by the due course of the law.[83]

This bold and extensive reformulation of the rule of law drew an indignant rebuke from Lord Ellesmere LC prior to Coke's downfall the following year:

> In giving excess of authority to the King's Bench, [Coke] doth as much as insinuate that this court is all sufficient in itself to manage the state. For if the King's Bench may reform any manner of misgovernment (as the words are), it seemeth that there is little or no use either of the king's royal care and authority exercised in his person and by his proclamations, ordinances and immediate directions, nor of the Council Table,[84] which under the king is the chief watch-tower for all points of misgovernment, nor of the Star Chamber, which hath ever been esteemed the highest court for extinguishment of all riots and public disorders and enormities.

He went on indignantly to accuse Coke of claiming for the King's Bench 'a superintendency over the government itself, and to judge wherein any of them do misgovern'.[85] That

[78] Baker (n 13) 203–206.

[79] *cf* the command 'praecipe' in, eg, a writ of debt.

[80] Here again the Common Pleas had led the way: *Middleton's Case* (1574) Dyer 332. But it was an isolated case.

[81] *R v Mayor of Cambridge*, ex parte *Tompson* (1606) KB 29/246, m 125; tr in Henderson (n 77) 163–67; judgment, KB 21/3, fo 72; reported in BL MS Lansdowne 1075, fo 189v; MS Add 35954, fo 444v; 1 Rolle Abr 456. Tompson was one of the bailiffs of Cambridge and had been displaced without good cause after a disagreement with the mayor.

[82] Most of the reported cases escaped the printing press: eg *R v Burgesses of Stamford*, ex parte *Loveday* (1609) KB 29/249, m 138d; reported in CUL MS Mm.6.69, fos 113, 117v; *R v Mayor of Lincoln*, ex parte *Shuttleworth* (1613) KB 29/255, m 23; *Calthorpe's Reports*, BL MS Hargrave 385, fo 115; *R v Mayor of Boston*, ex parte *Midlecott* (1615) KB 29/ 257, m 103; *Calthorpe's Reports*, fo 353v.

[83] *R v Mayor of Plymouth*, ex parte *Bagg* (1615) 11 Co Rep 98; also reported in 1 Rolle Rep 224; record in KB 29/259, m 76.

[84] ie Privy Council.

[85] Lord Ellesmere, 'Observations on Coke's Reports', BL MS Hargrave 254, fo 40, printed in LA Knafla (ed), *Law and Politics in Jacobean England: The Tracts of Lord Chancellor Ellesmere* (Cambridge University Press, 1977) 307 (here modernised).

was, indeed, exactly what Coke was claiming; and it has been the foundation of English administrative law ever since. It may have seemed preposterous to the lord chancellor in 1616. But leaving the review of misgovernment to the government itself, whether in the person of the king or through his Privy Council, or the Council in the Star Chamber,[86] was obviously not satisfactory to an aggrieved subject. In any case, his exasperation with Coke's sweeping claim, and his desire to be rid of him, had led Ellesmere to exaggerate the potential range of *mandamus*. The writ did not lie against the crown, or against a minister of the crown, and therefore was not (until 1968) available to challenge misgovernment at the highest level.[87] Moreover, it was still a writ of restitution, limited to public offices and positions, or freehold offices which existed 'for the common weal'.[88] It did not lie to enforce private contracts of employment or to compel the performance of official duties.

The last of the prerogative writs, *certiorari*, became established slightly later. The formula had long been used for removing indictments and other records into the King's Bench from lower courts of record,[89] and Coke found a year-book case in which something similar was used to review a decision by justices of the forest.[90] Like prohibition, it lay only to control courts; but there were several courts in the seventeenth century which exercised governmental functions. In the first half of that century it began to be used to review fines imposed by commissioners of sewers or convictions by justices of the peace exercising summary jurisdiction.[91] It operated formally in the same way as in the past, since the writ merely ordered that the record be sent up to the King's Bench, and the bare record was all that the return contained. But it began to be used to enable a judicial review of decisions and orders already made. For evidence of this newer function we are dependent on law reports. More or less invisible before the 1640s, it became a standard procedure during the later seventeenth century for challenging orders made by quarter sessions – in effect, the county local government – such as the assessment of rates, the settlement of paupers, and affiliation orders.[92]

The development may have been connected with the abandonment of oversight of local government by the assize judges in the middle of the seventeenth century, though that cannot be the full explanation.[93] The first reported debate about the extension of the remedy seems to have occurred in 1642, when *certiorari* was used successfully to remove

[86] These were closely similar bodies with much the same membership. The principal difference was that the Star Chamber usually sat in public and heard cases brought before it by a judicialised procedure.

[87] This was confirmed in *R v Treasury Commissioners* (1872) LR 7 QB 387; *R v Secretary of State for War* [1891] 2 QB 326. The position was changed by *Padfield v Ministry of Agriculture* [1968] AC 997.

[88] *Cock's Case* (1658) 2 Sid 112.

[89] For earlier uses see de Smith (n 4) 458. For its use in Chancery see WJ Jones, *The Elizabethan Court of Chancery* (Oxford University Press, 1969) 187–89.

[90] *Case of the Forest of Pickering* (1347) YB Mich 21 Edw 3, fo 48, pl 70; 4 Co Inst 294. It was not called *certiorari*, and the proceedings were initiated by *scire facias*. Coke called it a *venire facias recordum*.

[91] See K Costello, 'The Writ of Certiorari and Review of Summary Criminal Convictions 1600–1848' (2012) 128 *LQR* 443–65. It was presumably this use of the writ which occasioned complaints in 1621 that it was issued too frequently, resulting in judges' rules to regulate it: JF Larkin and PL Hughes (eds), *Stuart Royal Proclamations*, vol I (Oxford University Press, 1973) 513, no 217.

[92] See K Costello, 'The King's Bench and the Poor Law 1630–1800' (2014) 35 *Journal of Legal History* 3–26.

[93] See J Baker, 'Equity and Public Law in England' in J Baker, *Collected Papers on English Legal History*, vol II (Cambridge University Press, 2013) 956–60. The Star Chamber also had exercised some control over local government before its abolition in 1640, but it was chiefly concerned with criminal misconduct.

and quash an order made by commissioners of sewers. Although it was resisted as a new departure, once again the prevailing principle was that no inferior authority was beyond the scope of judicial review by the King's Bench.[94] Bramston CJ remarked in passing that he did not think the writ would be much used,[95] though in that prediction he was much deceived. The procedure rapidly gained a foothold because it suited all parties not to challenge it.[96] It relieved complainants from having to wait for an unlawful order to be enforced against them so that they could bring a civil action for damages or a replevin,[97] and it settled the status of the order itself rather than just the issue between the parties. Unlike *quo warranto* and *habeas corpus*, therefore, but like prohibition, *mandamus* and *certiorari* were purely public-law remedies. They lay only in respect of public authorities or courts.[98]

VI. JUDICIAL REVIEW OF THE CENTRAL GOVERNMENT

The five prerogative writs gave the King's Bench an extensive armoury to correct various forms of misgovernment. But there was one remaining obstacle to the court's judicial supremacy. The power of the Privy Council to imprison people without giving reasons, confirmed by the whole judiciary in 1592, was usually defended with reference to treasonous plots, since one of the major functions of the Council was to authorise and make preparations for state trials. Even Coke, both as law officer and as lord chief justice, accepted the need for secrecy in such cases.[99] But imprisonment could also be used in connection with more politically controversial ends, such as the enforcement of monopolies and extra-parliamentary taxation. Imprisonment for breaking monopolies was being challenged by 1595.[100] But the main battle-ground was to be taxation.

The first outcry over prerogative taxation concerned impositions. In *Customer Smyth's Case* (1598), concerning an imposition on alum, and in *Bate's Case* (1606), concerning an imposition on currants, the Court of Exchequer held that the king had an absolute prerogative power to lay impositions on imported merchandise.[101] As Fleming CB pointed out in

[94] *Comyns v Masham* (1642) March NR 196; HLS MS 113, 1705; KB 29/291, m 39 (writ and return); KB 21/13, fo 14 (decree affirmed); followed in *Re Newton and Tydd St Giles* (1648) Style 178, 184, 191; KB 29/297, m 33 (writ); KB 21/13, fos 120v–127v (rules). The 1642 case is discussed in Henderson (n 77) 101–106. For earlier but unreported precedents, see ibid 93–101. I am grateful to Paul Warchuk of St John's College, Cambridge, who is completing a dissertation on the history of *certiorari* (1600–1800), for a helpful discussion of the subject.

[95] From the citation of the case in *Re Newton*, as reported in *Barnard's Reports*, BL MS Add 25222, fo 166 (reversing).

[96] This was emphasised in *Comyns v Masham* (n 94). *cf Apsley's Case* (1648) Style 85, where the procedure seems to have gone unchallenged.

[97] Eg, in respect of commissioners of sewers, *Wythers* v *Rookes* (1598) *Coke's Notebooks*, 139 SS 844, 5 Co Rep 99 (replevin); *Keighley's Case* (1609) 10 Co Rep 139 (action on the case); *Hetly v Carryer* (1614) 2 Buls 197 (replevin). These were all brought in respect of distraints to enforce the orders.

[98] This was at first true de facto of *habeas corpus* also. No examples have been found of *habeas corpus* against private individuals before the time of Charles II, but it was then used (eg) to liberate wives from cruel husbands and young children from relatives seeking to force them into marriages.

[99] *Ruswell's Case* (1615) 118 SS 453; *Saltonstall's Case* (1615) 1 Rolle Rep 219; Baker (n 13) 401 n 342.

[100] *Leathersellers' Company v Darcy* (1598) Baker (n 13) 168, 196.

[101] *Att-Gen v Smyth* (1598) *Coke's Notebooks*, 139 SS 873; *Att-Gen v Bate* (1606) Lane 22. The imposition on alum was effected by the queen's letters under the privy signet. That on currants was effected by letters patent addressed to the lord treasurer, though a proclamation on the subject was later issued in 1615.

Bate's Case, the only losers were wealthy epicures who had to pay a little more for their currants; but the principle at stake was fundamental. The decision caused a major stir and was frequently debated in the Commons, where it was the subject of lengthy historical and legal discourses. Coke and Popham CJJ were of the view that new import duties could be imposed for the public good – for instance, in order to achieve parity with duties imposed by foreign governments – but that there was no general prerogative power of taxation.[102] Even more controversial were the forced loan of 1626, which caused a furore in Parliament and was not ruled upon decisively,[103] and the ship-money levy imposed in 1636, which was only upheld by a bare majority of the judiciary in 1638.[104] All these taxes were non-statutory, imposed under the king's prerogative, and earnestly contested. But by this time the judicial robustness of Coke's day had waned, not to mention the judges' independence. Coke had been dismissed from office in 1616, and his successor Sir Randall Crewe was dismissed 10 years later for opposing the loan. Those were heroic moments, but they fostered a sense that the judges who remained in office might no longer be as independent as in the past.

VII. CONCLUDING REFLECTIONS

The control of local government by means of *mandamus* and *certiorari* grew to become a major part of King's Bench business before 1700.[105] However, after the failure of the judges of the King's Bench in 1627 to strike down the forced loan, the protection of the subject from unconstitutional taxation and arbitrary imprisonment passed for a time to the High Court of Parliament, where the arguments of the lawyer members (some of whom had represented the Five Knights) stood a better chance of success. Coke had returned to Parliament in 1621, and – after being himself imprisoned without cause shown in 1621 and 1622[106] – he now recanted his former opinion about imprisonment by the king or the Privy Council.[107] In 1628 he was the chief promoter of the Petition of Right, which (with the king's grudging assent) guaranteed 'that no man hereafter be compelled to make or yield any gift, loan, benevolence, tax, or such like charge without common consent by Act of Parliament' and that no one could be imprisoned without cause shown.[108] That did not assist Hampden when he contested

[102] *Case of Impositions* (1606) 12 Co Rep 33.

[103] Its enforcement by imprisonment was contested in *The Five Knights' Case* (1627) 3 St Tr 1, but the returns to the writs of *habeas corpus* deliberately did not disclose the reason for the imprisonment, and therefore the only issue was whether the king could commit people to prison without giving reasons.

[104] *R v Hampden* (1638) 3 St Tr 1127 (Exchequer Chamber). Five judges supported Hampden, who had declined to pay a tax of £1 for the construction of warships, but seven voted for the crown.

[105] Some statutes which conferred new powers on justices of the peace contained provisions excluding judicial review, doubtless because the local magistrates serving in the Commons were anxious to protect their own autonomy.

[106] For his imprisonment in 1621 see *Coke's Notebooks*, 136 SS introduction, cx.

[107] He excused his former opinion on the grounds that 1615 was 'an ill time': 3 St Tr 81–2 (1628).

[108] The judges were equivocal when consulted by Charles I about the Petition of Right in May 1628. Not wishing to commit themselves extrajudicially, they advised him 'that by the general rule of law the cause of commitment by his majesty ought to be shown, yet some case may require such secrecy that the king may commit a subject without showing cause *for a convenient time*'; and that 'Every law after it is made hath its exposition, and so this petition and answer must have an exposition as the case in the nature thereof shall

ship-money;[109] but in 1640 Parliament reversed the judgment in the ship-money case and guaranteed the availability of *habeas corpus* in all cases of committal by the king or the council.[110] The role of the House of Commons in establishing these basic principles of public law during this turbulent period is well known and beyond the scope of the present chapter. It is enough to observe that it was a very different body from its successor today. It was not tied by party politics to do the Government's bidding. Its members came, in Selden's words, 'bound by the trust reposed in them by their country that sent them' to defend their freedoms.[111] Some of the members had themselves been imprisoned as loan-refusers. Most importantly, the House was full of distinguished lawyers, always chaired by a prominent lawyer, and frequently resounded with technical arguments of the highest quality, replete with legal and historical citations. Legal history was both a vocational subject and a force in politics. The lawyers in the Commons – and their lay supporters – thought they were defending an ancient inheritance represented by Magna Carta and *habeas corpus*, and they tried their utmost to ensure that the king (and Parliament itself) stayed within the rule of law. In that respect the Commons had taken over some of the initiative from the King's Bench. It was hardly surprising that kings should see Parliament as troublesome and seek to manage without it. As it turned out, that was a serious miscalculation. Constitutional monarchy had already been firmly implanted in the legal and political mind by the decisions of the courts in Westminster Hall, and by their inspired notion that the king's prerogative in executive action could be controlled by the king's higher prerogative in judicature.

require to stand with justice, which is to be left to the courts of justice to determine, which cannot particularly be discerned until such case shall happen': *Hyde CJ's Reports*, BL MS Hargrave 27, fo 105.

[109] Hampden was not imprisoned. The case arose from a *scire facias* to enforce the assessment upon him in the Exchequer.

[110] Ship Money Act 1640 (16 Car 1), cc 10, 14.

[111] Debate on the liberty of the subject (1628) 3 St Tr 145.

9

Good Counsel as a Constitutional Imperative

JANET McLEAN*

'[The] perfect courtier ... must always inform [the Prince] frankly of the truth of every matter meete for him to understand, without fear or peril to displease him'.[1]

I. INTRODUCTION

ARGUMENTS FOR THE desirability of good counsel described as 'free', 'frank' and 'fearless' can be traced back at least to Hoby's English translation of Castiglione's *Book of the Courtier* in 1561 and the associated humanist debates of the sixteenth century.[2] We can still find the traces of those debates in the cultural norms of the public service which have survived the New Public Management reforms. Sometimes the expectation of 'free', 'frank' and 'fearless' advice from public servants to ministers is given the status of constitutional convention and is regarded as deriving from the obligation on modern public servants to give impartial advice.[3] Most commonly, these days, the expression 'free and frank advice' appears in a deracinated form in freedom of information legislation which bluntly presumes that the non-disclosure of advice will in most cases preserve frankness.[4]

In this chapter I explain how the relationship of the counsellor to the ruler shifted from the centre to the margins of English constitutional and political thought, suggest when and how we have taken a wrong turning, and raise questions about the situation in which we currently find ourselves.

* This chapter forms part of a Marsden funded project. Thanks to Richard Mulgan, Paul Rishworth, Ben Yong, Joel Harrison and Helena Wiseman for comments on an earlier draft and to Jason Varuhas for his comments. All errors are mine.

[1] B Castiglione, *Book of the Courtier*, 1st edn (translated by T Hoby) (Wyllyam Seres, 1561) 261.

[2] ibid.

[3] This is the New Zealand approach: Department of the Prime Minister and Cabinet, 'Free and Frank Advice' (5 July 2022), available at https://dpmc.govt.nz/our-programmes/policy-project/policy-advice-themes/free-and-frank-advice#:~:text=Free%20and%20frank%20advice%20underpins,a%20politically%20neutral%20public%20service.

[4] See, eg, Official Information Act 1982 (NZ) s 9; Freedom of Information Act 2000 (UK) s 36; Freedom of Information Act 2002 (Scotland) s 30(b). There is a recent New Zealand instance of the term being revived more fully in unenforceable hortatory statutory provisions: Public Service Act (NZ) s 12.

The purpose of this historical chapter is unapologetically normative. It is part of a larger project which seeks to re-establish the centrality to constitutional and administrative law of the relationship between those who advise and counsel and those who enjoy the power of command – these days primarily but not exclusively the relationship between public servants and ministers. It does so by emphasising the continuities between the past and present controversies and their constitutional importance.

In the present day, populist presidents and prime ministers have encouraged a distrust of experts and 'insiders', short termism in politics is worse than ever, misinformation and conspiracy theories proliferate on the Internet, the New Public Management reforms of the previous century have privileged the responsiveness of certain parts of the public service while protecting others from political interference.[5] Within the former sphere any whiff of resistance has been demonised, and advice is increasingly outsourced. These factors have eroded the conditions under which public servants are able to give free, frank and fearless advice. The combination of these factors with the existential threats of climate change and pandemics we now face, is potentially calamitous and relationships between advisors and politicians are likely to be placed under increasing strain. In the larger project of which this is a part, I suggest that the doctrines of judicial review have a role to play in supporting the conditions necessary for good counsel.[6] In the language of the sixteenth century humanists, the contemporary law should assume the role of a 'lifeless prince' creating the conditions for good counsel to rulers.[7] This chapter seeks to revive a normative conception of good counsel from a time of Kingly rule which could inform contemporary political and legal norms and practices.

I begin in section II by establishing the constitutional centrality of the need for good counsel. Good counsel was considered to distinguish kings from tyrants and to be the means to lead omnipotent princes to knowledge and virtue. The conditions required for good counsel – namely equality and a licence to speak freely – indirectly challenged the natural order of authority.

Section III explains that by the seventeenth century the debates about good counsel took a direct institutional turn with both the judiciary and Parliament promoting their claims to be the best source of good counsel to kings in the events leading up to the civil war. During the eighteenth century arguments about counsel lost their constitutional currency and became more peripheral. That century's embrace of the mixed constitution of monarchy, aristocracy and democracy obscured issues of counsel at the same time as the ideas of 'balance' and 'influence' promised to be a cure for all constitutional ills.

Section IV examines Hobbes's seventeenth century writings, which predicted that the problems associated with bad counsel and flatterers would not be resolved by the elevation of sovereign assemblies but could in fact be made worse by them. He helpfully identified critical distinctions between advice and command and conceptual resources with which to imagine conciliar independence and licence to speak freely. Hobbes helps us to view afresh the role counsel plays in contemporary politics.

[5] There has been effort to protect certain financial areas from political interference.

[6] See for an early exploration J McLean, 'Administration in the Constitution: Disaggregating Power for Accountability Purposes' in C Harlow (ed), *A Research Agenda for Administrative Law* (Edward Elgar, 2023).

[7] B Tjällén, 'Teaching Virtue through the Law: Justice and Royal Authority in Giles of Rome's *De Regimine Principum* (c.1280)' in A Hellerstedt, *Virtue Ethics and Education From Late Antiquity to the Eighteenth Century* (Amsterdam University Press, 2018) 71.

In the final section I suggest some of the ways we remain vulnerable to bad counsel and identify some of the practices and conditions we should revisit or rethink.

II. THE HISTORICAL CENTRALITY OF COUNSEL IN CONSTITUTIONAL THOUGHT

A. Absolute Rule

From the medieval period until at least the seventeenth century, single person rule was considered to be the 'natural' form of government throughout Europe. Monarchy was viewed as reflecting the Godly order of nature in which creation was the expression of a single rational will and a 'principle of unity or headship prevailed throughout the universe'.[8] Kings were generally not considered to be bound by the laws of man. Hereditary monarchies claimed absolute power (in the sense of power that was unable to be shared) *regardless of* the fitness of the royal person for rule. Disobedience or resistance was treated as a kind of blasphemy and was never justifiable even in response to tyranny. However, neither the mirror-of-princes literature of the early middle-ages or the early modern works that followed, assumed that kings were *automatically* godly, infallible, or even competent. This view is apparent even among those who viewed single person rule as the best form of government and adhered to its more absolutist versions. Everyone acknowledged that monarchs were capable of tyrannical rule – classically defined as serving their own self-interest rather than the public interest – and were perhaps even predisposed to it.[9] As Lipsius quotes a character as saying in his translation of Tacitus, 'pray to God to send us good princes, and to tolerate them, however they are'[10] – or as the seventeenth century absolutist Calvinists would have it, 'the only recourse [is] to tears and prayers'.[11] James I/VI's rebuke to Parliament in 1610 evoked similar sentiments: '[i]f you have a good King you are to thank God, if an ill king he is a curse to his people but preces et lachrimae [prayers and tears] were ever their arms'.[12] In the early modern period, an unusual preponderance of childless monarchs, infant kings, and the reign of women, created a novel degree of instability in the natural order – a position made worse by religious schism.

[8] WH Greenleaf, 'The Thomasian Tradition and the Theory of Absolute Monarchy' (1964) 79 *English Historical Review* 747, 748.

[9] Tyranny was commonly associated with monarchy – in Polybius, Machiavelli and even Charles I's reply to Parliament's Nineteen Propositions 1641.

[10] Lipsius translations appeared in a series of editions 1574–1607, and there were also numerous commonplace books in circulation which contained quotes from the *Annals*. This translation into English is taken from A Gajda, 'Tacitus and Political Thought in Early Modern Europe c. 1530- c.1640' in WJ Woodman (ed), *Cambridge Companion to Tacitus* (Cambridge University Press, 2009) 253, 261. Gajda notes that in the original Tacitus this speech was from someone of questionable integrity. Machiavelli also quotes this passage: N Machiavelli, 'Discourses on Livy' in P Bondonella and M Musa (eds and trs), *The Portable Machiavelli* (Penguin, 1979) 358.

[11] IWS Campbell, 'Calvinist Absolutism: Archbishop James Ussher and Royal Power' (2014) 53 *Journal of British Studies* 588, 590.

[12] S R Gardiner Camden Society Parliamentary Debates 1610 (ed) ist series 81 (London, 1861) (as cited in D Colclough, *Freedom of Speech in Early Stuart England* (Cambridge University Press, 2005) 155).

Counsel was considered to be a cure for, or at least a mitigation of, such ills. The right counsel could inculcate virtue, educate, be a source of knowledge and aid stability in the succession. Even those who defended monarchy at its most absolute considered good counsel to be what differentiated kings from tyrants. Throughout Christian Europe, virtue – and the ability of virtuous men to play an active role in politics in the role of counsellors – had, since the early middle ages, been associated with successful rule. Giles of Rome's *De regimine principum* (c 1280) endorsed 'strong monarchical rule by a king who should make the law, but not be bound by it himself',[13] but premised such royal authority not in divine right but on the Prince's virtue, which could be taught and bestowed by divine grace, and by human agents in the form of royal confessors and counsellors.[14]

But as Thomas More later found to his cost, leading kings to virtue proved an increasingly dangerous business particularly during the Henrician reformation. In its aftermath, the Anglican bishops and clergy simultaneously promoted ideas of royal supremacy and their essential place as the appropriate channel for counsel. The Post-Reformation English clergy of all ranks claimed superior knowledge to the King on difficult doctrinal questions at the same time as they defended royal supremacy. This was explicitly for the reason that 'authoritie and knowledge doo not always ioyne'.[15] Christian parrhesia and advice relied on biblical texts such as Psalm 119:46, which recognised a religious duty to admonish hostile magistrates and to speak before kings and to not be ashamed, as well as on distinct historical examples such as Bishop Ambrose's rebuke of Emperor Theodosius.[16]

It was not the amount of power kings held that was considered to be the problem but the uses to which it was put.[17] Moral constraints on absolute power would primarily be effected through good counsel. Divine right theorists thought that kingship was unlimited by institutional or legal constraints, but they considered that *individual* counsel could ensure that monarchical rule was good rule. Good counsel would 'channel, assist but not impugn sovereignty',[18] be 'imperium's counterpart but not its contradiction'[19] and bring together 'royal will and royal goodness' – elements which were inseparable in God himself but could be separated in earthly rule.[20] Francis Bacon put the matter pithily, 'sovereignty is married to counsel'.[21] Bacon reassures us that this does not derogate from sovereignty:

> The wisest Princes neede not think it anie dimunition to their greatness, or derogation to their sufficiency, to rely upon councell. God himself is not without, but hath made it one of the great names of his blessed son the Counsellor.[22]

[13] Tjällén (n 7) 60.

[14] J Nelson, 'Kingship and Empire' in JH Burns (ed), *Cambridge History of Medieval Political Thought, c.350-c.1450* (Cambridge University Press, 1988) 227–28.

[15] A Nowell, *The Reproufe of M Dorman his Proufe of Certayne Articles in Religion et Cetera Continued* (first published 1566) (as cited in J Rose, 'Kingship and Counsel in Early Modern England' (2011) 54 *The Historical Journal* 47, 54).

[16] Rose (n 15) 51–52.

[17] ibid 53.

[18] ibid.

[19] ibid 54.

[20] ibid 53.

[21] F Bacon, *The Essayes or Counsels, Civill and Morall* (edited by M Kiernan) (Oxford University Press, 1985) 64.

[22] ibid.

Significantly, a Prince is unlike the trinitarian God in that, however learned, he could not know all that he needed to know.[23] The difficulties for a Prince in judging for himself what may be required for the common good had been acknowledged since medieval times. There was an important distinction to be made between omnipotence and omniscience.[24] Once that distinction is conceded, it must necessarily be envisaged that someone – a tutor, philosopher or confessor, or even the dead author of a particular text – could educate princes in the virtues, give them good counsel, and be their eyes and ears. As Sir Thomas Elyot said 'one mortal man cannot have knowledge of all thyngs done' so needs lesser magistrates in order to 'gouerne with the better advise, and consequently with more perfecte gouernance'.[25]

Princes also needed to be taught to rule via the law.[26] Like God who sets things in motion, the Prince would be the animating force – a fountain spring of power was the common metaphor – but he could not and *should not* play a personal role in everything. Bodin went further to separate sovereignty and government and suggested that direct government by the monarch personally was itself a kind of tyranny.[27] A King needed to rule through his officials and officials were the creation of law, the relationship between the King and his officials was regulated by law, and officials were answerable to the law.

Francis Bacon and later Innocent Gentillet suggested that the continuity of counsellors had a particular role to play in ensuring stability and in Gentillet's case this took the institutional form of a collective body of counsellors which survived changes of the monarch.[28] The role of officials in ensuring stability became all the more important in the early modern period during which there were numerous difficulties in the succession in England and elsewhere.

B. Humanist Counsel and Oblique Challenges to the Form of Government and Social Order

Rather than argue for fundamental change in the form of government directly, most humanists settled instead on using the insights of the ancients to civilise and educate princes and to encourage qualities and obligations of good counsel. We can still find in their writing evidence of a residual concern for the *political* and other conditions necessary for free and frank counsel.[29] By different means and degrees they suggested that counsel ought to have authority over the Prince. They valued participation of the laiety as well as clergy in public life. But how was a counsellor to speak freely and frankly to

[23] JP Kenyon, *The Stuart Constitution 1603–1688* (Cambridge University Press, 1986) 29.

[24] M Goldie, 'The Reception of Hobbes' in JH Burns and M Goldie (eds), *The Cambridge History of Political Thought 1450–1700* (Cambridge University Press, 1991) 594; Rose (n 15) 53.

[25] Sir Thomas Elyot, *The Boke Named the Gouernour*, vol 1 (edited by HHS Croft) (Kegan Paul, Trench & Co, 1883) 25–26, 262–63 (as cited in Rose (n 15) 49).

[26] Tjällén (n 7).

[27] See J McLean, 'Between Sovereign and Subject: The Constitutional Position of the Official' (2020) 70 *University of Toronto Law Journal* 167, discussing Jean Bodin.

[28] Bacon preferred a single individual counsellor: Bacon (n 21) 85. I Gentillet, *A Discourse Vpon the Means of Wel Governing* (first published 1576) (cited in J Paul, *Counsel and Command in Early Modern English Thought* (Cambridge University Press, 2020) 102–103).

[29] Rose (n 15) 58.

his superior in the natural order – and with what implications for the natural order itself? How was a counsellor to preserve his own position (and personal safety) and still speak truth to power? How was one to avoid flattering princes?

One answer was to give the Prince a proper humanist education from his infancy. But even a prince's education was susceptible to flattery. As Erasmus remarks:

> [R]oyal sons could not learn anything properly except horse riding: in all things everybody humoured or flattered them, but since a mere horse does not know whether he is being ridden … by a prince or a private individual, he throws off his back anyone who rides him incompetently.[30]

Humanists were thus concerned to ensure that a prince be educated so as to be able to detect flattery, and encouraged in sufficient self-reflection so as not to become his own flatterer. He should be taught to be able to recognise as well as to heed good counsel.[31]

More directly, humanists argued that it is incumbent upon the Prince himself to *create the conditions* under which good counsel could be given. It is the Prince who gives licence for candid advice:

> Nobody speaks the truth more honestly or more advantageously or more candidly than do books; but the Prince must nevertheless accustom his friends to the knowledge that they find favour by giving frank advice. Indeed, it is the job of those who keep the Prince company to advise him opportunely, advantageously, and amicably, but it will nevertheless be well to forgive those whose advice is given clumsily in order that no precedent may deter those who would advise him properly from doing his duty.[32]

There is a great deal in this quotation. The honesty of books is taken from Plutarch's *Moralia* in which Phalerious recommends that the Prince read books because he can learn from these what his friends will not dare to tell him.[33] Books by dead authors cannot flatter. Neither, by implication, does the law flatter. Both books and law endure and have a special role to play as sources of advice to princes. Before candid and frank advice will be forthcoming from living advisors, however, certain conditions of political freedom have to be met. Erasmus sets up a reciprocal set of obligations. The ruler must fulfil the conditions which make free and frank speech possible; and the counsellor is obliged to give frank advice. The counsellor has a *duty* to speak freely rather than a *right* to do so. Erasmus asks how it can demonstrate loyalty to humour a foolish prince but treason to oppose his shameful enterprises?[34] Frank speech should not be punished, and even when it has been conveyed ineptly on one occasion, should be received again the next time.

In this passage, Erasmus is adapting the political freedoms normally associated with democratic equality to relationships between social unequals. He uses the language of friendship and freedom of speech which were loaded concepts in Greek and Roman thought. For the Greeks, freedom of expression was built on egalitarian presumptions

[30] Erasmus, *The Education of a Christian Prince* (edited by L Jardine) (Cambridge University Press, 1997) 56.

[31] Erasmus mentions Plato's warning that an individual may be his own flatterer and lays himself open to other people doing the same thing as he did of own accord: ibid 58.

[32] ibid 64.

[33] ibid 60; Plutarch, *Moralia* (translated by FC Babbitt) (Heinemann, 1927) 189. The importance of books is later taken up by Francis Bacon who is explicit that books by those who have been advisors will be especially useful: 'books of such as themselves have been actors upon the stage': Bacon (n 21) 18.

[34] Erasmus (n 30) 90.

about freedom from dependence. Members of a koinonia (community or social group) were required to be equals (either absolutely or proportionally, according to Aristotle's terminology) in a way that equalised their contributions.[35] Cicero claimed that conditions of political freedom and the absence of absolute rule are necessary for great oratory.[36] However, in the Roman thought of later antiquity, such freedoms tended to be relegated to the private sphere to be enjoyed between true friends who were social equals rather than in public between equal citizens.[37] Candour is what might be expected of a true friend in private but, Plutarch warns, in relationships of patronage in which the advisor is clearly socially subordinate, what appears to be candid speech is more likely to be a 'cloak for flattery'.[38] Integrity may be the best that can be expected.

In the cited passage, Erasmus, drawing on the works of Philodemus and Plutarch,[39] makes frank speech between a patron and client possible and defines frank speech as the opposite of flattery.[40] In giving frank advice, subordinates acquire the rank of true friends – a condition of equality.[41] This has clear political implications for the natural order. As his readers would have been aware, Aristotle had noted the 'inconsistency of Kings in treating people as friends while denying them a share of power'.[42] Elsewhere, Erasmus suggests that flattery can also corrupt those who are clearly subordinate. Rulers also sometimes engage in flattery of the common people which has the effect of corrupting the people, just as men sometimes flatter their wives with gifts but fail to win their loyalty.[43]

The obligation of candour is not without important caveats about how, when, and by what means unwelcome advice should be given in order to preserve the dignity of the Prince. An important part of the debate was about whether flattery and deceit by the counsellor would be more likely to be checked if the advice were to be given individually or collectively, in private or in public – and was concerned to establish the degree of deference and candour appropriate to those different settings. Thomas Starkey preferred a governing council without whose counsel a King could not act.[44] Thomas Elyot suggested that the counsellor should both persuade, and 'govern' by example, mediating between the ruler and his subjects. The obligation on the good counsellor was such that he who was excluded from or not invited into the 'chambers of the mighty to correct their vices … must publish [the advice] publicly, so that shame may be a motivating factor for change to a vice-ridden leader'.[45] It was by no means to be assumed, that free and frank speech should or could only take place in private.

[35] R Mulgan, 'The Role of Friendship in Aristotle's Political Theory' (1999) 2(4) *Critical Review of International Social and Political Philosophy* 15, 18.

[36] S Bartsch, 'Praise and Doublespeak: Tacitus' *Dialogus*' in R Ash (ed), *Oxford Readings in Tacitus* (Oxford University Press, 2012) 132.

[37] Philodemus, *On Frank Criticism* (translated by D Konstan and others) (Scholars Press, 1998) 3.

[38] Quintilian, *Institutio Oratoria* (first published 95 AD) 494 (as cited in D Colclough, 'The Rhetoric of Free Speech in Early Modern England' (1999) 17(2) *Rhetorica: A Journal of the History of Rhetoric* 177, 186).

[39] Erasmus dedicated his translation of Plutarch to Henry VIII.

[40] He is inconsistent on this and elsewhere concedes that flattery is appropriate if it leads the Prince to virtue.

[41] See also Bacon (n 21) 85.

[42] Aristotle, *Politics* 1287b 30–35 (as cited in Mulgan (n 35) 16). Aristotle is ambivalent about whether friendship can exist between unequals such as between master and slave: Mulgan (n 35) 18.

[43] Erasmus (n 30) 66.

[44] For a discussion of Thomas Starkey, see Paul (n 28) 42–48.

[45] ibid 60.

There is a clear assumption by Erasmus and other of the humanists[46] that the tutor and counsellor is more likely to be capable, virtuous and less susceptible to passion, than the ruler. Indeed, while Castiglione laments that good counsel can never make a tyrannous prince truly good, he goes further than Erasmus, More, and Bodin to allow the possibility (through the voice of the Countesse in his dialogue) that a good counsellor may compete with the Prince for pre-eminence.[47] But what if the person competing for pre-eminence with the Prince is a bad rather than a good counsellor?

C. The Evil Counsellor

For Erasmus, it was more acceptable to the state if a prince were to be bad than if his friends were.[48] He thought that the state could better endure a single tyrant than satisfy a whole entourage of tyrants. This was one of many points on which he and Machiavelli disagreed.[49] Importantly, for Machiavelli it was much worse, as well as much more likely, for a counsellor to be more corrupt than the King. Counsel and courtiers are not motivated by virtue but by their own self-interest. They are their own tyrant.

Machiavelli whose work, *The Prince*, was first translated into English in 1562, but circulated in Italian much earlier, was an important interlocutor with and disrupter of these debates about good counsel.[50] He recognised the 'gap between how people actually live and how they ought to live'.[51] He rejected the basic humanist premise that virtue would necessarily lead to successful rule and suggested instead that virtue might be pursued at the risk of a ruler's survival.[52] Vice might be as important as virtue 'if [a ruler] is to hold onto power'.[53] Appearing to be virtuous by deceit rather than actually being so, may be more important to a ruler, or to someone seeking to rule;[54] appearing to act for the common good while securing your own power may be 'how things exist in reality'.[55]

According to Machiavelli, rulers, like everyone else, seek their own self-interest (defined as holding on to power and so maintaining the security of the state and safety of its citizens). Traditional virtue could frustrate this objective but so too could wanton self-indulgence. Hence the ruler's ministers should be chosen carefully – given wealth, honour and respect – and be made to 'see that [they] can't survive without the ruler' and that their self-interest is aligned with his.[56] Like Erasmus, Machiavelli warns against flatterers.

[46] Thomas More's history of Richard III is an exception.

[47] Castiglione (n 1) 332. Gentillet shared this view: Paul (n 28) 6.

[48] Erasmus (n 30) 71.

[49] ibid 94.

[50] See Paul (n 28) 84–86. In 1539 Henry Parker wrote to Thomas Cromwell recommending *Istorie Florentine* and *Il Principe*. Reginald Pole blamed the Henrician Reformation on the lack of good counsel at court, the timidity of the council and the 'vicious forwardness of Cromwell'. He suggested that Cromwell had been inspired by Machiavelli. We know that Machiavelli's works or works in translation were also purchased by other counsellor figures such as Thomas Smith, William Thomas, and William Cecil.

[51] N Machiavelli, *The Prince* (translated by T Parks) (Penguin, 2011) 60.

[52] ibid.

[53] ibid.

[54] ibid 70.

[55] ibid 60.

[56] ibid 92.

He suggests that the ruler should choose a few intelligent men and license only those chosen to be able to tell him the truth about specific issues.[57] Unasked for advice should be discouraged.[58] A ruler needs to show his advisors he is open to truthful advice, but not be ruled by advisors whom he cannot control. For Machiavelli, it is only the skilled ruler who can obtain good advice in the first instance – so there is no possibility that good advice could make the Prince skilled, let alone virtuous. If the ruler is not sensible or skilled, there is a real risk of appointing a shrewd counsellor who poses a threat to the ruler himself.[59]

In his *Discourses on Livy*,[60] Machiavelli adds important institutional context to these observations. He suggests it is more difficult to achieve good counsel in a monarchy than in other forms of government. Good counsel and the pursuit of virtue and the common good, he suggests, are much more likely in a republic than a monarchy. A republic, he argues, is more open to the advice of a single good man than an evil prince. (At another point he suggests that an 'ignorant populace', or an 'unruly and licentious people' can be brought back to the 'truth' or to 'the right path' by the advice of a single good man.[61]) The common good is

> observable only in republics, for in them everything that promotes it is practiced, and however much damage it does to this or that private individual, those who benefit from the said common good are so numerous that they are able to advance it in spite of the inclination of the few citizens who are oppressed by it.[62]

In a republic the counsellor's interests are naturally aligned with the common good and the counsellor is more likely to be virtuous, whereas under single person rule the counsellor must be bought off to align his interests with those of the Prince. The people too are better judges of the character of men running for office than princes are.[63] Machiavelli echoes Polybius in suggesting that a combination of the monarchical, aristocratic, and popular forms of government avoids the worst excesses of each.[64] The importance of good counsel to good rule, then, diminishes with the move away from monarchy.

Machiavelli's indictment of evil counsel to princes gained new political salience at the end of the reign of Elizabeth I. The accession of James I /IV and his Scottish entourage heralded a crisis relating to counsel. One contemporary report in 1603 compares James I to the late Queen who

> knew them [counsellors] and put up with them as a necessity but always kept an eye on their actions, the new King, on the contrary, seems almost to have forgotten he is King ... and leaves them with such absolute authority that beyond a doubt they are far more powerful than they were before.[65]

[57] ibid 93.
[58] ibid 94.
[59] ibid 94.
[60] Machiavelli (n 10).
[61] ibid 285.
[62] ibid 296.
[63] ibid 407.
[64] B Manin, *The Principles of Representative Government* (Cambridge University Press, 1997) 44.
[65] Giovanni Carlo Scarmelli, The Venetian Secretary in England describing James I/VI domination by counsel: C Perry, 'The Crisis of Counsel in Early Jacobean Political Tragedy' (1993) 24 *Renaissance Drama* 57, 57.

In contrast to Elizabeth I during whose reign access to the Bedchamber was separated from the enjoyment of formal office, the Scottish favourites of James I enjoyed a monopoly of access to the Bedchamber, Cecil continued to dominate the bureaucracy and the Privy Chamber was rendered largely ceremonial. Royal favourites threatened the authority of the King.

Contemporaneously, portrayals of flattery and bad counsel became a theme in Jacobean tragedy – including in Samuel Daniels' *The Tragedy of Philotas* (1605), Ben Jonson's *The Tragedy of Sejanus* (1603) and the revised version of Grevilles' *Mustapha* (1609), as well as Shakespeare's Polonious (*Hamlet*) (1603) and in the contrasting professions of esteem by King Lear's daughters (1606). Jonson's *Sejanus*, in particular, reasserts the important connection between sovereignty and good counsel: 'Learning needs rest: sovereignty gives it. Sovereignty needs counsel: Learning affords it'.[66] At a time when James I was asserting his supremacy in terms such as, 'Kings are not onely God's lieutenant upon earth, and sit upon God's throne, but even by God himself they are called Gods', these plays emphasise the 'powerlessness and isolation of the autocrat in the thrall of flatterers'.[67] Contrasting God's and man's justice, Isabella in Shakespeare's *Measure for Measure* reminds us that an outward appearance of virtue combined with private corruption is as inescapable in the ruler's surrogates as in the ruler himself. Indeed, brief authority may in fact be more corrupting than permanent authority: 'man, proud man, dressed in a little brief authority, most ignorant of what he has most assumed'.[68]

III. AN EXPLICIT TURN TO INSTITUTIONAL REFORM

We can see that Erasmus indirectly challenged the natural order when he obliquely referenced the importance of equality to free and frank advice. In the *Discourses* Machiavelli more directly suggests that it may be the form of government that is the cause of the problems relating to counsel. By the Elizabethan era, according to Rose, 'every plea to hear advice was an eruption of the classical republicanism bubbling away beneath the monarchist crust of Elizabeth's government'.[69] The seventeenth century saw a direct institutional turn in debates about good counsel. Both Parliament and the judges laid claim to be the best source of good, free and frank counsel. Individual and private counsel then, was less to be trusted than these more institutional forms. Both judges and Parliament were concerned about the conditions the ruler must create to encourage advice which is as free and frank as possible. This took various forms such as concerns about the tenure of judges and about who should control the limits of free and frank speech in Parliament.

A. Judges

The struggles for judicial independence can be viewed through the lens of good counsel. Unlike many other officials who held office for life, for a fixed term, or

[66] B Jonson, *Sejanus His Fall* (first published 1616) 8: 565.
[67] Referencing a 1609 speech to Parliament: Perry (n 65) 58.
[68] W Shakespeare, *Measure for Measure* (first published 1623) II: 116.
[69] ibid.

on good behaviour, judges held office at pleasure. The easy removal of judges was explained at the time by the need to make them answerable for their relative independence. Officials who merely carried out the King's orders tended to enjoy more secure tenure.[70] The institutional role of the judges and their relationship to the King came to a head during this time, especially under Coke CJ's short tenure. The King's judges were considered part of the executive (they executed the law), as well as acting as advisors to the King in private about the legality of his future actions.

In his now famous confrontations with James I as a member of Parliament in 1621, Sir Edward Coke drew directly on the humanist language of the previous century to suggest that judges drew on the authority of the law which did not flatter or feign friendship. Judicial counsel was premised on the idea of 'government not of men but of the laws', and informed by books which spoke across time. Coke declared it: '[b]est to ask counsel of the dead! ... For they will not flatter nor fawn to advance themselves, nor bribe, nor dissemble'.[71] The rule by law not man is, of course, from Aristotle. But the idea that books were the best source of advice (precisely because books did not flatter), originated in Plutarch and had been a theme taken up by Erasmus, Francis Bacon, and Ben Jonson in his play *Sejanus*. There is a direct connection, then, between the humanist scholarship of the sixteenth century and the assertions of judicial independence from the King in the seventeenth. In a rallying cry to Parliament, Coke invoked the law as endowing the individual official with the ability to discharge his duty:[72] 'The common law hath admeasured the King's prerogative. It is not I, Edward Coke, that speaks it but the records that speak it ... I am now the voice of the recorded law'.[73]

Coke CJ had, of course, been dismissed by the King from judicial office in 1616. But he continued his appeals to the law on the books as a way of depersonalising confrontations between judges and the King. Ideally, the advisory and executive actions of the judges (the distinction between the two was not always very clear) would become the exercise by the King of a kind of impersonal rule. Not everyone, however, would regard the authority of the law on the books as the best or only source of knowledge and counsel. Thomas Hobbes, for one, would later express his scepticism of the common law. He was suspicious of historical knowledge and its ability to apply in the present to predict future consequences – and also of the unchallenged authority of books (and by implication of the authoritative claims of the common law) which may simply ossify past mistakes. Hobbes cautions, '[b]ut they that trusting only to the authority of books follow the blind blindly'.[74] Nevertheless, the idea of the 'dead' 'unflattering' authority of the common law became something of a common law trope – illustrated most famously in the judgment of Lord Camden in the eighteenth-century case of *Entick v Carrington*: 'if it be law it will be in our books'.[75]

[70] GE Aylmer, *The King's Servants: The Civil Service of Charles I, 1625–1642* (Routledge and Kegal Paul, 1974) 96.

[71] C Bowen, *The Lion and the Throne: The Life and Times of Sir Edward Coke* (Little Brown and Co, 1956) 390.

[72] This is a paraphrase of J Orth, 'The Golden Metwand: The Measure of Justice in Shakespeare's *Measure for Measure*' (2010) 31 *Adelaide Law Review* 127, 140.

[73] Bowen (n 71) 418–19.

[74] T Hobbes, *Leviathan* (first published 1651, Clarendon Press, 1958) 37.

[75] *Entick v Carrington* (1765) 2 Wils 275, 95 ER 807.

As is well-known, the Star Chamber would be abolished by the Long Parliament in 1641 changing the nature of the advisory relationship between judges and the King. And in the Act of Settlement 1701 the power to dismiss judges would effectively move from the King to Parliament and be for cause. The independence of the judges would thereafter be better secured but their advisory function would be diminished.

B. Parliament

In the seventeenth century leading up to the English Civil War, Parliament (and more particularly the House of Commons) consistently promoted itself as the best source of counsel to kings. Members of the Commons emphasised the public and collective qualities of their advice and the alignment of their interests with the interests of the Commonweale – all matters considered by various of the humanist commentators to be necessary for good counsel and to avoid the flattery of princes. The Houses of Parliament replayed many of the issues raised earlier by Erasmus, More, Elyot, Castiglione, Gentillet and Machiavelli about the conditions necessary for frank advice through their direct confrontations with King James I/VI on the question of whether free speech could truly be enjoyed if it were dependent on the King's permission or licence at the beginning of each Parliament. Neither House would go so far as to claim that there should not be *any* restrictions on what should be able to be said in Parliament but rather asserted that the task of settling and enforcing the proper limits on and conditions of free speech and developing the proper ways to advise kings should be left to the Houses of Parliament themselves.[76]

At the same time, Parliament railed against rival sources of counsel and asserted its right to discipline evil counsellors. Its particular target was the private and individual counsel of close companions to the King. Parliament was ignominiously dissolved in 1626 just as it sought to impeach the King's favourite, the Duke of Buckingham.

The preoccupation of the Houses of Parliament with counsel remained at the forefront of their confrontations with Charles I. The first three grievances of Parliament's *Nineteen Propositions* presented to the King in 1642 directly concerned matters of counsel.[77] The first of these was that the great officers, ministers and members of the Privy Council should be approved by both Houses of Parliament, and be required to take a particular form of oath. The second proposed: 'That the great Affairs of the Kingdom may not be Concluded or Transacted by the Advise of private men, or by any unknown or unsworn Councellors.' Instead, the proposal was for matters of public concern to be transacted exclusively in Parliament and hence in public. The proposal went on to assert that Parliament should be able to censure those who do not comply, and to limit the number of members of the Privy Council. The advice and consent of the Privy Council so constituted, it claimed, should be required for the making of laws

[76] Colclough (n 12) 163.

[77] Constitution Society, 'Charles I, Propositions Made by Both Houses of Parliament … with His Majesties Answer Thereunto (1642)', available at https://constitution.org/1-History/eng/nineteen_propositions_1642.html.

under royal authority. The third proposition specifically listed some of the great officers of state and law whom parliamentarians considered should be chosen with the approbation of both Houses, or if Parliament was not meeting, by counsellors approved by Parliament.[78] The fourth proposition discussed a related humanist preoccupation – how princes were to be educated. It proposed that the Houses of Parliament should be required to approve the tutors and the education of the King's children.[79]

The King's response, written by two of his moderate advisors Sir John Colepepper and Lucius Cary Viscount Falkland, attempts to reassure in relation to the first three Propositions in terms reminiscent of the Magna Carta: the King will choose his advisors well from 'such persons in those places of trust, as shall have given good testimonies of their abilities and integrity'.[80] More tellingly, the King promises to 'hold' no one so 'near us in affection' that 'we will not leave [them] to the justice of the law'. But the King's Answer is very clear that it is for him to *choose* and not merely to *nominate* advisers and offices – otherwise, Colepepper and Falkland prophesise, his power would be rendered merely symbolic.

The King's Answer is now famous for its characterisation of the existing English constitution as balanced and as incorporating the monarchy, the aristocracy and democracy parts which have separate roles and limit each other. The King's reply repeats the Machiavellian tropes about the virtues and vices of each form of government and argues that it is *in the combination* of the three that all is held in balance.[81] Significantly, it attributes to the monarchy the power to *govern* according to law. The House of Commons acts as 'a conserver of and limitation on those powers',[82] 'but is not intended for any share in *government* or in choosing those who govern'. Accordingly, it is critical for the balance of the constitution that the King should be the one to choose and not merely to nominate advisors, and that he should be able freely to take advice and inform his understanding from whomsoever he chooses (and not only from the Privy Council). In particular, the monarch should be able to take advice from anyone he should choose about whether a Bill is fit to be passed, and not only from those who propose it. It was this tripartite characterisation of the English Constitution which drew Hobbes's ire in *Leviathan* (1651) and *Behemoth* (1681)[83] and provoked his defence of absolute and undivided sovereignty. Whether in fact sovereignty was effectively as divided as the advocates of a mixed constitution claimed, is another matter.

[78] ibid: 'III.That the Lord High Steward of England, Lord high Constable, Lord Chancellour, or Lord Keeper of the great Seal, Lord Treasurer, Lord Privie Seal, the Earle Marshall, Lord Admirall, Warden of the Cinque-Ports, chief Governour of Ireland, Chancellour of the Exchequer, Master of the Wards, Secretaries of State, two chief Justices, and chief Baron, may be alwayes chosen with the approbation of both Houses of Parliament: And in the Intervals of Parliaments by assent of the major part of the Councell, in such manner as is before expressed in the choice of Councellors'.

[79] Article X of the Propositions sought the reinstatement of particular officials lately removed. Others sought the removal and punishment of other officials: ibid.

[80] Online Library of Liberty, '1642: Propositions made by Parliament and Charles I's Answer', available at https://oll.libertyfund.org/page/1642-propositions-made-by-parliament-and-charles-i-s-answer.

[81] Taken from Polybius and Machiavelli: see JGA Pocock, *The Machiavellian Moment* (Princeton University Press, 1975) 364.

[82] The authors had tried to contain the expansion of prerogative powers during the Long Parliament.

[83] T Hobbes, *Behemoth* (first published 1681) (edited by F Tonnies) (Simpkin, Marshall and Co, 1889) 165; Hobbes (n 74).

Good counsel, its role in the constitution and its availability in different institutional forms was a central issue leading up to the English civil war. Some historians have suggested that the significant constitutional changes to the central institutions of government at the end of the seventeenth century giving greater power to Parliament and security of tenure to judges concluded serious debate about counsel.[84] They tend to suggest that arguments about counsel were merely subterfuge for arguments of a more republican kind. The real questions, they argue, were always about sovereignty and the proper form of government. What remains of these constitutional debates is only the relatively uninteresting psychological and prudential speculations about how and when to give unwanted advice.[85]

It is certainly true that during the eighteenth century good counsel lost its place as a central concern of the constitution and was replaced by theories of the mixed and balanced constitution and separation of powers. But the greatest theorist of sovereignty, Thomas Hobbes, did not think that changes to the form of government would make the problems associated with counsel go away. On the contrary, he argued that moving to a sovereign assembly would only likely exacerbate them – as we shall see in the next section.

IV. ILLUMINATING AND OBSCURING THE ROLE OF COUNSEL: HOBBES'S *LEVIATHAN* AND THE EIGHTEENTH CENTURY BALANCED CONSTITUTION

Given the regicide, civil war, establishment of a protectorate, restoration and revolution which followed, it is quite remarkable that the conception of the English constitution articulated by moderate royalists in defence of Charles I as a balance of the monarchy, aristocracy and democracy would become the orthodox description of the English Constitution in the eighteenth century. This idea of balance did not so much address the problems associated with counsel as obscure them. Hobbes' masterpiece *Leviathan* (1651)[86] speaks directly to the 19 Propositions and the King's Answer, as well as to many of the humanist debates about counsel from the previous century. Hobbes helps us to identify a wrong turning in constitutional thought and demonstrates the continuing relevance of the problems associated with counsel for democracy and indirectly for modern representative democracy.

Hobbes utterly rejects the idea of a mixed constitution in which sovereignty is distributed over the distinct institutions as described by Colepepper and Falkland. He thought sovereignty could not be so divided. By implication, Hobbes suspected that many of the seventeenth century proponents of the idea that Parliament was the best source of counsel to the King, did not so much want to counsel the King as to command him.[87] Hobbes insists instead that counsel which is always obeyed is not counsel at all but is rather a kind of command. If the person with the power of command always follows advice without any independent assessment of it, then advice becomes a form of rule and it is the advisor who has become the commander.

[84] See, eg, Joanne Paul tends to this view, while Jacqueline Rose is more equivocal: Paul (n 28).
[85] A Momigliano, 'Tacitus and the Tacitist Tradition' in Ash (n 36) 427.
[86] Hobbes (n 74).
[87] See Joanne Paul's discussion of Henry Parker: Paul (n 28) 174.

In this and much else Hobbes was prescient. As it transpired, the struggles of the eighteenth and nineteenth centuries would be to determine where sovereignty would ultimately lie as between the 'balanced estates'. Advisors nominally chosen by the King eventually came to be chosen in practice by Parliament as originally sought in the 19 Propositions. Ministers would become commanders in fact while remaining advisors in form (at least for most purposes).[88] I do not mean to suggest that that result was inevitable at the time Hobbes was writing *Leviathan*. Only later did the combined effect of the Bill of Rights 1689 and the Act of Settlement 1701 determine that it was within the Commons in which the contest for influence would play out. Once it was settled that Parliament could determine even the choice of monarch, including by the passing of legislation for the consent of its chosen monarch, the ability of a royal veto alone to restore balance to the monarchical aspect of the constitution was slim to non-existent. In any event, the formal checks and balances of one estate over another proved too blunt to be used regularly as a matter of practice. After Queen Anne, no monarch employed the legislative veto. The Houses' formal powers to impeach the King's Ministers were too uncertain and extreme when more subtle means could be used to oust them. The real political action would take place not between the formal estates but in the struggle for influence of the monarch and the aristocracy within the Commons.

The presence of the King's Ministers and officeholders in the Commons (a situation originally precluded by the Act of Settlement but subject to a compromise before the Act came into force)[89] could not readily be squared with the new theories of the balanced constitution or indeed with the later theory of the separation of powers. It was never the case that the Commons as a whole opposed the executive power, but rather that rival and opposing interests including the monarchical and aristocratic were represented *inside* the Commons. Influence was used to achieve 'balance' that could not be achieved by more formal mechanisms. And what was perceived as 'balance' by one person[90] was viewed as 'corruption' or overweening influence by those of a more republican disposition.[91] Hume, for example, approved of the King's placemen in the Commons as ensuring the monarchical interest was represented given the disuse of the royal veto. Ministerial responsibility to Parliament, on the other hand, was initially treated as a corrective to such 'undue influence'.[92] And while at first the King retained the power to appoint his own advisors, he began to be 'saddled with Ministers he did not want' (particularly in 1757 and 1761) and eventually a ministry nominally appointed by the King depended on the support of the Commons in order to govern.[93] All of these factors obscured the sources, choice of

[88] See, for an exception, *R (Miller) v Prime Minister; Cherry and Others v Advocate General for Scotland* [2019] UKSC 41 where the quality of counsel or of justification by Ministers to the Queen was tested and found wanting.

[89] The King's placemen included the Commissioners of Revenue, Lords of the Treasury and Secretaries of state. Other, more minor officials holding office from the King were by statute disqualified from election to the Commons. For the fullest discussion, see WE Hearn, *The Government of England: Its Structure and Development* (Longmans, Green, Reader and Dyer, 1867) 263–64.

[90] JAW Gunn, 'Influence, Parties and the Constitution: Changing Attitudes, 1783–1832' (1974) 17 *The Historical Journal* 301, 306.

[91] R Sparling, 'Political Corruption and the Concept of Dependence in Political Thought' (2013) 41 *Political Theory* 618, 622ff.

[92] Gunn (n 90) 328.

[93] ibid 303.

and role of counsel as well as the question of to whom counsel was being given. It was some time before constitutional theory would acknowledge what had long become fact.

In *Leviathan*, Hobbes further distinguished counsel from command on the basis of the former's need for justification. Command depends on nothing more than the authority of he who gives it. It requires no other justification than the authority of the will of he who is the commander. Counsel, by contrast, can be good or bad, justified or not and 'the reason to act in accordance with counsel cannot be separated from the reasons offered in its support'.[94] At the point at which ministers gave 'advice' to kings in name only, and the whips were able effectively to *enforce* the Minister's 'advice' and justifications on behalf of the government majority, the claims of ministers to be the source of counsel begin to look pretty thin. Counsel and command became entangled and thus obscured.

Hobbes thought that a balanced system of divided sovereignty was not possible, and was suspicious of command masquerading as counsel. As for the capacity of Parliament to act as a collective source of good counsel to the King, Hobbes is scathing. Indirectly addressing the fourth of the 19 Propositions from Parliament to Charles I (though without explicitly referring to it), he scolds that no one would want an assembly to advise him on 'the marriage of his children' or 'governing household matters' 'especially if there be among them those who do not wish his prosperity'.[95] An assembly is hardly likely then to be a source of good counsel on the education of a prince. Moreover, it is better to receive counsel from people individually because individuals in an assembly are likely to be swayed by each other's opinions.

Neither did Hobbes associate the problems of counsel solely with monarchical rule or consider that changing to a new form of government would solve such problems. Instead, he argued that the other forms of government were even more prone to bad counsel than monarchy. Unlike princes, rotating office holders in a sovereign assembly are not educated for the role from a young age. While he openly concedes the problems associated with the education and judgment of infant monarchs, he argues that the natural persons who constitute a sovereign assembly are likely to be equally ill-instructed in their positive duties. Indeed, he likens an assembly of sovereign representatives to a group of infant monarchs uneducated for their role, and susceptible to dictators.[96]

Monarchs, Hobbes says, can choose from whom and how to receive counsel – in whatever degree of secrecy they please. But a representative assembly is forced to receive counsel in public and can only hear from those who are admitted to it. Moreover, a sovereign assembly is as subject to evil counsel and the seduction of orators as is a monarch. Indeed, members of a sovereign assembly may in turns become one another's flatterer. And whereas the favourites of a monarch are few, the favourites or orators who may serve the private interests and kindred of a sovereign assembly are many.[97] It is, he suggests, much more difficult to counsel an assembly. In this way, Hobbes resists democratic exceptionalism. Like Isocrates, he understands that the demos too can become a tyrant, may attract demagogues, and may soon collapse into a monarchy or aristocracy of orators.

[94] M Walters, 'Judicial Review of Ministerial Advice to the Crown' (2016) 25 *Constitutional Forum* 33, 36.
[95] Hobbes (n 74) 202.
[96] ibid 146.
[97] ibid 200.

Hobbes was correct to predict that counsel *to* a sovereign assembly is likely to depend on rules of admittance. But it is also part of the confused legacy of the balanced constitution that today external advice to the sovereign assembly has to be channelled almost exclusively through ministers. Ministers are like monarchs in that they tend to receive their advice in private and are able to decide what should be revealed in public.[98]

In contemporary times it is the Osmotherly rules developed by the executive (though never approved by Parliament) which purport to prescribe the rules by which the Parliament in the United Kingdom (UK) and its Select Committees receive the advice of the civil service.[99] According to these rules, civil servants must be as helpful and open as possible and at the same time only represent the views of their ministers and only with ministerial agreement and under instruction. At the same time, however, civil servants are also subject to Parliament's own rules of contempt. By no means do civil servants have licence to speak freely. The availability of external advice to Parliament is thus severely curtailed.[100]

The Osmotherly rules[101] confirm that the primary object of counsel is not the sovereign assembly itself but the Minister. By the same token, William Pitt's eighteenth century orthodox understanding of the constitution explains why in the 1780s he treated urgent matters of administrative reform primarily as issues for the executive to deal with in the exercise of its prerogative rather than as the proper subject for Parliament and legislative reform. The cumulative effect has been to remove administrative reform and the public service advisory function from the direct constitutional gaze.[102]

Hobbes had much to say too about the necessary independence of the advisor from the ruler and the need for licence to speak freely.[103] In doing so, Hobbes makes a key distinction which has regrettably been lost to modern constitutional thought. A magistrate is an official who *represents* the sovereign and executes sovereign power directed by the sovereign will. Hobbes likens a magistrate to the artificial joints of the body politic. Counsellors, by contrast, are more like a body's memory. They are the repository of equity and the laws, artificial reason and will.[104] When officials are acting truly as counsellors to the sovereign they are not acting as his or her representatives: 'For the advice is addressed to the sovereign only, whose person cannot in his own presence be represented to him, by another'.[105]

Hobbes's solution to how the sovereign can remain in command but give licence for free and frank counsel which cannot be withdrawn is also innovative. The very

[98] Select committees are of course able to meet in private and privately to receive advice.

[99] Cabinet Office,' Giving Evidence to Select Committees: Guidance for Civil Servants' (October 2014), available at https://assets.publishing.service.gov.uk/government/uploads/system/uploads/attachment_data/file/364600/Osmotherly_Rules_October_2014.pdf.

[100] Expert advisors to select committees are sometimes appointed.

[101] In New Zealand it is the Cabinet Manual which sets out guidance about what evidence public servants can give to Parliament.

[102] JR Breihan, 'William Pitt and the Commission on Fees, 1785–1801' (1984) 27 *The Historical Journal* 59. The UK has long been an outlier among Westminster systems in leaving matters to do with the civil service to the prerogative. The Constitutional Governance and Reform Act 2010 (UK) now regulates some of these matters.

[103] I develop these ideas at length in a separate paper (manuscript available from author).

[104] Hobbes (n 74) 1, 196.

[105] ibid 88.

act of asking for counsel, he says, gives licence to the counsellor to speak freely: 'He that asked it, cannot in equity accuse or punish it'.[106] He goes further to say, 'And generally he that demandeth counsel, is the *author* of it and cannot punish it and what the sovereign cannot, no one else can [emphasis added].'[107] This use of the idea of authorship (which partially mirrors his discussion of authorship elsewhere to explain why subjects must obey the sovereign representative of whose actions they are authors) has the effect of maintaining sovereignty in the counselled but at the same time guaranteeing the conditions for free and frank advice explicitly even in cases in which the advice is contrary to majority opinion. An important condition is that the counsel be lawful.

Hobbes, like Machiavelli, is concerned about self-serving counsellors and flatterers. Recall that Machiavelli thought that it was necessary to align the private interests of the advisor with the private interests of the ruler. Hobbes's view is more nuanced again. The counsellor, Hobbes says, must advise the sovereign representative according to the sovereign's interests and not his own. The ends and interests of the counsellor should not be inconsistent with the ends and interests of 'him he counselleth'. But crucially, for Hobbes, the interests of the sovereign representative are two-fold. The natural person or persons who represent(s) the sovereign or 'bear(s) the person of the people'[108] seeks to procure *both* the common interest as well as their own private good. The interests of the people whom the sovereign representative 'bears' go much further than mere self-preservation and include prosperity, riches, honour and reputation.[109] If the public and private interests of the sovereign representative are in conflict, it is likely that it will be the private interests of the natural person who represents the sovereign that are more likely to be served. The answer to this problem, according to Hobbes, is not to make the advisor choose the public over the private interest but rather to align the sovereign representative's private interests with the public interest as much as is possible.[110] The implications are clear – institutional arrangements rather than individual virtue may best secure good counsel.

The mixed constitution seems to have been only marginally concerned about counsel as a component of good government – especially at the point at which the King's power had been severely weakened. Ministers effectively came to rule the monarch as Starkey had posited centuries before. Ministers are not so much counsellors to Parliament as commanders. The provision of counsel has reverted in the main to those who advise ministers, and to the courts. We need to pay close attention to the conditions by which these forms of counsel are given and whether and how the public have the benefit of it.

[106] ibid 196.
[107] ibid.
[108] ibid 142.
[109] ibid 145.
[110] Hobbes uses these arguments to suggest that public and private interests are best aligned in a monarch. This is because a king's riches honour and glory are likely to arise from the richness strength and reputation of his people. In a democracy or aristocracy by contrast 'the publique prosperity does not confer so much by way of private fortune on one who is corrupt' or ambitious. Perfidious advice, treacherous action or a civil war may better advance the private good of such natural persons (see ibid 145).

V. REFRAMING THE CONTEMPORARY ROLE OF COUNSEL

Good counsel has been considered central to good rule for centuries. Sovereignty needs counsel: omnipotence is not omniscience. But as Erasmus and Hobbes remind us, not all counsel is good. Conditions of equality between ruler and counsellor, and an independent licence to be frank without risk of such licence being withdrawn, help to foster advice that is truly free and frank and not merely a disguise for flattery. And counsel, truly deserving of the name, must be genuinely based on reason and justification and not just on power and authority. We should avoid, if possible, putting the advisor in a situation in which she has to choose between assisting the public and the private interests of those she counsels. One way to do so is to align the public and private interests of the ruler – law and convention can assist in this. Different forms of knowledge may help to inform better rule. And sometimes advice in public may be a better guarantee of frank speech than advice in private.

There are numerous opportunities for dangerous and flattering counsel in a modern Westminster representative democracy. Ministers, parliamentarians and the electorate are all prone to flattery in both public and private forums. If we were designing the system afresh, it is unlikely that we would channel the diverse knowledge resources of the public service exclusively to the executive branch (with counsel given predominately in private) and through ministers and thus severely restrict Parliament and the public's access to those resources. The people and Parliament are vested with a certain degree of omnipotence but can be misled and like princes should not be considered omniscient. We need repositories of institutional memory.

In recent years there has been an increase in political attacks on the judiciary, and, in some places, the politicisation of judicial appointments. The conditions under which public servants have been asked to give advice have significantly eroded over the past decades. The permanent tenure, which in the nineteenth century distinguished public servants from ministers in Parliament[111] and thence effected a degree of equality and independence between them and those they counselled, has gone. They are not protected when they are summoned to advise parliaments. Special advisors whose private interests are aligned with the private interests of ministers and whose careers rise and fall with their patrons have proliferated, especially at Westminster. Policy advice is increasingly outsourced to consultants. The rise of the public relations state and 24-hour media cycles puts a premium on public unity between ministers and public servants. Freedom of information regimes likely protect counsel that is neither objective nor impartial and amounts to flattery, as well as counsel which is free and frank. Major reforms to the public service itself are too constitutionally important to be left exclusively in the hands of the government of the day in the exercise of the prerogative – as they currently are

[111] In the late 18th century undersecretaries to the Admiralty and Treasury holding seats in the Commons more closely resembled permanent secretaries than ministers, in terms of their nature and tenure. Such officers were expressly excluded from the Place Act 1742. Even as late as 1830, Sir James Graham, the Secretary of the Admiralty, did not resign his seat in the Commons with the change of ministry. The difference between administrative officials and ministerial ones would eventually come to depend on their permanence or impermanence which was a matter to be worked out office by office. See G Kitson-Clark, '"Statesmen in Disguise": Reflexions on the History of Neutrality of the Civil Service' (1959) 2 *The Historical Journal* 19, 25, 28.

in the UK. Multi-party input is required with the goal of maintaining the capacity of the public service – including the ability to give advice to future governments.

Innovations which have been tried or at least mooted include: more frequent briefings to the public directly (as some jurisdictions tried during the worst phases of the Covid-19 pandemic); mandatory disclosure of the costs and benefits of policy and legislative measures to Parliament; access to (and disclosure of) Treasury advice in the costing of electoral promises; independent parliamentary budget offices, the use of public-facing commissions to provide information on matters of serious long term import such as climate change; and the provision of independent expertise to parliamentary select committees. Judicial declarations of inconsistency with human rights may also be considered an innovative from of judicial advice to Parliament.

The law can and should address the conditions necessary for good counsel and more directly than it does today. By law, I do not mean only to refer to legislation and institutions directly regulating the public service, but also challenge public lawyers to think more carefully about how we imagine the advisory function in judicial review doctrine. While we should retain the distinction between counsel and command we could be much more open and robust about separating the independent advisory function from the executive function and be prepared to look more closely at whether politicians are receiving bad advice, or are not receiving advice at all. Judicial review doctrines ought to be able to call out bad or flattering advice to ministers whether its source is temporary consultants or permanent advisors. This chapter is a call to revisit these and other related questions in light of modern-day politics and the existential crises we currently face.

10

Private Rights and Public Wrongs

BRIAN MURRAY

I. INTRODUCTION

FOR REASONS I explain in the course of this chapter, it seems to me to be clear that, historically, the common law viewed the unlawful and malicious interference by the State or its agents with a fundamental liberty of the citizen as a legally cognisable injury enabling an award of – at least – nominal damages. Specific trespassory torts, actionable *per se*, sought to protect particular interests in a similar way. As the constitutional law of those States with written Bills of Rights has evolved, the theory underlying these features of the common law has been applied in some of these jurisdictions to enable the award of damages for violation of protected constitutional rights – in many legal systems only against the State, in others also against non-State actors. As Brennan J explained in *Bivens v Six Unknown Agents of the Federal Narcotics Bureau*[1] – the first case in which the United States (US) Supreme Court recognised this jurisdiction – '[h]istorically, damages have been regarded as the ordinary remedy for an invasion of personal interests in liberty'.[2]

Over the past two decades that principle has, in different ways, in different legal contexts and in a variety of jurisdictions, waned. In *Watkins v Secretary of State for the Home Department*[3] the House of Lords held that the *mala fides* and unlawful interception by the authorities of a prisoner's correspondence with his lawyers and with a court did not disclose a cause of action at common law. This was found to be the case because the claimant was unable to prove resulting damage to person or property: interference with his rights of access to court was not in itself sufficient to complete the tort of misfeasance in public office. At the heart of that conclusion lay a more fundamental proposition and concern. It was framed thus by Lord Bingham: 'the primary role of the law of tort is to provide monetary compensation for those who have suffered material damage rather than to vindicate the rights of those who have not'.[4]

The same thinking underpinned the 2020 decision of the High Court of Australia in *Lewis v Australian Capital Territory*.[5] There, it was decided that a claimant in an action

[1] *Bivens v Six Unknown Agents of the Federal Narcotics Bureau* 403 US 388 (1971).
[2] ibid 395.
[3] *Watkins v Secretary of State for the Home Department* [2006] UKHL 17, [2006] 2 AC 395.
[4] ibid [9].
[5] *Lewis v Australian Capital Territory* [2020] HCA 26.

for false imprisonment who established that he or she had been unlawfully detained could only obtain an award of nominal damages if, but for the unlawful detention, the claimant could and would have been lawfully detained. The judgments relied on the decision of the United Kingdom (UK) Supreme Court in *R(WL) v Secretary of State for the Home Department*,[6] which has subsequently been interpreted in England and Wales[7] as limiting a claimant in an action for false imprisonment to nominal damages unless his unlawful detention could not have been effected lawfully, or the circumstances are such as to warrant an award of exemplary damages. To do otherwise, these courts have held, would compensate a claimant who – although unlawfully deprived of his liberty – has suffered no compensable loss. The decisions have obvious implications for other torts actionable *per se* in which such a 'but for' analysis has never traditionally been applied to the assessment of damages.

In June 2022, the US Supreme Court issued its decision in *Egbert v Boule*.[8] There, the Court has taken what may well prove the final step on a long path towards the dismemberment of the jurisdiction to award damages for violation of rights guaranteed by the Federal Constitution and established in *Bivens*.[9] Recognising a cause of action under *Bivens* was, the majority said, 'a disfavored judicial activity'.[10] In his separate opinion Gorsuch J explained that he would have over-ruled *Bivens* entirely: the court should, he said, 'exercise the truer modesty of ceding an ill-gotten gain, and forthrightly return the power to create new causes of action to the people's representatives in Congress'.[11]

In one sense these cases address different issues – the meaning of 'damage' for the purposes of a common law cause of action which is not actionable *per se* in the first, the rules of causation that should govern the award of damages in a case that is actionable *per se* in the second, and in the third, the principles that should govern the respective competencies of the legislature and the judiciary in ensuring that the law affords some remedy where there has been a breach of a constitutional right.

But viewed another way, they expose the same basic question: whether the violation of a fundamental liberty recognised by the common law or by any applicable constitutional law is an injury which itself perfects a tortious and or constitutionally based cause of action for damages and, where it is for that reason or otherwise actionable, whether the violation is compensatable in its own terms. That, in turn, raises important issues at the interface between private right and public wrong. The cases prompt reflection as to whether, how, when and why the law should afford compensation consequent upon an illegality of this kind and, in particular, the significance that should be attached to

[6] *(WL) v Secretary of State for the Home Department* [2011] UKSC 12, [2012] 1 AC 245.

[7] *Parker v Chief Constable of Essex Police* [2018] EWCA Civ 2788; *R (Hemmati) v Secretary of State for the Home Department* [2019] UKSC 56, [2021] AC 143.

[8] *Egbert v Boule* 596 US 482 (2022).

[9] As noted in the majority opinion, since 1983 there have been 11 cases in which the Court had refused, in a variety of situations, to imply this cause of action for other alleged constitutional violations: see *Chappell v Wallace* 462 US 296 (1983); *Bush v Lucas* 462 US 367 (1983); *United States v Stanley* 483 US 669 (1987); *Schweiker v Chilicky* 487 US 412 (1988); *FDIC v Meyer* 510 US 471 (1994); *Correctional Services Corp v Malesko* 534 US 61 (2001); *Wilkie v Robbins* 551 US 537 (2007); *Hui v Castaneda* 559 US 799 (2010); *Minneci v Pollard* 565 US 118 (2012); *Ziglar v Abbasi* 137 S Ct 1843 (2017); *Hernández v Mesa* 140 S Ct 735 (2020).

[10] *Egbert v Boule* (n 8) 60.

[11] ibid 74.

the fact that the State has not just acted unlawfully, but has by virtue of those unlawful actions, violated a fundamental constitutional entitlement.

II. *ASHBY v WHITE*

The judgments in some of the recent English, Australian and American cases ground their analysis in a dismissal of the relevance, authority and, at points, coherence of the decision in *Ashby v White*,[12] which has long been viewed as confirming the common law principle to which I have referred. Curiously, and at the same time, that decision is universally acknowledged as a critical building block in the evolution of the common law's only *public* tort, the cause of action for misfeasance in public office. *Ashby v White* was, Lord Steyn observed in *Three Rivers DC v Bank of England*, 'the first solid basis for this new head of tort liability'.[13] The question of what (if anything) *Ashby v White* can be said to have decided – is critical to an understanding of these developments.

Ashby, a burgess of the town of Aylesbury, sought to vote in the parliamentary election of January 1701. He was prevented from so doing by the defendant, a constable of the town. He sued, recovering damages of £5 from a jury. An application was successfully brought to arrest the verdict in the Court of Queen's Bench. In three separate judgments the majority in that Court found that the facts did not disclose a cause of action known to the law. Holt CJ dissented. The matter proceeded to the House of Lords on foot of a writ of error, the case there being dominated by a dispute as to whether the appellate jurisdiction lay with the Commons (it having arisen from a parliamentary election) or the Lords (in its capacity as the appellate tribunal having jurisdiction on a writ of error from the Queen's Bench). The House of Lords asserted jurisdiction, voting by a majority of 50 to 16 to reinstate the verdict.

There are different versions of Holt CJ's judgment, and indeed it appears that the version acted upon by the House of Lords had been revised by its author following the proceedings in the Queen's Bench. That consideration, combined with the fact that the decision was that of the lay members of the House of Lords in a highly political context, has generated some dispute as to the precise basis on which the case was decided.

[12] The reporting of this case has presented its own issues, as I explain in the text. The original report of Holt CJ's judgment is at (1703) 2 Ld Raym 938, 950, (1703) 92 ER 126, 134. There is a report of the House of Lords resolution at (1703) 1 Bro PC 62, (1703) 1 ER 417. The former was subsequently modified, according to a note in *Smith's Leading Cases*, 13th edn (Sweet & Maxwell, 1929) 253, 283 (which has been described as the best report, see Lord Steyn in *Three Rivers DC v Bank of England (No 3)* [2003] 2 AC 1, 190). The report of a committee appointed to report on the case by the House of Lords (principally drawn up by Holt CJ) appears at 14 Howell's State Trials 780, 789 (and see Clarke J in *Three Rivers DC v Bank of England* [1996] 3 All ER 558, 586). For ease of reference, I will rely here on the version of Holt CJ's judgment from *Smith's Leading Cases*. The extracts from the committee report I cite here are taken from *Cobbett's Parliamentary History of England*, vol 6 (London, 1810) 303 and following. Generally on the question of the reporting of the decision, see T Sampsell-Jones, 'The Myth of Ashby v White' (2010) 8 *University of St Thomas Law Review* 40, who refers to a version of Lord Holt's judgment published (seemingly on the direction of Lord Denman) as a pamphlet in 1838, 'The Judgments Delivered by the Lord Chief Justice Holt in the Case of Ashby v. White and others and in the Case of John Paty and Others'. Sampsell-Jones, ibid at 46, observes that the pamphlet report relied upon the Statute of Westminster I, and quotes the judgment as recording '[n]o action will lie for not giving a right, but surely it is law that an action will lie for defrauding and hindering a man to enjoy the right which he hath'.

[13] *Three Rivers DC v Bank of England (No 3)* [2003] 2 AC 1 [190].

Nonetheless, it is clear from the record that in determining the case in favour of Ashby, the Lords were heavily influenced by the rationale of Holt CJ's dissent. This is particularly evident from the committee report expressly adopted by the House, which was principally drawn up by Holt CJ[14] and is similar in structure and content to the judgment. It is probably correct to say that it does not adopt the dissent without at least a change in emphasis, placing greater stress on the requirement of malice than the early versions of the judgment.[15] This was acknowledged in some of the subsequent eighteenth century cases.[16] Nonetheless, it is to be stressed that the English courts have consistently looked to Holt CJ's judgment, subject to the qualification that the later versions of it attached particular importance to the requirement of malice.[17]

Notwithstanding these aspects of the case, there can in my view be no doubt as to three features of the decision.

First, the wrongful act generating the cause of action comprised the fraudulent and malicious act of the defendant in hindering the plaintiff from exercising his right to vote. It is now widely understood that the decision did *not* establish a broader and simpler principle of *ubi jus ibi remedium*. This, it should be repeated, is the point on which the original versions of the dissent and the proceedings before the House of Lords diverged, and certainly as the law has developed any doubt as to the requirement of malice has been removed.

Second, the consequence of these actions was that Ashby was awarded damages and costs of, respectively, £5 and £10. The former is often described as 'nominal', but one must query whether this is an accurate description of the award.[18]

Third, and most importantly for present purposes, the award of damages was made *because* of the injury entailed by the deprivation of the right. *Each* of the reports makes it clear that this was a central part of the judgment of Holt CJ, and the proceedings before and resolution of the House of Lords itself leaves no room for doubt in this regard. Holt CJ said, 'If the plaintiff has a right, he must of necessity have a means to vindicate and maintain it, and a remedy if he is injured in the exercise and enjoyment of it.'[19]

The Chief Justice specifically engaged – and in some detail – with the contention of the other judges that there was no cause of action because this was an action on the case and there was no damage. The terms in which he did so were, I think, significant, focussing as they did not merely on the nature of the damage and injury that would perfect an action on the case, but looking also to the trespassory torts and underlining the essential unity of purpose in the differing forms of action:

> My brother Power indeed thinks that an action upon the case is not maintainable because there is no hurt or damage to the plaintiff: but surely every injury imports a damage, though it is impossible to prove the contrary; for a damage is not merely pecuniary, but *an injury imports a damage, when a man is hindered of his right*. As in an action for slanderous words, though

[14] See the comments of Clarke J in *Three Rivers DC v Bank of England* [1996] 3 All ER 558, 586.

[15] See *Sampsell-Jones* (n 12) 47–49.

[16] In particular *Drewe v Coulton* reported as a note to *Harman v Tappenden* (1801) 102 ER 214, 217–18 and noted by *Sampsell-Jones* (n 12) 49.

[17] See, in particular, the judgment of Clarke J in *Three Rivers DC v Bank of England* [1996] 3 All ER 558, 586.

[18] Holt CJ's exhortation to the House of Lords suggests not: 'I will direct the jury to make him pay well for it'. In *Carey v Piphus* 435 US 247 (1978) 266, Powell J described the damages as awarded as 'substantial'.

[19] *Smith's Leading Cases* (n 12) 273.

> a man does not lose a penny by reason of the speaking of them, yet he shall have an action. So if a man gives another a cuff on the ear, though it cost him nothing, not so much as a little diachylon, yet he shall have his action, for it is a personal injury. So a man shall have an action against another for riding over his ground, though it do him no damage: for it is an invasion of his property and the other has no right to come there: and in these cases the action is brought vi et armis. *But for invasion of another's franchise trespass vi et armis does not lie, but an action of trespass on the case* [emphasis added].[20]

The short report of the argument articulated by Holt CJ in the House of Lords records the same point:

> Upon the arguments of this case, Holt Chief Justice said, the plaintiff has a particular right vested in him to vote. Is it not then a wrong *and an injury to that right*, to refuse to receive his vote? So, if a borough has a right of common and the freemen are hindered from enjoying it by inclusure or the like, every freeman may maintain his action. This action is brought by the plaintiff for the infringement of his franchise. You would have nothing to be a damage, but what is pecuniary, and a damage to property. If a man has retorna brevium, although no fees were due to him at common law, yet if the sheriff enters within his liberty, and executes process there, it is an invasion of his franchise *and he may bring his action, and there is the same reason in this case* ... if such an action comes to be tried before me. *I will direct the jury to make him pay well for it; it is denying a man his English right, and if his action be not allowed, a man may be forever deprived of it* ...[emphasis added].[21]

The report of the Committee appointed by the Lords on the state of the case (and approved in its eventual resolution) is replete with explanations by reference to the law of trespass and false imprisonment of how '*if a man is injured if he cannot bring an action to recover the thing he hath lost by the injury, the law will always give him damages in lieu thereof*'[22] The resolution approved by the House included this:

> It is resolved by the Lords Spiritual and temporal in parliament assembled, that by the laws of the Kingdom every freeholder, or other person, having a right to give his vote at the election of members to serve in parliament, and being wilfully denied or hindered so to do by the officer who ought to receive the same, *may maintain an action in the Queen's courts against such officer, to assert his right, and recover damages for injury* [emphasis added].[23]

The vagueness of – and tautology inherent in – the unqualified proposition with which the case is usually associated (*ubi jus ibi remedium*) has occluded the three important features of the case to which I have referred. In particular, the repeated – and correct – insistence that variations in the different versions of the judgment of Holt CJ has confused the issue of whether malice was an inherent and necessary aspect of the tort, has led to the – wholly incorrect – suggestion that there is some doubt about whether the case establishes that a malicious interference with the right was itself sufficient injury to ground a claim in damages. The finding that Ashby had an entitlement to damages simply because of the malicious impeding of his right to vote was central to the conclusion that he had a cause of action in the first place: the action was one on the case, in which proof of damage is

[20] ibid 274.
[21] ibid 279.
[22] *Cobbett's Parliamentary History of England* (n 12) 318.
[23] ibid 323.

necessary to the completion of the cause of action. Each of the judges whose decision was overturned by the House of Lords had stressed the absence of any, or any material, loss or damage as critical to their conclusion. None of the reports suggest that there was any damage *other* than that comprising the interference with Ashby's entitlement to vote.

Beecher v Lucas[24] put this aspect of the rationale of *Ashby v White* beyond doubt in Ireland. Lucas was chairman of a meeting convened for the election of a number of Conservators of Fisheries in accordance with various provisions of the Fisheries Acts. Beecher's vote was tendered by proxy and, he alleged, falsely and maliciously rejected by Lucas. Eventually, Beecher was instated as a Conservator following the bringing of proceedings in the Queen's Bench for a *qou warranto* and *mandamus*. His claim for damages was met with the defence that he had sustained no loss as any wrong inflicted had been redressed before commencement of the action, and at the most he had sustained a temporary damage. The plaintiff demurred. Lucas' contention that he had a right to vote, that it was unnecessary to allege or prove a mere damage, and that the mode of determining if damage had been sustained was to consider if any right had been infringed was accepted by the Exchequer Division. That the plaintiff had a cause of action without proof of special damage was, it was held, clear from *Ashby v White*.[25]

A similar interpretation of the decision proved influential in the US. Perhaps most famously in *Webb v Portland Mfg Co*,[26] Story J explained:

> I am not able to understand, how it can correctly be said, in a legal sense, that an action will not lie, even in case of a wrong or violation of a right, unless it is followed by some perceptible damage, which can be established, as a matter of fact; in other words, that *injuria sine damno* is not actionable.[27]

He concluded that when a party suffers a violation of a legal right that causes no pecuniary loss, or where it is 'impracticable' to prove actual damages, the party is 'entitled to maintain his action for nominal damages, in vindication of his right'.[28] Story J's explanation of the decision was subsequently brought back to English law *via* the judgment of Parke B in *Embrey v Owen*.[29]

Thereafter, a sequence of English authorities in the second half of the nineteenth and first half of the twentieth century stated and re-stated *Ashby v White* as authority for the proposition that upon the unlawful interference with certain rights at common law, no special damage was required.[30] Perhaps most significantly, this was the shared assumption of the members of the House of Lords in *Neville v London 'Express' Newspaper Ltd*,[31] where the judges split three to two on whether an action

[24] *Beecher v Lucas* (1877) 11 IR CL 517.

[25] ibid 520 (Fitzgerald B), 521 (Dowse B). See also *Sedley v McGowan* (1858) 7 ICLR 427.

[26] *Webb v Portland Mfg Co* 29 F Cas 506 (CCD Me 1838) (No 17, 322).

[27] ibid 507.

[28] ibid 508.

[29] *Embrey v Owen* (1851) 6 Exch 353, 368.

[30] *Quartz Hill Consolidated Gold Mining Co v Eyre* (1883) 11 QBD 674 (malicious presentation of a winding-up petition); *Fitzgerald v Firbank* [1897] 2 Ch 96 (whether special damage was required to maintain action by the holder of fishing rights against a river polluter); *Nicholls v Ely Beet Sugar Factory Ltd* [1936] Ch 343 (the rights of the owner of a several fishery against a party responsible for river pollution). The authorities were usefully surveyed by Birkett J in *Constantine v Imperial Hotels* [1944] KB 693 who concluded that the infringement of a common law right (there the wrongful refusal to accommodate a traveller), gave rise to an action maintainable without proof of special damage.

[31] *Neville v London 'Express' Newspaper Ltd* [1919] AC 368.

for maintenance lay in the absence of proof of such damage. The historical features of the tort were such that it was found that such damage was required. The analysis of the legal theory was, however, unequivocal. Referring to the judgment of Holt CJ in *Ashby v White* they variously observed 'if a right has been infringed … no proof of damage is necessary',[32] and 'where the right is … an absolute right … every infringement of such an absolute right gives rise to a claim to nominal damages, even though all actual loss or injury is disproved'.[33] There is Canadian authority to the same effect.[34]

It is unsurprising that the case was invoked – albeit often rhetorically – at an early point the evolution of damages remedies for violation of constitutional rights in those jurisdictions with Bills of Rights. It has been cited in cases applying that cause of action in Ireland,[35] New Zealand,[36] and indeed in the development of both the statutory constitutional tort remedy under the Civil Rights Act (42 USC § 1983) and of the remedial scheme enabled by *Bivens*.[37] Even before these developments, Louis L Jaffe had observed of *Ashby v White* 'the case has stood as a precedent and has had, as we know, tremendous generative force'.[38]

III. INFRINGEMENT OF RIGHTS, PROOF OF DAMAGE AND THE TORT OF MISFEASANCE IN PUBLIC OFFICE

This was the historical context in which the House of Lords came to decide *Watkins v Secretary of State for the Home Department*. There, the claimant's prison correspondence with his lawyers and with a court in which he had instituted proceedings against the relevant prison authorities was unlawfully opened by prison officers. The trial judge found that their actions were malicious but refused to impose liability in misfeasance in public office because the claimant had not established loss or damage in the form of injury to person or property which, he held, was an essential precondition to the cause of action. The Court of Appeal reversed the decision of the trial judge.[39] The nineteenth and early twentieth century English cases to which I have earlier referred were cited at some length, on the basis of which Brooke LJ concluded that *Ashby v White* showed

> that if there is a right which may be identified as a constitutional right, then there may be a cause of action for an infringement of that right without proof of special damage, provided there is something more than mere infringement.[40]

[32] ibid 380 (Lord Finlay LC).
[33] ibid 392 (Viscount Haldane).
[34] *Orchard v Tunney* [1957] SCR 436, 447.
[35] *Cosgrove v Ireland* [1982] ILRM 48.
[36] *Attorney General v Chapman* [2011] NZSC 110 [1] (per Elias CJ dissenting).
[37] *Carey v Piphus*, where earlier 20th century decisions of the US Supreme Court applying the case in the context of interferences with voting rights are noted. The judgment of Powell J interprets *Ashby v White* as enabling the award of 'substantial damages' upon a showing that a plaintiff was wrongfully deprived of that right. While *Carey v Piphus* was a section 1983 case, *Ashby v White* was also relied upon in determining when a plaintiff had standing to maintain an allegedly moot *Bivens* action in *Uzuegbunam v Preczewski* 141 S Ct 792, 209 L Ed 2d 94 (2021).
[38] LL Jaffe, 'Suits Against Governments and Officers: Sovereign Immunity' (1963) 77 *Harvard Law Review* 1, 14.
[39] *Watkins v Secretary of State for the Home Department* [2004] EWCA Civ 966, [2005] QB 883.
[40] ibid [48].

Laws LJ explained that the tort arose in two different situations: one was where the claimant had been exposed to economic or material injury by virtue of the public officer's wrongful and malicious act and in which it is inherent in the claim that there has been a quantifiable loss. The other was where the wrongful act 'interfered with a right of a kind which the law protects without proof of any loss'.[41] In that case, he said, the public officer's interference with the right will complete the tort and no actual damage needs to be shown. The right was both clear and fundamental: that of unimpeded access to the court, the breach arising from the *mala fides* interference with his legally privileged correspondence.[42] Nominal damages were awarded, and the matter was remitted for a determination as to whether exemplary damages were appropriate and, if so, as to the amount of same.

The principal judgment in the House of Lords was delivered by Lord Bingham. His treatment of *Ashby v White* involved a short, if 'remarkable' attack on the decision.[43] It was not, he said, easy to evaluate the authority given that Holt CJ had revised his judgment before the case went to the House of Lords. He noted that the case had been interpreted as one for the disturbance of miscellaneous rights, showed an affinity with nuisance and disturbance actions, and described as an action in quasi trespass for direct infringement of an incorporeal property right having all the attributes of trespass. The analogy with trespass, Lord Bingham said, 'may perhaps explain why material damage was not held to be a necessary ingredient of the tort, since trespass is of course the paradigm case of a tort actionable per se'.[44]

Citing a variety of cases in which reference was made to proof of damage in an action for misfeasance in general, and to the requirement in particular that the defendant appreciate the consequences for the plaintiff of his actions, Lord Bingham concluded that none of the authorities cited to the court supported the proposition that misfeasance in public office was actionable *per se*. *Ashby v White*, he said, 'is not reliable authority for that proposition'.[45] Lord Bingham moreover stressed the difficulty in English law of identifying fundamental or constitutional rights, given the absence of a written bill of rights, stating that while today the right to vote would be regarded as 'basic, fundamental or constitutional', none of these expressions was used by Holt CJ in the course of his judgment.[46]

In his speech, Lord Rodger noted frequent reference by Holt CJ in his judgment to the right in issue being 'a matter of property' or as 'a franchise'. This, he said, was fundamental to the judgment, and in particular to his defence of the jurisdiction of the House of Lords to entertain the case.[47]

As I explain shortly, the themes recited by Lord Bingham recur in subsequent cases – it is not clear what *Ashby v White* decided, the action was trespassory in

[41] ibid 67.
[42] ibid 3.
[43] C Harlow, 'A Punitive Role for Tort' in L Pearson et al (eds), *Administrative Law in a Changing State: Essays in Honour of Mark Aronson* (Hart Publishing, 2008) 261.
[44] *Watkins v Secretary of State for the Home Department* [2005] QB 883 [14].
[45] ibid 23.
[46] ibid 25.
[47] ibid 55.

nature, the authorities consistently demand proof of damage to complete the cause of action, and mere violation of a right does not achieve this. Three points should be made.

First, *Ashby v White* was not an action in trespass and at no point in any of the judgments was it suggested that it was. It was pleaded, argued and decided as an action on the case. I have earlier quoted that part of his judgment in which Holt CJ expressly stated that the action was *not* an action in trespass: 'for invasion of another's franchise trespass *vi et armis* does not lie, but an action of trespass on the case'. Had it been an action in trespass the question of whether Ashby had suffered legally cognisable damage would not have arisen. Clearly, it did. That was, at least in part, the basis on which the three judges in the majority in the King's Bench Division refused the plaintiff any relief. If anyone had believed the action was trespassory, that exegesis would have been unnecessary, and their conclusion misdirected.

For the same reason, the suggestion that the action was decided as it was because it was viewed as being in support of a property right is difficult to reconcile with any of the judgments. The report in *Smith's Leading Cases* differentiates the right in question from that annexed to an estate, describing it as 'a personal right and not a real one'.[48] It was the legal origin and nature of the right, not any perceived relationship with particular property that generated the cause of action: '[t]his right of voting is a right in the plaintiff by the common law, and consequently he shall maintain an action for the obstruction of it'.[49] That right may not have been expressed as 'constitutional' or 'fundamental' but it was described by Holt CJ as 'a most transcendent thing, and of a high nature'.[50]

Certainly, the relationship between voting and property was viewed in the House of Lords as relevant to the issue of jurisdiction, but not as dispositive of either that question or the cause of action itself. I have noted already that this feature of the right was stressed by Holt CJ, but it makes sense that in justifying jurisdiction generally to the House of Lords he, and the House, would refer to instances in which the right was based on property. Thus, the House of Lord's resolution was broadly based:

> the asserting, that a person having a right to give his vote at an election, and being hindered so to do by the officer, who ought to take the same, is without remedy for such wrong by the ordinary course of law, is destructive of the property of the subject, against the freedom of elections, and manifestly tends to encourage corruption or partiality in officers, who are to make returns to parliament, and to subject the freeholders and other electors to their arbitrary will and pleasure.[51]

Second, neither the fact of different versions of the judgment of Holt CJ, nor the political context and forum in which the case was decided, nor for that matter any difficulty in determining the basis for the ultimate decision in the House of Lords, have ever been suggested as detracting from its authority in laying the foundations for the tort of misfeasance in public office. It is hard to see how the decision can be sufficiently clear and authoritative to occupy the foundational position it does in that action, and yet be

[48] *Smith's Leading Cases* (n 12) 271.
[49] ibid 274.
[50] ibid 272.
[51] *Cobbett's Parliamentary History of England* (n 12) 318.

sufficiently unclear or uncertain as to the fact that damages were awarded without proof of any damage beyond the interference with the right in issue.

Third, the point was not as much that the tort was actionable *per se*, as that it was completed on violation of a right valuable in itself: Ashby obtained damages because the wrongful act 'was an interference with a political right and involved no trespass'.[52] To that extent, the fact that the authorities developing the tort of misfeasance in public office refer consistently to a requirement of damage as an element of the tort (as many of them certainly do) is question begging: what *Ashby v White* establishes is that the violation of the right in issue in that case was itself sufficient damage to perfect the cause of action.

As it happens, the approach adopted by Roberts CJ in *Uzuegbunam v Preczewski*[53] is remarkably similar to that reflected in Lord Bingham's judgment in *Watkins*. Uzuegbunam was a university student who was prevented by college authorities from distributing religious literature. Those steps were taken on foot of a policy adopted by the university that was changed shortly after the plaintiff initiated legal action challenging its legality and seeking nominal damages for a breach of his constitutional rights. The issue was whether the fact of the claim for nominal damages precluded a plea of mootness entered by the defendants. Roberts CJ, in a sole dissent, refused to accept that the law enabled the recovery of nominal damages without a claim of actual damage or prospective harm, dismissing reliance upon *Ashby v White* and the judgment of Story J in *Webb*. He said that 'the House of Lords likely paid scant attention to Lord Holt's analysis', noting the political context in which the decision was made. He said, 'Regardless, the House of Lords held that Ashby "should recover his damages assessed by the jury" at trial, suggesting that the fact of injury alone did not "import" them'.[54]

The examination by Thomas J (with whom the remaining seven members of the court agreed) is more conventional. The 'well established' rule at common law was 'that a party whose rights are invaded can always recover nominal damages without furnishing any evidence of actual damage'.[55] He continued:

> That this rule developed at common law is unsurprising in the light of the noneconomic rights that individuals had at that time. A contrary rule would have meant, in many cases, that there was no remedy at all for those rights, such as due process or voting rights, that were not readily reducible to monetary valuation .... By permitting plaintiffs to pursue nominal damages whenever they suffered a personal legal injury, the common law avoided the oddity of privileging small-dollar economic rights over important, but not easily quantifiable, nonpecuniary rights.[56]

IV. TORTS ACTIONABLE PER SE AND THE COMPENSATORY PRINCIPLE

R (Lumba) v Secretary of State for the Home Department[57] was a false imprisonment case, and to that extent there was no doubt that the claimant was entitled to nominal

[52] Jaffe (n 38) 14.
[53] *Uzuegbunam v Preczewski* (n 37).
[54] ibid 806.
[55] ibid 800.
[56] ibid.
[57] *R (Lumba) v Secretary of State for the Home Department* [2011] UKSC 12, [2012] 1 AC 245.

damages for the tortious conduct he alleged. Instead, what was at issue was whether more than nominal damages could be awarded where the claimant's detention – although technically unlawful – was inevitable and would have been effected lawfully had it not been effected unlawfully. The case shares some features with *Watkins* – the question of whether the law of torts is truly directed only to compensation for specific types of injury, or whether it also acknowledges and provides a remedy to reflect the inherent value of an important liberty when unlawfully violated. To put the matter another way, *Watkins* was concerned with whether an action could be brought relying solely upon a violation of a fundamental liberty, while *Lumba* addressed itself inter alia as to whether compensation could issue to reflect such a violation.

Lumba was a most unusual case in which the claimant was held to have been unlawfully detained when his continued imprisonment after the expiry of a sentence imposed upon him following his conviction of a criminal offence, was founded on an unlawful policy. Even had the lawful policy been applied, he would have been detained: because that detention was 'inevitable' he could obtain no damages. The case has been applied in the UK to preclude recovery of compensatory damages where detention was unlawful but lawful detention would and could have occurred,[58] and, as I have noted, has been interpreted similarly by the Australian High Court in *Lewis v Australian Capital Territories* (although there are differences in the principle formulated in the various judgments in that case).

At the heart of the majority judgments lie two propositions – that English law did not recognise a heading of 'vindicatory' damages in tort and that in determining the availability of compensatory damages for the tort of false imprisonment it was appropriate to adopt a 'counterfactual' analysis, asking whether 'but for' the wrongful detention there would and/or could and/or would *and* could (or perhaps 'inevitably') have been a lawful detention. Because the claimant's lawful detention was 'inevitable', because the court felt that awarding damages for deprivation of liberty in those circumstances would have involved compensating the claimant for something he had never lost,[59] and because English law did not recognise a heading of 'vindicatory' damages, the claimant's only entitlement was to nominal damages.[60]

That said, of the nine members of the Supreme Court who heard *Lumba*, five would have awarded the claimant more than nominal damages had they agreed that there had been a false imprisonment[61] (two members of the court felt that the tort was not made out at all).[62] Nonetheless – as in *Watkins* – central to the view of the majority was the thesis that English law did not enable an award of damages to reflect the fact of the violation of the claimant's fundamental right – in that case his right to liberty. To some extent, I think, the court's conclusions were affected by a misplaced emphasis by the claimant on the concept of 'vindicatory' damages and the accompanying suggestion that the court

[58] *Parker v Chief Constable of Essex Police* (n 7); *R (Hemmati) v Secretary of State for the Home Department* (n 7).

[59] *Lumba* (n 57) 95.

[60] ibid 101.

[61] Lords Hope, Walker, Brown, and Rodger and Lady Hale.

[62] Lord Brown and Lord Rodger dissented (as did Lord Phillips, although he said that had he concluded that there was a false imprisonment he would have agreed with the majority on damages).

was being asked to introduce a new concept into English law. Actually, as the judges in the minority stressed, English law had been awarding damages to reflect the fact of an unlawful violation of personal liberty, for centuries. Lord Walker's statement is more than a little redolent of the precise examples given by Holt CJ in his judgment in *Ashby v White*: 'the common law has always recognised that an award of more than nominal damages should be made to vindicate an assault on an individual's person or reputation, even if the claimant can prove no special damage'.[63]

In *GE v The Commissioner of An Garda Síochána*[64] the Irish Court of Appeal declined to follow *Lumba*, or *Lewis*, adopting the view that the limitation on the award of compensatory damages those decisions entailed had not formed part of the law of Ireland at the time of the adoption of the Constitution in 1937.[65] While in some respects the decision is the product of Irish constitutional law, the court felt it necessary to look first to the common law constituents of the tort. In that regard, it observed difficulties in identifying a consistent test in the post-*Lumba* decisions,[66] noted the lack of any authority before that case adopting the approach that ultimately found favour with the majority,[67] and expressed concern at the use of a 'counterfactual' that assumed that there could have been a lawful detention, when the point of the cause of action was that the detention giving rise to the claim had been unlawful.[68] The common law of false imprisonment, it concluded, had enabled an award of damages wherever there had been an unlawful detention, not only where there had been an unlawful detention that could not have been effected lawfully.

That view was shared by the Supreme Court,[69] where Hogan J agreed generally with the analysis conducted by the Court of Appeal, adding that 'vindicatory damages are … an established feature of the common law tradition, at least so far as trespassory torts such as false imprisonment are concerned'.[70] This was particularly so given that the Court had to view the cause of action in the light of the provisions of Article 40.3.2 of the Irish Constitution, which requires that the State 'in the case of injustice done … vindicate the life, person, good name and property rights of every citizen'.

As I have noted, unlike *Watkins*, the court in *Lumba* and its progeny were concerned with a trespassory tort, and to that extent the cases address different issues. However, the fundamental point remains the same. So, while the judgments in *Lumba* make no reference to either *Watkins* or *Ashby v White*, the judgment of Edelman J in *Lewis* referred to both. His treatment of *Ashby v White* was addressed to the submission on behalf of the claimant that 'substantial damages were available for the mere infringement of a right despite the absence of loss'.[71] He too stressed that the House of Lords

[63] *Lumba* (n 57) 195 (Lord Walker). There are a number of significant authorities from the Northern Ireland courts adopting the same approach, see *Oscar v Chief Constable of the RUC* [1992] NI 290; *Dodds v Chief Constable of the RUC* [1998] NI 393.

[64] *GE v The Commissioner of An Garda Síochána* [2021] IECA 113, [2021] 2 ILRM 442.

[65] ibid [147].

[66] ibid [52].

[67] ibid [49] and [86].

[68] ibid [112].

[69] *GE v The Commissioner of An Garda Síochána* [2022] IESC 51, [2022] 2 ILRM 393.

[70] ibid [39].

[71] *Lewis* (n 5) [163].

was not acting as a judicial body and expressed the view that it did not adopt the reported reasoning of Holt CJ.[72]

V. WHY DOES ANY OF THIS MATTER?

In *Watkins*, Lord Bingham explained that, notwithstanding the outcome of the case, the claimant was not without remedy. Prison officers who breached the rules and the governors of the prisons would be amenable to judicial review. Errant officers would be susceptible to disciplinary sanctions. Breaches of a fundamental human or constitutional right would, in all probability, found a claim under section 7 of the Human Rights Act 1998. Indeed, he suggested, it may well be that it could be inferred from the enactment of that statute that Parliament intended infringements of the core human and constitutional rights protected by the Human Rights Act to be remedied under it and not by the development of parallel remedies.[73]

To this there are some practical, if obvious, responses. Judicial review may enable the grant of vindicatory relief in some circumstances in which damages might (but for the rationale of *Watkins*) have been available, but not necessarily in all. The provisions of the Human Rights Act in the UK envisage significantly lower damages than those enabled at common law and, in particular, do not enable a grant of exemplary damages. But perhaps more importantly even if the Human Rights Act can, under English law, operate to narrow the scope of common law remedies, the essential thesis underlying *Watkins* is what delivered the outcome in *Lumba* and that, I fear, reflects a misconception as to the proper role of the law of torts at the intersection between private rights and public wrongs to which I have earlier referred.

The statement of Lord Bingham I mentioned above – that 'the primary role of the law of torts is to provide monetary compensation for those who have suffered material damage rather than to vindicate the rights of those who have not' – is both inherently (and uncertainly) qualified ('primary role'), in addition to being over-general. It is definitely true of the tort of negligence (which has been often said to have wielded a disproportionate influence in these cases), but it cannot be said with such certainty for other causes of action. It is, in particular, belied by the history of the trespassory torts. In *Grant v Roche*,[74] Hardiman J having surveyed the authorities observed:

> There is thus authority, both judicial and academic, for the proposition that the law of tort is, at least in certain circumstances, an important tool for the vindication of constitutional rights, and no authority whatever for the proposition that it is concerned exclusively for the allocation of damages and with nothing else whatsoever.[75]

The statement was made before *Lumba*, but the cases demonstrate the correctness of the assertion. In false imprisonment, it is clear that damages were awarded for any unlawful interference with liberty other than the merely fleeting, even where a detention could have

[72] ibid.
[73] *Watkins* (n 3) [26].
[74] *Grant v Roche* [2008] IESC 35, [2008] 4 IR 679.
[75] ibid [79].

been effected lawfully.[76] The cases show the award of damages in trespass to land or to chattels even though the plaintiff suffered no actual loss as a consequence of the wrong.[77] All of that, as I have alluded to earlier, was made clear in *Ashby v White* itself. To suggest that in these circumstances the law of torts does not have a role in vindicating at least certain rights of those who cannot point to personal injury or damage to property is to sidestep the history of these causes of action.[78]

The outcomes are also potentially unjust, and in a somewhat random way. This is in part because of the arbitrary – and accidental – distinction within the common law between torts actionable *per* se, and actions on the case. The plaintiff in *Watkins* had experienced an attack on his personal rights that was of such severity that the Court of Appeal felt the case should be remitted for a determination as to whether exemplary damages should be awarded and, if so, in what amount. Because that assault on his right was not 'damage', there was no cause of action on the back of which such an award could be even contemplated. The fact that the interference with those entitlements could cause distress, upset, or annoyance falling short of a recoverable personal injury becomes irrelevant.[79] The fact that had he been in a position to take his distress to the level required to constitute a personal injury, or indeed established any interference with his property, a claim for exemplary damages would have been possible, suggests the arbitrariness of the solution. That is particularly so in a context in which, by definition, the action for misfeasance in public office will often involve circumstances meriting the award of such damages.

The claimants in *Lumba* and the other false imprisonment cases had been subjected to forced confinement by the State without legal authority. The fact that such legal authority would inevitably have been granted had matters been done properly cannot affect the reality that they were not. Subsequent cases have suggested a test based on simply whether the detention *could* have been lawfully effected, meaning – precisely as Lord Brown predicted in the course of his dissent in *Lumba* – that in England the tort of false imprisonment may be committed merely in a technical way. That, he said, would seriously devalue the whole concept underpinning the cause of action.[80]

VI. DAMAGES FOLLOWING BREACH OF A CONSTITUTIONAL RIGHT[81]

I think that at least some of those jurisdictions that have acknowledged the viability of a claim for damages for a breach of constitutional rights have come closest to resolving these issues in a way that most effectively accommodates these concerns.[82]

[76] See *Dumbell v Roberts* [1944] 1 All ER 326; *Kuchenmeister v Home Office* [1958] 1 QB 496; *Christie v Leachinski* [1947] AC 573.

[77] *Morris Garner v One Step (Support) Ltd* [2018] UKSC 20, [2019] 1 AC 649.

[78] See generally on this theme and its relationship to the decisions in *Watkins* and *Lumba*, JNE Varuhas, *Damages and Human Rights* (Hart Publishing, 2016).

[79] See *Watkins* (n 3) [20], where Lord Bingham cited *Odhavji Estate v Woodhouse* [2003] 3 SCR 263 as authority for the proposition that 'while grief or emotional distress were insufficient injury to support a claim, visible and provable illness or recognisable physical or psychopathological harm were not'.

[80] *Lumba* (n 57) 343.

[81] I refer on occasion in the text to a 'constitutional tort'. Where I do so I am using this term in a generic rather than technical sense. In Ireland, the cause of action for damages for violation of a constitutional right is a tort so called, in others the remedy is viewed as *sui generis*.

[82] Apart from its recognition in the US, the availability of such a cause of action was confirmed by the New Zealand Court of Appeal in *Simpson v Attorney General (Baigent's case)* [1994] 3 NZLR 667, and by

In Ireland, in 1972, the Supreme Court decided that damages were available in at least some situations in which a plaintiff could establish a violation of his or her constitutional rights.[83] As the law has developed, the courts have interpreted that facility as operating only by way of default where no common law or statutory remedy is available to address the violation complained of.[84] So, for example, a plaintiff complaining of a violation of his or her constitutional rights as a consequence of an unlawful detention will be non-suited because the tort of false imprisonment affords a constitutionally adequate mechanism for obtaining damages.[85] Plaintiffs, however, who sought damages for violations of their rights to privacy arising from unauthorised and unlawful tapping of their telephones by the authorities could proceed with such an action – there being no common law tort covering their complaint.[86] Work remains to be done on the dividing line between circumstances in which the law of tort does, and does not, afford a 'constitutionally adequate remedy', this largely depending on issues of (sometimes uncertain) categorisation. In claims on the margins, there is an inclination to interpret the common law claims generously so as to render them constitutionally acceptable,[87] although there are cases in which the constitutional tort action has been preferred in the case of any doubt as to whether there is a common law claim.[88]

What matters here is how a constitutional remedy that closely follows the principles of tortious liability at common law provides a coherent basis for – certainly as I see it – maintaining the integrity of the principles originating in the common law. The decision in *Kearney v Minister for Justice*[89] provides a good example, and is a helpful contrast with *Watkins*. There, the plaintiff sued for damages for interference with his right to communicate when his prison correspondence (which had been lawfully opened) was not delivered to him. He was awarded nominal damages, but the court made it clear that exemplary damages would have been available had the interference been oppressive.

That case shows that for at least some rights the constitutional tort is actionable *per se*,[90] and other decisions confirm the ability of the courts to award exemplary damages in such proceedings.[91] While many actions have involved recovery for injury to property or person in a context that would be cognisable at common law, it is evident that a more relaxed threshold is applied in respect of injuries in the nature of

the Supreme Court of Canada in *Vancouver (City) v Ward* [2010] 2 SCR 28. The dissenting judgment of Elias CJ in *Attorney General v Chapman* (n 36) contains a most helpful summary of the consideration by the Privy Council of a similar jurisdiction in a range of Commonwealth legal systems, [41]–[45]. The judgment of Hardie-Boys J in *Baigent's case* considers the Irish decisions including those in *Meskell v CIE* [1973] IR 121 and *Kennedy v Ireland* [1987] IR 587. In *Fose v Minister of Safety and Security* (CCT14/96) [1997] ZACC 6, 1997 (7) BCLR 851, 1997 (3) SA 786 (5 June 1997), the South African Constitutional Court also recognised such a cause of action noting, again, the Irish decisions, see [50].

[83] *Meskell v CIE* [1973] IR 121; the decision and its subsequent development has attracted substantial literature. For one of the more recent and comprehensive examinations, see G Hogan, 'The Farthest – December 1972' (2019) 62 *Irish Jurist* 1.

[84] *W v Ireland (No 2)* [1997] 2 IR 141.

[85] *DF v Garda Commissioner* [2014] IEHC 213.

[86] *Kennedy v Ireland* [1987] IR 587.

[87] See *Carr v Olas* [2012] IEHC 59 [36].

[88] *Sullivan v Boylan* [2013] IEHC 104, [2013] 1 IR 510 [25].

[89] *Kearney v Minister for Justice* [1986] IR 116.

[90] As to which see B McMahon and W Binchy, *Law of Torts* (Bloomsbury, 2013) paras 1.96-1.100. This mirrors the conclusion reached by the majority in *Uzuegbunam v Preczewski* (n 37).

[91] *Conway v INTO* [1991] 2 IR 305.

distress and inconvenience than would be contemplated by the private law of tort.[92] Although the issue has never been directly confronted in the Supreme Court, it is not impossible that, in an appropriate case, more than nominal damages may be awarded to simply reflect the injury to the right itself in circumstances falling short of the requirements for a punitive award.[93] While the requirement of wrongful intent that must be established before the cause of action will be made out remains very much context dependent, it seems likely that in many circumstances in which the elements of the tort of misfeasance in public office are established, it will satisfy the constitutional requirement.[94] Conversely, when addressing public wrongdoing not contemplated by the common law actions (most notably in the form of loss caused by the operation of an unconstitutional statute), the courts have been inclined to limit the constitutional tort to circumstances of knowing and malicious or reckless indifference to that unconstitutionality,[95] with the Supreme Court in one case identifying an immunity from such liability where statutory decision-makers act *bona fide* and without negligence.[96] However, it follows from everything I have said that where a fundamental right is involved, in at least some circumstances this will be interpreted as requiring actionability without proof of special damage.

VII. SOME CONCLUDING THOUGHTS

Thus, and in one way strangely, the constitutional remedy presents a modern cause of action that is of considerable novelty, but which at the same time operates to return the law of tortious remedies to its original common law incarnation, functioning inter alia to identify fundamental liberties of the citizen and to enable the agitation of a claim in damages where specific categories of public wrongdoing result in the infringement of those interests. It is not impossible that in some jurisdictions it combines this with the power in appropriate cases to award damages reflecting the normative value of the right that has been breached, and it certainly treats the cause of action as one actionable per se in at least some circumstances.

This comes at the cost of a certain untidiness, but the sensible development of the law can abate this and, in any event, the trade-off may justify that cost. The remedy for damages for a breach of constitutional rights was judicially created partly because of the

[92] *Cosgrove v Ireland* (n 35), *Sullivan v Boylan* (n 88).

[93] The issue remains a controversial one in those jurisdictions that have recognised the cause of action: see in particular the discussion of the issue in *Fose v Minister of Safety and Security* (n 82) [67]–[68]. The judgment of Hogan J, and in particular noting his reference to Art 40.3.2 of the Irish Constitution, provides a strong indication that the making of an award of vindicatory damages (which Hogan J in *GE v The Commissioner of An Garda Síochána* (n 69) [42] described as 'damages which are not nominal but which are nonetheless intended to mark the importance of the right that has been infringed') is open to a Court when faced with a claim for damages for breach of a constitutional right. Having regard to the conclusion of the Court on the nature of the damages to be awarded for the tort of false imprisonment at common law, the statement may be *obiter* or, if not, may be limited to deprivations of liberty.

[94] *MC v Clinical Director of the Central Mental Hospital* [2020] IESC 28, [2020] 2 ILRM 309.

[95] *Blehein v Minister for Health and Children* [2018] IESC 40, but see *O'Callaghan v Ireland* [2021] IESC 68, [2021] 2 ILRM 397 in which damages were awarded for breach of the entitlement of the plaintiff to a criminal trial within a reasonable period of time.

[96] *Pine Valley Developments v Minister for the Environment* [1987] IR 23 [38].

historical fact that damages has always been the method of protecting interests in liberty, but primarily because the remedy reflects the importance of the entitlement at stake. Where the State acts unlawfully so as to engage the traditional law of torts – whether it be via a confinement without lawful authority, or a *mala fides* exercise of administrative power, or an entry upon property without warrant – and in the course of so doing interferes deliberately, directly and substantially with a vested constitutional right, the significance of the entitlement that has been violated demands at least the facility to award exemplary damages where warranted and in appropriate cases to compensate for the distress, inconvenience and insult arising from the breach. The analysis leading to that conclusion, and the variables required to sustain liability, are more complex than the proclamation *ubi jus ibi remedium* might suggest. There remain issues of principle to be resolved in its application – in particular in developing a structured model for calculating damages, and in determining when, if ever, it should be possible to award damages to reflect the inherent value of the right that has been infringed.

It is my own view that in many cases, much of this work can be done within the framework of the common law of torts, and I think it preferable that existing, established, and more clearly structured and certain remedies should be used where this is possible. Where it is not, however, the existence of a free-standing constitutional remedy that enables the courts to respond to novel infringements of basic liberties without awaiting legislative change, is vital to the dynamic of judicial protection of the basic rights of the citizen and the upholding and enforcement, of the rule of law.

11

Long Waves of Constitutional Principle in the Common Law

PHILIP SALES

I. INTRODUCTION

THIS CHAPTER SEEKS to explore the way in which constitutional law as embedded in and emerging from the common law addresses the problem of democratic time. It draws on analogies from states with written constitutions, which also have to address the problem of democratic time.

The governance regime in a liberal democratic polity has to accommodate different needs. It has to provide space for the fast-paced and reactive business of politics as carried on by the executive government, alongside the production of law through deliberation and legislation. To be effective, these functions have to have a constitutional framework which enables political actors to engage with each other and which secures legitimacy and acceptability of outcomes in the eyes of those subject to the regime. The constitutional framework provides a stable bedrock of law to make coherent political engagement possible. But in order to secure legitimacy as society changes, that bedrock itself has to be capable of change.

Reflection on the common law can explain how this occurs. The common law provides stability but is also capable of change over time without legislative intervention, as a necessary aspect of maintaining its legitimacy. In the same way, constitutional law as set out in common law rules has to fulfil the function of providing stability while also changing to maintain its ongoing legitimacy as the foundation for democratic politics. A similar process occurs where constitutional law is written down in instruments which are regarded as 'living'.

In a common law system like that in the United Kingdom (UK), constitutional law emerges from the judicial practice of statutory interpretation and the practice of judicial review of executive action. Statutory interpretation is carried out on the basis of a set of common law assumptions regarding how Parliament intends its legislation to be understood. The framing function of constitutional law requires this law to be stable, but constitutional law also has to ensure that it be kept in a good state of repair in terms of its alignment with background social values which give it legitimacy. The process of change to fulfil this repair function is slow and has to be, if constitutional law is to be able to provide the stability required of it and if the institutional limits on the judicial role in relation to effecting change in the law are to be respected. It is in this context that it is appropriate to speak of long waves of constitutional principle in the law, as pressure grows for legal change without legislation and then such change is recognised by courts as having occurred. I examine this process and discuss the criteria which govern such recognition.

II. THE TEMPO OF DEMOCRATIC TIME

Helen Thompson's book, *Disorder: Hard Times in the 21st Century*, addresses the concept of 'Democratic Time'.[1] She refers to the traditional understanding associated with, in particular, Machiavelli and Polybius, that time 'is the dimension of instability' in politics.[2] According to Polybius, government progresses between kingship, aristocracy and democracy, as each form of government is destroyed by its own excesses; '[t]he only way to check the cycle and allow for a long middle – what he called "a state of equilibrium" is to balance the three positive forms of government … and have them counteract each other'.[3] Transposing this idea to modern times, according to Thompson, a balance is required between the aristocratic element and the democratic element.[4] The aristocratic element tends to predominate in a representative democracy subject to the rule of law with strong protection for property rights, but can be balanced by the democratic element, involving equal voting rights. If liberal democracy is to survive, tendencies to either aristocratic excess – excessive control by rich elites[5] – or democratic excess – with a danger of decay, as feared by Max Weber, into authoritarianism through power acquired by a charismatic, demagogic leader[6] – have to be controlled and corrections made. She points out that Machiavelli 'started from the premise that states, including republics, had to change to sustain themselves against time'.[7]

Liberal democracies are forms of polity which seek to sustain themselves by drawing on various potential sources of legitimacy. One may debate how these should be identified and characterised, and the same value can sometimes have a tendency to pull in different directions. For example, liberal democracy is based on a moral and formal-legal concept of equality of citizens before the law and in their ability to participate in political life. But equality as a value can be invoked to emphasise individual rights and freedoms on the one hand, or by contrast to emphasise effective decision-making by the collectivity made up of individuals with an equal say in decisions. The relationship between equality and social solidarity, and the degree to which each depends on the other, is also important but contested. The same is true of the relationship between ideas of justice and

[1] H Thompson, *Disorder: Hard Times in the 21st Century* (Oxford University Press, 2022) ch 7.
[2] ibid 182, quoting JGA Pocock, *The Machiavellian Moment: Florentine Political Thought and the Atlantic Political Tradition* (Princeton University Press, 1975), 77.
[3] Thompson (n 1) 183.
[4] For discussion of the same theme running from Constant to Tocqueville to Habermas, see M Loughlin, *Against Constitutionalism* (Harvard University Press, 2022) ch 7.
[5] Thompson (n 1) 185.
[6] ibid 186.
[7] ibid 187. See N Machiavelli, *Discourses on Livy* (translated by J Bondanella and P Bondanella) ([1531], Oxford University Press, 1997).

community, and between respect for individuals and acceptance of their dependency and embeddedness in society. Such underlying issues are reflected in debates about what rights individuals should have and what duties they owe, or what limitations on their rights and freedoms they may reasonably be expected to accept. They are also reflected in debates about whether a constitution is or should be legal or political in nature or, if a mixture of these, where the balance should lie.

But a complex political regime like a liberal democracy cannot be reduced to simple ideas and slogans. The significance of particular elements which contribute to such a regime, and the need to reassert them or give them prominence, or on the contrary to de-emphasise them, is liable to fluctuate over time. It is also liable to vary according to the legal and political culture in which the issue arises.

However, having made the point that crude reductionism should be avoided, for the purposes of exposition it is fair to highlight a balance which a liberal democratic polity inevitably has to face up to, namely between the tradition of political liberalism – 'the rule of law, the separation of powers and the defence of individual freedom' – and the democratic tradition, 'whose central ideas are equality and popular sovereignty'.[8] To speak of these as traditions is to acknowledge that they are each constituted by clusters of ideas, not defined with precision or captured in exact logical relationships, but which nonetheless have a particular affinity in this context and hang together. This balance overlaps with, even if it does not exactly correspond to, the balance required between what Thompson calls the democratic and the aristocratic elements of the regime. If they are to retain their liberal democratic character, liberal democratic polities have to be able to engage in repair and reform across time in order to sustain the acceptability of the basic settlement they achieve between what is essentially a contingent compromise between the liberal tradition and the democratic tradition. One thinks of the marvellous line in Lampedusa's *The Leopard*,[9] '[i]f we want things to stay as they are, things will have to change'.

There are three tempos of time in a democracy embedded in a common law constitution. There is the need for an elected government which can respond at speed to events in the world as they unfold. This is executive time. It is characterised by a high level of discretion and flexibility for manoeuvre within very broad legal parameters. There is essentially an unavoidable need for a high degree of discretion in order to govern. As Raymond Geuss puts it: 'to attempt in a thoroughgoing and comprehensive way to oppose a discretionary power which is to some extent unpredictable is not a coherent project, because such discretionary power is of the essence of politics'.[10] A political order needs the capacity to react, and react quickly, to unpredictable changes in circumstances.

[8] C Mouffe, *For a Left Populism* (Verso, 2018) 14, citing CB Macpherson, *The Life and Times of Liberal Democracy* (Oxford University Press, 1977).

[9] GT di Lampedusa, *The Leopard* (first published 1958, translated by A Colquhoun) (Penguin, 2007); albeit that comment related to the old aristocratic order and the recognition that it had to change with the times to retain its power. See Machiavelli (n 7) 246, Book III, ch 1 'In Order for a Religion or a Republic to Have a Long Life, It Is Often Necessary to Bring it Back to its Beginnings': in a republic, this may be achieved by 'intrinsic prudence'. Also see J-W Müller, *Democracy Rules* (Allen Lane, 2021) 94, calling for a return to basics, 'another *riduzione verso il principio*' for democracy, to preserve its fundamental balance between a designated site for collectively binding decision-making involving the expression of political will through law-making and a protected place for 'the continuous formation of opinions and political judgments in society at large'.

[10] R Geuss, *History and Illusion in Politics* (Cambridge University Press, 2001) 107.

Then there is the need for the elected legislature to be able to consider proposals for reform of the law and to make decisions in light of what is judged to be the needs of the day. This is legislative time. It is slower and more measured than executive time. It generally involves a period of reflection and deliberation, proceeding from public debate out of which matters of public concern emerge, through refinement by application of democratic procedures (voting in elections on the basis of party manifestos, adoption of legislative proposals for presentation to Parliament) into enactment by Parliament as concrete laws.[11]

Then there is the need for basic ground-rules to be worked out to provide the framework for democratic contestation and engagement. This is the dimension of constitutional time. It is in the dimension of constitutional time that it is appropriate to speak of long waves of constitutional principle in the common law.

III. FRAMING AND REPAIR THROUGH CONSTITUTIONAL LAW IN THE LIBERAL DEMOCRATIC ORDER

Analysed in this way, the role of constitutional law is the framing and repair of the liberal democratic order. It frames that order because the ground-rules have to be taken to be fixed and stable to a high degree in order to make engagement in democratic politics comprehensible and effective. It contributes to repair of the order by adjusting it over time in an effort to keep the legal order aligned with social expectations and understandings.

In English law, the idea of constitutional law is indistinct. Speaking broadly, constitutional law is concerned with the generation and allocation of power to act, and with ensuring that it is exercised within proper bounds and subject to proper constraints. These aspects are inter-related. In part, ensuring that power is exercised within proper bounds involves policing how it is allocated. Power is generated by stipulating who may exercise it and specifying how their authority is constituted. Ensuring that power is exercised in the proper way also involves checking that this is done by the persons who have it assigned to them; and requiring them to respect certain values and standards when they do exercise it contributes to the generation of power by helping to secure public acceptance when it is exercised.[12] But partly because this is such a broad account of constitutional law, and partly because there is no comprehensive written constitution, there is no settled or rigorous definition of constitutional law. Constitutional law can be taken to extend from high principle to fine detail, such as the nuts and bolts of election law, so that where the limits of it are drawn is largely a matter of convenience, as Maitland put it.[13] He pointed out that it is difficult to discern where constitutional law ends and administrative law (the law governing the proper exercise of public power) begins; in the UK there is no sanctity attaching to constitutional law. Nonetheless, some aspects of constitutional/administrative law are more fundamental than others and may therefore be taken to be more constitutional in their impact. So I concentrate on these aspects in this chapter.

[11] J Habermas, *Between Facts and Norms* (translated by W Rehg) (MIT Press, 1996).

[12] S Holmes, *Passions and Constraint: On the Theory of Liberal Democracy* (University of Chicago Press, 1995).

[13] FW Maitland, *The Constitutional History of England* (edited by HAL Fisher) (Cambridge University Press, 1908) 526–39.

What contribution does the common law, specifically, make to these constitutional aspects of the law? In this context, common law is taken to be synonymous with judge-made law. I am concerned with the judicial contribution to the governing legal scheme, focusing on the position in the UK. The critical elements of this are the practice of and doctrine associated with statutory interpretation and the articulation of the principles of judicial review.

Speaking about the judicial contribution to constitutional law means that analogies can be drawn with jurisdictions which have a written constitution. In such jurisdictions, the judicial contribution to constitutional law remains considerable, because the application of a legal instrument in the form of a constitution calls for judicial interpretation in novel situations (as does the application of a legal instrument in the form of a statute) and because constitutional provisions (particularly those setting out fundamental rights[14]) are often in general terms, so that their application is under-determined by the instrument itself. Jurisdictions with written constitutions develop their own constitutional common law.

The framing function of constitutional law by setting the ground-rules of the liberal democratic order in constitutional law is not simply a matter of containment and restraint – though the rules do that as well; it is a matter of establishing the grammar of the system.[15] The ground-rules are power generating, in that they allow the joint formation of intentions which enables the taking of coherent action by the state according to a structure of authority which commands public acceptance.

The requirement that the executive and legislature respect constitutional norms means that the constitution slows down the tempo of executive time and legislative time, and so has a calming effect on politics. The standards imposed by the common law (and taken as implied into legislative provisions) require the executive to behave fairly, which may require them to seek and take account of representations from those affected by their actions. The executive may have to obtain legislative authorisation from Parliament for their actions. If Parliament wishes to legislate to override the implied constitutional standards such as those read into statutes pursuant to the principle of legality as discussed below, it has to ensure that it does this in particularly clear terms and pays the political price for doing so. This includes highlighting the issue for potentially hostile or sceptical debate which will take up time in the legislative process. The executive also has to give a political account of its actions to Parliament, and this and the need to seek legislative authorisation may take time and encourage reflection and moderation. This all aids legitimacy as well, and reinforces loser consent. It gives reassurance that minority views have been considered and not lost in the rush to get things done. As Jan-Werner Müller pithily puts it, the essence of liberal democracy is that the majority gets their way after the minority have their say,[16] and the slowing of the tempo of executive and legislative time allows for the minority's

[14] Judicial latitude in applying a constitutional provision will be considerably less in relation to those which are framed in concrete and specific terms: *Chandler v The State (No 2)* [2022] UKPC 19 [73]. *cf* J Balkin, *Living Originalism* (Harvard University Press, 2011) 24–25: 'Constitution drafters use rules because they want to limit discretion; they use standards or principles [sc expressed in vague language] because they want to channel politics but delegate the details to future generations'.

[15] Holmes (n 12) ch 5; P Sales, 'Legalism in Constitutional Law: Judging in a Democracy' (2018) *Public Law* 687, 691–95.

[16] Müller (n 9) 65, 72.

voice to be heard and be seen to be heard. It undercuts what Hannah Arendt called 'the contempt of the administrator', an impatience with procedural rules which, by requiring justifications to be given for action, gets in the way of pure executive fiat.[17]

The repair function of common law constitutional law is made possible by the judicial contribution to that law, which allows for adjustments over time to align constitutional norms with social expectations, so that they do not drift too far apart. Application of legal norms is a constant process, which can arise in the courts at any time. This distinguishes it from legislative action, where the focus is on a specific act at a particular time to define new laws to govern in the future. The judicial application of an already existing norm binds together past, present and future in a way that a legislative act does not. A judge has to understand how the norm to be applied came to exist in the past and its meaning then and decide what meaning it should bear in the present to govern the dispute before the court and (potentially) what meaning it should carry into the future to be derived from the precedential value of the decision.

The framing function of constitutional law suggests that the ground-rules comprised within it should be unchanging. In order to be able to participate fully and effectively in the exercise of public authority on behalf of the state, political actors need to understand clearly the grammar of the system, where they stand vis-à-vis other actors, what options are available in order to negotiate or engage with those others, what actions are open to them acting alone and what actions might be open to them acting with others. The executive needs to know what its powers are so that it can act with legitimacy and minimise the risk of getting into difficult and mutually damaging battles with the courts. But in practice a democratic system can function effectively so long as the ground-rules are *sufficiently* understood and are *reasonably* stable over time.[18]

This allows space for the repair function of constitutional law, which is also important.

IV. THE REPAIR FUNCTION IN LIBERAL DEMOCRACY

The liberal democratic system can only function effectively if respect for it and consequently for the laws it produces is maintained across time. As Hegel observed:

> How blind they are who may hope that institutions, constitutions, laws which no longer correspond to human manners, needs and opinions, from which the spirit has flown, can subsist any longer; or that forms in which intellect and feeling now take no interest are powerful enough to be any longer the bond of a nation![19]

The question of reasonable alignment potentially raises issues across the whole field of constitutional law. They extend from the balance between sources of authority stemming from the liberal and the democratic political traditions referred to above – is authority sufficiently democratic? Does it provide effective government? Does it provide effective protection of rights? – and hence how power is allocated between the different institutions

[17] C Volk, *Arendtian Constitutionalism: Law, Politics and the Order of Freedom* (Hart Publishing, 2015) 120.

[18] This point can be made generally about planning in the light of common law norms: *cf* MA Eisenberg, *The Nature of the Common Law* (Harvard University Press, 1988) 158: 'The greater part of the common law, although not certain, is nevertheless sufficiently determinate for planning purposes'.

[19] ZA Pełczyński (ed), *Hegel's Political Writings* (translated by TM Knox) (Clarendon Press, 1964) 243–44.

of the state, to the way in which public power is exercised – is it done fairly? Is there sufficient examination of relevant matters of the public interest? Is there effective recognition of individual rights? Is there sufficient opportunity for individuals' participation in decisions which affect them?

Four reasons why the work of repair through the maintenance of a reasonable alignment of the law (and constitutional law in particular) and social expectations is important may be emphasised. First, in order for its governance to be effective the state requires a high degree of cooperation from citizens, and this has to be secured by ensuring that they regard the law as legitimate.[20]

Secondly, since the balance between the two political traditions is inherently ambiguous and potentially liable to get out of kilter, thereby threatening one or other of the primary benefits conferred by liberal democracy (individual autonomy and participation in actions of collective autonomy), and hence the legitimacy of the whole system, work is required to adjust the tiller from time to time to ensure that both benefits are secured so far as possible in a self-reinforcing relationship. They cannot be allowed to descend into a spiral of growing mutual antagonism. Both are founded on an anti-paternalistic epistemological premise that there is no final truth about what is good for the individual, only what he or she decides upon, and there is no final truth about what is good for society; rather, the only criterion for the public good is what the people, freely organised and able to decide freely, will choose.[21] As Beetham observes, this ambiguity makes democratic critique of liberalism both necessary but also problematic, if it threatens the conditions of liberal democracy itself.[22] 'To be able to shape the course or conditions of one's life through sharing control over collective decisions is a necessary counterpart to exercising such control at the personal or individual level'.[23]

Thirdly, when they deliver their rulings courts represent society, and in order to preserve the legitimacy of their own function in the eyes of citizens, they have to be able to maintain the perception that they are doing this.[24] This too is important for preserving the legitimacy of the liberal democratic order since courts have to play such a central part in it by upholding individual rights while also ensuring that the government and legislature are able to rule.

Fourthly, by maintaining an appreciation of the legitimacy of the liberal democratic order, founded on the benefits it can and does provide, the courts make a significant contribution to ensuring that loser consent exists for democratic choices made by the majority under fair conditions. Loser consent is the essence of democracy, since without it majoritarian rule on a foundation of consensus cannot operate.[25] Responsiveness to changing expectations helps to maintain consent.[26]

[20] HLA Hart, *The Concept of Law*, 3rd edn (Oxford University Press, 2012) ch 4; TR Tyler, *Why People Obey The Law* (Princeton University Press, 2006).

[21] D Beetham, 'Liberal Democracy and the Limits of Democratization' (1992) *Political Studies XL*, Special Issue 40, 41–42.

[22] ibid 44.

[23] ibid 45.

[24] P Sales and F Wilmot-Smith, 'Justice for Foxes' (2022) 138 *LQR* 583, 600–02.

[25] Thompson (n 1) ch 7; A Przeworski, *Crises of Democracy* (Cambridge University Press, 2019).

[26] K Dyson, *The State Tradition in Western Europe: A Study of an Idea and an Institution* (Oxford University Press, 1980) 258. Hegel and Burke made similar points, as is noted in Loughlin (n 4) 36. He quotes Burke, 'A state without the means of some change is without the means of its conservation'.

V. WHY CHANGE IN COMMON LAW CONSTITUTIONAL PRINCIPLES COMES IN LONG WAVES

The framing function of constitutional law is also legitimacy-building, since it enables the democratic elements in the constitution to operate effectively. Coherent formation and exercise of democratic will would be frustrated if the ground-rules of constitutional law were liable to an excessive degree of unheralded and unexpected change, affecting the meaning and effect of choices made in the light of those rules. So they cannot be wholly overridden in the interests of repair. A reasonable balance between maintaining stability in the interests of the framing function and change in the interests of the repair function means that the changes ought to take place slowly and incrementally.

Executive time and legislative time produce changes according to high frequency wave-lengths, reacting to the high pace of the emergence of issues in the public sphere and the need for action to respond to them. Constitutional time produces changes according to low frequency, long wave-lengths. The framing function of constitutional common law means that it cannot change at such speed as executive and legislative time. The ground rules comprising constitutional law might appear unchanging, but in fact they are capable of change through the interpretive activity of judges, but at a far slower pace than executive action or legislative change. Since it provides the framework within which the high tempo engagement involved in executive time and legislative time is played out, constitutional law has to be stable enough to allow participants in democratic politics to be able to form coherent expectations about what actions are and are not permitted in the course of compromise, conflict and debate about how to proceed.

A requirement that change should occur at a slow pace and incrementally allows for the possibility of some notice that it is or may be on the way, so that political actors can allow for the risk that it may occur. In the common law, the way in which evidence may begin to mount in judicial statements and practice that a change might be on the cards can be likened to the way in which a wave begins to form and gather mass before it breaks.

In addition to this functional constraint on the development of common law constitutional norms, there are constraints on judges in the development of such norms stemming from judges' position and limited authority in a democratic order. Judges are appointed with guarantees of their independence and insulation from having to respond in the immediate term to shifts in public opinion. By contrast with the legislature, they do not have democratic legislative authority to change the law. Such legal change as judges can produce has to be carried out interstitially in the process of interpreting existing law, within comparatively narrow limits consonant with the legitimate exercise of judicial authority. This means that it has to be conducted at a slow pace, in such a way that it can be regarded as legitimately interpretive and not illegitimately legislative. Constitutional theory intersects here with a more general theory of the common law.

A significant constraint which reduces the legitimacy of law-making by courts is the problem of being able to identify with confidence what are the public expectations with which the law is to be brought into conformity. This relates to the epistemic point above. In times before the hegemony of liberal democracy, judges as leading members of their societies felt more confident of their role in laying down the law.[27] Now, the appeal to

[27] P Sales, 'Modern Statutory Interpretation' (2017) 38 *Statute Law Review* 125, 129.

natural law by a social elite has lost its persuasive force.[28] Democratic choice and selection of value is what remains, along with the recognition of legitimacy associated with maintaining in place and in healthy order the preconditions for the free exercise of such choice. In the absence of a clear written constitutional norm to which appeal can be made, the courts feel natural reticence in reviewing, criticising or modifying through interpretation laws passed according to democratic procedures.[29] A vote taken pursuant to democratic procedures appears to fill the epistemic gap: the people have spoken and have collectively declared the values to be promoted.

Courts looking to carry on their repair function by keeping the law aligned with social expectations therefore have to apply far more demanding criteria before they can have confidence that public opinion has changed so widely and so strongly or persistently that it is legitimate for them to act to change the law. It typically takes a long time for sufficient evidence to accumulate to allow the courts both to identify what action needs to be taken and to be sure that it will be regarded as legitimate for them to take it.

From the perspective of common law theory, Melvin Eisenberg argues that '[t]he common law should seek to satisfy three standards: social congruence, systemic consistency and doctrinal stability'.[30] By social congruence he means that the law should be made congruent with what he calls social propositions, ie moral norms, policies and experiential propositions about the way the world works.[31] As he says, '[t]he rules made by courts should be durable – generalizable over time as well as over persons – and therefore should not be based on policies that seem transitory'.[32] Also, because they are not representative institutions in the democratic sense, courts have to proceed slowly and taking care not to impose their own values: 'The legitimacy of the judicial establishment of legal rules therefore depends in large part on the employment of a process of reasoning that begins with existing legal and social standards rather than those standards the court thinks best'.[33] A judge is not free to employ those social propositions he or she thinks best, but acts in a position of trust for society as a whole.[34]

Benjamin Cardozo similarly described the compromise between rest and motion, stability and progress which lies at the heart of the common law.[35] The law needs both a spirit of change and a spirit of conservation.[36] If the law comes to depart from the 'norms and standards of behaviour' which previously legitimised it, the same process of legitimisation requires that it be changed and brought back into equilibrium with those norms and standards, 'without legislation, but by inherent energies of the judicial process'.[37]

[28] M Loughlin, *The Idea of Public Law* (Oxford University Press, 2003) 115–17. See also H Kelsen, *The Essence and Value of Democracy* ([1929] (edited by N Urbinati and C Invernizzi Accetti, translated by B Graf (Rowman and Littlefield, 2013) ch 10.

[29] See, eg, *R (SC) v Secretary of State for Work and Pensions* [2021] UKSC 6, [2022] AC 223 [208]–[209], *Suraj v Attorney General of Trinidad and Tobago* [2022] UKPC 26, [2023] AC 337 [93].

[30] Eisenberg (n 18) 50. For further discussion, see P Sales, 'Common Law: Context and Method' (2019) 135 *LQR* 47.

[31] Eisenberg (n 18) ch 4.

[32] ibid 31.

[33] ibid 150.

[34] ibid 2–3.

[35] BN Cardozo, *The Paradoxes of Legal Science* (Columbia University Press, 1928).

[36] ibid 7.

[37] ibid 14–15.

This is a statement of the repair function as something inherent generally in the common law legal process.

Cardozo addresses the problem of what criteria to apply before the courts can modify legal norms in the absence of legislation. He observes that while law has to reflect the morality of the community, that morality may vary between groups in a pluralistic society. So, he asks, when does the social pressure 'become strong enough to convert the moral norm into a jural one?'

According to Cardozo, the line should be drawn higher than the lowest level of moral principle or practice in society and lower than the highest; the law will strive to follow the principle and practice of the people of the community 'whom the social mind would rank as intelligent and virtuous'.[38] Law should follow public opinion, defined as 'critically thought out social judgments'.[39] It is the 'strong and preponderant opinion' which has capacity to turn desire into law. In Cardozo's formulation, '[t]he common will must have made itself known for so long a time as well as in so distinct a manner as to have gained stability and authority'; this may be difficult to identify, but a judge must try.[40]

Looking at the matter more broadly, the test for change in the law should not be that a judge has to wait to be satisfied that *everyone* in society would agree with it, since that would contemplate a situation in which the courts pressed on with an existing misaligned law which a substantial and stable majority regarded as illegitimate. The failure to adjust in such circumstances would risk discrediting the law in the eyes of the general public. But a judge has to be confident that there is a solid and sustained preponderance of view in favour of change, rather than react to more epiphenomenal shifts on the surface of public debate.

Turning more particularly to constitutional law, there are again accounts of how judges have a responsibility to maintain a degree of congruence between the law and social expectations, but again balanced by the need to maintain stability as part of the law's framing function.

In *Law and Public Opinion in England*, Dicey endorsed the law-making function of the courts. He pointed out that new cases require to be resolved by the application, meaning the extension, of established principles and sometimes by development of a new principle 'in harmony with the general spirit of the law' which is suitable to meet new social needs.[41] Courts are influenced by the beliefs of the time and public opinion, but this is refined and to a degree counterbalanced by professional ways of thinking.[42] In trying to sustain the values of the legal system, the ideas of expediency or policy accepted by the courts may differ from those of the general public.[43] According to Dicey, judicial legislation aims more at securing certainty and maintaining a fixed legal system with strong respect for precedent, than at amending the deficiencies of the law, for 'a law which was not certain would in reality be no law at all'.[44]

[38] ibid 37.
[39] ibid 50.
[40] ibid 51.
[41] AV Dicey, *Law and Public Opinion in England*, 2nd edn (Macmillan, 1914) 363.
[42] ibid 363–64.
[43] ibid 367–70.
[44] ibid 366–67.

Peter Cane offers this account of Dicey's approach:

> For Dicey, history was an important part of law's context; but the history that mattered to him was history that enabled students better to understand the law of the contemporary constitution – 'practically relevant' history, we might say. One of the social functions of norms, including legal norms, is to manage the relationship between a polity's (and a society's) past, present and future. Norms promote stability. In order to understand today's norms, it may be necessary to look to the past in which the norm was established and applied over the years. On the other hand, excessive stability may be dysfunctional. Norms may, and sometimes must, change in step with changes in the needs, interests and ideas of those whose conduct they regulate. … On the other hand, because too much radical change in a given period may itself be dysfunctional, normative change is typically, to a greater or lesser degree, incremental.[45]

The relative force of the social imperative for stability in the law is relevant to the discussion here. Dicey and Cardozo were commenting on the general legitimacy for the courts to change rules in common law. The extent to which that is acceptable turns to a significant degree on the importance of maintaining stability in a given situation, and the weight to be given to that factor varies according to context. Since constitutional norms provide the foundation for the whole legal and political order, the weight to be attached to their stability and continuity across time is high. This tends to limit the circumstances in which it may be legitimate for the courts to change them. But it does not eliminate the need to do so when that serves to preserve the fundamental legitimacy of the legal and political order.

Writing about the United States' (US) Constitution, Jack Balkin links the maintenance of a sense of the legitimacy of the Constitution to loser consent in a democracy. Government under the Constitution must be sufficiently effective to maintain security and social peace and sufficiently just to be deserving of co-operation. He points out that the legitimacy of a political and legal system makes it sufficiently worthy of respect so that people have good reasons to continue to accept its law and the coercion which goes with law even when they may disagree with aspects of that law, and may have tried to change it through the political process and lost.[46] To maintain the legitimacy of the system, there is a need to avoid constitutional idolatry and complacency, and allow for a degree of change in constitutional doctrine to reflect public opinion:[47]

> Constitutional argument relies on professional judgment, but professional judgment relies on assumptions about what both professionals and non-professionals think is reasonable at any point in history. The self-image of professionals is that of reasonable people who proceed through reasoned arguments; therefore professionals often care deeply about what others think is reasonable or beyond the pale. … But what is reasonable in this sense of the word depends on the practice of persuasion in public life, the institutions of public thought and expression, and the gradual development of public values and public opinions.[48]

[45] P Cane, 'AV Dicey as Legal Theorist' (2021) 85 *MLR* 247, 250.

[46] JM Balkin, *Constitutional Redemption: Political Faith in an Unjust World* (Harvard University Press, 2011) 34.

[47] ibid 11.

[48] ibid 12.

As Jon Elster writes, '[c]onstitutionalism ensures that constitutional change will be slow, compared to the fast lane of parliamentary politics. The constitution should be a framework for political action, not an instrument for action'.[49]

The fact that a constitution provides a framework for political action does not mean that it is itself completely immune from change. However, it occupies a place which means that it is embedded and more fixed than the more fluid processes of legal doctrinal development which it channels. In the realm of objective legal science, it provides the foundation for other rules and a vantage point from which they may be questioned.

Mary Midgley's comments about the general foundations for knowledge, based on Wittgenstein's analogy of a river and riverbed, are apposite here:

> … for every individual and every society, some set of propositions at any time must occupy this basic position. That set provides the background against which other things are questioned: it forms the underlying world picture. Its various elements are not themselves in principle incapable of being questioned. But they cannot be questioned unless some other set gains a special force and solidity, and supplies a ground adequate to make questions arise about them.[50]

This has a resonance with Cardozo's formulation, above. The fixedness of constitutional rules is especially marked where there is a written constitution, although the scope for change through interpretation is greater when they are formulated in open-textured language. In an unwritten constitution like that of the UK, the degree of their embeddedness in terms of congruence with the legal and political principles which underpin the operation of the governance system may be somewhat less clear, subject to more variation and hence may require more of an exercise in judgment to locate the importance and fixity of the rule. The more deeply a rule is embedded in this way, the more profound the process required to effect a change in it and the longer it may take for a wave to build to alter it.

VI. COMMON LAW CONSTITUTIONAL NORMS AND THE IDEA OF A LIVING CONSTITUTION

What is a common law constitution, in relation to which it makes sense to speak of constitutional norms? Even in the UK, which has no general written constitution, some norms with important status have a canonical written form, typically as statutes which have significance for constitutional framing such as the Bill of Rights of 1689 and, prior to Brexit, the European Communities Act 1972. Alongside these are norms developed as principles through judicial practice and recognition of their constitutional significance. These include the foundational norm of parliamentary sovereignty,[51] privilege in respect of parliamentary debates as a common law principle[52] and the responsibility of the executive for national security.[53] Some of these norms have legal effects, some are purely conventional and operate as a form of political custom or morality.

[49] J Elster, *Ulysses Unbound* (Cambridge University Press, 2000) 100.

[50] M Midgley, *Wisdom, Information and Wonder: What is Knowledge For?* (Routledge, 1989) 233–35; L Wittgenstein, *On Certainty* (translated by D Paul and G Anscombe) (Basil Blackwell, 1969), paras 95–98.

[51] *cf* the debate in *R (Privacy International) v Investigatory Powers Tribunal* [2020] AC 491.

[52] *Prebble v Television New Zealand Ltd* [1995] 1 AC 321.

[53] *R (Begum) v Special Immigration Appeals Commission* [2021] AC 765.

To treat norms as matters of convention makes for flexibility, but means they are particularly vulnerable to change and hence to aristocratic or democratic excess, to use Thompson's terminology. As the cultural conditions for a strong political morality based on conventions have been eroded,[54] there have been increased calls for elevation of norms into the legal sphere.[55] In part, Parliament has responded to reduced trust in government and reduced effectiveness of political processes to compel high standards of administrative conduct by legislating to impose such standards through law, for example by creating obligations of consultation. In part, the courts have responded over the longue durée, in constitutional time, by gradual change in legal doctrine. In some ways, this can be seen as a process of elevation of conventional norms into law.

Common law principles and political conventions also have a major role to play where there is a written constitution. The legal rules laid down by a constitution may be highly specific, but often they are expressed in general terms which means that their application is under-determined by the written rule itself. This creates a significant degree of discretion for the courts, through their interpretive practice, in determining the precise meaning and effect of the rules in concrete disputes. The guidance and framing functions of the rules and the supplementary principles laid down for their application then have to be reinforced by the authority structures inherent in court hierarchies and systems of precedent. If a superior court gives guidance regarding the concrete application of a constitutional norm, the public is entitled to expect that, absent good reason to the contrary, that guidance will be followed and applied.

The practical effect of this is that a form of common law develops around written constitutions which is not radically distinct from the common law constitutional approach in the UK. A typical way to express this is to say that a constitution or constitution-like instrument (such as the European Convention on Human Rights (ECHR)) is a living instrument. Its practical meaning and effect vary over time through judicial development of the law under the banner of interpretation.

In relation to the US, this point is made particularly clearly by David Strauss.[56] He observes that judicial interpretation of the Constitution offers a combination of constraint and the possibility of development. This combination can be said to be the essence of the common law. In constitutional terms, it allows the Constitution to be framed as a multi-generational project. He cites Thomas Jefferson in support of this idea: '[T]he earth belongs to the living, and not to the dead'.[57]

Even a conservative jurist like the former Chief Justice William Rehnquist acknowledged that there is an important sense in which the US Constitution could be seen as a living instrument, provided that this was not pushed too far to give excessive licence to judges to change the rules. As he put it, 'The framers of the Constitution wisely spoke in general language and left to succeeding generations the task of applying that language to the unceasingly changing environment in which they would live'.[58]

[54] L Siedentop, *Democracy in Europe* (Columbia University Press, 2001) chs 4 and 6; N Johnson, *In Search of the Constitution* (Pergamon Press, 1977) ch 3.

[55] See, eg, Johnson, ibid.

[56] DA Strauss, 'Common Law Constitutional Interpretation' (1996) 63 *University of Chicago Law Review* 877; DA Strauss, *The Living Constitution* (Oxford University Press, 2010).

[57] Strauss, *Living Constitution*, ibid 24.

[58] W Rehnquist, 'The Notion of a Living Constitution' (1976) 54 *Texas Law Review* 693, 694.

The same point can be made about the extensive jurisprudence developed by the Judicial Committee of the Privy Council in interpreting and applying the constitutions of the various jurisdictions for which it is the apex court. As early as 1930 the Board described the British North America Act in relation to Canada, a constitutional instrument, as 'a living tree capable of growth and expansion within its natural limits' and 'subject to development through usage and convention'.[59] In the landmark decision *Fisher v Minister for Home Affairs*, concerning the interpretation of the Bill of Rights in the Constitution of Bermuda, Lord Wilberforce pointed out it was 'drafted in a broad and ample style which lays down principles of width and generality'; this called for 'a generous interpretation avoiding what has been called "the austerity of tabulated legalism", suitable to give to individuals the full measure of the fundamental rights and freedoms referred to', while respecting 'the language which has been used and … the traditions and usages which have given meaning to that language'.[60]

This approach was powerfully reiterated by Lord Hoffmann in *Matadeen v Pointu*.[61] As he points out, a constitution is an attempt to lay down 'an enduring scheme of government in accordance with certain moral and political values'. In interpreting it, a judge is required to give effect to those values but does not have free rein in deciding what they are. The judge is constrained. The exercise is one of interpretation of the constitution having regard to its context.

Another well-known statement is that by Lord Bingham in *Reyes v The Queen*:

> A generous and purposive interpretation is to be given to constitutional provisions protecting human rights. The court has no licence to read its own predilections and moral values into the Constitution, but it is required to consider the substance of the fundamental right at issue and ensure contemporary protection of that right in the light of evolving standards of decency that mark the progress of a maturing society ….[62]

Similarly, the very extensive jurisprudence of the European Court of Human Rights regarding the meaning and effect of the ECHR is best seen as a form of common law which fleshes out the practical application of the very broadly drafted Convention rights. The argumentation presented to the Court and deployed in its judgments is strongly redolent of common law modes of reasoning. The Court has identified the ECHR as 'a living instrument', the meaning and effect of which is capable of being developed over time as social norms and expectations develop. Significant examples of this are the norms in relation to punishment of children[63] and the recognition of the family life of gay couples.[64]

Since constitutional development of this kind is recognised in the context of written constitutional instruments, it is not surprising that such development should also be possible in relation to the open-textured unwritten common law constitution in the UK. Development has occurred both in relation to the more positive identification of rights under the rubric of the principle of legality and in relation to the distribution of

[59] *Edwards v Attorney General for Canada* [1930] AC 124, 136.
[60] *Fisher v Minister for Home Affairs* [1980] AC 319, 328–29.
[61] *Matadeen v Pointu* [1999] 1 AC 98, 108.
[62] *Reyes v The Queen* [2002] 2 AC 235 [26].
[63] *Tyrer v United Kingdom* (1979–80) 2 EHRR 1 [31] 'the Convention is a living instrument which … must be interpreted in the light of present-day conditions'.
[64] *Schalk v Austria* (2011) 53 EHRR 20.

decision-making power and the extent of judicial control in relation to it. There is not a major distinction to be drawn between these movements. Where positive rights are developed this directly affects the distribution of power, since the effect is that government needs to do more to justify action which interferes with the rights.

In accordance with these ideas the courts have a limited role, interpreting constitutional norms (whether derived from the common law constitution or from a written instrument) in line with underlying constitutional traditions which are perceived to have current vibrancy and life. They are obliged not to legislate to impose the judiciary's own values, but instead are required to interpret the existing law to give effect to the long-term values of society.

VII. THE EMERGENCE OF CONSTITUTIONAL PRINCIPLE THROUGH THE DOCTRINE AND PRACTICE OF JUDICIAL REVIEW

I turn to sketch an account of long wave shifts in what can be called common law constitutional principle in the UK. Such principle regulates the extent to which political forces flow directly through the constitution through the medium of Parliament and executive government, the extent to which they are channelled and the extent to which they are (to some degree) arrested.

The UK has no foundational constitutional instrument. The distinction often drawn between constituent and constituted authority is collapsed into the authority of Parliament, as the supreme source of law. Therefore, in large part, identification of constitutional principle in the UK's legal system takes place under the overarching aegis of parliamentary sovereignty and within the practice of statutory interpretation. At the same time, statute exists alongside the common law, which is also oriented around certain basic principles and values, and to a degree statutes are taken to reflect these as well.

Since the terrain of public law is predominantly occupied by statute, a major context in which shifts in constitutional principle enter law is through the interaction of statute and common law. Statutory interpretation is a practice embedded in common law principles. Over the long term, the courts have gradually adjusted this practice to inject increasingly demanding standards of good administration and of the protection of individual interests against the action of the executive. In doing this the courts may be said to have shifted, to a degree, from a 'faithful agent' approach in interpreting the text of a statute towards locating it more in the context of underlying constitutional principles, of which the courts are interpreters and guardians, which come to the surface and affect its meaning.[65]

Major developments in the history of judicial review can be seen in this light, such as with the trilogy of *Ridge v Baldwin* (emphasis given to the obligation of fairness in the exercise of executive power),[66] *Padfield* (emphasis given to the obligation to use statutory powers for proper purposes)[67] and *Anisminic* (interpretation of statute in the light of the

[65] See K Greenawalt, *Statutory and Common Law Interpretation* (Oxford University Press, 2013) 8.

[66] *Ridge v Baldwin* [1964] AC 40. See S Juss and M Sunkin (eds), *Landmark Cases in Public Law* (Hart Publishing, 2017) ch 2.

[67] *Padfield v Minister of Agriculture, Fisheries and Food* [1968] AC 997. See Juss and Sunkin, ibid ch 3.

principle of access to justice).[68] These are regarded as landmark decisions because they signalled a significant shift in the way in which courts would approach the interpretation of powers in statute. As Lord Hodge has said:

> The development of administrative law in the second half of the twentieth century has indeed been a major legal development … as the incremental application and development of pre-existing principles in changed circumstances and in response to developing social needs.[69]

The changing social need to which legal doctrine responded was the greatly increased role of government and other executive bodies in the lives of citizens in the course of the twentieth century. Lord Hodge also suggests that changing social attitudes played a part: a decline in respect for and deference to established public institutions, and the rise of a more questioning attitude in society and a greater awareness of (or tendency to think in terms of) individual rights.[70] As Martin Loughlin points out, the 'positivization of the basic rights of citizens has the potential to reconfigure the architecture of public law'.[71] A coherent approach to administrative law was developed to reflect standards of good administration in the interest of citizens, as they came to be recognised by the courts.

One can identify earlier examples. Dicey wrote in 1915 about the development of administrative law, noting the application of new standards of administrative fairness to be applied by the courts, against a background where ministerial responsibility subject to political scrutiny was not perceived to be an adequate safeguard.[72]

Another significant shift in common law constitutional principle occurred towards the end of the twentieth century in the courts' approach to interpretation of tax statutes. There was a retreat from a highly restrictive interpretive approach which eschewed reference to the 'equity' of a statute and was protective of the rights of property-owners to seek to order their affairs, even by artificial adjustment, to avoid tax,[73] in favour of a far more purposive interpretive approach which gives emphasis to the basic intention of Parliament in imposing a tax (ie a reversion to a form of 'equity' of a statute) and is far more hostile to tax avoidance.[74]

Also in the late twentieth century, the courts developed the so-called principle of legality in the interpretation of statutes, to give legal effect to a range of individual rights identified by them with increasing specificity.[75] In broad terms, this was justified by the courts on the basis that Parliament is taken to legislate for a liberal democracy in a constitutional state which observes the rule of law.[76] However, if such broad concepts are regarded as capable of injecting determinate content into a

[68] *Anisminic Ltd v Foreign Compensation Commission* [1969] 2 AC 147. See Juss and Sunkin, ibid ch 4.

[69] PS Hodge, 'The Scope of Judicial Law-Making in Constitutional Law and Public Law' (2021) 26 *Judicial Review* 146, 148.

[70] See also PF Scott, 'Faith in Authority and the (Political) Constitution' (2019) 30 *King's Law Journal* 21.

[71] Loughlin (n 28) 114.

[72] AV Dicey, 'The Development of Administrative Law in England' (1915) 31 *LQR* 148.

[73] Exemplified in the *Duke of Westminster* case [1936] AC 1.

[74] *Furniss v Dawson* [1984] AC 474; *UBS AG v HMRC* [2016] 1 WLR 1005.

[75] See, eg, *R v Secretary of State for the Home Department, ex p Pierson* [1998] AC 539; *R v Secretary of State for the Home Department, ex p Simms* [2000] 2 AC 115, 131–32. For discussion see P Sales, 'A Comparison of the Principle of Legality and Section 3 of the Human Rights Act 1998' (2009) 125 *LQR* 598; J Varuhas, 'The Principle of Legality' [2020] 79 *CLJ* 578.

[76] *R (Anufrijeva) v Secretary of State for the Home Department* [2004] 1 AC 604 [28]–[31] (Lord Steyn).

statutory rule, the scope for the law to be affected by changes in the understanding of these concepts across time is clear.

As I put it elsewhere:

> The courts thus have a role to identify and give a degree of legal effect to slow waves of constitutional principle, which gradually cohere and form from the disparate materials of political practices and statements by a range of political actors and courts into distilled and concrete norms; and which may be capable of gradual dispersal too.[77]

An example of dispersal is the former constitutional presumption that women do not have the vote, referred to in *Nairn v University of St. Andrews*,[78] which could not be applied today.

A development parallel to the increasing prominence of the principle of legality is the identification of statutes with enhanced constitutional significance, such that ordinary principles of implied repeal do not apply in relation to them.[79] Such statutes are not declared to be such by Parliament; they are invested with such significance by the courts, by picking them out as running particularly closely with the grain of underlying constitutional principle.

Other general developments in judicial review reflect a similar process. The courts have to justify doctrinal change and they tend to do so by reference to underlying constitutional principle. The debate about whether or not to adopt proportionality as a general principle of judicial review largely takes place on this plane.[80] Similarly, by reference to arguments of constitutional principle, Jason Varuhas questions how far it is legitimate for courts to use the principle of legality to introduce a proportionality standard of review of executive action which has a tendency to supplant and undermine established standards of rationality review.[81]

The doctrine of legitimate expectations also developed in the late twentieth century as the courts gave legal protection to procedural and substantive legitimate expectations based on policies or assurances given by public authorities as to how they would exercise discretionary powers. The underlying justification for this development was increasingly put in terms of constitutional principle. At first emphasis was given to the abuse of power which was said would occur if there was a change of policy in circumstances where a person had relied upon it to their detriment, but this had to be balanced against the constitutional responsibilities of the authority in question.[82] Later, a distinct justification was given based on a constitutional principle of equality of treatment and protection against capricious and unjustified differentiation between persons falling within the scope of the policy; this has the effect that detrimental reliance is not required.[83]

[77] Sales (n 15) 968.

[78] *Nairn v University of St. Andrews* [1909] AC 147.

[79] *Thoburn v Sunderland City Council* [2003] QB 151.

[80] See the essays in H Wilberg and M Elliott (eds), *The Scope and Intensity of Substantive Review: Traversing Taggart's Rainbow* (Hart Publishing, 2015); P Sales, 'Rationality, Proportionality and the Development of the Law' (2013) 129 *LQR* 223.

[81] Varuhas (n 75).

[82] See, eg, *R (Begbie) v Department of Education* [2000] 1 WLR 1115.

[83] *Mandalia v Secretary of State for the Home Department* [2015] 1 WLR 4546; *Re Finucane* [2019] UKSC 7, [2019] NI 292.

There has also been a parallel development of judicial review of the exercise of prerogative powers through the extension of basic principles drawn from judicial review in the context of statutory powers. This has followed an arc from *ex parte Lain*,[84] through recognition in the *GCHQ* case[85] of the possibility of judicial control on the basis of underlying principles (which one could describe as fundamental or constitutional), to quashing of the prorogation of Parliament in the second *Miller* case.[86] The result in the latter case was justified explicitly in terms of the requirements of principles fundamental to a polity having the character of a parliamentary democracy, namely to ensure that Parliament should be able to carry out its constitutional functions as legislature and as the body responsible for supervision of the executive.[87]

However, the possibility of constitutional development of this character through change in doctrine carried on by the courts should in no way be taken to detract from constitutional responsibilities of maintenance and repair of the democratic polity which rest with Parliament and the executive government. The courts are secondary actors. By contrast with Parliament, they do not have ordinary democratic authority at an institutional level and can develop the law only slowly and incrementally.[88]

VIII. CONCLUSION

Common law constitutional law is something real, even though its precise parameters may be hazy. The courts have to identify and interpret the fundamental principles which constitute and govern the constitution. In doing so, they give effect to and hold in balance the framing and repair functions of constitutional law, to allow the governance system to operate effectively but also with legitimacy. This requires them to work at the tempo of constitutional time, through making incremental changes to constitutional norms to achieve a reasonable level of conformity with public opinion across time. By the courts recognising then giving effect to changes in public opinion which attain a sufficient degree of weight and force, the governance system embedded in the common law is subject to long waves of change in constitutional principle.

[84] *R v Criminal Injuries Compensation Board, ex parte Lain* [1967] 2 QB 864.

[85] *Council of Civil Service Unions v Minister for the Civil Service* [1985] AC 374. See P Sales, 'Crown Powers, the Royal Prerogative and Fundamental Rights' in Wilberg and Elliott (n 80).

[86] *R (Miller) v Prime Minister* [2020] AC 373.

[87] ibid [49]–[50].

[88] That circumstances may create a need for executive action to protect the constitution of the state (including to the point of displacing ordinary constitutional rules) was a theme of Carl Schmitt's argument in *Political Theology: Four Chapters on the Concept of Sovereignty* (first published 1922, translated by G Schwab) (University of Chicago Press, 2005), discussed in Loughlin (n 4) ch 11. The need for scope for effective executive action to uphold state interests is discussed in E Posner and A Vermeule, *The Executive Unbound: After the Madisonian Republic* (Oxford University Press, 2010).

12

Why Does Ireland Have a System of Judicial Review of Legislation? The Legacy of the Irish Free State Constitution of 1922

GERARD HOGAN

I. INTRODUCTION

On 10 August 1922 Felix Frankfurter (then a Professor at the Harvard Law School and future justice of the US Supreme Court from 1939 to 1962) wrote to a friend of his, Lionel Curtis, then a senior adviser to the British Government on Irish constitutional affairs. Frankfurter had just seen what was (then) Article 64 of the Irish Free State Constitution which provided for judicial review of legislation, with the express power to invalidate legislation enacted by the Oireachtas (Parliament) as unconstitutional. Frankfurter was intrigued as to why the Irish had adopted the US system of judicial review of legislation and desired to learn more about this:

> To a student of constitutional law – at least American law – the most arresting provision in the Irish Free State Constitution is Article 64 giving the High Court jurisdiction over the validity of any law having regard to the provisions of the Constitution – the familiar doctrine of judicial review. I write to trouble you for such information as you can give as to the purpose of Article 64. Was it urged by the Irish or by Great Britain and why by either? What part did American experience play in the proposal … The development is of vital significance.[1]

Curtis evidently passed on the letter to Hugh Kennedy KC, then legal adviser to the Provisional Government, because the letter was to be found in the latter's papers.[2]

Although Curtis had urged a full response to this senior American legal figure, there is no evidence that Kennedy had ever composed a letter in reply. This is not altogether surprising: the Irish Civil War had just commenced a few weeks previously and the two prominent leaders of the pro-Treaty side – Arthur Griffith and Michael Collins – were both to die within 10 days of each other in that month. Kennedy clearly had many things on his plate in that fateful month. But even if these dreadful events had not occurred, it is still not clear that the letter could easily have been answered. Indeed, 100 years later there is no simple answer to that question.

[1] UCD Archives, P4/1645.
[2] ibid. Kennedy was later Chief Justice between 1924 and 1936.

It is true, of course, that judicial review of legislation had been in the air in the course of the latter half of the nineteenth century. Various Home Rule Bills had provided for a system of protection for fundamental rights along with judicial review as part of the checks and balances designed for the protection of political and religious minorities.[3] But as ever it was all too little and too late, so that by the time Home Rule was finally placed on the statute-book via the Government of Ireland Act 1920, the British writ scarcely ran anymore in this part of the island of Ireland and the legislation was all but inoperable. Section 4 of the 1920 Act had placed significant limitations on the legislative capacity of the Parliament of Southern Ireland and section 5 introduced certain guarantees in relation to non-discrimination on grounds of religion. Section 50 of the 1920 Act envisaged the creation of a High Court of Ireland which would have had jurisdiction to pronounce on the validity of any legislation of that Parliament. Had the 1920 Act taken effect the type of judicial review thereby envisaged would probably largely have been along Australian lines, ie the judicial review challenges would have been largely directed to the scope of parliamentary and judicial powers with little by way of judicial review on the grounds of fundamental rights.

The Constitution of the Irish Free State which came into force on 6 December 1922 was different. Unlike what was envisaged for the (stillborn) House of Commons for Southern Ireland by the Government of Ireland Act 1920, the new Oireachtas created by the Constitution was now to have a full general legislative jurisdiction, save that it could not either infringe the Anglo-Irish Treaty of 1921 (which had led to the creation of the Irish Free State (IFS)) or infringe the Constitution. The IFS Constitution itself contained some basic fundamental rights guarantees,[4] along with the express powers of judicial review of legislation contained in Articles 65 and 66.

Some of these provisions were plainly inspired by a consideration of the inter-war constitutions from this period. There was clear borrowing from the 1919 Weimar Constitution, something which in time would be even more true of the present Constitution of 1937. Two examples may be given.

First, Article 6 of the IFS Constitution had provided that 'the liberty of the person is inviolable, and no person shall be deprived of his liberty except in accordance with law'. Compare this with Article 114 of the Weimar Constitution: 'Personal liberty is inviolable. Curtailment or deprivation of personal liberty by a public authority is permissible only by authority of law.' Second, Article 7 stated that 'the dwelling of each citizen is inviolable and shall not be forcibly entered except in accordance with law'. Now compare this with Article 115 of Weimar: 'The dwelling of every German is his sanctuary and is inviolable. Exceptions may be permitted by authority of law.'[5]

[3] See generally D O'Donnell, 'The Most Curious Forerunner' in B Ruane, D Barniville and J O'Callaghan (eds), *Law and Government: A Tribute to Rory Brady* (Round Hall, 2014) 139.

[4] Article 7 provided for the inviolability of the dwelling; Article 8 provided for freedom of conscience and religion; Article 9 provided for free expression and freedom of assembly; and Article 10 guaranteed the right to free primary education.

[5] 'Die Wohnung jedes Deutschen ist für ihn eine Freistatte und unverletzlich. Ausnahmen sind nur auf Grund von Gesetzen zulässig'. The reference to the 'inviolability' of the dwelling has, in fact, deep roots in the continental constitutional tradition. Article 3 of the (republican and short-lived) French Constitution of 1848 had provided that the 'residence [La demeure] of every person dwelling in French territory' was 'inviolable'. Article 14(1) and (2) of the Italian Constitution provides: '(1) Personal domicile shall be inviolable.

All of this was more or less tacitly acknowledged by the first Chief Justice of the IFS, Kennedy CJ, in his Foreword to Leo Kohn's *Constitution of the Irish Free State*:

> The Irish constitutional instrument was something different. [Kohn] recognised principles and theories with which he was familiar as a student of constitutions on the Continent of Europe breaking through and flowering in a soil long hardened to a surface of British appearance .... The [1922 Constitution] Committee was happily free from any obligation to accept existing British or Dominion models and could, on the one hand respond to guidance of Irish history and existing Irish conditions and, on the other hand, borrow of the experience of the constituted democracies of the worlds, looking for instance to the Constitution of the United States produced in circumstances of some analogy [to Ireland] and, on the other hand, to that of the German Republic, a political *tour de force* framed to work in contemporary conditions, as well as to those rules of law, affirmations and negations, enunciated from time to time over centuries, which make up collectively the unwritten constitution of Britain.[6]

Kohn was a distinguished German scholar whose book published in 1932 is a classical masterpiece of constitutional law scholarship. Kennedy CJ was himself a member of the 1922 Constitution Committee and his comments regarding Weimar ('a political *tour de force* framed to work in contemporary conditions') may be thought to be highly revealing of the Committee's attitude to that Constitution.

Returning, however, to Frankfurter's question: what was the inspiration for these powers of judicial review? There is no easy answer to this. Perhaps some form of judicial review was inevitable in 1922 given that the Oireachtas had no power to amend the Scheduled Treaty which was appended to the 1922 Constitution and this presupposed the existence of some entity which would have had the power to rule on questions of vires. Second, the drafters were clearly inspired by Weimar (and other inter-war continental constitutions), but even in those instances it was not clear the extent to which these constitutional guarantees were intended to be simply programmatic or, indeed, the extent to which the Weimar courts were permitted to exercise powers of judicial review. These very uncertainties were among the factors which led to the collapse of that Constitution.[7] Third, as Kennedy CJ hints in that quotation, the drafters were probably anxious to mark a break with the previous British legal tradition in Ireland and Provision for judicial review of legislation was as stark a statement of a desire for change as it was possible to

(2) No one's domicile shall be inspected, searched or seized save in cases and in the manner laid down by law in conformity with the guarantees prescribed for safeguarding personal freedom'. Article 15 of the Belgian Constitution provides: 'One's home is inviolable; no house search may take place except in the cases provided for by the law and in the form prescribed by the law.' The Danish Constitution of 1849 was clearly influenced by the developments in France (and elsewhere) in 1848, for it also provided for the inviolability of the dwelling: see generally, J Faerkel, 'Some Aspects of the Constitution of Denmark' (1982) 17 *The Irish Jurist* 1, 2–3. This is now numbered as Article 72 of the Danish Constitution: 'The dwelling shall be inviolable. Home searching, seizure and examination of letters and other papers as well as any breach of secrecy to be observed in postal, telegraph and telephone matters shall take place only under a judicial order unless particular exceptions are warranted by statute.'

[6] L Kohn, *Constitution of the Irish Free State* (G Allen & Unwin Limited, 1932) Foreword.

[7] This, essentially, was Kelsen's prediction with regard to the lack of a clear *Grundnorm* in the 1919 Weimar Constitution and the absence of a Constitutional Court to provide an effective means of protecting the workability of that Constitution: H Kelsen, 'Wer soll der Hüter der Verfassung sein?' (1931) 6 *Die Justiz* 576, 622–24. See generally, D Dyzenhaus, 'Legal Theory in the Collapse of Weimar: Contemporary Lessons?' (1997) 91 *American Political Science Review* 121, 127–28.

make. Fourth, the IFS was determined to show that it could and would protect religious and political minorities and judicial review was a further safeguard against the possible tyranny of the majority in the new Oireachtas.

II. THE JUDICIAL REVIEW EXPERIENCE 1922–1937

The judicial review powers of the 1922 Constitution did not prove to be a success and these powers seem to have been exercised at most twice during the period of the IFS between 1922 and 1937. Part of the reason was political: the 1922 Constitution had embodied the Treaty and as that Treaty had essentially caused a Civil War and riven Irish politics, it meant that that Constitution could never really obtain widespread acceptance. The other reason was essentially a legal one: the 1922 Constitution contained essentially the same internal legal flaws as Weimar: an uncertainty as to the ultimate *Grundnorm*[8] and the lack of an effective body which could rule authoritatively on such questions.

Article 50 of the IFS Constitution had originally provided that every amendment to the Constitution could only be made by way of a referendum. A last minute amendment to Article 50 was, however, made in the course of the Dáil Debates so that as a result the Constitution could be amended by ordinary legislation for an initial eight-year period. This well-intentioned amendment ultimately proved disastrous for the long term stability of the Constitution. The courts took their cue from this and reverted to traditional thinking, regarding the Constitution almost as a statute which could be implicitly amended. As O'Connor MR stated in the last judgment of the (old) Irish Court of Appeal in May 1924 in *R (Cooney) v Clinton*:[9]

> … It is difficult to see how, during the period of eight years, any Act passed by the Oireachtas can be impeached as ultra vires so long as it is within the terms of the Scheduled Treaty. It was urged that any Act of Parliament purporting to amend the Constitution should declare that it was so intended, but I cannot accede to the argument in view of the express provision that any amendment made within the period may be made by ordinary legislation.[10]

This trend was to continue throughout the life of the IFS, with judges ultimately accepting what came to be known as the 'implicit amendment' theory, ie, that if there was a conflict between the Constitution and a statute, the Constitution must be taken to have been implicitly amended.[11] Article 50 was itself amended by the Constitution (Amendment No 16) Act 1929 which extended the original eight-year period for a further eight years

[8] ie, the ultimate basic law. In the context of the IFS there was always uncertainty as to whether the ultimate *Grundnorm* lay. Was it the Scheduled Treaty (ie, the 1921 Anglo-Irish Treaty) or the Constitution of the IFS? In the case of the former, the British considered that the Statute of Westminster could be amended by the Oireachtas, but in *The State (Ryan) v Lennon* [1935] IR 170 the Irish Supreme Court disagreed. So far as the latter was concerned, were there any real limits to the capacity of the Oireachtas to amend the Constitution given the 'implicit amendment' doctrine? None of the matters were ever authoritatively resolved during the lifetime of the IFS Constitution.

[9] Belatedly reported at *R (Cooney) v Clinton* [1935] IR 247.

[10] ibid 247.

[11] See, eg, *Attorney General v McBride* [1928] IR 451, 456 (Hanna J); *Lynham v Butler (No 2)* [1933] IR 74, 112. See generally, L Cahillane, *Drafting the Irish Free State Constitution* (Manchester University Press, 2016) 157–62.

to 1938. When the validity of this constitutional amendment was upheld by a majority of the Supreme Court in December 1934 in *The State (Ryan) v Lennon*,[12] this had the consequence that during the entire period of its existence the Constitution of the IFS was totally vulnerable to legislative change, thereby rendering totally ineffective the idea of judicial review of legislation.

III. JUDICIAL REVIEW AND THE CONSTITUTION OF 1937

What is perhaps just as interesting a question is why the drafters of the Constitution of 1937 not only continued with the experiment of judicial review of legislation, but actually took the opportunity to strengthen and copper-fasten these powers in a manner I will shortly describe. Planning for a new constitution had commenced in earnest in 1934. This was not in itself a particular surprise as the new political party – Fianna Fáil – which had been formed in 1926 by Mr de Valera and others who were opposed to the 1922 Treaty and had come to power following the March 1932 general election. That period between 1932 to 1936 was notable for the enactment of various constitutional amendments designed to undo the Treaty settlement, not least the oath of allegiance,[13] the appeal to the Privy Council[14] and (later) the Governor General. The validity of these amendments was ultimately upheld by the Privy Council in June 1935 in *Moore v Attorney General of the Irish Free State*[15] on the basis that the Statute of Westminster 1931 had given the Oireachtas (as a Dominion Parliament) the power to amend the Irish Free State Agreement Act 1922.[16]

Writing shortly afterwards, Hood Phillips thought that it followed from the Privy Council's decision in *Moore* that the Oireachtas was free to repeal '*ex post facto* Article 65 and part of Article 66 of the Constitution which give the Courts their power to review legislation'.[17] Yet unbeknownst to him, events were already moving decisively in the opposite direction. Mr de Valera had no intention at all of removing these powers of judicial review: if anything, he went about strengthening it. To this end he had already established a Committee drawn from the senior echelons of the civil service whose task it was to examine the existing Constitution with a view:

> to ascertaining what Articles should be regarded as fundamental on the grounds that they safeguard democratic rights, and to make recommendations as to steps which should be taken to ensure that such Articles should not be capable of being altered by ordinary processes of legislation.[18]

The Committee duly reported to Mr de Valera and its report ultimately paved the way for the introduction of a new Constitution. The draft was approved by a unicameral

[12] *The State (Ryan) v Lennon* [1935] IR 70.

[13] Constitution (Removal of Oath) Act 1933. This Act had purported to amend Article 50 of the IFS Constitution which had provided that the Oireachtas had no power to amend the Scheduled Treaty.

[14] Constitution (Amendment No 22) Act 1933.

[15] *Moore v Attorney General of the Irish Free State* [1935] IR 472.

[16] ibid 486–87. As Viscount Sankey LC put it, 'The simplest way of stating the situation is to say that the Statute of Westminster gave to the Irish Free State a power under which they could abrogate the Treaty, and that, as a matter of law, they have availed themselves of that power.'

[17] O Hood Phillips, 'Ryan's Case' (1936) 52 *Law Quarterly Review* 241, 244.

[18] National Archives of Ireland, Document S 2979.

Oireachtas between May and June 1937, with the draft Constitution being approved by a plebiscite held in conjunction with the general election which was held on 2 July 1937. The Constitution itself came into force on 29 December 1937.

While an account of the complex drafting history of the Constitution lies well beyond this chapter, there are three striking features of that document's organisation. First, the drafters took great pains to ensure that, henceforth, it could not be easily amended. There were to be no further implicit amendments, as Article 46.3 stipulated that every bill to amend the Constitution must expressly be so described and Article 46.4 states that a Bill containing a proposal to amend the Constitution 'shall not contain any other proposal'. Article 46.2 provided that the only way of amending the Constitution was by way of referendum.[19]

The second was that the power of judicial review of legislation was actually strengthened. So far as judicial review powers are concerned, Article 34.3.2° expressly and unambiguously conferred the right of judicial review of legislation on the High Court and the Supreme Court.[20] Article 26 introduced the entirely new procedure of ex ante judicial review in that the President was enabled, following consultation with the Council of State, to refer Bills passed by both Houses of the Oireachtas to the Supreme Court so that their consistency with the Constitution may be determined. These powers of judicial review are reinforced by the prohibition on the enactment of unconstitutional litigation contained in Article 15.4[21] and by the statement contained in Article 28.2 that the executive power of the State may only be exercised in a manner which is consistent with the Constitution itself.[22] Neither Article 15.4 nor Article 28.2 had any counterpart in the 1922 Constitution. It might, of course, be said that both of these provisions did no more than expressly state a principle which is in any event inherent in a system of judicial review where legislative enactments and executive action are subjected to examination for consistency with the higher law contained in the Constitution itself.

Third, the list of enumerated fundamental rights was much extended, including for the first time guarantees as to equality before the law (Article 40.1), property rights (Article 40.3.2° and Article 43), family and education (Article 41 and Article 42). Critically, there was also a provision – Article 40.3.1° and Article 40.3.2° – which imposed a general obligation on the State 'as best it may' to defend and vindicate constitutional rights, including in particular the right to life, person, good name and property. The Preamble to the Constitution also sought to protect the 'freedom and dignity of the individual'.[23]

[19] It is true that Article 51 allowed as a transitional measure the Constitution (other than Article 46 itself and Article 51) to be amended by ordinary legislation in certain circumstances for a period of three years from the date on which the first President took office. That period lapsed on 25 June 1941 so that henceforth the Constitution can only be amended by referendum. See G Hogan, G Whyte, D Kenny and R Walsh (eds), *Kelly, The Irish Constitution*, 5th edn (Bloomsbury Professional, 2018) 2605–10.

[20] And the Court of Appeal since its establishment in October 2014: see 33rd Amendment of the Constitution Act 2013.

[21] '1. The Oireachtas shall not enact any law which is in any respect repugnant to the Constitution or any provision thereof. 2. Every law enacted by the Oireachtas which is in any respect repugnant to this Constitution or to any provision thereof shall, but only to the extent of such repugnancy, be invalid.'

[22] Article 28.2 provides that, 'The executive power of the State shall, subject to the provisions of this Constitution, be exercised by or on the authority of the Government.'

[23] See generally S Moyn, 'The Secret History of Constitutional Dignity' (2014) 17 *Yale Human Rights and Development Law Journal* 39; C McCrudden, 'Where Did Human Dignity Come From? Drafting the Preamble to the Irish Constitution' (2020) 60 *American Journal of Legal History* 485.

Against that background, the contention that the Constitution does not adequately protect fundamental rights is a somewhat puzzling one. How, for example, could the elaborate guarantees for *habeas corpus* in Article 40.4.2° be better improved? What is so wrong with the guarantee of trial 'in due course of law' in Article 38.1? Article 8 of the European Convention on Human Rights (ECHR) famously guarantees that Contracting States must have 'respect' for the dwelling and family life, but Article 40.5 of the Constitution proclaims the dwelling to be 'inviolable'[24] and Article 41 speaks of the 'inalienable and imprescriptible'[25] right to family life and to that extent these constitutional provisions go even further than the ECHR. In a similar vein one may say that in many respects the due process guarantees of the 14th Amendment of the US Constitution seem altogether slender compared with the comparable provisions contained in Article 40.3.1° and Article 40.3.2° of the Irish Constitution with the latter's guarantees to respect, defend and vindicate constitutional rights, including 'in particular' the rights to life, person, good name and property. As I have previously argued:

> Perhaps it was not realized in 1937, but the wording of the latter provisions in particular *do* give the Irish courts even wider powers of judicial review than that accorded to their US counterparts. In some ways, therefore, it is striking that the US Supreme Court has gone further in terms of judicial decision-making given the more slender basis of the 14th Amendment. It may seem curious to say so, but in January 1973 the US Supreme Court might have been better – indeed, far better – able to justify its decision in *Roe v Wade* had it the greater firepower of Article 40.3.1 and Article 40.3.2 or, for that matter, the ancillary provisions of the dignity clause in the Preamble or Article 40.5 or Article 41 at its disposal.[26]

IV. WHY WAS A SYSTEM OF JUDICIAL REVIEW OF LEGISLATION ADOPTED IN 1937?

So why, then, did the drafters adopt a system of judicial review legislation? I think that a real clue is to be found in a document prepared by John Hearne,[27] one of the principal drafters – if not *the* principal drafter – of the Constitution which was prepared on 4 April 1937. This detailed note formed the basis of de Valera's radio address and press statement on the occasion of the publication of the Constitution some four weeks later on 1 May 1937. The following passage did not find its way into the final version of the address – it was evidently considered to be too technical – it nonetheless provides clear evidence of Hearne's thinking:

> In a list of 52 countries, I find that the courts of 14 of these countries have powers comparable to those of the Supreme Court of the United States to pass on the constitutionality of laws, that the courts of 17 [such countries] have limited powers in this regard and that the courts of 21 have no power to pass on the question at all. Where the Constitution of a country is written down and the legislative powers of the Parliament are declared to be subject to the Constitution, there must be authority to determine the question as to the constitutionality of laws. The view on which the draft proposal in the draft Constitution is based is that

[24] See, eg, *Clare County Council v McDonagh* [2022] IESC 2.
[25] See, eg, *Gorry v Minister for Justice and Equality* [2020] IESC 55.
[26] G Hogan, 'Re-examining *McGee, Norris* and the X case' (2021) 65 *The Irish Jurist* 25, 62.
[27] See generally, E Broderick, *John Hearne: Architect of the 1937 Constitution* (Irish Academic Press, 2017).

> constitutional issues should be determined expeditiously and finally on the authority of the highest tribunal in the land.[28]

The only reference which de Valera made in this context in his subsequent radio address was in respect of the powers of the President to refer Bills to the Supreme Court which is contained in Article 26 of the Constitution where he is quoted as saying:

> These powers are undoubtedly great powers and will call for the exercise of a wise discretion. The due exercise of these powers will, however, provide a safeguard for the Constitution itself and a protection for the people against legislation contrary to the public interest.[29]

What, then, do these passages tell us? They reflect orthodox Kelsenian theory from which it may be predicted that any internal legal system without a clear hierarchy of norms and a body – such as a Supreme Court or a Constitutional Court – with a power to determine and apply those norms in a manner which would secure public acceptance would ultimately suffer from internal collapse.[30] Indeed, the Constitution of the IFS provides a paradigmatical example of this, because there was (in practice) no clear *Grundnorm* and no clear hierarchy of norms. De Valera and the drafting Committee had seen this happen before their very own eyes and they were determined not to let it happen again.

I think that there were two other reasons. First, in both 1922 and 1937, there was a conscious decision to move away from the traditional British system of parliamentary supremacy. Second, there was also a determination to show that religious and political minorities would be fairly treated by the new State and a system of judicial review of legislation was part of what might now be termed as a 'confidence building' measure.

V. HAS THE SYSTEM OF JUDICIAL REVIEW OF LEGISLATION MADE ANY DIFFERENCE?

The final question is: what difference has the existence of a system of judicial review of legislation actually made? I suppose that I am not here called upon to rehearse the weakness and faults of the original document: these are well known and often emphasised in public discourse, not least the fact that some elements of the original too faithfully reflected the (then prevailing) Catholic, nationalist ethos of the State. Many of the constitutional changes which has taken place since 1972 have sought to effect the gradual secularisation of the original document.[31] The 19th Amendment of the Constitution Act 1998 has given effect to the Belfast Agreement and dropped the original territorial claim to Northern Ireland reflected in the (original) Article 2 and Article 3.

The other part of the ledger gets insufficient attention. The drafting, lay-out and structure of the 1937 Constitution was (generally) superb and far-sighted. Just as is the case with the original Treaty of Rome 1957, subsequent amendments have struggled to match the elegant simplicity of the original. At almost every level the Constitution strengthened

[28] National Archives of Ireland, Document S 9868.

[29] 'Mr De Valera's Broadcast' *The Irish Times* (Dublin, 1 May 1937).

[30] See Kelsen (n 7).

[31] See, eg, 5th Amendment of the Constitution Act 1972 (removing references to the Catholic Churches and other religious faiths); 15th Amendment of the Constitution Act 1995 (removing constitutional prohibition on divorce).

and enhanced the democratic character of the State and bolstered its institutions, often by prescribing clear rules as to what was and was not legally permissible. As Doyle puts it:

> Across a range of metrics the Constitution of 1937 has proved remarkably successful and resilient ....The 2016 democracy ranking of the Economist Intelligence Unit ranks Ireland as the sixth most democratic country of the world. The freedom ranking for 2015 accords Ireland a number one grade for its freedom rating, political rights and civil rights. Ireland is a country with many problems but the Constitution seems to have successfully performed its most basic task: the establishment and continuation of a stable democratic system of government that respects minority rights and political freedoms.[32]

Writing in 2015, David Kenny, Rachael Walsh and myself identified some 93 instances of where Acts of the Oireachtas (Parliament) were found unconstitutional.[33] This figure includes Acts of the Oireachtas of the IFS between 1922 and 1937 and – perhaps intriguingly for UK constitutional scholars – pre-1922 legislation enacted by Westminster and a variety of common law rules[34] as well. That figure now exceeds 100 instances of findings of unconstitutionality.[35]

One might then ask: does the existence of this power of judicial review of legislation really make any difference? On the whole I think it does. Writing in 1980, our greatest constitutional law scholar, JM Kelly, delivered this verdict:

> If the judgment of the average liberal observer were asked for, he would probably say that the overall impact of the courts on modern Irish life, in their handling of constitutional issues, had been beneficial, rational, progressive and fair: as witness the decisions in *O'Donovan's, Ryan's, Macauley's*,[36] *Byrne's*,[37] *McGee's*,[38] and *de* Burca's[39] cases (the list could be much extended).[40]

[32] O Doyle, *The Constitution of Ireland: A Contextual Analysis* (Hart Publishing, 2018) 2.

[33] G Hogan, D Kenny and R Walsh, 'An Anthology of Unconstitutionality' (2015) 54 *The Irish Jurist* 1.

[34] See, eg, *S v S* [1983] IR 68 (holding that the common law rule in *Russell v Russell* was unconstitutional).

[35] The other additional subsequent findings of unconstitutionality post-2015 are *Moore v Minister for Justice* [2016] IEHC 244 (arbitrary legislation governing the imposition of suspended sentences held to be unconstitutional); *NHV v Minister for Justice* [2017] IESC 35, [2018] 1 IR 146 (holding absolute ban on asylum seekers working to be unconstitutional); *PC v Minister for Social Welfare* [2018] IESC 57 (denial of contributory State pension to prisoners held to be unconstitutional); *AB v Clinical Director of St Loman's Hospital* [2018] IECA 123, [2018] 3 IR 531; *Ellis v Minister for Justice* [2019] IESC 30, [2019] 3 IR 511 (mandatory sentencing for certain forearms offences disproportionately interfered with judicial independence); *Damache v Minister for Justice* [2021] IESC 6 (legislation providing for revocation of citizenship of naturalised persons held to be unconstitutional); *Zalewski v Workplace Relations Commission* [2021] IESC 24 (finding absolute ban on publicity in Workplace Relations Commission to be unconstitutional); *Costello v Ireland* [2022] IESC 44 (ratification of EU Canada trade deal ('CETA') held to be unconstitutional); *Heneghan v Minister for Housing, Planning and Local Government* [2023] IESC 7, [2023] 2 ILRM 1 (failure to give effect to requirements of Article 18 regarding university franchise to Seanad Éireann held to be unconstitutional); *CW v Minister for Justice* [2022] IEHC 336 (legislation requiring defence of honest belief to be proved by the defence in a criminal case to the civil standard before it could be accepted by a jury held to contravene the guarantee of trial in due course of law in Article 38.1). *O'Meara v Minister for Social Protection* [2024] IESC 1 (exclusion of unmarried couple from widower's pension unconstitutional).

[36] *Macauley v Minister for Posts and Telegraphs* [1966] IR 345 (holding unconstitutional the requirement contained in s 2 of the Ministers and Secretaries Act 1966 that a plaintiff obtain the prior *fiat* of the Attorney General before commencing proceedings against a government minister).

[37] *Byrne v Ireland* [1972] IR 241 (holding that the common law rule of State immunity was unconstitutional).

[38] *McGee v Attorney General* [1974] IR 284 (holding that a statutory rule prohibiting the importation of contraceptives was unconstitutional).

[39] *De Burca v Attorney General* [1976] IR 38 (holding that the *de facto* exclusion of women and non-ratepayers from juries was unconstitutional).

[40] JM Kelly, *Preface to The Irish Constitution* (Jurist Publishing, 1980).

This verdict was, however, delivered towards what turned out to be the end of the greatest era of judicial activism in our constitutional history. Aided by the presence on the Supreme Court of two outstanding judges in particular,[41] the courts coaxed and prodded the other branches of government into legislative action. While these decisions were in some respects counter- majoritarian, they were nonetheless often notable contributions to the cause of personal liberty at a time when such was not often a political priority. Other decisions served to strengthen the political process.[42]

Since that period, the role of constitutional review of legislation – while still very important – has not perhaps been absolutely central to Irish political life in the way that it is with the US Supreme Court or the German Constitutional Court. In that respect, the Irish Supreme Court is perhaps closer in this respect to its Italian, Spanish, Belgian and (more recently) French cousins. At the same time, Irish constitutional review remains a distinctive and (in some respects) unique feature of Irish political life which has served to cut the moorings of the Irish legal system from the common law. This in turn has facilitated the development of an interesting jurisprudence which mixes a common law inheritance with what we like to believe is a sophisticated system of constitutional review.

As the Danish physicist, Niels Bohr, once said, predictions are difficult, especially about the future. But one may venture this prediction: constitutional review is now such an embedded feature of Irish political and legal life that even if – for example – some form of unification of the island of Ireland were ever to come about – this feature would still be retained. Perhaps the true lesson of all of this is that it has taken 100 years to be able to answer the question posed in Felix Frankfurter's letter.

[41] Mr Justice Brian Walsh and Mr Justice Seamus Henchy. See generally, G Hogan, 'The Judicial Thought and Prose of Mr Justice Seamus Henchy' (2011) 46 *The Irish Jurist* 96; G Hogan, 'Mr Justice Brian Walsh: The Legacy of Experiment and the Triumph of Judicial Imagination' (2017) 60 *The Irish Jurist* 1.

[42] See, eg, *O'Donovan v Attorney General* [1961] IR 114 (holding Electoral Act 1959 unconstitutional on the ground that the constituency boundaries were not fairly drawn).

Part III

Re-Making Public Law: Contemporary Challenges and the Future

13

Legislating for Emergencies: Insights from the Pandemic

CHERYL SAUNDERS

I. INTRODUCTION

THE COVID-19 PANDEMIC that swept the world from 2020–22 had a profound impact across the field of public law. It called for effective action by states, reinforcing the significance of the core protective function of states, globalisation notwithstanding.[1] Many of the actions taken, however, made inroads into norms and practices of public law that generally are taken for granted, with implications for the protected spheres of individual rights and the functioning of democratic institutions. Government responses to the pandemic also had consequences for the operations of multi-level government within states, with effects that varied across the spectrum from centralisation to decentralisation of authority.[2]

Experiences with the pandemic merit study and assessment, to capture insights that may be useful in the future for public law. Much has been written on the subject already.[3] To avoid traversing familiar ground, this chapter focusses on one significant systemic public law issue exposed by the pandemic that has attracted relatively less scholarly attention: the use of legislation to respond to an emergency.

The constitutions of many states provide a framework for government in emergency conditions. Typically, the framework seeks to guard against abuse of emergency powers. States that make no constitutional provision for emergencies, if they have considered the matter at all, presumably assume that, if emergencies occur, they can be handled adequately within the normal processes of constitutional government. The implications of this choice, which effectively is made by default, are likely to be overlooked unless and until an emergency arises that is sufficiently serious to draw attention to them.

In the context of the pandemic, emergency legislation was widely used in jurisdictions across the world without invoking constitutional emergency provisions, even where

[1] D Grimm, 'The Protective Function of the State' in G Nolte (ed), *European and US Constitutionalism* (Cambridge University Press, 2005).

[2] C Saunders, 'Grappling with the Pandemic: Rich Insights into Intergovernmental Relations' in N Steytler (ed), *Comparative Federalism and Covid-19: Combating the Pandemic* (Routledge, 2021).

[3] For one recent publication, spanning a range of jurisdictions, see J Grogan and A Donald (eds), *Routledge Handbook of Law and the COVID-19 Pandemic* (Routledge, 2022).

these existed. Emergency conditions persisted for lengthy periods of time and prompted actions by states that normally would be regarded as extraordinary. Inevitably, exactly how legislation was used and with what consequences varied considerably between jurisdictions, depending on constitutional, political, social and economic context, as well as the severity of the impact of the pandemic on the health of the population and the public health system. To make the study both manageable and less abstract, therefore, the chapter develops a case study based on experience with emergency legislation in the Australian State of Victoria, where new pandemic-specific legislation was enacted in 2021 to take the place of more generic legislation for managing health emergencies, generating insights into two quite different approaches.[4] While all the usual caveats against extrapolation from single instances necessarily apply to the conclusions drawn until they have been considered and tested in other contexts, the insights that emerge are sufficiently plausible to suggest at least potential application elsewhere.

The COVID-19 pandemic had distinctive characteristics that justified its treatment as an emergency and shaped the response of governments everywhere, in varying ways. While its characteristics are familiar, it is worth recalling them briefly.[5] COVID-19 had very serious effects on human health and life and was highly contagious. Infection was hard to control and illness was difficult to manage until vaccines and new forms of treatment began to come on stream, well into the pandemic years. As a result, at its intermittent peaks, the virus put severe strain on hospitals and other public services, threatening to overwhelm them and, in some cases doing so. While features of this kind might be claimed for any infectious disease of epidemic proportions, COVID-19 had additional properties that made it particularly challenging. The manner in which it was transmitted was not fully understood at the outset. The virus mutated in any event, sometimes dramatically, further complicating the scientific and medical response. At least in its early phases, the virus disproportionately affected older people. The vaccines that were produced relatively quickly in the scheme of things had some, admittedly rare, side effects that contributed to suspicion of immunisation and active resistance in some quarters. The pandemic persisted for a long time, although in peaks and troughs. And while it appeared to be nearing its end-phase in late 2022, levels of infection and death remained high into 2023. In another worrying development, significant numbers of those infected had lingering symptoms, described as 'long Covid', that in some cases are debilitating and even now are not well understood.

The primary focus of this chapter is the regulatory framework for responding to the pandemic. Regulation alone is unlikely to be effective in responding to any emergency, however. In the case of the COVID-19 pandemic, an effective response required at least two other components. One was the availability of social and economic support, tailored to the needs of different segments of the community, to enable regulatory measures to be observed.[6] The other was a willingness on the part of the population to comply with

[4] Public Health and Wellbeing Act 2008 (Vic); Public Health and Wellbeing Amendment (Pandemic Management) Act 2021 (Vic), now Public Health and Wellbeing Act 2008 (Vic) pt 8A.

[5] For one of many detailed accounts, see K McIntosh, 'COVID-19: Epidemiology, Virology and Prevention' (*UpToDate*, 16 February 2023), available at www.uptodate.com/contents/covid-19-epidemiology-virology-and-prevention.

[6] Victorian Department of Health COVID-19 Writing Group, 'Population-based Analysis of the Epidemiological Features of COVID-19 epidemics in Victoria, Australia, January 2020-March 2021, and Their

restrictive measures, either as a complement to regulation or, in appropriate cases, as an alternative to it.[7] The mix of these strategies differed between jurisdictions for reasons that ranged from economic capacity to cultural preferences and practice, including ideological predisposition. Why a particular mix of strategies was pursued in each jurisdiction and how well they worked would be an instructive comparative project in its own right. In what follows, these other dimensions of an emergency response are assumed but not specifically examined unless they are relevant to the regulatory choices made.

Section II of the chapter examines the characteristics of emergency regulation and the options for putting it in place. This section also helps to explain why legislation was the favoured regulatory option in so many jurisdictions grappling with the pandemic. Section III considers the implications of the choice of legislation, with particular reference to its impact on constitutional government in both the short and longer term. Section IV demonstrates how these considerations played out through the two sets of legislation on which the sub-national response to the pandemic relied in the Australian State of Victoria. A final section of the chapter reaches some tentative conclusions about matters that may require attention in developing emergency legislation.

II. GOVERNING IN EMERGENCIES

COVID-19 created conditions that, in many and perhaps most countries, were considered to constitute a crisis that called for the exercise of emergency powers. For present purposes, I draw on the useful conceptualisation of emergency powers by Ferejohn and Pasquino, as an 'exception or derogation' from constitutional government, in the sense of 'normal or ordinary government', on a basis that is justified in terms of the circumstances that have arisen and with the intention, implicit or explicit, of return to normality in due course.[8] Constitutional government should be understood here in a small 'c' sense. It is intended to convey the idea that, while action in response to an emergency complies with any written constitution with the status of fundamental law, it is not consistent with the principles and practices normally observed in the conduct of government in the jurisdiction in question.

Government responses to the COVID-19 pandemic met this conception at least superficially during the times at which the pandemic was at its height. They involved a departure from normal government in various ways. Typically, power was concentrated in the executive branch and, sometimes, in a small segment of the executive branch, to a much greater degree than usual. Law-making authority was used to impinge significantly on liberty, privacy, and often equality through, for example, quarantine requirements, stay-at-home orders, mobility restrictions, check-in procedures and mask-wearing

Suppression Through Comprehensive Control Strategies' (*The Lancet Regional Health-Western Pacific*, 25 October 2021), available at www.thelancet.com/action/showPdf?pii=S2666-6065%2821%2900206-6.

[7] Paul Daly has usefully characterised these as imperium, dominium, and suasion: P Daly, 'COVID-19 in Canada: The Legal Framework' (2022) Ottawa Faculty of Law Working Paper No 2022-07, available at https://papers.ssrn.com/sol3/papers.cfm?abstract_id=4016632.

[8] J Ferejohn and P Pasquino, 'The Law of the Exception: A Typology of Emergency Powers' (2004) 2 *International Journal of Constitutional Law* 210, 222.

mandates. Legislatures met less frequently, if at all. Judicial review tended to be more deferential than usual. All these measures, and related developments, were publicly justified by the need to protect the health and lives of the community from the worst effects of the virus and, often, by the need to protect the viability of health systems as well. Even as the pandemic dragged on, there was a general assumption that these measures were exceptional and would end as the conditions that gave rise to them died away.

This approach to identifying and understanding emergency powers also suggests some criteria by which their form and the manner of their exercise might be evaluated in particular contexts.

First and most obviously, the powers should enable an adequate response to the crisis that has arisen. Handling existential threats to the community goes to the raison d'être of a state and feeds into the sociological legitimacy of governing institutions. This criterion is complicated where the existence or severity of the crisis is contested, or there is disagreement about how it is appropriately handled. The significance of contestation varies with the character of the claimed crisis. In the case of COVID-19, the existence of a threat to health of unusual proportions was widely accepted. Disagreements over what was 'adequate' in the circumstances were rife, but did not negate the need for effective action.

Secondly, the inroads that are made into 'normal' constitutional practice should be proportionate to the crisis, in both depth and duration. Proportionality, in a general rather than a technical sense, requires the maintenance of normality unless that is inconsistent with managing the emergency situation, and a return to normality as soon as reasonably practicable. It also suggests the need for checks and balances to reinforce proportionality as long, again, as they do not preclude managing the crisis in hand.

Thirdly, the exceptional nature of emergency governance requires public trust, as a matter of principle and in practice. What is involved in public acceptance of a departure from constitutional normality might even be conceived in terms of a social licence, hesitant as I am to introduce concepts generated in other contexts into public law.[9] How such trust is sought in emergency conditions and how readily it is given may vary with attitudes towards the role of the state and understanding of what is involved in membership of a community. This criterion may have implications, however, for the way in which emergency powers are exercised in terms of, for example, transparency, accountability, and fairness.

Emergencies are often categorised by reference to the characteristics of the trigger that may elicit an emergency response. A familiar typology distinguishes four types of trigger: immediate threats to the political order; serious economic crises; natural disasters; and health emergencies, of which the COVID-19 pandemic is an example.[10] There are similarities across these categories. Each of these types of crises demands effective action by the state as long, at least, as the claim of a crisis is genuine and sufficiently serious. The action that is taken may need to depart from public law norms. There is scope for misjudgement in dealing with what, by definition, are exceptional circumstances. There are differences between these types of crisis as well, however, in terms of the types of response needed

[9] J Lacey, 'Can you Legislate a Social Licence to Operate' (*The Conversation*, 27 February 2013), available at https://theconversation.com/can-you-legislate-a-social-licence-to-operate-10948.

[10] Jon Elster reduces these to three, combining the last two as 'natural (as opposed to man-made) disasters': J Elster 'Comments on the Paper by Ferejohn and Pasquino' (2004) 2 *International Journal of Constitutional Law* 240, 241.

from the state, the potential for manipulation or opportunism in political self-interest, the types of safeguards against abuse that might be effective and are likely to be available, and community reaction to government intervention. Much of the received wisdom on emergencies has been forged in reaction to or anticipation of political emergencies, which themselves have mutated in recent years to absorb threats of terrorist violence. Other types of emergencies also are familiar, however. Those involving natural disasters or health seem likely to become more frequent. Each of these has properties that distinguish them both from political emergencies and from each other.

The response of state institutions to emergencies may take a variety of forms, from the standpoint of law. In some cases, the action taken may be unauthorised by existing law and, in that sense, will lie outside the legal order. In such cases, the action may represent the classic 'state of exception' theorised by Schmitt,[11] or may retrospectively be validated, where such a possibility exists in law, as envisaged by Dicey, in conditions of parliamentary sovereignty.[12] Typically, however, in the twenty-first century, public law seeks to anticipate emergencies, so as to manage excess and abuse, and to try to ensure a return to normality. This may be done in the formal constitution itself; it has been estimated that 'nine out of ten modern constitutions contain explicit emergency provisions' of some kind.[13]

Constitutional emergency provisions may recognise a range of emergencies, but the procedures they prescribe often appear to be drafted with political emergencies in mind, including the suspicion that such emergencies typically generate. Section 37 of the Constitution of South Africa is a case in point. While expressed to apply to any 'public emergency', a declaration is authorised only if 'necessary to restore peace and order' and action taken in response to it is strictly time-limited to 21 days in the first instance, extendable by the National Assembly for three months at a time, requiring supermajorities after the first extension.

Whatever the merits of provisions of this kind for responding to emergencies of an essentially political kind, they may be problematic in practice in dealing with a health emergency, to the extent that they are applicable to such an emergency at all. To take an obvious example, a constitutional procedure that calls for frequent renewal of an emergency declaration by parliamentary resolutions, as in South Africa, is hard to apply in the context of a pandemic that dragged on for several years, proved highly infectious in indoor settings, and inhibited travel in a variety of ways. It is unsurprising in these circumstances that many countries instead relied on legislation as a framework for action in responding to the pandemic, even where constitutional emergency procedures theoretically were available. Where, as in Australia and other, older, common law countries, constitutional emergency procedures were not available, legislation necessarily was used when a crisis was deemed to require an emergency response. It appears that, in any event, there is a more general trend to rely on legislative, rather than constitutional, emergency procedures, initially prompted by ongoing threats of terrorism.[14]

[11] C Schmitt, *Verfassungslehre* (Drucker & Humblot, 1928).

[12] AV Dicey, *An Introduction to the Study of the Law of the Constitution* (MacMillan & Co, 1908) 396.

[13] C Bjørnskov, S Voigt and M Khesali, 'Unconstitutional States of Emergency' (2022) 61 *Journal of Legal Studies* 455. As the title of this piece suggests, such provisions may be exercised in an unconstitutional way, creating a 'de jure/de facto gap'.

[14] Ferejohn and Pasquino (n 8).

In these circumstances, emergency legislation presents a genre that deserves attention in its own right. In what follows, I examine it by reference to the criteria of effectiveness, proportionality and trust against which, it was suggested earlier, an emergency framework needs to be measured.

III. EMERGENCY LEGISLATION

A legal framework provided by legislation alone has advantages in managing an emergency, in terms of flexibility and fit. It can readily be enacted in advance, or after a crisis materialises. It can be adapted as circumstances change, subject to the exigencies of the emergency. It can be tailored to the type of emergency, including the nature of the action that is required and the checks and balances that might appropriately be used. It thus has the potential to be effective in framing an emergency response.

On the face of it, a response to an emergency under legislation, rather than constitutional emergency procedures, also presents less of a concern for public law in terms of proportionality and trust. The normal constitution remains in force, and so legislation must comply with it. All the institutions of the polity retain the responsibilities conferred on them by whatever form of constitutional separation of powers, including checks and balances, applies.[15] Reliance on ordinary legislation avoids the drama potentially triggered by a constitutional emergency and to that extent may also encourage trust or, at least, avoid mistrust.

This superficial impression may be misleading, however, and merits closer attention to the typical modalities of emergency legislation and the dynamics encouraged by emergency conditions.

The principal mechanism on which emergency legislation relies to meet a significant crisis is the conferral of extensive legislative and discretionary authority on the executive branch, within the limits that the constitution allows. In common law constitutional systems, this leeway may be considerable. Typically, there are relatively few constraints on the extent of legislative power that can be delegated to the executive, and although parliamentary scrutiny mechanisms may be somewhat more stringent, they tend to operate after delegation has occurred, if they are operative at all. Statutory discretions are subject to the principles and practices of judicial review but may also be both broad and subjective, empowering the decision-maker and inhibiting review. Inherent executive power, exercisable without legislative support, also is a notable feature of common law constitutions, drawing on the ancient concept of the prerogative in addition to other executive powers recognised by the common law. Both of these categories are broad, and liable to further expansion in times of emergency.

Rather than presenting a transitory departure from a norm, therefore, emergency legislation risks normalising the already advanced tendency to concentrate power in the executive branch, including through the delegation of legislative power. The risk is augmented where, in the usual case, emergency legislation is standing legislation.

[15] C Saunders, 'Theoretical Underpinnings of Separation of Powers' in G Jacobsohn and M Schor (eds), *Comparative Constitutional Theory* (Edward Elgar, 2018) 66.

Measures to underpin a proportionate use of the power in legislation enacted to anticipate emergencies will be tailored to the need to ensure that crisis conditions that as yet are unknown can be handled. Parliaments, through which accountability for executive action can systemically be enforced, at least in principle, may be prevented from meeting regularly by emergency conditions. Even when they meet, legislatures may be inclined to deference, so as not to undermine the emergency response. Depending on the form of emergency to which legislation is directed, authority may be conferred on experts both for functional purposes and to diminish the potential for political manipulation at the cost, however, of further attenuating political accountability. Judicial review of both constitutionality and legality remains available in principle but in practice is likely to be restrained, accepting considerable inroads into liberty, privacy, mobility, and other rights as authorised by the generalised terms of emergency legislation.

These considerations suggest that the risks presented for public law by emergency legislation need to be better appreciated and ways in which they might be diminished examined. The case study that follows draws insights for both purposes from one particular experience with emergency legislation during the pandemic.

IV. CASE STUDY

Both the challenges for public law potentially presented by emergency legislation and ways in which they might be anticipated and minimised can be exemplified by experience with two sets of legislative measures during the pandemic in the Australian State of Victoria. One was standing health emergency legislation, the Public Health and Wellbeing Act 2008 (Vic) ('the 2008 Act') put in place in the wake of global experiences with Ebola and SARS.[16] The second was pandemic-specific legislation, the Public Health and Wellbeing Amendment (Pandemic Management) Act 2021 (Vic) ('the 2021 Act') enacted in the course of the COVID-19 pandemic, as the Victorian Parliament lost patience with the need for repeated amendment of the 2008 Act.[17] These legislative events offer the opportunity to compare two different approaches to legislation to deal with the same emergency in the same jurisdiction, and to draw some insights from them.[18]

Local context affected the ways in which the pandemic was handled, in Australia as elsewhere, and needs brief description here.

In Australia, distance, from the rest of the world and internally, was a key factor in the approach to management of the pandemic. By the time the virus attracted attention in Australia, early in 2020, its impact elsewhere in the world was familiar and alarming. It was practicable for the Commonwealth to close Australia's external borders, thus enabling a strategy of exclusion of the virus from Australian territory and internal suppression of any outbreaks that occurred. Border closures, both between and within sub-national

[16] The Commonwealth and all other states and territories also had standing health emergency legislation, the design of which varied in some significant ways: H Mclean and B Huf, 'Emergency Powers, Public Health and COVID-19' (2020) Victorian Parliamentary Library and Information Service Research Paper No 2, 50.

[17] Several other jurisdictions also enacted pandemic specific legislation during this period: ibid.

[18] Like other states and territories, Victoria also has generic 'Emergency Management' legislation: ibid, 6–7. While this also was engaged at various times during the pandemic, it is not the primary focus of this chapter.

jurisdictions, also were used internally by the states and territories, to the same end. Most other regulatory measures taken were consistent with this overall strategy. They included quarantine of affected or potentially affected persons; isolation of members of the population from each other during pandemic peaks, including through stay-at-home orders; testing and contact tracing; mask mandates; and action to enhance high take-up of vaccines once they became available, including through mandates.

This Australian approach proved broadly effective, at least from a health perspective, despite mishaps along the way.[19] The strategy of exclusion and suppression lasted until the highly infectious omicron variant emerged in 2021, by which stage vaccines were available. While the roll-out was slower than it needed to be, once it occurred, it eased transition to a new phase of 'living with' the virus. The costs were significant, in human as well as economic terms, in ways that differed across the country. Even so, as a generalisation, the actions of Australian governments in responding to the pandemic were broadly supported by the residential population, waning over the course of 2021.

Features of the Australian system of government are contextually relevant too, for present purposes. Australia is a federation, in which the federal division of power leaves health and general emergency power primarily with the states and self-governing territories, which exercised significant authority during the pandemic.[20] Parliamentary government, in a form originally derived from Westminster, operates in all jurisdictions, most of which, including the State of Victoria, have bicameral Parliaments.[21] Australia has no – or almost no – constitutionally protected rights, but there are statutory charters of rights in some states and territories, including Victoria.[22] Over the course of the pandemic, there were occasional judicial challenges on constitutional, charter and administrative law grounds, (almost) none of which succeeded.[23] Australians have a developed rule of law culture, which affects both the extent to which law is used to influence behaviour and the extent of compliance with it.

Different experiences with the pandemic in different parts of the country were attributable to geography, demography, politics, and the constitutional and legal setting. The pandemic presented particular challenges in cooler, more densely populated Victoria, where border restrictions inevitably were less effective. Over the course of 2020–21, the capital city, Melbourne, had six lockdowns, totalling more than 250 days, some of which applied in regional Victoria as well. These and other measures were implemented

[19] Two high profile issues were the management of disembarkation of the cruise ship Ruby Princess in Sydney and the management of hotel quarantine in Melbourne in the early months of the pandemic: Mclean and Huf (n 16) 46–47. Each cast light on other issues for public law: in the case of the Ruby Princess, the co-ordination of Commonwealth and State authority in relation to disembarkation and in the case of hotel quarantine, the risks and limitations of government reliance on outsourcing.

[20] Mclean and Huf (n 16).

[21] The State of Queensland and the two self-governing territories, the Northern Territory and the Australian Capital Territory, are exceptions.

[22] Charter of Human Rights and Responsibilities Act 2006 (Vic).

[23] Australia was not alone in this in the common law world: B Chen, 'COVID-19 Stay at Home Restrictions and the Interpretation of Emergency Powers: A Comparative Analysis' (2023) 44 *Statute Law Review* 102. The first *Djokovic* case was a high profile exception in which, however, the respondent Minister conceded unreasonableness: see the description in *Djokovic v Minister for Immigration, Citizenship, Migrant Services and Multicultural Affairs* (2022) 289 FCR 21, 23–24 [3]–[5] (Allsop CJ, Besanko and O'Callaghan JJ).

primarily under the 2008 Act, including its emergency provisions.[24] Public patience was wearing thin by the time amending legislation was mooted, leading to difficult negotiations in the second chamber of the Parliament and loud protests from groups outside, representing a small but growing minority.

Objectively, the 2008 Act was a fair attempt at striking a balance between enabling an effective response to an unknown health emergency and ensuring that the response was proportionate.[25] The Act identified principles, including accountability, proportionality and collaboration, to guide the administration and implementation of the legislation, including the emergency provisions.[26] The emergency procedures that it prescribed required 'a serious risk to public health' and had regard to the safeguards of transparency, justification, accountability, and compensation for damage if powers were exercised on insufficient grounds.[27] The Act also used the familiar device of time limits to offset the impact of emergency powers, initially providing for renewal of the declaration of a continuing emergency every four weeks, to a maximum of six months.[28]

Nevertheless, the Act clearly assumed a different kind of health emergency: more confined, more manageable and shorter in duration than the COVID-19 pandemic. The powers triggered by a declaration of emergency were generic and broad including, for example, powers to detain and restrict movement and to 'give any other direction' considered 'reasonably necessary to protect public health'.[29] The power to make the declaration was vested only in the line Minister, albeit after consultation with the Minister and Commissioner for Emergency Management and an official, the Chief Health Officer ('the CHO'). The power to issue directives was vested in the CHO, prioritising expertise over political accountability. The terms in which emergency power was conferred enabled it to be exercised in relation to either individuals or entire communities, blurring the boundary between administrative and delegated legislative power.[30]

Most telling of all were the time limits. A declaration could be renewed by the Minister every four weeks, with appropriate notification to Parliament and the public. The maximum term, with extensions, was initially six months. However, legislative change was soon required to manage a pandemic that spanned several years. The relevant section of the 2008 Act was amended twice in the course of the pandemic: initially to extend the maximum period to 12 months and then to 21 months. Passage of these changes through the second parliamentary chamber, the Legislative Council, was complicated by the lack of a government majority, leaving final decisions in the hands of a small number of crossbenchers who were under significant pressure, both within and outside the Parliament. In dealing with the Government's proposal for a

[24] The 2008 Act, pt 10, div 3. Other parts of the 2008 Act were engaged as well, including pt 8, dealing with the management and control of infectious diseases and the other divisions of pt 10, dealing with protection and enforcement.

[25] See, generally, the observations of the Victorian Court of Appeal in *Cotterill v Romanes* [2023] VSCA 7 [33]–[41], [116]–[117] (Emerton P, McLeish and Kennedy JJA).

[26] 2008 Act, ss 8, 9, 10. Additional principles applied to the administration of pt 8: ss 11, 111.

[27] ibid s 198 (1), 198(5)–(7), 201(3) and 204 respectively.

[28] ibid s 198(7).

[29] ibid s 200(1).

[30] ibid.

second extension, Members of the Legislative Council demanded pandemic-specific legislation if further extensions were required.

What became the 2021 Act[31] was drafted and negotiated over the latter part of 2021, spanning two separate lockdowns in a jurisdiction already weary of pandemic restrictions. The new legislation amended the 2008 Act, by inserting a new Part 8A, 'Protection of life and public health during pandemics'. As that title implies, the Act as amended also purports to be standing legislation, for use in future pandemics, in the light of experience with COVID-19. The 2021 Act was hard fought in the upper House, the Legislative Council, where the same beleaguered crossbenchers tried hard to secure agreement on a version that satisfied as many as possible of the competing pressures on them. In the circumstances, it is not surprising that they had no appetite for limiting the legislation to the pandemic in hand, notwithstanding the lessons from the past. Coming relatively late in the COVID-19 pandemic that, with the benefit of hindsight, was beginning to wind down, those actively involved in the legislative process also had the opportunity to draw on what were perceived elsewhere as good practices for pandemic emergency management, in polities ranging from Taiwan to New Zealand.[32] The result was broadly positive, both in its own right and by comparison with the regime it replaced, at least for the context to which it was responding.

Distinctive features of the new legislation include the following. The procedures under the new Part 8A are triggered by the making of a 'pandemic declaration' by the Premier, as the chief Minister of the Government of Victoria.[33] The declaration is time-limited to an initial four weeks but can be extended by the Premier for three months at a time.[34] There is no fixed overall time-limit for the duration of a declaration, which instead is bounded by a requirement that the Premier is 'satisfied on reasonable grounds' that there is a 'serious risk to public health' arising from pandemic conditions.[35] In reaching this state of satisfaction, the Premier is required to 'consult with and consider the advice' of both the line Minister and the CHO.[36] The initial pandemic declaration and extensions of it are hedged around by elaborate requirements for consultation, publication, and detailed reporting to Parliament of both the reasoning on which the Premier's decision is based and on the health and other advice provided for the purpose.[37]

Once a declaration is in place, orders may be made to protect life and health. What now are called pandemic orders are made by the Minister with line responsibility for health, rather than by the CHO.[38] Requirements similar to those that apply to making a declaration are prescribed, in terms of consultation, publication, and reporting to

[31] Public Health and Wellbeing Amendment (Pandemic Management) Act 2021 (Vic), now Public Health and Wellbeing Act 2008 (Vic), pt 8A.

[32] Wen-Chen Chang, 'Taiwan's Fight against COVID-19: Constitutionalism, Laws, and the Global Pandemic' (*Verfassungsblog*, 21 March 2020), available at https://verfassungsblog.de/taiwans-fight-against-covid-19-constitutionalism-laws-and-the-global-pandemic/; D Knight, 'Stamping out COVID-19 in New Zealand: Legal Pragmatism and Democratic Legitimacy' [2021] *Public Law* 241.

[33] 2008 Act (as amended in 2021), s 165AB.

[34] ibid ss 165AC, 165AE.

[35] ibid s 165AE(3).

[36] ibid s 165AE(4).

[37] ibid 165AG.

[38] ibid s 165AI.

Parliament.[39] The powers exercisable under the Act are specified in a degree of detail that assists both political and legal accountability. Any exercise of power that involves 'detention', as broadly delineated (section 165AI), is subject to an additional accountability regime, involving independent review and appeal.[40] Explicit privacy safeguards are put in place.[41] The Charter of Human Rights and Responsibilities Act 2006 ('the Charter') is specifically made applicable; a matter that was unclear under the original 2008 Act.[42] A free and accessible register of pandemic orders is mandated.[43] An 'Independent Pandemic Management Advisory Committee' comprising experts in fields ranging from public health to emergencies, to human rights, to vulnerable communities is required to be established once a pandemic declaration is first extended, to provide advice to the Minister, including on its own motion.[44] The operation of the Act is to be independently reviewed, two years after it comes into force.[45]

The feature of the new legislation that was most fiercely contested was the role of Parliament in the review of the pandemic orders, as delegated legislation. There is a long-established, although by no means universal, practice in Australia whereby delegated legislation may be disallowed by either House of a bicameral Parliament. The significance of an arrangement whereby the second chamber can impugn secondary legislation lies in the typical lack of control of the second chamber by the Government and the correspondingly greater willingness of such a chamber to scrutinise delegated legislation. This contrasts with lower Houses that are substantially and, it seems, increasingly, dominated by the executive branch. These and other features of bicameralism in Australia lend reality to claims of a separation of executive and legislative power[46] and have caused what is claimed as a 'new political system' to be characterised as 'semi-parliamentary government'.[47]

However this may be, it presents a dilemma in an emergency, as reflection on the criteria for evaluating emergency powers suggests.[48] If a pandemic order is deemed necessary by a government, informed by health advice, there is risk involved in procedures that might result in disallowance by an Opposition intent on pursuing political advantage, or even by a combination of the Opposition and a crossbench, the makeup of which is hard to predict from election to election. While the example of the role accorded to the Opposition in New Zealand was much cited in debate, both within and outside the Parliament, the unicameral Parliament in New Zealand means that, by definition, the view of the Opposition is unlikely to prevail unless the Government loses support of the chamber from which it is formed.[49]

[39] ibid ss 165AI–165AR.
[40] ibid pt 8A, div 6.
[41] ibid pt 8A, divs 7, 8.
[42] ibid s 165A(2).
[43] ibid s 165CS.
[44] ibid pt 8A, div 9.
[45] ibid s 165CX.
[46] C Saunders, 'Separation of Legislative and Executive Power' in C Saunders and A Stone (eds), *Oxford Handbook of the Australian Constitution* (Oxford University Press, 2018).
[47] S Ganghof, 'A New Political System Model: Semi-Parliamentary Government' (2018) 57 *European Journal of Political Research* 261.
[48] The first of these criteria, identified earlier, necessitated an adequate response to the crisis.
[49] DR Knight, 'Accountability through Dialogue: New Zealand's Experience During the First Year of the COVID-19 Pandemic' in Grogan and Donald (eds) (n 3).

In the end, the agreed solution was to establish a new joint committee of the two Houses, with a majority of non-government members, to scrutinise pandemic orders by reference to particular criteria, including consistency with the Charter.[50] The Committee has a power to recommend disallowance, after consideration of the advice of the Independent Pandemic Management Advisory Committee. Disallowance requires majority acceptance of a resolution by a joint sitting of the two Houses, rendering Victoria unicameral, at least for this purpose. This arrangement was able to strike the right balance between accountability and the effectiveness of the Government response to the emergency in the Parliament that enacted the 2021 Act. The composition of the two Houses in this Parliament ensured that neither the Government nor the opposition had a majority on the Committee and that, in a joint sitting, the view of the Government would be likely to prevail. It may also prove to be a satisfactory arrangement in a differently constituted Parliament, although this cannot be guaranteed, and the dynamics undoubtedly would change.

V. CONCLUSIONS

The amendments to the Victorian pandemic emergency legislation effected by the 2021 Act were the product of particular political negotiations, in a particular jurisdiction, in light of particular experience with the pandemic. These events in Victoria may nevertheless offer insights with broader relevance for the design and operation of emergency legislation elsewhere to achieve the twin goals of emergency management and proportionality on which, in the end, public trust also depends.

The following four conclusions are tentatively drawn.

First, generic emergency legislation may not suit all emergency conditions, however carefully considered at the time it is made. Legislation targeted to managing the specific emergency in hand is preferable in principle. Emergency-specific legislation also has the advantage of enabling powers to be structured in ways that take account of prevailing conditions in designing procedures for both political and legal accountability and imposing workable time limits. This option also may be fraught, however, as experience with COVID-19 showed, requiring other factors to be weighed in the balance. In particular, as with COVID-19, the full exigencies of an emergency may not be adequately understood at the outset. Negotiating new legislation when a crisis already is underway also may be challenging, even when political consensus can be forged. It may also lead to overreach, if the panic induced by an emerging crisis causes measures to be put in place that in fact are not necessary to respond adequately to the crisis as it develops.

Secondly, on balance, Ministers, rather than unelected officials, should be responsible and held accountable for key decisions, including declaring an emergency, renewing an emergency, and imposing legal requirements to manage an emergency through the exercise of delegated legislative power. Reliance on health experts has advantages, in terms of helping to ensure that decisions are evidence-based and reducing the opportunity for governments to take advantage of the emergency for political gain. They cannot so readily

[50] Pt 8, div 4.

be held accountable, however, through either political or legal processes and reliance on them as the primary decision-makers becomes increasingly problematic if the emergency is prolonged. Even in a health emergency, moreover, scientific and medical considerations need to be weighed against other factors, including economic and social considerations, in the exercise of political judgement and in conditions of political accountability. The advantages of health and scientific expertise can be secured in other ways, through requirements for effective consultation and the transparency of advice.

A third set of conclusions concerns the legislature, as the most broadly representative, elected body. Legislatures are a critical accountability mechanism in an emergency. Logistical impediments to their operation, of the kind exposed by the COVID-19 pandemic, should be eased for the future by procedural frameworks that enable remote or hybrid sittings, if only as a last resort.

A more challenging aspect of the role of the legislature in emergencies, however, is the potential unwillingness of the primary chamber to scrutinise executive activity. A familiar problem in most parliamentary systems in the Westminster tradition, the reluctance of this chamber to hold government to account takes on greater significance in an emergency. Whether and how this can be overcome is a matter for consideration in each jurisdiction. Second chambers, where they exist, offer an additional check, but one that requires cautious deployment, so as not to destabilise the emergency response. Experience with the pandemic suggests that both the operations of bicameralism and the role and functions of an Opposition in emergency conditions are public law projects that deserve more attention.

Finally, departures from the normal and expected approaches to government that are justified by response to an emergency should be balanced by other mechanisms conducive to proportionality in the broad sense in which the term has been used here. These mechanisms include the transparency of decisions, reasoning, and the evidence base; the accessibility, in both senses of the word, of law and relevant policy, including intergovernmental agreements, where applicable; the ready availability of key decision-makers to public and media; meaningful and mandatory consultation with communities and experts of all relevant kinds; and requirements for ongoing public justification of particular and continuing operation under emergency powers.

Global experience with the pandemic has already identified many such alternative mechanisms. The full range of these could usefully be harvested for future reference as the pandemic winds down and introspection, almost inevitably, gears up.

14

Administrative Law and the Pandemic

GILLIAN E METZGER

American administrative law's relationship to change is, as they say, complicated.[1] On the one hand, continual evolution has been an endemic feature of American administrative law.[2] Doctrines such as *Chevron* deference[3] to agency statutory interpretations were born, grew, and declined in just the period from the 1980s to today.[4] On the other, the United States (US) Supreme Court regularly rejects such common law development in administrative law as illegitimate and insists that federal judges must adhere to the original terms of the 1946 Administrative Procedure Act (APA) and other statutes, unless the Constitution requires otherwise.[5] And to this day scholars disagree over the merits of each approach.[6]

It is clear, moreover, that American administrative law is in a period of change. Some developments are overtly constitutional, such as increased judicial resistance to removal protections for executive branch officers. Others are more common-law based even if constitutionally inspired – such as new limits on agency claims of authority under the major questions doctrine, greater scrutiny of agency reasoning on claims of pretext, and an overall rollback in agency deference.[7] Yet whether it occurs through common law evolution rather than radical constitutional transformations, the impact of this change is already dramatic, with multiple agencies and administrative initiatives under substantial fire in the courts.[8]

[1] See J Doll, 'The Cut: The Long Linguistic Life of It's Complicated' *New York Magazine* (New York, 19 November 2014).

[2] See GE Metzger, 'Embracing Administrative Common Law' (2012) 80 *George Washington Law Review* 1293.

[3] *Chevron USA Inc v Natural Resources Defense Council Inc* 467 US 837 (1984).

[4] See GE Metzger, 'The Roberts Court and Administrative Law' (2020) *Supreme Court Review* 1.

[5] See *Vermont Yankee v NRDC*, 435 US 519 (1978); see Metzger (n 2) 1298–1304.

[6] Indeed, in recent years administrative law originalism has been the subject of active debate, see ED Bernick, 'Envisioning Administrative Procedure Act Originalism' (2018) 70 *Administrative Law Review* 807; compare R M Levin, 'The Evolving APA and the Originalist Challenge' (2022) 97 Chicago-Kent Law Review with KE Kovacs, 'Superstatute Theory and Administrative Common Law' (2015) 90 *Indiana Law Journal* 1207. For my own views defending administrative common law as inevitable and legitimate, see Metzger (n 2).

[7] See section III.A.

[8] See, eg, *West Va v EPA*, 142 S Ct 2587 (2022) (holding that US environmental agency lacked statutory authority to adopt regulations incorporating generation shifting as a means of addressing climate change); *Community Fin Servs Association v CFPB*, 2022 WL 11054082 (5th Cir, October 22, 2022) (invalidating the funding scheme for US consumer finance agency); L Heinzerling, 'How Government Ends' (*Boston Review*, September 2022), available at www.bostonreview.net/articles/how-government-ends/.

A recent context for such developments was the Supreme Court's administrative law jurisprudence arising from the COVID-19 pandemic. Examining this case law provides a good window on the forces behind transformations in American administrative law, a heady brew of constitutional, ideological and political factors united by a shared theme: resistance to the state. A strong anti-statist orientation and skepticism of administrative power emanates from the Court's pandemic administrative law opinions. This resistance to the administrative state was also evident in the pre-pandemic jurisprudence of the Supreme Court under Chief Justice John Roberts (conventionally called the Roberts Court).[9] Yet its continued surfacing and intensification in the face of the worst public health crisis in generations is particularly striking. Such administrative skepticism is also present in many pandemic decisions addressing individual right claims, reinforcing its importance as a central theme of the Roberts Court.

This feature notably differentiates American pandemic jurisprudence from that of common-law jurisdictions, where the judicial response was far more deferential and accommodating of unprecedented executive actions – even though these jurisdictions imposed similar or more draconian measures (more extensive and long-lasting lockdowns, for example) than were used in the US.[10] The contrast is all the more notable because US and common law courts apply facially similar analytic frameworks: both examine whether executive pandemic actions are based in legal authority and whether these actions violate protected rights (although the standards governing these analyses diverge at times). Moreover, while US courts have fashioned a new requirement of specific authorisation of administrative actions that affect matters of particular importance, common law jurisdictions already have such a requirement with respect to rights intrusions in the principle of legality.

In what follows, I begin with an overview of the Roberts Court's pandemic jurisprudence, focusing in particular on its administrative law pandemic cases. I then examine how this case law compares to the pandemic jurisprudence in common law countries, and seek to explain what is driving the Roberts Court's distinct approach. I close with some thoughts on what this example suggests about change in American administrative law more broadly.

I. THE US PANDEMIC JURISPRUDENCE

The sheer scope of US federal court case law addressing COVID-19 is impressive. Many aspects of the US pandemic response, such as the massive vaccine development effort or major fiscal measures like the Coronavirus Aid, Relief, and Economic Security (CARES) Act and the American Rescue Plan (ARPA), sparked relatively limited legal challenge.[11]

[9] See GE Metzger, 'The Supreme Court, 2016 Term – Foreword: 1930s Redux: The Administrative State Under Siege' (2017) 131 *Harvard Law Review* 1.

[10] For a description of some of these measures, characterised as instances where 'a strong case can be made that those actions were unlawful', see NJ McBride, 'Ill Fares the Land: Has COVID-19 Killed the Principle of Legality' (*SSRN*, February 2022), available at https://papers.ssrn.com/sol3/papers.cfm?abstract_id=4023242.

[11] Although some significant legal challenges were brought against these fiscal measures, the federal Government was able to disburse the funds they authorised largely unimpeded by litigation. For exceptions, see, eg, *Texas v Yellin* 2022 WL 1063088, *4-*6 (N.D. Tex., Apr. 8, 2022) (concluding that ARPA's prohibition on using

But others encountered substantial litigation, with federal administrative pandemic measures challenged as exceeding statutory authority, deviating from administrative law reasoning and procedural requirements, and violating the separation of powers. Other lawsuits involved attacks on federal, state, and local restrictions as violating individual constitutional rights. The resulting jurisprudence demonstrates growing judicial skepticism of, and resistance to, administrative action.

A. Administrative Law Pandemic Cases

The Supreme Court's pandemic case law arose almost entirely on its 'shadow docket', addressing requests for emergency relief. As a result, these cases were often decided based on limited briefing and without argument.[12] A prime example is *Alabama Association of Realtors v Department of Health and Human Services*,[13] which involved a challenge to a nationwide eviction moratorium imposed by the Centers for Disease Control (CDC) using its powers under the Public Health Service Act (PHSA).[14] That Act has a long lineage; its earliest forebear dates back to 1796, when the Fourth Congress enacted an act that authorised the President to direct revenue and military officers to 'aid in the execution of quarantine, and also in the execution of the health laws of the states, in such manner as may to him appear necessary'.[15] The current version came on the books in 1944, at a time when Congress thought venereal disease particularly required a federal authority to quarantine and isolate, but also recognised 'the impossibility of foreseeing what preventive measures may become necessary' and therefore wrote the provisions 'broadly enough to apply to any disease listed by the President as quarantinable'.[16] Notwithstanding the PHSA, however, public health has long been primarily an area of state regulation.[17] The same is true of landlord-tenant law, and thus the CDC moratorium was a novelty.

Initially, Congress enacted a nationwide eviction moratorium as part of the CARES Act, but that moratorium lasted only for 120 days.[18] Shortly before it was to expire, the CDC issued an order adopting a similar temporary moratorium which was repeatedly

its funds to offset tax reductions was coercive and unconstitutionally commandeers the states); *Miller v Vilsack* 2021 WL 1115194 (ND Tex, July 1, 2021) (preliminarily enjoining sec 1005 CARES, providing for payments to Black farmers, on equal protection grounds); *DV Diamond Club v SBA*, 459 F Supp 3d 943 (ED Mich 2020), stay denied, 960 F 3d 743 (6th Cir 2020) (invalidating SBA rule excluding sexually oriented businesses from obtaining loans under the Paycheck Protection Act); *Vitolo v Guzman* 999 F 3d 353 (6th Cir 2021) (race and sex preferences in Restaurant Revitalization Funds under American Rescue Plan Act violated equal protection); *Scholl v Mnuchin* 494 F Supp 3d 661 (ND Cal 2020) (IRS decision to exclude incarcerated individuals from economic impact payments under the CARES Act violated statute and was arbitrary and capricious).

[12] SI Vladeck, 'Essay: The Solicitor General And The Shadow Docket' (2019) 133 *Harvard Law Review* 123. These cases are part of a contentious development of the shadow docket as a tool to make new law. See *Merrill v Milligan* 142 S Ct 879 (2022), 887–89 (Kagan J, dissenting).

[13] 141 S Ct 2485 (2021).

[14] 42 USC s 264(a); 42 CFR § 70.2; HHS, Temporary Halt in Residential Evictions to Prevent the Further Spread of COVID-19, 85 Fed Reg 55292 (2020).

[15] Act of May 27, 1796, ch 31, 4th Cong, Sess 1; see also Act of February 25, 1799, ch 12, sec 1, 5th Cong.

[16] H Rep No 1364, 78th Cong 2d Sess (1944), 25.

[17] See *Compagnie Francaise de Navigation a Vapeur v Board of Health* 186 US 380 (1902), 387, 390–92; WJ Novak, *The People's Welfare* (UNC Press, 1996) 191–233 (describing early state public health regulation).

[18] CARES Act, Pub L 116–136, 134 Stat 281, Sec 4024(b).

extended over the next year, including once by Congress.[19] CDC relied on its powers under section 361(a) of the PHSA,[20] which broadly authorises the CDC Director[21] 'to make and enforce such regulations as in his judgment are necessary to prevent the introduction, transmission, or spread of communicable diseases' from foreign countries into the US or from one state into another. Section 361(a) further states that '[f]or purposes of carrying out and enforcing such regulations', the CDC

> may provide for such inspection, fumigation, disinfection, sanitation, pest extermination, destruction of animals or articles found to be so infected of contaminated as to be sources of dangerous infection to human beings, and other measures, as in [its] judgment may be necessary.[22]

The moratorium faced mounting legal challenges, and was ultimately invalidated by the Supreme Court in a *per curiam* opinion at the end of August 2021.[23] The Court held that the moratorium exceeded CDC's statutory authority.[24] According to the Court, § 361(a)'s illustration of 'the kinds of measures' that CDC could adopt made clear that § 361(a) only authorised the CDC to take measures that 'directly relate to preventing the interstate spread of disease'.[25] But the moratorium 'relates to interstate infection far more indirectly: If eviction were to occur, some subset of tenants might move from one State to another, and some subset of that group might do so while infested with COVID-19'.[26]

The Court's reading of the statutory text is hardly obvious. An alternative view would see the examples in the second sentence as setting a floor on the agency's authority, not a ceiling.[27] This alternative reading is supported by the permissive language used with respect to the listed actions ('may') and the broad catch-all language at the end of the § 361(a) authorising CDC to adopt 'other measures, as in [its] judgment may be necessary'.[28] But the Court did not rest on its cursory statutory analysis alone. It also argued that

[19] Consolidated Appropriations Act, 2021, Pub L 116–260, § 534, 134 Stat 2078–79; *Alabama Association*, 141 S Ct, 2487.

[20] Fighting the Spread of COVID-19 by Providing Assistance to Renters and Homeowners, Executive Order 13,945, 85 Fed Reg 49,935, 49,936 (Aug 8 2020).

[21] Although the statutory text actually references the Surgeon General, as a result of subsequent reorganisation the power now resides with the CDC Director 42 CFR § 70.2.

[22] 42 US § 264(a).

[23] *Alabama Association of Realtors v HHS* 141 S Ct 2485 (2021), 2490. The Court first considered the moratorium in June, at which point it denied the emergency relief the moratorium's challengers sought, but it was clear a majority considered the moratorium to be outside of CDC's powers. See *Alabama Association of Realtors v HHS*, 141 S Ct 2320 (2021), 2320; see also ibid 2321 (Kavanaugh J, concurring).

[24] ibid.

[25] *Alabama Association* (n 23) 2488.

[26] ibid.

[27] *Alabama Association of Realtors v HHS*, 2021 WL 2221646 at *2 (DC Cir 2021) ('That language makes clear that HHS has even the exceptional authority to take measures carrying out its regulations that Congress in 1944 had reason to believe required express congressional authorization under the Fourth Amendment.'). But see *Tiger Lily LLC v HUD*, 5 F 4th 666 (5th Cir 2021) 670–71 (rejecting this view of the second sentence and the claim of special Fourth Amendment concerns).

[28] *Alabama Association* (n 23) 2491–92 (Breyer, Sotomayor, and Kagan JJ, dissenting); see also text accompanying n 16. Moreover, as the dissenting justices emphasised, § 361 expressly authorises quarantines, which 'arguably impose greater restrictions on individuals and state[s] … than do limits on evictions', ibid 2492. The dissenters also emphasised that Congress had extended CDC's moratorium in 2020 rather than repudiated it as unauthorised, ibid.

> [e]ven if the text were ambiguous, the sheer scope of the CDC's claimed authority under § 361(a) would counsel against the Government's interpretation. We expect Congress to speak clearly when authorizing an agency to exercise powers of "vast economic and political significance'.[29]

Emphasising the moratorium's novelty, broad applicability, and hefty financial cost – as well as its intrusion on the states' traditional domain of landlord-tenant law – the Court warned that reading § 361(a) to allow the moratorium would confer 'a breathtaking amount of authority' on CDC and made it 'hard to see what measures would … [be] outside of CDC's reach'.[30] In the Court's words, '[i]f a federally imposed eviction moratorium is to continue, Congress must specifically authorize it'.[31]

To be sure, the Court certainly could have questioned the CDC's about-face in extending the moratorium after repeatedly saying it would not do so – and after the Biden Administration had suggested CDC might lack authority to extend it.[32] In addition, ample grounds existed for critiquing the CDC's response in the early months of the pandemic, and perhaps deny its factual determinations and policy conclusions the deference that they might ordinarily receive.[33] But the *per curiam* majority did not fault the agency on these bases.

Separate from the opinion's reasoning, it is important to underscore the practical effect of the Court's decision. In the midst of a pandemic – indeed, at a point when COVID-19 cases were surging as a result of the Delta variant – the Court adopted a reading of CDC's core authority that limited the ability of the nation's premier public health agency to respond to an urgent public health crisis. Yet the Court ignored this critical ramification. Instead, in assessing whether the public interest was affected by granting an emergency stay, it focused only on the agency's interest in preserving the eviction moratorium and concluded that the equities plainly favoured the moratorium's challengers.[34]

Five months later, in *National Federation of Independent Business (NFIB) v Occupational Safety and Health Administration (OSHA)*, the Court took a very similar approach in staying a vaccinate-or-test emergency temporary standard (ETS) for workplaces. Applicable to employers with at least 100 employees, the standard required employers to have their employees get vaccinated for COVID-19 or mask and test regularly. Under the Occupational Safety and Health (OSH) Act, OSHA has broad power to promulgate occupational safety and health standards, and an ETS is authorised if 'necessary to protect employees' from a 'grave danger from exposure to substances or agents determined to be toxic or physically harmful or from new hazards'.[35] Unlike section 361(a) at issue in *Alabama Association*, however, the OSH Act lacks language that

[29] ibid 2489 (quoting *Utility Air Regulatory Grp v EPA*, 573 US 302 (2014), 324).

[30] ibid (noting that the moratorium applied to '[a]t least 80% of the country, including between 6 and 17 million tenants,' and could be claimed to cost nearly $50 billion).

[31] ibid 2490.

[32] See CDC, *Temporary Halt in Residential Evictions To Prevent the Further Spread of COVID–19*, 86 Fed Reg 34010, 34015 (2021); MD Shear, G Thrush, C Savage and A Rappeport, 'As Democrats Seethed, White House Struggled to Contain Eviction Fallout' *The New York Times* (New York, 7 August 2021).

[33] E Lipton, A Goodnough, MD Shear, M Twohey, A Mandavilli, S Fink and M Walker, 'The CDC Waited "Its Entire Existence for This Moment." What Went Wrong?' *The New York Times* (New York, 3 June 2020); RP Baird, 'What Went Wrong with Coronavirus Testing in the US' *The New Yorker* (New York, 16 March 2020).

[34] 141 S Ct 2489–90; see also ibid 2492–93 (Breyer, Sotomayor, and Kagan JJ, dissenting) (emphasising the dangers of limiting CDC authority).

[35] 29 USC §§ 655(b)–(c).

could be read to cabin the broad scope of these terms. Instead, an 'occupational safety and health standard' is defined quite capaciously as one that 'requires conditions, or the adoption or use of one or more practices, means, methods, operations, or processes, reasonably necessary or appropriate to provide safe or healthful employment and places of employment'.[36]

Nonetheless, the Court stayed the ETS on the ground that it was likely outside OSHA's authority.[37] The *per curiam* majority opinion again began with a narrow reading of the statutory text, drawing a distinction between '*occupational* risk' and the ordinary 'day-to-day dangers that all face' like COVID-19, concluding that OSHA could only regulate the former.[38] And '[a]lthough COVID-19 is a risk that occurs in many workplaces, it is not an *occupational* hazard in most'.[39] This analysis relied more on italicisation than argument.[40] Among other things, the Court made no effort to square its definition of occupational risks as excluding everyday risks in the workplace with the statute's definition of occupational standards in terms of 'safe or healthful employment and places of employment' more generally.[41] In response to the dissent's complaint that OSHA had long regulated risks of a type that arise 'both inside and outside of the workplace', such as fire or excessive noise, the majority claimed that a workplace vaccination requirement was different because it 'cannot be undone at the end of the workday'.[42] Although this suggested that an occupational standard cannot extend outside of a workplace, the majority's acknowledgement that OSHA could adopt a COVID-19 occupational standard '[w]here the virus poses a special danger because of the particular features of an employee's job or workplace' undermined any such a definitional line.[43]

At the end of the day, what drove the majority opinion in *NFIB* was not statutory text but the Court's insistence that 'imposing a vaccine mandate on 84 million Americans in response to a worldwide pandemic is simply not part of what [OSHA] was built for'.[44] Not surprisingly, in this regard the Court invoked *Alabama Association* and its requirement that Congress must specifically authorise agency actions with vast economic and political significance. In concluding the ETS was such an action, the Court emphasised the huge number of employees it covered, the intrusiveness of vaccination in employees' lives and health, and the fact in 'its half century of existence' OSHA had 'never before adopted a broad public health regulation of this kind'.[45] Concurring, Justice Gorsuch went further, arguing that '[if the statut[e] … really *did* endow OSHA with the power it asserts, that law would likely constitute an unconstitutional delegation of legislative

[36] ibid § 652(8). The limitations on OSHA are instead procedural and institutional; for example, any ETS must be issued as a permanent standard within six months, affected parties have a right to a public hearing on a proposed permanent standard, enforcement actions are adjudicated by a separate entity, and judicial review has often been rigorous. ibid §§ 655(b)–(c), 658–61.

[37] 142 S Ct 661 (2022) 665.

[38] ibid 665–66.

[39] ibid 665.

[40] See A Krishnakumar, 'Some Brief Thoughts on Gorsuch's Opinion in NFIB v OSHA' (*Election Law Blog*, 15 January 2022), available at https://electionlawblog.org/?p=126944.

[41] 29 USC § 652(8).

[42] *NFIB*, 142 S Ct 665; ibid 673 (Breyer, Sotomayor, and Kagan JJ, dissenting).

[43] ibid 665–66.

[44] ibid 665.

[45] ibid 665–66.

authority'.[46] A companion case, *Biden v Missouri*, reinforced the lack of a majority for the view that Congress could not delegate authority to impose such a vaccination mandate.[47] There, a five to four Court upheld a vaccination requirement imposed by the Department of Health and Human Services (HHS) on staff at healthcare facilities participating in the federal Medicaid and Medicare programmes, covering 10 million workers. To say that *Biden* is hard to square with *Alabama Association* and *NFIB* is putting it mildly. The *Biden per curiam* majority emphasised the breadth of the governing statutory language, which authorised the HHS Secretary 'to impose conditions on the receipt of Medicaid and Medicare funds that "the Secretary finds necessary in the interest of the health and safety of individuals who are furnished services".'[48] That language is indeed broad, but surely no broader than the language in § 361(a) or the OSH Act. Even more extraordinary was the majority's statement that although 'the [HHS] vaccine mandate goes further than what the Secretary has done in the past to implement infection control, … he has never had to address an infection problem of this scale and scope before'.[49] Surely the same point applies to the CDC and OSHA. Perhaps the best explanation of this incongruity is again the majority's sense of what types of action were appropriate for the Secretary of HHS to take, with the Court concluding that 'there can be no doubt that addressing infection problems in Medicare and Medicaid is what [the Secretary] does'.[50] In fact, however, four justices did indeed doubt just that, viewing the statutes invoked by the majority as textually limited 'ancillary provisions' and insisting that '[h]ad Congress wanted to grant … power to impose a vaccine mandate across all facility types, it would have … specifically authorize[d] one'.[51]

Notwithstanding *Biden*'s willingness to uphold the HHS vaccination requirement, the most important effect of these pandemic cases came in their endorsement of the claim that Congress must specifically authorise agency actions deemed sufficiently important, dubbed the major questions doctrine. Although reference to the economic and political significance of an agency action had surfaced in a few cases before *Alabama Association*, the import of this factor was unclear. In most instances up to this point, the fact that an agency action addressed a matter of major political or economic significance was primarily used as a reason not to grant *Chevron* deference to an agency interpretation of an ambiguous statutory provision the agency was charged with implementing.[52] Yet in 2015 the Court invoked such significance in a different fashion, as a basis for demanding specific statutory authorisation for the agency actions in question.[53] The pandemic decisions paved the way for the Court's full decision later in the same term, *West Virginia v EPA*, expressly adopting the specific authorisation version of the major questions doctrine. There, citing both *Alabama Association* and *NFIB*, the Court stated that 'in

[46] ibid 669 (Gorsuch J, concurring).
[47] *Biden v Missouri* 142 S Ct 647 (2022).
[48] ibid 652 (2022) (quoting 42 USC § 1395x(e)(9)).
[49] ibid 653.
[50] ibid.
[51] ibid 656–58 (Thomas J, dissenting).
[52] See *King v Burwell*, 576 US 473, 486 (2015); *FDA v Brown & Williamson Tobacco Corp.*, 529 US 120, 159–160 (2000); *MCI Telecomms. Corp v American Tel. & Tel. Co.*, 512 US 218, 231–232 (1994).
[53] *See Utility Air Regulatory Group (UARG) v Environmental Protection Agency*, 575 US 902 (2015).

certain extraordinary cases … an agency instead must point to "clear congressional authorization" for the power it claims'.[54]

Another notable shift in these cases is the justices' reliance on their own intuitions about these agencies' proper roles, rather than deferring to the agencies' views. Just a few years earlier, in a 2013 decision, the Court had deferred to an agency's determination that it had jurisdiction to act in an area when its governing statute was ambiguous.[55] Whether or not the statutes in *Alabama Association*, *NFIB*, and *Biden* clearly authorise the actions at issue, at a minimum they are ambiguous on that question, yet the Court refused to defer to the relevant agencies' interpretations. Interestingly, in these pandemic cases the Court for the most part ignored the ordinary bread-and-butter administrative law questions of whether the agency's policy choices were adequately explained, supported by the record, and reasonable. For example, it did not engage at all with the voluminous record OSHA created to defend its ETS or the justifications the CDC provided for the eviction moratorium, treating those cases as simply turning on questions of statutory authority. The one exception is *Biden*, where – having upheld HHS's authority to act – the Court also rejected the claim that HHS's vaccination policy was arbitrary and capricious, but its review of the record was fairly cursory.[56]

Finally, these pandemic cases stand out for the suspicion of agency decisions and motivations that often lies just below the surface. Such suspicion rose to the fore in *NFIB* oral argument, when Chief Justice Roberts complained that the Biden administration was 'trying to work across the waterfront' by 'just going agency by agency', adding that as 'more and more mandates … pop up in different agencies … I wonder if it's not fair for us to look at … [this] as a general exercise of power by the federal government'.[57] The implicit suggestion was that workplaces didn't actually present a special risk of COVID-19, as OSHA claimed, and instead the administration was engaged in a broad 'work-around' to exercise power Congress had not seen fit to give.[58] And the *per curiam* eviction moratorium decision portrayed the CDC as seeking 'sweeping power', including potentially authority to '[o]rder telecommunications companies to provide free high-speed Internet service to facilitate remote work'.[59] Lower court decisions on pandemic administrative law challenges often displayed similar skepticism of federal agency justifications and narrow views of agency authority. Indeed, often lower courts have been more extreme that the Supreme Court. A prime example is the Fifth Circuit's decision enjoining the OSHA rule, which even rejected OSHA's determination that COVID-19 presented a 'grave danger' to worker health.[60] The Sixth Circuit, in turn, enjoined the federal

[54] 142 S Ct. 2587, 2609 (2022) (quoting *Utility Air*, 573 US at 324). In *Biden v Nebraska*, 143 S Ct 2355 (2023), a decision issued after this chapter was submitted, the Roberts Court subsequently applied *West Virginia* and the major question doctrine to invalidate a pandemic-based measure that would have cancelled $430 billion in student loans owed to the federal Government. ibid at 2372–75.

[55] *City of Arlington v FCC*, 569 US 290 (2013).

[56] 142 S Ct 653–54. But see ibid at 659–60 (Alito, J, dissenting) (concluding that HHS had violated procedural requirements).

[57] Transcript of Oral Argument at 79–81, *NFIB v DOL*, 142 S Ct 661 (2022); see also Transcript of Oral Argument at 11–12, *Biden v Missouri*, 142 S Ct 647 (2022).

[58] Transcript of Oral Argument at 79–80, *NFIB v DOL*, 142 S Ct 661 (2022).

[59] *Alabama Assn of Realtors v HHS*, 141 S Ct 2485 (2021), 2489.

[60] *BST Holdings, LLC v OSHA*, 17 F 4th 604 (5th Cir 2021).

Government from requiring that federal contractors be vaccinated, invoking *Alabama Association* and the new demand for specific congressional authorisation and accusing the Government of using its contracting authority as 'a naked pretext' to increase vaccination.[61] And a Florida district court invalidated CDC's requirement that passengers must wear masks in transportation contexts, going beyond *Alabama Association* to conclude that that CDC could take the specific actions listed in § 361's second sentence only with respect to property and (even more dubiously) that a mask requirement was not a 'sanitation' measure notwithstanding that it helped keep transportation areas clean.[62] There were also lower court decisions rejecting administrative law challenges to federal agency actions related to the pandemic, but the overall trend goes in the opposite direction.[63]

B. Individual Rights Pandemic Challenges

Although the focus here is on transformations in administrative law, it is also worth considering individual rights challenges to pandemic measures, which constitute much of the COVID-19 litigation in federal courts. Most of these challenges were to state government actions and questions of authority to act were largely not in play; instead, the focus was on whether otherwise authorised state actions were unlawful because they were unconstitutional.[64] Here, the Supreme Court's responses varied over time and even more by the constitutional right involved. Of particular note are challenges involving religious freedom rights, the right to obtain abortion, and the right to vote.

A significant portion of federal pandemic litigation involved religious freedom claims, again decided on an expedited basis on the Court's shadow docket. Although these cases initially challenged limits on how many people could attend in-person religious services, a second round targeted vaccination requirements. Separately from the pandemic, constitutional religious freedom protections have expanded significantly in recent years, with the Roberts Court invalidating prohibitions on public funds going to religious institutions and reading the federal Religious Freedom Restoration Act quite capaciously.[65] The Court used religious freedom challenges to COVID-19 restrictions to expand Free Exercise Clause protections further. *Roman Catholic Diocese v Cuomo*[66]

[61] *Kentucky v Biden*, 23 F 4th 585, 609 & n 16 (6th Cir 2022).

[62] *Health Freedom Defense Fund, Inc. v Biden*, 2022 WL 1134138 (M.D.Fla. Apr. 18, 2022).

[63] See, eg, *Corbett v TSA*, 19 F.4th 478 (D.C. Cir 2021) (upholding TSA mask mandate in transportation contexts); *In Re: MCP* No 165, 21 F 4th 357 (6th Cir 2021) (in consolidated multidistrict litigation, upholding the OSHA rule and reversing the Fifth Circuit's injunction), *rev'd*, *NFIB v OSHA*, 142 S Ct 661 (2022); *League of Independent Fitness Facilities & Trainers Inc v Whitmer* 814 Fed Appx 125 (June 24, 2020) (upholding governor's executive order closing indoor fitness facilities in response to the pandemic).

[64] See, eg, *Marciano v de Blasio* 2022 WL 678779 at *6-*8, *9 (SDNY 8 March 2022) (rejecting the claim that NYC vaccination order was ultra vires based on a long history of state and local vaccination requirements and noting that 'a state's delegation of its police power to an administrator is not subject to review as a matter of federal constitutional law').

[65] See, eg, *Espinoza v Montana Dept of Revenue*, 140 S Ct 2246 (2020); *Trinity Lutheran Church v Comer*, 137 S Ct 2012 (2017); *Burwell v Hobby Lobby Stores Inc* 573 US 682 (2014).

[66] *Roman Catholic Diocese v Cuomo* 141 S Ct 63 (2020).

and *Tandon v Newsom*[67] were particularly significant in this regard. In *Roman Catholic Diocese*, the Court invalidated an executive order from New York's governor that limited attendance at religious services in red zone areas (where COVID-19 was highly prevalent) to no more than 10 people and attendance in orange zones (where COVID-19 rates were slightly lower) to no more than 25. The *per curiam* majority opinion held that the restrictions were not neutral or generally applicable, because essential businesses in red zones – and both essential and non-essential businesses in orange zones – could 'admit as many people as they wish[ed]'.[68] As a result, the Court subjected the attendance limits to strict scrutiny, emphasised that they were more restrictive than limits imposed by other jurisdictions, and concluded they were not narrowly tailored as constitutionally required.[69] Although prior jurisprudence established that the Government cannot target or discriminate against religion without triggering strict scrutiny, the novel move in the pandemic cases was the Court's dramatic expansion in what counts as discrimination.[70] In *Tandon*, the Court insisted that not discriminating against religion meant treating religious activities as well as '*any* comparable secular activity', with comparability determined by judges exercising independent judgment and not deferring to risk assessments by public health authorities.[71]

This refusal to defer to state and local public health assessments in religious freedom challenges marked a change in the Roberts Court's approach to the COVID-19 pandemic. In *South Bay United Pentecostal Church v Newsom*, a decision from May 2020 at the outset of the pandemic, the Court refused to enjoin an order from the California Governor that limited in-person religious services to 25 per cent of capacity. Concurring, Chief Justice Roberts noted that similar restrictions applied to secular gatherings and offered a strong defence of deference to state officials who bore primary responsibility for protecting public health:

> The precise question of when restrictions on particular social activities should be lifted during the pandemic is a dynamic and fact-intensive matter subject to reasonable disagreement. Our Constitution principally entrusts '[t]he safety and the health of the people' to the politically accountable officials of the States 'to guard and protect.' *Jacobson v Massachusetts*,

[67] *Tandon v Newsom* 141 S Ct 1294 (2021).

[68] *Roman Catholic Diocese* (n 66) 66–67.

[69] ibid 67. Prior to *Roman Catholic Diocese*, the Court had refused to enjoin similar governor orders limiting attendance at religious services over strong dissents. *Calvary Chapel v Sisolak* 140 S Ct 2603 (2020); *South Bay United Pentecostal Church v Newsom* 140 S Ct 1613 (2020). Some lower courts enjoined more extreme limits on religious services. *Roberts v Neace*, 958 F 3d 409, 414–16 (6th Cir 2020) (enjoining total prohibition on in-person religious services, but expressly noting the possibility of capping attendance as a less restrictive alternative).

[70] See A Koppelman, 'The Increasingly Dangerous Variants of the "Most-Favored-Nation" Theory of Religious Liberty' (2023) 108 *Iowa Law Review* 2237, 2267–69, 2271–74.

[71] *Tandon v Newsom* (n 67) 1296 (relying on *Roman Catholic Diocese*); ibid 1298–99 (Kagan J, dissenting) (noting that California imposed the same three-family limit on in-home secular gathering as the Court held was unconstitutional as applied to in-home religious gatherings); see also VD Amar and AE Brownstein, 'Exploring the Meaning of and Problems with the Supreme Court's (Apparent) Adoption of a "Most Favored Nation" Approach to Protecting Religious Liberty Under the Free Exercise Clause: Part One in a Series' *Verdict* (30 April 2021) (arguing that the Court was expanding religious protections by according religion the equivalent of 'most favored nation' status).

> 197 US 11, 38 (1905). When those officials 'undertake[] to act in areas fraught with medical and scientific uncertainties,' their latitude 'must be especially broad.' *Marshall v United States*, 414 US 417, 427 (1974). Where those broad limits are not exceeded, they should not be subject to second-guessing by an 'unelected federal judiciary,' which lacks the background, competence, and expertise to assess public health and is not accountable to the people.[72]

Yet even at that early point several justices were unwilling to defer to state public health determinations restricting religion,[73] and by *Roman Catholic Diocese* in November 2020 they had secured a majority for their views.[74] Although these justices argued that their refusal to defer was justified because 'even in a pandemic, the Constitution cannot be put away and forgotten',[75] the reality is that deference has regularly characterised constitutional challenges to public health measures, including measures that were quite restrictive of individual liberty.[76]

The emblematic citation for such traditional public health deference, relied on by Chief Justice Roberts in *South Bay*, is the famous 1905 decision in *Jacobsen v Massachusetts* that rejected the claim that a smallpox vaccination requirement enforced by a criminal fine violated substantive due process.[77] Efforts to challenge state vaccination requirements on similar grounds, for example claiming that the requirements violate bodily autonomy, have consequently failed.[78] So far, lower courts have also largely rejected religious freedom challenges to vaccination requirements and the Supreme Court has gone along, although at least three justices have argued that such requirements are unconstitutional when governments provide medical but not religious exemptions.[79]

The Supreme Court was more deferential when it came to constitutional rights other than religious free exercise. For example, the Court stayed a lower court decision that prohibited the Food and Drug Administration (FDA) from requiring in-person dispensing of the drug used in medication abortion, notwithstanding that the FDA had waived

[72] *South Bay* 140 S Ct, 1613–14; see also *SH3 Health Consulting LLC v Page*, 459 F Supp 3d 1212 (ED Mo 2020), 1220–21 ('[I]in our constitutional republic, the decisions of whether, when, and how to exercise emergency powers amidst a global pandemic belong not to the unelected members of the judicial branch but to the elected officials of the executive branch.'); WE Parmet, 'The Covid Cases: A Preliminary Assessment of Judicial Review of Public Health Powers During A Partisan and Polarized Pandemic' (2020) 53 *San Diego Law Review* 999, 1016–26 (describing lower court pandemic cases that deferred to public health determinations).

[73] *Calvary Chapel* 140 S Ct 2603 (2020), 2603 (Alito J, dissenting from denial, joined by Thomas and Kavanaugh JJ); ibid 2609 (Gorsuch J, dissenting from denial); *South Bay* 140 S Ct, 1614 (Kavanaugh J, dissenting from denial, joined by Thomas and Gorsuch JJ).

[74] *Roman Catholic Diocese* (n 66() 67–68 (noting that '[m]embers of this Court are not public health experts, and we should respect the judgment of those with special expertise and responsibility in this area' but proceeding to enjoin occupancy limit, noting 'there is no evidence that [church and synagogue seeking relief] have contributed to the spread of COVID-19,' and identifying 'many other less restrictive rules that could be adopted').

[75] ibid 68.

[76] *Liberian Community Association v Lamont*, 970 F 3d 174 (2d Cir 2020), 187–91; *Hickox v Christie*, 205 F Supp 3d 579 (DNJ 2016), 591.

[77] *Jacobsen v Massachusetts* 197 US 11 (1905).

[78] eg, *Legaretta v Macias 2022 WL 1443014* (D Mex, May 6, 2022); *Troogstad v City of Chicago* 2021 WL 6049975 (ND Ill. Dec 21, 2021); see also *Philips v City of New York* 775 F 3d 538 (2d Cir 2015) (upholding requirement that children must be vaccinated to attend school).

[79] See *Dr A v Hochul*, 142 S Ct 552 (2021) (Gorsuch J, joined by Alito J, dissenting from denial of injunctive relief): *Does 1-3 v Mills* 142 S Ct 17 (2021) (Gorsuch J, joined by Alito and Thomas, JJ, dissenting from denial of injunctive relief).

in-person requirements for many other drugs.[80] Similarly, several lower courts upheld application of state gubernatorial orders prohibiting all non-essential surgeries or procedures to most abortions.[81] In these decisions, which occurred before the Supreme Court overruled *Roe v Wade's* constitutional protection for abortion,[82] courts leaned heavily on the deference due public health officials' determinations of needs.[83] On the other hand, the liberal justices – who dissented strongly in *Alabama Association*, *NFIB*, *Roman Catholic Diocese* and elsewhere criticising the majorities in these cases for failing to defer to governmental public health determinations – here complained that the rest of the Court was being too deferential and failing to protect fundamental constitutional rights.[84]

An analogous scenario unfolded with respect to elections. The early months of the pandemic in 2020 coincided with presidential primaries in many states, and the pandemic also impacted the presidential election in November. A number of states were sued on the grounds that their requirements for obtaining or counting absentee ballots, gaining access to ballot drop boxes, and similar measures failed to adequately accommodate the risks posed by the pandemic and violated the right to vote. Unlike most pandemic cases, which targeted government measures as too restrictive, here the claim was that states had not done enough to adjust their existing election law regimes to account for the risks posed by COVID-19. Such claims found some support in lower courts, but ran into strong resistance at the Supreme Court.[85] Yet while COVID-19 provided the impetus for these suits, they were largely adjudicated under established doctrines, especially the *Purcell* doctrine that sharply limits the ability of federal courts to alter election rules close to an election.[86] Moreover, the rejection of these suits is again part of a broader trend at the Court of declining protection for the right to vote and deference to state legislative choices respecting voting.[87] And again, the liberal justices, who have also opposed this broader rollback of voting rights, dissented.[88]

[80] *FDA v Am Coll of Obstetricians & Gynecologists* 141 S Ct 578 (2021) 578. Subsequently, FDA waived enforcement of the in-person requirement during the pandemic and then determined that in-person dispensing was not necessary for safe use. See L McGinley and K Shepherd, 'FDA Eliminates Key Restriction on Abortion Pill as Supreme Court Weighs Case that Challenges Roe v Wade' *The Washington Post* (16 December 2021, available at www.washingtonpost.com/health/2021/12/16/abortion-pill-fda/.

[81] *In re Abbott* 954 F.3d 772, 784–87 (5th Cir 2020) (staying lower court injunction of the order as applied to abortions except as to women who would be past the legal limit for abortion in Texas if prohibited to have an abortion while the order was in force), *vacated & dismissed as moot*, 2021 WL 231539 (US Jan 25, 2021); *In re Rutledge* 956 F 3d 1018 (8th Cir 2020), 1028.

[82] See *Dobbs v Jackson Women's Health Org* 142 S Ct 2228, 2242 (2022) (overruling *Roe v Wade*, 410 US 113 (1973)).

[83] 141 S Ct 578–79 (Roberts, CJ, concurring); *In re Abbott*, 954 F.3d at 716–18.

[84] See *FDA* 141 S Ct at 581–85 (Sotomayor J, dissenting).

[85] See, eg, *Democratic National Comm v Wisconsin State Leg* 141 S Ct 28 (2020) (refusing to lift stay of district court order extending time within which absentee ballots could be returned); see also *Mi Familia Vota v Abbott* 834 Fed Appx 860 (5th Cir 2020); *Mi Familia Vota v Hobbs* 977 F 3d 948 (9th Cir 2020). Grants of relief by state courts were allowed to stand. *Republican Party of Pennsylvania v Boockvar* 141 S Ct 1 (2020) (refusing to stay Pennsylvania Supreme Court decision extending the period within which absentee ballots could be received).

[86] See, eg, *RNC v DNC* 140 S Ct 1205 (2020).

[87] See, eg, *Brnovich v DNC* 141 S Ct 2321 (2021) (upholding voting restrictions); *Rucho v Common Cause* 139 S Ct 2484 (2019) (concluding that political gerrymandering claims are not justiciable); *Shelby Cty v Holder* 570 US 529 (2013) (invalidating § 4 of the Voting Rights Act).

[88] See *Wisconsin State Leg.*, 141 S Ct at 240–46 (Kagan, J, dissenting); *RNC*, 140 S Ct at 1208–11 (Ginsburg, J, dissenting).

II. PUTTING US PANDEMIC JURISPRUDENCE IN COMPARATIVE COMMON LAW PERSPECTIVE

This US pandemic jurisprudence stands in sharp contrast to pandemic case law that emerged elsewhere, especially in Australia, Canada, New Zealand and the United Kingdom (UK). One obvious difference is the dramatically lower rate of litigation challenging pandemic restrictions in these common law countries. Others have noted the relatively sidelined role common law courts have played in the pandemic,[89] and one global database of COVID-19 litigation suggests a similar tale, with the number of cases listed from the US being nearly double the number listed for these four common law countries combined.[90] Even more striking is the extent to which the Government has won in these common law pandemic cases, with courts often rejecting the narrow readings of statutory authority that have prevailed in the US and adopting a far more deferential stance towards executive decision-making.

As in the US, much of the pandemic jurisprudence in these countries has involved claims that pandemic restrictions were not legally authorised or violated individual rights. Moreover, these challenges to legal authority similarly centred on claims that the underlying legislation did not support the executive action at issue. A UK decision, *R (Dolan) v Secretary of State for Health and Social Care* provides a prime example. *Dolan* involved, inter alia, the claim that the Public Health (Control of Disease) Act 1984 only authorised measures targeting specific individuals, groups of individuals, or premises, and not measures applicable to the general population.[91] The Court of Appeal granted the applicant permission to bring this claim but rejected it on the merits, emphasising the Act's broad textual authorisation for the Secretary of State to issue regulations 'preventing, protecting against, controlling or providing a public health response to the incidence or spread of infection', including through regulations 'imposing or enabling imposition of restrictions or requirements or in relation to persons, things, or premises in the event of, or in response to, a threat to public health'.[92] It also repeatedly emphasised that amendments

[89] See S Bateman and A Stone, 'COVID-19 and Constitutional Law' in JM Serna de la Garza (ed), *Covid-19 and Constitutional Law* (National Autonomous University of Mexico, 2020) 223, 231 (observing that 'compared with the very prominent role played by Australia's executive governments, and the, albeit diminished, but still important role played by the Parliaments at least to authorise executive action, the Australian judiciary has thus far played a fairly limited role in the early part of the pandemic'); P Daly, 'COVID-19 in Canada: The Legal Framework' (*SSRN*, 24 February 2022) 2, available at https://papers.ssrn.com/sol3/papers.cfm?abstract_id=4016632 (noting that 'executive government has been in the driving seat', with legislatures and courts playing 'a marginal role'); G MacLay and DR Knight, 'New Zealand Courts and COVID-19: Navigating the Tensions Between Necessity, Legality, and the Rule of Law' (*SSRN*, 23 March 2022) 16, available at https://papers.ssrn.com/sol3/papers.cfm?abstract_id=3989243 (remarking on the 'paucity' of cases for much of the pandemic and suggesting this 'perhaps reflects the high degree of social consensus over the government's response to COVID-19').

[90] COVID-19 Litigation Open Access Database, available at www.covid19litigation.org/ (listing 236 decisions from the US, compared to 39 from the UK, 27 from Canada, 43 from Australia and 19 from New Zealand). Many lawyers expect a surge in other litigation related to COVID-19, such as contractual disputes or insolvency cases. J Croft, 'London Lawyers Expect New Wave of Covid Litigation' *Financial Times* (London, 10 April 2022).

[91] *R (Dolan) v Secretary of State for Health and Social Care* [2020] EWCA Civ 1605 [1].

[92] ibid [45], [62]–[63] (quoting section 45C of the 1984 Act); see also ibid [61] (noting that the subsequent subsection expressly limits the Secretary from taking only a subset of the actions it included, suggesting the Secretary was authorised to pursue the remainder).

in 2008 were intended to ensure the Act would be able to meet the demands of a modern epidemic.[93] In contrast to *Alabama Association*, the Court of Appeal refused to read the immediately following provisions that listed particular authorised actions as limiting this broad grant of authority, emphasising that the use of open-ended permissive language at the outset of the list – 'may in particular include' – demonstrated that the list was 'not exhaustive' and should not be read to 'cut[] down the generality of the power' earlier conferred on the Secretary.[94] And in contrast to *NFIB*, the Court of Appeal was unmoved by the suggestion that Parliament should have to expressly authorise the general population regulations at issue. This suggestion was based on the principle of legality's insistence that '[f]undamental rights cannot be overridden by general or ambiguous words' because 'Parliament must squarely confront what it is doing and accept the political cost'.[95] Rejecting this argument, the Court of Appeal insisted the section's language was not ambiguous, that a necessary implication would suffice, and that other enactments provided similar powers.[96]

Dolan's refusal to read a broad grant of authority narrowly in light of surrounding provisions hardly stands alone. At issue in *LibertyWorks v Commonweath* was the Australian Health Minister's prohibition on overseas travel by all Australian citizens and permanent residents, issued under section 477 of the Biosecurity Act 2015 (Cth). Section 477 provides that the Minister could 'determine any requirement that he or she is satisfied is necessary … to prevent or control:… the entry of the … listed human disease' or 'the emergence, establishment, or spread of the … disease into Australian territory' or 'another country', but also provided that such a determination could not 'require an individual to be subject to a biosecurity measure of a kind' set out in a separate part of the Act.[97] LibertyWorks contended that because that part expressly authorised an order prohibiting an individual from leaving Australian territory, the section 477 authority could not be used to similar effect, even if the prohibition took the form of an across-the-board ban on overseas travel and not an order targeting a particular individual. In rejecting this argument, the High Court emphasised section 477's broad text and even more the fact that LibertyWorks' reading would 'emasculate' section 477 and frustrate Parliament's purpose in granting the emergency powers, concluding that 'it defies belief' that Parliament intended to hamstring the Minister by requiring issuance of an order 'made with respect to every single would-be [overseas] traveler'.[98]

Several decisions addressing ultra vires challenges to New Zealand's lockdown strike a similar note of reading empowering legislation capaciously and not requiring specific authorisation. In the first of these, *Borrowdale v Director-General of Health*, a full court of the High Court held that the Health Act 1956 authorised the Government's imposition of a national lockdown, although it further held that some initial restrictions were not prescribed by law.[99] In upholding the legality of the lockdown, the High Court rejected an effort to read the Act's language narrowly in a way that would preclude the Government

[93] ibid [59], [65], [69]–[71].
[94] ibid [62]–[63].
[95] ibid [66].
[96] ibid [66], [68].
[97] Biosecurity Act 2015 (Cth) s 477(1)(a)–(b), (6).
[98] [2021] FCAFC 90 [58], [62]–[66].
[99] *Borrowdale v Director-General of Health* [2020] NZHC 2090 [139], [225], [2020] 2 NZLR 864.

from imposing a national measure applicable to the population at large.[100] In dismissing an appeal from the decision, the Court of Appeal emphasised that Parliament 'intended to confer on the Director-General and Medical Officers of Health wide-ranging powers to prevent the outbreak of infectious disease' and '[t]he breadth of the statutory language and the context in which the powers fall to be exercised weigh against a narrow construction of those powers'.[101] Subsequently, in *Four Midwives v Minister for COVID-19 Response*, the High Court ruled that an order requiring workers in the health and disability sector to receive the COVID-19 vaccine was authorised by the COVID-19 Public Health Response (Vaccination) Act 2021.[102] In so holding, the Court concluded that the relevant section's list of specific examples should not be read as limiting its otherwise broad framing and refused to read the section's authorisation narrowly to avoid limiting the right to refuse medical treatment.[103] And in *Four Aviation Security Employees v Minister for COVID-19 Response*, the High Court rejected the argument that, given the significance of vaccination, the Government should not be able to require vaccination unless the empowering legislation expressly references it – exactly the argument that carried the day in *NFIB*.[104] In all of these decisions, the New Zealand courts stressed the need to interpret the measures at issue with attention to their purpose of empowering the Government to respond to COVID-19 and public health emergencies more generally.[105]

A central theme running through many common law COVID-19 decisions is the importance of deference to governmental expertise and decision-making, given the conflicting interests and uncertainties public officials had to consider in determining which restrictions to impose. In *Dolan*, for example, the Court of Appeal denied permission to appeal on the ordinary public law grounds that the Secretary of State acted irrationally in adopting the regulations, emphasising that

> the Secretary … had to make difficult judgements about medical and scientific issues and did so after taking advice from relevant experts …. This was quintessentially a matter of political judgment for the Government, which is accountable to Parliament, and is not suited to determination by the courts.[106]

Or, as the High Court put the point in a subsequent case, '[i]t is not for a court to make, or assess the correctness of … assessments of what measures should be adopted to address the public health problems posed by coronavirus.'[107] Similarly, a leading Canadian decision, *Taylor v Newfoundland and Labrador*, emphasised that 'courts do not have the specialized expertise to second guess the decisions of public health officials', in holding that violation of the Charter right to mobility resulting from the province's restrictions on entry were demonstrably justified.[108] Another Canadian judge emphasised that her

[100] ibid [113]–[116], [127]–[130].
[101] [2021] NZCA 520 [142].
[102] *Four Midwives v Minister for COVID-19 Response* [2021] NZHC 3064 [2].
[103] ibid [26]–[30], [51]–[54], [64].
[104] *Four Aviation Security Employees v Minister for COVID-19 Response* [2021] NZHC 3012 [60]–[63].
[105] [2021] NZCA 520 [100], [103], [114]; [2021] NZHC 3064 [27], [32]–[33].
[106] *Dolan* (n 91) [89]–[90].
[107] *Manchester Airports Holdings Ltd v Secretary of State* [2021] EWHC 2031 [38] (Admin); see also *Kassam v Hazzard* [2021] NSWSC 1320 [235].
[108] *Taylor v Newfoundland and Labrador* 2020 NLSC 125 [458]–[471], [493] NJ No 191; see also *Beaudoin v British Columbia*, 2021 BCSC 512 [120], [124], [244].

'role [wa]s not that of an armchair epidemiologist'.[109] Ironically, often these courts quote Chief Justice Roberts' paean to deference in *South Bay*, sometimes even in decisions issued after the Roberts Court had switched to far more aggressive scrutiny in *Roman Catholic Diocese*.[110]

Some decisions suggest that over time common law courts became more searching and skeptical in their review.[111] In a February 2022 decision, *Grounded Kiwis Group Inc v Minister of Health*, the New Zealand High Court concluded that the government-managed isolation system for entry into New Zealand had 'operated as an unjustified limit on the right of New Zealand citizens to enter their country' because it 'did not sufficiently allow individual circumstances to be considered and prioritised where necessary'.[112] Another New Zealand High Court decision from February 2022 rejected a vaccination requirement as not demonstrably justified, albeit emphasising that the requirement had been justified solely as a means of ensuring continuity of affected services and not also as needed to limit transmission.[113] And in March 2022, the High Court for England and Wales read the COVID-19 regulations and *Dolan* as requiring that the police determine 'that a conviction would be a necessary and proportionate measure in pursuit of the aim of protecting public health' – before taking an enforcement action against a protest. The Court concluded that the police had failed to do so with respect to a request for a vigil to protest the murder of Sarah Everard, and hence their decisions 'were legally flawed'.[114] Yet even in these decisions, the courts have signalled their reluctance to second-guess government public health measures. In *Grounded Kiwis*, for example, the Court went out of its way to praise the New Zealand isolation system as 'a critical component of the Government's elimination strategy that was highly successful in achieving positive health outcomes'.[115]

The different approach some common law courts took to religious freedom claims is also noteworthy. Canadian courts in particular rejected several challenges to prohibitions on in-person religious gatherings such as the US Supreme Court upheld in *Roman Catholic Diocese*. Although concluding that the COVID-19 restrictions in question infringed the fundamental guarantee of freedom of religion in section 2(a) of the Canadian Charter, these courts also determined that the limits imposed on section 2(a) were 'reasonable limits prescribed by law' and 'demonstrably justified in a free and democratic society' under section 1. In reaching these determinations, these courts rejected the claim that in-person religious gatherings presented the same risk as allowed secular activities, such that the prohibitions on religious gatherings were arbitrary or represented discrimination

[109] *Ontario v Trinity Bible Chapel et al*, 2022 ONSC 1344 [6].

[110] ibid [122]–[128]; *Taylor* (n 108) [459].

[111] Some courts have also been more sympathetic to individuals' claims for exemptions from regulations, particularly stringent quarantine requirements, even if not to challenges to the regulations themselves. MacLay and Knight (n 89).

[112] *Grounded Kiwis Group Inc v Minister of Health* [2022] NZHC 832 [22], [429]; see also *NZDSOS Inc v Minister for Covid-19 Response* [2022] NZHC 716 [72], [75]–[81], [105], [157]–[164]; (questioning some of the justifications offered for the vaccination requirements, although ultimately upholding the requirements in question).

[113] *Yardley v Minister for Workplace Relations and Safety* [2022] NZHC 291.

[114] *Leigh v Commissioner of the Police of the Metropolis* [2022] EWHC 527 (Admin) [79], [107].

[115] *Grounded Kiwis* (n 112) [22].

against religion.[116] Not surprisingly, deference to public officials' decisions on matters of medical and scientific uncertainty, especially decisions made during the height of the pressures of a pandemic, were central to these rejections of religious freedom claims.[117] The Federal Court of Australia similarly referenced its very limited power to grant relief to religious groups seeking exceptions from COVID-19 restrictions, declining to upset orders issued using powers delegated under the Biosecurity Act.[118] On the other hand, the Scottish Court of Session upheld a challenge to regulations closing places of worship and prohibiting communal worship in Scotland, faulting Scottish officials for 'fail[ing] to show that no less intrusive means were available to address their aim of reducing risk to a significant extent'.[119] The driving force behind the decision was the Court of Session's application of more searching scrutiny and reluctance to defer, with the Court emphasising the greater justificatory burden on Scottish officials because of their having granted exceptions to other situations it deemed analogous to religious communal worship, such as going to the cinema or serving on a jury.[120] In so holding, the Court of Session sounded a theme much closer to that of the Roberts Court in *Roman Catholic Diocese*.[121] Even with this Scottish variation, however, the overall contrast between common law and US courts in reviewing pandemic measures is striking.

III. EXPLAINING US PANDEMIC JURISPRUDENCE

The US pandemic jurisprudence described above is remarkable. Past experience – including recently with the war on terror – does not suggest that US courts would robustly restrict executive power and strongly defend individual rights in an emergency context.[122] Yet the Roberts Court not only enforced existing limits on executive action, it significantly expanded these limits at both the federal and state levels. The contrasting deferential stance of common law courts elsewhere reinforces how unusual the US approach has been.

To be sure, the COVID-19 pandemic was a public health emergency, not (or not primarily) a national security one,[123] and many Americans quickly rejected the claim that

[116] *Beaudoin* (n 108) [226], [229], [233]–[234]; 2022 ONSC 1344 [151]–[153]; *Gateway Bible Baptist Church et al v Manitoba et al* 2021 MBQB 218 [269]–[270], [273]–[274].

[117] *Beaudoin* (n 108) [244]; 2022 ONSC 1344 [126]–[127]; *Gateway Bible Baptist Church* (n 116) [280], [283], [292], [299]–[300]; *Hudson's Bay Company ULC v Ontario* 2020 ONSC 8046 [4].

[118] *Athavle v State of New South Wales* [2021] FCA 1075 [115].

[119] *Reverend Dr William J U Philip and others for Judicial Review of the closure of places of worship in Scotland* [2021] CSOH 32 [115].

[120] ibid [111]–[114]; see also ibid [119]–[126] (assessing that the Regulations had a disproportionate effect on the right to worship).

[121] See *Roman Catholic Diocese* (n 66) 66–67, see also 69 (Gorsuch J, concurring).

[122] The classic cite is *Korematsu v United States* 324 US 885 (1945). For a particularly skeptical view of legal constraints in emergencies, see E Posner and A Vermeule, *The Executive Unbound: After the Madisonian Republic* (Oxford University Press, 2010) 4–5, 34–41. President Trump declared a national emergency on 13 March 2020, after the Secretary of HHS declared a public health emergency on 31 January 2020. See Proclamation 9994 of 13 March 2020, Declaring a National Emergency Concerning the Novel Coronavirus Disease (COVID-19) Outbreak, 85 Fed Reg 15337 (2020).

[123] That said, many countries (including the US) have responded to COVID-19 by imposing national security-type measures, such as tight border control restrictions, so this distinction should not be exaggerated. For an interesting discussion of how national security and public health emergencies differ, see G Abiria and S Guidiaa, 'The Pandemic Constitution' (2021) 60 *Columbia Journal of Transnational Law* 68.

it was an emergency at all. Pandemic restrictions targeted all aspects of domestic life, not just US actions abroad or in separate territory such as Guantanamo Bay. In addition, those challenging pandemic restrictions were often sympathetic plaintiffs: pastors and churches challenging in-person attendance limits or first responders and teachers challenging vaccine requirements.[124] The states' traditional dominant role in public health emergencies make major federal agency interventions seem suspect from a federalism perspective.[125] And of particular note, the pandemic became a political fault line in the US early on, with many Republicans strongly rejecting pandemic restrictions and former President Trump as well as conservative groups urging challenges to state stay at home orders.[126] The politicisation of COVID-19 litigation is evident from the number of Republican-led states seeking to challenge COVID-19 restrictions imposed by the Democratic Biden Administration. It is further reinforced by the fact that challengers carefully choose where they file suit to maximise their odds of obtaining a sympathetic conservative judge – leading to a heavy presence of such litigation in Texas and Louisiana district courts and the now notoriously conservative Fifth Circuit.

These factors unquestionably played a substantial role in the US courts' greater receptivity to legal challenges to pandemic measures. But they do not tell the full story. Instead, also underlying the US courts' response is an attack on the federal administrative state that the Roberts Court has been waging for more than a decade. Viewed against this background, the Court's response is not anomalous at all. Rather, the executive actions taken to confront the pandemic have simply allowed the Court's newly consolidated conservative block to advance this attack more rapidly and dramatically than it might otherwise have done. Although different legal approaches complicate the comparison, this US judicial resistance to administrative governance may also explain some of the contrast between US and common law courts' response to the pandemic.

A. Resistance to the State in Contemporary US Administrative Law

A signal feature of the Roberts Court is what I have elsewhere termed its anti-administrativism: an effort to rein in federal administrative power that stands out for its rhetorical bureaucracy-bashing, formalist account of the separation-of-powers, and insistence on expanding judicial power to enforce that structural model and check administrative excess.[127] This attack on the administrative state claims to reflect

[124] *cf Does 1-3 v Mills* 142 S Ct 17 (2021) 18 (Gorsuch J) dissenting from denial of application for injunctive relief, 'No one questions that these individuals have served patients on the front line of the COVID–19 pandemic with bravery and grace for 18 months now.'

[125] See *NFIB v DOL* 142 S Ct 661 (2022) 667–68 (Gorsuch J) concurring emphasising that '[h]istorically, such matters have been regulated at the state level by authorities who enjoy broader and more general governmental powers').

[126] See, eg, KP Vogel, J Rutenberg and L Lerer, 'The Quiet Hand of Conservative Groups in the Anti-Lockdown Protests' *The New York Times* (New York, 21 April 2020). For partisan division over COVID over time, see P Bump, 'The Partisan Divide on Covid isn't Simply Two Groups Pulling in Separate Directions' *The Washington Post* (Washington, 25 January 2022), available at www.washingtonpost.com/politics/2022/01/25/covid-partisan-divide/; D Goldberg, R Roubein and AM Ollstein, 'Red State Governors Reject Biden on Mask Orders' *Politico* (Washington, 14 November 2020), available at www.politico.com/news/2020/11/13/republican-governors-reject-biden-mask-orders-436385.

[127] See Metzger (n 9) 34–44.

original understandings and a founding commitment to protecting liberty by dividing power and making legislating difficult. But its originalism operates at a highly generalised level and has run into increasing historical scholarship to the contrary.[128] Meanwhile, its libertarian vision of constitutional structure is one-sided, focusing only on government as a threat to liberty and ignoring constitutional arguments in favour of effective and flexible government.[129] It is also deeply at odds with established precedent and if fully adopted by the Court would likely entail a massive transformation in how the federal Government operates today.[130] As that suggests, despite proclaiming political accountability as a central constitutional goal, implementation of this anti-administrative vision would be undemocratic in many ways and entail a significant expansion of judicial power at the expense of the political branches.

Yet for all these flaws, this anti-administrative account appears ascendant and surfaces in a broad array of contexts, from judicial opinions undermining broad delegation,[131] to decisions rejecting removal protections for agency heads,[132] limiting administrative adjudication,[133] pulling back on deference to administrative interpretations,[134] and asserting individual rights protections against government regulation.[135] Although analytically distinct from efforts to curtail federal power writ large, which often focus more on congressional than administrative authority, there are synergies between these two impulses; both seek to limit the federal Government's imprint. Significantly, however, this anti-administrativism is not an attack on all forms of executive power. The Roberts Court has expanded presidential authority over agencies by invalidating for-cause removal protections at the same time as it has pulled back on agency authority. In this sense, it is Congress's ability to empower and structure agencies as it sees fit that is

[128] See ibid 44–46; CR *Sunstein and A Vermeule, 'The New Coke: On the Plural Aims of Administrative Law' (2015) Supreme Court Review* 41, 85–87. This historical scholarship has focused on demonstrating the broad extent of delegation to the executive branch at the founding. See, eg, J Mortenson and N Bagley, 'Delegation at the Founding' (2021) 121 *Columbia Law Review* 277; NR Parillo, 'A Critical Assessment of the Originalist Case Against Administrative Regulatory Power: New Evidence from the Federal Tax on Private Real Estate in the 1790s' (2021) 130 *Yale Law Journal* 1208. These works have, not surprisingly, sparked rejoinders seeking to explain away their evidence. See, eg, I Wurman, 'Nondelegation at the Founding' (2021) 130 *Yale Law Journal* 1490.

[129] See Metzger (n 9) 43–45, 77–95; see also *Gundy v United States*, 139 S Ct 2116 (2019) 2130 (plurality op) (emphasising Congress's 'need to give discretion to executive officials to implement its programs'); B Emerson, 'Liberty and Democracy through the Administrative State: A Critique of the Roberts Court's Political Theory' (2022) 73 *Hastings Law Journal* 371, 380–81, 389–99 (describing the multiple dimensions of liberty that the Roberts Court's opinions ignore).

[130] See Mortenson and Bagley (n 128) 288.

[131] ibid 287 (noting there may be five votes for new limits on delegation).

[132] See, eg, *Free Enterp Fund v PCAOB* 561 US 477 (2010) 499 ('One can have a government that functions without being ruled by functionaries, and a government that benefits from expertise without being ruled by experts .... The growth of the Executive Branch, which now wields vast power and touches almost every aspect of daily life, heightens the concern that it may slip from the Executive's control, and thus from that of the people.').

[133] See *Stern v Marshall* 64 US 462 (2011); see also *Jarkesy v SEC* 34 F 4th 446 (5th Cir 2022). But see *Oil States Energy Services LLC v Greene's Energy Group LLC*, 138 S Ct 1365 (2018) (upholding administrative adjudication regime for challenging patents).

[134] See *Kisor v Wilkie*, 139 S Ct 2400 (2019) (narrowing deference to agency regulatory interpretations); see also Metzger (n 9) 26–28 (describing criticism of Chevron deference).

[135] See, eg, *Cedar Point Nursery v Hadid* 141 S Ct 2063 (2021) (invalidating labour organising regulation as an uncompensated taking of private property); Metzger (n 9) 28–31.

the Court's prime target.[136] But given the extent to which contemporary Presidents rely on administrative action to advance their policies, a pull-back on agency authority also translates into a curtailment of presidential authority – at least when a President wants to pursue a pro-regulatory agenda and needs to rely on authorities granted to agencies. The Court has also rejected efforts to impose new judicially-crafted procedural requirements on agencies[137] and at times emphasised deference to agency discretionary choices, but its approach to the latter has been inconsistent.[138]

The Roberts Court's pandemic administrative law cases fit with this anti-administrative pattern. Indeed, the combination of constant challenges to pandemic restrictions and the fact that these cases are decided on an expedited basis put the Court's anti-administrative campaign on steroids. These cases contain their fair share of anti-administrative rhetoric, painting the agency actions in question as sweeping assertions of power,[139] and the doctrinal changes they wreak have potential to substantially constrict the authority of federal agencies. One difference from some of the Court's other recent anti-administrative decisions is that here only concurrences and dissents expressly invoke constitutional separation of powers concerns, with the *per curiam* majorities appearing to operate at the subconstitutional level of statutory interpretation. But separation of powers concerns lie just below the surface of the majority opinions in these cases, with their narrow readings of statutory authority and otherwise unsupported assertions that Congress would speak explicitly if it wanted to delegate authority for an agency to take an action with vast economic or political significance. As others have noted, the specific authorisation version of the major questions doctrine operates as a super-strong substantive canon of statutory interpretation, much like federalism clear statement rules or the canon of constitutional avoidance.[140] It holds great potential to be a significant barrier to agency action.[141] And in their imposition of this requirement and insistence on independently determining what it is that a particular agency 'does', these cases all represent significant expansion of judicial power at the expense of the executive branch.[142] The pandemic individual rights cases are more complicated to categorise as anti-administrative and obviously relate to separate legal analyses, such as free exercise doctrine. Yet these cases share aspects of the anti-administrative framing, most specifically in their skepticism of – and sometimes scorn for – public health agencies' determinations of risk and their insistence on courts

[136] Emerson (n 129) 380, 386–87 (noting this tension and the inconsistency in how Congress is treated in this case law).

[137] See *Little Sisters of the Poor v Pennsylvania* 140 S Ct 2367 (2020); *Perez v Mortgage Bankers Association* 575 US 92 (2015).

[138] *Compare FCC v Prometheus Radio* 141 S Ct 1150 (2021) (adopting a deferential form of arbitrary and capriciousness review); *Department of Commerce v New York* 139 S Ct 2551 (2019) 2569–71 (same) with *DHS v Regents*, 140 S Ct 1891 (2020) (rejecting agency rationale as arbitrary and capricious); *Department of Commerce*, 139 S Ct, 2573–76 (scrutinising agency action for pretext).

[139] See text accompanying n 30, 57–58.

[140] See N Richardson, 'Essay: Antideference: COVID, Climate, and the Rise of the Major Questions Canon' (2022) 108 *Virginia Law Review Online* 174.

[141] See Heinzerling (n 8); CR Sunstein, 'There are Two "Major Questions" Doctrines' (2021) 73 *Administrative Law Review* 475, 477–80; LM Littman and DT Deacon, 'The New Major Questions Doctrine' (2023) 109 *Virginia Law Review*^ 1009, 1011.

[142] Littman and Deacon, ibid; Heinzerling (n 8).

determining when religious and non-religious activities are comparable.[143] The anti-administrative thread also helps explain why the US courts have treated this emergency so differently from other emergencies and in addition connects the pandemic litigation to broader ideological and political opposition to COVID-19 restrictions. The fact that the prime actors are paradigmatic domestic administrative agencies, responsible for regulating everyday life, frames COVID-19 responses as different from emergencies involving the military or national security agencies.[144] Meanwhile, anti-administrativism is certainly not limited to the courts, but also manifests in the political sphere and was strongly evident in the Trump Administration's attacks on agency capacity.[145] The same political and ideological basis that animates anti-administrativism writ large – an anti-regulatory and libertarian limited government orientation – also drives public opposition to pandemic restrictions. Indeed, often it is the same conservative organisations are involved in both the political and judicial realms.[146]

B. Common-Law Contrasts on Administrative Power

This anti-administrativism also may help to explain the contrast between US and common law courts' approaches to COVID-19 restrictions. The common law courts' greater invocation of deference and general unwillingness to second-guess public health officials' risk determinations at a minimum suggest a different stance than that of US courts; trust in the state appears more the dominant mode. In New Zealand and Australia this is particularly evident: approximately three quarters of the population agreed in early 2021 that administrative management of the pandemic increased their trust in the central government.[147]

To be sure, there are other factors contributing to the US-common law divergence. One is the different legal analyses and standards applicable in the US compared to many common law systems. For example, broad statements of the need to interpret statutes to achieve their underlying purposes are a rarity in US case law today, with the emphasis on textualism and castigation of free-floating purposivism that now dominate federal statutory interpretation.[148] Thus, it was left to the dissenters in *Alabama Association* and *NFIB* to complain that the majority's interpretations of the statutes at issue were at odds

[143] They also contain some of the most extreme rhetoric of the COVID-19 case law. For a particularly egregious example, see *On Fire Christian Center Inc v Fischer* 453 F Supp 3d 901 (WD Ky 2020) 905 ('On Holy Thursday, an American mayor criminalized the communal celebration of Easter.').

[144] Although the military is of course an agency of the US Government, it is often viewed as distinct from ordinary administrative agencies. For example, the APA expressly puts certain military activities outside of its scope. See 5 USC §§ 551(a)(1)(F)-(G); 5 USC § 553(a)(1).

[145] See J Freeman and S Jacobs, 'Structural Deregulation' (2021) 135 *Harvard Law Review* 585, 592–94; Metzger (n 9) 9–17, 66–69.

[146] See Vogel et al (n 126); E Kilgore, 'The Lockdown Backlash May Be the New Tea Party Movement' (*New York Magazine*, New York, 16 April 2020).

[147] Goldfinch et al, 'Trust in Government Increased During the COVID-19 Pandemic in Australia and New Zealand' (2021) 80(1) *Australian Journal of Public Administration* 10. See also 'Trust in Government Soars in Australia and New Zealand During Pandemic', *The Conversation* (11 February 2021), available at https://theconversation.com/trust-in-government-soars-in-australia-and-new-zealand-during-pandemic-154948.

[148] Justice Kagan has famously commented that 'w[e are] all textualists now', 'The 2015 Scalia Lecture: A Dialogue with Justice Elena Kagan on the Reading of Statutes' (Harvard Law School, 25 November 2015), available at www.youtube.com/watch?v=dpEtszFT0Tg; see also Metzger (n 4) 54.

with the goals Congress enacted them to achieve.[149] In addition, the common law test governing determinations of whether a rights violation has occurred – whether challenged measures represent 'reasonable limits prescribed by law as can be demonstrably justified in a free and democratic society' – incorporates more room for governmental choices than the rigorous strict scrutiny that the US Supreme Court now applies to religious free exercise claims.[150] Moreover, these courts' respective stances might reflect background administrative law differences; in particular, common law courts have traditionally resisted reviewing the substance of administrative decisions except in truly extreme cases of unreasonableness, whereas US courts sometimes apply fairly searching arbitrary and capriciousness review.[151] A final factor is the precautionary principle, which surfaced in some common law cases to provide additional support for restrictions imposed by public officials and lacks a US analogue.[152]

Yet these doctrinal differences seem easily exaggerated and fail to explain the divergence here. There is plenty of purposivism that still creeps into Supreme Court opinions, and one of the marked features of *NFIB* is the extent to which the supposedly textualist Roberts Court refused to credit the broad terms of the OSH Act. Further – as Chief Justice Roberts' infamous *South Bay* concurrence demonstrates – the US approach to religious freedom claims is compatible with granting deference to public health judgments, provided that deference occurs at the initial step of determining whether religious and secular activities are analogous.[153] Not only have many common law courts embraced more substantive scrutiny in recent decades (in practice if not in formal doctrine), but also most of the pandemic cases expressly invoke substantive scrutiny in the form of proportionality review because of the rights violations asserted.[154] In any event, as noted above,[155] a conspicuous feature of the US pandemic administrative law jurisprudence is that courts have largely avoided arbitrary and capriciousness review, focusing instead on statutory authority. And it is not clear that the precautionary principle would provide greater benefit to US agencies in these cases than ordinary deference, were the courts actually willing to defer.

A further difference is structural rather than doctrinal: the greater role parliaments play in enacting specific COVID-19 legislation and approving (or disapproving)

[149] 141 S Ct, 2491–2492.

[150] VC Jackson, 'Constitutional Law in an Age of Proportionality' (2015) 124 *Yale Law Journal* 3094, 31111. See ibid 3104–3106 (That said, US constitutional rights analysis incorporates proportionality analysis at times, more perhaps than is generally acknowledged). See also J Greene, *How Rights Went Wrong* (Houghton Mifflin Harcourt, 2021) 92–94.

[151] *Compare Associated Provincial Picture Houses Ltd v Wednesbury Corporation* [1948] 1 KB 223 (CA) *with Motor Vehicle Mfrs Association of United States Inc v State Farm Mut Automobile Ins Co*, 463 US 29 (1983) 43.

[152] NZSOS [2022] NZHC [136]; *Taylor* 2020 NLSC [60], [411], [467].

[153] See text accompanying n 71–72.

[154] See M Aronson, 'The Growth of Substantive Review: The Changes, their Causes and their Consequences' in J Bell, M Elliott, JNE Varuhas, and P Murray (eds), *Public Law Adjudication in Common Law Systems: Process and Substance* (Hart Publishing, 2016) 113, 114–23; T Poole, 'The Reformation of English Administrative Law' (2009) 68 *Cambridge Law Journal* 142, 142 ('The language of *Wednesbury* unreasonableness and *ultra vires* increasingly gives way to talk about rights, proportionality, and deference'); see also P Daly, *Understanding Administrative Law in the Common Law World* (Oxford University Press, 2021) 128–39 (describing the current range of approaches to reasonableness review and their relationship to underlying administrative law values).

[155] See text accompanying n 56.

COVID-19 regulations compared to the US Congress.[156] This reflects in part the greater institutional barriers to enacting legislation in the US system, with its political separation of the executive and legislative branches, requirements of bicameralism and presentment, institutional practices such as the Senate filibuster, and prohibition on Congress overturning administrative actions through less arduous methods.[157] By contrast, in parliamentary systems like that of the UK, controversial matters are often dealt with in primary legislation, as the ruling party has little trouble pushing its statutes through Parliament.[158] Still, a notable feature of COVID-19 is the extent to which Congress *did* act, repeatedly enacting dramatic funding packages to stem the economic fallout from the pandemic and ensure that governments had the resources necessary to respond. Congress has also endorsed specific pandemic restrictions, such as its 30-day extension of the CDC's eviction moratorium. This limited extension could be read as precluding further CDC extensions, as the Court suggested in *Alabama Association*, but it could alternatively be seen as a congressional endorsement of the moratorium and not forestalling further extension. Indeed, the very fact that enacting legislation is difficult might be grounds for reading measures that are enacted more capaciously, so as not to undercut administrative power in ways that would be challenging to remedy. Alternatively, courts could give greater weight to funding enactments or oversight actions, both of which occur regularly, as signals of congressional intentions. And by contrast, the greater ease of parliamentary action might be thought to justify requiring clearer authorisation of particular COVID-19 restrictions, rather than a willingness to read legislation broadly. Hence, how courts respond to legislative involvement seems inseparable from their overall approach to administrative action.

This suggests that the different stances towards administrative action may explain much of the differences in the US and common law approaches. If so, that just pushes the relevant questions back a step. Why is there greater acceptance of pandemic administrative action in these common law systems? Is it a reflection of broader acceptance of the state across the political spectrum, greater social consensus on pandemic response, or a lesser role of the courts in matters of public dispute – or entirely separate causes? These are complicated questions that go well beyond what I can address here. At a minimum, however, this comparison of pandemic jurisprudence suggests that the determinants of administrative law decisions cannot be understood by looking just to the decisions on their own, separate from the political, social, and economic contexts from which they emerge.

[156] See MacLay and Knight (n 89) ('Parliament was heavily involved in holding the government to account during the pandemic.'); see also G Hellyer, 'Assessing Parliament's Response to the COVID-19 Pandemic' (2021) 17(1) *Policy Quarterly* 20 (in New Zealand, between 25 March and 6 September 2020, Parliament passed 14 bills explicitly relating to COVID); see also J Brown and E Kirk-Wade, 'Coronavirus: A History of 'Lockdown Laws' in England' (House of Commons Library, Briefing Paper, 2021), available at https://commonslibrary.parliament.uk/research-briefings/cbp-9068/ (detailing the timeline of House of Commons COVID enactments throughout the pandemic); see also Government of Canada, 'Government of Canada's Response to COVID-19', available at www.justice.gc.ca/eng/csj-sjc/covid.html (listing Canadian legislative enactments throughout the pandemic); see also Australian Parliament, 'Timeline of Key Decisions and Milestones', available at www.aph.gov.au/Parliamentary_Business/Committees/Senate/COVID-19/COVID19/Report/section?id=committees%2freportsen%2f024920%2f79485 (detailing enactments and extensions of Australian Parliament under the Biosecurity Act of 2015).

[157] US Const art I, §7; *INS v Chadha* 462 US 919 (1983).

[158] M Asimow, 'Delegated Legislation: United States and United Kingdom' (1983) 3(2) *OJLS* 270; S Lindquist and D Searle, 'Comparative Administrative Law: The View from Political Science' in P Cane, H Hofmann, E Ip and P Lindseth (eds), *Comparative Administrative Law* (Oxford University Press, 2021) 205–206.

IV. CONCLUSION: LESSONS FOR PUBLIC LAW CHANGE

A final task is to consider what this foray into the US pandemic jurisprudence might tell us about change in public law. That change has occurred is clear; the pandemic cases have led to important doctrinal developments on both the major questions and free exercise fronts. These developments are in line with broader trends, but without the opportunities the pandemic provided these changes might have taken longer and occurred in more developed and perhaps more nuanced opinions. That said, the Roberts Court's willingness to push public law so aggressively in expedited cases is itself telling, suggesting that one important factor behind doctrinal transformation is the presence of judges committed to achieving change.

More generally, despite their constitutional and statutory overlay, politics and ideology appear the central drivers behind the US pandemic cases and the transformation of US public law these decisions portend. In particular, these decisions embody the strong anti-administrative and conservative turn that marks the current rightward shift of the federal judiciary, and they also reflect the strongly anti-administrative and conservative politics of the current Republican party. Nor can these transformations be viewed as accidental. Instead, they represent a careful conservative strategy to take control of the courts, one that has a long history and is now bearing notable success.[159]

Yet it is also important to note that this is not the first time that US courts developed administrative law as a mechanism to check perceived dangers of excess administrative power or to serve a political agenda. In the 1960s and 1970s, courts developed more robust procedural requirements for agencies and more searching substantive review in part out of concern about agencies' new authority to issue rules with nationwide scope and major impact.[160] Fears of the state were voiced at the time more by liberals like Charles Reich, who sounded notes remarkably similar to contemporary conservatives.[161] Equally important to the development of administrative law in this period was the perception that agencies were captured by the industries and interests they regulated, and could not be trusted to implement the new environmental, health, and safety statutes Congress was enacting on their own.[162] Fast forward a decade or so, and it was the Republican deregulatory agenda that first benefitted from the ascendancy of *Chevron* deference, and then subsequently such deference served the more activist government goals of Democratic administrations. It is now clear that battles over deference are political battles at root.[163] In short, when it comes to changes in US administrative law, ideology and politics, as well background constitutional concerns, have long played a starring role.

[159] See Metzger (n 9) 51–71; see also *Dobbs v Jackson's Women's Health Org* 142 S Ct 2228 (2022).

[160] See GE Metzger, 'Ordinary Administrative Law as Constitutional Common Law' (2010) 110 *Columbia Law Review* 479, 491–92.

[161] See R Schiller, 'Regulation and the Collapse of the New Deal Order or How I Learned to Stop Worrying and Love the Market' in G Gerstle, N Lichtenstein and A O'Connor (eds) *Beyond the New Deal Order* (University of Pennsylvania Press, 2019) 168, 178–80.

[162] See RL Rabin, 'Federal Regulation in Historical Perspective' (1986) 38 *Stanford Law Review* 1189, 1296–1309; see also R Schiller, 'The Curious Origins of Airline Deregulation: Economic Deregulation and the American Left' (2020) 93 *Business History Review* 729, 732–43.

[163] See GA Elinson and J Gould, 'The Politics of Deference' (2022) 75 *Vanderbilt Law Review* 475, 478–82, 508–23; see also TW Merrill, 'The Story of Chevron: The Making of an Accidental Landmark' (2014) 66 *Administrative Law Review* 253, 275–82 (analysing various factors behind the *Chevron* rise).

15

Populism and Administrative Law

CAROL HARLOW AND RICHARD RAWLINGS

I. INTRODUCTION

THE WIDESPREAD RESURGENCE of populist discourse and influence is a familiar matter of public debate. The role and place of administrative law is however generally neglected in the burgeoning literature, despite bearing directly on the form and quality of relations between government and governed. This short contribution is intended to open up the topic, with a view to making good the deficiency.[1]

We are administrative lawyers, and our primary interest is in the way that administration operates, the uses made of law by the administration and the interplay with law generated by courts.[2] We do not wish for populist government, but we think it important not to close our ears to all lines of populist argument. Rather, in light of a long-held concern for the human face of government, we consider there are some important messages for administrative lawyers to digest and act on.

The chapter adopts several different angles of approach. They represent a mix of theoretical and practical perspectives as befits the highly challenging nature of the subject-matter. In section II, we draw out key themes from the wider literature on populism of particular relevance for administrative law. Section III highlights potential implications for administrative law of populist government, emphasising the practical dimension. Reversing the lens, we consider in section IV how classic models or 'poles' of administrative law sit with populism. Section V expands on this form of inquiry, factoring in liberal constitutionalism and market ideology and managerialism as chief contemporary 'poles' of our subject, as well as the burgeoning role of automation. In the final section (section VI), we express our concern over a major 'disconnect' between government and governed and stress the importance of constructive responses from administrative law to the populist challenge. We consider how administrative law might contribute to a less depersonalised and more participatory system of public administration.

[1] We are grateful to commentators and participants for their views at meetings in Dublin, London, Melbourne and York. The text of this chapter was finalised on 10 April 2023 and first published as an LSE Working Paper (WPS 12/2023).

[2] C Harlow and R Rawlings, *Law and Administration*, 1st edn (Weidenfeld and Nicolson, 1984).

II. POPULISM: SOME KEY THEMES

Populism as a war cry belongs more to the world of politics than law and as a concept less to legal literature than to that of political science. Its meanings are, however, quite as contestable as those attributed to the rule of law or its sister concept of democracy. For their part, administrative law thinkers should not shy away or be intimidated. A grasp of certain key ideas and influential visualisations is important, not least when shaping practical responses. The so-called populist revival in many countries demands nothing less.[3]

Demonisation is a recurring theme in the populist narrative. It is highlighted in the ideational perspective of Cas Mudde, for whom populism is

> an ideology that considers society to be ultimately separated into two homogeneous and antagonistic groups, 'the pure people' versus 'the corrupt elite', and which argues that politics should be an expression of the … general will … of the people.

Populism, defined in this way, has two opposites: elitism and pluralism. 'Elitism is populism's mirror-image: it shares its Manichean world view, but wants politics to be an expression of the views of the moral elite, instead of the amoral people.' Pluralism, on the other hand, 'rejects the homogeneity of both populism and elitism, seeing society as a heterogeneous collection of groups and individuals with often fundamentally different views and wishes'.[4]

Centred around a common core of struggle in which populist leaders claim that they, and only they, represent what populists often refer to as 'the real people',[5] this depiction of populism is perhaps the best-known.[6] It is an important starting point for exploring the relationship between populism and administrative law systems. We have long stressed the plural nature of administrative law, a living form of human construction which can have many different focal points. Mudde's definition is significant for our project because it puts in issue as populism's arch-enemies, elitism, which underlies the significance of the judiciary and judicial review in much administrative law theory, and pluralism, which for us represents a key dimension of administrative and legal process.

Lawyers, whose interest in the subject dates in the United Kingdom (UK) largely to the divisive Brexit debate, have often been less than scrupulous in their terminology. There has been a tendency to 'stick the label of populism on all kinds of phenomena for which we have perfectly good and precise concepts',[7] to extend it to political views that one opposes, or to classify it simply as a right-wing ideology.

[3] For overviews, see CR Kaltwasser, P Taggart, PO Espejo, and P Ostiguy (eds), *The Oxford Handbook of Populism* (Oxford University Press, 2017); C de la Torre (ed), *Routledge Handbook of Global Populism* (Routledge, 2019).

[4] C Mudde, 'The Populist Zeitgeist' (2004) 39(4) *Government and Opposition* 541, 543–44; C Mudde, 'Populism in Europe: An Illiberal Democratic Response to Undemocratic Liberalism' (2021) 56 *Government and Opposition* 577.

[5] The associated theoretical debate around 'the will of the people' naturally reaches back through political philosophy. For classic illustration, see G Ionescu and E Gellner (eds), *Populism: Its Meaning and National Characteristics* (Macmillan, 1969).

[6] J Ramos-González and P Ortiz, 'Radicalism and Populism: Do They Always Go Hand by Hand?' (2022) 27 *Journal of Political Ideologies* 1, 3. But see K Weyland, 'Populism: A Political-Strategic Approach' in Kaltwasser, Taggart, Espejo, and Ostiguy (eds) (n 3).

[7] J-W Müller, 'Rawls and Right-Wing Populism – A Qualified Defense of the Former,' (2021) 19 *International Journal of Constitutional Law* 419, 420. See also N Lacey, 'Populism and the Rule of Law' (2019) 11 *Annual Review of Law and Social Science* 79, 90–92.

A second main theme is the chameleon-like, even parasitical, nature of populism. As Chantal Mouffe puts it, populism is 'a way of doing politics that can take various ideological forms according to both time and place, and is compatible with a variety of institutional frameworks'.[8] Mudde and Rovira Kaltwasser present populism as a 'thin-centred ideology … attached to – and sometimes even assimilated into – other ideologies'.[9] Put simply, there is space within populism for both left- and right-wing policy, as well as a nationalistic and/or exclusionary zeitgeist.[10] The so-called redemptive aspect of populist discourse calls attention to alienated and marginalised groups[11] and by extension to artificial barriers on citizen engagement in the governmental process. And though authoritarianism may be an accommodating 'host' ideology,[12] populism should not necessarily be paired with authoritarianism.

Richard Bellamy, exploring the variable relationship with political and legal types of constitutionalism, underscores this theme. Recent comparative studies talk in terms of 'a gamut of populisms' extending between 'a predominately right-wing authoritarian populism' and 'a more left-wing, democratic populism', and 'in certain cases combining elements of each'.[13] Issues of (national) identity and (woke) culture, and pressing socio-economic concerns, feature prominently. While familiar features such as an 'anti-system politics' read across.

Administrative law, we asserted many years ago, can only be properly understood in the context of the state.[14] Alongside institutional changes come changes in public administration and law as these shift their focus in response to changing political, economic and social conditions. Varying forms and instances of populism should be viewed accordingly as part of the contemporary milieu of our subject. Different strains of populism may in turn have variable connotations for administrative law and theorists and practitioners should be alert to the different potentials in administrative law to foster and support, and avoid and dilute, populist criticism and influence. The populist revival is attributed to a number of causes. Some are deep-rooted and far-reaching, as with 'cartelisation' of political parties and cultural 'backlash', and of course the globalised forces of financial and technological disruption.[15] Others appear more contingent or context specific. Populist forms of nationalism are seen to varying degrees inside the European Union.[16] Meanwhile, the self-justifying imagery of the

[8] C Mouffe, *For a Left Populism* (Verso, 2018) 11. See also E Laclau and C Mouffe, *Hegemony and Socialist Strategy*, 2nd edn (Verso, 2001).

[9] C Mudde and CR Kaltwasser, *Populism: A Very Short Introduction* (Oxford University Press, 2017) 6.

[10] P Taggart, *Populism* (Oxford University Press, 2000).

[11] M Canovan, *Populism* (Harcourt Brace Jovanovich, 1981); M Canovan, 'Trust the People! Populism and the Two Faces of Democracy' (1999) 47 *Political Studies* 2. And see on 'inclusionary populism', J Mansbridge and S Macedo, 'Populism and Democratic Theory' (2019) 15 *Annual Review of Law and Social Science* 59.

[12] G Halmai, 'Populism, Authoritarianism and Constitutionalism' (2019) 20 *German Law Journal* 296.

[13] R Bellamy, 'Political Constitutionalism and Populism' (2023) 50 *Journal of Law and Society*. And see M Tushnet and B Bugarič, *Power to the People: Constitutionalism in the Age of Populism* (Oxford University Press, 2022).

[14] Harlow and Rawlings (n 2) 1.

[15] Eg, J Hopkin, *Anti-system Politics: The Crisis of Market Liberalism in Rich Democracies* (Oxford University Press, 2020).

[16] See especially, S Kukovič and P Just, *The Rise of Populism in Central and Eastern Europe* (Edward Elgar, 2022).

strong leader directly attuned to the 'common sense' of 'the heartland' has been exemplified in America with President Trump.[17]

The complex relation and interplay of populist tendencies with precepts of liberal democracy, in the broad sense of party competition, representative and accountable government, the rule of law and individual rights, constitute other major themes in the literature.[18] Giving tangible expression to the notion of a thin-centred ideology, we hear today of 'populist constitutionalism', epitomised by the use of formally valid constitutional methods to promote reform in the name of collective identity and purpose.[19] Likewise, 'abusive constitutionalism' references the disruptive art of trumping constitutional checks through other constitutional techniques.[20] With deep historical echoes, and inevitably encompassing administrative law matter, appropriation or colonisation of the state apparatus by political actors claiming to articulate the general will is a litmus test for authoritarian forms of populism.

A recognition that tension between the demands of popular democracy and constraint on the power of popular sovereignty may feed a populist mind-set is a noteworthy feature of the public discussion.[21] This connects for present purposes with the issue of 'fit' between populist views and different models of administrative law, which, as we discuss in section V, today include treating the subject as a vehicle for assertive forms of liberal constitutionalist ideology. An anti-institutionalist impulse in populist discourse, hostile to checks on executive power exercised in the name of 'the people', is also demonstrated, an aspect to which we return in section III.

Populism, Jan-Werner Müller suggests, is most dangerous when it combines the language of democratic values with innately anti-pluralist sentiment.[22] His alternative visualisation of populism as 'a dynamic process'[23] opens up the question of the practical implications of populist tendencies for established institutional and policy frameworks. Widening the perspective, the notion of a 'spectrum' or 'dial' of populist leanings and influence in the shared constitutional context of liberal democracy provides a basic analytical framework for political scientists. For our more modest purposes, this type of approach has the particular virtue of directing attention to the important place of administrative process not only as the essential day-to-day apparatus of public power but also as a repository of governance values.

The revival of populist discourse raises further questions about what might be expected of populist government. Here the literature has been surprisingly limited, being again largely concerned with the political side of governance (elections, political parties, etc).[24] Complaint has indeed been made of failure, at least until recently, 'to address in any

[17] M Kazin, *The Populist Persuasion: An American History* (Basic Books, 1995) gives the longer view.

[18] With no sign of slackening: M Krygier, A Czarnota and W Sadurski (eds), *Anti-Constitutional Populism* (Cambridge University Press, 2022).

[19] P Blokker, B Bugarič and G Halmai (eds), *Populist Constitutionalism: Varieties, Complexities and Contradictions* (2019) 20 *German Law Journal Special Issue* 3.

[20] D Landau, 'Abusive Constitutionalism' (2013) 47 *University of California, Davis Law Review* 189.

[21] C Mouffe, *The Democratic Paradox* (Verso, 2000); N Walker, 'Populism and Constitutional Tension' (2019) 17 *International Journal of Constitutional Law* 515.

[22] J-W Müller, *What Is Populism?* (Republished Penguin Books, 2017) 6.

[23] J-W Müller, 'The People Must Be Extracted from Within the People: Reflections on Populism' (2014) 21 *Constellations* 483, 484.

[24] Though see M Caiani and P Graziano, 'The Three Faces of Populism in Power: Polity, Policies and Politics' (2022) 57 *Government and Opposition* 569.

detail … the impact of populism on public administration and the State more generally'.[25] The same can be said of administrative law even though it too is a basic feature of the exercise of public power. Possible 'thickenings' of a thin-centred model of populist government that have special reference to administrative law are an important aspect of our inquiry.

A different but related theme concerns possible strategic responses to populism, using legal and constitutional techniques. The typical prompt is worry or lament over populist political advance against the backdrop of post Second World War achievements in constitutionalism and human rights and also regional (European) integration. The evident propensity of the European Union to foster populist mobilisation at Member State level, not least by way of protest against cosmopolitanism and technocracy, or cosy forms of supranational consensus and overarching constraint on domestic forms of political and regulatory space, provides a good illustration.[26] Mark Dawson explores a set of possible strategic responses. The first he calls 'bracketing' or insulating areas of EU law and policy from contestation; the second, 'accommodation', a reverse approach that favours allowing populist challenge within the parameters of EU law; the third, 'confrontation', or using EU law to combat populist tendencies and steer the development of conflict within the national law of Member States. These responses are highly context-specific and dependent in part on the distinctive, supranational quality of the EU, but we do not dismiss them entirely. In a federal state system, variations on the themes of 'bracketing' and 'confrontation' might be possible,[27] while 'accommodation' in Dawson's limited meaning is always a possibility. Experience confirms, however, that there is no 'magic wand' to wish the populists away – far from it.

While this type of strategy may allow of mixes of approach, they hardly exhaust the field. As Müller observes, rather than treat populism simply as a threat, the problems populists complain about can be taken seriously without adopting the political framework in which they are articulated.[28] In this chapter we stress the importance of heeding messages. Concerned as we are with administrative law rather than high constitutional law, this more reflective approach involves grappling with the potential of public administration to foster the spread of populism, distilling elements of populist concern with day-to-day governance and using them as a prompt for rethinking aspects of our subject.

III. POPULIST GOVERNMENT: EXPECTATIONS AND PRESSURE POINTS

As administrative lawyers with a keen interest in governmental process and the relations of citizen and state, we next consider what might be experienced from populist government in the field of governance and what the pressure points and impacts might be for law and administration. How might an insistence that the voice of 'the real people' is

[25] BG Peters and J Pierre, 'Populism and Public Administration: Confronting the Administrative State' (2019) 51 *Administration and Society* 1521, 1524.

[26] F Bignami (ed), *EU Law in Populist Times* (Cambridge University Press, 2019); IT Berend, *The Economics and Politics of European Integration: Populism, Nationalism and the History of the EU* (Routledge, 2020).

[27] A Benz, *Constitutional Policy in Multilevel Government: The Art of Keeping the Balance* (Oxford University Press, 2016).

[28] Müller (n 23) 491.

commonly distorted – even drowned out – by a homogeneous and morally corrupt elite and/or a multiplicity of special interests, find tangible expression in the manner and approach of executive authority? More prosaically, how might a populist government seek to counter 'establishment' and/or discordant views and what are the everyday relations likely to be between a populist government and independent courts?

In highlighting these issues, we are concerned to sketch some possible lines of development in pre-existing conditions of representative and responsible government, leaving space to others to elaborate the argument by exemplifying from different constitutional settings and jurisdictions. Other structural and contingent factors may of course be in play, pointing in similar directions; then again, populist government might also exploit such tendencies, perhaps of considerable historical pedigree. Most of the materials we reference are from the UK, our home turf. The distinctive constitutional milieu featuring parliamentary sovereignty and lack of codified structure is useful for highlighting the broader potentials of populist government in liberal democratic settings. We should not however be taken to say that recent UK governments are or have been populist ones. Rather, we see some recent tendencies in this direction despite, or perhaps in part because of, traditional modes of parliamentary government. In addition, we shall suggest in section V that the growing influence of constitutionalism may have escalated a growth in populist reaction against the precepts of liberal democracy.

In this short account, we home in on three main sets of expectation. Indicative of enhanced executive authority and influence, they are characterised by much overlap and interlock. The first grouping concerns the style and structure of governance, extending through aspects of institutional culture to the use of particular law and policy forms. In the second grouping, the focus is on contemporary forms of public messaging, administrative process and engagement. The third grouping involves the possible harnessing and/or neutralising of alternative sources of authority and influence, more particularly the judiciary. The populist concern with conformity to 'the general will' is a recurring theme.

A. Style, Structure and Forms

The prospect of strong executive government tending to authoritarianism looms large here. One element is the propensity for greater internal centralisation of power, so underwriting nostrums of direct linkage between political leadership and 'the real people'.[29] This in turn suggests a more personalised style and form of authority, and not only in presidential systems of government.[30] The growth of core institutional structures and stronger centralised inputs into the general policy-making are relevant steps. Likewise, significant changes may be anticipated to the internal nexuses of executive power, the proverbial 'hidden wiring' of government. With elite forms of bureaucratic organisation and culture being seen as remote or hostile by populists, very possibly for good reason, enhanced politicisation of the administration is clearly on the cards. Indicative of an

[29] M Bauer and S Becker, 'Democratic Backsliding, Populism and Public Administration' (2019) 3 *Perspectives on Public Management and Governance* 19.

[30] A Blick, *Populism and the UK Constitution* (Constitution Society, 2019).

increasing level of patronage within government, a powerful coterie of special advisers and temporary secondments may be thought necessary: more true believers and/or disruptors of the 'old, corrupt system'.[31] Elsewhere, a populist-style testing of hard and soft law precepts of official conduct suggests friction with the expansive 'integrity branch' of government, in which autonomous bodies and actors are charged with accountability functions and grouped together as an identifiable branch of government with responsibility for maintaining standards in public life.[32]

In such conditions, executive primacy, in the general sense of blocking up power and dominant position among state institutions, may be demonstrated in various ways.[33] Take for example the major design question in public administration of regulatory structures. Independent agencies are centre stage today in multiple administrative law systems, a reflection in part of late twentieth century cultures of privatisation and managerialism. The deep forces of technological change and seemingly never-ending demands for social and professional regulation continue to drive the institutional development in the sprawling conditions of contemporary governance. As a large scale exercise in depoliticisation, this is an evident source of concern for populists, and the more so in view of expansive developments on the international plane framed by powerful forces of economic liberalism.[34] Whereas expertise and specialism is classically seen to justify administrative agencies, contesting technocracy in the guise of an 'out-of-touch' or 'self-serving' elite, is another recurring theme in populist discourse.[35] Curtailment of the agency model, perhaps by 'bonfire', perhaps through more patronage, may well fit a populist zeitgeist, especially under right-wing regimes imbued with notions of 'less government'. On the other hand, this may pose a particular challenge for populist government of effective policy delivery with less expert support.

The use of prerogative-type powers remains a familiar executive technique, and indeed was unsuccessfully attempted in the well-known 'Brexit cases' discussed below. Cast in terms of strong centralised authority and avoiding or downplaying parliamentary process, it may have particular appeal for a populist government. Large-scale invocation of the wealth-based power of government in the name of 'the real people' may also be envisaged, not least when exploiting the potential of public contract as a policy and regulatory vehicle.[36] While typically involving much by way of co-dependency with big business, historically a chief villain in the populist canon, the widespread phenomenon of

[31] See T Durrant, N Blacklaws and K Zodgekar, *Special Advisers and the Johnson Government* (Institute for Government, 2020).

[32] Best developed in Australia: see AJ Brown, 'The Integrity Branch: A "System", an "Industry", or a Sensible Emerging Fourth Arm of Government?' in M Groves (ed), *Modern Administrative Law in Australia: Concepts and Context* (Cambridge University Press, 2014). See also M Tushnet (ed), *The New Fourth Branch: Institutions for Protecting Constitutional Democracy* (Cambridge University Press, 2021).

[33] P Cane, 'The Resurgence of Executive Primacy in the Age of Populism' (2019) 28 *Washington International Law Journal* 311.

[34] A White and M Neblo, 'Capturing the Public: Beyond Technocracy & Populism in the U.S. Administrative State' (2021) 150 *Daedalus* 172; M Zürn, 'How Non-Majoritarian Institutions Make Silent Majorities Vocal: A Popular Explanation of Authoritarian Populism' (2022) 20 *Perspectives on Politics* 788.

[35] T Nichols, *The Death of Expertise: The Campaign Against Established Knowledge and Why it Matters* (Oxford University Press, 2017). Though see C Bickerton and C Accetti, *Technopopulism: The New Logic of Democratic Politics* (Oxford University Press, 2021).

[36] See further, A Perry, 'The Crown's Administrative Powers' (2015) 131 *LQR* 652.

'the commissioning state', where much of what the administration does is procurement,[37] magnifies such potentials in contemporary administrative law systems.

A particularly heavy use of statutory forms of executive legislation appears par for the course, including perhaps under the innately dangerous rubric of 'emergency powers'. Future populist regimes interested in streamlined process would certainly have much precedent to go on around the common law world and mass government initiatives in a global pandemic have highlighted the crowd of techniques lying ready to hand.[38] Repeated, even desperate complaints by representative institutions of 'government by diktat' or 'democracy denied' confirm the wide, discretionary potential of this form of executive output. Some devices are familiar if perpetually challenging, such as broad enabling or 'skeleton' statutes and so-called 'Henry VIII clause' powers to amend or repeal primary legislation. Others serve to draw attention to the continued scope for pushing boundaries, for example, by legislative sub-delegation of powers to a tertiary level.[39] Further exploiting the strong potential of 'soft law' policy forms might also prove particularly attractive for populist regimes in view of the evident limitations on judicial control and legislative scrutiny in this field.[40]

B. Communication, Engagement and Process

Turning to methods of engagement, a propensity for government by popular feel cuts against the key administrative law ideal of rational decision-making. Contemporary forms of populist government can be expected to feature direct and personalised forms of messaging: mass electronic communication via the immediacy of social media.[41] At one with the general theme of demonisation, a strong performative element – picking fights with all those special interests and/or 'the corrupt elite' – is facilitated. Fashionable methods for testing public opinion can be combined. Indicative of a different form of governance, one in which so-called 'establishment' views may be countered or suppressed, this is the stuff of vague or aspirational policy suggestions, of reaction via (trusted) media and (carefully selected) focus groups, and of dictated forms of government response. This is, in short, one way for populist regimes to weaponise 'the real people'.[42]

[37] R Rawlings, 'Addressing Contractual Governance' in C Harlow (ed), *A Research Agenda for Administrative Law* (Edward Elgar, 2023).

[38] See J King and O Ferraz (eds), 'Oxford Compendium of National Legal Responses to Covid-19' (Oxford University Press, online), available at https://oxcon.ouplaw.com/home/occ19; and in the UK context, Hansard Society, 'Coronavirus Statutory Instruments Dashboard' (2020–2022, online), available at www.hansardsociety.org.uk/publications/data/coronavirus-statutory-instruments-dashboard.

[39] Hansard Society, 'Proposals for a New System for Delegated Legislation: A Working Paper' (2023), available at www.hansardsociety.org.uk/publications/reports/proposals-for-a-new-system-for-delegated-legislation-a-working-paper.

[40] R Rawlings, 'Soft Law Never Dies' in M Elliott and D Feldman (eds), *The Cambridge Companion to Public Law* (Cambridge University Press, 2015).

[41] B Moffitt, *The Global Rise of Populism: Performance, Political Style and Representation* (Stanford University Press, 2016). See also M Fenster, 'Populism and Transparency: The Political Core of an Administrative Norm' (2021) 89 *University of Cincinnati Law Review* 286.

[42] See further, P Norris and R Inglehart, *Cultural Backlash: Trump, Brexit, and Authoritarian Populism* (Cambridge University Press, 2019).

A burgeoning feature of the administrative law landscape in recent times, consultation procedure presents something of a dilemma for populist government. Drawing decision-making closer to 'the heartland' may clearly appeal, while the formal process requirements may also serve as a useful counterweight to an inwards-looking institutional culture. But as well as the enervating elements of cost and delay, there is the practical experience of privileged access and well-heeled domination, and the potential for manipulation by an official elite, to grapple with. A populist government can be expected to prefer statute-based consultation procedures to more free-ranging common law demands founded on judicial notions of fairness and openness.[43]

A basic disdain for process is suggested in the mantra 'get things done'. Popularly viewed as the enervating and obfuscating product of officialdom, 'red-tape' is a label ripe for exploitation by populist regimes operating in the declared – impatient – service of 'the real people'. A populist government concerned to (be seen to) make a difference will have to navigate, circumnavigate or cut through much administrative procedure accordingly. Planning law, with its familiar delays and distribution of power between assorted groups and interests within the planning process, is an obvious target. Seemingly ubiquitous regulatory-type procedures such as impact assessments, which are often elongated and replete with technical assessment and expert judgement,[44] are the kind of procedural paraphernalia which may well be looked at askance. More generally, the often clunky style of modern public administration, based on a complex framework of detailed regulation and heavy proceduralisation, helps to foster, we argue in section V, a serious disconnect between government and governed.

C. Alternative Power Centres: Taming the Judiciary?

For populist regimes to be uninterested in harnessing and/or neutralising alternative sources of authority and influence would be strange indeed.[45] Intermediate interests represent a plurality of political views, conflicting with the idea of the general will. The status of opposed elites may leave them well-placed to shape the discourse, while in separation of powers terms external 'checks and balances' may be precisely that. As regards the 'dial' of populist tendencies in conditions of liberal democracy, possible government actions range through different degrees of mobilisation and control. An array of potential targets immediately present themselves. The control of information sources via state broadcasting and/or restrictions on press freedom are all too familiar strategies, as is pushing back on the discrete advocacy role of powerful civil society organisations, or effectively co-opting them, in increasingly authoritarian contexts of administrative law.[46] Campaigning litigation or 'pressure through law', the use of test case strategies, etc for

[43] For competing judicial views on this point, see *R(Moseley) v London Borough of Haringey* [2014] UKSC 56.

[44] See C Dunlop and C Radaelli. *Handbook of Regulatory Impact Assessment* (Edward Elgar, 2017).

[45] For contemporary comparative perspective, see W Sadurski, *A Pandemic of Populists* (Cambridge University Press, 2022).

[46] P Kenny, '"The Enemy of the People": Populists and Press Freedom' (2020) 73 *Political Research Quarterly* 261; A Arato and J Cohen, *Populism and Civil Society* (Oxford University Press, 2021).

obtaining wider group objectives, is a centuries-old feature of the common law tradition.[47] In recent times it has gained fresh impetus, facilitated in the UK by major developments in human rights and equality law and expansive parameters of judicial review process and procedure. Particularly for right-wing populists, this is pluralist-type anathema: a realm of self-appointed 'public interest advocates' looking for maximum 'impact' at the expense of executive authority through complex legal means and on behalf of minority and special interests. They are liable to find themselves on the receiving end of counter-measures from populist governments, financial disincentive (costs) for example.

Alternative power centres may continue to do their work but be increasingly required to play according to new rules. Populist regimes can be expected to embrace certain key elements of the judicial function, beginning with that essential ingredient for strong executive authority, firm law enforcement. There is a good fit with demands for strict or highly textual forms of legislative interpretation, and for limited forms of procedural review, recalling the role of judicial review as a source of legitimacy: constitutional symbolism and legal authority, government under law, stamp of approval for lawful decision-making. At the authoritarian end of the populist 'spectrum', the courts themselves may be deployed against electoral democracy, contrary to comfortable liberal democratic assumptions of representation reinforcement.[48] Conversely, inherently elite forms of judicial review, perhaps increasingly substantive in form and rights focused, perhaps avowedly constitutionalist in character, may jar, to put it mildly, with governments featuring populist ideology, especially where matters of high policy are involved or in high-profile cases involving unpopular minority interests.

Numerous techniques exist in a liberal constitutional framework for constraining the judicial power, starting with negative statutory reactions to inconvenient case law and validatory legislation or nullification. A broader 'fire-prevention' stance means taking steps to reorder the judicial process in restrictive or more government-friendly fashion. Preclusive or ouster clauses offer a classic blocking strategy, for example in immigration control, which is not only a familiar matter of public concern but also a bulk field of administrative law challenge in multiple jurisdictions. Standard institutional variations include diversion to inferior adjudicative bodies and curtailment of appeal rights. More subtle procedural techniques, such as heightened thresholds for cases to proceed, or less potent versions of remedy, may also be deployed in the face of enhanced judicial review challenge.[49] For political leaders driven by the perception of an activist judiciary that may dispute 'the general will', further attempts at patronage, and hence greater pressure on established process for maintaining judicial independence, may be another option.

International courts, with constitutionalist proclivities, standing for the vertical dimension to the spread of law, are susceptible to populist criticism as innately cosmopolitan, 'interfering' and remote from 'the heartland'. This is epitomised in the regional context by the interplay over many years between national courts and authorities with the

[47] C Harlow and R Rawlings, *Pressure through Law* (Routledge, 1992).

[48] D Landau and R Dixon, 'Abusive Judicial Review: Courts Against Democracy' (2020) 53 *University of California, Davis Law Review* 1313.

[49] For illustration in the UK context, see Senior Courts Act 1981, ss 29A and 31, as elaborated by Criminal Courts and Justice Act 2015 and Judicial Review and Courts Act 2022. And see Ministry of Justice, *Judicial Review Reform Consultation: The Government Response* (CP 477, 2021).

European Court of Human Rights (ECtHR) and Court of Justice of the European Union (CJEU): policy-makers on a grand scale sometimes portrayed as enemies of democracy.[50] Severing or replacing linkage with international courts with home anchoring – from a populist standpoint, a less lofty form of institutional 'dialogue' – is a foreseeable populist strategy. Recent controversies in the UK illuminate the possibilities. The powerful integrationist role of the CJEU featured prominently in the bitter Brexit debates as a wish to 'take back control from foreign judges'. Nationalistic in character, the Conservative Government's Bill of Rights Bill introduced in June 2022 targeted the Human Rights Act 1998, with a view to rebalancing the relationship between the domestic courts, the ECtHR and Parliament, giving primacy to decision-making by Parliament where competing rights and interests are at stake and underwriting the UK Supreme Court's role as the ultimate judicial authority for domestic law purposes.[51]

Techniques of 'striking back' and 'clamping down' on judicial review are naturally shaped and driven by local constitutional and political conditions.[52] Some may be frustrated by the very judicial authority and influence they are designed to curb. Others, packaged perhaps as tweaks to legal practice and procedure, may be subtly cumulative. In our own jurisdiction, parliamentary sovereignty magnifies the opportunities, and more obviously so in the light of Brexit and continued vigorous reassertion of the doctrine at Supreme Court level.[53] Yet the UK experience also confirms that taming the judges through formal legal means may be far more easily said than done, whether because of careful husbanding of judicial discretion and common law technique, or of high profile opposition under the banner of 'rule of law' and threats of escalating constitutional conflict.[54] An alternative expectation of government featuring populist ideology is strident and mass-communicated forms of 'soft pressure' on the judges to be more executive-minded – or else![55]

IV. 'POLES' OF ADMINISTRATIVE LAW: THE CLASSIC FRAMEWORK

There is no inherent reason why administrative law and populism should be at odds. Populism does not purport to dictate the content of the general will nor precisely how it is to be expressed.

It does, however, require the content to be homogeneous and, as indicated above, populist governments generally claim to represent the voice of the people. Like populism, administrative law is 'thin-centred' in the sense that it is not tied to any particular political

[50] E Voeten, 'Populism and Backlashes against International Courts' (2020) 18 *Perspectives on Politics* 207.

[51] Ministry of Justice, *Human Rights Act Reform: A Modern Bill of Rights* (CP 588, 2021). The Bill was withdrawn in June 2023.

[52] C Harlow and R Rawlings, '"Striking Back" and "Clamping Down": An Alternative Perspective on Judicial Review' in J Bell, M Elliott, J Varuhas and P Murray (eds), *Public Law Adjudication in Public Law Systems* (Hart Publishing, 2016).

[53] See, eg, *References by the Attorney General and the Advocate General for Scotland – United Nations Convention on the Rights of the Child (Incorporation) (Scotland) Bill and European Charter of Local Self-Government (Incorporation) (Scotland) Bill* [2021] UKSC 42.

[54] R Rawlings, 'Review, Revenge and Retreat' (2005) 68 *MLR* 378.

[55] See, eg, All Party Parliamentary Group on Democracy and the Constitution, *An Independent Judiciary – Challenges since 2016* (2022).

persuasion; it operates as a set of tools at the disposal of any government for the efficient conduct of its public administration and execution of its policies.[56] And although both populism and administrative law customarily 'speak the language of democratic values', neither is irrevocably democratic in character; both can be used to support authoritarian and even tyrannical systems of government.[57]

For Sabino Cassese, administrative law is a subject in continuous tension or 'oscillation' between three 'poles': an authoritarian pole, where administrative law acts as 'an instrument of public power' on rather than for the people; an instrumentalist pole, in which administrative law is simply the machinery of public administration used by society to realise its collective goals; and a liberal pole, which Cassese traces to the nineteenth century Kantian ideal of the *Rechtsstaat*.[58]

Cassese perhaps gives the impression that the authoritarian pole is, if not obsolete, at least obsolescent, having morphed into the instrumentalist pole. But we should not be too quick to dismiss administrative law's authoritarian possibilities. In the common law world, vestiges of the authoritarian tradition persist in the remnants of the prerogative powers of the Crown, and although unrestrained prerogative power is generally seen as on its way out,[59] this is by no means always the case.[60] Nor are we alone in discerning an upsurge in authoritarian uses of administrative law.[61] Counter-terrorism laws and security measures are multiplying, police powers are routinely expanded, the 'surveillance state' is burgeoning, 'conditionality' is increasingly a prerequisite for access to welfare benefits and other privileges, the will of government is imposed on civil society by the widespread use of contract and civil and regulatory sanctions, and much, much more. Such developments are not peculiar to authoritarian or populist regimes; they are also manifest within overtly liberal democratic systems. Thus Cassese's tripolar model stands as a valuable warning of the dangerous nexus between administrative law and authoritarianism.

Cassese calls the instrumentalist or functionalist approach to administrative law 'transformative' and 'socialistic'. Pioneered by academics to justify the use of state power to carry through social reform, it emerged in the common law world as strongly linked to left-wing reformism. It came to the fore in the United States (US) with the advent of President Roosevelt's New Deal and travelled from there through many Anglophone jurisdictions.[62] This instrumentalist model downplayed the place of courts and judges and up-played the role of 'impartial' technical expertise in the administrative state,[63] making

[56] E Fisher and S Shapiro, *Administrative Competence: Reimagining Administrative Law* (Cambridge University Press, 2020).

[57] Müller (n 22) 6.

[58] S Cassese, '"Le droit tout puissant et unique de la société": Paradoxes of Administrative Law' (2010) 22 *European Review of Public Law* 171.

[59] T Poole, 'The Strange Death of the Prerogative in England' (2018) 43 *University of Western Australia Law Review* 42.

[60] Notably, the Chagos Islanders' case: *R (Bancoult) v Secretary of State for Foreign and Commonwealth Affairs* [2008] UKHL 61.

[61] B Schotel, 'Administrative Law as a Dual State. Authoritarian Elements of Administrative Law' (2021) 13 *Hague Journal on the Rule of Law* 195. And see, eg, from a criminological perspective, I Koch, *Personalizing the State: An Anthropology of Law, Politics and Welfare in Austerity Britain* (Oxford University Press, 2018).

[62] R Gordon, 'Willis's American Counterparts: The Legal Realists' Defence of Administration' (2005) 55 *University of Toronto Law Journal* 405. See on the wider connections, C Harlow, 'The Influence of Léon Duguit on Anglo-American Legal Thought' in F Melleray (ed), *Autour du Léon Duguit* (Bruylant, 2011).

[63] J Landis, *The Administrative Process* (Yale University Press, 1938).

it at one and the same time a partial fit with the thin-centred ideology of populism and a suspect instrument of elitist experts.

Cassese's third 'pole' is a 'control' or rights-based model of administrative law that operates on behalf of the individual to 'define the limits of public power, inspire the notion of administrative review, and oblige administrative bodies to comply with the principle of transparency and provide reasons for its decisions'.[64] There is much common ground here with the rights-based and individualistic model that has been the orthodoxy in English administrative law since the subject was first recognised in the nineteenth century. Control of the executive by the 'ordinary' courts administering general principles derived from the common law was a key aspect of Dicey's formulation of the rule of law doctrine,[65] garnished with a strong anti-executive streak and suspicion of 'wide, arbitrary or discretionary powers'.[66] In Wade and Forsyth's contemporary definition, administrative law is 'the law relating to the control of governmental power', its primary purpose being 'to keep the powers of government within their legal bounds, so as to protect the citizen against their abuse'.[67]

Here the fit with Mudde's ideational view of populism is less close than is the case with the instrumentalist pole of administrative law. The focus is on the legal interests and rights of individuals, while the focus of populism is on the people as a collective whole. Moreover, the role of populism is to champion the people against the governing elite, while the anti-executive dimension of the control and rights-based approach has led to an emphasis on the role of courts, judges and the case law they create. Senior judges, by definition members of an elite, play an important part in developing general principles of administrative law and setting its values. As emphasised in section III, judges also form an influential power block perhaps capable of blocking the 'general will' as formulated by the government. We noted too the weaponisation of legal action for political purposes, generating the potential for judges to collide with populist governments by moving onto terrain that the latter see as primarily political and resent.

Two celebrated cases involving the divisive Brexit struggle illustrate this point. When the High Court in London was asked in *Miller (No 1)* to decide whether the Government needed authority from Parliament before notifying the EU of UK intention to withdraw from the Union, the Court was conscious that it was on dangerous ground. The three senior judges who heard the case were careful to underline that the Court's ruling in favour of parliamentary approval was purely legal and in no way political.[68] Yet after the decision, the *Daily Mail* published a front page article under the banner headline 'Enemies of the People', accusing the judges of defying 17.4 million Brexit voters in a referendum.[69] There could hardly be a clearer illustration of 'the people versus the corrupt elite' dichotomy central to populist beliefs.

[64] Cassese (n 58) 176.

[65] JWF Allison, 'Turning the Rule of Law into an English Constitutional Idea' in C May and A Winchester (eds), *Handbook on the Rule of Law* (Edward Elgar, 2018).

[66] AV Dicey, *The Law of the Constitution* (edited by JWF Allison) (Oxford University Press, 2013); AV Dicey, *Introduction to the Study of the Law of the Constitution*, 10th edn (Macmillan, 1959).

[67] C Forsyth and J Ghosh, *Wade & Forsyth's Administrative Law*, 12th edn (Oxford University Press, 2023) 4.

[68] *R (Miller) v The Secretary of State for Exiting the European Union* (*Miller No 1*) [2016] EWHC 2768 (Admin) [5], later confirmed by the Supreme Court at [2017] UKSC 5.

[69] J Slack, 'Enemies of the People' *Daily Mail* (4 November 2016). The Conservative Government's subsequent efforts at 'clamping down' on judicial review were noted previously.

Miller and Cherry[70] concerned the prerogative power to prorogue Parliament, exercised by the monarch on advice from the Prime Minister. A legal challenge to the prorogation succeeded in Scotland on the ground of improper purpose but was ruled by the High Court in London to be non-justiciable.[71] On appeal, the Supreme Court ruled that the issue was the limits of the prerogative power to prorogue over which the courts unquestionably had jurisdiction. Perhaps more questionable was their further ruling that the Prime Minister's advice was unlawful, a point to which we shall return. The case represents an extreme example of the blocking power of an independent judiciary, in populist terms a 'veto point' occupied by the elites.[72]

V. NEW POLES, NEW DYNAMICS

For our purposes, Cassese's analysis is incomplete.[73] Although he mentions 'new concepts and models' such as 'governance', 'new public management' and 'expert bodies', Cassese observes only that they are 'difficult to understand and to classify in terms of traditional paradigms'.[74] This, in our view, is to underplay the two most potent twentieth century influences on administrative law: on one side, the pull towards constitutionalism associated with the global human rights movement; on the other, the legalisation of social relations ('juridification') and rise of managerialist public administration, commonly framed and underwritten by the international market ideology of economic liberalism. As we argue below, constitutionalism has acted as an important driver of juridification, creating a link with administrative law in its instrumentalist sense of the machinery of public administration.

The addition of new rights to the list of judicially protected interests or the amplification of judicial power through a more intensive style of judicial review might be regarded merely as an extension of the classical rights-based pole of administrative law. However, we prefer to acknowledge two new poles for administrative law. The incursion of liberal constitutionalist and market-oriented/managerialist ideologies into administrative law is a step change so considerable that to ignore it would be to underplay the cumulative significance of constitutional and legal invention in our own historical period.

In a similar vein, we feel that such is the scale and force of new technology in public administration that it moves beyond earlier instrumentalist conceptions: it too might be termed a distinct new pole for the administrative law of the twenty-first century.[75] Yet although its drawing power is certainly magnetic, technology is neither an abstraction nor (as yet) an ideology, For the time being therefore, we leave this question open.

[70] *R (Miller and Cherry) v The Prime Minister* [2019] UKSC 41.

[71] *R (Miller) v The Prime Minister* [2019] EWHC 2381; *Cherry and others v Advocate General for Scotland* [2019] CSIH 49. The unusual length of the prorogation was allegedly designed to avoid further parliamentary debate in the run up to the then prescribed UK 'exit day'.

[72] M Tushnet, 'Varieties of Populism' (2019) 20 *German Law Journal* 382.

[73] Cassese goes on to discuss 'four unresolved tensions' of contemporary administrative law: politics and administration; public/private; statal and universal; national and transnational.

[74] Cassese (n 58) 171–72.

[75] See along similar lines, R Brownsword, *Law, Technology and Society: Reimagining the Regulatory Environment* (Routledge, 2019).

A. Liberal Constitutionalist Ideology

Constitutionalism classically translates as the belief that the most effective safeguard for individual liberty and democracy lies in a constitution, ideally a documentary text. This sets the parameters of governmental activity and, like the rule of law with which constitutionalism has close connections, binds all the organs of government including the legislature. Constitutionalism is normative in the sense that it contains a set of ideas that defines what a constitution is or ought to be.[76] The standing of the constitution as a 'higher law', 'elevated above the ordinary cut and thrust of politics', is justified by its acceptance as 'the authoritative expression of the regime's collective political identity' and its permanence.[77]

The genesis of modern constitutionalism is in the US Constitution, which remains paradigmatic. It rose to pre-eminence after the Second World War, a period of change when, partly due to US influence in world affairs, partly to the winding down of colonialism, written constitutions and human rights texts proliferated. By the end of the century, constitutionalism had gained sufficient traction to render a 'rights and review tandem … an essential, even obligatory component of any move toward constitutional democracy'.[78] The ingredients of modern constitutionalism are typically: a written text with a heightened threshold for constitutional amendment; a textual enumeration of individual rights, rights-based judicial review; and a commitment to the rule of law and to democracy in the shape of periodic democratic elections.[79] This formula provides a double layer of protection: the constitution and a power of review by an independent judiciary for enforcement.

Constitutionalism can co-exist with authoritarian government; authoritarian regimes often possess a seemingly democratic constitution with a generous human rights charter, which lends the regime a legal legitimacy of sorts.[80] But just as instrumentalist administrative law is generally considered 'socialistic', so it is hard to decouple constitutionalism from its essentially liberal purposes of protecting individual liberty and representative democracy. Thus, Martin Loughlin lists amongst the aspirations of constitutionalism the imposition of curbs on the exercise of arbitrary power, advancement of the rule of law, establishing a regime of limited government and ensuring the protection of a citizen's basic rights,[81] all characteristic components of liberalism. The spread of these ideas owes much to the influence of liberal philosophers such as Ronald Dworkin, whose work reinstated law's ethical dimension, restored the link between law and morals and strengthened the arm of the judiciary with an infusion of principled reasoning.[82] As an interpretivist who believed that law should be interpreted by reference to a 'coherent set

[76] R Schutze, 'Constitutionalism(s)' in R Masterman and R Schutze (eds), *The Cambridge Companion to Comparative Constitutional Law* (Cambridge University Press, 2019).

[77] M Loughlin, *Against Constitutionalism* (Harvard University Press, 2022) ix, 6–7.

[78] M Shapiro and AS Sweet, *On Law, Politics and Judicialization* (Oxford University Press, 2002) 136.

[79] T Ginsburg, AZ Huq and M Versteeg, *'The Coming Demise of Liberal Constitutionalism?'* (2018) 85 *University of Chicago Law Review* 239.

[80] KL Scheppele, 'Autocratic Legalism' (2018) 85 *University of Chicago Law Review* 545.

[81] Loughlin (n 77) ix.

[82] R Dworkin, *Law's Empire* (Harvard University Press, 1986); R Dworkin, *Freedom's Law: The Moral Reading of the American Constitution* (Harvard University Press, 1996).

of principles about people's rights and duties',[83] Dworkin opened the way for a 'thickened' rights-oriented system of judicial review with a legitimate basis in values. Over time, these aspirations have thickened into a liberal democratic ideology that has spilled over into administrative law.

Best suited to a society with a modern documentary constitution, this essentially American model poses problems for the historic UK constitution, where sovereignty rests with Parliament and constitutional principles are largely unwritten. This does not mean that there has been no interest in constitutionalism in the UK. Common law constitutionalism, a theory that postulates a set of public law values that temper, though they do not overthrow the foundational principle of parliamentary sovereignty, has made some headway. The core idea common to the many variants is of the common law as an embodiment of the fundamental values of the community and the common law courts as 'primary guardian' of these values.[84] Thus, common law principles and values such as 'higher-order duties of good administration' or 'high principles of constitutional morality' are to be regarded as a 'higher-order of law'.[85]

Although this belief is central to common law constitutionalism, it is by no means certain what these values are and how far they are capable of countering the doctrine of parliamentary sovereignty. Sir John Laws prioritised the value of human autonomy and proffered reason, fairness and the presumption of liberty as 'three horizons of the law of the constitution [that] provide the higher premise or at least part of it that mandates obedience to the law'.[86] Like many judges, he believed that the principles of judicial review were 'accepted across the party political divide as an uncontentious and necessary element in the conduct of public life in England'.[87] In this he was almost certainly mistaken and his ideas were forcefully attacked by John Griffith from the Left.[88] Later, after *Miller and Cherry*, where the UK Supreme Court asserted that 'the courts have the responsibility of upholding the values and principles of our constitution and making them effective',[89] Jason Varuhas expressed alarm about a shift that had the effect of 'lifting values from the substrata that underpins legal norms to the surface level of the law, themselves now having the status of legal norms and, where engaged, having direct legal consequences'.[90] In a more direct echo of populist theory, Richard Ekins accused the judges of 'simply enforce[ing] their own view of what good constitutional practice consisted in'.[91]

For some political scientists, liberal constitutionalism is the unremitting enemy of democracy, responsible for an 'ever-accelerating reliance on courts and judicial means for

[83] Dworkin, *Laws Empire*, ibid 155.

[84] T Poole, 'Back to the Future? Unearthing the Theory of Common Law Constitutionalism' (2003) 23 *OJLS* 435, 439.

[85] D Oliver, 'The Underlying Values of Public and Private Law' in M Taggart (ed), *The Province of Administrative Law* (Hart Publishing, 1997) 230; J Laws, 'Law and Democracy' [1995] *Public Law* 72, 84. And see TRS Allan, *Law, Liberty and Justice, The Legal Foundations of British Constitutionalism* (Oxford University Press, 1993).

[86] J Laws, *The Constitutional Balance* (Hart Publishing, 2021) 153.

[87] Laws (n 85) 79.

[88] JAG Griffith, 'The Brave New World of Sir John Laws' (2000) 63 *MLR* 159.

[89] *Miller and Cherry* (n 70) [39].

[90] J Varuhas, 'The Principle of Legality' (2020) 79 *Cambridge Law Journal* 578.

[91] R Ekins, 'Protecting the Constitution: How and Why Parliament Should Limit Judicial Power' (Policy Exchange 2019) 11–13.

addressing core moral predicaments, public policy questions, and political controversies'.[92] We observe a constitutionalist administrative law developing in the shadow of liberal constitutionalism with many of the same features. Constitutionalist administrative law puts such great trust in judges and legal method that judicial review appears a chief defence against populism. With a markedly liberal ethos and expansionist character, constitutionalist administrative law is essentially a system with a basis in human rights, thickened interpretations of the rule of law and at least some principles generally recognised as 'constitutional' in nature, such as access to justice.[93] There have been hints too in UK case law that the right to a court may be a 'constitutional fundamental' so foundational as to be incapable of abolition.[94] The thickened form of constitutionalism has a disproportionate strength and magnetic attraction in the legal academy and for some members of the judiciary. This lends it something of the character of an ideology, which cannot be obscured by the mundane nature of much judicial review practice and particular mood swings on the Bench.

B. Public Administration Transformed

Looking back at the linked trajectories of public administration and administrative law over half-a-century, we find a wide-ranging series of developments that are cumulative in character. The basic dynamics are increasing reliance on rules and formalised procedures at the expense of customary looser and more flexible administrative processes. Squeezing individual elements of discretion, this process has taken on a momentum of its own in a seemingly never-ending quest to make public administration more economical, efficient and effective, accelerated by a rapid adoption of automation.[95]

The tone was set in the 1980s, an important decade in the development of our subject in which bracing forms of market ideology increasingly took hold and, as famously demonstrated in the UK in the context of an extended administrative state, governments set about downsizing and reinventing government through financial constraint, privatisation and outsourcing.[96] These were fertile conditions for populist appeal to 'the heartland' based on economic and social protection, a theme later magnified in the light of a global financial crisis and the politics of austerity ('the shrinking state').[97] In effectively reshaping public administration and hence the basic contours of administrative law,[98] this new main 'pole' in our subject of market ideology/managerialism also

[92] R Hirschl, 'The New Constitutionalism and the Judicialization of Pure Politics Worldwide' (2006) 75 *Fordham Law Review* 721, 721. And see R Bellamy, *Political Constitutionalism* (Cambridge University Press, 2007).

[93] T Bingham, *The Rule of Law* (reprint edn) (Penguin Books, 2011).

[94] See *Jackson v Attorney General* [2005] UKHL 56 [102] (Lord Steyn). See also *R (Privacy International) v Investigatory Powers Tribunal* [2019] UKSC 22 [144] where Lord Carnwath opined obiter that a statutory clause purporting 'wholly to exclude the supervisory jurisdiction of the High Court to review a decision of an inferior court or tribunal' might not be recognised by the courts.

[95] C Harlow and R Rawlings, 'Proceduralism and Automation. Challenges to the Values of Administrative Law' in E Fisher, A Young and J King (eds), *The Foundations and Future of Public Law* (Oxford University Press, 2020).

[96] D Osborne and T Gaebler, *Reinventing Government* (Addison Wesley, 1992); R Vinen, *Thatcher's Britain* (Simon & Schuster, 2009).

[97] H Kriesi and TS Pappas (eds), *European Populism in the Shadow of the Great Recession* (Rowman & Littlefield, 2015).

[98] M Taggart (ed), *The Province of Administrative Law* (Hart Publishing, 1997).

produced new and elitist methodologies of formalised decision-making seemingly ever more distanced from people.

The intake of managerial and statistical disciplines under the rubric of 'New Public Management' (NPM)[99] came together with the dogma of privatisation and outsourcing. Beginning with target-setting and performance indicators, NPM drove proceduralisation throughout the administrative process, the more so as the task of public administration increasingly came to be perceived in terms of risk assessment.[100] Increased reliance on elaborate and contestable tools of governance, such as detailed cost benefit analysis or value for money audit, was reflected in the prevalence of off-putting expert and technical jargon.[101] As outsourcing became the norm in the delivery of many public services, established systems were fragmented and public service ethos undercut. The backdrop of contemporary governance was also becoming more arcane and obfuscatory and harder for people to navigate.

In the landscape of administrative law, a general tendency in modern and post-modern societies for social relationships to be encapsulated in formal legal rules – a process labelled 'juridification' by Gunther Teubner[102] – has proved ongoing. Emerging in the market sphere, the 'regulatory state' quickly extended its reach into the realms of professional and social regulation where it impacted directly on personal lives.[103] Much administrative law could now be characterised in terms of 'cycles of juridification': repeated and interactive forms of executive rule-making, interpretation and application by the administration and challenge, rule interpretation and review in the courts. In the EU, charged with transnational regulation, the expansive thickets of well-nigh impenetrable regulation fit the populist critique all too well.[104] Juridified public administration has fed into judicial review, making it often less a question of propounding general principles and standard-setting and more a question of legal experts seeking to understand complex and opaque regulation.[105] We should factor in too how processes of juridification are fostered by liberal constitutionalism and its contemporary engagement with human rights and the equality principle. This dynamic is apt to be intensified on the international stage by the absence of a clear demos and established political structures and the role played by transnational courts, so again feeding domestic concerns about a 'judicialisation of politics'.[106]

[99] M Barzelay, *Breaking Through Bureaucracy: A New Vision for Managing in Government* (University of California Press, 1992); C Pollitt and G Bouckaert, *Public Management Reform, A Comparative Analysis – Into the Age of Austerity*, 4th edn (Oxford University Press, 2017).

[100] E Fisher, *Risk, Regulation and Administrative Constitutionalism* (Hart Publishing, 2007).

[101] M Power, *The Audit Society: Rituals of Verification* (Oxford University Press, 1997); M Power, *Organised Uncertainty: Designing a World of Risk Management* (Oxford University Press, 2007).

[102] G Teubner, 'Juridification: Concepts, Aspects, Limits, Solutions' in G Teubner (ed), *Juridification of Social Spheres* (de Gruyter, 1987).

[103] M Moran, *The British Regulatory State: High Modernism and Hyper-Innovation* (Oxford University Press, 2003); T Prosser, *The Regulatory Enterprise: Government, Regulation, and Legitimacy* (Oxford University Press, 2010).

[104] C Harlow and R Rawlings, *Process and Procedure in European Union Administration* (Hart Publishing, 2014).

[105] A trend highlighted by J Bell, *The Anatomy of Administrative Law* (Hart Publishing, 2020).

[106] C Harlow, 'Global Administrative Law: The Quest for Principles and Values' (2006) 17 *European Journal of International Law* 187.

In the long view, the emergence in the 1990s of automated public services and use of information and communication technology inside government may well be seen as heralding a paradigm shift in our subject as great as that signalled earlier by the rise of economic liberalism. The official discourse was soon notably upbeat in emphasising prospective efficiency gains. For the Organisation for Economic Co-operation and Development (OECD), remarkable prospects of higher quality services were heightened by easy online access to information and greater engagement with citizens.[107] The case for citizen enablement was echoed in the UK, where a government policy paper spoke of automation and ICT in terms not only of modernising government but of citizen empowerment via democratic engagement in 'open policy making'.[108] Yet as the new century began, researchers were already cautioning that decision-making processes on the frontline were being depersonalised by the new technology: the 'street-level bureaucrat' was disappearing to be replaced by the systematised bureaucratic power of computer code.[109] There was a rapidly dawning realisation of new institutional cultures in a digital age.

The DNA of administrative law derives from the age of pen and print. Basic structures and processes and standard legal values with which we are familiar are apt to be sorely tested in a dizzying era of algorithms, machine learning and beyond.[110] Science and technology move rapidly and just two decades on, much in the dynamics of public administration looks different. Showing the force of this in administrative law, online administration is already an everyday experience for people. An abundant literature draws our attention to the extent of government reliance on automation, to the spread of algorithmic decision-making and to rapid developments in the field of artificial intelligence.[111] While offering major new opportunities for public policy analysis and implementation, the rise of big data and artificial intelligence is already generating a host of challenges around information retention, system bias and regulation, etc.[112] Familiar problems of transparency, accountability and participation and accessibility are being reinvented.

Alienation from or lack of stake in public institutions, lack of trust in government, and limited citizen engagement in depersonalised and often distant administrative processes make fertile breeding grounds for populism.[113] To help repair the 'disconnect' and preserve the 'human face' of governance as it progresses into a digital, perhaps even a robotic age, administrative law will need to up its game.

[107] OECD, 'The e-Government Imperative' (OECD e-Government Studies, 2003); OECD, 'e-Government for Better Government' (OECD e-Government Studies, 2005).

[108] See J Morison, 'Modernising Government and the E-Government Revolution' in N Bamforth and P Leyland (eds), *Public Law in a Multi-Layered Constitution* (Hart Publishing, 2003).

[109] M Bovens and S Zouridis, 'From Street-Level to System-Level Bureaucracies: How Information and Communication Technology Is Transforming Administrative Discretion and Constitutional Control' (2002) 62 *Public Administration Review* 174.

[110] R Williams, 'Rethinking Administrative Law for Algorithmic Decision-Making' (2022) 42 *OJLS* 468; P Daly, J Raso and J Tomlinson, 'Administrative Law in the Digital World' in Harlow (n 37).

[111] For pioneering legal studies, see J Tomlinson, *Justice in the Digital State* (Bristol University Press, 2019); J Boughey and K Miller (eds), *The Automated State* (Federation Press, 2021).

[112] S Chesterman, *We, the Robots? Regulating Artificial Intelligence and the Limits of the Law* (Cambridge University Press, 2021); K Yeung, 'The New Public Analytics as an Emerging Paradigm in Public Sector Administration' (2022) 27(2) *Tilburg Law Review* 1.

[113] Illuminated by eg, P Mair, *Ruling the Void: The Hollowing of Western Democracy*, 2nd edn (Verso, 2023); D Runciman, *How Democracy Ends* (Profile, 2018).

VI. UPPING THE GAME

Our aim in this chapter has been to explore ideas of populism and consider their potential relationship with administrative law. We were dissatisfied with the legal discourse, where the concept of populism tended to be treated dismissively, used merely as a term of abuse and conflated with right-wing authoritarianism. We settled for a thin definition of populism as 'a thin-centred ideology' (Cas Mudde) or 'a way of doing politics' (Chantal Mousse) that can host or be hosted by political ideologies of the left or right.

Populism can appear in widely different forms and situations and in different political contexts, but in this chapter we have focused on certain core features. Populism purports to represent the 'general will' of the 'pure' or 'real' people as against 'corrupt elites', which govern and control them. It contests elites in all their forms: the aristocratic, meritocratic and political elites who make up 'the establishment' and elites composed of experts such as regulators and other technocrats who are seen to deprive the people of democratic decision-making powers and exploit their position in their own interests. Populism is in short anti-elitist, anti-expert and anti-establishment. It is also commonly anti-pluralist. The 'general will' is a monolithic concept, embodied in the government and unchallengeable, except perhaps at election time, Thus, although populism is not necessarily authoritarian in nature, populist government is apt to be executive-centred: an executive that purports to speak in the name of the people, and so teeters on the edge of authoritarianism.

We have presented administrative law as a plural discipline oscillating between various poles some of which sit more comfortably with populism than others. In an instrumentalist model of administrative law, the focus is on the provision of the processes and technical devices necessary for the efficient implementation of policy, and it is left to government to provide the policies and values. In a classical, rights-based and control model, where the primary function is the provision of justice for individuals, the principles incorporated in legal judgments encapsulate values, which supposedly reflect the legal and political culture of the community but are in reality judge-made. This carries the risk of strike-back. The court-centred constitutionalist model, more open about its promotion of liberal values and often aggressively anti-populist, is yet more likely to become an active target of populism.

We are not advocates of populism, but we see in its rise a warning for administrative law. In many ways, administrative law is a top-down subject: it is for the people but not of the people. In recent years too, there has been a trend in governance towards juridification and proceduralisation accentuated by the introduction of automation. Public administration and the administrative law that frames it are in danger of becoming overly formulaic and depersonalised.

In thinking about the relationship of populism and administrative law, we turned to Albert Hirschman's theory of Exit, Voice and Loyalty, developed in the field of employer/employee relations but equally applicable in political contexts.[114] In a stripped-down version, Hirschman points to two courses of action open to dissatisfied members of

[114] AO Hirschman, *Exit, Voice, and Loyalty: Responses to Decline in Firms, Organizations, and States* (Harvard University Press, 1970).

an organisation: they may articulate their concerns and seek change (Voice) or they may terminate the relationship (Exit). Loyalty, in many ways the most important of Hirschman's three concepts, comprises the relationship of trust in any organisation and degree of support from its members that allows it to function effectively. Loyalty is the normality of a working democracy, which encourages its citizens to participate constructively in the governance system. While Loyalty remains strong, discontented citizens express their discontent through Voice, by complaining, protesting, seeking legal redress or, in the political arena, by campaigning, participating in demonstrations and other forms of organised political action. When Loyalty breaks down, citizens may seek to Exit. One way to characterise populism might be as the Exit point on Hirschman's model. For dissatisfied consumers of public services, however, the choices are limited. Exit may be impossible or impractical, more especially for those highly dependent on welfare support or subject to authoritarian tools of social control. Thus, the better and more usual choice is Voice.

We are not of course arguing that loyalty has broken down across western political democracies. We are suggesting that a 'disconnect' has arisen between the state and its citizens and that trust has weakened.[115] It is not that the 'disconnect' has been caused by administrative law, but administrative law has contributed to it. There is a need to reassert the importance of responsiveness in public administration, not only to treat people with dignity and respect, but also to engage more directly with individuals, groups and communities and hear what they are saying. Paul Daly has argued that a set of non-prescriptive but implicit 'values' latent within common law judicial review systems operates as 'signposts' pointing judges to the direction judicial review ought to be taking,[116] We see a signpost role for administrative law in pointing public administration in a more participatory direction.

Together with accountability and transparency, participation is one of a triad of 'good governance values' recognised on a global basis and serving as a benchmark for the evaluation of democratic systems of governance.[117] Participation theory attracted interest from political scientists in the mid-twentieth century but suffered a partial eclipse due to perceived links with totalitarianism.[118] On the international scene, it has underpinned influential international instruments, most notably the Aarhus Convention, which protects public participation in decision-making and access to justice in environmental matters.[119] It has to be said, however, that the concept of participation has not (as yet) figured widely in our domestic administrative law system; today, it is still commonly associated with land-use planning.[120]

Widely used in political science for analysis of citizen/state relations, the Exit, Voice and Loyalty framework is less familiar in law. Voice is nonetheless implicit in many legal

[115] See, eg, H Quilter-Pinner, R Statham, W Jennings and V Valgarðsson, 'Trust Issues. Dealing with Distrust in Politics' (Institute for Public Policy Research, 2021).

[116] P Daly, *Understanding Administrative Law in the Common Law World* (Oxford University Press, 2021) 111–13, 259–62.

[117] See Harlow (n 106).

[118] C Pateman, *Participation and Democratic Theory* (Cambridge University Press, 1970).

[119] The UNECE Convention on Access to Information, Public Participation in Decision-Making and Access to Justice in Environmental Matters (adopted 25 June 1998, entered into force 30 October 2001) 2161 UNTS 447 to which the UK is a signatory.

[120] For historical perspective, see P McAuslan, *Ideologies of Planning Law* (Pergamon Press, 1980).

concepts and processes. In terms of Hirschman's model, open justice is important not only in permitting individuals to voice their claims but also in promoting loyalty to the justice system more generally. As the House of Commons Justice Committee recently observed, it is essential that the public should 'reach its own judgment on whether the courts are delivering justice' and 'axiomatic that the public cannot assure itself of having confidence in the courts if it does not have access to court proceedings or to information on those proceedings'.[121]

The voice-enabling values of free speech and opinion central to liberalism are fundamental constitutional rights strongly represented in the human rights charters venerated by liberal constitutionalists. Again, a copious jurisprudence throughout the common law world establishes ways for individuals to participate in decisions that affect them through the legal principles of natural justice and fairness. In this way, they may contribute, albeit indirectly, to administrative policy-making.

The judicial process is inherently participatory, a point made trenchantly by Kathleen Bell in the context of administrative tribunals. Individual participation helps in Bell's view to 'foster civic competence, personal responsibility and active involvement rather than over-dependency on professionals and a belief that people are not able to cope'. Equally important, the presence of lay members to represent the public on tribunals as ordinary members of the community, like juries and lay magistrates, is essential for public engagement. Participation is, in other words, not only an opportunity for voice, it also gives tribunal users a sense of ownership of 'their' justice system and thus helps to promote loyalty.[122] This is something to think about when contemplating the steady judicialisation of the tribunal system experienced in the UK in recent years, where lay members have largely disappeared[123] to be replaced by legally qualified judges and members with 'special expertise' supervised by a Senior President who is very much part of the judicial elite[124] – a development that populists might not altogether approve of. The current plan is for tribunals to be 'digital by default with easy to use and intuitive online processes' and assistance provided for those who need it.[125] We shall see.

The early work of American scholar Jerry Mashaw highlighted the importance of front-line decision-making in administrative justice; his later work underlines the need to treat people with dignity and respect.[126] For sociologist Michael Adler, this necessitates a holistic conception of administrative justice that reflects the consumer's view of justice

[121] House of Commons Justice Committee, *Open Justice: Court Reporting in the Digital Age* (HC 2022–23, 339) para 11.

[122] K Bell, 'Social Security Tribunals – A General Perspective' (1982) 33 *Northern Ireland Legal Quarterly* 132, 147.

[123] See N Wikeley and R Young, 'The Marginalisation of Lay Members in Social Security Appeal Tribunals' (1992) 14 *Journal of Social Welfare and Family Law* 127.

[124] Introduced by the Tribunals, Courts and Enforcement Act 2007, which applies to tribunals that cover the UK and England. The devolved nations have their own tribunal services.

[125] UK Ministry of Justice, *Transforming Our Justice System* (2016) 15. And see House of Commons Justice Committee, *Court and Tribunal Reforms* (HC 2019, 190).

[126] J Mashaw, *Bureaucratic Justice* (Yale University Press, 1983); RA Kagan, 'Varieties of Bureaucratic Justice' in NR Padrillo (ed), *Administrative Law from the Inside Out, Essays on Themes in the Work of Jerry Mashaw* (Cambridge University Press, 2017).

as securing one's just entitlement and is listening, responsive and user-friendly.[127] A key challenge for the next generation of administrative lawyers is to use automation to shape administrative procedures that enable individuals to participate and exercise voice.

The concept of voice crept into administrative justice via the managerial ethos that swept through public administration in the 1990s when complaining began to be viewed as an opportunity to make contact with public service 'consumers' and complaints systems were a tool for scrutiny and appraisal of front-line, decision-making systems. It is nowadays a principle of good administration that public bodies should utilise feedback to improve their public service delivery and performance. They are advised to 'actively seek and welcome all feedback, both compliments and complaints' and 'capture and review' lessons learned from complaints so as to contribute to service development.[128] A Parliamentary Committee reviewing complaints procedures asked for 'More complaints please!' and 'lots of ways for people to give feedback'– an essentially instrumental use of voice in the interests of good governance with the hope perhaps of stoking loyalty. As the Committee also recognised, complaints are a method of public engagement with democratic institutions. They show that 'people think it's worth complaining and that they will be listened to, and that they believe that they have power to influence the system. and to encourage public participation. They are a good sign of democracy in action'.[129] There is a close link here to Hirschman's model.

In the ex ante field of executive law-making, where administrative law has consistently shown weakness, there are serious problems of control. Parliamentary scrutiny is tenuous,[130] a feature that populist governments may be particularly ready to exploit. There are missed opportunities also to gather some much-needed input legitimacy by encouraging participation and voice. Regulations are shaped in a disparate fashion at different times in different government offices, the outcome being a lack both of coherence and transparency. Consultation, the main technique for securing popular voice, is sometimes a statutory requirement. Voluntary consultation is another possibility, when the shape of the consultation and the way in which it is conducted remain largely a public service responsibility subject only to guidelines and promises to use digital methods for easier public access.[131] The judiciary has been hesitant to make a decisive contribution.[132] The main choice is between a 'staged exercise' aimed only at those considered to be stakeholders or an 'at large' consultation, where a wider public may have its say. But even if it is true that departments 'generally make serious

[127] M Adler, 'Understanding and Analysing Administrative Justice' in M Adler (ed), *Administrative Justice in Context* (Hart Publishing, 2010). And see G McKeever, 'A Ladder of Legal Participation for Tribunal Users' [2013] *Public Law* 575, drawing on the famous paper by S Arnstein, 'A Ladder of Citizen Participation' (1969) 35 *Journal of the American Planning Association* 216.

[128] UK Parliamentary and Health Service Ombudsman, 'Principles of Good Administration' (PHSO, 10 February 2009), available at www.ombudsman.org.uk/sites/default/files/page/0188-Principles-of-Good-Administration-bookletweb.pdf. And see R Simmons and C Brennan, *Grumbles, Gripes and Grievances: The Role of Complaints in Transforming Public Services* (Nesta, 2013).

[129] House of Commons Public Administration Committee, *More Complaints Please!* (HC 2013–14, 229) para 12, Box 3.

[130] See A Horne and M Torrance, 'Parliament as Scrutineer: Parliamentary Oversight of the Law-Making Process', in Harlow (n 37).

[131] UK Cabinet Office, 'Consultation Principles: Guidance' (2012, updated 2018).

[132] See *R(Moseley)* (n 43).

efforts to consult relevant groups' and 'will generally consult anyone interested in the legislation',[133] this is in essence a top-down process and the quality of consultations is variable. Little may be known about the contributors and even less about their impact.

Some recent initiatives suggest a different approach. When, for example, the Law Commission was asked to give expert advice on restructuring the complex and unwieldy Immigration Rules,[134] it underlined the importance of building public trust in administrative decision-making and the final draft of its proposal for a new set of coordinated Immigration Rules took account of its open consultation, which formed an integral part of the project. Considerable space was devoted also to the question of public access. The Report went to some lengths to point to online systems that the Home Office could use to achieve wider access for the Rules. Moreover, the formal Rules should be clearly linked to guidance written in simple language easily accessible to users and to non-expert readers at least for purposes of information.[135] Disappointingly, there is no specific provision for citizen input as and when the Department needs to make changes.

In much the same way, the Hansard Society, in its praiseworthy project to survey and make proposals for a complete reshaping of the parliamentary arrangements for scrutiny of delegated legislation, emphasised the need for transparency and accessibility. The preliminary proposals suggest that explanatory memoranda are 'not meant for lawyers' but intended to provide 'a plain English, free-standing, explanation of the effect of an instrument and how it is intended to operate',[136] an objective that is not always achieved. All statutory instruments should be published in draft on Parliament's website together with all supporting documentation: explanatory memoranda, consultations and supporting documents, which would provide a platform for citizen input, albeit unsolicited. Once again, however, there are no proposals for voice in the shape of mandatory consultation on drafts of statutory instruments laid before Parliament.

There are signs too that parliaments may themselves be conscious of a new need for democratic engagement with the public capable of encouraging loyalty. Several Westminster-style parliaments have shown a wish to fold new-found techniques from the world of politics, such as citizen forums and assemblies[137] and participation in social media groups, into law-making. Recently, they have come together in the Connected Parliaments Project to share experiences and look at different ways of 'connecting the people to public law-making'.[138] A Digital Democracy Commission was set up by the previous Speaker of the House of Commons to inquire into the use of automation to connect Members of Parliament more closely with the people they represent. The Commission recommended a digital 'Open House' to hold regular digital public discussion forums. As a response to public demands to 'have their say' in debates, such a move would 'enhance'

[133] EC Page, *Governing by Numbers* (Hart Publishing, 2001) 142.

[134] Law Commission for England and Wales, *Simplification of the Immigration Rules* (Law Comm No 388, 2020). The Commission is currently working with the Home Office on a project to consolidate the primary legislation on immigration.

[135] ibid chs 10–12, app 1.

[136] Hansard Society (n 39) 39.

[137] See, eg, L Patriquin, *Permanent Citizens' Assemblies: A New Model for Public Deliberation* (Rowman & Littlefield International, 2019).

[138] S Moulds, 'Connected Parliaments: Evaluating the Impact of Parliamentary Public Engagement on Public Lawmaking in Australia, New Zealand, Ireland and the UK' (2021) 38 *Australasian Parliamentary Review* 109.

debates, though it might also provide a useful resource for Members. More daringly, the Commission mooted the idea that members of the public might be allowed to put parliamentary questions or 'contribute to different stages of the law-making process', primarily by digital means.[139] Nothing further has been heard.

Our analysis of the relationship between populism and administrative law serves to highlight the problem of disconnect, its relationship with populism and the potential contribution of administrative law to ameliorating it. Public administration can seem increasingly impersonal and distant, an elitist enterprise managed in the name of the people though not always for their benefit or with their involvement. We have envisaged a response in terms of voice, using illustrations that suggest administrative law could do more to secure the human face of governance. We would welcome a participatory turn in administrative law.

[139] Speaker's Commission on Digital Democracy, 'Open Up!' (2015).

16

Populism and Constitutional Democracy: Feature or Bug?

NEIL WALKER*

I. INTRODUCTION: POPULISM AND CONSTITUTIONAL ANXIETY

As is true of contested political concepts in general, controversy over the practical and normative implications of contemporary populism is bound up with disagreement over its full meaning and scope.[1] A rough consensus does hold, however, over a core minimum understanding of the concept.[2] According to that consensus, populism speaks to a political world-view, and where that world-view is successfully sponsored, also to a style of government, in which a singular conception of the People is invoked as the proper source of political authority against, and in replacement for, an elite Establishment of vested interests. Understood in these thin and capaciously inclusive terms, there is no doubt that the wave of populist sentiment and practice that has washed over the global political landscape in recent years poses new and pressing challenges to certain dominant approaches within constitutional thought and design. One consequence of this has been an explosion of writing on the topic, both from those who see populism as a threat to constitutional virtue and from those who are more sympathetic to its motivations and manifestations.[3] But as we shall see, the terms of debate between these positions often leave little scope for mutual enlightenment. The aim of the present chapter is to try to shift these terms onto more fruitful territory, a move that involves focusing less on what supposedly distinguishes constitutional and populist perspectives and forms of government, and more on their points of intersection.

Some of the challenges posed to proponents of constitutional government by the recent rise in populist movements and in the profile of their leaders are practical. Does the new populism necessarily embrace or invite forms of rule inconsistent with or even antithetical to the structures and values of constitutional government as broadly understood?

* Thanks to Bojan Bugaric for generous comments on an early draft.

[1] See, eg, W Bryce Gallie, 'Essentially Contested Concepts' (1955–1956) New Series 56 Proceedings of the Aristotelian Society 167.

[2] See, eg, M Tushnet and B Bugaric, *Power to the People: Constitutionalism in the Age of Populism* (Oxford University Press, 2022) ch 2; J-W Muller, *What is Populism?* (University of Pennsylvania Press, 2016).

[3] Two recent rich (and reasonably nuanced) additions to this massive literature are: on the anti-populist side (though with dissenting contributions), M Krygier, A Czarnota and W Sadurski, *Anti-Constitutional Populism* (Cambridge University Press, 2022); and on the more sympathetic side, Tushnet and Bugaric (n 2).

Is there anything in the constitutional toolbox that can prevent, resist or counter the worst impulses of populism? How do we prevent some populist forms of government developing into full-blown authoritarianism? Other challenges are conceptual or theoretical. A first echoes our opening caution. Is populism a single species or, on closer inspection, is it simply a loose label for a range of disparate phenomena? Relatedly, can we distinguish 'good' from 'bad' populism, and, if we can, to what extent, if at all, does that distinction turn on the presence or absence of certain constitutional criteria or standards? And, if, as is clearly the case, populists embrace their own vision(s) of constitutional government, on what grounds, if any, might we nevertheless retain the 'c' word or any of its derivatives, notably *constitutionalism* – the term that we tend to use to refer to the endorsement or promotion of what is deemed to be of general value in constitutional government[4] – as an independent analytical standard to assess and compare the good government credentials of populist and non-populist regimes?

If we put these various concerns together, we begin to see why the whole of the challenge offered by populism may appear greater than the sum of its parts. For populism doesn't simply figure as a common factor in a loose set of questions. Rather, it has become the focus of a general apprehension amongst a key constituency. This is the constituency of those who see populism as a test of – but also as a threat to – their affirmation of constitutional government in constitutionalist terms, as categorically separate from and superior to other forms of public authority or power. More specifically, they see populism as a sharp challenge to the idea of constitutional government as a *distinct form or standard of rule that is both worth defending and capable of being defended*. For in casting doubt on the various aspects of this categorical claim, the populist surge, and the arguments raised in its promotion or defence, is at once the source of an anxiety of meaning, of justification, and of relevance.

The anxiety of meaning concerns the difficulty of drawing a bright line distinction between constitutional forms of government and those that exhibit populist characteristics. On the one hand, we may make the normative claim as to what is *properly* of constitutional standard in the democratic age[5] – and so constitutionalist – in minimal terms, to include, say, the institutionalisation of procedures of majority rule, the entrenchment of some basic rights and decision-making structures, the independence of judges from direct political control, and the protection of the freedom of different political parties to seek to obtain popular support for their policy programmes.[6] But if

[4] See, eg, Tushnet and Bugaric (n 2); R Schutze, 'Constitutionalism(s)' in R Masterman and R Schutze (eds), *The Cambridge Companion to Comparative Constitutional Law* (Cambridge University Press, 2019); J Waldron, *Political Political Theory* (Harvard University Press, 2016) ch 2; M Loughlin, *Against Constitutionalism* (Harvard University Press, 2022) ch 2.

[5] While most definitions of constitutionalism embrace constitutional democracy, some writers insist on a difference not only of degree, but even of type, between modern constitutionalism *tout court* and constitutional democracy. Where this is the case, it tends to follow from a definition of constitutionalism *tout court* that emphasises constraint on governmental power and protection of individual rights over an expansive sense of popular sovereignty; see in particular Loughlin (n 4) introduction, chs 2 and 7; and Waldron (n 4) ch 2. Some of the reasons for this tension are explored in section V of the text below. My own preference is to treat the distinction as a matter of degree, based upon a fluid but always internally conflicted and balanced range of responses to the deep and continuing modern tension between individual and collective conceptions of the good (just as the distinction between constitutionalist and non-constitutionalist government is also a matter of degree).

[6] See, eg, Tushnet and Bugaric (n 2) ch 2.

we confine ourselves to that elementary blend of collective democratic goods and protections of individual rights, then many so-called populist regimes can still tick all or at least some of the necessary formal constitutional boxes. Indeed, the record of populists in government, from Trump to Erdogan, and from Orban to Bolsonaro, far from involving a denial or wholesale evasion of constitutional method, suggests its strong endorsement both as an instrument of governmental reform and a symbol of renewed national identity and purpose.[7] In these and other presumptively populist regimes, sufficient has remained of the constitutional edifice sketched by the thin democratic constitutionalist to allow the populist insurgent to claim a constitutional authority that, while distinctive, retains plausible links with the mainstream tradition. If, on the other hand, one thickens out the definition of constitutionalism to embrace a much greater degree of 'specification'[8] of constitutional controls, including, say, the requirement of a high degree of entrenchment, the need for robust types of institutional checks and balances to guarantee effective judicial protection from executive interference or sanction and the defence of basic rights, or the imperative of strong forms of safeguarding and promotion (through rights and other means) of speech, association and media diversity necessary to nurture political pluralism, then many forms of populism might be excluded by definitional fiat. It seems, then, that those in the constitutionalist camp are faced with opposite dangers. Too thin a definition of democratic constitutionalism, and too many populist-leaning regimes may be allowed into the tent. Too thick a definition, and exclusion follows from the application of a rigidly Procrustean method in which specifications of various aspects of formal design may become proxies for substantive regime-type preferences that should instead require independent recognition and justification.

What, then, of that anxiety of justification? This manifests itself in various ways and provokes a number of different responses, not necessarily mutually exclusive. One, as just noted, is to fall back on a thin formal legal-institutional definition of constitutional health that, while itself involving a normative endorsement (however minimal), simply avoids broader questions of philosophical justification. Another approach, quite often in tandem, is to use highly abstract labels which gesture towards such deeper justification. So terms such as 'liberal democracy', or 'constitutional democracy' are invoked in opposition to populism, or broad meta-constitutional norms such as the 'separation of powers', or 'responsible government', or 'Rule of Law' (as opposed to 'Rule *by* Law') are claimed as distinguishing standards. But these too can be highly question-begging. Their content and justifying standards are vague, and also, on most understandings, a matter of degree rather than a simple binary. And to the extent that they are linked to detailed formal criteria, this is a matter of stipulative definition, or at best contestable specification.

A third way of dealing with the anxiety of justification is to focus on the other side of the equation, and so to thicken the definition of populism in ways that are more likely to dramatise the incompatibility or uneasy relationship of at least some of its variants with constitutional standards of government, even where relatively thinly defined. Building on the core notion of an opposition between the 'real' People and the self-appointed Elite,

[7] See, eg, P Blokker, 'Populist Constitutionalism' in C de la Torre (ed), *Routledge Handbook of Global Populism* (Routledge, 2019) ch 7.

[8] Tushnet and Bugaric (n 2) ch 2.

we find the definition of Populism being filled out to embrace various selections from a much wider menu of ideas. These include the moral righteousness of the People's vision, their homogeneity of culture or of belief, affirmation of an exclusive national identity, treatment of the political opposition as illegitimate, vilification of minorities, identification of a strong single leader with a special capacity to shape or interpret the People's mission, impatience with institutional constraints, and a preference for direct forms of popular rule.[9] And alongside this spectrum of more or less anti-elitist and anti-pluralist attitudes and methods of rule, populism can also differ in terms of its capacity to accommodate a variety of 'host' ideologies that reflect different substantive political projects; so producing variants such as agrarian populism, socio-economic populism, (left) progressive populism and (right) reactionary populism. Noting that positions on these two axes of variation – governance method and substantive ideology – can be combined in different mixes, we can appreciate just how wide is the diversity of populism types. Yet for the advocate of constitutionalism as a philosophy of government that necessarily stands against populism this is a double edged sword. While it may make it easier to justify the critique of the more strongly power-concentrating and anti-pluralist versions of populism on constitutional grounds, by the same token it makes it more difficult to find reasons to be critical of populism in *all* its diversity.

What, finally, of the anxiety of relevance? Even if we were able to claim that constitutional government speaks to a (constitutionalist) form or standard of rule that is distinct from that of some or all forms of populist government, and even if we were able to demonstrate that constitutional government is worth defending over some or all of the populist alternatives, the question remains whether it is *capable* of being maintained against populist tendencies. This anxiety centres on the textualist and institutional bias of constitutional thought. There are two separate (but connected) concerns here. One relates to the flimsiness of 'parchment barriers'[10] before a regime intent on evading legal constraints or monopolising the levers of power. Strategies of *circumvention*, such as ruling by executive decree, clientelism in executive appointments, and emergency powers, may be liberally employed. Or where the populist government has enjoyed sustained electoral support, as in the Hungarian case, the approach may instead involve a broader *commandeering* of the constitutional machinery. This may take the form of the liberal use of constitutional amendments or the exerting of increasing influence over the apex court(s) as the key interpreters of the Constitution.[11] These various strategies have been labelled 'abusive constitutionalism',[12] a term that nicely captures how methods themselves technically constitutionally valid can be used to avoid, erode or override supposedly core constitutional checks and standards.

A second concern relates to the gap between formal institutions and constitutional culture. Even where some of the classic features of constitutionalism remain inscribed in

[9] ibid ch 3.

[10] In James Madison's famous phrase, from 'The Federalist' 48, available at https://guides.loc.gov/federalist-papers/text-41-50.

[11] See N Walker, 'Populism and Constitutional Tension' (2019) 17 *International Journal of Constitutional Law* 515, 519–22.

[12] D Landau, 'Abusive Constitutionalism' (2013) 47 *UC Davis Law Review* 189; see also R Dixon and D Landau, *Abusive Constitutional Borrowing: Legal Globalization and the Subversion of Liberal Democracy* (Oxford University Press, 2022).

the formal constitution and are not subject to systematic abuse, this does not necessarily translate into the kinds of attitudes and practices amongst governing elites and their supporters that will be resistant to populist tendencies. The basic point here is that there is more to the development or sustenance of a way of governing than making formal textual provision or even supplying the basic institutions charged with the operationalisation of such provision. Beyond this, there has to be a set of attitudes and sensibilities that is supportive of the relevant measures and their institutionalisation. Crudely put, whereas one type of problem arises when exploitation of the political power to amend the text or to influence its authoritative interpretation leads to a pattern of 'abuse', an associated type of problem, often deriving from the same mindset, arises where the letter of the constitutional law is not altered but the culture of governance is one of non- or irregular compliance, so reducing the text and the formal institutions to a 'sham'.[13] Martin Krygier seeks to make sense of this phenomenon by reference to the idea of 'the spirit of constitutionalism', which he claims to be 'manifest in an overarching concern to temper power, to moderate it so it is not available for arbitrary use'.[14] When the requisite spirit or constitutional culture is deficient amongst the governing class and other relevant constituencies within the population, Krygier argues, then even where this does not lead to clear patterns and practices of circumvention and commandeering, constitutionalism is in danger of degenerating into a façade. Its key function may descend into that of providing cover for more narrowly partisan forms of rule, amongst which would number certain populist approaches.

The counterposing of the spirit of the constitution to the letter, or the culture to the form, may be indispensable in exposing the anxiety of relevance, yet it also connects back to the problems of meaning and justification and their associated anxieties in ways that are at once both promising and problematic. For if constitutionalism in its fullest sense is irreducible to a check list of textual provisions and their formal institutionalisation, then this inevitably goes to the question of meaning and justification too. On the one hand, if neither the meaning of constitutionalism, nor the justification tied to that meaning, is reducible to constitutional text, then, equally, our efforts to meet the challenges we identified in showing the distinctiveness of constitutionalism from populist forms of governance and demonstrating the superiority of the former over the latter need not necessarily be prejudiced by our being restricted to an entirely text-bound understanding. On the other hand, the supplement suggested by the 'spirit' of constitutionalism in general and a notion such as 'tempering power' in particular, is not without problems. 'Tempering' may be a suggestive idea. It is a term sufficiently nuanced and balanced to go beyond the long held exclusive association of many versions of constitutionalism with the notion of limiting what the state can do. It embraces not just this negative register – the curbing of public power, but also a positive constitutional register, the 'constituting' and granting of collective power and positive rights in suitably legally conditioned and

[13] See, eg, D Law and M Versteeg, 'Constitutional Variation Among Strains of Authoritarianism' in T Ginsburg and A Simpser, *Constitutions in Authoritarian Regimes* (Cambridge University Press, 2013) 165; DS Law and M Versteeg, 'Sham Constitutions' (2013) 101 *California Law Review* 863.

[14] 'Introduction' in Krygier et al (n 3) 16; see further, M Krygier, 'Tempering Power' in M Adams, E Hirsch Ballin and A Meuwese (eds), *Constitutionalism and the Rule of Law: Bridging Idealism and Realism* (Cambridge University Press, 2017).

'tempered' form. Yet perhaps even more so than some of the more general ideas associated with constitutionalism we mentioned earlier, as a single capsule term for the whole of constitutionalism the notion of a constitutional spirit that embraces a disposition to temper public power suffers from a problem of vagueness and a consequent lack of clear grounds and firmly sketched lines for excluding populist types.

II. POPULISM ON THE CONSTITUTIONAL SPECTRUM

If we pull all of these anxieties together – anxieties of meaning, of justification and of relevance – populism can seem like the waves crashing against the crumbling edge of a cliff upon which a certain type of received understanding and investment in constitutionalism is precariously perched. Yet is there not something askew with this 'cliff-edge' image? The danger is that preoccupation with viewing and demonstrating populism as the stark counterpoint to and 'other' of constitutional government – a task that, as we have seen, faces difficult, perhaps insurmountable, obstacles – both feeds and is fed by a tribal attachment to the supposed merits of the constitutionalist way. This can produce an intellectual dynamic that is both self-perpetuating in its pursuit of an elusive constitutional purity and polarising in its exclusion of anything that does not meet a standard that is itself problematically vague and contested. But how might we frame matters differently and more productively? How, if at all, can we move beyond the idea of populism as posing a standing contrast and particular threat to constitutional patterns of thought and practice, while holding on to the idea that there are important differences between certain types of constitutional perspective and certain types of populism along a spectrum of political authority?

We can begin to do so, I contend, by viewing the relationship between constitutionalism and populism in less starkly oppositional terms. It is a relationship that certainly produces tensions, but it also involves certain continuities and overlaps, and taken together these contrasting features can raise sharper questions and tell us something of more general importance about the conditions and difficulties of modern constitutional rule. To make this argument requires a number of steps. First, we need to overcome the tendency, and the assumptions behind the tendency, to treat the 'constitutionalist' approach to government – thinner or thicker, spirit or letter – as describing what is common across modern systems of rule. It does not. There is a much wider spectrum of actually existing constitutional types, and those that embrace constitutionalist values and institutions in any strong sense occupy one modest and precarious space towards one end of that spectrum. They are, in short, the exception rather than the constitutional norm. Secondly, populist types are widely distributed across this spectrum, and at least some stand closely adjacent to or overlap the constitutionalist types, with the point of closest adjacency, or overlap, relating to those features of both constitutionalist and populist thought that stress the importance of democratic values. Thirdly, in consequence of this overlap, the key intellectual and practical question concerning populism's relationship to constitutionalism is whether or in what circumstances populism may be viewed as a normal feature of the variant of constitutional government known as constitutional democracy or as its destructive bug – or perhaps even as both. Let us now take these three steps in turn.

III. THE FULL CONSTITUTIONAL SPECTRUM

Any attempt to describe and distinguish across the full spectrum of constitutional government is of course prey to many of the definitional problems already identified above. Yet the Economist Intelligence Unit (EIU) annual Democracy Index offers a good general picture, and meets at least some of these objections.[15] The Democracy Index covers all countries and regime types, from the highest standard of 'full democracy'[16] through' flawed democracies'[17] and 'hybrid regimes'[18] to the lowest standard of 'authoritarian regimes'.[19] In addition, the constitutional standards central to most definitions of constitutionalism are embedded within the Index's definition of full democracy, just as the relative absence of these standards figures strongly in the defining features of the various democratically deficient regimes. Moreover, the Index does not use the holistic category of populism, or anything that might be a proxy for populism, and so runs with no preconceived sense of what is entailed by populism. Instead, it uses a wide range of highly particular criteria to build an aggregate picture, and this allows it to be sensitive to the variety of populisms. What is more, and with reference to the concerns, noted above, about the relevance of purely formal constitutional indices, these criteria have a broad ambit. They cover not only 'rules in the book' such as these dealing with electoral process and party pluralism, but also indices of effectiveness associated with government functioning, and aspects of political culture such as political participation, citizen involvement in holding political elites to account, and public and political willingness to accept the peaceful transfer of power after elections.

What emerges from the most recent (2023) Democracy Index, is that only 24 of the world's 167 independent polities – which is 14.4 per cent, and only 7.8 per cent of the world's population, live in 'full democracies'. Flawed democracies account for

[15] Economist Intelligence Unit, 'Democracy Index 2023: The Age of Conflict' (2024), available at https://pages.eiu.com/rs/753-RIQ-438/images/Democracy-Index-2023-Final-report.pdf. Freedom House has developed a similar approach, and with similar results. See, eg, Freedom House, 'Freedom in the World 2024: The Mounting Damage of Flawed Elections and Armed Conflict' available at https://freedomhouse.org/sites/default/files/2024-02/FIW_2024_DigitalBooklet.pdf.

[16] 'Full democracies' are nations where civil liberties and fundamental political freedoms are not only respected but also reinforced by a political culture conducive to the thriving of democratic principles. These nations have a valid system of governmental checks and balances, an independent judiciary whose decisions are enforced, governments that function adequately, and diverse and independent media. These nations have only limited problems in democratic functioning.

[17] 'Flawed democracies' are nations where elections are fair and free and basic civil liberties are honoured but may have issues (eg media freedom infringement and minor suppression of political opposition and critics). These nations have significant faults in other democratic aspects, including underdeveloped political culture, low levels of participation in politics, and issues in the functioning of governance.

[18] 'Hybrid regimes' are nations with regular electoral frauds, preventing them from being fair and free democracies. These nations commonly have governments that apply pressure on political opposition, non-independent judiciaries, widespread corruption, harassment and pressure placed on the media, anaemic rule of law, and more pronounced faults than flawed democracies in the realms of underdeveloped political culture, low levels of participation in politics, and issues in the functioning of governance.

[19] 'Authoritarian regimes' are nations where political pluralism is non-existent or severely limited. These nations are often absolute monarchies or dictatorships, may have some conventional institutions of democracy but with meagre significance, infringements and abuses of civil liberties are commonplace, elections (if they take place) are not fair or free (including sham elections), the media is often state-owned or controlled by groups associated with the ruling regime, the judiciary is not independent, and censorship and suppression of governmental criticism are commonplace.

another 50 (29.9 per cent) countries, and another 37.6 per cent of the global population. This means that, according to the Index, less than half of countries (44.3 per cent) are basically democratic, and less than half of the world's population (45.4 per cent) live under basically democratic conditions. And of the rest, as many as 59 (35.3 per cent) covering 39.4 per cent of the population (the majority in China) are classified as fully authoritarian regimes, while 34 (20.4 per cent) countries covering 15.2 per cent of the world's population live in hybrid or semi-authoritarian regimes.

It transpires, then, that full democracies are very thin on the ground. These are regimes, where, to paraphrase the Democracy Index's definition, civil liberties and fundamental political freedoms are reinforced by a political culture conducive to the thriving of democratic principles, and supplemented by a valid system of governmental checks and balances, an independent judiciary whose decisions are enforced, governments that function adequately, and diverse and independent media. If this type of democracy, which invests heavily in the basic constitutionalist criteria set out earlier, is the gold standard against which all are compared, then the great majority of national constitutional systems are severely lacking. There are well over twice as many fully authoritarian regimes as there are fully democratic ones. Yet all these fully authoritarian regimes, as also the hybrid and flawed democratic regimes, have their own self-styled constitutional texts and operating systems, and their own ambient constitutional culture or cultures, all of which are quite different from those favoured within the constitutionalist approach.

What is more, whereas much of the constitutionalist critique of populism is concerned with the supposed authoritarian tendencies that are encouraged by the anti-pluralist, executive-centred, demagogic and anti-institutional features of populist movements, most of the well populated category of fully authoritarian regimes lacks such populist features. In their analysis of authoritarian constitutions, David Law and Mila Versteeg identify three types – monarchical, military and civilian.[20] The monarchical systems tend to rely on historically grounded kinship networks, generally involving traditionalistic forms of social and political hierarchy, sometimes within a theocratic framework. Military dictatorships typically seize power with the help of the generals, thereafter drawing upon the organisational apparatus of the armed forces to consolidate their rule. Civilian authoritarian systems, which are the most common of the three,[21] normally rely on a dominant or exclusive political party organisation to mobilise popular support, to offer patronage to clients and collaborators, and to keep regime opponents in check. In all three categories the authoritarianism tended to be strongly 'embedded'.[22] The claim to provide the only authentic leadership, typically backed up by military power, dynastic privilege or longstanding party hegemony, is largely independent of any populist-style claim to represent and respond to the people as a concrete entity, nor does it rest on a proto-democratic conception of constituent power. The partial exception to this tendency is civilian, party-based systems. In the case of mass parties, their origins may be linked to a notion of popular sovereignty, though that claim, where it has been made, has typically atrophied as top-down one party bureaucratic rule has become consolidated.

[20] Law and Versteeg, 'Constitutional Variation' (n 13).

[21] According to Law and Versteeg, ibid, as of 2008, of the 70 authoritarian regimes worldwide in their estimation, 11 were of the monarchical type, 23 were military and 36 were civilian.

[22] Walker (n 11) 526–28.

For the most part, therefore, strongly authoritarian constitutional regimes simply do not depend on populist methods of rule. The few exceptions from the Democracy Index, notably Putin's Russia and Maduro's Venezuela, stand out as cases where the descent from a position where populist methods were heavily employed, drawing on democratic constitutionalist rhetoric and structures, has been particularly precipitous. However, most of the cases which have been the focus of the constitutionalist critique of populism figure instead in the 'hybrid' category, or, more frequently, the 'flawed democracy' category. We shall discuss these cases in a moment, but first it is worth underlining two indisputable but nevertheless largely unremarked conclusions. First, full democratic constitutionalism is very much a marginal case globally, even though most self-styled constitutionalists treat it as paradigmatic. Secondly, the deepest and most common contrast with the democratically constitutionalist case is with the authoritarian constitution, a category that in fact owes little to the populist tendency, yet has received rather less recent attention in its own right in recent constitutional thought than has populism.[23]

IV. THE ADJACENCY OF POPULISM

On the face of it, this second conclusion represents something of a conundrum. Why focus on anything other than the starkest contrast and the deepest repudiation of constitutionalist mores when seeking to depict the threat to constitutionalism? Two explanations are possible. First, it may simply reflect a certain Western-centric myopia. The vast majority of the cases of authoritarian regimes, 53 out of 59,[24] are located in Asia and Africa, as, indeed, are a significant majority of the hybrid cases (24 out of 34). To put it crudely, through a Western lens this non-Western world may be largely invisible, or viewed as involving such distinct traditions of rule as to be somehow impervious to constitutional analysis. Neither of these attitudes, ignorance or exotic othering – flatters its holder. Also, to the extent that such attitudes do arise, they can breed both complacency and alarm. Complacency, that the democratically troubled experience of Africa and Asia is somehow irrelevant to our appreciation of the global success or otherwise of constitutional democracy. Alarm, to the extent that this narrowness of vision encourages the homing in on populism as the arch-enemy, and so highlights the particularly close challenge that populism offers.

A second explanation is more reasonable, and more palatable. For there are also good reasons – reasons other than ignorance or exotic othering – for focusing on the closeness of the challenge offered by populism. While some forms of authoritarianism are embedded, and largely unacquainted with populist tendencies, there are two other types we should attend to. In both cases certain lesser or incipiently authoritarian tendencies can be identified, here alongside certain populist traits. These traits, moreover, speak to a significant democratic legacy. Tellingly, within the Democracy Index all these cases fall

[23] Although there is also growing interest in authoritarian constitutionalism: eg Ginsburg and Simpser (n 13); G Frankenberg, *Authoritarianism: Constitutional Perspectives* (Edward Elgar, 2020); M Tushnet, 'Authoritarian Constitutionalism' (2014) 100 *Cornell Law Review* 391.

[24] The six exceptions being Russia, Belarus, Nicaragua, Cuba, Venezuela and Haiti.

within the two intermediate categories – either as hybrid regimes or, more commonly, as flawed democracies.[25]

On the one hand, there are *reversionist* types.[26] These include those, such as Turkey, Hungary, Poland and Brazil, where a more pluralistic political system has been introduced against an authoritarian historical backdrop, but there is a tendency towards reversion or 'backsliding'[27] in accordance with the reassertion of party, military or dynastic power. The new clothes of democratically pluralist constitutionalism tend to be discarded in the name of a rediscovery of the 'true essence' of the people by a leader and political movement (often articulated through the creation of a new vanguard party) positioned against a supposedly hegemonic establishment. Perhaps this may be done through a recovery or re-emphasis of a particular constitutional heritage associated with a regime characterised by a greater concentration of power,[28] and perhaps also, or alternatively, through a process of constitutional renewal that involves a reconcentration of power.[29]

On the other hand, there are *emergent* types; these range from India to Italy and from Bolivia and Ecuador to the United States (US), although such regimes are often marked by volatile politics and fast changing political fortunes.[30] In addition, emergent traits also present in minor, aspirational or oppositional form in many other systems worldwide, North and South, East and West, including the United Kingdom and many of the West European members of the European Union (EU). Indeed, these fledgling or merely aspirational populisms nevertheless receive a lot of attention, and are the focus of much constitutional anxiety. In the more developed emergent cases, there are two pathways; either, as in the case of India or the US, authoritarian drift from – and emergence out of – a long established democratic tradition, through the gradual reworking of a constitutional order from its pluralistic pedigree; or, as, for example, in the case of the 'progressive' populism of Morales in Bolivia (2006–19), Correa in Ecuador (2007–17) and

[25] So, eg, Turkey, Bolivia and Ecuador figure in the hybrid category, while the US, Hungary, Poland, Slovenia, India, Italy and Brazil are assessed as flawed democracies.

[26] Walker (n 11) 526–28. There is terminological overlap but also a difference of emphasis between my reversionist-emergent distinction and Huq and Ginsberg's distinction between 'authoritarian reversion' and 'constitutional retrogression'. While their 'constitutional retrogression' type fits closely my 'emergent' type, their 'authoritarian reversion' type differs from my 'reversionist' type in its primary focus on output factors (the rapid and near complete collapse of democratic institutions), rather than input factors (the significance of the authoritarian tradition in enabling reversionist tendencies): A Huq and T Ginsberg, 'How to Lose a Constitutional Democracy' (2018) 65 *UCLA Law Review* 78.

[27] See, eg, R Dixon and D Landau, 'Tiered Constitutional Design' (2018) 86 *George Washington Law Review* 438.

[28] On this aspect of the Turkish experience, see T Isiksel, 'Between Text and Context: Turkey's Tradition of Authoritarian Constitutionalism' (2013) 11 *International Journal of Constitutional Law* 702, 710.

[29] As in the case of the Hungarian Constitution, already amended nine times following its renewal under Orban in 2010. See, eg, A Arato, *Post-Sovereign Constitution Making: Learning And Legitimacy* (Oxford University Press, 2016) ch 4. See also V Makszimov, 'Orban to Change Constitution, Again' (*EURACTIV*, 22 April 2022), available at www.euractiv.com/section/politics/short_news/orban-to-change-the-constitution-again/.

[30] For example, the US' recent populist leaning is tied up with the volatile fortunes of Donald Trump, President from 2016–2020, and of 'Trumpian' ideology going forward. Italy has had recent uneven experience of populist movements in power, with the populist Five Star Movement part of the governing coalition between 2018–2021, followed by a technocratic government led by Mario Draghi, which in turn was followed by the electoral success of another populist party, Fratelli d'Italia, and the appointment of their leader Georgia Meloni as Prime Minister in the Autumn of 2022. The Slovenian case is also one of uneven recent populist success. Ivan Jansa, the populist Prime Minister, leader of the Slovenian Democratic Party, and close ally of Hungary's populist Victor Orban, having been defeated in an election in April 2022 after two years in office.

Maduro's predecessor Chavez in Venezuela (1999–2013), a more clearly discontinuous new constitutional order that combines certain pluralist features with a populist ideology and programme.[31] In emergent scenarios, then, unlike the reversionist case, the pluralist dimension within the constitutional order is recognised as a deeper and longer tradition, or at least as a parallel theme; but it is also criticised as one that, supportive of and exploited or exploitable by an elite, is out of sympathy with the 'real' people. The (re)assertion of the interests of the populace is a trust assumed by the new populist leadership. It is a trust that is likely to involve either or both significant circumvention of the extant constitutional framework and a fuller commandeering and renewal.

In either case, whether reversionist or emergent, the populist moment *may* harbour an authoritarian susceptibility. It is important to underline that there is no causal *necessity* involved here. We can find recent examples of episodes of populists in government, such as the ascent of Syriza in Greece,[32] or Podemos power-sharing in Spain, where there is no discernible authoritarian shift or drift. And there may well be *particular* indicators, such as a liberal Left emphasis on the popular renewal of democratic methods, which make it less rather than more likely that a populist movement will acquire authoritarian overtones.[33] Yet it is arguable that, if we are required to view matters prospectively rather than permitted to explain them retrospectively – with the luxury of the detailed knowledge of case-specific pathways that hindsight allows – we may still talk of a *general* authoritarian propensity within populist thought and practice. Even if the populism in question involves a *bona fide* investment in 'plebeian politics that appeals to ordinary people'[34] rather than the ideological projection of the wishes of a dominant populist leader, or leadership corps, onto the masses, the risk remains. For as Camila Vergara argues, *any* 'project of popular empowerment demands an extraordinary authority that goes beyond the electoral legitimacy conferred by ordinary forms of representation'.[35] It involves a claim to renewed constitutional legitimacy in the name of an encompassing people and a popular manifesto that tends to be defined as an indispensable anchor of such renewed legitimacy. And this may justify both a concentration of power upon the means and actors necessary to fill out and execute this singular project, and the marginalisation or suppression of those constituencies deemed to be opposed to the project.

The relative proximity of both the reversionist and the emergent types to the model of constitutional democracy allows us to return to the constitutional anxieties associated with populism, but now with a clearer sense of what is at stake. For the vital concerns associated with populism are revealed to flow not from the starkness or vividness of its contrast with constitutional democracy; to the contrary, such concerns flow from their contiguity to and overlap with constitutional democracy. In the first place,

[31] See, eg, C de la Torre, 'Latin American Populist Authoritarian Inclusion' (2021) 1 *Comparative Political Theory* 187.

[32] See, eg, C Mudde, *Syriza: The Failure of the Populist Promise* (Palgrave, 2016).

[33] See, eg, C Mouffe, *For a Left Populism* (Verso, 2018); see also Tushnet and Bugaric, above (n 2) ch 3, and B Bugaric, 'The Two Faces of Populism: Between Authoritarian and Democratic Populism' (2019) 20 *German Law Journal* 390, emphasising the importance of looking for more granular explanations of the types of circumstances and the kinds of populist traits that lead to authoritarian outcomes.

[34] C Vergera, 'Populism as Plebeian Politics: Inequality, Domination and Popular Empowerment' (2020) 28 *The Journal of Political Philosophy* 222, 246.

[35] ibid.

both the reversionist and the emergent types reveal the ease, fluidity and continuity of movement between the pluralist model of constitutional democracy and an anti-pluralist and potentially authoritarian populism. Here we find the language of 'drift',[36] 'decay',[37] retrogression',[38] etc in liberal use within the literature. This speaks to a concern both that populism has tended to grow out of constitutional democracy rather than any other regime type, and that in this process the valued attributes of constitutional democracy are lost more by slow erosion and gradual eclipse than by rupture and revolution.[39]

Behind and informing this practical concern, however, there is a deeper question about the overlap between constitutional democracy and populism. What if adjacency can be best explained by there being an *internal* relation between constitutional democracy and populism? What if the difficulties of identifying a bright line simply obscure the truth that there is no clear line, and that the two not only blend into one another but *presuppose* one another? Perhaps we simply cannot have constitutional democracy *without* populism. To that inquiry we now turn.

V. FEATURE OR BUG?

In order to make the argument for overlap between constitutional democracy and populism we need to say something about the origins of our modern constitutional tradition. We should begin by recognising that the twin aspects that make up that tradition are not naturally reconciled. On the one hand, there is the belief in the constitution as a superordinate ordering device for government. On the other, there is the belief in democracy – the rule of the many. From Aristotle to Alexander Hamilton, however, democracy in this pure form was seen as a deficient and dangerous form of government, as akin to mob rule and in danger of descending into tyranny or anarchy.[40]

The rise of modern constitutionalism under the design pioneered in the late eighteenth century North Atlantic was partly in response to this. To the extent that it had an overarching justification, it was as an emancipatory project intended to subordinate the exercise of governmental power to the rule of law.[41] Yet the core meaning and dominant emphasis of this emancipatory project was contested. The authority of the rule of (constitutional) law could contain the abuses and cure the excesses of undiluted forms of rule such as monarchy and aristocracy. Crucially, however, this left the position of democracy under the rule of law unresolved. It could, on the one hand, be viewed as a key means of diluting and overcoming these old forms of hierarchy and the abuses and excesses they

[36] See, eg, K Weyland, 'Latin America's Authoritarian Drift: The Threat from the Populist Left' (2013) 24 *Journal of Democracy* 18.

[37] See, eg, the Dem-Dec Resource, 'Democratic Decay', available at www.democratic-decay.org/democratic-decay-as-the-organising-concept.

[38] See, eg, Huq and Ginsburg (n 26).

[39] See, eg, B Bugaric, 'Could Populism Be Good for Constitutional Democracy?' (2019) 15 *Annual Review of Law and Social Science* 41.

[40] See, eg, Loughlin (n 4); N Walker, 'Constitutionalism and the Incompleteness of Democracy' (2010) 39 *Netherlands Journal of Legal Philosophy* 206.

[41] See, eg, G Frankenberg, *Comparative Constitutional Studies: Between Magic and Deceit* (Edward Elgar, 2018) ch 2.

allowed.[42] Yet on the other hand, as already noted, democracy could also itself be seen as a form of power in need of dilution, and of the establishment of safeguards against *its* abuse and excess.[43] Over time, as the case for democracy (as opposed to the other pure forms of rule) became stronger within a modern political imaginary that increasingly affirmed the autonomy and equality of human agency over pre-modern conceptions of hierarchy and cosmic order, the particular combination of constitutional and democratic authority that would eventually become paradigmatic of Western constitutional government took a double form. And in this double form something of the earlier ambivalence towards democracy remained. At the highest level, the idea of popular sovereignty, based on popular endorsement (or subsequent homologation) of the founding constitutional text itself, inaugurated a republican system of self-government. At the second level of everyday government, the system of democratic authority, as guided and constrained by the popularly self-authorised constitutional rules, involved both structural and substantive checks and limitations. It did so in the form (respectively) of the separation and balance of governmental branches and institutions, and the affirmation of individual rights. Within that mediated framework, democratic authority itself became indirect, organised through the representative channels of political parties.

Within this dual system, the relationship between the two dimensions, between constitutional 'law-rule' and democratic 'self-rule'[44] – between the 'order' and the 'self-government' of ordered self-government – has remained perennially unresolved. We see this tension, for example, in repeated disputes over the respective credentials of judges and legislators, individual protections and collective capacities, rights and voice, etc. But, more importantly for present purposes, we also see it in a residual sense, present within all modern democratically-inclined political cultures, that the fuller promise of democratic self-rule – offered abstractly in the idea of a popular constituent power and present often only as a latent possibility in quotidian political discourse – supplies an exacting critical standard against which the shortcomings of actually existing forms of government practice can be measured and highlighted. What the vindication of that promise might mean as a matter of government method is often vague, frequently contested, its positive force subordinated to its critical power. It has been persuasively argued, however, that, at least considered ideal typically, the most uncompromisingly 'democratic' alternatives to the constrained 'law-rule' of a representative democracy hedged by liberal checks and balances fall into two basic streams: Jacobinism, where the competitive struggles of representative democracy within a pluralist framework are replaced by a vision of collective consensus based upon nature, reason and virtue, and Caesarism, where the affirmation of cultural identity, homogeneity and unity allows a 'strongman' to gain popular support for his particular vision of the collective good.[45]

[42] See, eg, L Kramer, *The People Themselves: Popular Constitutionalism and Judicial Review* (Oxford University Press, 2005).

[43] See, eg, G Sartori, 'Constitutionalism: A Preliminary Discussion' (1962) 56 *American Political Science Review* 853.

[44] See Frankenberg (n 41) 20.

[45] U Wagrandl, 'A Theory of Illiberal Democracy' in A Sajo, R Uitz and S Holmes (eds), *Routledge Handbook of Illiberalism* (Routledge, 2022) 94, 95.

Of these two options, the Caesarist tradition in particular, which in the modern age reaches back as far as Napoleon Bonaparte, shows strong affinities with the methods and presuppositions of populism – or at least those forms of populism that focus on the charismatic authority of the political leader. Yet a broader point can be made about the relevance of populism to the unfulfilled promise of democratic self-rule. For as Jan-Werner Muller puts it, populism, more emphatically so in its critical and aspirational role than in its positive governmental role, styles itself as 'the permanent shadow of representative politics'[46] – promising and promoting a severe reaction against all supposed compromises of democratic purity and distortions of the voice of 'We, the People'. Or, as Margaret Canovan has explained, democracy always has two faces. It has a pragmatic face, a way, typically through representative party politics, of coping peacefully with the conflicts of modern pluralist societies. But it also has a redemptive face, 'kin to the family of modern ideologies that promise salvation through politics'.[47] Populism thrives in the permanent tension between the pragmatic reality and the redemptive ideal.

This tension, integral to the very idea of democracy, provides us with a first *structural* account of populism's internal relationship to constitutional democracy. It is inevitable, in other words, that constitutional democracy will carry a populist echo. Its pragmatism will always feed the more radical redemptive impulses associated with the democratic tradition. For all the attention paid to the latest twenty-first century wave of populism, it is no narrow time-bound pathology. Rather, it speaks to a tradition as old as modern constitutionalism itself (indeed, as the Caesarist handle suggest, much older). What is more – to repeat a point – as the popularity of the term as a party-political label in nineteenth century America suggests,[48] and as the contemporary emergence of some non-authoritarian strains of populism reinforces, it is not a term which *need* carry the negative implications that have tended to attach to it in much of today's commentaries.

We might conclude, therefore, that populism is a standard feature of constitutional democracy, at least in the sense that it answers to a standard and unavoidable concern of constitutional democracy with its deeper credentials of self-rule. If not always in its manifest appearance, then certainly in its latent and lurking possibility, therefore, populism is the inevitable accompaniment of the constitutional machinery and culture. When it speaks it tends to do so in an urgently assertive voice to an aspect – namely the democratic aspect – that is internal to constitutional democracy. What is more, and vitally importantly so, the connection sounds not just in the realm of ideas and philosophical reflection, but also of practice. The success or otherwise of our constitutional order depends, as we noted earlier, on culture as well as institutions and rules. In particular, it depends, in a self-reinforcing dynamic, upon whether the system generates trust and confidence to a level such that those over whom its authority is claimed come to understand themselves and to act as a community of engagement in a common form of political life sufficiently for the system's institutions to operate effectively. It depends,

[46] Muller (n 2) 101.

[47] M Canovan, 'Trust the People! Populism and the Two Faces of Democracy' (1999) 47 *Political Studies* 2, 10. Canovan draws heavily on Michael Oakeshott's distinction between the politics of scepticism and the politics of faith in developing her arguments. See M Oakeshott, *The Politics of Faith and the Politics of Scepticism* (Yale University Press, 1996) 21.

[48] See, eg, C Postel, *The Populist Vision* (Oxford University Press, 2007).

in other words, on the adequacy of the *political capital* recurrently generated by the system.[49] Importantly, the development of populist side narratives or counter narratives typically offers an alternative source of political capital, and the pursuit of that offer can either stimulate (by competition), undermine or diminish the existing stock of political capital. And to the extent that it diminishes that capital, the populist element can be seen to be a bug as well as a feature of constitutional democracy.

Whether or not this is the case remains of course an empirical question. Again to repeat a point, what populism delivers depends on the background context of each particular constitutional system and the balance of motivating forces within each populist movement.[50] Yet, allowing for that large caveat, we can say something in general about contemporary populist trends – the very trends that have generated the surge of anxious attention with regard to which we began this chapter. An assessment of these trends provides us with a second and *contingent* account of populism's internal relationship to constitutional democracy to set alongside and in development of the more basic structural account.

We can begin with a recent pithy summary of the contemporary situation by Claus Offe. According to him, 'we may … say that abstract liberal democracy is celebrating its near-global victory, while concrete and existing democracies are widely looked at with discontent and frustration over failures of both the legitimacy and effectiveness of democratic rule'.[51] If we excuse the typically significant overestimation of global investment in liberal or constitutional democracy, Offe makes a good point about the way in which the systems of rule associated with constitutional democracy attract only tepid support. But what are the more particular factors feeding this general discontent?

Much of this is captured in the notion of the 'hollowing'[52] of contemporary democracy, an idea that speaks directly to the theme of political capital. On the one hand, the passivity that is a structural feature of representative democracy can morph into expressions of apathy and alienation. This is especially so in those political systems that are long established, and so frequently adept at suppressing the very triggers of violence or disorder that have often provided democratic government's formative impetus, while failing to address the tenacious underlying roots of unrest.[53] These attitudes of withdrawal are particularly prevalent within the most disadvantaged sectors of the population. Those suffering from economic or educational inequality, or from structural discrimination on the basis of gender, race, age or other minority status, are less likely to feel a stake in the democratic system and more likely to opt out of participation as party members, or even as voters. On the other hand, and contributing to a self-reinforcing cycle, governing elites within and beyond the political parties become gradually disconnected from these sectors. Policy priorities are increasingly set by groups whose privileged access to the levers of political influence is as entrenched as is the exclusion of other

[49] On the idea of political capital, see, eg, E Banfield, *Political Influence* (The Free Press, 1961) 241–42; P Bourdieu, 'The Forms of Capital' in J Richardson (ed), *Handbook of Theory and Research for the Sociology of Education* (Greenwood Press, 1986) 241.

[50] See Tushnet and Bugaric (n 2); Bugaric (n 33).

[51] C Offe, 'Referendum versus Institutionalized Deliberation: What Democratic Theorists Can Learn from the 2016 Brexit Decision' (2017) 146 *Daedalus* 14, 15.

[52] P Mair, *Ruling the Void: The Hollowing of Western Democracy* (Verso, 2013).

[53] D Runciman, *How Democracy Ends* (Profile, 2018) ch 2.

groups. In particular, employers, investors and various other organised interests possess the economic resources, the strategic know-how and the cultural confidence to shape the political agenda in ways that secure their privilege and respond to their own concerns at the expense of others.

The 'void'[54] that opens up between rulers and ruled not only leads to the disempowerment of certain types of constituency and their interests, but contributes to a general depletion of democratic political capital and a general erosion of the steering capacity of the political system in its traditional home of the nation state. Confidence in the capacity, and trust in the willingness of the political system and its leaders to respond to major social and economic problems and promote effective social change declines across all constituencies. Once more, a self-fulfilling dynamic comes into play. As issues such as social exclusion, deepening inequality, environmental degradation and international conflict – both old wars between states and the 'new wars'[55] of non-state actors – are increasingly seen as beyond the policy reach of any particular governing party or coalition, 'the perceived political purchasing power of the ballot declines'.[56] Citizens of all stripes are less likely to invest their efforts in making the system more fully fit for purpose, or to respond to the overtures of governing elites to make the kinds of collective commitments necessary to deliver social reform. Major political parties, with declining room for manoeuvre, provide a narrowing and increasingly similar menu of outcomes, and even of aspirations.

Another key contributory factor to the narrowing of political vision is the impact of economic globalisation. Through its latest wave which began with the post-war development of the Breton Woods institutions, globalisation was reinforced by the growing influence of neo-liberal governing ideologies in leading Western polities from the 1970s onwards. Transnational imperatives of competitiveness, capital mobility and tax competition, and the associated disciplines of debt consolidation and austerity generally prevailed. This has dovetailed with a rescaling of economic decision-making from national to the supranational level. And in the gradual transfer of authority from the democratic state to supranational technocratic elites, we see, yet again, a self-reinforcing feedback. Yet for all their new ascendancy, the room to manoeuvre of these new elites also remains restricted. Even in the relatively broadly purposed and democratically accountable case of the EU, supranational capacity has tended to be limited to mitigating some of the harsher effects of the operation of transnational markets on workers, savers or public service-recipients.[57]

Overall, the hollowing of democracy has led to a situation where the governing capacity of nation states becomes less adequate and less responsive to the aspirations and well-being of the citizenry as a whole. Terms such as 'post-democracy'[58] and 'competitive authoritarianism'[59] have been coined to capture some of the diverse consequences

[54] Mair (n 52).

[55] M Kaldor, *New and Old Wars: Organized Violence in a Global Era*, 3rd edn (Polity, 2012).

[56] Offe (n 51) 16.

[57] On the roots of populist responses to the EU, see, eg, J Zielonka, *Counter-Revolution: Liberal Europe in Retreat* (Oxford University Press, 2018).

[58] C Crouch, *Post-Democracy* (Polity, 2014).

[59] S Levitsky and L Way, *Competitive Authoritarianism: Hybrid Regimes after the Cold War* (Cambridge University Press, 2010).

of this drift. These include the technocratic turn to 'output legitimacy' over 'input legitimacy'[60] but also, and crucially for present purposes, the development of more selective, culturally specific emotionally charged forms of electoral coalition-building that falls under the rubric of populism. For in a context of limited and apparently declining political capital, citizens may come to be re-addressed by political elites in two ways: Merely as the rationally self-interested consumers of a finite pool of public goods and private benefits; or, partly in reaction to the arms-length, deracinating style and its distributive patterns, a particular category of citizens may instead be mobilised and rewarded as holders of a privileged social and political identity.

Political leadership is emphasised in either case, both in the 'cool' technocratic mode and, more emphatically, in the recently resurgent 'hot' populist form. Contemporary populism, as we have seen, comes in many shades. Boosted by the recruitment to its cause of the leaders of global or regional powers such as Trump, Putin, Bolsonaro, Modi, Erdogan and Orban, however, in some of its most vivid colours it works by explicitly rejecting an inclusive and ecumenical conception of the common good. Instead, it often appeals to the ethical particularity of 'left behind' nativist identities, setting these in confrontation with cosmopolitan elites, internal minorities, 'foreign' forces and others who have frustrated and would continue to deny the birthright of the 'real' people. Populist movements and parties often foreground an expressive agenda of identity assertion. They not only target marginal groups but, as we have seen, they also frame an amorphous 'Establishment' or 'deep state' as the scapegoat for the longstanding failure of 'normal' politics to recognise them or their aspirations. 'Strongman' leaders are an important part of this package. They offer both a galvanising force to set in performative contrast with the complacent conservatism or cramped ambition of the political mainstream, and a way of lending shape and coherence to an approach that may lack clear policy vision. Such leaders, moreover, tend to treat the classic constraints of liberal constitutionalism, including the separation of powers and minority rights, with casual regard. They are at best rules to be strategically managed and at worst impediments to a project of electoral authoritarianism that seeks to sustain itself more by the acclamation of its base than the acceptance of the wider population.[61]

To present 'cool' technocratic and 'hot' populist forms of governance merely as neatly framed alternatives, however, would be too simple and too stylised.[62] As already suggested, both styles of governance respond to weaknesses in representative democracy. In particular, both respond to, and in their turn reinforce, the increasing vulnerability of mass representative democracy in the face of the declining hold of generic political identities based on Left/Right affiliations of class and ideology. While the technocratic response tends to present itself as *post-political*, and the populist response as *meta-political* – as a reassertion of a popular political identity and imaginary prior to and tending to eclipse differences over political programmes – there is a common attraction to the idea of the

[60] F Scharpf, *Governing in Europe: Effective and Democratic?* (Oxford University Press, 2010).

[61] Populist leaders also focus on 'wedge' issues that can be seen to dramatise the distinction between the identity and mores of the 'real' people and those of others. On one key recent instance of this – populist responses to the coronavirus pandemic, see W Sadurski, *A Pandemic of Populists* (Cambridge University Press, 2022).

[62] Staying with the contrast for a moment, we can see a clear link to the deeper and older contrast between Jacobin and Caesarist approaches: see Wagrandl (n 45).

common good as something *that either evidently* (in the case of technocracy) *or self-evidently* (in the case of leader-centred populism) trumps ideological divisions.[63]

VI. CONCLUSION

The progressive hollowing out of democracy places the democratic constitutional order, already a precarious outlier on the global scene, in a more critical spotlight. Democratic governance is seen to become less close, less capacious, less responsive, less trusted, less recognisably representative of those it is intended to represent, yet still the only form of governance that many citizens would wish to contemplate. In consequence, the burden falls on political projects and their leaders to turn the tide – to offer a fuller and more appetizing version of the same dish. But the problems remain structural, concerning the limited traction that political decision-making, treating all citizens as formal equals, has over circuits of economic and social power that are unequally possessed and distributed, and that in any case stretch well beyond the decision-making purview of the nation state. And since, in addition, those who steer the system often exhibit the very 'elitist' qualities that for many citizens indict the system as a whole, democratic leadership always treads a treacherous path. In the name of efficiency, there may be a retreat into a technocratic style that increases the affective disconnect with the democratic audience and undermines the capacity to mobilise future political capital. Alternatively, in the name of popular identification, there may be a retreat by its populist critics into a connective style that draws its political capital from a limited section of the population, becomes careless of the broader framework of constitutional controls, and undermines the classic democratic ambition to represent the people as a whole.

This more restrictive lens is not the inevitable expression of new populist initiatives in and against constitutional democracy. But it is definitely a temptation. To the extent that it is succumbed to, making enemies out of adversaries, and rendering the sources of political capital (mutually) exclusionary rather than (competitively) inclusionary, it must be seen as a bug that increasingly accompanies the system of constitutional democracy; one that both highlights and contributes to the inherent precariousness of that system. In so doing, it offers an immediate and recurrent challenge and threat to set alongside the even more profound global danger and injustice of authoritarian rule.

[63] In turn, this structural convergence may encourage strategic blending. Populist governments, like any other, can see the political advantages that may accrue from association with the legitimating power of scientific expertise. And the post-ideological orientation of both styles may in certain contexts ease the process of convergence. See, eg, C Bickerton and C Invernizzi Accetti, 'Populism and Technocracy' in C R Kaltwasser, PA Taggart, P Ochoa Espejo and P Ostiguy (eds), *The Oxford Handbook of Populism* (Oxford University Press, 2017) 319; see also CJ Bickerton and C Invernizzi Accetti, *Technopopulism: The New Logic of Democratic Politics* (Oxford University Press, 2021).

17

'You Can't Go Home Again': Constitutional Fidelity and Change in Post-Brexit Britain

COLM Ó CINNÉIDE

I. INTRODUCTION

'CONSTITUTIONAL UNSETTLEMENT', TO borrow a phrase from Neil Walker,[1] has become a feature of the comparative public law landscape. In many states, laws and practices introduced as byproducts of the liberal constitutionalist boom of the last few decades, which were assumed to have become established parts of the national constitutional order, have instead become the focus of sustained legal and political contestation.[2] Such contestation often takes the form of demands for a return to the original and 'authentic' norms of the domestic constitutional system, and for a correction of certain strands of allegedly deviant public law development – usually involving perceived judicial and regulatory over-reach, encouraged by the influence of foreign legal thinking, which is supposed to have undermined the integrity of more political, 'democratic' and autochthonous methods of controlling the exercise of public power.[3] In response, defenders of the liberal constitutionalist status quo have tended to accuse its critics of dabbling in 'populism', and of seeking to erode not only the stability and integrity of the established constitutional order but also basic rule of law and separation of powers norms.[4] And so battle is joined over what 'constitutional fidelity' requires, ie fidelity to the core principles and values that are supposed to underpin the national constitutional order, or what Gary Jacobsohn has described as its fundamental 'identity'.[5]

The United Kingdom (UK) is currently experiencing this type of constitutional unsettlement. It used to be famous for the relative placidity and unobtrusiveness of its constitutional arrangements (if one set aside issues related to Ireland/Northern Ireland).

[1] N Walker, 'Our Constitutional Unsettlement' (2014) *Public Law* 529.
[2] M Loughlin, 'The Contemporary Crisis of Constitutional Democracy' (2018) 39(2) *OJLS* 435–54.
[3] For a taste of such criticism, see, eg, J Sumption, *Trials of the State: Law and the Decline of Politics* (Profile, 2019).
[4] For a useful comparative and conceptual analysis of this dynamic, see N Walker, 'Populism and Constitutional Tension' (2019) 17(2) *OJLS* 515–35.
[5] G Jacobsohn, *Constitutional Identity* (Harvard University Press, 2010).

Moreover, its constitution tended to be viewed in functional terms, as a pragmatic and inherently flexible set of rules, practices and conventions which loosely structured how political and legal power was exercised – and was not expected to maintain rigid alignment with any specific framework of underlying principles and values.[6] But things have changed. In recent years, thanks in part to the political dynamics unleashed by Brexit, aspects of its uncodified constitution have become the focus of sustained controversy. And much of the debate has revolved around questions of constitutional fidelity, and whether legal and political actors are faithfully adhering to foundational norms that allegedly make up the identitarian core of the UK's constitutional order.

Much of this controversy has been driven by critics objecting to elements of the 'thickening' of the UK constitutional order as it has evolved over the last few decades, ie the new layers of constitutional governance engendered by devolution, the extension of legal and quasi-legal controls on the exercise of executive power, and the persisting entanglement of domestic UK law with European Union (EU), European Convention on Human Rights (ECHR) and other European or international law norms.[7] These critics, who include prominent academics, ex-judges and former government ministers, claim that this 'thickening' process has imposed excessive constraints on political decision-making, as channelled in particular through the institutional framework of the Westminster Parliament.[8] In their eyes, this runs counter to democratic first principles and threatens to corrode parliamentary sovereignty – which they regard as the dominant underpinning structural norm of the British constitution. And such criticism has generated calls for a process of 'constitutional rebalancing', which would strip away undesirable aspects of current public law and restore the integrity of the UK's 'political constitution'.[9] These calls for reform have often been linked to Brexit, but have not been confined in scope to the EU influence on UK law: at the time of writing, the debate about the alleged need for a return to constitutional fundamentals has been mainly focused on devolution and the UK's relationship with the ECHR.

However, supporters of the status quo have pushed back against these calls for constitutional reclamation. They have defended the democratic legitimacy of the contested thicker elements of the existing constitutional order, and highlighted the flaws of various concrete 'rebalancing' initiatives proposed by government ministers.[10] They have also argued that critics of thicker constitutionalism downplay the importance of rule of law, separation of powers and respect for human rights – values generally acknowledged to also form part of the normative core of the UK constitutional order, sitting alongside its foundational commitment to democratic self-government.[11] More generally, critics of the

[6] This view of the UK constitution is perhaps best encapsulated by John Griffith's classic quip to the effect that the British constitution was 'no more and no less than what happens' – a quote that will be returned to later: see JAG Griffith, 'The Political Constitution' (1979) 42 *MLR* 1–21, at 19.

[7] For an excellent overview of this process, see E Delaney, 'Judiciary Rising: Constitutional Change in the United Kingdom' (2014) *Northwestern University Law Review* 543–606.

[8] In conversation, Erin Delaney has suggested these critics could be described as 'neo-Diceyans'.

[9] See, eg, J McConalogue, *Rebalancing the British Constitution: The Future for Human Rights Law* (Civitas, 2020).

[10] For further detail, see sections II and III below.

[11] For a descriptive analysis of the underpinning values that animate the UK constitutional order, see J Jowell and C O'Cinneide, 'Values in the UK Constitution' in D Davis, A Richter and C Saunders (eds), *An Inquiry into the Existence of Global Values: Through the Lens of Comparative Constitutional Law* (Hart Publishing, 2015) 357–92.

status quo have also been accused of pandering to populism, and risking the erosion of important constitutional safeguards.[12]

Two competing narratives are thus in play. Critics of the status quo claim it is out of alignment with democratic fundamentals, while supporters argue that rebalancing initiatives risk corroding key underpinning principles like respect for rights and rule of law. In other words, mirroring trends elsewhere, sharp dividing lines have opened up as to what constitutional fidelity entails in the specific context of the UK. Faultline issues like reform of the Human Rights Act 1998 (HRA), compliance with the European Court of Human Rights (ECtHR) judgments, the outcome of the *Miller* cases[13] and the scope of competency of the Scottish Parliament have become the focus of particular controversy – often channelled through sharp-edged rhetoric, and garnished with accusations of betrayal, bad faith and disregard of the 'will of the people'.[14]

Successive Conservative governments have taken active steps to dilute some of the thicker elements of the current constitutional order and to bring it back into alignment with what they regard as its underpinning core values.[15] Their efforts in this regard have had limited success, in terms of formal law reform: for example, the attempt to replace the HRA with a 'British Bill of Rights' has floundered.[16] However, taken in tandem with the influence of other critical voices, this push back seems to have changed some of the dynamics of UK constitutional debate. Identarian' concerns have been spotlighted, certain existing aspects of the constitutional order have been problematised, and supporters of 'thicker' elements of the status quo have been put on the back foot. Furthermore, this push back has been paralleled by some significant and controversial shifts in the relevant case law of the British courts. In particular, the UK Supreme Court (UKSC) appears to have embarked on a doctrinal 'rebalancing' project of its own, involving a reassertion of the centrality of parliamentary sovereignty and political modes of accountability to the UK's constitutional order.[17] In so doing, the Court may be attempting to root its public law jurisprudence in what it perceives to be solid constitutional ground, in a time of clashing narratives and unsettling debate about the status of fundamental norms. However, it remains to be seen how convincing and sustainable the Court's recent doctrinal shifts prove to be.

This chapter sets out to explore the underlying dynamics of this current bout of constitutional unsettlement, and how appeals to concepts of constitutional fidelity have formed a central part of the argumentative matrix. Section II explores how the 'thickening' of UK constitutional norms over the last few decades has triggered a sharp backlash, amplified by the legal and political tensions generated by Brexit. Section III examines the attempts of

[12] See the nuanced discussion of these dynamics in A Young, 'Populism and the UK Constitution' (2018) 71 *Current Legal Problems* 17–52. See also A Blick, *Populism and the UK Constitution* (Constitutional Society, 2019).

[13] *R (Miller) v Secretary of State for Exiting the European Union* [2017] UKSC 5; *R (Miller) v The Prime Minister and Cherry v Advocate General for Scotland* [2019] UKSC 41.

[14] C Phipps, 'British Newspapers React to Judges' Brexit Ruling: "Enemies of the people"' *The Guardian* (4 November 2016), available at www.theguardian.com/politics/2016/nov/04/enemies-of-the-people-british-newspapers-react-judges-brexit-ruling.

[15] See further section III below.

[16] M Dathan, 'Dominic Raab's Bill of Rights will be Scrapped for a Third Time' *The Times* (8 May 2023), available at www.thetimes.co.uk/article/dominic-raabs-bill-of-rights-will-be-scrapped-for-a-third-time-nqqfl3sq7.

[17] See section IV below.

recent Conservative governments to 'rebalance' the constitutional order, in particular the reform initiatives undertaken by the Boris Johnson Government of 2019–22. Section IV outlines the recent doctrinal developments in the jurisprudence of the Supreme Court, which arguably represent a response to this background context of constitutional unsettlement and concerns about a loss of fidelity to first principles. Section V analyses the factors that have helped to drive this general 'identitarian' turn in UK constitutional discourse, and identifies some of its problematic features – in particular the difficulty in identifying the existence of an authentic, fixed and settled normative core to the UK's unwritten constitution, given its historically flexible and malleable character. Finally, by way of conclusion, this chapter critiques how notions of constitutional fidelity have been invoked in recent debates about the content of UK public law. In the British context, attempts to foreclose constitutional debates by invoking fundamental norms should be treated with a healthy dose of scepticism. So too should attempts to turn functional rules of the game into foundational normative commitments, or to insist that the contemporary evolution of UK public law should always fit within a static and backwards-facing model of how the constitution should work.

II. THE CONTEMPORARY DYNAMIC OF CONSTITUTIONAL SETTLEMENT

As already indicated, the roots of the current bout of constitutional unsettlement can be traced back to how the British constitutional order has evolved over the last few decades. Developments such as: (i) the incremental expansion of the reach of judicial review since the 1960s; (ii) the influence exerted by both EU and ECHR law over British law; (iii) the enactment of the HRA; (iv) the establishment of devolved governance structures in Northern Ireland, Scotland and Wales; and (v) the emergence of various 'fourth branch' institutions designed to regulate ministerial conduct and other aspects of political life have 'thickened' UK constitutional governance, ie added new institutional structures, legal requirements and normative expectations to what had previously been a relatively 'thin' regulatory framework.[18]

This 'thickening' process has imposed certain constraints on political decision-making, even as they have created new layers of democratically representative institutions in the devolved regions. In particular, it has imposed new limitations on the powers of central government, whose freedom of action is more hemmed in now by constitutional controls than was historically the case.[19] It has also helped to mould the scope and content of UK political debate, even though the Westminster Parliament retains its ultimate sovereign

[18] Delaney (n 7). For a comprehensive overview of the New Labour reforms that drove many (but not all) of these developments, see M Gordon and A Tucker (eds), *The New Labour Constitution: Twenty Years On* (Hart Publishing, 2021). For the concept of 'fourth branch' institutions, see T Khaitan, 'A Fourth Branch of the State? On Constitutional Guarantors in the UK' (*UK Constitutional Law Blog*, 30 March 2023), available at https://ukconstitutionallaw.org/.

[19] Delaney (n 7). Note that it is important to distinguish 'constitutional controls' in this context, ie authoritative or even legally binding norms pertaining to matters of constitutional structure and functioning, from political, economic or social factors which may limit the freedom of action of central government in a de facto sense. For example, the political power wielded by British trade unions in the 1970s arguably had more of a constraining effect on government policy than any of the 'thicker' constitutional norms currently the focus of debate – a point returned to later in this chapter.

decision-making authority.[20] As a result, British public governance is now structured by legal and political norms of a constitutional character in ways that differ significantly from the operating conditions of the post-war 'political constitution', which imposed significantly fewer constraints on how power was exercised – at least when viewed from the perspective of Westminster and Whitehall.

This 'thickening' of UK constitutionalism has generated significant controversy. An assortment of critics claim that this process has gone too far, and created a situation where the constitutional constraints imposed on political decision-making are excessive. This in turn has generated calls for a return to a more authentically British form of constitutionalism, and a reversion to what are claimed to be the primordial first principles of the constitutional order – specifically, the primacy that is supposed to be given to political decision-making, as channelled through the fused executive-legislature institutional framework built around the functioning of the sovereign Westminster Parliament.[21]

For example, Richard Ekins and other commentators associated with the influential Judicial Power Project (JPP) have spent the best part of a decade calling for legal constraints on the exercise of political power to be minimised.[22] They argue that containing judicial power in this way is a necessary step towards the restoration of the authentic UK constitutional order, as embodied in the operating practices of the post-war political constitution.[23] Similar opinions were aired in Lord Sumption's high-profile 2019 Reith Lectures, which criticised how the 'empire of law' had started to annex the realm of politics.[24] Other commentators have similarly lamented how constitutional thickening has diluted the democratic integrity of the political process, and called for a return to the prelapsarian days of the historic political constitution.[25]

A similar refrain can be heard at times from former government ministers and MPs, especially from those on the right wing of British politics. This reflects over a decade's worth of discontent within the Conservative Party at the constraints imposed by the new constitutional order – including in particular those related to judicial review and the requirements of the ECHR and HRA. It became common during this time for ministers to talk about the need for 'constitutional rebalancing', and to lament how authority had seeped away from democratically elected politicians into the hands of judges, civil servants and other allegedly unaccountable functionaries. Thus, for example, speaking in August 2022, Suella Braverman MP (then the Attorney General) acclaimed the 'thought

[20] See, eg, the discussion of parliamentary responses to declarations of incompatibility issued under the HRA in J King, 'Parliament's Role following Declarations of Incompatibility under the Human Rights Act' in H Hooper, M Hunt and P Yowell (eds), *Parliaments and Human Rights* (Hart Publishing, 2015) 165–92.

[21] See generally the essays contained in R Johnson and YY Zhu (eds), *Sceptical Perspectives on the Changing Constitution of the United Kingdom* (Hart Publishing, 2023).

[22] See in general the archive of JPP publications, available at http://judicialpowerproject.org.uk/publications/. See also R Ekins and G Gee, 'Putting Judicial Power in its Place' (2015) 36(2) *University of Queensland Law Journal* 1–25.

[23] See in particular R Ekins, *Protecting the Constitution: How and Why Parliament Should Limit Judicial Power* (Policy Exchange, 2019).

[24] J Sumption, *Trials of the State: Law and the Decline of Politics* (Profile, 2019).

[25] See, eg McConalogue (n 9); N Malcolm, *Human Rights and Political Wrongs* (Policy Exchange, 2017); D Nicol, 'Supreme Court Against the People' (*UK Constitutional Law Blog*, 25 September 2019), available at https://ukconstitutionallaw.org/; more generally, P Yowell, *Constitutional Rights and Constitutional Design* (Hart Publishing, 2018).

leadership' of the JPP in defending a 'clear, Diceyan view of our constitution'; expressed concern about the 'alarming constitutional and practical consequences' of the expansion of the judicial role in protecting rights; and called for a return to political- and parliamentary-led law-making in this sphere and others.[26]

The legal and political dynamics surrounding Brexit have also contributed to this sense of constitutional malaise. In the eyes of many Brexit enthusiasts, the UK leaving the EU was a potential 'constitutional moment', to use Ackerman's terminology:[27] an opportunity to cast aside some of the legal constraints that had previously circumscribed the free exercise of political power through the institutional framework of the sovereign Westminster Parliament.[28] However, some of the most prominent public controversies post-Brexit have involved government policies, often framed as pro-Leave measures giving effect to the 'will of the people', running up against constitutional buffers.[29] This has helped to reinforce a sense among Brexit enthusiasts that the existing 'thicker' constitutional order is insufficiently responsive to popular opinion and the dynamism of the political process. It also fuels sweeping accusations that constitutional norms have fallen out of alignment with democratic first principles, and are being manipulated by political and legal elites hostile to change – views which align with key tropes of the global right-populist turn against liberal constitutionalism.[30]

Thus, the academic and political pushback against constitutional thickening has been fuelled to some degree by right-populist energy. This has helped to heighten the rhetorical intensity of UK constitutional debates over the last few years.[31] Calls for 'constitutional rebalancing' increasingly go further than conventional forms of political backlash against judicial encroachment, or the usual skirmishing between political and legal constitutionalism. Many contemporary critics of the status quo are not just trying to protect current boundaries, but are also seeking to bring about a broader project of constitutional reclamation. Furthermore, their ambitions are not always confined to diluting the impact of legal controls like the HRA, but also extend to non-legal manifestations of thicker constitutionalism – such as how elements of the devolution settlement have functioned in practice,[32] or even at times the framing of the non-binding provisions of the Ministerial Code.[33]

[26] S Braverman MP, 'Equalities and Rights: Conflict and the Need for Clarity', speech delivered at Policy Exchange on 10 August 2022, available at www.gov.uk/government/speeches/equalities-and-rights-conflict-and-the-need-for-clarity.

[27] B Ackerman, *We the People: Foundations* (Belknap Press, 1991) 3–5.

[28] See McConalogue (n 9); Nicol (n 25); F Nelson, 'Suella Braverman: "Brexit isn't a Revolution – it's a Restoration"' *The Spectator* (8 October 2022).

[29] See the *Miller* cases, cited at n 13.

[30] See, eg, R Littlejohn, 'Nothing Less than a Coup is Taking Place in Britain …' *Daily Mail* (26 May 2023), available at www.dailymail.co.uk/debate/article-12129859/RICHARD-LITTLEJOHN-coup-taking-place-Britain.html.

[31] Young (n 12).

[32] See, eg, the recent use of s 35 of the Scotland Act 1998 by the UK central Government to prevent the Gender Recognition Reform (Scotland) Bill passed by the Scottish Parliament from receiving Royal Assent: P Walker and L Brooks, 'Court Battle Looms as UK Ministers Block Scottish Gender Recognition Law' *The Guardian* (17 January 2023), available at www.theguardian.com/uk-news/2023/jan/17/uk-government-formally-blocks-scotlands-gender-recognition-legislation.

[33] R Ekins and G Verdirame, 'The Ministerial Code and the Rule of Law' (*UK Constitutional Law Blog*, 6th November 2015), available at https://ukconstitutionallaw.org/.

This tendency was particularly evident in the approach to constitutional issues adopted by Boris Johnson's Government between 2019 and 2022, as discussed further below in section III. But it has also resonated to some degree beyond party political circles, and helped to generate a sense of constitutional malaise within certain sectors of British political opinion – in particular among the political right, broadly defined.

Having said that, the constitutional status quo also attracts passionate support. Its thicker content is widely viewed as playing an important role in: (i) ensuring that government is held to account; (ii) protecting fundamental rights; (iii) improving the quality and transparency of public decision-making; (iv) regulating the conduct of ministers; (v) and ensuring compliance with basic rule of law norms.[34] More generally, it gives effect to the mainstream liberal constitutionalist view that a structural system of checks and balances should be imposed on the exercise of public power, including a comprehensive framework of legal controls, so as to reduce the possibility of such power being abused – a view which retains a firm grip on both the political and legal imagination in the UK as elsewhere.[35] This thickening process is closely bound up with particular constitutional design projects, which attract plenty of both expert-elite and popular support – including the establishment of devolved governance, the embedding of human rights protection into domestic law, and the attempt to regulate ministerial conduct in office.[36]

All this helps to explain why attempts to roll back elements of thicker constitutionalism have attracted plenty of resistance, as detailed further below in section III. Defenders of the status quo have been quick to highlight the problematic elements of any proposed reforms, including their potential risk in terms of unintended consequences, futility, collateral damage and so on.[37] But they have also appealed to ideas of constitutional fidelity – arguing that the thicker elements of the status quo reflect and reinforce core constitutional commitments, especially principles such as respect for rule of law and fundamental rights.[38] By extension, attempts to roll back the status quo get framed as a form of norm-corroding populism. Politicians supporting reform are often accused of pushing a simplistic, partial and distorted narrative about democratic representation, while disregarding the importance of rule of law and other constitutional controls on the exercise of public power.[39] In other words, a counter-narrative has been generated, in response to claims that the status quo is out of alignment with first principles – with constitutional fidelity thus defined in terms of fidelity to the status quo.

[34] See, eg, A Young, 'The Relationship between Parliament, the Executive and the Judiciary' in J Jowell and C O'Cinneide (eds), *The Changing Constitution*, 9th edn (Oxford University Press, 2019), 325–57.

[35] For a critique of such mainstream liberal constitutionalism, see M Loughlin, *Against Constitutionalism* (Harvard University Press, 2022).

[36] See, eg, C O'Cinneide, 'Human Rights and the UK Constitution' in Jowell and O'Cinneide (n 34) 58–93; M Elliott, 'Parliamentary Sovereignty in a Changing Constitutional Landscape' in Jowell and O'Cinneide, ibid 29–57, and further chapters in Parts I–III more generally.

[37] Mark Tushnet on Facebook has made the provocative point that constitutional status quo defenders often deploy arguments that resemble the categories of 'reactionary' narrative sketched out in A Hirschman, *The Rhetoric of Reaction* (Harvard University Press, 1991), available at www.facebook.com/mark.tushnet/posts/pfbid02tZzNuvDY9JeXf1tqECiSKd83wAEnTwXvg7Ct9iAbDZUHyR9xDBjL5sC1zARDzkapl.

[38] The HRA, for example, has been defended on the basis that it both helps to protect rights and also ensures better compliance with the UK's international treaty obligations arising under the ECHR: see O'Cinneide (n 36).

[39] See, eg, Blick (n 12).

Now, in outlining this dichotomy, it is worth noting that plenty of political and legal actors are not irrevocably committed to one camp or the other.[40] Also, given the inherent flexibility of the UK's uncodified constitutional order, one person's constitutional rebalancing project is another person's return to orthodoxy. Critics of the constitutional thickening of the last few decades often claim to be attempting to restore UK public law to its proper and authentic operating conditions, rather than being engaged in a project of constitutional revision as such – with many of those critics viewing the thickening of the UK constitutional order as the product of an unhealthy ideological attachment to liberal rationalism, which they consider to be inherently difficult to reconcile with its underlying normative orientation.[41] Similarly, many defenders of the status quo see themselves as promoting adherence to core rule of law and separation of powers values, which have become embedded within the framework of UK public law through a slow process of incremental constitutional transformation[42] – and thus, when responding to the type of critique advanced by the JPP or Lord Sumption, claim to be advocating fidelity to the established rules of the constitutional game. However, in general, the critic/defender dichotomy outlined here arguably be viewed as representing the complementary magnetic poles of current UK constitutional debates.[43]

Given the tension generated by these two poles, it is unsurprising that UK constitutional debate has become so divisive and unsettled over recent years. Allegiance to first principles seem to be on the line, along with fundamental issues of constitutional fidelity. But, given the passion stirred up by this antagonism, it is also unsurprising that this constitutional unsettlement has not been easily resolved, one way or the other. To properly grasp the underlying dynamics of this process, we need to examine its impact on both the political and judicial branches of the state – focusing initially on the active embrace by the Boris Johnson Government of 2019–22 of a constitutional rebalancing agenda.

III. FIDELITY AND REBALANCING IN THE CONSTITUTIONAL REFORM AGENDA OF THE JOHNSON AND SUNAK GOVERNMENTS

When Boris Johnson took over as Prime Minister in 2019, and subsequently prevailed in the December 2019 general election on the platform of 'Get Brexit Done', it seemed as if the way was open for a substantive programme of constitutional reform to be implemented. The Government had a big majority in the House of Commons; right-wing discontent with the state of the constitution had reached an elevated pitch in the aftermath of the Government's defeat in *Miller (No 2)*; the process of Brexit was complete; and the Conservative Party's 2019 general election manifesto had undertaken to 'look at the

[40] See further section III below.

[41] G Gee and G Webber, 'Rationalism in Public Law' (2013) 76(4) *MLR* 708–34. See also the essays in Johnson and Zhu (n 21).

[42] J Murkens, 'Preservative or Transformative? Theorizing the U.K. Constitution Using Comparative Method' (2020) 68(2) *American Journal of Comparative Law* 412–40.

[43] For a perceptive analysis of analogous dynamics elsewhere, see P Blokker, 'Populist Counter-Constitutionalism, Conservatism, and Legal Fundamentalism' (2019) 15(3) *European Constitutional Law Review* 519–43.

broader aspects of our constitution' and update UK human rights and administrative law with a view to restoring 'trust in our institutions and in how our democracy operates'.[44] Constitutional rebalancing reflecting the views of the JPP and other critics of the status quo thus appeared to be inevitable.

It was thus unsurprising when senior ministers began to call for a substantive recalibration of the constitutional relationship between law and politics, using the language of constitutional fidelity. For example, Robert Buckland MP, the then Lord Chancellor and Secretary of State for Justice, stated in 2021 that the Government was 'attempting to return to the political constitution model that was the orthodoxy for much of the 20th century'.[45] Particular criticism was directed at the HRA, as well as recent judicial review judgments which had further thickened the framework of administrative law controls on government action – such as the 'ouster clause' judgments of *Evans* and *Privacy International*, which have been subject to sustained critical attack by JPP commentators and others on the basis that they involved judicial reading down of the clearly expressed will of Parliament.[46] Consultation papers reflecting this rebalancing agenda were subsequently published in respect of judicial review and human rights law,[47] independent expert review bodies were established to assess the case for reform,[48] and government rhetoric was ramped up on the need for a rebalancing of the relationship between the executive, legislative and judicial branches. Concrete legislative proposals followed soon afterwards, in the form of the bill that became the Judicial Review and Courts Act 2022 and the ultimately ill-fated proposal to replace the HRA with a new Bill of Rights.

All this followed on from the deployment of similar rhetoric in the wake of the two *Miller* judgments.[49] It also echoed how Brexit itself had been framed as a project of constitutional restoration, as discussed above, as well as the harsh criticism directed by previous Conservative prime ministers against both the HRA and ECtHR.[50] However, the Johnson Government was the first of the post-2010 Conservative administrations which set out to achieve wholescale constitutional rebalancing. By 2002, the Prime Minister was claiming that this programme of constitutional rebalancing constituted a key element of his administration's post-Brexit policy agenda.[51]

The Johnson Government also broke new ground in extending its constitutional reclamation project beyond the specific issues surrounding the scope of judicial authority.

[44] Conservative & Unionist Party Manifesto 2019, *Get Brexit Done: Unleash Britain's Potential*, 48.

[45] See R Buckland, 'Judicial Review and the Rule of Law', speech delivered to the UCL Constitutional Unity 2021 Conference, 17 June 2021, available at www.gov.uk/government/speeches/lord-chancellor-speaks-at-ucl-conference-on-the-constitution, citing a blogpost written by the author of this chapter.

[46] See, eg, S Braverman, 'Accountability and the Constitution', speech delivered to the 2021 Public Law Project Conference, 19 October 2021, available at www.gov.uk/government/speeches/judicial-review-trends-and-forecasts-2021-accountability-and-the-constitution.

[47] Ministry of Justice, *Judicial Review Reform: The Government Response to the Independent Review of Administrative Law*, March 2021, CP 408; Ministry of Justice, *Human Rights Act Reform: A Modern Bill of Rights*, December 2021, CP 588.

[48] The Independent Review of Administrative Law and the Independent Human Rights Act Review, whose proceedings and final reports are available at www.gov.uk/government/groups/independent-review-of-administrative-law and www.gov.uk/guidance/independent-human-rights-act-review respectively.

[49] Braverman (n 46).

[50] O'Cinneide (n 36).

[51] A Forsyth, 'Boris Johnson "Actively Thinking About" Third Term as PM' (*BBC News*, 25 June 2022, available at www.bbc.com/news/uk-politics-61939938.

In the first few months of Johnson's time in power, government ministers were quick to criticise the actions of the Commons majority in passing the European Union (Withdrawal) (No 2) Act 2019 (aka the 'Benn Act'), which restricted the Government's ability to exit the EU on a 'no deal' basis: this allegedly broke with established constitutional practice by tying the hands of the Government on a matter of important national policy instead of denying it confidence, and thus disregarded the established division of roles between the executive and legislature that had historically underpinned the functioning of Westminster-style democracy.[52] After the 2019 general election, ministers also began to push back against what they saw as attempts to juridify the Ministerial Code and other soft law instruments designed to regulate their conduct, emphasising the overriding importance of political accountability in this context.[53] Similarly, the functioning of the devolution settlement began to be the subject of controversy, with ministers challenging assumptions about the desirability of maximising the scope of authority and competency of the devolved institutions.[54]

Once again the concept of constitution rebalancing, of a return to allegedly more authentic modes of public governance, underpinned all these distinct points of contention. As with its push to reform judicial review and the HRA, the Johnson Government was claiming to be acting with fidelity to the deep structure of the constitutional order – specifically to the basic DNA of the UK's political constitution, founded upon the concept of the Crown-in-Parliament. In contrast, the legal and political thickening of the constitutional order in its different facets, including non-judicial elements such as ministerial conduct codes, was increasingly framed as representing an artificial, abstract and alien understanding of separation of powers.[55]

The fidelity framing of the Government's constitutional reform package is reflected in the highly unorthodox 'introductory clause' contained in Clause 1 of the Bill of Rights Bill, as originally introduced into Parliament in 2021. The key passage reads as follows:

> 1(2) In particular, this Act clarifies and re-balances the relationship between courts in the United Kingdom, the European Court of Human Rights and Parliament by ensuring …
>
> (c) that courts must give the greatest possible weight to the principle that, in a Parliamentary democracy, decisions about the balance between different policy aims, different Convention rights and Convention rights of different persons are properly made by Parliament …

In other words, the purpose of the proposed new Bill of Rights was framed explicitly as an exercise in constitutional rebalancing – a rectification of the legal status quo, to

[52] J Rees-Mogg MP, then Leader of the House of Commons, described the Benn Act as 'constitutionally irregular': HC Deb 3 September 2019, vol 664, col 90.

[53] See the revisions to the Ministerial Code and the Terms of Reference of the Independent Adviser on Ministers' Interests announced in May 2022: Cabinet Office, *Statement of Government Policy: Standards in Public Life*, 27 May 2022, available at www.gov.uk/government/publications/revisions-to-the-ministerial-code-and-the-role-of-the-independent-adviser-on-ministers-interests/statement-of-government-policy-standards-in-public-life.

[54] See the analysis of the difference between pre-2019 'plain vanilla unionism' and the 'muscular unionism' of the Johnson Government in I MacLean, 'Can Muscular Unionism Save the Union?' (*Constitution Unit Blog*, 3 November 2023), available at https://constitution-unit.com/2022/11/03/can-muscular-unionism-save-the-union/.

[55] This was sometimes blamed on evil influences emanating from continental Europe: See Lord Frost's comments to the Public Administration and Constitutional Affairs Committee of the House of Commons, 7 June 2022, Qs 79–81.

ensure it better aligns with the core identitarian features of a 'Parliamentary democracy' (note the capitalisation).[56]

However, ambition failed to reflect reality. The Johnson Government's constitutional rebalancing project quickly ran into difficulties. To start with, it soon became clear that different views existed within the Conservative party as to how far this rebalancing process should go. Robert Buckland MP, who as Secretary of State for Justice had initially taken a lead role in pushing for reform of judicial review and the HRA, soon showed a preference for achieving incremental and targeted reforms rather than trying to pull down big chunks of the existing constitutional structure. Thus, the Judicial Review and Courts Act 2022 which he piloted through Parliament achieved the symbolically important objective of reversing the *Cart* judgment of the Supreme Court[57] and insulating decisions of the Upper Tribunal from further review by the senior appellate courts[58] – thereby in effect imposing an ouster clause, and asserting the final authority of Parliament over the courts. However, his reluctance to more fully embrace the wider reclamation narrative appeared to cost him his job, when he was replaced by Dominic Raab MP as Justice Secretary in September 2021. Raab then proceeded to try and replace the HRA with his own Bill of Rights scheme, of which Buckland was critical.[59] This doomed project was rather quixotic from its inception, due to the UK's commitment to remain a good faith member of the ECHR.[60] But this switch in direction and personnel also exposed clear divisions of opinion within the Conservative party as to how much constitutional reconstruction was desirable.

Furthermore, external opposition proved to be serious and sustained. Defenders of the status quo rallied around the thicker elements of the constitutional order that had come under attack, and started to accuse the Government of disrespecting constitutional fundamentals and indulging in crude populism across much of its policy agenda.[61] Ministers were alleged to have arrogated too much power to themselves;[62] failed to show sufficient respect for parliamentary scrutiny procedures;[63] disregarded constitutional conventions related to ministerial responsibility and ethical conduct;[64] disrespected the Sewel Convention and other constitutional conventions relating to devolution;[65] and failed to comply with international law commitments and thus undermined respect for rule of law.[66]

[56] See also Dominic Raab's criticisms of human rights 'mission creep' in his statement introducing the Bill: HC Deb 22 June 2022, vol 716, cols 42–44.

[57] *Cart v The Upper Tribunal* [2011] UKSC 28 (21 June 2011).

[58] Judicial Review and Courts Act 2022, s 2.

[59] C Baksi, 'Bill Blasted as a Blow to Human Rights' *The Times* (24 November 2022), available at www.thetimes.co.uk/article/bill-blasted-as-a-blow-to-human-rights-7rg6c76nz.

[60] C O'Cinneide, 'Having its (Strasbourg) Cake, and Eating It: The UK Government's Proposals for a New "Bill of Rights"' (*Völkerrechtsblog*, 26 January 2022), available at https://voelkerrechtsblog.org/having-its-strasbourg-cake-and-eating-it/.

[61] P Hennessy, *The Bonfire of Decencies* (Haus, 2022).

[62] House of Lords Constitutional Committee, *Brexit Legislation: Constitutional Issues*, 6th Report of Session 2019–21, 9 June 2000, HL Paper 71.

[63] See, eg, D Lock, 'Three Ways the Bill of Rights Bill Undermines UK Sovereignty' (*UK Constitutional Law Blog*, 27 June 2022), available at https://ukconstitutionallaw.org/.

[64] R Brazier, 'Contempt for the Constitution?' (*UK Constitutional Law Blog*, 6 October 2020), available at https://ukconstitutionallaw.org/.

[65] Scottish Government, *After Brexit: The UK Internal Market Act and Devolution*, Parts IV & V, 8 March 2021, available at www.gov.scot/publications/brexit-uk-internal-market-act-devolution/pages/5/.

[66] J Rozenberg, 'Johnson's Disrespect for the Law' (*The Critic*, August/September 2022), available at https://thecritic.co.uk/issues/august-september-2022/johnsons-disrespect-for-the-law/.

These attacks seem to have helped undermine the Johnson Government. In particular, accusations that Boris Johnson had misled Parliament played a key role in crystallising political opposition to his rule, both within and outside the Tory Party, and helped to bring about his resignation in July 2022. This resulted in his Government's constitutional reform project grinding to a halt. Both his successors – the soon to be deposed Liz Truss MP and the seemingly more pragmatic Rishi Sunak MP – showed much less enthusiasm for wholescale constitutional reform.[67]

However, in line with the dynamic outlined in section II, discontent with the thicker elements of the constitutional status quo remained strong. Sunak's Government started to chip away at the scope of the HRA, narrowing its impact through a number of incremental, issue-specific legislative provisions.[68] Senior ministers continued to hammer away at what they see as the constitutionally disreputable nature of the UK's relationship with the ECtHR. And the UK Government adopted a more confrontational approach to Scottish devolved legislation which it viewed as intruding into reserved areas of competence.[69] Constitutional unsettlement persisted, and continues to do so at the time of writing (just before the July 2024 general election).

IV. FIDELITY AND REBALANCING IN CONSTITUTIONAL JURISPRUDENCE: THE UK SUPREME COURT'S 'RECLAMATION PROJECT'

Such unsettlement inevitably shines a spotlight on relevant doctrinal issues. Courts are effectively required to respond to this turbulence, if only by how they interpret and apply relevant public law norms. And, given the accusations of constitutional infidelity that have been flying around over the last few years, it is noteworthy that the upper courts of the UK, and in particular the Supreme Court, seem to have embarked on their own specific project of constitutional rebalancing. Since Lord Reed assumed the Presidency of the Supreme Court in 2020, the Court has shown considerable eagerness to protect the core of the political constitution, embodied in the doctrine of parliamentary sovereignty, against allegedly corrupting influences such as the threat of excessive juridification. In so doing, it has deviated sharply from some elements of its former jurisprudence – justifying this divergence by the need to maintain fidelity with constitutional first principles.

Thus, in a number of recent judgments, notable for their unanimity, the Court has reined in elements of the HRA case law which in its view encroached too far upon legislative authority. Specifically, in *SC*,[70] the Court concluded that legislation in the social welfare field would be afforded extensive and even perhaps overriding deference, even in the context of Article 14 sex discrimination challenges – effectively departing from the approach it had previously taken, with different personnel, in similar cases,[71] rowing back

[67] Alison Young described the Sunak Government as adopting a 'pragmatically populist' approach to constitutional issues: A Young, 'The Queen's Speech – Another Example of Pragmatic Populism' (*UK in a Changing Europe*, 17 May 2022), available at https://ukandeu.ac.uk/the-queens-speech-another-example-of-pragmatic-populism/.

[68] S Wallace, 'Death by a Thousand Cuts: The Human Rights Act' (*UK Constitution Society Blog*,), available at https://consoc.org.uk/death-by-a-thousand-cuts/.

[69] See the recent use of s 35 of the Scotland Act 1998, referred to in n 32.

[70] *R (SC) v Secretary of State for Work and Pensions* [2021] UKSC 26.

[71] *cf* eg *Mathieson v Secretary of State for Work and Pensions* [2015] UKSC 47.

on some of its own previous case law. In *AB*[72] and *Elan-Cane*,[73] the Court made it clear that domestic courts should not interpret ECHR rights as having a wider scope than indicated by the established case law of the Strasbourg Court. In *Elan-Cane*, the Court also specifically disowned Lord Hoffmann's view expressed in 2008 in *In re G* that UK courts could find a violation of Convention rights even in respect of an issue that the Strasbourg Court had concluded lay within the margin of appreciation.[74]

As individual judgments, these decisions concern specific and discrete issues of HRA interpretation. Taken collectively, they represent a significant narrowing of the scope of the judicial role under the HRA. This has attracted both praise and criticism.[75] However, for the purposes of this chapter, what is striking about these judgments is that they share a common rationale. In each case, the scope of HRA rights protection was interpreted narrowly, on the basis of a presumption that it was not constitutionally appropriate for judicial power to intrude upon the terrain of parliamentary decision-making – even though the HRA does not disturb Parliament's power to have the 'final say' over any human rights matter, and no court is given the power to suspend the operation of an Act of Parliament. This specific interpretation of the doctrine of parliamentary sovereignty – understood not just as a 'who decides' rule, but rather as a general protective shield for the political process insofar as it is channelled through the legislature – is now treated by the Court as foundational to the UK's constitutional order. Furthermore, case law that deviates from it is purged accordingly.

Thus, in *Elan-Cane*, the Supreme Court took the view that, if the HRA were interpreted as permitting UK courts to make findings of a breach of Convention rights when the Strasbourg Court would not have done so, this would 'represent a substantial expansion of the constitutional powers of the judiciary at the expense of Parliament', and 'undermine the constitutional principle of Parliamentary sovereignty'.[76] As a consequence, the Court concluded that Parliament was unlikely to have intended such an 'encroachment upon Parliamentary sovereignty'.[77] In so deciding, the Court dismissed the argument that *Rights Brought Home*, the White Paper that preceded the Act, had seemed to envisage that UK courts would have this power by noting that '[i]n future, our judges will be able to contribute to this dynamic and evolving interpretation of the Convention'.[78] It also effectively overruled dicta in *Nicklinson* and other cases that seemed to suggest an alternative view,[79] and did not engage in any depth with some of the concerns expressed by judges and academics that confining the scope of HRA rights protection within the bounds of existing ECHR case law would make the UK courts mere 'underwriters' of the Strasbourg Court.[80] Instead, what might be described as

[72] *R (AB) v Secretary of State for Justice* [2021] UKSC 282.

[73] *R (Elan-Cane) v Secretary of State for the Home Department* [2021] UKSC 56.

[74] *In re G (Adoption: Unmarried Couples)* [2008] UKHL 38.

[75] See the exchange of views in the *London Review of Books* between Conor Gearty ('In the Shallow End', 27 January 2022) and Lord Sumption ('On the Court', 10 February 2022).

[76] *Elan-Cane* (n 73) [90]–[92] *per* Lord Reed.

[77] ibid [108].

[78] *Rights Brought Home: The Human Rights Bill*, Cm 3782 (1997), para 2.5.

[79] *Elan-Cane* (n 73) [105]–[107].

[80] See, eg, Lady Hale, '*Argentoratum Locutum*: Is Strasbourg or the Supreme Court Supreme' (2012) 12(1) *Human Rights Law Review* 65–78.

the 'presumption of non-intrusion' was applied, framed essentially as a constitutional syllogism – and contradictory case law was rectified accordingly.

A similar approach was applied in *SC*, with the Court ruling that any judicial assessment of the social welfare legislation under challenge – the controversial 'two child' benefit cap – would resolve itself 'into a question as to whether Parliament made the right choice ... a question of intense political controversy, which cannot be answered by any process of legal reasoning'.[81] In other words, the Court concluded that the 'separation of powers under our constitution' precluded British courts assessing the proportionality of a piece of welfare legislation, even when the legislation was being challenged on the basis of alleged sex discrimination – a 'suspect ground' under Article 14 ECHR.[82] In so doing, the Court effectively narrowed the approach it had applied in its previous case law, and (unconvincingly) distinguished a recent Strasbourg judgment.[83] Fidelity to parliamentary sovereignty was understood to require almost total judicial self-abnegation in this context, and the deviant tendencies of previous jurisprudence was corrected.[84]

The Supreme Court has also applied a similar approach in a number of non-HRA cases. In *UNCRC Reference*,[85] the scope of devolved powers was read down so as to prevent the Scottish Parliament requiring Scottish courts to interpret Westminster legislation in line with the UN Convention on the Rights of the Child (CRC), or even to comment on such legislation by issuing non-binding declarations of incompatibility. In *AB*, the Court confirmed that unincorporated international human rights treaties had little if any status in UK law, even as non-binding reference points, noting that any doctrinal shift in this regard could only be brought about via legislation.[86] In *Citizenship Fees*, the Court applied the principle of legality narrowly, significantly restricting the circumstances in which the courts would be prepared to apply an interpretative gloss to 'clear legislative words'.[87] Notably, Saini J in the High Court adopted a similar approach in refusing to read down the abovementioned de facto ouster clause set out in section 2 of the Judicial Review and Courts Act 2022: he emphasised that the judicial role was to give effect to the clearly expressed intention of Parliament, and previous UKSC judgments like *Evans* and *Privacy International* which suggested a contrary approach were effectively disregarded.[88]

[81] *SC* (n 70) [208].

[82] ibid [209].

[83] *JD & A v UK* App nos 32949/17 and 34614/17 (ECtHR, 24 October 2019).

[84] The Court in passing also depreciated attempts by non-governmental organisations (NGOs) to use the HRA to challenge measures they had lobbied against in Parliament, seeming to regard such tactics as also representing a questionable legal intrusion into political space – although this part of the judgment is probably best regarded as a misplaced piece of political editorialising, as it conflates the campaigning role of NGOs with their role as legal representatives for claimants. See *SC* (n 70) [162].

[85] *Reference by the Attorney General and the Advocate General for Scotland – United Nations Convention on the Rights of the Child (Incorporation) (Scotland) Bill* [2021] UKSC 42 [23]–[28], [48]–[54].

[86] *R(AB) v Secretary of State for Justice* [2021] UKSC 28.

[87] *R (O (a minor, by her litigation friend AO)) v Secretary of State for the Home Department; R (The Project for the Registration of Children as British Citizens) v Secretary of State for the Home Department* [2022] UKSC 3.

[88] *R (Oceana) v Upper Tribunal (Immigration and Asylum Chamber)* [2023] EWHC 791 (Admin). Note, referring back to section III, that Robert Buckland MP tweeted approval of this judgment: https://twitter.com/RobertBuckland/status/1643282678425309187.

Again, all these decisions are linked by a common theme – namely the need to maintain fidelity with a specific concept of parliamentary sovereignty, which assumes that the courts should (i) give effect to the presumed will of the Westminster Parliament without applying much if anything by way of an interpretative gloss, unless specifically mandated to do so by primary legislation such as the HRA and (ii) interpret and apply legal norms, including devolved legislation, in ways that shield the law-making power of the Westminster Parliament from extraneous legal influences. Throughout all these judgments, this 'radiating' take on parliamentary sovereignty has been presented in axiomatic terms, as a giving effect to a core constitutional norm – with anything casting a shadow over the authority of the Westminster Parliament treated as prima facie suspect.

Some commentary on this case law has framed this jurisprudential turn as a response to political pressure.[89] There may be some truth to that – although it is worth noting that this shift adheres closely to the considered views of at last one new member of the Court,[90] may reflect a generational shift in judicial attitudes,[91] and has a solid conceptual foundation in political constitutionalist views as to how the UK constitution should work. More generally, it is perhaps best understood as a reaction to the dynamics of constitutional unsettlement discussed here. At a time when the constitutional order has become the subject of fraught debate, there is an obvious attraction in attempting to identify constitutional first principles and to try to build a jurisprudence around that core framework – while clearing away deviant case law that does not sit comfortably with it. And, for the current Supreme Court, parliamentary sovereignty seems to fit that bill. Thus the Court has embarked on its own particular rebalancing project, adjusting existing case law and legal norms to conform to what it considers to be the authentic core of the UK constitutional order.

Space prevents detailed discussion of this judicially-driven doctrinal turn – which is in any case still a work in progress. It remains to be seen how radical the Supreme Court's 'reclamation project' will prove to be, and how it might differ in focus from the form of rebalancing advocated by the JPP and others.[92] However, it is worth noting that this project is controversial. The specific understanding of parliamentary sovereignty that underpins the Court's new direction is obviously difficult to reconcile with plenty of previous case law, including some very recent judgments of the Court.[93] As with any sharp change in judicial trajectory, this raises issues as to the legitimacy of such an abrupt about turn and the judicial politics that underpin it.[94] The approach to parliamentary sovereignty adopted by the Court also differs from how the doctrine has been conventionally

[89] See, eg, All-Party Parliamentary Group (APPG) on Democracy and the Constitution, *An Independent Judiciary – Challenges Since 2016* (8 June 2022).

[90] G Tan, 'Children's Rights and the Influence of Lord Sales in the UKSC's Political Constitutionalist Turn' (2022) 26(1) *Edinburgh Law Review* 93–100.

[91] See Lord Sumption (n 75).

[92] The 'radiating' impact of parliamentary sovereignty was in essence first recognised in *Miller No 2*, and deployed to limit the permissive scope of the executive prerogative power to prorogue Parliament – a judgment which attracted much excitable criticism from JPP commentators.

[93] *cf* eg the judgments of Lady Hale and Lord Kerr in *In the Matter of an Application by the Northern Ireland Human Rights Commission for Judicial Review* [2018] UKSC 27 (the '*NIHRC* judgment'), in particular the views expressed by Lady Hale at [37]–[40].

[94] See, eg, C Murphy, 'Human Rights Advocacy after *AB* and the Supreme Court's "Conservative Approach"' [2021] 5 *European Human Rights Law Review* 465–75.

understood by many legal scholars and commentators, who have generally not viewed it as having a wider radiating effect of the sort the Court endorses in cases such as *SC* and *UNCRC Reference*.[95] Alternative understandings of the normative underpinnings of the constitutional order exist – in particular those that emphasise the role of the judiciary as a protector of important fundamental values such as rights and rule of law, and view the separation of powers system (including the role of the devolved institutions) as collaborative rather than hierarchical.[96] Concerns also exist as to whether the Court's approach is reconcilable with the internal logic of the devolution settlement.[97] These perspectives are currently sidelined in the Court's jurisprudence. It remains to be seen how much dissent this will generate going forward, and how settled the Court's current understanding of what constitutional fidelity requires will prove to be. But, for now, it is worth noting that its recent doctrinal turn has interesting echoes of wider constitutional debates.

V. FIDELITY AND CONSTITUTIONAL CHANGE: 'YOU CAN'T GO HOME AGAIN'

So, to recapitulate, it is possible to identify a pattern – a thematic structure – in current UK constitutional debates. Various rebalancing projects are underway, which set out to restore fidelity to particular political constitutionalist understandings of how the constitution should work. These projects are framed as involving a return to the authentic underpinning values and identity of the UK constitutional order. However, alternative takes exist as to what constitutional fidelity actually requires. This results in a clash of values, which in turn fuel constitutional unsettlement.

A. What to Make of this Clash? What Does it Tell Us about UK Constitutionalism, and How it has Developed Over Time?

First of all, it is worth noting that these debates about fidelity and change are explicitly playing out in a constitutional register. They are framed as first order conflicts about what adherence to abstract constitutional values entails – in interesting contrast to how similar issues tended to be analysed and debated in the past, which often involved greater focus on the concrete points of contestation at issue and the particular legal, political and material context in which they were embedded.[98]

Furthermore, the appeal to authenticity, to the idea that the UK has a stable, fixed constitutional core underpinning the quotidian flux of law and politics, is striking. John Griffith's famous dictum, that the British constitution 'is no more and no less than what happens', referenced in passing in the Introduction, now seems outmoded – if it is taken

[95] Elliott (n 36).

[96] See, eg, A Kavanagh, 'Recasting the Political Constitution: From Rivals to Relationships' (2019) 30(1) *King's Law Journal* 43–73.

[97] A McHarg, 'Giving Substance to Sovereignty: Parliamentary Sovereignty and Parliamentary Effectiveness' in B Dickson and C McCormick (eds), *In The Judicial Mind: A Festschrift for Lord Kerr of Tonaghmore* (Bloomsbury, 2021) 203–22.

[98] A point developed to good effect in M Loughlin, 'What Would John Griffith Have Made of Jonathan Sumption's Reith Lectures?' (2019) 90(4) *Political Quarterly* 785–93.

as a description of the attitude of key actors. Even political constitutionalists who invoke Griffith's work with enthusiasm now like to claim their views reflect the deep order of the UK's unwritten framework – thereby producing a narrative of constitutional authenticity that resembles a strange mirror image of the competing claims put forward by their 'legal constitutionalist' antagonists.[99]

It is interesting to speculate why this turn to constitutionalism, as channelled through claims of fidelity and authenticity, has happened. Expanding expectations as to what constitutions should do; an erosion of expert-elite consensus about how the UK should be governed; the challenges of co-ordinating governance between Westminster and the devolved regions; the increasing salience of international law and the challenges it poses for national sovereignty; growing inter-institutional tension across the legislative/executive/judicial axes; greater political divisiveness – all arguably play a role. Constitutional 'steering', whether political, legal or a combination of both, has become necessary. Hence the search for the ultimate, authentic rules of the game, in the hope that they can provide a fixed framework for resolving these increasingly vexed issues.

However, all these current debates suggest that there is ample raw material within the UK's constitutional sandbox from which to construct competing accounts of its 'true' essence. For example, both critics and defenders of the constitutional status quo can dredge up creditable arguments in favour of their respective positions – as demonstrated by the divergences in respectable academic opinion on these issues.[100] Similarly, the current Supreme Court does a good job in producing plausible opinions setting out its specific take on parliamentary sovereignty as the governing principle of UK separation of powers – but so too did the majority of the Supreme Court when it adopted a radically different position only four years ago.[101]

Certain claims are inevitably more creditable than others, in the sense that they better fit established legal norms and prevailing understanding about how the constitution works. But this leaves plenty of room for competing claims of authenticity. As Martin Loughlin has argued, 'the British constitution is not a "thing" to be discovered so much as a battleground in which material interests are fought out through abstract ideas'.[102] Furthermore, many of these claims of authenticity are overplayed, or rest on a very dubious basis – even allowing for the tenuous nature of constitutional authority claims more generally.

This is a problem that afflicts both sides in current constitutional debates. For example, many defenders of the status quo exaggerate the degree to which their fidelity claims rest on a solid bedrock of established principle. The status of the Ministerial Code has always been ambivalent; devolution is necessarily a moveable feast; views legitimately differ as to what respect for rule of law entails; and certain aspects of judicial review and human rights law are clearly vulnerable to claims of over-stretch.[103] More generally,

[99] ibid. But see also eg Martin Loughlin's trenchant critique of the *Miller No 2* judgment, which ultimately slips into the questionable form of a 'fidelity/authenticity' claim as analysed here: M Loughlin, *The Case of Prorogation* (Policy Exchange, 2019).

[100] See the academic commentary cited in section II.

[101] See, eg, the *NIHRC* judgment (n 93).

[102] M Loughlin, 'In Search of the Constitution', *LSE Legal Studies Working Paper No. 19/2019*, 9 December, 201, available at https://ssrn.com/abstract=3501014.

[103] See, eg, Jason Varuhas's critique of how certain aspects of the 'principle of legality' have been over-extended: J Varuhas, 'The Principle of Legality' (2020) 79(3) *Cambridge Law Journal* 578–614.

much of the post-1997 constitutional landscape, and the norms and expectations associated with it, has always been contested – and elected politicians are entitled to challenge the status quo, and push back against alleged judicial over-reach and other forms of constitutional thickening.[104] The tendency of status quo defenders to tar proponents of constitutional change with the 'populist' tag is very questionable – as is the tendency of many legal commentators to be sweepingly dismissive of the views of the JPP and other critics of thickened constitutionalism.

However, similar criticisms can be directed at the other side of the fence. The JPP and its political interlocutors overstate the extent to which there ever was a prelapsarian 'political constitutionalist' consensus aligned with its position. The assumption that political power should be exercised with restraint, and that judges had some role to play in refereeing the fairness of its exercise, has been a persisting part of the framework of norms and expectations that have shaped UK constitutional governance over the years.[105] The emergence of modern judicial review in the 1960s did not originate in a vacuum – and any serious description of the 'good old days' of political constitutionalism would need to factor in the presence of multiple constraining factors that limited the exercise of political authority back then.[106]

Furthermore, the UK constitutional order has evolved over the last few decades. Devolution is a reality, approved by popular referendums. Fidelity to voluntarily (necessarily?) assumed international law commitments inevitably requires some dilution of state sovereignty – particularly in respect of rights protective instruments such as the ECHR, which have come to play an important authority-legitimating function in Northern Ireland and elsewhere. Separation of powers dynamics have evolved over time, not least along the executive/legislature axis.[107] The corrosion of elite consensus about how the UK should be governed, and the fracturing of traditional deferential relationships between the governed and the governors, also need to borne in mind if one is tempted to assume that there is a past form of public governance that somehow represents the 'true' or 'authentic' mode of UK constitutionalism.[108]

All of this makes it difficult to argue the case for some sort of originalist-style analysis, which insists for example that the political constitution of the post-1945 period represents the authentic mode of UK constitutional governance. Plenty of water has flowed under the bridge since then, and the UK has experimented and continues to experiment with different modes of 'Parliamentary democracy' (to revert to the phrase used in section 1 of the Bill of Rights Bill). Claims that constitutional fidelity necessarily requires a return to the past should be resisted – not least because it cuts against the grain of that strand of UK political constitutionalist thought that has always viewed legal and political governance as a perpetual project in flux, ripe for reflexive revision and change going forward,

[104] A point made very well in B Bugaric and M Tushnet, *Power to the People* (Oxford University Press, 2022).

[105] See, eg, the context provided by the essays contained in T Arvind et al (eds), *Executive Decision-Making and the Courts: Revisiting the Origins of Modern Judicial Review* (Hart Publishing, 2021).

[106] See the point about trade union power made at n 19.

[107] Note that even leading JPP commentators are often quick to cite changing patterns of public governance in support of shifts in constitutional norms of which they approve: see, eg, S Laws, *The Future for Constitutional Reform* (Policy Exchange, 2020).

[108] See the excellent discussion on this point by P Scott, 'Faith in Authority and the (Political) Constitution' (2019) 30(1) *King's Law Journal* 21–42.

rather than being stuck in a backwards-facing, small-c conservative orientation.[109] As Mark Elliott puts it, the UK constitution 'supplies neither a decisive statement of the periphery of what is constitutionally legitimate nor a roadmap for determining what should happen in the event of the transgression of any such boundary'.[110]

None of this precludes critics of the status quo advocating reforms that hearken back to old practices and institutional modes of ordering. However, in the UK context, such changes should be fought for and justified on their appropriateness in current conditions, or on the basis of their fit with what Jonathan Crowe describes as the functions and purposes that contemporary constitutional governance is expected to discharge.[111] In contrast, claims that the UK constitutional governance must necessarily remain faithful to historic modes of constitutional design – whether put forward by critics or defenders of the status quo – are highly questionable. They ascribe a solidity, embeddedness and inflexibility to the UK constitutional order that is largely a myth.[112]

Similar objections can be made to the Supreme Court's recent rebalancing project, based as it is around a particular take on parliamentary sovereignty. As discussed in section IV, this take does not have a clear basis in existing precedent or a clearly established constitutional consensus. In particular, the idea that any form of 'intrusion' upon the legislative function of the Westminster Parliament is inherently problematic, as mapped out in judgments like *SC* and *UNCRC Reference*, arguably lacks a solid foundation in pre-existing case law or doctrine.[113]

This is not to dismiss the Court's reasoning out of hand. It may be the case that such doctrinal developments can be normatively justified, or framed as a 'best fit' with conventional contemporary understandings of how the UK constitution works. However, the Court's axiomatic reasoning in this respect, which treats these conclusions as necessarily mandated by the UK's historically established model of separation of powers, is very questionable. Furthermore, the Court's reasoning also risks eliding the normative choices that may be underpinning its decisions, and their practical impact on separation of powers and accountability mechanisms.[114] The Court appears to assume that its preferred take on parliamentary sovereignty flows naturally from a commitment to fixed, embedded and settled constitutionalist norms. However, where the Court sees authenticity and fidelity, others may see artifice and inconstancy.

VI. CONCLUSION

In general, recent UK constitutional debates have featured plenty of appeals to the notion of constitutional fidelity, and demands for political and legal actors to conform to

[109] M Goldoni and C McCorkindale, 'Three Waves of Political Constitutionalism' (2019) 30(1) *King's Law Journal* 74–96.

[110] Elliott (n 36) 54–55.

[111] J Crowe, 'Functions, Context and Constitutional Values' in R Dixon (ed), *Australian Constitutional Values* (Hart Publishing, 2018) 61–73.

[112] M Gordon, 'Parliamentary Sovereignty and the Political Constitution(s): From Griffith to Brexit' (2019) 30(1) *King's Law Journal* 125–47.

[113] McHarg (n 97).

[114] Gearty (n 75).

allegedly fixed and settled norms. However, such appeals often hearken back to an imagined past – a prelapsarian era of settled constitutional bedrock, which never existed.[115] It is tempting to fetishise particular constitutional approaches, and frame them as part of the identitarian core of the UK constitutional order – especially in the current period of constitutional unsettlement. However, this temptation should be resisted. There is obviously a need to take account of past practices, which provide a key reference point for current interpretative debates.[116] However, the UK's unwritten constitution is ultimately committed to interpretative openness, change and flexibility – as distinct from fixed fidelity to a pre-existing set of standards. And this approach has much to commend it.[117]

As such, it should be borne in mind that authenticity claims may obscure the reality that contemporary constitutional debates are really about the present and future – and that there is no fixed and settled constitutional 'home' to return to. Furthermore, this should encourage a certain degree of modesty in such debates, and a greater concern with incrementalism, compromise and nuance on all sides. Heated allegations of constitutional heresy are misplaced when there is no pre-established true faith to betray.

[115] M Hickford, 'Historicity and the Political Constitution' (2019) 30(1) *King's Law Journal* 97–124.

[116] See in this regard Ming-Sung Kuo's nuanced analysis of the unavoidable centrality of the 'transtemporal concept of constitutional authorship' to any form of constitutional interpretation: 'Cutting the Gordian Knot of Legitimacy Theory?' (2009) 7(4) *International Journal of Constitutional Law* 683–714.

[117] Note John Gardner's argument that this may well be true of all constitutions: 'Can there be a Written Constitution?' (2011) *Oxford Studies in Philosophy of Law* 162–94.

18

Public Faces: Indigenous Law Today and Through the Futuristic Looking Glass

VAL NAPOLEON*

Many of the starting points for understanding Indigenous law are laden with colonial interventions and yet, as a process of rebuilding and self-determination, Indigenous law research seeks Indigenous self-understandings that are not (or are not overly) coloured by that colonial history.[1]

I. INTRODUCTION

HISTORICALLY, INDIGENOUS SOCIETIES in Canada and the world over were complete with legal, political, social and economic ordering. My basic argument is that while many or even most of these Indigenous societies were non-state, it stands to reason that the decentralised structuring of authorities and the institutions through which law operated would nonetheless have had public and private dimensions in order to constitute complete legal orders.[2] When contrasting the Indigenous public-private law divide to that of Canadian state law, what is different is not that there was and is a public-private divide, but about where and why the dividing line is drawn.

Another way to think about this divide, is to simply differentiate between those things that more people must know about from those things that fewer people must know about in any given Indigenous legal order.[3] Within this approach, there will be further category divisions and variations depending on societal structures as explained below with the Gitxsan example. This 'who needs to know' perspective does have the advantage of

* I am grateful for the generous and insightful feedback received from my colleague, Dr Janna Promislow, Faculty of Law, University of Victoria.

[1] Janna Promislow, law professor, Faculty of Law, University of Victoria. Private conversation with the author (summer 2022).

[2] There is public law scholarship concerned with the emergence of the divide between public and private law in the 16th and late 17th centuries as generated by the industrial revolution, changes to the monarchy, secularisation, and the emergence of the state. See, eg, M Loughlin, *Foundations of Public Law* (Oxford University Press, 2010) ch 2.

[3] Thanks to Hoi Kong, Professor at the Peter A Allard School of Law, UBC for this suggested perspective.

avoiding the heavily politically laden private-public divide that exists within the common law discourse, and it is likely helpful to avoid importing that dichotomy into Indigenous law discussions.

Much of the scholarship about the private and public law divide in the common law occurs in the field of administrative law which according to Paul Daly is concerned with, 'the distinctively judicial public law task … [of protecting] individual rights and interests against undue encroachment in the name of social interests'.[4] However, it is important to note that without the equivalent state structuring, the law of Indigenous societies is also concerned with legitimate public purposes, the common good, and balancing individual and collective interests.[5]

There is little scholarship on the public law questions of Indigenous law except for Janna Promislow who provides a cautionary perspective for approaching the complex and developing field of Indigenous public law:

> [R]esearching a distinctive 'public law' within an Indigenous legal order already presumes several distinctions and institutions within Indigenous legal orders, which are themselves questions to consider in defining the research. In Indigenous legal orders, is there a public law that might be identified as apart from and in relation to multiple areas of community and family decision-making and dispute resolution, such as resource and territorial stewardship, care for family and community members, and property and ownership of cultural heritage and intellectual property? In other words, whether the problems and concerns addressed by (common law) public law form a distinct category or type of law within a particular Indigenous legal order is itself a question that deserves attention before the research questions are settled.[6]

While I agree with Promislow's suggestion for further thought and research into the public law questions in each Indigenous legal order, I still begin this chapter with the presumption that historic and present-day Indigenous legal orders include public law dimensions that operate according to the legalities, structures and institutions, norms, legal practices and principles of each Indigenous society across a range of subject areas. From my experience in engaging with 'Indigenous legal orders', there are common law categories that are helpful to at least begin conversations about the scope and specific areas of Indigenous law, and its practice. Not surprisingly, there are major differences between common law and Indigenous law, but these are not so much in the functions of law, but rather in the purposes of law and organisation of law, particularly with differing foundational economic purposes such as those concerning forms of property and ownership.

It is important in this conversation to consider who the legal actors are in both state legal orders and in Indigenous legal orders as a point of contrast. In states, there are often two categories of legal actor: the state (the Crown in Canada) and the individual person, who may be a natural person or a pseudo-person such as a corporation. Private law then governs issues between persons and public law governs issues between persons and the state.

[4] P Daly, 'Administrative Law: A Values-Based Approach' in J Bell, M Elliott, J Varuhas and P Murray (eds), *Public Law Adjudication in Common Law Systems: Process and Substance* (Hart Publishing, 2016) (citations omitted).

[5] See V Napoleon, 'Living Together: Gitksan Legal Reasoning as a Foundation for Consent' in J Webber and C McLeod (eds), *Challenges of Consent: Consent as the Foundation of Political Community in Indigenous/Non-Indigenous Contexts* (UBC Press, 2009).

[6] Promislow (n 1).

In Indigenous societies, such as the Gitxsan, there is generally one legal actor, which is a kinship group of one sort or another. Indigenous law seems to exclusively concern itself with coordination and conflict resolution among groups of collective agents, which always includes a public legal process to confirm its legitimacy. Usually, coordination and dispute-resolution within a collective agent group are not public and thus not recorded. For example, a Gitxsan House group will hold an in-House feast (*liliget*) to confirm an internal House decision, which decision will be carried forward to a public feast with other relevant House groups at a public feast (*yukw*).[7] The in-House feast can be considered private, and only those members of the House need to 'know' and participate in the decision-making. The public feast is where the other kinship groups then need to 'know' and need to witness and record the proceedings publicly.

My starting place is that Indigenous law must first be comprehended and seriously engaged with as law. Here I set out my working premises for Indigenous law and legal orders to provide a frame of reference for readers unfamiliar with Indigenous peoples and legal orders in Canada. I will then provide three small discussions from several Indigenous legal orders about critical aspects of Indigenous public-private law – or those things that varying numbers of people need to know. My overall purpose is to illustrate that Indigenous law is public with corresponding and differentiated public and private law functions. Further, I propose that Indigenous law's public dimension is a continuing and essential Indigenous legality across Indigenous legal orders. To a limited extent, these examples will also serve to demonstrate how Indigenous law interacts and contrasts with Canadian law.

II. WORKING PREMISE

> A legal tradition ... is a set of deeply rooted, historically conditioned attitudes about the nature of law, about the role of law in the society and the polity, about the proper organization and operation of a legal system, and about the way law is or should be made, applied, studied, perfected, and taught.[8]

The above description of a legal tradition is instructive in thinking about what comprises an Indigenous legal order as well as the common law. For example, the Dunne-za and Cree[9] legal traditions, as with other legal traditions, include all of the intellectual elements

[7] My thanks to Richard Overstall, lawyer, author and former evidence director for the Gitxsan aboriginal title case, *Delgamuukw v The Queen* (1991) 79 D.L.R. (4th) 185 (B.C.S.C.) 36; *Delgamuukw v British Columbia* (1993) 104 D.L.R. (4th) 470 (B.C.C.A.); and *Delgamuukw v British Columbia* [1997] 3 S.C.R. 1010. Private communication with author (21 November 2022).

[8] JH Merryman and R Pérez-Perdomo, *The Civil Law Tradition: An Introduction to the Legal Systems of Europe and Latin America*, 3rd edn (Stanford University Press, 2007) 2.

[9] See generally, R Ridington, *Trail to Heaven: Knowledge and Narrative in a Northern Native Community* (University of Iowa Press, 1988); R Ridington, *Little Bit Know Something: Stories in a Language of Anthropology* (Douglas & McIntyre, 1990); R Ridington and J Ridington, *When you Sing It Now, Just Like New: First Nations Poetics, Voices, and Representations* (University of Nebraska Press, 2006); and R Ridington and J Ridington, *Where Happiness Dwells: A History of the Dane-Zaa First Nations* (UBC Press, 2013). Also see H Friedland, *Cree Legal Traditions Report* (UVIC, 2014); Cree Legal Summary (A Part of the Cree Legal Traditions Report), available at www.ILRU.ca; and H Friedland, *The Wetiko Legal Principles* (University of Toronto Press, 2018).

referred to in Merryman's definition, as well as the full complex that is a legal order with implicit and explicit laws, legal relationships and authorities, remedies and sanctions, collaborative legal reasoning processes (eg, legal norms, obligations, and principles), and precedent and public legal memories (eg, forms of oral histories, and expressions of law such as songs, crests, etc). Following Merryman's lead, it is possible to conceptualise a Dunne-za or Cree (or other) legal tradition that broadly encompasses the history and attitudes about the nature of law, the ideas about the role of law in Dunne-za or Cree society and as part of governance, the proper structure and operation of the Dunne-za or Cree legal orders, and the necessary ongoing public contestation about the way law should be made, applied, studied, perfected and taught.[10]

As with other legal orders, Dunne-za or Cree legal orders require standards of legitimacy and coherence just as Canadian law does. The legitimacy and efficacy of any stable legal order requires an ongoing collective and authoritative capacity to determine the substance of law as well as its: (1) ascertainment (agreement of what law is); (2) change (when and how law is changed and why); and (3) application of law (when law is broken and determination of an appropriate legal response).[11] Added to this, Matthew Fletcher, an Indigenous tribal judge, argues that legitimacy and coherence requires that Indigenous law is accessible, understandable and applicable.[12]

From what we know of Indigenous legal orders today, historically these would have been bottom-up, horizontally structured with collaborative, public decision-making processes, and collective public memories or precedent. Within the present nation state of Canada, Indigenous peoples are organised in 11 major linguistic groups, each with numerous regional dialects. Within these larger linguistic groups, there are about 60 Indigenous societies in Canada, each with its own legal, economic, social and political ordering but which are often closely related with adjacent peoples. For example, the Nisga'a, Tsimshian and Gitxsan comprise the Tsimshian linguistic group, and their legal and political orders interrelate as necessary to maintain close societal connections. The Royal Commission on Aboriginal Peoples commented on the importance of comprehending Indigenous polities at this larger societal scale rather than at the ahistorical, but nonetheless prevailing current notion of Indigenous peoples as being solely organised in small separate, independent communities known as bands or First Nations.

Generally, the linguistic divisions reflect larger collectives, or societies, with common sets of recognised legal principles that enabled the member groups to interact with each other, through time, for resource sharing, trade, marriage and so on. For example, the Nisga'a, Tsimshian and Gitxsan peoples are all part of the larger Tsimshian linguistic group but each of these peoples have shared legal principles and deliberate

[10] Interestingly, much of Merryman's description (n 8) formed the body of evidence provided by Gitxsan plaintiffs, testifying on their own behalf in their seminal title court action, *Delgamuukw v The Queen* (1991) 79 DLR (4th) 185 (BCSC); *Delgamuukw v British Columbia* (1993) 104 DLR (4th) 470 (BCCA) (this decision is actually erroneously cited as *Uukw v British Columbia*); *Delgamuukw v British Columbia* [1997] 3 SCR 1010.

[11] HLA Hart, *The Concept of Law*, 2nd edn (Oxford University Press, 1994).

[12] See M Fletcher, 'Rethinking Customary Law in Tribal Court Jurisprudence' (2007) 13 *Michigan Journal of Race & Law* 57.

ongoing intersocietal relationships through trade and marriage.[13] According to the Royal Commission on Aboriginal Peoples, an Indigenous society or, in the language of the report, a nation, is a:

> 4. … a sizeable body of Aboriginal people with a shared sense of national identity that constitutes the predominant population in a certain territory or group of territories ….
>
> 5. The more specific attributes …
>
> the nation has a collective sense of national identity that is evinced in a common history, language, culture, traditions, political consciousness, laws, governmental structures, spirituality, ancestry and homeland;
>
> it is of sufficient size and capacity to enable it to assume and exercise powers and responsibilities flowing from the right of self-determination in an effective manner; and
>
> it constitutes a majority of the permanent population of a certain territory or collection of territories and, in the future, will operate from a defined territorial base.[14]

The boundaries around 'Indian' reserves created by the Indian Act[15] divided Indigenous peoples into over 600 bands in Canada[16] that have no correlation with their larger societies or Indigenous legal orders. For example, Tsimshian people on the Pacific north coast are divided into seven Indian Act bands with a number of small additional reserves. As with most other Indigenous peoples, many Tsimshian people live off reserve mainly in British Columbia, but elsewhere in the world as well. This colonial division of Indigenous peoples and lands has seriously undermined the cohesion and efficacy of the larger legal orders and has continued to curtail the application and practice of Indigenous laws today. Furthermore, according to Richard Overstall, 'More important is than the societal fragmentation is the result of the *Indian Act*'s imposition of command-and-control governance, which is particularly corrosive in small, interrelated and intermarried communities. It generally leads to patronage, nepotism and corruption'.[17]

These factors create the current challenging realities that are part of the rebuilding of Indigenous law today. I have written elsewhere that Indigenous law has not disappeared in

[13] These three societies share a common ancient heritage, and there are many similarities among their laws and languages. See S Marsden, M Anderson and D Nyce, 'Tsimshian' in PR Magosci (ed), *Aboriginal Peoples of Canada: A Short Introduction* (University of Toronto Press, 2002) 264. Overstall (n 7) explains that each of these peoples would have legal relations with Athapaskan-speaking Wet'suwet'en, Tahltan and Sekani peoples, Wakashan-speaking Haisla and Heiltsuk peoples, and with Tlingit and Haida peoples, each with their distinctive language and clan system. Such interactions include marriage alliances, legally-regulated warfare, legally-regulated economic exchanges, etc.

[14] Canada Privy Council Office, *Report of the Royal Commission on Aboriginal Peoples: Restructuring the Relationship volume 2* (Canada Communication Group – Publishing, 1996) 35.

[15] The federal Indian Act RSC 1985, c I-5, only concerns those Indigenous peoples registered as status under its terms. It does not affect Inuit peoples, Metis peoples, or Indigenous people (often called First Nations) who are unregistered.

[16] For a critical examination of changing Indigenous and Canadian legal identities off-reserve and in urban settings, see: Yale D Belanger, *Breaching Reserve Boundaries: Canada v Misquadis and the Legal Creation of the Urban Aboriginal Community* in Evelyn Peters and Chris Andersen (eds), *Indigenous in the City: Contemporary Identities and Cultural Innovation* (UBC Press 2013) 69.

[17] Overstall (n 7).

Canada, and that there are no completely intact Indigenous legal orders ready to spring to life in response to its mere recognition.[18] The colonial suppression of Indigenous laws has meant that today, there are gaps and distortions. However, Indigenous peoples across North America are engaged in the hard work of rebuilding their legal orders.[19]

Dunne-za and Cree legal orders (and other Indigenous legal orders) each have their own internal modes of argumentation and legitimisation, and collective reason and accountability – all of which is evident in both the Dunne-za and Cree oral histories. To treat Indigenous law more simplistically reduces it from a normative order[20] that requires collaborative intellectual engagement and reasoning, to mere behaviour. Without such a comprehensive and critical perspective, one cannot see how Indigenous legal orders manage and resolve arguments to solve human problems – essential elements in the actual practice of law.[21] What a sustained and dynamic practice of Indigenous law requires, as do other legal orders, is the adherence to public processes and the demand that the practitioners seek common judgment on a case-by-case basis despite disagreement and dispute. It is the shared common knowledge and its shared interpretation, as is evidenced in Indigenous oral histories and precedential memory commons, that is the essence of legal reasoning.[22] As Gerald Postema has argued:

> The use and acceptance of the law rested on a shared sense of its reasonableness and historical appropriateness. It was thought insufficient that each member of the law community believes the rules reasonable, or wise; they acted from the conviction that this sense was shared, a sensus communis. This learned capacity for reflective judgment – jurisprudence, we might call it – is a social capacity: the ability to reason from a body of shared experiences with normative significance to solutions for new practical problems.[23]

I have argued elsewhere that the Gitxsan legal reasoning process, as an example, meets Postema's standards for the form and structure of common law reasoning in a public forum. Specifically, Postema describes distinctive features of common law reasoning: (i) pragmatic focus on problem solving; (ii) self-conscious regard for the public good; (iii) contextual competence of the adjudicators; (iv) system-resistant nature; (v) discoursive-deliberative reasoning and argument in an interlocutory context; and (vi) reason that is considered common or shared.[24] In a 1945 case involving a crest dispute, I applied

[18] V Napoleon and H Friedland, 'An Inside Job: Engaging with Indigenous Legal Traditions through Stories' (2016) 61(4) *McGill Law Journal* 725.

[19] For example, see the Indigenous Law Research Unit, available at www.ilru.ca; the Wahkohtowin Law and Governance Lodge at the Faculty of Law, University of Alberta, available at www.ualberta.ca/wahkohtowin/index.html; and the Indigenous Legal Orders Institute at the Faculty of Law, University of Windsor, available at www.uwindsor.ca/law/Indigenous-Legal-Orders-Institute.

[20] J Webber, 'Naturalism and Agency in the Living Law' in M Hertogh (ed), *Living Law: Reconsidering Eugen Ehrlich* (Hart Publishing, 2009). Webber defines a normative order as 'a natural dimension of any human interaction, generated through the day-to-day business of human life, perhaps even definitional of the existence of society', ibid 201.

[21] V Napoleon, 'Legal Pluralism and Reconciliation: Journey or Arrival' (2019) *November Maori Law Review* 1.

[22] Napoleon (n 5) 62.

[23] GJ Postema, 'Classical Common Law Jurisprudence (Part II)' (2003) 3(1) *Oxford University Commonwealth Law Journal* 1, 9.

[24] Napoleon (n 5) 62. Also see R Overstall, 'Encountering the Spirit in the Land: "Property" in a Kinship-Based Legal Order' in J McLaren (ed), *Despotic Dominion: Property Rights in British Settler Societies* (UBC Press, 2005).

Postema's criteria and argued that while the legal processes and expressions of Gitxsan law looked different from those taking place in Canadian courtrooms, the Gitxsan legal functions and reasoning were clearly recognisable and equivalent in practice.[25] Through this example of multi-party dispute management, each level of decision-making required consideration of the principles for the common good.

In each Indigenous society, citizens and their legal institutions, organised in various ways were, and are, responsible for the maintenance and operation of their legal order.[26] For example, in Cree society, there are four decision-making groups, and their role and authority depends on the type of legal decision required: the family, medicine people, elders and the community.[27] In Dunne-za society, depending on the type of legal problem, the authoritative decision-makers are families, family members, individuals, medicine people or dreamers. Another example is Gitxsan society where law operates through the institutions of matrilineal kinship units of extended families and the four overarching clans.[28]

Indigenous peoples were and are reasonable and reasoning peoples.[29] Jeremy Webber argues that it is law that enables large groups of people to collectively manage themselves 'against a backdrop of deep-seated normative disagreement' and to fashion 'collective positions out of the welter of disagreement'.[30] Law is an intellectual process that people must actively engage in to manage the full range of collective human life including all aspects of political, economic and social life – families, governance, harvesting fish and game, accessing and distributing resources, managing lands and waters, etc.

Indigenous law is not perfect, nor does it have to be because no legal system ever lives up to its aspirations. Nonetheless, a people's collective aspirations inform standards and ethics, and they help to maintain the power of hope. As with all law, Indigenous law contains thinking processes and intellectual resources that necessarily adapt though time to solve the problems of each new generational era.[31] Today, as in the past, there is no room for romanticisation of Indigenous law or peoples. Brunée and Toope provide this helpful caution, 'Communities of practice are

[25] Napoleon (n 5) 64–66.

[26] For an important discussion about questions and issues concerning non-state law at an international level, see J Brunnée and SJ Toope, *Legitimacy and Legality in International Law: and International Account* (Cambridge University Press, 2010). For a broad discussion about non-state law from a range of non-Indigenous perspectives, see H Dedek and S Van Praagh (eds), *Stateless Law: Evolving Boundaries of a Discipline* (Routledge, 2015).

[27] Friedland, *Cree Legal Traditions Report* (n 9). Also see Friedland, *The Wetiko Legal Principles* (n 9) fn 26.

[28] For an exploration into questions of Gitxsan democracy see, V Napoleon, 'Gitxsan Democracy: On Its Own Terms' in J Tully, K Cherry, F Forman, J Morefield, J Nichols, P Ouziel, D Owen and O Schmidtke (eds), *Democratic Multiplicity: Perceiving, Enacting, and Integrating Democratic Diversity* (Cambridge University Press, 2022).

[29] Friedland referring to the importance of John Borrows' scholarship, 'Certainly, his starting assumptions of (1) reasoning people and traditions, his focus on (2) contemporary application of legal principles, and (3) on legitimate social reasoning processes, rather than individual pathology, help here.' Friedland, *The Wetiko Legal Principles* (n 9) 41.

[30] Webber (n 20) 202.

[31] V Napoleon, A Cameron, C Arcand and D Scott, 'Where is the Law in Restorative Justice?' in Y Belanger (ed), *Aboriginal Self-Government in Canada: Current Trends and Issues*, 3rd edn (Purich Press, 2008) 348–72.

not intrinsically positive; practices emerge that can undermine legality, just as they can support it.'[32]

There are a number of sources or authorities of Indigenous law. According to internationally renowned Indigenous legal scholar John Borrows:

> Not all law flows from courts, legislatures, or parliaments. Law was made in varied local settings before nation-state formation. Law is also developed in these locations after state formation too, particularly in Indigenous contexts where state law is ineffective because of its imposed, foreign, authoritarian, or dismissive nature. The failure of state law to be persuasive and credible within Indigenous contexts propels people to turn to their own authorities, standards, measures, precedents, and norms to regulate behaviour and resolve disputes.[33]

Borrows argues that Indigenous societies have at least five sources of law: sacred; deliberative; custom; positive; and natural.[34] Drawing on Lon Fuller, I have argued that there is another source of law, human interaction deriving from the general patterns of how we treat one another through time.[35] Borrows cautions, and I agree, against treating these sources or authorities as separate or artificially watertight because, in actuality, 'Indigenous legal traditions usually involve the interaction of two or more ... sources'.[36] All sources or authorities of law require collaborative interpretive choices about precedent and its application on a pragmatic case-by-case basis. It is through this sustained engagement with law[37] that people create the necessary intellectual space to critically examine norms, power, and assumptions – a healthy exercise of citizenship and individual and collective legal agency and so integral to healthy societies.

III. INDIGENOUS PUBLIC-PRIVATE LAW – SEVERAL EXAMPLES

In this section, I set out three small explorations of what might be considered Indigenous public law. Ultimately, each Indigenous people must attend to what Promislow calls the markers of public law values and concerns, namely decision-making processes, decision-makers, institutions, transparency, accountability and fairness.[38] Further, Promislow argues that this requires Indigenous communities to:

> [M]ake explicit their self-knowledge of the laws and values that shape decision-making and dispute resolution in particular contexts in their legal orders, ... so that state questions in self-government negotiations relating to public law (e.g., expressions of fairness, respect for the rule of law and democracy, accountability, transparency) can be responded to, deflected, and re-oriented as appropriate, in efforts to avoid further impositions.

[32] See J Brunnée and SJ Toope's important discussion on torture: *Legitimacy and Legality in International Law: An Interactional Account* (Cambridge University Press, 2010) 262.
[33] John Borrows in Friedland, *The Wetiko Legal Principles* (n 9) xii.
[34] J Borrows, *Canada's Indigenous Constitution* (University of Toronto Press, 2010) 23.
[35] V Napoleon, 'Thinking About Indigenous Legal Orders' in R Provist and C Sheppard (eds), *Dialogues on Human Rights and Legal Pluralism* (Springer, 2012) 242.
[36] Borrows (n 34) 55.
[37] Promislow (n 1).
[38] ibid.

A. Impact Benefit Agreements

Commonly referred to as IBAs, the simplest Canadian legal description of impact benefit agreements is that they are contracts made between Indigenous communities and private companies, or between Indian Act bands and both the company and the government, in order to allow a range of industrial type projects to proceed with Indigenous consent.[39] There are many types of similar agreements variously referred to as participation agreements, supraregulatory agreements, and benefits sharing agreements.[40] I am using the IBAs as a placeholder in this discussion, but my analysis applies more broadly to other forms of agreements between Indigenous peoples and industry. While appearing simple if one simply accepts the Canadian legal definition, what actually becomes clear on closer examination is that IBAs are complex because they concern issues of paramount importance to Indigenous peoples and which span environmental protection, territories, land and resource rights in Canadian law, resource jurisdiction, treaties, governance, economies, and social/cultural health as well as constitutional rights in Canadian law. In contrast to these paramount Indigenous concerns, are the basic goals and purposes of industry, namely that of resource development and extraction usually backed by more financial resources beyond what Indigenous communities and groups have access to.

IBAs themselves are a moving target – they are continually being reshaped by the ongoing legal and political activism of Indigenous peoples, the Canadian political and legal climate, and the goals of industries as determined by world markets.[41] There is an important critical scholarship about IBAs and since IBAs have now been around for some years, there are some assessments drawing from the actual experiences of Indigenous peoples, state government, and industry.[42]

There are a host of issues that have been identified as to the scope and rigour of IBA assessments, the methodologies and standards for these assessments, the extent and power of the state's role, the extent and power of industry's role, whether and how long-term sustainability is accounted for, and the widely varying levels of direct local Indigenous community engagement.[43] There are a number of serious concerns relating to the lack

[39] G Gibson and C O'Faircheallaigh, *IBA Community Toolkit, Negotiation and Implementation of Impact Benefit Agreements* (*Gordon Foundation*, 2015) 10, available at www.gordonfoundation.ca/sites/default/files/publications/IBAToolkit.pdf.

[40] ibid.

[41] For example, the IBA resources have been expanded beyond employment and contracting opportunities to capture recent changes and additions such as royalty payments, profit sharing, equity stakes, greater transparency and disclosure as per new federal requirements for Indigenous communities, and prevention measures and compensation in the event of environmental problems. For a range of examples, see https://gordonfoundation.ca/imitiatives/iba-toolkit/.

[42] For example, M Langton and J Longbottom (eds), *Community Futures, Legal Architecture: Foundations for Indigenous Peoples in the Mining Boom* (Routledge, 2012); M Langton, O Mazel, L Palmer, K Shain and M Tehan, *Settling With Indigenous People* (The Federation Press, 2006); M Langton, L Palmer, M Tehan and K Shain, *Honour Among Nations? Treaties and Agreements with Indigenous People* (Melbourne University Press, 2004). Also see references listed in the IBA Database, available at www.impactbenefit.com. This website provides a list of Canadian IBAs and other information about IBAs in Canada.

[43] IBA Database.

of transparency and the typical confidentiality requirements of IBAs with Indigenous communities. There are also Indigenous worries about whether the IBAs create or are part of a reactive stance as opposed to facilitating forward planning, about the internal community tensions regarding the IBA arrangements, and for some communities, the political and economic vulnerability created by the dire need for local employment and contracting opportunities.[44]

While all these concerns are important, one of the critical issues is that they are characterised as private agreements according to Canadian law – contracts – negotiated between industry and Indigenous communities. It is worthwhile noting that private law is still law, so it necessarily involves public legal institutions. To assert a private claim against another is to direct this demand through those public state institutions of law, though as I argue above, the public aspect of a state's legal institutions is a requirement for all law. However, it is also arguable that IBAs are private law because the principles that would be adjudicated in a court (ie, a public forum, unless the IBA included a provision for arbitration in a different forum) would be private law about the nature and meaning of the contract, and in what conditions. My colleague, Kathy Chan, helpfully notes that:

> For private persons, the rule is that you may do anything you choose which the law does not prohibit … But for public bodies the rule is opposite, and so of another character altogether. It is that any action to be taken must be justified by positive law.[45]

If we understand law, including Indigenous law, to be a public collaborative process through which legitimate legal decisions are made, can we understand the characterisation of IBAs as private from an Indigenous perspective?[46] Again, it is usually Indigenous public governments that are negotiating IBAs with industry, arguably about Indigenous public issues, so they cannot be considered private insofar as Indigenous law. If IBAs are considered private according to Canadian law, does this locate them outside of Indigenous law? What might be the consequence of taking issues of paramount importance (ie, lands, environment, etc) to Indigenous peoples out of their Indigenous public legal processes? Does this place IBAs beyond the reach of legitimate and lawful Indigenous processes, and beyond accountability and lawfulness according to the applicable Indigenous legal order? At the end of the day, does this strengthen or undermine Indigenous legal traditions and their efficacy? There are of course Canadian public law processes such as judicial review that might be available to a band member (as per the Indian Act) to challenge their government's (ie, Indian Band) decision to enter into an IBA without proper process in the community.

IBAs are treated as an unavoidable, but necessary everyday aspect of doing business as usual by governments, third parties, and often by Indigenous communities. Consequently, IBAs are either taken for granted without a larger critical analysis, and if Indigenous community members are suspicious of the IBA, it is often because they do not believe they had a meaningful voice or role in their negotiation and implementation. The question of the legality of IBA's under Indigenous law is not addressed, and this continues the same old colonial dynamic of undermining and rendering invisible Indigenous legal orders.

[44] KJ Caine and N Krogman, 'Powerful or Just Plain Power-Full? A Power Analysis of Impact Benefit Agreements in Canada's North' (2010) 23(1) *Organization and Environment* 76.

[45] K Chan, course notes, quoting from *R v Somerset County Council, ex parte Fewings* [1995] 1 All ER 513.

[46] The public/private divide in Western law is murky. For example, the law of torts, contracts, and property are considered private, but again they are regulated and operated within public law and government.

So what if we took Indigenous law seriously as law? This would mean not presupposing the outcomes of Indigenous legal processes according to any predetermined political expectation of Indigenous peoples and what they 'should' do to meet those expectations. Again, there are legitimate legal processes of deliberation and reasoning through which Indigenous communities have and will continue to make hard decisions about lands, governance and resources. To foreclose the outcomes of Indigenous legal decisions by assuming what such decisions would be or should be without the actual engagement of Indigenous law is to fundamentally disregard that law. One should certainly be critical, and one can disagree with Indigenous decisions, but the actual decisions should stand if they meet the terms of Indigenous legalities and legitimacy. As stated earlier, critique, debate and disagreement are a necessary part of any healthy human society and this should continue to be a part of an active Indigenous public discourse about law, its aspirations, operation and function, application and interpretations. What I am advocating here is that Indigenous legal processes be fully engaged, that their integrity be maintained, that change is explicit and public, that accountability is factored in, and that decisions are public and form part of an accessible public record, at least within Indigenous communities. Clearly these are all public law concerns or values.

I want to make two final points here. First, it is not fair or accurate to categorically say that all IBAs are simply neoliberal constructs that Indigenous peoples are either forced or simply duped into signing. Indigenous peoples, as with other peoples, are individual and collective agents with reasons for the decisions they make. In other words, Indigenous peoples are managing as best as they can despite colonial history and within the relations of power that they are a part of. However, if left unexamined, IBAs may well be another way to neoliberalise Indigenous relationships to their lands, and this is fine if that is what they deliberately choose to do, ideally according to their own laws and within the bounds of their Indigenous law norms concerning harms and constraints to future generations. Second, Indigenous peoples do have historic legal and political intellectual resources from which to draw to constructively resist the relentless pressures that seek to displace them from their lands – and many Indigenous peoples are doing just that – resisting and protecting their lands.

B. Gitxsan Compensation Law

I turn now to the Gitxsan law of compensation, which is rarely but sometimes, in the form of land. This area of law demonstrates another public-private divide, and which provides an interesting contrast with Canadian law. The importance of examining compensation cases provides some insight into the on-the-ground practice of Gitxsan law. How do people understand and work with injury, liability and compensation? To gain an understanding of Gitxsan law and legal practices, I examined a number of ancient cases as well as some that are more recent. The challenge in the later cases is the varying degrees of involvement by Canadian law or state authorities.[47] In all, these cases serve to demonstrate the continuing resilience of the Gitxsan legal traditions since European arrival.

[47] V Napoleon, 'Ayook: Gitksan Legal Order, Law, and Legal Theory', Doctoral thesis (UVIC, 2009).

The law governing land compensation, particularly permanent alienation from one society to another, is called *xsiisxw*, and it is applied only in the most serious of situations involving loss of life or a major debt, and it is formally announced and witnessed in a public feast[48] hall after the requisite private deliberations. *Xsiisxw* (compensation/cleansing) may be applied when a life is taken either accidentally or with intent, in which case the offending House[49] may publicly transfer land to the wronged House. The principle behind land as compensation is that land does not wear out and the compensation must last at least a lifetime, often more. If and when the land is to be returned to the original owner, the head chief of the House that received the land as compensation will announce its return at the main public forum of the Feast. Gitxsan Chief Xamlaxyeltxw, Solomon Marsden, explains:

> This is when a person's life is taken, and it's a serious matter to ... give compensation to the ... family. And a life has been taken here, and that's what they look at. This is why they have to – to give a lifetime thing, like the land, another person they would give, because the – the life of a person has been taken.[50]

Richard Overstall provides an overview of *xsiisxw* and its significance to Gitxsan territories and operation of law:

> Once acquired, a relationship with territory is inalienable unless the House is unable to produce sufficient wealth to perform its feast responsibilities or is required to relinquish one of its territories as compensation. The compensation system, known as *xsiisxw*, requires a House to relinquish wealth, names, crests, or territory to repay an offence committed against another House. The amount paid is gauged more to settle the disquiet felt by the other party than to replace the lost value. In the past, if the compensation process was not started quickly, homicides and other serious offences could escalate into feuds, as retaliation killings were lawful after warnings had been given.
>
> For the death of an individual, compensation might involve a gift of material wealth; for the intentional death of an important chief, it might involve the transfer of territory for the lifetime of the immediate family of the deceased; and for a series of unprovoked attacks on a neighbouring people, it might involve the permanent transfer of territory to the innocent party. The legal principle coming into play in the latter case is that not only has an offence been committed against an innocent human party, but also against the laws of respect for the land itself. In such cases, the original bond [with the land] is broken and divorce is the sole remedy.[51]

[48] The Feast (often referred to outside Gitksan circles as the potlatch) is a complex political, legal, economic and social institution in which the main business of the hosting House is transacted and formally witnessed by the guest Houses. Jurisdiction among the Gitksan is exercised through the Feast. In former times, feasts were held for all major legal, social and political transactions. See generally R Daly, *Our Box Was Full: An Ethnography for the Delgamuukw Plaintiffs* (UBC Press, 2005) 57–106.

[49] A House (English name) is a matrilineal kinship unit, the Gitxsan term is *wilp*. The *wilp* is the basic conceptual political, social, economic and legal unit in Gitxsan society. Each Gitxsan person is born into his or her mother's House, a group of around 150 persons who share a common ancestry. The term 'House' originates from the historical longhouses, although members of the same House did not actually live under one roof. Rather, they were and are widely scattered by marriage and occupation. House members have rights and responsibilities in other Houses by virtue of their roles as spouses and clan members. See R Daly and V Napoleon, 'A Dialogue on the Effects of Aboriginal Rights Litigation and Activism on Aboriginal Communities in Northwestern British Columbia' (2003) 47(3) *Social Analysis: The International Journal of Cultural and Social Practice* 108.

[50] Solomon Marsden (Xamlaxyeltxw) 9 May 1988, BCSC trial transcript, 5932, 5938, evidence for *Delgamuukw v The Queen* [1991] BCJ No 525, 79 DLR (4th) 185, 5957.

[51] Overstall (n 24) 40.

According to the oral histories or *adaawk*,[52] land is the ultimate compensation payment. In order for land to be paid as compensation for varying periods of time – sometimes generations – a well organised system was required that allowed those with recognised legal authority for land to transfer it to another House. These compensation payments in land would have to be publicly and widely communicated, through precedent over generations, so that everyone affected would be informed of the ownership changes (ie, original transfer of land and the possible return of that land). These transfers are not restricted to the distant past but are recalled and dealt with in today's Feasts.

In this example, Gitxsan Chief Guuhadakw Thomas Wright from the House of 'Wiik'aax (*wolf/lax gibuu*), described an accidental death that occurred in Kisgagas 'a long time ago' for which no compensation was paid.[53] In this case, while the families were eating, the nephew of Yagosip died when he accidentally fell onto Yagosip's knife. Because Yagosip and the nephew were both members of the House of 'Wiik'aax there was no need for a *xsiisxw*. According to Thomas Wright, 'It was resolved. There was peace. Nobody mentioned it.'[54] Mr Wright explained that a *xsiisxw* would have been held if Yagosip and the nephew were from two different Houses, '[T]here will be Xsiisxw if that person was from a different house [and different clan]; there will be an exchange of blood.'[55]

The case of Yagosip reveals a division between those matters that are dealt with publicly, in the sense of being out in the open and in the nature of being a public concern, as opposed to those matters that are dealt with privately within the House which are not for external consumption. Again, we can see how some things concern more people, whereas others do not, thereby determining who must know. Admittedly, this is a different cast on the question of the Indigenous public as the focus is not on an actor delegated by the state and whether they acted within the grant of that authority. Nonetheless, it is my contention that the grounding of such decisions lies in the commitment to the public good which is necessary to maintain the chief's public authority in this system.

A central Gitxsan governing concept, *daxgyet*,[56] illustrates just how important upholding the public good is to the integrity and maintenance of Gitxsan law and political ordering. Literally *daxgyet* means chief's power and authority, and the strength of a people.[57] Each matrilineal kinship unit, the *Wilp*,[58] has the legal and political responsibility to maintain its power relationship, its *daxgyet* – its fundamental relationship to the

[52] The *adaawk* (collective oral history) is a formal and primary Gitxsan intellectual governing institution that each House owns. It is the *adaawk* that links each House to its territories and establishes ownership of the land and resources. The *adaawk* tell of the origins and migrations of groups to their current territories, explorations, covenants established with the land, and songs, crests and names that result from the spiritual connection between people and their land.

[53] Olive Ryan (Gwaans) 15 June 1987, BCSC trial transcript, 5932 at 5938, evidence for *Delgamuukw v The Queen*, [1991] BCJ No 525, 79 DLR (4th) 185, 1252.

[54] ibid.

[55] ibid.

[56] Napoleon (n 48) xi.

[57] According to R Overstall, *daxgyet means* a 'firmly bound person', and is a 'concept not easily translated although the English term "powers" is often used'. See R Overstall, 'A People of Themselves: Some Field Notes On Gitxsan Law' in V Napoleon, R Johnson, R Overstall and D McKenzie, *An Interrupted Intergenerational Conversation: Indigenous Art and Societal/Cultural Expressions* (University of Toronto Press, forthcoming) 9 (pre-publication draft).

[58] Napoleon (n 48) xv.

land. *Daxgyet* is a relational concept in that it derives from the public fulfillment of legal, political and economic obligations that are essential for the health, strength, continuation, and wealth of the matrilineal kinship units – whether those obligations are internal (private) or external (public). The loss of *daxgyet*, caused by profound disrespect or loss of face correlates to a diminishment of *daxgyet* for the *Wilp*, the most serious loss any *Wilp* can experience as it is essentially a loss of relational political power.

According to Gitxsan Chief Hanamuxw Don Ryan, if one House member intentionally harmed another member from the same House, this matter would be considered an internal matter but could, depending on the seriousness of the injury, involve the father's side of the person that was harmed at which time it would become a public matter, a matter of *daxgyet*. Mr Ryan explains: 'The injury would have to be dealt with, and the father's side would try to be involved, but it would be dealt with internally, not publicly in a feast'.[59] Because of this, the witnesses did not provide the Court with any examples of internal (ie, private) House legal processes for such injuries.

C. Administrative Law

In this section, I take up the question of how we might imagine Indigenous law being practised through the various current administrative tribunals. One question is about how Indigenous law might reshape the design and structures of tribunals. How will Indigenous administrative law continue to develop in various Indigenous legal orders? What are the various expectations of Indigenous law in this field?[60]

Over the years, there has been much productive discussion about tribunals and administrative law. We know that in this country, tribunals are a very important and integral part of the Canadian legal fabric and the operation of Canadian law. We know that it is the legislative frameworks and terms for statutory interpretation that enables tribunals today. We also know that it is easier to talk about procedural matters and access than about substantive Indigenous law. More information or data is needed as to how the various tribunals: (1) serve Indigenous communities and what rights are involved; (2) serve Indigenous individuals and in what tribunals; and (3) how to deal with access questions and what access issues remain to be addressed.[61]

The field of administrative law and the development of tribunals has been within and in response to Canadian law and its operational needs. Given this, if and when Indigenous

[59] Telephone conversation with Don Ryan (Hanamuxw) and author, 16 May 2008.

[60] I do not take up the many further questions about how the obligations of the Declaration on the Rights of Indigenous Peoples Act (DRIPA) and United Nations Declaration on the Rights of Indigenous Peoples should be acted on in the field of administrative tribunals(DRIPA BC 2019).

[61] A couple of papers with related calls for more information on who tribunals serve, 'user' oriented design (an access to justice project) (and see the cites at the end of this comment too): L Sossin, 'Designing Administrative Justice' (2017) 34 *Windsor Year Book Access to Justice* 87; and L Jacobs and S Tomkinson, 'Examining the Social Security Tribunal's Navigator Service: Access to Administrative Justice for Marginalized Communities', Report (University of Windsor, 2022), available at https://scholar.uwindsor.ca/lawpub/133. Here I am not distinguishing between administrative bodies that serve the general population (eg, human rights, residential tenancies, income support, workers' compensation, or environmental appeals contexts) and those that are involved in planning and decision-making related to Indigenous agreements (eg, co-management, joint management, or Indigenous treaty governments.

law is considered, it is primarily as an add-on to an existing, hard-wired Canadian legal system. The consequence of not explicitly considering Indigenous law is that the terms of reference for administrative law continues to be Canadian law though there a several notable exceptions to this with the Haida Nation and the Deline Judicial Council.[62]

Taking Indigenous law seriously as law, means considering both the substantive and procedural issues from an Indigenous legal perspective from a specific legal order. Given that administrative law is a creature of the state, we cannot ask what Indigenous administrative law might have been historically, but rather, what it is in the present day. However, Janna Promislow has helpfully suggested asking, 'What is the law of how the community administered its governance? How are public decisions made and enforced? And what Indigenous law (procedural or substantive) would be relevant to governance bodies making decisions that affect Indigenous people and communities today?'[63] Such inquiries mean asking which legal order is involved? Is it Wet'suwet'en? Or Secwepemc? Is it Gitxsan? Or Cree? It also means determining what is the legal issue according to that Indigenous legal order and that law, and who the Indigenous authoritative decision-makers (past and present) are. Finally, one needs to ask about the legal processes for determining a response to the identified legal issue, what that range of legitimate legal responses are according to the specified Indigenous legal order, and what the appropriate range of past and present sanctions and remedies are.[64]

Turning to the question of expectations, Indigenous law has not gone anywhere in multi-juridical Canada, but as previously stated, it has been severely undermined and curtailed. The work today is fundamentally that of rebuilding – that is what we see taking place across Canada.[65] Indigenous peoples need support to continue this rebuilding – this absolutely must be a central part of reconciliation and meeting the obligations of UNDRIP – whether this is for administrative law challenges or matters relating to governance, citizenries or healthy communities.

In 2013, the then Chief Justice Beverly McLachlin said,

> [W]ithout administrative tribunals, the rule of law in the modern regulatory state would falter and fail. Tribunals offer flexible, swift, and relevant justice. In an age when access to justice is increasingly lacking, they help to fill the gap. And there is no going back.[66]

In 2017, Lorne Sossin wrote that, every tribunal that has been established reflects a core premise that an alternative to court, on the one hand, and government, on the other, is both necessary and beneficial.[67]

There are at least two ways to think about these statements. First, Indigenous communities and individuals need these alternatives to present day courts. However, I am more

[62] Council of the Haida Nation, available at www.haidanation.ca/, and Deline Justice Council, available at www.deline.ca/en/justicecouncil/.

[63] Promislow (n 1).

[64] This methodology is more fully described in H Friedland and V Napoleon, 'Gathering the Threads: Indigenous Legal Methodology' (2015) 1(1) *Lakehead Law Journal* 33.

[65] See, eg, the Indigenous Law Research Unit, available at, www.ilru.ca. Also see the *Truth and Reconciliation Commission of Canada, Calls to Action* (Truth and Reconciliation Commission of Canada, 2015), available at www.trc.ca.

[66] B McLachlin, former Chief Justice, Supreme Court of Canada, quoted in Sossin (n 62) 88.

[67] ibid.

interested in a second idea which needs much more exploration than what I am going to be able to offer here. My preliminary approach is this:

- If we are to consider what Indigenous administrative law is, then what is it an alternative to insofar as Indigenous adjudication and governance?
- What governance problems should Indigenous administrative law and tribunal processes deal with?

Context and history matter here. A historic answer must be contextualised by non-state Indigenous societies with political and legal authorities that were distributed horizontally, and which operated through decentralised institutions. These were and are institutions such as clans, lineage groups, families, governance structures, delegated groups, etc. In the past, the relationships that mattered were horizontal rather than vertical like today with Indigenous communities upwardly hardwired into the Canadian state through recent history, legislation, agreements and funding.[68]

As with state societies, Indigenous law is also a public process that operates through legal institutions and to apply law, one draws from patterns and dissimilarities of past applications. It would appear that given the historic non-state organisation of Indigenous societies, it is unlikely or less likely that there would be a need for a 'Canadian-like' substantial and procedural administrative law. I could be wrong of course.

In contrast, asking this question in the present day, with many of today's forms of governance and the vertical changes to historic Indigenous political and legal institutions, would present a different picture. This is, fundamentally, a question of which public – that of the past or that of today – and of course there is further complication in that these are overlapping, sometimes conflicting publics. There is also the question of whether the tribunals' reasons are public and available to add to the public memories of each legal order. This is an important area that would benefit from a critical inquiry and further research.

So here is the thing, Indigenous administrative law that would deal with contemporary governing institutions can draw on historic Indigenous law and legal principles for application in a present-day context. This work is not about going back in time, but rather drawing on historic legal resources to manage the problems of each generation.

IV. CONCLUSION

With this chapter, my intent is to create a conversation about finding ways to broaden the state-based meaning of 'public law', and to find ways to consider and work with Indigenous 'constraints of public power'. While I am not taking up the 'special' coercive power of the state, I am still talking about Indigenous publics in relation to the existence of politics, community and accessibility/public nature of law as an essential part of the character of legality.

Rundle's relationship theory is very helpful to my intention as she argues that relationships and their demands were necessary to and constituted Lon Fuller's legalities. Further, that a society's institutional forms have carriage for those relationships because they

[68] I address this question more fully in Napoleon (n 21).

hold the 'responsibilities and opportunities for the authority of law itself'.[69] According to Rundle, Fuller's jurisprudence applies to all governing relationships not just to a state's legislative function. This insight frees Rundle's analysis from being state-centric and releases its potential application to non-state societies such as the Gitxsan. It is this authority of law, captured by Gitxsan *daxgyet*, that is the enduring public imperative for Gitxsan society.

The challenge for Indigenous peoples is to rebuild their legal orders by the hard work of critically and collaboratively rearticulating and restating their historic legal resources. This approach will enable Indigenous peoples to restore the best practices of their historic forms of democracies complete with inclusive and active citizenship for today's political and legal negotiations, and self-determination and governance demands. To conclude, Richard Overstall offers an interesting thought as to how legal history must be an explicit and continuing part of rebuilding Indigenous legal orders:

> Historic indigenous law is important in that, when fully described, it demonstrably was a functional, integrated order of norms, relationships and legal process that dealt with all the coordination and conflicts that the society encountered. To be useful in present-day societal contexts, a historical legal order requires empirical evidence and legal reasoning to figure out which parts can be tinkered with, and which parts are keystones that either must be left in place or substituted with other keystones.[70]

[69] K Rundle, 'Fuller's Relationships' in H Takikawa (ed), *The Rule of Law and Democracy* (Archiv für Rechts-und Sozialphilosophie/Archives for Philosophy of Law and Social Philosophy, 2019) 19. Also helpful is K Rundle, *Forms Liberate: Reclaiming the Jurisprudence of Lon L Fuller* (Hart Publishing, 2013).

[70] Overstall (n 7).

19

Public Law and the Future: A Sustainable Jurisprudence?

PETER C OLIVER*

I. INTRODUCTION

THIS CHAPTER USES the example of Irish independence[1] in order to get at a number of important issues regarding how we theorise about law; notably, our reluctance to bring consideration of the future, of sustainable legal futures, into the frame, despite their necessary role, or so I argue, in our considered theoretical and practical work on law generally, and public law in particular.

Section II describes how competing understandings of parliamentary sovereignty and of the (dis)continuity of legal systems presented genuinely hard cases for Irish (and other Commonwealth) constitutional lawyers a century ago, in their attempts to anticipate, achieve and then explain constitutional independence.[2] It will be argued that, despite the claims of those already dug into opposing legal trenches, existing legal rules did not dictate a clear answer with respect to independence, and principles (such as democracy and the rule of law) while structuring the range of possible answers did not point to a single, clear solution – in fact, it could be said that the same principle (democracy, for example) justified quite different solutions depending on the context. More will be said about this below.

As it happened, it was only consideration of Ireland's sustainable futures that made the choice of a solution obvious. One narrative regarding Ireland's future pointed to ongoing Westminster parliamentary sovereignty, with increasing autonomy, though still within the legal system of the British Empire and Commonwealth. Another narrative pointed to a future of Irish popular sovereignty and the not-too-distant prospect of full

* I am very grateful to participants in the Ottawa-Queens works-in-progress workshop in May 2022 and to those attending the Public Law Conference in Dublin in July 2022 for comments and suggestions on an earlier draft of this chapter. I am particularly grateful to Vanessa MacDonnell and Grégoire Webber who provided detailed written feedback. Of course, I alone am responsible for any errors or lack of clarity in the final version. This chapter relies on ongoing research supported by the Social Sciences and Humanities Research Council.

[1] While discussing Irish independence, I also discuss Canadian independence, with which I am more familiar.

[2] In PC Oliver, *The Constitution of Independence: The Development of Constitutional Theory in Australia, Canada and New Zealand* (Oxford University Press, 2005) 1–2, I discuss the progression through political, international, judicial and, finally, *constitutional* independence. I define 'constitutional independence' as the 'ability in formal terms to determine with finality all the rules, constitutional and other, in [the] legal system'. Unless otherwise indicated, references to 'independence' in this chapter should be understood to mean 'constitutional independence'.

constitutional independence. Both narratives were theoretically coherent, but only one was truly sustainable, given the socio-political context in Ireland at the time. I will have more to say about what I mean by 'sustainable' below. The key point, for now, is that consideration of the future, in particular *sustainable* futures, seems to be a vital part, a *necessary* part, of working through hard cases in public law.

Section III sets out to discover whether future-focussed, sustainability considerations are already a part of our legal and public law jurisprudence. On the whole, because of the dominance of the positivist-inspired rule-book model of law, the answer appears to be 'no', though there are occasional intimations of future-focussed concerns if we look for them.

First, we see that even the main proponents of the rule-book picture of law saw need to mention that which is fundamental to a sustainable jurisprudence of law: that our considered use of the word law includes an *ongoing* aspect. Assuming, then, that something in a public law jurisprudence must account for that ongoing aspect of law, we see, secondly, that the (so it is said) essential requirement of 'efficacy' can only account for that ongoing quality if, contrary to its deployment by positivists such as Hart and Kelsen, it too looks forward to the future and to the sustainability of law. We see, thirdly, that positivist accounts of normativity are inadequate to explain how or why law is sustainable. Somewhat ironically, we see, fourthly that positivist theorists had a good deal to say about making good, sustainable judgements when they spoke of *non-legal* discretion, wherein wisdom and non-legal knowledge (including with regard to the future) were clearly seen to be relevant.

We see, fifthly, that neither anti-positivist nor natural law theories (or at least the ones that are prominent in the common law world) provide a forward-focussed perspective. Ronald Dworkin's theory is promising in terms of sustainability, in that it includes forthright consideration of what I will refer to as the *quality* of our laws, but his description of the back-and-forth reasoning before reaching reflective equilibrium expressly rules out consideration of social-scientific, real-world factors, the ingredients most likely to inform a future-focussed, sustainability approach. We will see that John Finnis's understanding of practical reasoning and reflective equilibrium expressly includes social-scientific, real-world factors, but crucially his account of law and legal reasoning does not.

Finally, moving away from case law and judging, we see with respect to legislation that even democratically-sanctioned measures emerging from a recognised source (eg Parliament) may nonetheless be lacking in *quality* or *appropriateness to a changing context* and lacking in sustainability for those reasons (just as a decision by an unelected judge may be lacking in *source-based* authority but be excellent in terms of its intrinsic *quality* and *appropriateness to the ongoing context*). In order to explain why I think considerations of *source*, *quality* and *appropriateness to a changing context* are relevant to a sustainable jurisprudence, I need to say something more about what I mean by the term 'sustainability'. I do so initially by means of a medical analogy (to which I will return occasionally in the discussion that follows).

A. Thinking about Sustainability

As just discussed, this chapter considers, in part through a theoretical prism, the extent to which we have or should have a sustainable jurisprudence of public law. I use 'sustainability' primarily in the straightforward dictionary sense of 'able to continue over a period of time',[3] but a further, related sense well-known to many Indigenous cultures[4] and to local and global environmental movements[5] is also relevant: 'meeting the needs of the present without compromising the ability of future generations to meet their own needs'.[6]

B. A Medical Analogy

If we take a medical example for the purposes of illustration, we can identify three elements that might have an effect on the sustainability of 'medical treatments' (that is, medications or medical procedures): the fact that treatments come from medical professionals rather than from untrained individuals (*the source*); the intrinsic qualities of the recommended treatments (*the quality*); and the appropriateness of such treatments given the (frequently evolving) context into which they will take effect (*appropriateness to ongoing context*[7]). We might also observe that these elements are related. At the moment, patients in most countries trust medical professionals and the health care system more generally. If those same professionals make a practice of recommending ineffective or otherwise inadequate (low *quality*) treatments out of laziness or a desire to cut corners, those treatments would be less sustainable in themselves, in the sense of failing to endure and to meet the future needs of patients, but they would also have knock-on or feedback effects[8] with respect to the trust in medical professionals, medical treatments and the health care system more generally – not immediately or dramatically but gradually and insidiously. Furthermore, if respected medical professionals instead make great efforts to recommend excellent (high *quality*) clinically proven treatments but ignore the *ongoing context* into which the treatments must inevitably take effect (eg, that the ideal medication is increasingly difficult to obtain, or that the recommended physical therapy is unobtainable due to a public health crisis), the theoretically excellent treatments would in fact be less sustainable or entirely unsustainable. This unsustainability potentially also

[3] *Cambridge Dictionary Online*, available at www.dictionary.cambridge.org/dictionary/english/sustainable.

[4] See, eg, O Lyons, 'Looking Toward the Seventh Generation' (University of Arizona, 17 April 2008), 11.35 onwards, available at www.nnigovernance.arizona.edu/oren-lyons-looking-toward-seventh-generation.

[5] See, eg, GH Brundtland, *Our Common Future: Report of the World Commission on Environment and Development* (United Nations Documents, 1987) ('Brundtland Report') and United Nations, *The UN Sustainable Development Goals* (United Nations, 2015).

[6] R Nissenbaum, *Sustainable Solutions: Problem Solving for Current and Future Generations* (Oxford University Press, 2020). Nissenbaum's definition is largely based on the Brundtland Report, however he applies it not only to environmental issues but also to problem-solving (for current and future generations) more generally.

[7] For the moment, the ongoing context is understood to refer to practical matters, such as the availability of certain drugs when supply chain issues exist, or the practicality of obtaining particular physical therapies due to public health regulations in a global pandemic. But the future context can also be articulated in less tangible terms, relating to the purpose and meaning of *life* and *health*, or to the presence of competing norms in that regard. More concretely, treatments that are perfectly well suited to curing a particular physical ailment might, for example, interfere with mental health at a level that is normally within an acceptable range but that is likely to fall outside that range in the context of developments that are already placing great stress on mental health, such as an economic or public health crisis. Or, to take an example relating to competing norms, treatments that are medically recommended generally speaking may run into new and difficult issues of appropriate application where they conflict with family, community or religious norms. Each of these scenarios has a legal analogue, and some of these will be touched on later in this chapter.

[8] 'Feedback' refers to the phenomenon in sound technology where the output source is affected not only by the original input but by the looping effect of the sound emanating from that source.

has knock-on or feedback effects regarding the way in which medical professionals, medical treatments and the health care system are viewed, and therefore on the sustainability more generally speaking of the care provided by those same components in the future.

If the teaching and practice of medicine proceeded on the basis that something is a 'medical treatment' simply because it emanates from a medical professional (its *source*), regardless of the intrinsic *quality* of that treatment and regardless of the *ongoing context* into which that treatment takes effect, that would have consequences for the sustainability of the overall project of health care – not suddenly or immediately, but incrementally and insidiously, as just noted. Teaching and practice that takes in not only the authority of medical professionals (*source*-related considerations) and the *quality* of medical treatments, but also the difficult judgements involved in ensuring that treatments are *appropriate to often changing contexts* would seem to have more sustainable prospects and less negative knock-on or feedback effects for the overall project of health care, both in terms of individuals treatments and for the health-care goals more generally.

C. The Relevance of the Medical Analogy to Law

This chapter considers whether the same sustainability-focussed analysis is true for law, notably for public law. Implicit in the discussion of the medical example was the sense that a medical treatment is not just a discrete medication or procedure but a dynamic process including follow-on effects. Is the same true of our understanding of law? Is public law sustainable simply by virtue of that fact that it emanates from a *source* that is for the moment recognised as having the authority to generate law: a constituent process, a legislature or a court judgment for example. Is the *quality* of that legal measure not just relevant but in some sense essential to the ongoing authority of law? And even if a legal measure comes from an authoritatively recognised *source* and is perfectly justifiable in terms of the pre-existing legal and abstract moral standards (*quality*), is it sustainable if it ignores or significantly misapprehends the *ongoing context* into which that otherwise 'perfect' law is to play out? Would any lack of sustainability as a result of ongoing contextual factors have knock-on or feedback implications in relation to the sustainability of not just the legal measure in question, but other laws and the law project as a whole?

If it is indeed the case, as in the medical example, that the *quality* and the *ongoing context* into which all legal 'treatments' play out affect the sustainability of that 'treatment', and that ignoring such considerations risks incremental and insidious undermining effects to the sustainability of the discrete legal treatment and to the law project as a whole, should not the teaching and practice of law take this into account? This chapter considers the extent to which our public law requires a sustainable jurisprudence, and it attempts to identify some of the questions that looking at public law in this way brings into sharper relief. It reserves for subsequent elaboration the detailed account of what a truly sustainable jurisprudence of public law might entail.[9]

[9] I have made a first, brief attempt at summarising what a sustainable jurisprudence might mean in P Oliver, 'A Constitution Similar in Principle to that of the United Kingdom: The Preamble, Constitutional Principles, and a Sustainable Jurisprudence' (2019) 65 *McGill Law Journal* 207, 255 onwards. That article and this chapter form part of a larger project.

I turn now to the topic of Irish independence, the context (seen from a wider Commonwealth perspective) in which I initially identified what I take to be the unavoidable need to bring future-focussed legal considerations to bear on hard constitutional cases.[10]

II. EXPLAINING CONSTITUTIONAL INDEPENDENCE

A. Two Competing Narratives of Irish Independence: Sovereignty of the UK Parliament and Sovereignty of the Irish People

In the past I have written at considerable length about the acquisition of constitutional independence in Australia, Canada and New Zealand,[11] and in particular about a central part of that story: the sovereignty of the Imperial, United Kingdom (UK) (or, more neutrally, Westminster) Parliament. By the end of the nineteenth century, legal understandings of parliamentary sovereignty had come to be defined by Professor AV Dicey's highly influential *Lectures Introductory to the Study of the Law of the Constitution*, first published in 1885.[12] Dicey communicated widely and effectively certain core propositions, neatly summarised in a publication regarding Irish Home Rule that appeared just two years after the first edition of *The Law of the Constitution*. These propositions can be paraphrased as follows:[13]

1. The Westminster Parliament is the sovereign law-making body of the British Empire.
2. The Westminster Parliament, as a sovereign body, can make laws for every part of the British Empire, and make or unmake any law.
3. The Westminster Parliament cannot, while retaining its sovereignty, be bound by any Act of Parliament whatever.

[10] For further discussion, see P Oliver, 'Change in the Ultimate Rules of a Legal System: Hard Cases, Uncertainty, Commonwealth Precedents and the Importance of Context' (2015) 26 *King's Law Journal* 367.

[11] Oliver (n 2).

[12] AV Dicey, *Lectures Introductory to the Study of the Law of the Constitution* (Macmillan, 1885), now more easily found in its 10th edition, edited by ECS Wade (Macmillan, 1959) (*The Law of the Constitution*). On Dicey and his contribution to legal and constitutional ideas more generally, see M Walters, *AV Dicey and the Common Law Constitutional Tradition* (Cambridge University Press, 2021).

[13] AV Dicey, *England's Case Against Home Rule* (Richmond Publishing Co, 1886) pt IV, 'Home Rule under the Gladstonian Constitution' – '1st Question – Is sovereignty of Parliament preserved?'. Dicey, *The Law of the Constitution* (n 12), acknowledged that even a sovereign Parliament could abdicate its sovereignty, but he had in mind total abdication rather than the sort of partial limitation contemplated by Home Rule. Dicey also set out the basics of parliamentary sovereignty in an 1893 publication regarding Irish Home Rule, AV Dicey, *A Leap in the Dark: A Criticism of the Principles of Home Rule as Illustrated by the Bill of 1893* (John Murray, 1893) (2nd edn, John Murray, 1911) (3rd edn, John Murray, 1912) (dedicated to 'Irish Unionists Whose Noble And Strenuous Defence Of Their Own Rights And Liberties As Citizens Of Great Britain And Ireland Will I Trust Preserve The Political Unity Of The United Kingdom'): 'Of the legislative authority of Parliament … it is scarcely necessary to speak. Any law … not only lawfully may, but can in fact be changed by … Parliament. Of the unlimited legislative authority ascribed to, and exercised by, Parliament … the Home Rule Bill itself is sufficient evidence; and the Gladstonian Ministry, at any rate, see no reason why Parliament should not within the course of a few weeks remodel the fundamental laws of the realm' (at 2–3); 'As a matter of legal theory Parliament has the right to legislate for any part of the Crown's dominions' (at 4).

For Dicey, whose preference was clearly to hold true to these core constitutional propositions, Irish Home Rule proposals represented an undesirable level of legal and political confusion. The Gladstone Government disagreed regarding the politics, but held to substantially similar legal understandings. James Bryce, himself a scholar and friend of Dicey, and for the time being Under Secretary of State for Foreign Affairs, set out the Government's view of the legal situation under the proposed Home Rule Bill of 1886. One can hear echoes of Dicey throughout Bryce's speech before Parliament:

> We shall retain as a matter of pure right the powers to legislate for Ireland, for all purposes whatsoever, for the simple reason that we cannot divest ourselves of it. There is no principle more universally admitted by constitutional jurists than the absolute omnipotence of Parliament. This omnipotence exists because there is nothing beyond Parliament, or behind Parliament ... There is one limitation and one only upon our omnipotence, and that is that we cannot bind our successors. If we pass a statute annihilating our right to legislate it may be repudiated by our successors.[14]

As a formal legal matter, at least as seen through the eyes of British jurists of the period, there seemed to be no way for those in favour of autonomy and ultimate independence for Ireland to both respect constitutional continuity *and* achieve that constitutional independence. Therefore, for both legal and political reasons, it made sense for Irish public lawyers to explore alternative foundations for independent Irish constitutional authority, even if that required a constitutional novation (or disguised legal revolution) from the perspective of British constitutional theory of the period.

The process that eventually resulted in the creation of the Irish Free State in 1922 had within it two competing legal narratives, one that would be familiar to British constitutional lawyers, and another more congenial to Irish nationalists and to the future that so many imagined for their new state. The Treaty between Great Britain and Ireland of 1921 was, *first*, given force of law under an *Act* of the Imperial Parliament,[15] and *second*, enacted as a schedule to the new Irish Free State Constitution Act, 1922 by a single-chamber Irish Parliament sitting as a constituent assembly (the Third *Dáil Éireann*). A first narrative gave precedence to the UK *Act* and was later preferred by the Judicial Committee of the Privy Council;[16] whereas a second narrative emphasised Irish events and was eventually adopted by the Supreme Court of Ireland.[17] Once appeals from Ireland to the Judicial Committee of the Privy Council ended,[18] Irish courts were free to affirm the second narrative as providing an outlet from the apparent constitutional one-way street of Westminster parliamentary sovereignty, as well as an appropriate account of the authority and legitimacy of the Irish Constitution given the independent, later republican, course that the Irish nation had set for itself.

[14] United Kingdom Parliament, *Parliamentary Debates* (10 May 1886), quoted in G Marshall, *Parliamentary Sovereignty and the Commonwealth* (Clarendon Press, 1957) 65–66. Bryce's speech is also quoted and discussed in HWR Wade, 'The Basis of Legal Sovereignty' [1955] *Cambridge Law Journal* 155, 194.

[15] See Irish Free State (Agreement) Act 1922 (12 & 13 Geo 5 c 4), s 1 referring to the Treaty in a Schedule.

[16] See *Moore v AG Irish Free State* [1935] AC 484.

[17] See, eg, *The State (Ryan) and others v Lennon* [1935] IR 70 (Kennedy CJ and Fitzgibbon J).

[18] As confirmed in *Moore* (n 16).

B. The Opening Up of New Routes to Independence

By the late 1950s and early 1960s, compelling legal accounts for the acquisition of independence, including some within the British constitutional tradition, were more readily available, and examples of apparently successful transitions to independence more plentiful.[19] According to a Kelsenian analysis, constitutional independence ultimately defying the sovereignty of the Westminster Parliament involved the positing of an independent local *Grundnorm* or Basic Norm;[20] and according to a Hartian account, the allegiance of local officials to a new local Constitution (to the exclusion of the Westminster Parliament that had enacted that Constitution) signalled the arrival of a new ultimate rule of recognition.[21] What these accounts lacked, however, was any explanation of the significance of the scrupulous respect for constitutional propriety represented by most independence legislation.[22] Those explanations were not long in coming. They focussed not only on features of the concept of law, but also on the concept of legal systems, and they did so in ways that took into account both formal legal mechanisms and an ongoing local context.

Hart's writing on uncertainty in the ultimate rule of recognition finally made clear that Dicey's version of parliamentary sovereignty was only one possible understanding of sovereignty. So while it was still possible to assert as a logical and legal proposition that a sovereign parliament could not bind future parliaments and remain absolutely sovereign (Hart called this 'continuing sovereignty'), it was also possible to assert as an equally logical, legal proposition that a sovereign parliament could do whatever it wished with that sovereignty, *including* binding future parliaments (Hart referred to this as 'self-embracing sovereignty').[23] Furthermore in his discussion of the 'pathology of legal systems', Hart reminded us that it was possible, in the context of independence, for one legal system (the UK) to cling to one version of sovereignty ('continuing') and for another legal system (the newly independent former colony) to adopt another, almost invariably more congenial version of sovereignty ('self-embracing'), even with regard to the same legal process (involving Westminster-enacted independence legislation).[24]

That which Hart did not explain was the sorts of legal and constitutional considerations that should determine whether a newly independent nation should prefer continuing sovereignty and the maintenance of the same ultimate rule of recognition

[19] The independence process for India and Pakistan followed the staged approach modelled on the Irish example – Dominion status followed only later by full independence – whereas later independence processes (involving African former colonies, for example) sought to achieve independence in one critical constitutional moment. On India and Pakistan (and the Irish model), see: 'Symposium: New Dominion Constitutionalism' in (2019) 17 *International Journal of Constitutional Law* 1166–1300, especially articles by L McDonagh, R De and M Malagodi. On later independence processes see, eg, SA de Smith, *The New Commonwealth and its Constitutions* (Stevens, 1964).

[20] H Kelsen, *General Theory of Law and State* (translated by A Wedberg) (Harvard University Press, 1949) and H Kelsen, *Pure Theory of Law* (translated by M Knight) (University of California Press, 1967) 200.

[21] HLA Hart, *The Concept of Law*, 3rd edn (Clarendon Press, 2012) 120–21.

[22] See J Finnis, 'Revolutions and Continuity of Law' in AWB Simpson (ed), *Oxford Essays in Jurisprudence*, 2nd Series (Clarendon Press, 1973) 44, 52 onwards.

[23] Hart (n 21) 147–54.

[24] ibid 120–21.

(the ongoing sovereignty of the Westminster Parliament) or self-embracing sovereignty and the substitution of a new ultimate rule of recognition (usually the supremacy of the new Constitution including a new, exclusive, domestic amending formula). The Canadian example pushed the need for an explanation to the extreme given that the Supreme Court of Canada both recognised the ultimate sovereignty of the Westminster Parliament with respect to Canada in 1981,[25] and one year later, after the enactment by the Westminster Parliament of the Canada Act 1982, confirmed that the new Constitution and its new amending formula had 'entirely replace[d]' the old Westminster-based process.[26] How can we explain Canada's apparent choice of a self-embracing understanding of the Westminster Parliament's sovereignty ahead of the continuing understanding that would have preserved a ghostly presence for that Parliament over Canadian constitutional affairs?

C. Competing Narratives of Independence

The practically-minded lawyer is of course inclined to reply that the self-embracing interpretation of the events of 1982 is the only one that corresponds with contemporary Canadian expectations of the final step in its independence process. However, it is quite possible to conjure up a counterfactual in which Canada's desire to remain part of a single Commonwealth political, economic and social Union (with Westminster as a convenient central rule-maker) would have made the continuing interpretation just as or more compelling.[27]

What we appear to be seeing here is that while the ultimate rule of a legal system can be clear in important respects (eg, that officials should recognise an enactment of the Westminster Parliament as law in relation to Canada as opposed to, say, a ruling by the Speaker of that Parliament), it can be uncertain in other vital respects as we have just seen (eg, should Canadian officials post-1982 interpret the Westminster Parliament's powers as continuing or self-embracing?). As was the case with Ireland, Canada's constitutional independence turned on the choice of one legally-available narrative over another. It would seem that post-1982 legal understandings of the 1982 patriation process were guided both by formal legal indicators (recognition of the power of the Westminster Parliament to legislate for Canada in 1982), and by ongoing contextual factors relating to Canada's lived past and imagined future (that appeared to indicate a preference for an independent social, political and economic future rather than any sort of Commonwealth Union of the kind just mentioned).

Even leading, influential positivist and natural law thinkers such as Joseph Raz and John Finnis, normally committed to the importance of law as a clear guide in a complex society,[28] acknowledge that we need to reach outside the legal system, formally understood,

[25] *Reference re Resolution to Amend the Constitution* [1981] 1 SCR 753, 194–95.

[26] *Reference re Objection to a Resolution to Amend the Constitution* [1982] 2 SCR 793, 806.

[27] I discuss this sort of counter-factual more fully (using New Zealand rather than Canada as an example) in Oliver, (n 10) pt III.

[28] See J Raz, *Practical Reason and Norms* (Oxford University Press, 1990) 159 and J Finnis, *Natural Law and Natural Rights*, 2nd edn (Oxford University Press, 2011) 8, 267.

in order to analyse scenarios such as the one just discussed.[29] An anti-positivist thinker such as Ronald Dworkin would be no better off than Hart in terms of the open-and-shut guidance of existing rules, given that they are inconclusive in our examples; and even at the level of principle-led moral reasoning preferred by his theoretical approach, it would seem difficult to arrive at the best interpretation possible without knowing more about the ongoing context of the legal systems in question, notably the future that the citizens of that legal system appeared to have charted for themselves.[30] As the factual and counter-factual scenarios noted earlier indicate, a principle such as 'democracy' could, in practical terms, point one way in the context of a wish by the majority of Canadians for complete independence and quite another way in the context of a wish by Canadians to pursue a Commonwealth Union with the Westminster Parliament as the designated central legislator.[31]

D. Concluding Observations Regarding the Acquisition of Constitutional Independence

Let us assume for sake of argument (though such matters are inevitably controversial) that this partial account of Commonwealth constitutional history justifies the following observations:

1. That Irish and Canadian examples involved in each case two compelling though competing legal narratives regarding the proper *source* of new constitutional rules, that is, the ultimate rule of the respective legal systems:
   a. The sovereignty of the Westminster Parliament versus the sovereignty of the people in the Irish example; and
   b. The continuing sovereignty versus the self-embracing sovereignty of the Westminster Parliament in the Canadian example.
2. That the intrinsic *qualities* of each of these narratives, from the perspective of constitutional rules, principles and even abstract political morality, were on 'a par'.[32]
3. That the most *appropriate* (and therefore sustainable) narratives were discoverable by reference to the *ongoing contexts* for Ireland and Canada, respectively,

[29] See J Raz, *The Concept of a Legal System: An Introduction to the Theory of Legal System*, 2nd edn (Clarendon Press, 1980) 188–89: '[N]either the "constitutional continuity" of the laws nor their content are necessary or sufficient conditions for establishing the continuity or lack of continuity of legal systems. … The identity of legal systems depends on the identity of the social forms to which they belong. The criterion of identity of legal systems is therefore determined not only by jurisprudential or legal considerations but by other considerations as well, considerations belonging to other social sciences.' See also Finnis (n 22) 69, 72: '[T]he continuity and identity of a legal system is a function of the continuity and identity of the society in whose ordered existence in time the legal system participates … "History" and "ethics" (the latter subsuming much of political philosophy) are the "social sciences" concerned with the identity of the societies and legal systems with which jurisprudence is concerned.'

[30] For further elaboration of this counter-factual and discussion of how the ultimate rule of a legal system changes, see Oliver (n 10) pt III.

[31] ibid.

[32] This is the vocabulary of the present holder of the Oxford Chair of Jurisprudence, Ruth Chang. See R Chang, 'Hard Choices' (2017) 3 *Journal of the American Philosophical Association* 1.

> that is, popular sovereignty in the Irish case and self-embracing sovereignty in the Canadian case.[33]

We know that these last-mentioned narratives are indeed those that were eventually chosen. We also know that the highest Irish or Canadian courts declaring this to be the case made it so, legally speaking. However, arguably we deprive our public law jurisprudence of important insight if we focus only on formal sources: the final enactments and the court-sanctioned interpretations. If the sustainability of our legal systems, and our legal rules, is a function not just of their pronouncement by constituent processes, legislatures and courts, but of the *quality* of those determinations, and of their *appropriateness* from the perspective of the relevant *ongoing context*, then should our jurisprudential account not say as much?

III. IS SUSTAINABILITY ALREADY A PART OF OUR EXISTING (PUBLIC LAW AND OTHER) JURISPRUDENCE?

This section seeks to identify the extent to which sustainability (related to *source*, *quality* and, most notably, *appropriateness to an ongoing context*) is already present in mainstream jurisprudential accounts, if perhaps under different names. For example, the way that we use the word 'law' points in the direction of a static rule-book picture; however, that image appears to assume that the rule-book somehow *endures*, that it is a *moving* picture, so to speak, not a photograph. Also, most positivist accounts of law include discussions of the necessary efficacy of law, which would seem to be a close cousin to sustainability. As we shall see, however, those accounts tend to have a backward-looking orientation rather than the forward-looking perspective that a sustainable public law jurisprudence would seem to require. More will be said about this below.

Normativity is another consideration that relates to sustainability, and it too will be considered. Some accounts of normativity (anti-positivist and natural law) let questions of *quality* (or morality) into the legal calculus, but we will see that these too appear to de-emphasise forward-looking, sustainability-related considerations such as real-world *quality* and *appropriateness to an ongoing context*. Section III concludes with a discussion of the place of sustainability in legal reasoning in hard cases, and in the making of legislation (or constitutions).

A. Our Standard Use of the Word 'Law': Does it Have a Rule-Book Aspect *and* A Dynamic Forward-Looking Aspect, and, if so, are Both Essential to Our Concept of Law?

HLA Hart famously explored the concept of law by focussing on the 'standard uses' of that term in what he somewhat misleadingly referred to as an exercise in 'descriptive

[33] Chang refers to the importance of 'commitment' in the context of hard choices where two options are on 'a par', ibid 2, 16. From a sustainability perspective, it is easier to commit oneself to choices that are appropriate or compatible with an ongoing context rather than destined, sooner or later, to perhaps undeserved but contextually determined failure.

sociology'.[34] In what follows, I propose a second-look or 'considered' version of that standard use that, while not emphasised by Hart, is not entirely ignored.[35]

What comes to mind when we think of law in its most common or standard use? The simple rule-book version of law has considerable immediate appeal. Hart and others employ it by way of analogy on multiple occasions, whether we think of the rules of cricket or baseball, or the rules of chess.[36] The rules in a statute book look a lot like those kinds of rules, even if they are often much longer and usually less interesting.

I think that on my first few readings of Hart's *The Concept of Law* I was reasonably satisfied or comfortable with this picture of law. However, for reasons perhaps connected to the independence-related questions explored in section II of this chapter, I eventually found myself questioning Hart's account. If our concept of legal systems needs to be dynamic rather than static, sustainable rather than stumbling, might the same not be true of our concept of law? In fact, is it not the case that even when we focus on the static rule-book version of law we are assuming that neither the individual rules nor the rule-book as a whole are here one second and gone or in the process of evaporating the next? To my mind, the only possible answer is 'yes'.[37] The picture of private laws that allow us to make wills and contracts, or of public laws that empower a legislature to enact laws that make murder and assault crimes, but that then evaporates or declines in relevance in the moments or months that follow, does not correspond with our standard use of the word 'law'. It seems that in the original conception of law I was *assuming* that the rules and rule-book that have a static image in my mind's eye would have to have some quality of endurance or sustainability. The rules and rule-book that were here one moment and gone, or beginning to evaporate, the next would not just be poor examples of law, but rather not the right picture of law at all, or at least not in the standard use that I (and others, I believe[38]) regularly employ. By this I mean

[34] Hart (n 21) Preface, vi. I say that this is somewhat misleading because, as will become clear by way of contrast with a sustainable jurisprudence, Hart's positivism seems, relatively speaking, largely disinterested in the real-life context into which law plays out. I put aside for the moment whether Hart's conceptual focus is a sufficient inquiry, or merely a pre-interpretive move, as it is viewed in the Dworkinian model. As I indicate below, even the Dworkinian interpretative approach is lacking from the future-focussed sustainable perspective that I emphasise in this chapter.

[35] By referring to 'standard use' I do not deny that law is used in ways that differ from the standard use, such as explored in legal pluralism. See, eg, RA Macdonald, 'L'hypothèse du pluralisme juridique dans les sociétés avancés' (2002–2003) *Revue de droit de Sherbrooke* 135 and J-G Belley, 'Le pluralisme juridique comme doctrine de la science du droit' dans Jean Kellerhals et al (eds), *Pour un droit pluriel : Études offertes au professeur Jean-François Perrin* (Helbing & Lichtenhahn, 2002) 135. For the purposes of this chapter, I am mostly interested in examining 'law' as it is most often used and understood by public lawyers. We will see that if I am right about the sorts of questions that we need to ask and answer regarding our standard use of the word 'law', then the existence of plural normativities may be one of the social-scientific facts with which 'state law' must be cognizant as it faces the future.

[36] See, eg, Hart (n 21) 9, 40, 56–57, 89, 102–103, 142–45. R Dworkin, *Taking Rights Seriously* (Duckworth, 1977) 24.

[37] In hearing a paper that I presented on a related theme, Professor Farrah Ahmed of the University of Melbourne helpfully pointed out that a hypothetical nomadic community might have laws that only endure for the time spent, say, at a particular oasis, and that this might be a very short time indeed. To my mind this helpful example shows that there is no identifiable *minimum* duration that allows something to qualify as law, the endurance factor being relative to that which law or laws set out to do. But some degree of endurance or sustainability is nonetheless necessary. A law that appears and disappears in the same instant cannot accomplish anything. A law that appears and then begins a process of evaporation accomplishes less and less, a matter that is a concern for the project of law.

[38] It is perhaps important at this point to note that one's conception of law may well depend upon the perspective one has in mind. The rule-book version of law naturally appeals to the lawyer advising a client and to the citizen seeking to respect that law and/or avoid imprisonment. It perhaps has less resonance for the appeal-court

that, while the enduring or sustainable nature of law may often be overlooked, it is nonetheless an essential feature of the law we have in mind. In emphasising the future-focussed, sustainability element in law, in addition to the past-focussed rule-in-the-rule-book element, I am not suggesting that a conception favouring only the latter is impossible. I am instead asserting that it does not fit our considered version of a standard use.[39]

What is the 'considered use' of 'law'? As I indicated earlier, the rule-book version of law was one that I associated with Hart. And yet, in re-reading the first few chapters of *The Concept of Law* with a future-focussed, sustainability question in mind, I found that Hart alludes to what I have referred to as a more considered version. Unlike the Austin-inspired gunman's threat that need only be temporary, laws must have an 'enduring character', according to Hart:[40] ('the gunman does not issue … *standing orders* to be followed time after time';[41] 'laws pre-eminently have this "standing" or *persistent* characteristic' (emphasis added)).[42] Still with the gunman situation in mind, Hart asserts that '[m]ere *temporary* ascendancy of one person over another is naturally thought of as the polar opposite of law, with its *relatively enduring and settled* character' (emphasis added).[43] Further along, in his famously critical discussion of Austin's sovereign, Hart emphasises two particularly important features of most legal systems: 'the *continuity* of the authority to make law possessed by a succession of different legislators, and the *persistence* of laws long after their maker … [has] perished'.[44]

It would seem then that the full, considered way in which we use the word 'law' has two aspects: first, an aspect that corresponds with the rule-book conception of law and that allows us to identify for the most part the rules that are valid (or invalid); and second, a future-focussed, sustainability aspect that is equally necessary according to the considered use of law, though often measurable only according to a necessarily tentative, relative standard. It is perhaps this difficulty to gauge or measure that explains why it is often overlooked. As we have seen, Hart makes passing references to the second aspect, viewing it as essential to law's enduring character, but his focus, as is the case for most positivist scholars, is clearly on the first aspect.

If we assume for the moment that our concept of law necessarily includes *both* of these aspects – that it is rule-like, but that those rules also have to somehow endure for

judge deciding a hard case, or for the legislator or framer making difficult drafting choices, perspectives that, when conceptualised in a manner that is sustainable, include but also extend beyond the moment of judgment or enactment. It is argued here that even the practising lawyer and the citizen are implicitly also relying on the enduring aspect of law, though they are temporarily and habitually focussed on the static, rule-book aspect.

[39] What do I mean by a 'considered' version of standard use? Returning to the medical analogy employed in the Introduction, let us assume that the medical profession makes frequent use of the term 'medical "treatment"' in both the teaching and in the practice of medicine. When asked to consider their standard use of the term, health professionals might well say something along the lines of 'a medical *treatment* is a pill or procedure administered to a patient'. If those same professionals were asked whether what they had in mind included the pill or procedure *and* their ongoing future effects, it would be open to them to say 'no, we mean only that which is administered on the day'. However, it strikes me that both the teaching and practice of medicine make more sense if 'treatment' also includes both the administration of the pill or procedure *and* the ongoing effects, and I suspect that the considered view of health professionals would confirm that.

[40] Hart (n 21) 23–24.

[41] ibid 23. Hart is here giving primary emphasis to the generality of law but the need for all laws to have an enduring quality is also apparent.

[42] ibid.

[43] ibid 24.

[44] ibid 51.

a time in order to deliver what we expect from law – then we might ask what it is in our concept of law that accounts for this second necessary aspect? A new rule for a game, like a new 'legal' rule can appear in written form and yet have no, or weak, enduring effects, generally or sectorally,[45] for a multitude of reasons. The enduring quality of law would seem at first glance to be related to a familiar, apparently essential, feature of Hart and others' discussion of the concept of law: efficacy (or effectiveness).

B. Is Efficacy a Proxy for Future-Focussed Sustainability?

Efficacy[46] is commonly said by positivists to be an essential component of the concepts of law and legal system.[47] Perhaps here lies the element of our public law jurisprudence that accounts for the future-focussed, enduring or sustainability aspect of law.

Austin famously referred to the commands of the sovereign to which 'the bulk of the given society are in *a habit of obedience*', that habit suggesting a relatively high level of efficacy (emphasis added).[48] Hart placed greater emphasis on the conduct of officials, but he allowed that 'those rules of behaviour which are valid according the system's ultimate criteria of validity must be generally obeyed'.[49] He referred to this as 'a necessary condition'.[50] Kelsen stated that 'the efficacy of the total legal order is a necessary condition for the validity of every single norm of the order',[51] and furthermore that a legal order is considered valid 'if its norms are by and large effective'.[52]

All of this would seem to be germane to the issue of law's future sustainability until one realises that each of these positivist scholars is referring to efficacy from the perspective of the past-until-present rather than from the difficult-to-determine but essential perspective of the present going forward into the future.[53] The former perspective

[45] By 'sectorally', I mean 'in a certain sector of the targeted community to which the rules or laws apply'. A legal rule might work passably well in the polity as a whole but very badly, for example, in Indigenous communities or in certain specialised business sectors. I say more about this below in the discussion of efficacy in Kelsen's writings.

[46] 'Efficacy has different meanings within legal discourse. It may, eg, refer to the capacity of legal norms to produce legal effects (eg, rights, duties, liabilities, etc) or to their capacity to realize the goals for which they were produced or to the fact that their addressees actually behave as they require of them', L Burazin, 'The Concept of Law and Efficacy' in M Sellers and S Kirste (eds), *Encyclopedia of the Philosophy of Law and Social Philosophy* (Springer, 2017), available at www.link.springer.com/referenceworkentry/10.1007/978-94-007-6730-0_231-1. Either meaning is acceptable for the purposes of the discussion in this chapter so long as the implied word 'ongoing' is rendered explicit, as in: 'the [ongoing] capacity …'.

[47] The efficacy condition has recently been considered by Thomas Adams, who rightfully points out that '[d]espite widespread recognition that efficacy is a condition of the existence of law … little time has been spent analyzing the notion': T Adams, 'The Efficacy Condition' (2020) 25 *Legal Theory* 225, 225.

[48] J Austin, *The Province of Jurisprudence Determined* (Cambridge University Press, 1995) Lecture 1.

[49] Hart (n 21) 116.

[50] ibid 112 and 116.

[51] Kelsen, *General Theory of Law and State* (n 20) 119.

[52] Kelsen, *Pure Theory of Law* (n 20) 212.

[53] See, eg, Kelsen, *Pure Theory of Law* (n 20) 212 referring to whether 'the Constitution is *actually* established and effective' (emphasis added). In Kelsen, *General Theory of Law and State* (n 20) 172–73, he discusses efficacy from the perspective of normative and sociological jurisprudence and notes the possibility of considering future efficacy. He appears to be disinterested in the sorts of considerations considered below regarding *declining* efficacy/health, preferring to view things as a general matter pertaining to the legal order as a whole. 'It would hardly be possible to foresee at the moment of enactment … As long as the legal order as a whole retains its

does not explicitly exclude the latter; rather it appears to *assume* that past efficacy still observed in the present is determinative of future efficacy, something that is contingent rather than truly worthy of that assumption, given the fast-changing world in which we live. In the Austinian and Kelsenian conceptions of law, threats or sanctions have a prominent place, which perhaps explains why past efficacy is assumed to persist into the future. However, not only is the sustainability of *bad* and *inappropriate* laws unclear even when combined with sanctions, but, as will be discussed in the following section, Hart convincingly pointed out that important parts of law, notably public law, involve the *conferral* of power rather than the imposition of duties backed by threat.[54] One can try to look at the legislative delegation to a minister as threat or sanctioned based, but that arguably deforms rather than informs legal analysis, as Hart himself concluded.[55]

The past-until-present perspective on efficacy is consistent with the rule-book focus of positivist scholars. Once the existence of a valid rule is established according to some version of the sources thesis (common to most or all positivist conceptions of law[56]), the rule is 'in the book', so to speak, and the necessary (though on this version artificially limited) efficacy requirement is usually easily satisfied, both because it is a weak, past-focussed standard and because it is assessed in only the most general, society-wide terms.

This past, society-wide focus is particularly clear in Kelsen, who is committed to driving a middle path between two extremes that he views as untenable. On one extreme (labelled 'idealistic') is the view that the validity of law is entirely independent of its efficacy; and on the other extreme (labelled 'realistic') is the view that validity and efficacy run together.[57] For Kelsen, one should not be forced to choose between the poles of validity *independent of* efficacy, or validity *amounting to* efficacy, any more than one should have to choose between life *only* meaning birth and life *only* meaning nourishment.[58]

Focussing on the latter half of Kelsen's health-related analogy for the moment, we can observe that efficacy is clearly vital to law just as nourishment is vital to life, but that neither law nor life is *equivalent* to efficacy/nourishment. The upshot of this analysis would seem to be that at any moment after creation or birth, it is possible to identify both law and life even where there are marginal levels of efficacy or nourishment (provided, that is, that one focusses, as Kelsen does, on law and life at the present moment and averts one gaze from the more precarious, even marginal prospects for the future on this scenario). It is hard to see this approach as sustainable, whether one is ignoring the future consequences altogether, or minimising the ongoing importance of efficacy or nourishment for the future. For the doctor as for the jurist, declining health, not just the fact of life at any given moment, is always a matter of concern.

efficacy, as long as the government is able generally to obtain obedience, of all possibilities the most likely seems to be that a regulation issued by the competent authorities will actually be carried out.' See also Hart (n 21) 104 ('a system of rules which *had* … never actually been effective', 'that the system *is* generally efficacious'); 105 ('for, though … the judge presupposes but does not state the general efficacy of the system, he plainly is not concerned to predict …').

[54] See nn 63 and 64) and accompanying text.

[55] See Hart (n 21) 38.

[56] J Raz, *The Authority of Law* (Clarendon Press, 1979) 46 onwards.

[57] Kelsen, *Pure Theory of Law* (n 20) 208–14.

[58] ibid.

So much for Kelsen's problematic focus on the past. What about the drawbacks in his general, society-wide perspective on efficacy? As noted above, Kelsen's criterion for efficacy refers to a general ('*by and large*' (emphasis added[59]) assessment. Similarly, Austin refers to general obedience in 'the *bulk of … society*' (emphasis added)[60] and Hart to 'rules of behaviour … *generally* obeyed' (emphasis added).[61] Combining the observations regarding the past-present and society-wide focus, and continuing with the health care analogy, this would seem to indicate that for Kelsen's purposes, law, like life, can be measured and confirmed in the present on the basis of *general* vital statistics while ignoring, as non-essential, the legal equivalent of future atrophy, partial paralysis, undernourishment, mental illness or, in the extreme, self-destructive and suicidal tendencies, even if any or all of these are already foreseeable.

The considered conception of law included a necessary future-focussed, sustainability aspect that would certainly have taken into account, at least in relative, difficult-to-measure terms, the pathological factors just alluded to. It is tempting to insist immediately that *future* efficacy, both generally *and* sectorally, is a necessary component of a considered concept of law absent from leading jurisprudential accounts. But perhaps it is too early to come to that conclusion.

Perhaps other components in existing conceptions of law can serve that purpose. If, for the moment, we hang onto the idea that efficacy as commonly understood is not the place to consider law's sustainability, due to the past-present rather than present-future focus, perhaps the matter of 'normativity'[62] or obligation can do better.

C. Is Normativity a Proxy for Future-Focussed Sustainability?

Positivist theories of law are particularly good at helping us to explain that which constitutes valid law; however, they are on the whole less adept at accounting for law's normativity, keeping in mind that both of these elements – validity and normativity – correspond with the standard rule-book model of law. (That is, we assume that any concept of law worth its salt will provide an account for, first, how we identify valid law, and, second, the sense in which that law is in some sense obligatory.)

Austin's command theory is an exception to the statement that positivism struggles to provide an account for normativity or obligation. 'Commands' backed by 'threats' would seem to explain law's normativity so far as that goes. As noted in the previous section, one of the most telling criticisms that Hart made of Austin was that much of law does not fit the duty-imposing 'command and threat' model.[63] Much of law, including much of public law, is power-conferring rather than duty-imposing.[64] One thinks, for example, of the power-conferring nature of the law of federalism or of public administration.

[59] ibid 212.
[60] Austin (n 48).
[61] Hart (n 21) 116.
[62] Understood as 'law's capacity to guide our conduct'. See S Delacroix, 'Understanding Normativity' (2019) 37 *Journal for Constitutional Theory and Philosophy of Law* 17.
[63] Hart (n 21) ch 3.
[64] ibid 33.

Kelsen's and, especially, Hart's theories could account for a more representative variety of laws, but it is hard to see their accounts of normativity filling the explanatory need that we have identified regarding law's future sustainability. Using Raz's vocabulary we can describe Kelsen's account as a form of '*justified* normativity',[65] though as we shall see the word 'justified' is used here in the most watered-down manner. In the by-now familiar logical-normative ascent up through the hierarchy of norms and back through the chain of validity until one reaches the first historical constitution and, behind it, the *Grundnorm* or Basic Norm, one finds Kelsen's account for both the validity and the normativity of, say, a local city by-law; however, this normative thread is impossibly thin and weak if one is searching for an account of the future sustainability of that by-law. According to Raz's description of justified normativity 'an individual can consider a legal system as normative only if he endorses it as morally just and good'; however, '[l]egal theory considers legal systems as normative in the same sense of "normative" but in a different sense of "consider" which does not commit it to accepting the laws as just'.[66] It is the fact that the Basic Norm is presupposed that injects the legal system with (justified) normativity, not any particular *quality* of normative content or consideration of *appropriateness to context*, and therefore there is nothing here that accounts for law's endurance or sustainability, unless one reverts to Austin's partial threat-based account.

Raz classifies Hart's account as a form of 'social normativity' according to which 'standards of behaviour can be considered norms ... in so far as they are socially upheld', and therefore 'regardless of their merit'.[67] Those who *participate* in games like cricket, baseball or chess provide examples of social normativity, viewed from the internal point of view.[68] So too do those who queue for a London bus, though Hart is agnostic as to the explanations that each person in the queue might have for their conforming behaviour. One person might feel a full sense of social obligation, another might be following what others in the queue are doing, another may simply be daydreaming, and so on. And so too for law, on Hart's account. As Hart stated, '[citizens] may obey each "for his part only" and from any motive whatever'.[69] Hart was famously anxious about the adequacy of his own account of normativity and legal obligation,[70] and one can see why, given its lack of any 'justification', even remaining with Raz's watered-down use of the term 'normativity'. Raz was able to recast Hart's social normativity as a statement from the legal point of view, thereby transforming it into a type of justified normativity, but Hart's account recast in this way by Raz is no more useful to explain law's endurance or sustainability than Kelsen's is. Even an anarchist with no genuine commitment to law whatsoever could adopt the legal point of view, as a mere citizen or even as an official, on this account,[71] just as a medical science sceptic or charlatan could adopt the medical point of view. It is hard to see how considerations of *quality* and *appropriateness to ongoing context* get

[65] Raz (n 56) 134 ('According to one view [justified normativity] legal standards of behaviour are norms only if and in so far as they are justified' (emphasis added)).

[66] ibid 134–35.

[67] ibid 134.

[68] On the importance of the internal point of view, see Hart (n 21) 89–91.

[69] ibid 116.

[70] See N Lacey, *A Life of HLA Hart: The Nightmare and the Noble Dream* (Oxford University Press, 2004) 228: '[Hart] was never convinced that he had satisfactorily resolved this dilemma about the restricted, but genuinely normative, notion of obligation'.

[71] Raz (n 56) 138.

taken seriously in this sort of pantomime, by which I mean that the latter requirements, as opposed to merely identifying source-based law, would seem to require some level of commitment to and understanding of the task at hand.

Somewhat counterintuitively, one place where one can find a glimpse of analysis that might feed into an account of law's future-focussed sustainability is in positivists' description of what happens when no law is available, or where the law is unsettled – what happens in 'hard cases', in other words.

D. What Does an Account of 'Hard Cases' Tell Us in Relation to Future-Focussed Sustainability?

We usually associate the term 'hard cases' with Ronald Dworkin, whose legal philosophy will be addressed (in necessarily summary terms) in the next subsection. Dworkin began the chapter entitled 'Hard Cases' in *Taking Rights Seriously* by presenting the positivist view with which he disagreed. '[L]egal positivism provides a theory of hard cases': '[w]hen a particular law-suit cannot be brought under a clear rule of law, laid down by some institution in advance, then the judge has, according to that theory, a 'discretion' to decide the case either way'.[72]

Even those positivists most disposed to the view that law must be clear (in order to serve as a second-order exclusionary reason in Raz's authority-focussed terminology)[73] acknowledge that there are cases where there is no law that determines an answer, and that judges must exercise discretion.[74] Hart accepts that in hard cases, 'at the margin of rules and in the fields left open by the theory of precedents',[75] judges exercise a 'rule-producing' rather than a 'rule-following' function.[76] Without succumbing to anything like full-blown scepticism, Hart nonetheless acknowledges that, in by far the greatest number of cases, the law is *not* clear and the judge has to exercise *a degree of discretion*. 'It is only the tradition that judges "find" and do not "make" law that conceals this and presents their decisions as if they were deductions smoothly made from clear pre-existing rules without intrusion of the judge's choice.'[77] Hart notes that uncertainty is particularly present in constitutional law.[78] We have seen in section II of this chapter, that uncertainty can extend to the ultimate rules of the legal system. Hart comments on how it is a mistake – 'a formalist error'[79] – to '[think] that every step taken by a court is covered

[72] Dworkin (n 36) 81.

[73] Raz (n 28) 35–48. Much like the way an arbitrator's decision, whether understood or approved by both parties, provides a basis on which to move forward, law represents a second-order, exclusionary means of putting first-order debates about the morality of certain options in the rear-view mirror and consequently a means of moving on, guided by the authoritative legal rule. This allows law to perform its vital coordinating function.

[74] Dworkin (n 36) 33, describing the positivist point of view, puts it this way: '[T]he positivist doctrine of judicial discretion … argues that if a case is not controlled by an established rule, the judge must decide it by exercising discretion.'

[75] Hart (n 21) 135.

[76] ibid.

[77] ibid. Hart famously goes on to state that '[l]egal rules may have a central core of undisputed meaning … [y]et all rules have a penumbra of uncertainty where the judge must choose between alternatives'.

[78] ibid 13.

[79] ibid 153.

by some general rule conferring in advance the authority to take it'.[80] In cases where there is uncertainty at level of the ultimate rule of recognition, for example, 'all that succeeds is success'.[81] If the reality of discretion in hard cases is apparent in these comments, the way in which officials such as judges should go about answering such cases is less clear. Raz is more forthcoming than Hart on this point.

According to Raz, 'if a legal question is not answered by standards deriving from legal sources then it lacks a legal answer'.[82] As a positivist, Raz is committed to the relevance of the 'sources thesis'.[83] In his discussion on 'gaps' in the law, Raz clarifies that '[t]he point of the sources thesis is not that courts never rely on sourceless considerations, but rather that when doing so they are not relying on legally binding considerations but *exercising their own discretion*' (emphasis added).[84] How is that discretion exercised? Raz goes on to say that where legal sources provide no answer '[n]aturally, [courts'] decisions in such cases rely at least partly on *moral* and *other extra-legal* considerations' (emphasis added).[85] '[I]n deciding cases regarding which the law is unsettled … judges … develop the law using *moral, social, and other non-legal* arguments (emphasis added)'.[86] It is for this reason that, '[w]hen discussing appointment to the Bench' we look not just for 'legal experience and expertise' but also for '*wisdom* and *understanding of human nature … moral sensibility … enlightened approach*, etc' (emphasis added).[87] Though clearly acknowledging the importance of 'wisdom and understanding' in hard cases, Raz remains generally committed to the sources thesis, causing him to persist in separating out criticism of a decision into what are traditionally referred to as legal considerations (it is 'legally defective') and policy considerations (it 'betray[s] gross insensitivity to current social conditions').[88] However, if our considered conception of law includes both rule-book and essential future-focussed, sustainability-related aspects, then both considerations are properly viewed as legal (even if the former is measured in clear, binary terms and the latter in less clear, relative terms).

It may be helpful if we use a categorisation of legal cases provided by Hart to reprise what may be going on when courts decide easy and hard cases, but if we look at that categorisation from the perspective of a sustainable jurisprudence. In 'easy' or 'simple cases' it may well be true, according to Hart, that 'decisions are the necessary consequence of predetermined rules whose meaning is fixed and clear'.[89] As all lawyers are aware, it is this certainty and predictability that is said in many[90] legal cultures to contribute in important ways to its durability, that is, to its sustainability.

[80] ibid.
[81] ibid.
[82] Raz(n 56) 50.
[83] See (n 56) and accompanying text.
[84] Raz (n 56) 59.
[85] ibid.
[86] ibid 49.
[87] ibid 48.
[88] ibid.
[89] Hart (n 21) 12.
[90] It is easy to imagine a legal culture in which the sustainability of law is based not on the certainty and predictability of pre-existing (ie, *source*-focussed) law, but on accumulation of wise (ie, high *quality*) case-by-case decisions taken by enlightened decision-makers. Positivist thinkers often emphasise the need for certainty and predictability in order to coordinate complex societies. See n 73 and accompanying text.

Hart continues: '[b]ut in the vast majority of cases ... neither statutes nor precedents allow of one result'.[91] Nonetheless, 'courts so frame their judgments as to give the impression that their decisions are the necessary consequence'[92] of predetermined, clear rules. From the perspective of a forward-looking sustainable jurisprudence, presenting something that is unclear as clear *can* be positive. Just as the average patient may not want to know what parts of a diagnosis and treatment are based on medical science and what parts are based on the health professionals' experience and judgement, so too the average citizen may not want to know how much of a legal decision was clearly predetermined by a fixed rule and how much was necessarily based on a discretionary judgement. However, it would be dangerous, it is argued here, both to medical and to legal education and to a sustainable practice of medicine and law, if dogmatic assertions of medical and legal certainty supplanted frank acknowledgment of the role of a wider range of considerations and judgements in medicine and law. At the end of Hart's categorisation, of course, we return to the 'important' or hard cases where 'there is *always* a choice' (emphasis added).[93]

In all of the cases that do not qualify as 'simple' or straightforward, a choice presents itself for our concept of law. We can either say, with Hart and Raz, that hard cases involve to varying degrees choice, discretion, judgement and wisdom rather than the mere application of law, and focus on the fact that the discretion *once exercised* becomes part of the corpus of law, a new *source* of law; or, from the perspective of an emerging sustainable jurisprudence, we can acknowledge all of that *and* note that the *quality* and the *ongoing contextual appropriateness* of that discretion or judgement will inevitably have an impact on the ability of that new law to endure, including possible knock-on or feedback effects on the very authority of law that positivists prize, and that therefore the whole category should be considered 'legal'.

While leading positivist accounts of law provide refreshing honesty regarding the various elements that go into decision-making in hard cases, these accounts persist in separating out the supposedly non-legal (including *quality* and *ongoing contextual appropriateness*) from the supposedly legal. If future-focussed sustainability is a *necessary* component of law, then the former cannot be considered non-legal even if they can only be measured in difficult-to-assess relative terms rather than the clear binary of rule-book law.

Traditional natural law and contemporary anti-positivist theories explicitly acknowledge the importance to a concept of law of moral considerations, or what have been referred to thus far as sustainability-related considerations regarding *quality*. As we will see, however, such moral or quality-related considerations tend to involve either backward-looking inquiry in the case of Ronald Dworkin's anti-positivism, or preliminary moral inquiry culminating in an essentially positivist version of law in the case of John Finnis' natural law. Another way of putting this is that neither of these accounts appear to make room in their accounts of law for sustainability-related consideration of real-world, social-scientific elements of *quality* or the *appropriateness* of law *for ongoing*, often changing *contexts*. But let us examine that assertion.

[91] Hart (n 21) 12.
[92] ibid.
[93] ibid.

E. Do Anti-Positivist and Natural Law Concepts of Law Make Room for Future-Focussed Sustainability Considerations?

i. Discretion and Reflective Equilibrium

On Ronald Dworkin's anti-positivist account of law, scholars such as Hart deceive themselves by thinking that we can all agree on relevant legal criteria such as a shared concept of law,[94] and by thinking that discretion in hard cases is independent of legal considerations and constraints.[95] When Dworkin first introduced his principle-led, interpretive, jurisprudential theory, he indicated that judges in hard cases engage in a sort of reflective equilibrium[96] in developing the common law (in public law or otherwise), moving back-and-forth, or to-and-fro, between the underlying *legal* principles, on the one hand, and the more particularised intuitions represented by existing case law on the other.[97] The more recent and better-known version of this approach is Dworkin's famous chain novel analogy, according to which judges are seen metaphorically to be providing a new chapter in a novel each time they decide a case, while remaining faithful to the chapters written by judges in earlier cases.[98]

In a contrasting version of reflective equilibrium, that of John Finnis, the back-and-forth of reflective equilibrium is between (natural law or other) principles on the one hand and *social scientific context*[99] on the other.[100] This variation on reflective equilibrium is expressly rejected by Dworkin.[101] Is there any important difference between the

[94] Dworkin famously employs the expression 'semantic sting' to describe this form of self-deception: R Dworkin, *Law's Empire* (Fontana, 1986) 45.

[95] Dworkin (n 36) 31–39.

[96] 'Viewed most generally, a "reflective equilibrium" is the end-point of a deliberative process in which we reflect on and revise our beliefs about an area of inquiry, moral or non-moral.' N Daniels, 'Reflective Equilibrium' in EN Zalta (ed), *The Stanford Encyclopedia of Philosophy* (archived Spring 2010 Edition), available at https://plato.stanford.edu/archives/spr2010/entries/reflective-equilibrium/.

[97] Dworkin (n 36) 155–68.

[98] Dworkin (n 94) 228–38.

[99] Finnis (n 28) 17–18: 'explanatory descriptions (using all appropriate historical, experimental, and statistical techniques to trace all relevant causal interrelationships of the human context in which human well-being is variously realized and variously ruined'; 'descriptive social science'; 'knowledge of the facts of the human situation'.

[100] See, eg, the reflective equilibrium described (though not always applied, I would argue) by John Finnis (ibid). Finnis uses this form of advanced practical reasoning in order to work through the moral considerations that lead us to the conclusion that Law is required in order to achieve basic forms of human good. However, once we are within the sphere of Law, reflective equilibrium appears to play no further part in Finnis' account. Finnis quietly acknowledges that there are (hard) cases where the law does not provide an obvious answer ('"legislator"… includes any judiciary that, like the judge at common law, enjoys a creative role' (ibid 286)), and where the court must presumably exercise the sort of judgment that both Hart and Raz acknowledge, as we have seen, and that in Finnis' initial take (ibid 17–18) clearly involves practical reasoning and reflective equilibrium. One looks in vain, at least in his *magnum opus*, for a fuller exploration of this scenario. A clue as to the reason for the absence of such an exploration may be where Finnis notes (ibid 269), that lawyers rely on the admittedly fictitious postulate that there are 'no gaps' in the law, that is, that 'every present practical question … has, in every respect, been … "provided for" by some … past juridical act or acts', concluding that there is 'no need to labour the point' (ibid). A sustainable jurisprudence would seem to require labouring this point if only to explain how judicial legislation that does not consider 'extra-legal considerations' (Raz (n 56) 59) can speak to what that approach deems to be the essential requirement of future sustainability. See also the discussion below (n 110) and accompanying text of Finnis's understanding of *determinationes* or concretisations of general (natural law) principles.

[101] See Dworkin (n 36) 159–66, where he distinguishes between moral and common law forms of reasoning, the former taking facts (context) into account and the latter confined to something akin to specifications of general principle.

two variations? To my mind there is, and crucially so, especially from the perspective of a sustainable jurisprudence. One can adapt the chain novel metaphor to make the point.

In Dworkin's version, the judge seized with a hard question must ensure fidelity to the themes, setting, and characterisations that have been developed in past chapters, with no necessary concern for how those relate to life in the polity. While this may not seem odd when we are talking about novels, which can be as fantastical as they like, it is a surprising assertion when talking about law, an institution that is designed not to entertain or divert but to regulate real people in real, multi-sectored societies, and to do so on a sustainable basis. Dworkin's model had the advantage, formally speaking, of confining judges' tools to rules, principles, and even political morality developed in the past and applied in the present. As we have seen, so many of our immediate, perhaps insufficiently considered, legal instincts tell us that this past-focussed emphasis is the proper way for law to work. The problem with Dworkin's version of reflective equilibrium is that, by excluding from consideration the social-scientific context, law risks becoming less relevant and less effective in the future in the society, or in sectors of the society, to which it is meant to apply. Laws and legal systems, unlike chain novels, have to be relevant and effective (and sustainable) in the real world, for if it is otherwise the promise of the rule of law cannot be realised. With that in mind, it would seem to make more sense, *contra* Dworkin, to move in reflective equilibrium between principles and the real, variable, ongoing context.

ii. Discretion and Hard Cases

The foregoing discussion is also of course relevant to Dworkin's criticism of the positivist account of discretion and hard cases.[102] Dworkin disagrees with what he takes to be positivists' adoption of a strong sense of discretion with regard to hard cases, according to which the decision-maker is not bound by legal standards at all, as we saw in the previous section.[103] He attributes this erroneous view to positivists' focus on rules to the exclusion of other relevant legal tools such as principles.[104] According to Dworkin, if what positivists mean by discretion is that principles do not '*determine* a particular result' then they have said nothing more pertinent than that 'principles are not rules' (emphasis added).[105] 'Only rules *dictate* results ….' (emphasis added)[106] 'Principles do not work in that way; they incline a decision one way, though not conclusively'.[107]

> If a judge believes that principles he is bound to recognize point in one direction and … principles pointing in another direction … are not of equal weight, then he must decide accordingly, just as he must follow what he believes to be a binding rule.[108]

We see here that, on Dworkin's account, principles do indeed guide adjudication; but we also see that principles, by their very nature, do not 'determine a particular result'. Something other than the principles themselves is at work in Dworkin's model of

[102] Dworkin (n 36) 31–39.
[103] ibid 32.
[104] ibid 38.
[105] ibid 35.
[106] ibid.
[107] ibid.
[108] ibid 35–36.

adjudication; hence the relevance of the discussion regarding reflective equilibrium, and the status of social science considerations (the particularities of morality (or *quality*) and the *appropriateness of the ongoing context*) to that reasoning process.

iii. Discretion and Determinationes

Dworkin's observations regarding discretion bring to mind a familiar form of analysis that appears prominently in natural law scholarship. Natural law scholars point out that legal sceptics of all kinds exaggerate the discretionary nature of adjudication because the latter fail to make a distinction, fundamental to natural lawyers, between general principles of natural law and the concretisation of those general principles in the form of more precise rules (*determinationes*).[109] Finnis, for example, illustrates this phenomenon by means of an analogy taken from architecture. In architecture:

> [A] general idea of 'form' (say 'house', 'door', 'door-knob') has to be made determinate … with specifications which are certainly derived from and shaped by the general idea but which could have been more or less different in many (even in every!) particular dimension and aspect, and which therefore require of the artificer a multitude of choices.

These choices may appear to be discretionary in the strong sense, but they are not: 'the (making of the) artefact is controlled but not fully determined by the basic idea'.[110] And, of course, the same is said to be true, by analogy, in the making of concrete legal rules, 'controlled but not fully determined' in this case by more general principles.

If we bring the architectural and the legal examples together, we might ask how a judge should approach a hard case regarding whether a particular building owner should be allowed to install throughout the building particularly creative door-handles that are in practice (according to social-scientific research) unusable by disabled users of the premises, perhaps in circumstances where the existing law refers only to a requirement that all doors have handles. Both Dworkin and Finnis acknowledge that principles do not determine a particular result, but in their insistence on underlining the role of those pre-existing principles, they do not explain what other factors ensure that the eventual decision is not just consistent with pre-existing principles but particularised for all members of society, including the disabled, and generally appropriate to a changing context in which mobility is increasingly vital to freedom. In Dworkin's case, we have seen that his reflective equilibrium deliberately ignores the social-scientific context. Finnis' general, working version of reflective equilibrium includes principles *and* social-scientific context,[111] but he appears to reserve reflective equilibrium for the moral reasoning that leads us to Law, not for the elaboration of the laws themselves. When he comes to discuss reasoning in the law context, the back-and-forth involving social scientific context is gone, even in the sorts of hard cases that were discussed in looking at the positivist account.[112] The result of a failure to consider context from the perspective of a sustainable jurisprudence is that, in

[109] See Finnis (n 28) 281 onwards. See also J Finnis, 'The Critical Legal Studies Movement' (1985) 30 *American Journal of Jurisprudence* 21, 22–26.
[110] Finnis (n 28) 284.
[111] ibid 17–18.
[112] ibid 260 and discussion in n 101.

a society where disabled issues have been invisible in the past, a decision in favour of full discretion in the choice of door-handles is available, despite the unsustainability of that choice for an important if frequently neglected section of society. Such a decision would clearly now be law in the source-focussed, rule-book sense of that concept, but it could be said to be sorely lacking in terms of its future sustainability for an important part of the polity, with difficult to measure knock-on and feedback implications for the authority of law, sectorally and more widely.

F. What Bearing, if Any, do Future-Focussed, Sustainability Considerations have on Legislating (Primary and Secondary) and on Constitution Making?

The foregoing discussion has been in relation to 'law' generally, without distinction between, for example, constitutions, legislation, regulations and case law. Consistent with the tendency in the common-law legal tradition, that jurisprudential inquiry placed case law in the foreground in a way that is relevant to public law but not fully representative. Constitutions, legislation and regulations dominate public law and can claim democratic legitimacy in a way that is unavailable to case law. In fact, not only does case law lack democratic legitimacy, but judicial power is frequently feared or criticised for its lack of the same.[113] One way or the other, such democratic legitimacy contributes to the initial source-based authority of those legislative (and other) instruments and is therefore relevant to our discussion of sustainability.

This chapter has already explored how the sustainability of case law varies in relation to *source*, *quality* and *appropriateness to an ongoing context*. Even undemocratic decisions by judges can be sustainable if the authority of the judicial *source* continues to be recognised, if the *quality* of decisions is good, and if those decisions are reasonably *appropriate to a changing context* (both generally and sectorally).

What of the sustainability of legal measures that have initial democratic legitimacy? Source-based authority should benefit from such legitimacy, as already noted. But what if such measures are simply based on wedge politics and other partisan interests, or are deliberately designed to benefit only the sectors of society that generally support the party in power, and are otherwise lacking in merit. Such measures might well lack *quality* and *appropriateness to a changing context*, with all that that means for the ongoing sustainability of particular laws and, through knock-on or feedback effects, the legal system as a whole. We can observe that the measures are formally valid but otherwise deficient in qualities that will affect their future prospects. All this to say that while legal measures are different in important ways, including the extent to which they have or lack democratic legitimacy, future-focussed, sustainability considerations remain relevant. A one-dimensional rule-book picture of law tends to hide that relevance.

From the perspective of the rule-book picture, law-making in the form of legislation (supreme, primary and secondary) is a straightforward matter. All concepts

[113] See, eg, J Finnis, 'Judicial Power: Past, Present and Future' (*Judicial Power Project*, 2 February 2018), available at www.judicialpowerproject.org.uk/john-finnis-judicial-power-past-present-and-future/.

of law designate legislation as a valid source of law. It is this clarity and certainty, as compared to the uncertainties and vagaries of adjudication and legal reasoning, that makes law reform such a popular route for legal stakeholders, ranging from gun controllers/promoters, to environmental protectors/greenwashers, to feminist/race-based/disability advocates or to wider movements attempting to promote a 'just society' or to make it 'great again'.[114]

From the perspective of future sustainability, the act of legislating should appear far more difficult, sobering and consequential, just as a medical treatment appears to require far more in the way of humility-inspiring judgement when seen as in part an ongoing future-directed matter rather than a relatively speaking more straightforward present-focussed task involving the recommendation by a medical professional of a standard treatment from a medical manual.

In some instances, legislation is problematic from a sustainability perspective from the outset. South Africa's *apartheid* laws and Canada's laws attempting to assimilate Indigenous peoples through a residential school programme were 'laws' by the legal and constitutional source-based standards of their time, but they were filled with negative implications from a future-focussed, sustainability perspective as a result of their intrinsic lack of *quality* and their radical *inappropriateness to* important sectors of ongoing South African and Canadian *contexts*.[115]

In other instances, laws may be adequate when enacted but increasingly unsustainable given changing technological, public health or ecological developments, to take three prominent contemporary examples. As already noted, respect for democratically enacted legislation has value from both rule-book and sustainability perspectives. However, when new facts present genuinely difficult, sobering and consequential new questions, the rule-book model tempts jurists to present the hard case as nothing of the kind in the name of certainty, with negative consequences in terms of future sustainability, either because the legislation in question is not interpreted in a sustainable manner or because it is not amended with a similar end in mind.

As Ranchorda and Roznai state in a recent publication, '[l]aws that become obsolete put at stake the trust of citizens in the ability of laws to solve the problems for which they were enacted'.[116] While the stability and persistence of laws may be either a good and desirable thing or the product of inertia or neglect, 'this persistence becomes problematic when there are no rational reasons to maintain a law in place', as occurs, for example, when jurists of all kinds deliberately ignore the facts of technological, public health or ecological crisis. As Ranchorda and Roznai rightly point out, a further locus for these insights is in

[114] PE Trudeau, the former Prime Minister and father of present Canadian Prime Minister, Justin Trudeau, famously campaigned on the basis that he would create a 'Just Society'. Of course, Donald Trump has popularised the idea of making a polity 'great again'.

[115] South Africa, *Truth and Reconciliation Commission of South Africa Report* (The Commission, 1999); Canada, Truth and Reconciliation Commission, *They Came for the Children: Canada, Aboriginal People and Residential Schools* (Truth and Reconciliation Commission, 2012).

[116] S Ranchorda and Y Roznai (eds), *Time, Law, and Change: An Interdisciplinary Study* (Hart Publishing, 2020) 1.

the debate between originalism and living tree constitutional interpretation,[117] though the many dimensions to that debate cannot be explored here.

IV. CONCLUSION

A. Recap

Section II, the discussion of Irish (and Canadian) independence, highlighted the importance of looking to the future in order to arrive at a sustainable account of those legal systems' evolution. Sustainability, it was argued, takes in, at the very least, considerations of *source*, *quality* and *appropriateness to ongoing conditions*, the last of these being particularly important in the independence story.

Section III set out to identify the extent to which these considerations – *source*, *quality* and *appropriateness to ongoing conditions* – are already taken into account by leading jurisprudential theories. We saw that positivists are committed as a primary consideration to focussing on whether a legal measure emanates from a recognised *source*.[118] A second consideration, the *quality* of the legal measure, is not relevant to whether a measure counts as law according to the positivist account (clarificatory jurisprudence[119]), though positivists are of course interested in discussing a legal measure's relative qualities, so long as that discussion is understood to be a separate inquiry (evaluative or normative jurisprudence). Anti-positivists take the *quality* of the legal measure to be relevant to the legal inquiry, but the most influential expositor of this jurisprudential approach, Ronald Dworkin, would limit that inquiry so as to exclude the third consideration noted above, that is, the *appropriateness* of that measure *to the ongoing context* into which it must play out.[120] A natural lawyer such as John Finnis accepts that, generally speaking, practical reasoning must involve consideration of both governing principle and social scientific *context*,[121] but when he comes to discuss the law project, he too excludes from his conception of law any need to take into account the context into which positive law (itself required by natural law) will take effect. He is particularly adamant that courts not do so.[122]

Before considering what a truly sustainable jurisprudence might have to offer public law, it may be appropriate to identify very briefly what some readers may already have identified as the potential drawbacks of such an approach. Given that *source*-based considerations are already deemed to be acceptable in mainstream jurisprudential accounts, the focus will be on the merits, questionable to some, of considering *quality* and, especially, *appropriateness to an ongoing context*.

[117] ibid, citing G-F Mait, 'Dynamic Interpretation, Spatial and Temporal Aspects in Interpretation' in J Bjarup and M Blegvad (eds), *Time, Law and Society* (Franz Steiner, 1995) 85.

[118] Raz (n 56) 46 onwards.

[119] Clarificatory jurisprudence is usually associated with Hart (n 21).

[120] Dworkin (n 36) 159–66. For further discussion see (n 94) and accompanying text.

[121] Finnis (n 28) 17–18.

[122] Finnis (n 113).

B. Perceived Drawbacks of a Future-Focussed, Sustainable Jurisprudence and Potential Replies

Amongst the perceived drawbacks to considering future-focussed, sustainability-related factors such as the relative *quality* of our laws and their relative *appropriateness given an ongoing and changing context* are the following:

1. Quality and appropriateness to an ongoing context are difficult to measure.
2. Difficulty of measurement is not compatible with the designation of clear criteria for what is and is not law.
3. If law is to perform many of its most important roles, such as providing a means to coordinate a complex society, those clear criteria are essential.
4. Therefore law must be an end in itself (the rule of law), not an instrument of some other moral or contextual ends.

These are the sorts of considerations that draw positivists and others to identify clear, source-based criteria for legal validity, leaving questions of *quality* and *appropriateness to ongoing context* in a separate domain of non-legal inquiry. According to this view, those same considerations can be used to distinguish between law and morality, between legal arguments and policy arguments.

If we assume that the discussion in this chapter gives us reason (notably in the dimension of sustainability) to at least question these familiar divisions (law/morality; law/policy), we might then want to consider some of the following points:

1. Even those who promote clear criteria and clear distinctions acknowledge that there are many cases where legal guidance runs thin and a smaller number of truly hard cases where it runs out, and that in such circumstances it is inevitable that partially legal, or non-legal, judgments occur. Leading positivists such as Hart and Raz acknowledge as much, as we have seen.
2. Even if clear criteria are available that allow us to identify those legal instruments that ultimately count as law (in that they emanate from recognised *sources* such as Parliament or the courts), the factors that go into the making of such instruments (legislation or case law) in the harder and hardest cases, including context-based, future-focussed considerations, are also integral to jurisprudential inquiry.
3. Even if clear criteria allow us to identify that which constitute legal instruments in the rule-book aspect of that term, with the benefits (including sustainability benefits) that such clarity thereby provides, each of those same instruments can at the same time vary in terms of *quality* and *appropriateness for an ongoing context* (with inevitable, if difficult-to-measure negative knock-on or feedback effects even for law in its rule-book sense).
4. Even if a jurisprudential account acknowledges the importance of clear criteria in the name of the rule of law, that same account must, in reflective equilibrium, look to *quality* and *appropriateness to ongoing context* in order to promote the sustainability of that same rule of law.

In other words, even if one believes that our public law jurisprudence must include an account of law in its *binary* (law/not law), rule-book aspect, and that this *binary* calculus must not be muddied with considerations of *quality* and *appropriateness*, one is not precluded from believing that any law so identified must also be considered from a *relative* (better/worse; more/less appropriate) sustainability aspect. The argument in this chapter is that not only is the future-focussed aspect not precluded, it is a necessary component of a sustainable jurisprudence of public law. That was true in the case of Irish independence, and it is true for public law as a whole.

C. Does a Sustainable Jurisprudence Open Up Any New Questions for Public Law?

Rather than conclude with a list of assertions regarding the importance of a sustainable jurisprudence for public law, it seems more appropriate, given the early stage of development of this account, to identify at least a few of the sorts of questions that such an account may open up.

- What contributes to the sustainability of public law? Source, quality, appropriateness to ongoing context, as argued here? Other more aspirational factors of an abstract (seven basic forms of human good[123]), or more concrete kind (17 United Nations Sustainable Development Goals[124])? Other values?
- Should appropriateness to an ongoing context include taking cognizance of other competing normativities identified with the aid of a legal pluralist perspective,[125] given that such normativities are as likely to affect the way in which state law plays out in the future as the more concrete, factual context?
- Should jurists draft legal opinions, pleadings, judgments, regulations, legislation and constitutions with future-focussed sustainability considerations in mind?
- What is the effect (for individual laws and for the rule of law) of using the force of law (in the sense of orders backed by threats) to impose laws that have sustainability-related deficiencies, great or small? What is the effect of such a dynamic if it is particularly acute in certain sectors of a society rather than in others?
- Would we teach, practice, make, interpret and apply law differently if we embraced what was presented here as a considered understanding of law (eg, rule book *and* future-focussed considerations) rather than the standard understanding of law (the rule book alone)?
- Does a sustainable jurisprudence assist in explaining the relevance of socio-legal research to more doctrinal legal research, and vice versa?[126]
- If many legal rules developed over the past 250 years were made on the (usually implicit) assumption that industrial development would increase the overall well-being of a

[123] See, eg, Finnis (n 28) ch 4.
[124] *United Nations Sustainable Development Goals*, available at https://sdgs.un.org./goals.
[125] See, eg, Macdonald and Belley (n 35).
[126] DJ Galligan, 'The Paradox of Constitutionalism or the Potential of Constitutional Theory' (2008) 28 *OJLS* 343.

polity,[127] does the reality of a global environmental crisis now alter both the straightforward nature of that assumption and the way that we view the sustainability of those laws and future laws?

Some of these questions give rise to obvious answers and a need for immediate action. Others may require more research and more reflection. It is hoped that the present chapter points to fruitful directions for that research and reflection in the area of public law.

[127] For American examples, see MJ Horwitz, *The Transformation of American Law 1870–1860* (Harvard University Press, 1979).

Index

abortion:
Canada, 73
Northern Ireland, 17–18, 61
procedural deadlock, 66
US, 255, 257–58
absolute monarchy, 303
good counsel, 167–69
abuse of power, 219
South Africa, 92, 111
Act of Union (Ireland) 1800, 10, 15
administrative action, right to:
South Africa, 109–10
constitutional entrenchment, 112–15, 115–17, 118–19
legality principle, 117–18
US
COVID-19 pandemic, 268–69
anti-institutionalism, 274, 304
Aotearoa New Zealand, 48–49
background, 30–31
constitutional culture, 32–33
constitutional settlement, 31–32
international law, role of, 30, 46–48
statutory bill of rights, 30, 32
see also New Zealand Bill of Rights Act 1990
Te Tiriti o Waitangi, 30–31
see also Te Tiriti o Waitangi
tikanga, 30
see also tikanga
Waitangi Tribunal, 31
see also Te Tiriti o Waitangi
apartheid era (South Africa), 87
common law, 89–90, 110
courts' role, 90–93
housing, 99–100
judicial review, 111
parliamentary sovereignty doctrine, 87–89
remedies, 110
states of emergency, 111
Aristotle:
constitutional democracy, 308
good counsel, 170–71
rule of law, 175
Austin, John, 364, 365–66
command theory, 367–68
efficacy, 367
Australia:
COVID-19 emergency legislation, 239–40
accountability mechanism, 244–45
bicameralism, 240, 243, 245
delegated legislation, 243
distinctive features, 242–43
federalism, impact of, 240–41
generic emergency legislation, value of, 244
pandemic declarations, 242–43
pandemic orders, 243
proportionality, 245
scrutiny of executive activity, 245
time limits and extensions, 241–42

Bacon, Francis:
good counsel, 168–69, 175
Belfast Agreement 1998, 51–52
Brexit:
Northern Ireland, 67
populism, 272, 277, 281, 283–84
UK constitutional order, 315–18
constitutional (un)settlement, 318–22
rebalancing through reform, 322–26
Supreme Court's reclamation project, 326–30
burden of proof:
habeas corpus proceedings, 92
onus shifting, 12–14

Canada, 69–70
Canadian federalism, 71
Constitution Act 1867, 71–72
Constitution Act 1982, 33–34, 72
indigenous rights, 78–79
Constitutional history, 70–72
Dominion of Canada, 71–72
Indigenous law, 3, 4–5, 72–73, 335–37, 350–51
administrative law, 348–50
Constitution Act 1982 (s. 35), 78–79
Gitxsan law of compensation, 345–48
impact benefit agreements, 343–45
understanding Indigenous law, 337–42
legal pluralism, 73, 80–81, 83–84
Quebec, position of, 72
Supreme Court, 11–12
'three-nation Canada', 80–83
Truth and Reconciliation Commission of Canada, 81–83

Canadian Charter of Rights and Freedoms, 12–14, 32, 69–70, 72–78, 262–63
Cardozo, Benjamin, 211–14
Cassese, Sabino, 282–83, 284
***certiorari*,** 59, 147–48, 153, 159, 161–62, 163–64
challenges, public law's response to, 4–5
Charter of Fundamental Rights of the EU, 28
climate change, 4–5, 166, 184
codification:
  Canadian Constitution Act 1982, 75
  constitutional entrenchment in South Africa, 110, 112, 119
  UK's uncodified constitution, 276, 316, 322
Coke, Sir Edward, 148–49, 151–52, 154–59, 160–61, 175
common law constitutionalism, 214–15, 286
  emergency legislation, 238–39
  framing function, 203, 206–8, 210, 212, 215, 220
  judicial review, relationship with, 217–20
  repair function, 208, 208–9, 210, 211–12, 220
common law tradition, diversity of, 4
compensation, 159, 185–87, 195, 197, 241
  expropriation of land, 135–36, 142
  Gitxsan law of compensation
  see also damages
constituent versus constituted authority, 3–4, 217
constitutional abolitionism, 121–23, 131–33, 137
constitutional democracy:
  populism, relationship with, 297–302, 310–14
    authoritarian regimes, 303, 304–5
    constitutional 'law-rule' versus democratic 'self-rule', 309–10
    democratically deficient regimes, 303
    emergent populism, 306–8
    flawed democracies, 303
    full democracies, 303, 304
    reversionist populism, 306–8
  thick constitutionalism, 285–86, 287
    UK constitutional order, 316–17, 318–22, 325–26, 331–32
  thin constitutionalism, 281, 282–83, 299–300, 302, 318
constitutional identity, 3
  Canada, 72
constitutional independence (Ireland), 353–54, 359–60
  competing narratives, 360–62
    sovereignty of Irish people, 358
    sovereignty of UK Parliament, 357–58
constitutional rebalancing, 316
  Johnson/Sunak reform agenda, 322–25
  judicial encroachment, 319–22
  Supreme Court's reclamation project, 326–27
constitutional transitions or transformations, *see* **transformative constitutions**
constraints of public power, 350–51
Convention against Torture, 47
Convention for a Democratic South Africa (CODESA), 93
Council of Europe, 22
Court of Justice of the European Union (CJEU), 10, 11–12, 280–81
COVID-19 and public health emergencies, 4–5, 233–35
  Australian emergency legislation, 239–40
    accountability mechanism, 244–45
    bicameralism, 240, 243, 245
    delegated legislation, 243
    distinctive features, 242–43
    federalism, impact of, 240–41
    generic emergency legislation, value of, 244
    pandemic declarations, 242–43
    pandemic orders, 243
    proportionality, 245
    scrutiny of executive activity, 245
    time limits and extensions, 241–42
  lack of trust in government, 254–55, 264–67
  South Africa
    affirmative action measures, 140–41
  US administrative law, 247–48, 248–49, 259–60, 270
    anti-administrativism, 254–55, 264–67
    Australia compared, 260, 263
    Canada compared, 261–62, 262–63
    CDC moratoria, 249–51
    common law, contrasts with, 267–69
    individual rights challenges to pandemic measures, 255–58
    New Zealand compared, 260–61, 262
    politicisation of COVID-19 litigation, 263–64
    requests for emergency relief, 249
    suspicion of agency decisions and motivations, 254–55, 264–67
    vaccinate-or-test emergency temporary standard, 251–54
  see also emergency legislation

damages:
  compensatory damages, 194–96
  exemplary damages, 186, 192, 197–98, 199–200, 201
  nominal damages, 185–86, 188, 190–91, 192, 194, 194–96, 199–200

vindicatory damages, 195–96, 197–98
violations of protected constitutional rights, 199–200
Ashby v White, 187–91
actionable *per se*, 186, 199–200
causation, 186
false imprisonment, 185–86
see also false imprisonment
misfeasance in public office, 185
see also misfeasance in public office
remedies, 186
tortious versus constitutional actions for damages, 186–87
unlawful interception of prisoners' correspondence, 185
see also unlawful interception of prisoners' correspondence
wrongful intent, 200
democracy:
constitutional democracy
authoritarian regimes, 303, 304–5
constitutional 'law-rule' versus democratic 'self-rule', 309–10
democratically deficient regimes, 303
emergent populism, 306–8
flawed democracies, 303
full democracies, 303, 304
populism, relationship with, 297–14
reversionist populism, 306–8
thick constitutionalism, 285–86, 287, 316–17, 318–22, 325–26, 331–32
thin constitutionalism, 281, 282–83, 299–300, 302, 318
equality and equal participation, 76–77
liberal democracy, 204–6
framing function of constitutional law, 203, 206–8, 210, 212, 215, 220
repair function of common law constitutional law, 208, 208–9, 210, 211–12, 220
representative democracy, 183–84
Polybius, 204–6
democratic time concept, 203, 204–6
devolution issues:
Brexit, 316, 320, 324, 325, 330, 331–32
Northern Ireland, 51–52, 61–62, 65–66
Dicey, A.V.:
administrative fairness, 218
constitutional rebalancing, 319–20
Irish Home Rule, 357–58
law-making function of courts, 87–88, 212–13
parliamentary supremacy, 2–3, 87–88, 237, 359
rule of law doctrine, 283
direct rule in Northern Ireland, 51, 52–53, 54–55
division of powers doctrine, 75, 78, 206, 240
Australia, 45
Canada, 13–14, 69–70
checks and balances, 279
emergency legislation, 238, 248–49
political liberalism, 205
populism, 279, 299, 313, 315–17, 322, 324, 328
South Africa, 96, 131
UK
good counsel, 178, 179
judicial review, 113, 118
parliamentary sovereignty, 331, 332–33
US, 264–66
see also parliamentary sovereignty
duty of care, 89
duty to interpret and enforce the US Constitution, 24–27
Dworkin, Ronald, 285–86, 354, 360–61, 363
anti-positivism, 377
discretion and *determinations*, 374–75
discretion and hard cases, 373–74
discretion and reflective equilibrium, 372–73
hard cases, 369, 371, 373–74

emergency legislation:
concentration of power, 238
conceptualisation of emergency powers, 235–36
adequacy of response, 236
proportionality of response, 236
transparency, accountability, fairness and public trust, 236
types of emergencies, 236–37
conferral of extensive authority on executive, 238
COVID-19, 239–44
see also COVID-19 and public health emergencies
delegation of legislative power, 238–39
English law:
constitutional law, 206
damages, 190, 195–96, 197
South Africa, 89–91
equal participation, 19, 76–77, 292
equal treatment, 97, 219
equality, 76–77, 85–86, 89–90, 219, 226
democracy, relationship with, 76–77, 93–94, 97, 101, 170–71, 204–5, 309
emergency measures, 235–36
gender equality
Canada, 73
Ireland, 10
South Africa, 135–36
good counsel, 183

legitimate expectations, 219
legislative equality of Commonwealth nations, 72
liberalism, 126–27, 288
transformative adjudication, 128–31
transformative constitutionalism, 121–22, 124–26, 142–43
Erasmus, Desiderius:
good counsel, 170–72, 174, 175, 176, 183
European Convention on Human Rights (ECHR), 28, 316
common law constitutional approach, 215
Ireland's accession, 10
judicial review, 227, 315–16, 319–20, 325
living instrument doctrine, 215, 216
UK's relationship with, 21, 326–28
European Court of Human Rights (ECtHR), 10, 11–12, 20, 22, 280–81, 317, 323, 325–26
European Union (EU), 275
Ireland's accession, 10
Executive authority:
Northern Ireland, 52–54, 61, 62–64
populism, 275–76, 279–80

false imprisonment, 153, 185–86, 189
damages, 199
Lumba case, 194–97
impact, 197–98
Finnis, John:
natural law, 360–61, 371, 377
reflective equilibrium, 372–73, 374
framing function of constitutional law, 203, 206–8, 210, 212, 215, 220
France:
Canada
Quebec, 70, 72, 73, 81
three-nation Canada, 78–81
two-nation theory, 70, 81–82
Seven Years' War, 70
Fuller, Lon, 342, 350–51
future-proofing public law, *see* **sustainability of public law**

Gitxsan law of compensation, 345–48
good counsel, 165–66
absolute rule, 167–69
Hobbes' *Leviathan*, 178–80
counsel versus command, 180–82
Osmotherly rules, 181
humanist counsel, 169–72
independence, 183–4
institutional reform
judicial independence, 174–76
parliamentary reform, 176–78
Machiavelli, 172–74
obligation of candour, 170–71
representative democracy, 183–84
Good Friday Agreement 1998, 51–52
Gorz, Andre, *see* **non-reformist reform**

***habeas corpus*,** 15, 227
judicial review, 147, 153–54, 159–60, 164
Elizabethan age, 154–59
South Africa, 90–91, 92
Hart, H.L.A., 354, 378
concept of law, 362–63, 364–65, 372
conferral of power, 366
continuing sovereignty, 359–60
hard cases, 369–71
social normativity, 368–69
Hobbes, Thomas (*Leviathan*), 166, 175, 177–78
counsel's role, 178–80
counsel versus command, 180–82
self-serving counsellors and flatterers, 182
Osmotherly rules, 181
housing:
South Africa
apartheid era, 99–100
Constitution 1996, 100–5
constitutional damages, 104
dignity and equality, 101
reasonableness approach, 103–5
right to access to adequate housing, 100–1
South African Constitutional Court, 100–5
Human Rights Act 1998, 20–22, 43, 45–46, 197, 281, 317

Indigenous law, 3, 4–5
Canada, 72–73, 335–37, 350–51
administrative law, 348–50
Constitution Act 1982 (s. 35), 78–79
Gitxsan law of compensation, 345–48
impact benefit agreements, 343–45
understanding Indigenous law, 337–42
constraints of public power, 350–51
International Covenant on Civil and Political Rights (ICCPR):
New Zealand's Bill of Rights, 32, 43, 47
International Covenant on Economic, Social and Cultural Rights (ICESCR):
South Africa, 103
international law, 103–4
New Zealand, impact on, 46–48, 49
UK, 21, 316, 325, 331–32
interpretive approach, 16, 19–20, 30
duty to interpret and enforce the US Constitution, 24–27

Good Friday/Belfast Agreement 1998, 51–52, 63–64, 65
Ministerial Code, 56–57
judicial restraint, 24–25
margin of appreciation, 20–22
parliamentary sovereignty and literalist interpretive approach, 91
statutory interpretation, 203–4, 217
Te Tiriti o Waitangi, 36–37, 41–42, 46–48
three-nation Canada, 78–81
Ireland, 1–2
constitutional independence, 359–60
competing narratives, 360–62
foreign jurisprudence, impact of, 14–15
illegally obtained evidence, 16
importation/sale of contraceptives, 16–17
right to abortion, 17–18
surrender of suspects, 15–16
judicial review, 221–24
1922 Constitution, 224–25
1937 Constitution, 225–27
judicial review of legislation, 227–30
legal future of public law, 353–54
medical analogy, 355–57
sustainability, 354–55
proportionality, 10–12
Canadian approach distinguished, 12–14
sovereignty
constitutional independence, 359–60
Irish people, 358
UK Parliament, 357–58
written constitutionalism, 2–3
Irish Free State Constitution 1922, 221–23
judicial review, 224–25
Irish Home Rule, 357–58

judicial activism, 23–24, 76, 229–30
judicial decision-making, 28, 216–17, 227
judicial deference, 33, 332
emergency legislation, 235–36
US approach to COVID-19 pandemic, 248, 257–58, 263–64, 268, 270
judicial discretion, 205, 215, 281, 283, 287
determinations, 374–75
emergency legislation, 238
hard cases, 369–71, 373–74
legitimate expectations, 219
presumption of consistency, 47, 48
reflective equilibrium, 372–73
tikanga values, 41
judicial enforcement of rights, 22–23, 27–28
judicial independence, 162–63, 280
good counsel, 174–76, 183–4
judicial restraint, 23–24, 33, 128, 332
judicial review, 147–49, 203–4
Canada, 75–76
common law constitutional norms, relationship with, 217–20
damages and infringement of rights, 197
Ireland, 221–24
1922 Constitution, 224–25
1937 Constitution, 225–27
judicial review of legislation, 227–30
Magna Carta, 149–51
prerogative powers, 220
writ of *certiorari*, 161–62, 163–64
writ of *habeas corpus*, 153–54, 164
writ of *mandamus*, 159–61, 163–64
writ of *prohibition*, 161
royal prerogatives
absolute prerogatives, 151–52
ordinary prerogatives, 151, 152
South Africa
entrenchment of rights, 112–14
limitations on judicial review, 113, 114
time limits, 118
judicialisation of politics, 288
justice, equality and fairness, 90

Kant, Immanuel:
Rechtsstaat doctrine, 282
Kelsen, Hans:
constitutional independence, 223, 227–28, 359
efficacy, 354, 365–67
Grundnorms, 223, 227–28, 359, 368
justified normativity, 368
Klare, Karl:
transformative adjudication, 128–31
transformative constitutionalism, 93, 125, 126–28, 132, 137

law, concept of, 362–65
efficacy, 365–67
hard cases, 369–71
natural law concepts of law
discretion and *determinations*, 374–75
discretion and hard cases, 372, 373–74
discretion and reflective equilibrium, 372–73
normativity, 366–69
legal positivism, 354, 360–61, 362, 377–79
anti-positivism, 377
discretion and *determinations*, 374–75
discretion and hard cases, 373–74
discretion and reflective equilibrium, 372–73
command theory, 367–68
efficacy, 365–66
hard cases, 369–72

legal subjecthood:
Indigenous populations of Canada, 78–79
legality principle:
New Zealand, 37, 43–44, 47
South Africa, 115–16, 117–18
UK, 216–17, 218–20, 328
US, 248, 260
legitimacy of courts, 203–4, 338
domestication of constitutions, impact of, 86, 97–98, 107
judicial review, role of, 280
see also judicial review
Indigenisation of constitutions, impact of, 97–98
liberal constitutionalism, 285
liberal democracy, 220
framing function, 210–11, 213
repair function, 209
rights of minorities, 76–77
sustainability of legal measures, 375–76
legitimate expectations, 219
liberal constitutionalism, 123–24, 131–32
departure from, 126–28, 130–31, 140–41, 142–43
juridification, 288
limitations, 133, 313
populism, relationship with, 271, 280, 284, 285–87, 315, 320–21
liberal democracy, 204–6
framing function of constitutional law, 203, 206–8, 210, 212, 215, 220
repair function of common law constitutional law, 208, 208–9, 210, 211–12, 220
liberal legalism, 121–22, 128–31
living instrument doctrine:
Canada, 77–78, 216
common law constitutionalism, 215–17
ECHR, 215, 216

Machiavelli, Niccolo, 172–74, 176, 177, 182, 204
***mandamus*,** 147, 159–62, 163
Beecher v Lucas, 190
margin of appreciation, 20, 326–27
ministerial resignations and appointments:
Northern Ireland, 55
minority rights, 72–73
COVID-19 and public health emergencies, 4–5
affirmative action measures, 140–41
South Africa, 140–41
see also Indigenous rights
misfeasance in public office, 185
Ashby v White, 187–91
impact, 191–94
ubi jus ibi remedium, 189–90, 201
More, Thomas:
good counsel, 168, 172, 176

national identity, 3, 273, 299–300, 339
national security, 20, 47, 214, 263–64, 267
natural justice, 90, 113, 292
natural law, 210–11, 354, 360–61, 362, 371, 377
determinations, 374
reflective equilibrium, 372–73
see also anti-positivism
New Public Management (NPM), 165–66, 288
New Zealand, ***see*** **Aotearoa New Zealand**
New Zealand Bill of Rights Act 1990, 43–44
declarations of inconsistency, 44–46
remedies for breach, 44–46
New Zealand Supreme Court, 32
non-interference with parliamentary proceedings:
Ngāti Whātua Ōrākei Trust case, 39–40
non-reformist reform, 122–24, 143
conditions, 139–40
definition, 138
departures from classic liberal constitutions, 142–43
affirmative action measures, 140–41
horizontal application of rights, 141
protection of private property, 141–42
goals, 138–39
transformative constitutionalism, 137–38
Northern Ireland:
absence of power-sharing
legal challenges, 62–64
assembly, 60
constitutional structure, 67
cross-community representation, 53–54
direct rule, 51, 54
Executive authority, 53–54, 60
Good Friday/Belfast Agreement 1998, 51–52
Government of Ireland Act 1920, 51
individual ministerial responsibility, 52–53, 54, 59–60
Northern Ireland Act 1998, 51–52
transferred matters, 52
devolution issues, 65–66
First Minister/deputy First Minister joint working, 56, 60
ministerial code, 56–60
ministerial decision-making, 57–58
ministerial resignations and appointments, 55
Minister of Justice, 55
North–South relations, 58–59
procedural deadlock, 60–61
reintroduction of direct rule, 54
St Andrews Agreement 2006, 54–55
sovereignty issues, 64–65
standing
individual ministerial responsibility, 59–60
Northern Ireland (Executive Formation etc) Act 2019, 61–62, 63–64

onus of proof, *see* **burden of proof**
ouster clauses, 280, 323, 325, 328
South Africa, 93, 113, 114

parliament:
government, parliament and courts, relationship between, 20–22, 176–78
non-interference with parliamentary proceedings
Ngāti Whātua Ōrākei Trust case, 39–40
parliamentary scrutiny, 48
emergency legislation, 238
populism, 293–94, 325
transformative constitutionalism, 131
parliamentary sovereignty doctrine, 357–58, 359
constitutional principle, 214, 217
constitutional rebalancing, 316–18, 326–30
emergency legislation, 237
populism, 276, 281, 286–87
separation of powers, 331, 333
South African
apartheid era, 87–89, 91
constitutional democracy, 93
parliamentary supremacy:
Canada, 71, 75
Diceyan model of parliamentary supremacy, 2–3
Ireland, 2–3, 228
pluralism:
Canada, 73, 80–81, 83–84
populism, 272, 290, 299–300, 304, 306–8, 310
sustainability, 379
plurality of public law, 4, 76–77, 279–81
political constitutionalism, 3, 32–33, 329, 330, 331–33
Polybius:
kingship, aristocracy and democracy, relationship between, 204–6
populism, 4–5, 271
administrative law and, 273–75, 281–82, 290–91
alienation and lack of trust in government, 289
alternative sources of authority and influence, taming/neutralising, 279–81
anti-institutionalism, 274
authoritarian pole, 282
Brexit cases, 283–84
demonisation narrative, 272
executive law-making, 293–95
exit, voice and loyalty framework, 290–93
features of, 272–73
instrumentalist/functionalist pole, 282–83
law and policy forms, 277–78
liberal constitutionalism, 284, 285–87
liberal pole, 283
market-oriented managerialism, 284, 287–89
parliamentary scrutiny, tenuous nature of, 293–94
public messaging, administrative process and engagement, 278–79
redemptive aspect of populist discourse, 273
struggle and the 'real' people, 272, 273–74, 275–76
style and structure of governance, 276–78
Caesarist tradition, 309–10
constitutional democracy, 297–302, 310–14
authoritarian regimes, 304–5
constitutional 'law-rule' versus democratic 'self-rule', 309–10
democratically deficient regimes, 303
emergent populism, 306–8
full democracies, 304
relationship between, 302–8
reversionist populism, 306–8
economic globalisation, relationship with, 312–13
prerogative writs:
certiorari, 161–62, 163–64
habeas corpus, 153–54, 164
mandamus, 159–61, 163–64
prohibition, 161
quo warranto, 154, 162
prisoners' right to vote:
New Zealand, 44–45
Privy Council's powers, 153, 158–59, 162–63, 176–77, 216
Canada, 77–78
Ireland, 225–26, 358
New Zealand, 32
procedural deadlock:
Northern Ireland, 60–61
abortion, 61
same-sex marriage, 61
welfare reform, 61–62
procedural fairness:
Diceyean administrative fairness, 218
emergency powers
transparency, accountability, fairness and public trust, 236
justice, equality and fairness, 90
South Africa, 112, 113, 114–15, 118
tikanga, 43
prohibition, writ of, 154, 161–62
proportionality:
Canada, 74
constitutional principle, 219
emergency legislation, 236, 238, 241, 244–45
EU law, 10–11
Irish approach distinguished, 12–14
separation of powers, 328
substantive scrutiny and proportionality reviews, 268

prorogation of Parliament, 152, 220, 284
Public Law Conference, 1

quo warranto, 154, 162
Beecher v Lucas, 190

rationality principle:
South Africa, 117–18, 138
Raz, Joseph, 360–61
hard cases, 369–70, 371
justified normativity, 368–69
social normativity, 368–69
reasonableness, 12
constitutional entrenchment, 114–15
executive prerogative, 87
reasonable man concept, 89
South Africa, 102–3, 104–5
religious identity, 3
repair function of common law constitutional law, 208, 208–9, 210, 211–12, 220
reproductive rights, *see* **abortion**
right to vote:
constitutional democracy, 105–6, 188, 189–90, 192
COVID-19 pandemic challenges, 255, 258
English law, 89–91
equality and equal participation, 76–77
prisoners, 44–45
ubi jus ibi remedium principle, 188, 189–90
Roman-Dutch law:
South Africa, 89, 90–91, 110
royal prerogatives, 148–49
absolute prerogatives, 151–52
ordinary prerogatives, 151, 152
prerogative courts, 158
rule of law, 22, 321–22, 331–32
administrative action, 115
Australia, 240
balancing elements of government, 204–5
constitutional independence, 353
constitutional rebalancing, 330
habeas corpus, 156, 160, 163–64
hard cases, 369
judicial review, 113
legal certainty, 96, 119
legality principle, 218–19
parliamentary scrutiny, 325
populism, 272, 274, 315, 316–17
common law judicial discretion, 281, 283
liberal constitutionalism, 285–87, 308–9
reflective equilibrium, 373
separation of powers, 322
South Africa, 86, 95–96, 107–8, 115, 131–32
St Andrews Agreement, 55
sustainable jurisprudence, 378–79

St Andrews Agreement 2006, 54–55
same sex marriage:
Canada, 76–77
procedural deadlock in Northern Ireland, 61
self-determination:
Indigenous rights, 82–83, 339, 351
separation of powers, *see* **division of powers doctrine**
Seven Years' War, 70
sexual orientation, 73, 76
same sex marriage
Canada, 76–77
procedural deadlock in Northern Ireland, 61
social and political challenges, 3–4, 18–20, 31, 34, 132, 304–5, 313, 338
social contract, 128
South Africa, 85–86
apartheid era, 87
common law, 89–90, 110
courts' role, 90–93
judicial review, 111
parliamentary sovereignty doctrine, 87–89
remedies, 110
states of emergency, 111
Constitution 1996, 93–94, 109
constitutional supremacy, 94–96
entrenchment of rights, 109–10
indigenisation of Constitution, 97–99
judiciary, powers of, 96–97
English law, 89–91
entrenchment of rights, 109–10, 112
judicial review, 112–14
limitations on judicial review, 113, 114
ouster clauses, 113
procedural fairness, 113, 114–15
scope of administrative action, 115–17
housing crisis, 99–105
judicial review
entrenchment of rights, 112–14
limitations on judicial review, 113, 114
time limits, 118
'never again' principle, 107–8
political rights, 105–7
Roman-Dutch law, 89, 90–91, 110
transitional Constitution 1993, 93–94, 109, 111
constitutional supremacy, 94–96
indigenisation of Constitution, 97–99
judiciary, powers of, 96–97
South African Constitutional Court:
housing cases
constitutional damages, 104
dignity and equality, 101
reasonableness approach, 103–5
right to access to adequate housing, 100–1
political rights, 105–7

sovereignty or authority, challenges to, 3–4
Northern Ireland, 64–65
standard-setting, 288
standing:
New Zealand, 29–30
Northern Ireland
individual ministerial responsibility, 59–60
South Africa, 140–41
statutory interpretation, 19–20
Canada, 348
New Zealand, 46
Te Tiriti o Waitangi, 30, 36–37
Trans-Tasman case, 41–42
South Africa
constitutional entrenchment, 115–16
UK, 203–4, 207, 217
US
Chevron deference to agency, 247
separation of powers, 266–67
purposivism, 267–68
substantive rights:
Canada, 77–78
sustainability of private law, 377
constitution-making, 375–76
drawbacks of future-focussed, sustainable jurisprudence, 378–79
importance for public law, 379–80
law, concept of, 362–65
discretion and *determinations*, 374–75
discretion and hard cases, 372, 373–74
discretion and reflective equilibrium, 372–73
efficacy, 365–67
hard cases, 369–71
natural law concepts of law, 372–75
normativity, 366–69

Te Tiriti o Waitangi, 30–31, 33–34
constitutional comity, 37–40
courts' engagement with the Treaty, 34–35
constitutional comity, 37–40
future relationships, 40
statutory interpretation, 36–37
free-floating Treaty principles, 34
future relationships, 40
Lands case, 34–35
Ngāti Whātua Ōrākei Trust case, 39–40
non-interference with parliamentary proceedings, 39–40
Sealords case, 38–39
statutory interpretation, 36–37
Te Heuheu Tūkino case, 34
Waitangi Tribunal, 34–35
thick constitutionalism, 285–86, 287
UK constitutional order, 316–17, 318–22, 325–26, 331–32
thin constitutionalism, 281, 282–83, 299–300, 302, 318
tikanga as a source of law, 30, 40–42
Ellis v R, 41–42
future relationships, 42–43
Trans-Tasman case, 36, 41–42
tort:
actionable *per se*, 186, 199–200
false imprisonment
Lumba case, 194–97
see also false imprisonment
misfeasance in public office, 185
Ashby v White, 187–94
ubi jus ibi remedium, 189–90, 201
see also misfeasance in public office
unlawful interception of prisoners' correspondence
Watkins case, 185, 191–92, 195–98
see also unlawful interception of prisoners' correspondence
transformative adjudication, 123–24, 128–31
transformative constitutions, 3, 143
abolitionist critique, 131–33
definition, 124–26
classical liberal constitutions, departure from, 126–28, 131–32
transformative adjudication, 128–31, 132–33
institutional critique, 132–33, 137
judicial review powers, 123–24
non-reformist reform, 121–24, 137–43
see also non-reformist reform
postcolonial criticism, 134–37
South Africa, 93–94, 121–24
decolonisation of the Constitution, 135
democratisation framework, 134–35
constitutional supremacy, 94–96
indigenisation of Constitution, 97–99
judiciary, powers of, 96–97
non-reformist reform, 123, 137–43
transformative adjudication, 128–31
transgender discrimination, 19
Truth and Reconciliation Commission of Canada, 81–83
Truth and Reconciliation Commission of South Africa, 117–18

***ubi jus ibi remedium*,** 188, 189–90, 201
***ubuntu* principle (South Africa),** 86, 98–99
UN Committee on Economic, Social and Cultural Rights (UNCESCR), 103
UN Convention against Torture and Other Cruel, Inhuman or Degrading Treatment or Punishment (CAT), 47
UN Declaration on the Rights of Indigenous Peoples (UNDRIP), 82–83

United Kingdom:
Brexit, *see* Brexit
courts
ECtHR, relationship with, 20–21
influence in Ireland, 14–15
constitutional order, 315–18
constitutional (un)settlement, 318–22
rebalancing through reform, 322–26
Supreme Court's reclamation project, 326–30
good counsel, 178, 179
government, parliament and courts, relationship between, 20–22
Human Rights Act, 20–22, 43, 45–46, 197, 281, 317
judicial review, 113, 118
legality principle, 216–17, 218–20, 328
parliamentary sovereignty, 331, 332–33, 357–58
statutory interpretation, 203–4, 207, 217
thick constitutionalism, 316–17, 318–22, 325–26, 331–32
uncodified constitution, 276, 316, 322
United States:
COVID-19 and administrative law, 247–48, 248–49, 259–60, 270
anti-administrativism, 254–55, 264–67
Australia compared, 260, 263
Canada compared, 261–62, 262–63
CDC moratoria, 249–51
common law, contrasts with, 267–69
individual rights challenges to pandemic measures, 255–58
New Zealand compared, 260–61, 262
politicisation of COVID-19 litigation, 263–64
requests for emergency relief, 249
suspicion of agency decisions and motivations, 254–55, 264–67
vaccinate-or-test emergency temporary standard, 251–54
Supreme Court
citation of foreign precedents, 9
desegregation cases, 26
influence in Ireland, 15–17
unlawful interception of prisoners' correspondence:
Watkins case, 185, 191–92, 197–98
impact, 195–97

Weber, Max, 204
Wechsler, Herbert, 24–26
welfare reform:
procedural deadlock in Northern Ireland, 61–62

www.ingramcontent.com/pod-product-compliance
Ingram Content Group UK Ltd.
Pitfield, Milton Keynes, MK11 3LW, UK
UKHW050649200926
475560UK00005BA/347

9 781509 970056